D1600490

Between Containment and Rollback

INTERNATIONAL HISTORY
PROJECT SERIES

James G. Hershberg
series editor

 Published in collaboration with the Woodrow
Wilson International Center for Scholars

BETWEEN CONTAINMENT AND ROLLBACK

THE UNITED STATES AND THE COLD WAR IN GERMANY

Christian F. Ostermann

Stanford University Press

Stanford, California

STANFORD UNIVERSITY PRESS
Stanford, California

Printed in the United States of America on acid-free, archival-quality paper

Library of Congress Cataloging-in-Publication Data

Names: Ostermann, Christian F., author.
Title: Between containment and rollback : the United States and the Cold War in Germany / Christian F. Ostermann.
Description: Stanford, California : Stanford University Press, 2021 | Series: Cold war international history project | Includes bibliographical references and index.
Identifiers: LCCN 2019051240 (print) | LCCN 2019051241 (ebook) | ISBN 9781503606784 (cloth) | ISBN 9781503607637 (ebook)
Subjects: LCSH: Cold War. | United States—Foreign relations—Germany (East) | Germany (East)—Foreign relations—United States. | United States—Foreign relations—1945-1953. | Germany—Foreign relations—1945- | Germany (East)—History.
Classification: LCC E183.8.G3 O83 2019 (print) | LCC E183.8.G3 (ebook) | DDC 327.73043/109045—dc23
LC record available at https://lccn.loc.gov/2019051240
LC ebook record available at https://lccn.loc.gov/2019051241

Cover photo: June 17, 1953 Uprising—strikers on Leipziger Strasse on the way to Potsdamer Platz. Courtesy of Gert Schütz/Landesarchiv Berlin.

Cover design: Rob Ehle

Typeset by Kevin Barrett Kane in 10.2/14 Adobe Garamond Pro

To my parents, Elisabeth and Friedrich Ostermann

Contents

Writing East Germany into Cold War History

On February 9, 1990, U.S. president George H. W. Bush sat down to pen a personal letter to West German federal chancellor Helmut Kohl. He wanted Kohl to know that he wholeheartedly supported the chancellor's accelerated drive toward German unification. The situation in the German Democratic Republic (GDR) had been deteriorating. For many East Germans, change in the wake of the fall of the Berlin Wall on November 9, 1989, could not come fast enough. Thousands of East Germans went west, putting pressure on Kohl for fast-track unification. The West German leader was about to confront Soviet Communist Party secretary general Mikhail Gorbachev, who, by all accounts, held the key to Germany's unity. Bush assured his German counterpart of "the complete readiness of the United States to see the fulfillment of the deepest national aspirations of the German people. If events are moving faster than expected, it just means that our common goal for all these years of German unity will be realized even sooner than we had hoped."[1]

In characterizing his support of Kohl, Bush was on the mark. Sooner than other European leaders, the American president had developed a "comfort level" with the idea of German unification: "I'd love to see Germany reunited," Bush told the *Washington Times* on May 16, 1989.[2] It reflected his belief, as Robert Gates, the then–deputy national security adviser, later recalled, that "the Germans had changed, and he was prepared to gamble a great deal on that faith."[3] The president's conviction that West Germany had become a stable democracy and a reliable ally positioned him and his administration to embrace the idea of a united Germany sooner than others, including the Germans themselves. His advisers, too, believed that "there

is no German of any age who does not dream of it in his soul."[4] But it was more
than sympathy for the Germans that motivated the Bush administration in its support for German unity: it made the alliance with West Germany the centerpiece
of its strategy to preserve U.S. preeminence on the European continent. The Bush
administration's support for German unification, Robert Hutchings, a National
Security Council (NSC) official at the time, recalled, was "genuine, consistent with
our principles and based on careful consideration of our interests."[5]

Yet the grand narrative of Americans and Germans standing side by side "for
all these years" in the pursuit of Germany unity, so evocatively suggested by Bush's
letter to Kohl, reduces the complex story of U.S. policy toward the German question since the end of World War II. This study looks at that story's early years,
from Allied occupation to the early 1950s, when both West Germany and East
Germany became members of the politico-military pacts facing off against each
other in Europe. It does so through the prism of American attitudes and policy
toward the Soviet-controlled part of Germany. It was these Germans, caught by
the post-1945 geopolitical fallout of the war that Nazi Germany had launched in
1939, who most dearly paid the price of the country's division.[6] Histories of the
American–German relationships in the postwar era have left these Germans largely
out of the narrative. This book seeks to write the East Germans—leadership and
populace—back into history, certainly as objects of American policy, at times even
as historical agents of their own.

Was there an American policy toward East Germany? Two major intellectual-
political projects for a long time relegated the answer to this question to a footnote. One was the perception, prevailing for most of the Cold War, of the USSR's
dominating role in the Soviet occupation zone and later the German Democratic
Republic. In this view, generally speaking, the GDR as part of the Soviet-led eastern bloc lacked historical agency. American policy was thus directed at the Soviets
in Germany; based on the "supreme authority" the four occupation powers had
assumed in Germany in June 1945, the United States held the USSR responsible
for events in the Soviet zone and GDR.. If there was a distinctive U.S. approach
to East Germany in this perspective, it was one of diplomatic non-recognition of
the Communist German regime after 1949, a policy that sought to deprive that
regime of any legitimacy and aligned with the West German "Hallstein Doctrine,"
which punished recognition of the GDR by other countries. During the Cold
War and beyond, many historians unconsciously echoed the dominant political
view in the West by denying the GDR historical agency. Not until 1989 did a
book by a political scientist address the topic more fully, although it focused on

the period after the resumption of relations between the United States and the GDR in 1974.[7]

The more important reason for the lack of inquiries into U.S. policy toward East Germany was the primacy of the American relationship with "its" Germany. To this day, the alliance the United States forged with the Federal Republic of Germany (FRG) "represents one of the most successful endeavors in the history of U.S. diplomacy." Turning the western part of Germany from a wartime adversary to an economically and politically pluralistic, vibrant, and peaceful ally was and is considered critical to the post–World War II reconstruction and stabilization of Western Europe and the global liberal-capitalist system, vital to America's prevailing in the Cold War, and central to assuring U.S. predominance on the European continent once the Soviet empire had crumbled.[8]

Emblematic of the importance of West Germany to the United States, President Bush in May 1989 called for both countries to become "partners in leadership." With a great deal of merit, generations of historians in the United States and Germany and beyond have written libraries full of books exploring every aspect of America's relationship with the Federal Republic. Whether supportive of the relationship in which both countries had invested so much, or critical of the mistakes, failures, and moral or political compromises that had been involved, however, these bodies of work were by and large united in their neglect of East Germany as a serious factor in forging the relationship.[9]

This book is made possible by two recent historiographic shifts, both facilitated in part by access to declassified documents. First, a greater appreciation for the fact that U.S. foreign policy in the early phase of the Cold War was far more assertive in nature than the defensive posture implied by the notion of "containment." Since the late 1940s, reactive, defensive notions of "containing" this new Soviet threat mixed in the political discourse in Washington with more activist and offensively conceived notions of "liberation" and of "rollback" of Soviet power. Benefiting from increased declassification of formerly secret documents in the 1980s, Melvyn Leffler's *Preponderance of Power* (1992) finally provided persuasive documentation that U.S. objectives had been more far-reaching than previously acknowledged. American planners, Leffler argued, wanted to redraw Russia's borders to their pre-1939 status, destroy the Cominform, "retract" influence of the Soviet Union, and eventually cause the Soviet system to weaken and decay. Given time and strength, containment could evolve into a "rollback" of Soviet power. On the basis of declassified top-level U.S. planning papers, Gregory Mitrovich and Peter Grose pushed this notion even further: Rollback did not await successful containment. The Truman administration embarked on a strategy to "compel" the Soviet Union to abandon its international ambitions in sync with its containment policy.[10]

Notions of "rollback" and "liberation" struck a deeper chord because, as Bernd Stöver has demonstrated, they related to traditional American political paradigms of liberty and Manifest Destiny, linked to the religiously infused ideology of American exceptionalism and America's moral superiority that had motivated U.S. interventionism from the nineteenth century until the world wars of the twentieth. Faced with yet another "totalitarian challenge" to its very concept of modernity in the wake of the German Reich's defeat, the United States saw itself as assisting the "natural" or "divine" trends of world history and defending its own security at the same time as it sought to expand the domains of freedom abroad. The United States, therefore, could not limit itself to the "long-term, patient but firm and vigilant containment of Russian expansive tendencies" alone, as U.S. diplomat George F. Kennan had—now famously—demanded in his 1947 *Foreign Affairs* article "The Sources of Soviet Conduct."

Led in fact by Kennan himself, American officials had set out in 1947–48 to destabilize the Soviet regime and its East European "satellites" through a concerted "psychological warfare" effort—termed "counteroffensive"—that sought to further exploit "vulnerabilities" of the Soviet system, particularly its pervasive distrust and suspicion, and "rollback" Soviet domination from Central Europe. East Germany constituted an important target in this "counteroffensive" strategy, especially after the North Korean invasion of South Korea led to a dramatic rise in Cold War tensions globally. This study benefited from the unprecedented openness and declassification of U.S. government records through the Freedom of Information Act (FOIA)—including records on covert operations and psychological warfare. More recently, new scholarship based on exclusive access to the archives of West Germany's foreign intelligence service, led by German historians Jost Dülfer, Klaus-Dietmar Henke, Wofgang Krieger, and Rolf-Dieter Müller, has enriched the Western perspective.[11]

Second, with the end of the Cold War, the implosion of the Communist regimes in east-central Europe, the disintegration of the Soviet Union, and the ensuing opening of archives of the former Communist world, historians have also sought to internationalize the history of the Cold War. Gaining access to the innermost chambers of secrets of the formerly ruling Communist parties from Moscow to Berlin has allowed historians to recast the Cold War in ways that were unthinkable beforehand: the narrative could now be reconstructed from an international perspective, on a multi-archival basis, overcoming the one-sided, largely Western-centered perspectives that had dominated scholarship in East and West.[12] The sudden end of the Cold War confrontation posed the challenge to historians to write its history knowing the outcome, yet it also allowed them to escape the ideological and political parameters that it seemed to have set while it was ongoing.

The German battleground of the Cold War has always formed an important sub-narrative. Reflecting the larger debate on the origins of the Cold War, during the Cold War (and beyond) historians fought and refought the battle over who was to blame for the division of Germany. During the height of the Cold War, most Western accounts laid the blame squarely at Stalin's doorstep. Much of the late Cold War–era scholarship had firmly grounded American policy toward postwar Germany in the containment paradigm. To be sure, the notion of a "double" or "dual" containment developed by Wolfram Hanrieder and Thomas Alan Schwartz added subtlety to the notion that Washington was solely preoccupied with countering Soviet expansionism into Europe.[13] With the U.S. and British sources well exploited by the late 1980s, the study of American policy in Germany during the first postwar decade took a cultural and transnational turn in the 1990s. Reflecting similar trends in other fields, major works of the 1990s emphasize the significance of ideological or cultural agendas and discourse as well as the importance of nonstate, nongovernmental actors in the international arena of the postwar period.[14]

Though over time historians came to question the Cold War consensus, only Carolyn Eisenberg finally turned the historiographic tables, with her 1996 work *Drawing the Line: The American Decision to Divide Germany, 1944–1949.* The United States—along with Britain and France, not the Soviet Union—Eisenberg argued in what has become the standard account of the subject, was the architect of Germany's partition. Lacking access to archival sources in Germany and Russia, Eisenberg's brilliant account, however, tended to underestimate Soviet responsibility. In other ways, it did not go far enough in analyzing U.S. responsibility. This study is meant to complement Eisenberg's account in the light of new Russian and German documentation. It also builds on Marc Trachtenberg's pathbreaking work, especially his *A Constructed Peace* (1999).[15]

What these new and important contributions, including works by Hermann Josef Rupieper and Frank Schumacher, had in common—and indeed what united them with landmark earlier studies such as John Lewis Gaddis's *The Long Peace: Inquiries into the History of the Cold War* (1987) and Melvyn Leffler's *Preponderance of Power* (1992)—was the fact that they paid little attention to East Germany, as either an object or an actor in the story that unfolded. Still mirroring the American political vantage point, much of the scholarship focused on West Germany and, in line with the longtime denial of diplomatic recognition, ignored the eastern part of the country and treated it as a negligible appendage. Other studies subsumed the

GDR as a Soviet "satellite," as part of the political east-central Europe, famously written off to Soviet domination by American "non-policy."[16] Even in works on German-American relations, including classics by John H. Backer, Frank Ninkovich, Wolfgang Krieger, and Thomas Schwartz, developments in eastern Germany found scant mention.[17] Only recently have a number of new publications—among them work by Anjana Buckow, Schanett Riller, and Burton C. Gaida—focused greater attention on certain aspects of the American approach to the "other" Germany.[18]

The scholarship deficit on the GDR diminished when the doors of the archives of the Socialist Unity Party of Germany (Sozialistische Einheitspartei Deutschlands, or SED), and the government that it ran were flung open in the wake of the fall of the Berlin Wall.[19] To be sure, the GDR had been a subject of serious study in West Germany before reunification, particularly by the Mannheimer Arbeitskreis "Geschichte und Politik der DDR," led by Hermann Weber, as well as other experts, such as Karl Wilhelm Fricke, Gisela Helwig, Peter Christian Ludz, Ilse Spittmann, and Carola Stern, but it remained handicapped by the dearth of sources.[20] Much like the broader debate about the Cold War in the United States, the study of the GDR reflected the political debate and exigencies in the Federal Republic about *Deutschlandpolitik*, from the early totalitarian critique of the 1950s to the "systemic" understanding of the GDR as a modernizing society in the détente years. Only access to the archives in eastern Germany (and Russia) after 1989–90 allowed historians in East and West Germany to begin a critical reassessment of the political and social history, the "historicization" of the "second German state."[21]

Since the early 1990s, the history of East Germany (and the relations between both German states) has witnessed an explosion of new research. In this process, a new generation of historians born and/or educated in the GDR—in particular Ilko-Sascha Kowalczuk, Michael Lemke, Andreas Malycha, Armin Mitter, and Stefan Wolle, liberated from the prerequisites of Marxist-Leninist ideological framework—have played a leading role in reassessing GDR history.[22] International historians have joined this proliferation of research on postwar eastern Germany, with landmark studies by Timothy Garton Ash, Catherine Epstein, Hope Harrison, Konrad Jarausch, and Norman Naimark.[23] *Between Containment and Rollback* builds on this rich archival corpus of documents and analytical literature to show how American policy affected events in East Germany; access to these resources has allowed this study to give historical agency to the East German leaders and "masses" as they faced the West.

While the events of June 1953 and the Soviet occupation period drew much public and scholarly attention, research on international history based on the former East German records preoccupied itself largely with German-German relations, with an emphasis on the period after 1960.[24] Studies of GDR foreign policy generally suffered from two circumstances: First, despite the setting up of a foreign ministry in the GDR in 1949, international affairs remained a tightly guarded prerogative of the Soviet occupation power, particularly in the immediate postwar period, but to a great degree into the 1950s as well. Thus the German record, exemplified by the important but often cryptic Pieck diary notes, has been fragmentary at best.[25] Second, until the early 2000s, Russian records for the early postwar period in Germany remained inaccessible in the Presidential Archive and the Russian Foreign Ministry Archive in Moscow.[26] Thanks to the patient efforts of Jochen Laufer, Elke Scherstjanoi, Jan Foitzik, and others at the Zentrum für zeithistorische Forschung in Potsdam and the Institute for Contemporary Research in Munich/Berlin, Russian records on occupied Germany have begun to be published in cooperation with the Russian Foreign Ministry Archive. Norman Naimark, Bernd Bonwetsch Gennadij Bordjugov and Gerhard Wettig published additional important Russian documentation for the period under consideration in this study. Though far from complete, these records, supplemented with Russian records relating to Germany from other collections and archives, have informed this study to the extent that they allow, for the first time in a fairly systematic fashion, insights into Soviet (and German) intentions and actions vis-à-vis the United States and its allies.[27]

ACKNOWLEDGMENTS

This book is the result of research over a number of years, more than I care to admit. I am indebted first and foremost to Thomas A. Schwartz, dear friend and mentor, without whose encouragement, steadfast support, and inspiration this book would not have seen the light of day. The late Erich Angermann and then Norbert Finzsch, leading German historians of the United States, played a foundational role in forging my historical tradecraft. My mentor, colleague, and friend Robert Litwak at the Wilson Center provided me with cherished opportunities away from program management. I am grateful to my dear friend Hope Harrison for encouragement, close reading, and stimulating conversations about our respective book manuscripts. Her work on the history of the Berlin Wall has been an inspiration for me.

Friends and colleagues Chen Jian, Warren Cohen, Frank Costigliola, John Lewis Gaddis, William Gray, Jamil Hasanli, James Hershberg, Mark Kramer, Konrad Jarausch, Melvyn Leffler, Li Danhui, W. R. Louis, Charles Maier, William Stivers, Thomas Boghardt, Vladimir Pechatnov, Sergey Radchenko, Shen Zhihua, William Taubman, Odd Arne Westad, and Vladislav Zubok supported me throughout the process. Thomas Boghardt, Marc Frey, William G. Gray, Hope Harrison, Jim Hershberg, Mark Kramer, Melvyn Leffler, Vladimir Pechatnov, Thomas Schwartz, and William Stivers read early versions of the manuscript; I benefited greatly from their comments.

At the Wilson Center many other colleagues encouraged, supported, and critiqued along the way: besides Rob Litwak, the Honorable Lee H. Hamilton, the Honorable Jane Harman, Michael H. Van Dusen, Samuel F. Wells Jr., Haleh

Esfandiari, Robert Hathaway, Blair Ruble, Cynthia Arnson, Diana Negroponte, and Joseph Brinley. My talented and dedicated staff and generations of interns assisted in a variety of ways in the completion of the manuscript: I thank especially Charles Kraus, Laura Deal, Nancy Meyers, Mircea Munteanu, Pieter Biersteker, Evan Pikulski, Allison Lylakov, Martha "Dee" Beutel, Kayla Orta, Kristina Terzieva, Kian Byrne, Ryan Gage, and Timothy McDonnell.

This study began under the auspices of the U.S.-Soviet Flashpoints Project of the National Security Archive, of which I am to this day a proud senior fellow. I gained access to many documents as a result of the archive's Freedom of Information Act (FOIA) requests and am indebted to the archive's amazing staff, led by Thomas Blanton, Malcolm Byrne, William Burr, and Svetlana Savranskaya. Thanks also to my research assistants Gregory Domber, now a published historian in his own right, and Peter Voth. I owe enormous gratitude to the Cold War International History Project under its first director, Jim Hershberg, for encouraging, editing, and publishing my research on the 1953 uprising.

For a historian working in a public policy institution, quasi-sabbaticals that allow time for thinking and writing are rare and hence precious. Geir Lundestad, Odd Arne Westad, and Olaf Njolstad allowed me to start working on this project during a research fellowship at the Norwegian Nobel Institute. The institute's librarian, Anne Kjelling, was incredibly helpful. I am grateful to the American Academy in Berlin for giving me time to put the finishing touches on the project. Librarians Yolande Korb and Kelly Pocklington fanned out across Berlin to fulfill my numerous research requests. In Oslo and Berlin, my co-fellows inspired me to be a better historian and writer.

I also gratefully acknowledge the financial support of the Society of Historians of American Foreign Relations, the Gerda Henkel Foundation (Düsseldorf), and the Harry S. Truman Presidential Library and Museum (Independence, MO). My thanks also go to the archivists and other staff at the National Archives (College Park, MD), the U.S. Department of State, the Truman Library, the Dwight D. Eisenhower Library, the Bundesarchiv (Koblenz/Berlin), and the Political Archive of the German Foreign Ministry (Bonn/Berlin), as well as to the Public Record Office/UK National Archives for providing access to the records. I am grateful to Ulrich von Hehl and Stephan Kieninger for their assistance with the Bundesarchiv records in the final stage of the manuscript.

I am deeply grateful to Margo Irvin, Nora Spiegel, and Emily Smith at Stanford University Press for their superb editorial assistance.

Unfailing in their encouragement, support, inspiring diversions, and nagging questions, my friends, near and far, have helped make this book possible: Carol Ann

Adamcik, Keith Allen, Lynn Brallier, Harold and Clemencia Cohen, Katharina Dahl, Joan Dobkin, Jordan Fried, Axel Frohn, Marilena Gala, Francis Gavin, Massimiliano Guderzo, Eva Kleedermann, Paweł and Anka Machcewicz, Jürgen Martschukat, Leopoldo and Teresa Nuti, Mark R. Pennington, Lynda Pilgrim, Maria Stella Rognoni, Ruud van Dijk, Elena Vitenberg, Sherrill Wells, Andrea Williams, and Chris and Angela Willmore.

This book is dedicated to my parents, Elisabeth and Friedrich Ostermann, whose love, support, and life story formed the foundation for the passion and effort that went into this project. My American families—the Wilsons and the Katchkas—extended that foundation to the United States. And all of them will be pleased that this book will now no longer be a topic of increasingly painful conversations at family reunions and vacations.

I remember when my partner and love of my life, Elizabeth H. Katchka, first read an early version of the chapter on the failed East German rebellion of 1953. Lisa was moved to tears by the tale of the workers and students who took to the streets for freedom and democracy, by the human story. Long before and even longer afterward, she believed that their story would finally see the light of day. It is to her I owe my greatest and unending debt.

Map of Allied Occupation Zones, 1945–1949

1

"Toward a Line down the Middle of Germany"

Containment at Potsdam, 1945

BERLIN WAS A DESOLATE PLACE when President Harry S. Truman and his
entourage arrived there on July 15, 1945. Truman planned to discuss the future
of Germany with the leaders of the Soviet Union and Great Britain, his wartime
allies, on the outskirts of a city largely in ruins. Berlin had absorbed more bombs
and shells in World War II than any other metropolis. The scale of the wreckage
and mass of rubble defied measurement.[1] "For mile after mile through Berlin
and its suburbs," one member of Truman's party remembered, "every building
was shattered beyond habitation. Some were still smoldering. . . . The stench of
death was everywhere."[2] To another, former Moscow ambassador Joseph E. Davies,
Berlin seemed like "a spectral, ghost city" with "scorched and burned-out wrecks
of buildings."[3] Yet another, John J. McCloy, the assistant secretary of war and
future U.S. high commissioner in Germany, noted driving "past dogged looking
people trudging along the road—most of them without shoes" on his way into
Berlin on the autobahn. Everything in the center of town was "stark ruin—it
[went] on as far as you [could] see and the deeper we proceeded through the city,
the worse it became." There was a "stink of broken sewers," people in the streets
looked "grey and dull. A conquered, devastated and depressed city—so different
from the vigor of Berlin and its neat if heavy character in peace time that it is
almost unbelievable."[4] McCloy and most of the American delegation, headed by
Truman and Secretary of State James F. Byrnes, stayed more than two weeks in
these almost surreal surroundings.

This chapter argues that the two weeks that U.S. leaders and their foreign policy advisers spent in Potsdam in the Soviet zone were critical for the transformation of American policy. Truman and Byrnes had arrived in Germany prepared to work out some kind of joint governance of the territory they had occupied. But the core deal struck between Truman and his counterparts at Potsdam was a dramatic reversal of the plan to treat Germany as an economic unit and in good measure a result of their experience in the Soviet zone: an agreement that allowed each occupation power to serve its reparations needs from its own zone. Buried in a thicket of pronouncements on the unitary political treatment of Germany by the World War II allies, the zonal solution to the reparations question had profound ramifications for the future of Germany: it set the eastern and western occupation zones on different economic and political trajectories. While recent historiography has rightly placed this American-inspired plan in the context of broader fears about socioeconomic turmoil in Europe, internal administration debates over occupation priorities, or a broader sphere-of-influence approach to relations with the Soviet Union, it is important to emphasize that this zonal approach to the reparations problem owed much to the preemptive Soviet campaign of dismantling that had taken place since the Red Army entered German territory. In Potsdam the results of that campaign were staring the Americans in the face.

The Evolution of American Policy

"We have to remember that in their occupied territory they will do more or less what they wish."[5] President Franklin D. Roosevelt (FDR) had a sober and somewhat ambivalent view of what to expect from the Red Army occupation of eastern Germany. He acknowledged the geopolitical reality that the Soviet government would run the zone of Germany that it would come to occupy with an essentially free hand. And probably a heavy one as well. No one had any "idea as yet what they have in mind," but disagreements were to be expected. American leverage to ensure Soviet cooperation was minimal—though not entirely ruled out. We could "not afford to get into a position of merely recording protests on our part unless there [was] some chance of some of [the] protests being heeded." FDR hastened to add that he did "not intend by this to break off or delay negotiations with the Soviet government over lend-lease, the wartime program that had supplied matériel to the USSR since 1941."[6]

The presidential statement, a rare intrusion into the postwar planning debates within his bureaucracy for a president who, as late as October 1944, famously expressed his dislike for "making detailed plans for a country . . . which we do not yet occupy,"[7] encapsulated Roosevelt's wartime priorities: defeating Germany and

FIGURE 1. Pedestrians walk down a street in Berlin lined with buildings destroyed or damaged by bombing during World War II, circa July 1945. Courtesy of Harry S. Truman Library and Museum.

Japan and securing Soviet cooperation for the postwar world. If he had any inkling of what was awaiting the German population that came under Red Army control, he showed no qualms. He had been inclined toward draconian treatment of the Germans after the war, and he was convinced that it needed to be "driven home to the German people" that their "nation has been engaged in a lawless conspiracy against the decencies of modern civilization." Worried that the Germans might rise again to unleash another war, he had suggested that "we either have to castrate the German people or you have got to treat them in such a manner so they can't just go on reproducing people who want to continue the way they have in the past."[8] As late as November 1944, FDR professed to still be "in a tough mood." He was "determined to be tough with Germany."[9]

His attitude on Germany let him and his New Deal advisers consider the deindustrialization, dismemberment, and harsh punishment of the country that had engulfed the world twice in a global conflagration.[10] For a few weeks in late 1944 he had supported a scheme, pushed by Secretary of the Treasury Henry Morgenthau, for the "complete eradication of German industrial productive capacity in the Ruhr and Saar," though he later denied doing so.[11] He had also been enthralled with the idea, first proposed by Soviet leader Joseph Stalin, of dismembering the German Reich into five to seven parts, and he and British prime minister Winston Churchill strongly supported dismemberment at the first "Big Three" Conference in Tehran in October 1943. Roosevelt hung on to the idea as late as the Yalta Conference in February 1945, despite opposition from within his administration and Churchill.[12]

At Yalta, the Big Three leaders (Churchill, Roosevelt, and Stalin) also confirmed Germany's obligation to compensate the Allied nations for damages, through dismantling, reparations from current production as well as the use of German labor. There was broad understanding that the Soviet Union would receive the lion's share, given its tremendous wartime losses. To be sure, when Stalin requested $10 billion of a proposed total of $20 billion as the Soviet portion in reparations from Germany, with the deputy Soviet foreign minister, Ambassador Ivan Maisky, adding a demand for 75 percent of dismantled German industrial equipment, both Churchill and Roosevelt balked at fixing the amount. But Roosevelt had at least implicitly acknowledged the validity of the Soviet request by agreeing to use the Soviet proposal as a basis for discussion in the Allied Reparations Commission in Moscow, which was tasked with resolving the matter.[13]

In Roosevelt's view, assuring Soviet cooperation for the postwar peace required accommodating reasonable Soviet security interests, especially in central and eastern Europe. Roosevelt had therefore quietly endorsed the October 1944 percentage agreement in which Churchill and Stalin had divided southeastern Europe into spheres of influence (British dominance in Greece, Soviet dominance in Bulgaria and Romania), and he had consented to Soviet control over the Baltic republics and eastern Poland (which the USSR had annexed as a result of the Molotov-Ribbentrop Pact of 1939). But FDR had stopped just short of giving Stalin a completely free hand in the region, especially in what would constitute postwar Poland. He and Churchill had insisted at Yalta that the Communist-dominated Lublin Committee, which Stalin had recognized as the provisional Polish government, be reorganized on a broader basis by including democratic leaders from inside and outside of the country. A new government facilitated by Allied negotiations in Moscow would be pledged to holding free elections. The solution reflected a broader approach to central Europe: acknowledging Soviet security concerns in an area that had been the gateway for the German invasion, Roosevelt aimed at a region made up of countries that aligned with Russia strategically but preserved autonomy in their domestic affairs. It implied some degree of political openness.[14]

The Moscow negotiations on a reconstituted Polish government soon stalled. In Poland, the Soviets proceeded to impose a Communist police state. Unwilling to "whitewash" the Lublin Committee, Roosevelt sought to increase public pressure on Moscow—in vain, as it turned out. Roosevelt's death on April 12 left the issue to his successor to deal with. Truman, lacking full details of Roosevelt's negotiations with Stalin (and Churchill), warned of a violation of the Yalta agreements, telling Soviet foreign minister Vyacheslav Molotov on April 23, 1945, that the issue would "be the symbol of future collaboration" between the countries. The Polish issue—and Soviet communization in Eastern Europe more broadly—threatened to undermine Allied relations at the very moment when the three countries set out to run occupied Germany collectively. Unwilling to allow a complete break with Moscow, Truman dispatched Roosevelt's confidant Harry Hopkins to Moscow in May. Following quick agreement on the composition of the new Polish government and assurances of free elections, the Truman administration recognized the still Communist-dominated government.[15]

The ruthless sovietization of Poland and much of eastern Europe frustrated U.S. officials. But "what was truly alarming" to the Truman administration, Melvyn Leffler has argued, was that Soviet imposition of Communist rule in Poland and elsewhere in the region was occurring "at the same time as economic chaos, social turmoil, and political upheaval were spreading in southern and western Europe."[16] While the Kremlin may not have instigated these developments, U.S. officials were certain that the Soviet government could capitalize on the unrest. As World War II ended in Europe in early May 1945, Leffler contends, the Truman administration did not consider anything of greater strategic significance, excluding the defeat of Japan, than "dealing with the potential for revolution in European areas not under Soviet occupation."[17]

German coal resources in particular were quickly identified as critical for the stabilization and reconstruction of all of western Europe. This in turn meant that the United States and Great Britain would have to import substantial amounts of food, clothing, and machinery in order to resuscitate German coal production and its distribution to western Europe. The funds necessary to pay for these imports, top policy makers within the administration decided well before the Potsdam Conference, were to be the "first charge" on all German exports from current production and stocks. This arrangement would require reparations to be deferred until the payments for imports necessary to rehabilitate the German coal industry had been recovered. By the time Truman arrived in Potsdam in mid-July 1945, the need to revive German coal production was firmly entrenched in the minds of his top advisers.[18]

The priority that these "rebuilders" (Carolyn Eisenberg) within the administration, most of them conservatives at the State and War Departments whose influence was eclipsing that of the New Deal liberals under the new president, ascribed to resuscitating German coal production over reparations reflected a view of reparations that starkly contrasted with the Soviet position: they valued the punitive effects of reparations only to the extent that they fostered a "controlled demobilization of German self-sufficiency," but not "economic disarmament." These officials felt that penalizing and crippling Germany permanently through harsh reparations or dismemberment would fail. They considered the punitive reparations regime after World War I to be one of the most fundamental sources of conflict and tension. Instead, they wanted reparations to become a tool for economic integration. Preventing future German aggression, from their perspective, was less a matter of emasculating German industrial might than creating inextricable interdependencies with other economies. They regarded integrating German economic potential with the economies of neighboring countries as the best way to undercut German nationalistic propensies for autarky and hegemony. This in turn would facilitate the restoration of a multilateral capitalist world trade system deemed vital to assuring American preponderance and to sustaining peaceful international order.[19]

If the idea of the centrality of Germany's coal and steel industrial complex—located as it was largely in the western Rhein-Ruhr Valley—to the revival of the European economy thoroughly pervaded American postwar planning in the spring of 1945, most officials still looked at the former Reich as an economic whole. Roosevelt's sustained interest in various dismemberment schemes had raised the specter of Germany's political division, but not one along ideological lines. Few at this stage would go so far as the U.S. chargé d'affaires in Moscow, George F. Kennan, who, just before the Yalta Conference advocated Germany's division into a Soviet zone and a U.S. zone. Key American officials in fact felt that reviving prewar trade patterns within Germany was critical to supplying the western zones as well as serving as leverage vis-à-vis the Soviet interest in reparations. In their view, treating Germany as a single economic unit would be the only way to address the food shortages, economic dislocations, and trade imbalances. Thus the "first charge" principle would be applied to trade in all zones, including the traditionally export-rich east.[20]

The economy of the German Reich had in fact been marked by a high degree of sectoral interdependence and interregional exchanges. Traditionally, eastern Germany had been the country's bread basket and had depended extensively on imports of hard coal and steel from the heavily industrial Rhein-Ruhr heartland region (and

to a lesser extent from Upper Silesia, which had come under Polish administration);
in turn, it processed these imports into finished and semi-finished goods. Eastern
Germany's thin raw-materials base was largely limited to brown coal, allowing it
to boast extensive highly developed and export-oriented manufacturing capacities
centered on textiles, ceramics and glass, optics and fine mechanics, paper, and printing machines, as well as cars. The wartime economy had only accelerated eastern
Germany's degree of specialization in processing industrial goods—and its dependence on the rest of the Reich. By 1945–46, the Soviet zone was almost completely
dependent on the West for iron and coal, for 92 percent of its pressed metal, and
for 84 percent of its concrete supplies.[21]

Truman, his newly appointed secretary of state, James F. Byrnes, and his other
top advisers used the ten-day voyage to Potsdam to hammer out final negotiating
positions for the Big Three meeting. Aside from securing Soviet entry into the ongoing war against Japan, their most important and most controversial positions at
Potsdam related to the economic treatment of Germany. Given the new emphasis
on reviving German coal production, they first aimed at reducing the Soviet demand
for $10 billion in reparations extractions from Germany, tentatively agreed to by
Roosevelt at Yalta. Second, they sought to ensure that any capital or production
extracted from Germany would first pay for Allied imports required to restart coal
production, thus deferring reparation payments. Administration officials had also
had second thoughts about the internationalization and separation of the Rhein-
Ruhr Valley, possibly involving a Soviet role, as had been envisioned in Yalta. That
idea was now off the table. Truman's party was fully aware that the U.S. priorities
clashed with Soviet interests in compensation for their enormous war-induced losses,
in long-term "economic demilitarization" of Germany's industrial-military might,
and in participation in controlling and exploiting the Rhein-Ruhr.

The U.S. concerns reflected not just a preoccupation with German coal as the
motor for western Europe's survival and recovery, and a shrinking conception of
the utility and value of reparations. They also betrayed at the highest levels of the
administration deeply held ideological convictions that called into question the possibility of cooperation with the Soviets. Secretary of War Henry Stimson professed
to be "much troubled about the fundamental difficulty with the Russians—theirs a
totalitarian political concept—a secret police regime with subordination of all to the
State and the use of the one-party system." Perhaps no one epitomized that belief
more than Byrnes. Marc Trachtenberg has emphasized Byrnes's conviction by the
time of Potsdam that there was "too much difference in the ideologies of the U.S.
and Russia to work out a long-term program of cooperation."[22]

That belief was increasingly shared among the inner circle of foreign policy advisers that the new president gathered for his diplomatic debut among the "Big Three." U.S. ambassador to Moscow Averell Harriman and Edwin Pauley, Truman's lead negotiator on the Allied Reparations Commission, joining Truman's party from Moscow, were both reportedly "violently critical"[23] of Russian behavior. General Lucius DuBignon Clay, slated to take over as General Dwight D. Eisenhower's deputy to run the U.S. occupation government in Germany (OMGUS), arrived from U.S. headquarters in Frankfurt and told of reports of "the excesses in the Russian area." Assistant Secretary of War John J. McCloy, who accompanied Stimson to Berlin for the conference, bemoaned his country's hesitancy about "setting our 'ideology' against hers [the USSR's]," allowing the Russians to pose as democrats "in spite of practicing totalitarianism in its most complete form."[24] Joseph E. Davies, FDR's former ambassador to Moscow who had been invited by Truman to serve as his personal adviser during the conference, was among the few in the delegation who were more optimistic about the prospects for Soviet cooperation. He quickly noticed the anti-Soviet "temper of many about the PRESIDENT." He felt "the hostility towards Russia" was "bitter and surprisingly open" among the delegation.[25]

Soviet behavior in eastern Europe seemed to reinforce this skepticism. But the posture at Potsdam also suggested that American policy makers were cognizant of Soviet vulnerabilities in the wake of the war. News of the successful U.S. atomic test, which reached Truman on July 16, the morning after he got to Potsdam, could only strengthen a sense of the hand they had to play even further.[26]

The Soviet Approach

By the time Truman encountered Stalin in Potsdam, the fundamental thrust of American policy ran counter to the Soviet approach to the German problem. The German invasion in June 1941 had brought Stalin's regime to the brink of collapse. The existential threat and the staggering human and material losses the country suffered at the hands of the Germans had a profound impact on the international outlook of the Soviet leadership and people. An estimated 26.6 million Soviet citizens had lost their lives in the war. Millions of buildings, tens of thousands of industrial plants, agricultural production cooperatives, train tracks and stations, postal and telegraph stations, thousands of schools, universities, and research institutions, hundreds of museums, libraries, theaters, and hospitals had been destroyed or damaged. By mid-1944, internal Soviet estimates figured that direct physical damage caused by the war alone amounted to $130–$150 billion. Consequently, the Soviet government planned to assert a right to compensation from Germany and its allies as "the highest possible priority." Historical lessons influenced that view as well: arguing that reparations in the form of financial transfers had proved unworkable after World War I, Soviet planners demanded reparations in the form of one-time removals of industrial plants and goods, annual deliveries of industrial and other products over a span of ten years, and German labor.[27]

In the Soviet view, reparations were crucial not only to the country's postwar recovery but also to the goal of emasculating Germany's potential for future aggression. It was a common assumption in Moscow's foreign policy circles that Germany, if unchecked, would quickly recover from its 1945 defeat.[28] In July 1944 the Soviet Foreign Ministry's Commission on Reparations, led by Maisky, had called for scaling down Germany's living standard to a minimum that would not exceed the average postwar central European standard, estimated to be half that of the German prewar standard. Industrial disarmament would reduce Germany's heavy industry, such as iron and steel production, to 25 percent of prewar levels. Overall, Soviet planners anticipated halving Germany's total industrial capacity. Given the huge discrepancy between Soviet losses and Germany's capacity for compensation, the "most practicable" method was "to extract from Germany everything that can possibly be extracted from this country."[29]

While the Western powers had recognized the Soviet right to compensation and also considered it necessary to disarm Germany completely, it had not been lost on Soviet officials that American and British officials almost never spoke of "industrial disarmament." The notion of reparations as a tool of guaranteeing security in Europe was completely lacking in the Anglo-American approach, Maisky told Soviet foreign minister Vyacheslav Molotov in the fall of 1944, and so he expected them to oppose the expansive Soviet program that linked reparations to the reduction of German war potential.[30] Soviet diplomats considered Treasury Secretary Henry Morgenthau's "deindustrialization plan" to be a step in the right direction but remained skeptical. The Soviet ambassador in Washington, Andrej A. Gromyko, was well aware that Secretary of War Henry Stimson was emphatically opposed and that the majority of those State Department officials who dealt with postwar Germany were "strictly set against" any plans to weaken Germany economically. In his view, the Allies wanted to preserve Germany as a "developed industrial country." Though Roosevelt's final decision was still pending, it was becoming clear, Gromyko reported in the fall of 1944, that influential groups inside and outside of the administration favored a "softer policy" toward Germany.[31]

These warnings aligned with those of Eugene Varga, an influential Soviet economist who advised Stalin that reparations among capitalist countries could not be implemented given "the insuperable contradiction" between reparations and the need to "protect the capitalist social order." Marxist-Leninist ideology thus fed Soviet officials' doubts that the Western powers would be willing to impose a harsh reparation regime on Germany.[32]

The logic of the Soviet approach to reparations took all of Germany into view. As they advocated for a zone-by-zone occupation of Germany, Soviet officials emphasized that these zones should be simply administrative, not economic entities. One should not consider them "property" of the Allied power that occupied them, the deputy chairman of the Council of People's Commissars, Kliment Voroshilov, a confidant of Stalin, emphasized in the internal deliberations of spring 1944. After all, in that case the Ruhr and Saar areas would become British property, which was "not acceptable under any circumstances." Future reparation capacity could not be the decisive consideration underlying the zonal division "since the Allies would receive reparations from Germany as whole."[33]

Yet throughout the discussions in the tripartite European Advisory Commission meetings in London charged with planning for the armistice period in Germany, the Soviet government pushed for the zone commanders—not an interallied executive organ—to have exclusive authority to implement the armistice agreement. They were worried that American and, even more so, British proposals for a centralized, complicated, and possibly omnipotent interallied control mechanism would lead to "confusion, misunderstandings and weakened authority of the supreme commanders."[34] Behind these very practical concerns lurked suspicions about Western interference in Soviet zone affairs and fears of being outnumbered in any joint occupation agencies. Protecting their zone from Western influence became an obsession for Soviet officials even before they had occupied their part of Germany. Strikingly, Soviet planning documents on more than one occasion referred to the American and British zones as the "western zone," reflecting a mental map with deep ideological fault lines. As late as August 1944, such documents denied relinquishing even the most rudimentary executive and administrative functions to any central inter-Allied authority proposed by the Americans to coordinate matters pertaining to all of Germany and supervise a future German government; at most, Moscow officials wanted to concede some form of regular consultations between the supreme commanders within a "control council" whose decisions had to be unanimous.[35]

To be sure, American and British officials took little time to recognize the advantages of a military government that operated primarily at the zonal level. American planners still favored creating a three-power entity in Berlin that would act on the orders of the three governments in all matters concerning Germany as a whole. But the final Zonal Protocol agreed upon by the European Advisory Commission on September 12, 1944, reflected the basic predilection for zonal control and decentralization shared by all three powers: Allied control in postwar Germany would be divided between joint central authority vested in the "Allied Control Council" and the authority of the individual zonal commanders for administration in their zone, with the weight of power gravitating toward the latter.[36] Moreover, in May 1945, after France had been ceded its own occupation zone in southwestern Germany, American negotiators advanced the idea that while the Allied Control Council's authority would be supreme in all of Germany, in cases where the Allies would not be able to agree, each military commandant would be free to proceed unilaterally in his own zone.[37] Germany's capital, Berlin, was to become in effect a "fifth zone," stay undivided, and come under joint Allied control, with sector lines of rather "platonic significance." Supreme Allied Commander Dwight D. Eisenhower's decision in the spring not to advance directly toward Berlin made the Soviets the "sole masters of the city" for a full two months.[38]

The Soviet insistence on a free hand in their zone was crucial for understanding the Soviet attitude toward reparations. The formal Allied recognition at Yalta of Germany's responsibility to pay reparations in kind from its national wealth, along with the acknowledgment that the lion's share would fall to those Allied nations that had suffered most and had contributed most to defeating the Germans (which meant above all the Soviet Union) was to Stalin far more important than the actual amount that became the focus of endless Allied discussions. His ideas about what the USSR required in compensation had shifted significantly over the years. Early in the war he had stated: "40,000 machine tools—that is all we want in reparations from Germany!"[39] As late as Yalta, Stalin was apparently willing to ask for no more than $5 billion in reparations, causing Ambassador Ivan Maisky, the head of the Soviet Reparations Commission that had been developing a Soviet reparations plan for more than a year, to produce panicked memos arguing for twice that amount, which he considered the absolute minimum.[40] When Roosevelt and Churchill pushed back on a $10 billion commitment at the Yalta Conference, Stalin was apparently ready to back down to $7 billion, though the figure was never officially tabled.[41] Despite the lack of a firm Western agreement on overall amounts for reparations, the Soviet leadership considered the "Crimea Conference" a success—especially with regard to reparations![42] The reasons would soon become apparent: a massive unilateral dismantling program for their zone.

What Stalin wanted to avoid at all costs was for the negotiations over a precise reparations plan to curtail the Soviet dismantling effort that had been long prepared and began to unfold in the weeks after Yalta. He thus dragged out till mid-March the appointment of Maisky as Soviet representative to the Allied Reparations Commission, which the Big Three had agreed was to finalize a countrywide reparations plan, and then he blocked the beginning of the commission's work over the inclusion of France as supported by the United States and Great Britain. When Edwin Pauley, the head of the U.S. delegation to the Allied Reparations Commission, called for a joint inspection trip through Germany's industrial zones, Molotov refused to let Maisky participate. Maisky was also forced to stall in responding to Western demands that the Soviets provide details on their reparations plans, specifically from what sources they expected to draw reparation deliveries in the amount of $10 billion.[43] Without instructions from the leadership, Soviet officials hedged on specifics. Internally, Maisky acknowledged that further delays on these long-standing Western requests put him in a position that was "awkward to the highest degree."[44]

As the Potsdam Conference drew near, Maisky prodded his leadership to accept a request by Pauley, put forward in a private discussion, to agree at least to a percentage key and to a joint mechanism for early removal of certain plants and goods prior to finalizing an overall reparations agreement. Such a mechanism had the advantage that "we could begin with certain removals in the Anglo-American zone where particularly many German industrial plants were concentrated." There was, however, a "negative aspect," Maisky conceded: such a mechanism would "inevitably also extend to our zone," given that Pauley "was steadfast in emphasizing that Germany had to be considered as a unified economic whole" when it came to reparations. Could not a solution to this dilemma be found, Maisky suggested, "by taking the most important items out of our zone during, let's say, the next month and a half, and simultaneously maneuver so that the mechanism proposed by Pauley actually begins functioning no earlier than the middle of August?"[45] But the Soviet leadership had little interest in restricting its free hand in its zone, and by mid-July refused to discuss the issue at all.[46]

Indeed, Maisky's disingenuous suggestion to preempt removals under an Allied reparations plan by unilateral early dismantling in the Soviet zone spelled out the very strategy Stalin had pursued since Yalta by creating faits accomplis on the ground.[47] Two weeks after Yalta, the State Defense Committee, the highest Soviet governmental decision body during the war, established a "Special Committee," headed by Georgy Malenkov, to end the organizational confusion and competition over war trophies that mounted in the wake of the Red Army's push into central Europe. The committee was to coordinate "special removals" in order to carry away industrial plants and equipment in large quantities, as fast and as secretly as possible.

FIGURE 2. Dismantled railroad tracks at the Potsdam Station in Berlin, July 1945. Credit: Gerhard Gronefeld/Deutsches Historisches Museum, Berlin.

Soviet reparation planning had emphasized the need for a fast-track removal of industrial equipment and trains since early 1944, and by February of that year plans had been drawn up anticipating deployment of five thousand agents representing some eighty-five people's commissariats and other institutions to Germany. In March 1945, thousands of Soviet agents (some 70,000 by one estimate) from the Special Committee, various people's commissariats, scientific and academic institutions in Moscow, and even from individual industrial plants began to "sweep" the zone in search of materials and installations that could be transported to the Soviet Union. With their commissariat's interests uppermost in mind, these agents often fiercely competed with one another and the Soviet occupation authorities. Contrasting sharply with Soviet inertia in the Reparations Commission, Stalin signed off on hundreds of dismantling orders within a few weeks.[48]

The first wave focused on the greater Berlin area, where months earlier, Soviet agents had identified 122 large plants for removal. Under the banner "Ship Off Everything" (Alles auf die Räder), the agents dismantled (or destroyed) large quantities of industrial equipment, particularly in Berlin's western parts, which were expected to come under Western control according to the Allied agreement. So rushed was the Soviet removal effort in Berlin in May and June 1945 that Moscow officials could not keep up with approvals. The dismantling frenzy during the eight weeks when western Berlin was under Soviet occupation resulted in the loss of half of its industrial capacity. It would amount to 8 percent of the total Soviet removals from its occupation zone in Germany![49]

The American delegation to the Big Three conference arrived in Berlin in the immediate aftermath of this feverish dismantling effort. By the time the conference convened, nearly 50 percent of the total number of plants to be dismantled by the USSR in the aftermath of the war had been approved for removal and largely shipped off.[50] Charged with assuring the self-sufficiency of the zone, the freshly appointed head of the Soviet Military Administration (SMA) in Germany, Marshal Georgy Zhukov, was concerned about the "beginning deindustrialization" of eastern Germany as a result of the unrestrained removals; leading Soviet officials fretted that the relentless dismantling effort was creating "an economic vacuum" in the zone. German historian Jochen Laufer has persuasively argued that Stalin's unilateral trophy removals effectively preempted the zonal reparations scheme that would be agreed to at Potsdam.[51]

Decision at Potsdam

Reports of the Red Army ravaging the lands that it occupied had alarmed Truman administration officials in the weeks leading up to Potsdam. But it was not until Truman's entourage had arrived in Berlin that the extent of the removals became shockingly evident to the president and his advisers. After the several-mile drive from the airport, Truman's group reached Babelsberg, the "movie colony district" of Potsdam, where the American delegation was dispersed among thirty-eight houses that had been requisitioned. The Berlin White House, a dirty yellow damaged French château that had been fixed up for Truman, had been "stripped of everything by the Russians." The president marveled in his diary on July 16: "not even a tin spoon left!" But the American commander in charge, the president was told, had "caught the Russian loot train and recovered enough furniture to make the place livable."[52] In the afternoon, Truman, Byrnes, and Admiral William D. Leahy were driven into Berlin, witnessing "absolute ruin" and "sorrowful sight[s]," including the "deluded Hitlerian populace." "*Of course* [my emphasis] the Russians have kidnapped the able bodied and I suppose have made involuntary workmen of them. They have also looted every house left standing and have sent the loot to Russia." Truman acknowledged that "Hitler did the same thing to them."[53]

Trips into Berlin—ironically, often to hunt for souvenirs themselves—left members of the U.S. conference delegation reeling from the evidence of Russian removals. American officials surmised the extent of what had been taken in the areas occupied by the Red Army "from the conditions we find in the Berlin area,"[54] as McCloy noted in his diary. Averell Harriman, who had arrived for the Potsdam Conference from war-torn Moscow, recalled being impressed by "how completely the Russians had stripped every factory they could get their hands on." The Soviet conception of "surplus" to be taken from Germany was evidently far tougher than what the Americans could agree to. The Allied Reparations Commission had been meeting in Moscow and "talking endlessly about percentages, and all this time the Russians had been helping themselves to everything of any value in the Eastern Zone and in Berlin. I decided after seeing the situation for myself that while there was nothing we could do to stop the Russians from taking whatever they wanted out of their own zone, we ought to give them nothing from the Western Zones."[55] Stimson seemed to have been affected as well: Davies detected "quite a change in his attitude towards the Russians." It was "quite the contrast to the opinions he had expressed in Washington."[56]

Soviet dismantling practices thus had a profound impact on the American delegation: "There is constant repetition of the whispered suggestions of how ruthless the Russian Army had been in looting and shipping back vast quantities of everything from cattle to plumbing fixtures taken from houses etc," Davies confided to his journal. "It is being sedulously circulated. The atmosphere is poisoned with it."[57] Davies grew so concerned about the possibility that the issue would prevent an agreement at Potsdam that he met with Soviet deputy foreign minister Andrei Vyshinski on July 29 to emphasize that "there had been a great deal of discussion over alleged removal of plants by the Russians in the Berlin area by so-called 'looting.'" Later that day, he impressed Molotov, in a handwritten diary passage that was not transcribed until years later, when much of the material was prepared for publication, that "it would be very harmful if the correspondents in Berlin, after being [bottled?—illegible] up, when censorship no longer tied their hand [sic], would make a scandal over alleged looting in the Russian zone which would be followed by countercharges by Russian papers."[58] Davies understood the explosive nature of the Soviet removals.

U.S. officials' concerns over Soviet dismantling in the eastern zone were aggravated by arguments that Maisky advanced in the Potsdam discussions to consider all removals taken thus far as war booty rather than reparations, without any accounting. Ignoring far more limited proposals for war booty and reparations

FIGURE 3. President Harry S. Truman, Secretary of State James Byrnes, and Fleet Admiral William Leahy (left to right in the rear seat of the car) inspect the ruins of Hitler's Chancellery in Berlin, July 16, 1945. Credit: U.S. Army Signal Corps, Courtesy of Harry S. Truman Library.

developed internally in mid-July by Eugene Varga, official Soviet conference documents presumed an expansive definition of trophy removals. Moreover, Varga had distanced himself from a complete destruction of German war potential as an unrealistic goal, yet the official Soviet claim for war trophies included all of Germany's armaments-related industries, whether already removed or still standing but slated for dismantling.[59] In light of such a broad definition of trophies, "the matter of the treatment of Germany as an economic unit," John McCloy observed, "rather goes by the boards."[60] Exasperated by the Soviet fait accompli, Pauley warned of the dire consequences of Soviet (and French) policies: "After they have looted their own zone, they will come around and ask for 'their share' of our zones. Is the horse being stolen?"[61] American officials were determined not to finance imports into the Soviet zone necessitated by the rapid depletion of that zone. If Germany were now treated as one economic unit, American and British taxpayers would essentially pay for Soviet removals in the east.[62]

Even worse from a U.S. perspective, the Soviet government claimed a role in the Rhein-Ruhr industrial complex by suggesting a trusteeship for the area. Truman's advisers agreed that Stalin's hands ought to be kept out of the Ruhr, a region whose strategic economic importance grew with every removal from the Soviet zone to the east. Upon learning about the Soviet proposal, McCloy argued that the United States should counter with a trusteeship or internationalization of the Chemnitz area in the north of the Soviet zone: "I do not see how we can possibly agree to Russian participation in the Ruhr if we do not participate in the East to some degree," probably recognizing that this would be a non-starter for Moscow.[63] Within days it became clear that the Americans were resolved not to let Stalin get his fingers on the Ruhr: McCloy expected a "few yells if we do not go along with the Russians on the Ruhr," but "it may have a healthy result."[64]

"After long discussion and a consideration of the consequences," Truman's team settled on the idea to let the Soviet Union satisfy its need for reparations exclusively from its own zone: "we had to let the Russians look to their zone for reparations and we look to ours for reparations for other countries."[65] Prewar statistics dug up by the Allied Reparations Commission could be interpreted to suggest that the economic value of the territory under Soviet administration equaled roughly 40 percent to 50 percent of the total, about the same percentage of reparations that the USSR could have expected in an agreement covering all of Germany. Rather than endlessly quarreling over the removals—whether "war booty" should be counted as reparations, about how much Germany should pay, and what forms these payments would take—each side would take whatever it wanted from the areas it controlled.[66]

FIGURE 4. Soviet Foreign Minister Vyacheslav Molotov (left, back to camera) shaking hands with Secretary of State James Byrnes during the Potsdam Conference, July 27, 1945. Credit: U.S. Army Signal Corps, Courtesy of Harry S. Truman Library.

On July 23, Byrnes tabled the zonal approach as the core principle to resolve the reparations conundrum. As Pauley told his Soviet counterpart, the reparations program could "best be conducted on a zonal basis" and "not by treating Germany as a single economic unit." Pauley noted that "here in Berlin it has been impossible not to observe that extensive removals of capital equipment of all kinds have been made by the Soviet Government both from the American zone of occupation prior to our occupation, and from the Soviet zone." Moscow's rejection of the first-charge principle forced the United States and the UK to import food and other supplies into Germany without compensation. As a result, the Western powers would essentially be advancing funds to provide for German reparations deliveries (the bulk of which were slated to go to the USSR). Unwilling to foot the bill for Germany's reparations as it had done after World War I, the United States would "deal with [its] reparations along the same lines" as the Soviets had. The zonal approach was portrayed as the "regrettable but inescapable" result of the Soviet unilateralism in its zone.[67]

In the conception of Byrnes and his advisers, Marc Trachtenberg has argued, this zonal approach was not limited to reparations alone; it would also govern Germany's foreign trade and would allow each zonal authority to control exports and imports—and not just with other countries, but even with the other zones. The Soviet Union, Byrnes assured Molotov in Potsdam, would not have to worry about financing imports into western zones and be hamstrung by the first-charge principle. In the minds of some in the American delegation, the scheme also implied some form of "three-party economic rule" in Western Germany, "a sort of politico-economic grouping in the West." It was better to have a "clear line of distinction and negotiate across that line." McCloy aptly underlined the very pragmatic advantages of the zonal formula: "This situation is better than the constant distrust and difficulty we would have with the Russians over their being in our zones, knowing what goes on in theirs and we not being in theirs." But the broader geopolitical ramifications of the new arrangement were clear: "It has tremendous significance for Europe," the U.S. assistant secretary of war acknowledged, but the alternative carried even "more sinister" risks, considering "the atmosphere in which negotiations are conducted in Berlin today."[68]

Soviet officials knew that the "American plan" carried considerable risks for their side, particularly by shutting the door to the industrial riches of the Ruhr. Experts from the renowned Institute of World Economy and World Politics in Moscow had estimated that as much as one-third of the total German military-industrial potential was located in the Ruhr area alone. A commission led by the Soviet people's commissar for industry, Ivan F. Tevosyan, suggested that the Ruhr district had suffered comparatively little from Allied military operations. According to the Tevosyan Commission, about 35 percent of the buildings and structures of the enterprises were damaged or destroyed but only about 5–15 percent of the equipment was put out of operation. They presumed that the Ruhr's production capacity had been reduced by only about 20 percent.

These estimates raised the specter of restoring the Ruhr region's productive capacity before too long. From Isador Lubin, the deputy U.S. representative on the Allied Reparations Commission who had visited western Germany earlier that year, Maisky had learned that the Americans expected the Rhein-Ruhr industry to recover completely within a year. He promptly passed that information to Molotov. Maxim M. Litvinov, a former Soviet ambassador to the United States who now chaired the Soviet Commission for the Preparation of the Peace Treaties and Postwar Order, warned that it was absolutely clear that there was "a tendency in the West not to destroy the industry of the Ruhr district but to put it under international administration or control, intending to concentrate this control in the hands of the Western countries."[69]

The strongest objections to the zonal solution continued to come from Eugene Varga. Shortly after Byrnes had advanced the zonal-formula idea, Georgy P. Arkadeev, deputy head of the Soviet Foreign Ministry's economic department, sought to stiffen "our arguments against the existing American plan."[70] Basing his analysis on Varga's estimates, he warned Molotov that only 30 percent of all materials available for dismantling were located in the Soviet zone and that the USSR was entitled to some $7 billion worth of deliveries from the western "zone."[71] When Molotov seemed nonetheless agreeable to apply the zonal principle not just to one-time removals but also to annual deliveries from current production, Maisky made a final pitch to Molotov to prevent its application to the latter, given the "Americans' adamant insistence" on the former. In view of the "relative poverty of our zone," the USSR would not be able to cover its share of reparations from current production if the zonal principle applied.[72]

It was not to be. The American reparations formula played to Stalin's predilections for retaining a free hand in the Soviet zone. Molotov consented to Byrnes's plan and signaled his readiness to negotiate on the basis of the zonal principle that very same day. "The basis for an agreement" was there, McCloy noted in his diary, but several days of "great horse trading" ensued over the question of the relative value of the zones and respective import needs. The negotiators went "round and round the mulberry bush" until the wee hours.[73] Molotov finally agreed to a package deal mediated by Davies, which sweetened the agreement by including American recognition of the western borders of Poland.[74] Further negotiations also assured the Soviet Union 25 percent of all reparations that could be extracted from the western zones (15 percent in exchange for food, coal, potash, timber, and other products from eastern Germany). Stalin, in turn, dropped his insistence on shares in stocks of those enterprises to remain in the western zones and German gold and foreign assets, removing the last obstacle to the deal.[75] Firm Soviet control of the occupation zone trumped broader economic and political interests. The Soviet leadership felt that the "Berlin Conference" decisions on reparations presented a "step forward."[76]

Byrnes's efforts at Potsdam to work out a modus vivendi with the Soviets based on the idea of autonomous zonal development were rooted in his belief, shared by Truman and a growing number of administration officials, that lasting cooperation was not possible. The American leadership accepted that much of the region would become a sphere in which the Soviets would run the show. At the London Council of Foreign Ministers meeting in September, Byrnes signed off on Soviet dominance in Romania and Bulgaria. For all intents and purposes Byrnes was writing off much of east-central Europe, including eastern Germany, as a Soviet domain.[77]

By mid-1945, Byrnes's views of the relationship with the Soviets—and his conclusions for joint control of Germany—were, however, not yet shared by everyone within the administration. Truman himself appeared to condone the feelings of his secretary of state at times, while at other moments he seemed convinced that he could work out a deal with the Soviet leader. One of Truman's aides aptly captured this ambivalent feeling, noting that Stalin was considered by most on the delegation as "the most likable horse thief I have ever seen."[78] Unease and uncertainty about the implications of the reparations deal persisted even among Truman's closest advisers: While some thought zonal separation was "inevitable," others, like McCloy, confessed to be "undecided" and "hate[d] to give up the idea of treating Germany as a single economic unit."[79] Even a skeptic such as McCloy felt that "we shall get somewhere in trying to work out with the Russians the things they should take out of their zone."[80] Most importantly for a politician so attuned to congressional and media opinion as Byrnes was, much of the American public was not yet ready to abandon hopes for Soviet-American amity in running Germany. Hence the Potsdam Conference declaration buried the essential Byrnes-Molotov deal on reparations in calls for a unitary treatment of Germany.

The "Big Three" called for the unified treatment of Germany by the Allies in matters of de-nazification, democratization, de-cartelization, de-militarization, and economic policy, and envisioned the establishment of central German administrations in the fields of finance, transport, communications, foreign trade, and industry, headed by German state secretaries under the control of the Allied Control Council. The conference documents mandated Allied agreement within six months on a country-wide level of industry plan based on a minimum living standard for Germany that was not to exceed the European average (excluding the UK and the USSR).[81]

But the reparations formula adopted at Potsdam split Germany into two economic zones. Playing to the desires of both sides for a free hand in occupation policy, it set eastern and western Germany on very different economic trajectories that would make quadripartite governance (after France was granted its own occupation zone in western Germany) difficult at best. It reflected and reinforced the binary thinking that increasingly pervaded the discourse in Allied capitals. "Eastern and Western Germany are two separate economic units, run by Russia and the three Western powers respectively," noted a British official later that year.[82] Soviet officials more frequently spoke of the "western zone" (rather than "zones") when referring to the three Western Allied territories. Such thinking was not limited to the economic sphere alone: diverging political futures for both parts of Germany seemed in the offing. "There will be two Germanies," Stalin told German Communist leaders as early as June 1945.[83] John J. McCloy confessed to his diary that "[w]e are drifting towards a line down the middle of Germany."[84]

"Western Democracy on the Elbe"?

Rollback through Cooperation

IN THE WAKE OF THE POTSDAM CONFERENCE, the U.S. military government in Germany, led by General Dwight D. Eisenhower and his deputy military governor, Lucius D. Clay, emerged as the decisive proponent of cooperation with the Soviets in Germany. Conceptually this put Eisenhower and Clay in stark opposition to Secretary of State Byrnes, whose championing of a zonal reparations solution had been based on the conviction, shared by many within the State Department, that long-term cooperation with the USSR was not possible. Eisenhower, Clay, and the new political adviser to the U.S. Military Government, Robert D. Murphy, who had served as chief diplomatic adviser at Eisenhower's wartime headquarters, viewed common Allied economic interests in Germany as the best strategy for preventing a "walling off" of the occupation zones and—ambitiously—therefore to "roll back" Soviet power in the eastern part of the country.

Conscious of the hardships that the Soviet people had endured during the war, Eisenhower believed deeply that they had earned America's trust. Few Americans had as much a sense as Eisenhower did of the paramount role that the USSR had played in the defeat of Germany; now he held Soviet-American partnership to be a key to the postwar peace. He wanted four-power government to succeed, and he regarded Berlin as an experimental laboratory for the development of international accord and quadripartite agencies as the catalyst: "The more contact we have with the Russians," he told his naval aide, Harry Butcher, "the more they will understand us and the greater will be the co-operation."[1] In May, presidential adviser Harry

Hopkins had conveyed to Stalin, in person, Eisenhower's desire to visit Moscow—
a request that the Soviet leader welcomed warmly. On June 5, 1945, the very day
that the Allied powers assumed supreme authority in Germany, the presidium of
the Supreme Soviet of the USSR awarded Eisenhower the "Order of Victory" for
his contribution to the Allied victory over Germany. Two months later, Eisenhower
visited Moscow and Leningrad at the invitation of the Red Army leadership, meeting
Stalin on August 13. The trip reinforced the enormous respect that Soviet leaders
felt for the general.[2]

On the day-to-day occupation operations, it fell to General Clay to implement
Eisenhower's approach, and Clay made it his mission.[3] President Franklin Roosevelt
had "acquiesced" to Clay's appointment to the "Germany job" just days before he
died. A Jeffersonian liberal, Clay was committed to the president's concept of a single
postwar world.[4] He had come to the Germany job after three years of operating at the
peak of the vast U.S. war mobilization effort, "a vantage point that afforded human
understanding of how a major industrial economy functions."[5] He brought to his
post an outstanding mind, "a legendary capacity for relentless hard-driving work,
the ability to make swift independent decisions and extensive experience in dealing
with top civilian leaders."[6] Without much prior knowledge about Germany, and
certainly unfamiliar with the policies and tripartite agreements that were to govern
the occupation, Clay essentially took the Potsdam communiqué as a directive by
his new commander in chief, President Truman. Confronted with suspicions about
Soviet intentions to fulfill the Potsdam program voiced by senior State Department
officials H. Freeman Matthews and James Riddleberger, who briefed him on the
negotiations shortly after the conference, Clay bristled: not abiding by the Potsdam
agreements "would mean that I should deviate from what the President determined
at the conference."[7]

What had been determined in Potsdam was, in fact, not entirely clear. Even
within the Truman administration, there was considerable uncertainty about what
had been decided, especially on economic matters. During the conference, decision-
making had been disjointed and at times ad hoc in response to events on the ground.
Assistant Secretary of War John J. McCloy, praised by Byrnes as the person within
the administration who was most knowledgeable about German affairs, was initially not privy to many of the State Department consultations or included in the
conference sessions dealing with Germany. "The place," McCloy noted during the
early stages of the Potsdam Conference, "is full of rumors." Instead of a coherent
discussion among the key American officials, such as Byrnes, Clay, Assistant Secretary of State William Clayton, and McCloy, and their British counterparts, the

FIGURE 5. General Dwight D. Eisenhower (left) talks with Lieutenant General Lucius D. Clay at Gatow Field, Berlin, July 20, 1945. They are attending the Potsdam Conference. From Potsdam album, 1945. Credit: U.S. Army Signal Corps, Courtesy of Harry S. Truman Library.

zonal reparations solution had evolved out of a "series of talks, rather unrelated," McCloy felt, "to the real problems, and with only one point of view expressed at a time." The disjointed nature of the decision-making on Germany in Potsdam mirrored to his mind an acute lack of integration of "our whole policy with respect to Russia." McCloy himself struggled to understand the full measure of what had been decided, confessing to his diary toward the end of the Potsdam Conference that "where Clay stands, I do not exactly know."[8]

Clay had arrived in Europe in early April and been impressed with the practical challenges facing the United States in Germany—especially the calamitous food situation. By the time the Big Three convened in Potsdam, Clay had concluded that treating Germany as a single "economic unit" was the only way to address the food shortages, economic dislocations, and trade imbalances that beset the American occupation mission. Clay was convinced—and McCloy apparently agreed—that it would be critical to revive trade within the old Reich and that coal surplus in Silesia, even as it was slated to come under Polish administration, should become available

for German needs, to be paid for by export proceeds. He had asked McCloy to make
sure that Assistant Secretary of State William Clayton and Political Adviser Robert
Murphy fully understood his views on the matter.[9] His post-conference briefing by
the State Department suggested that the "hands-off policy" initially envisioned in
occupation directive JCS #1067—which had become effective on July 15, 1945—
had been overtaken by the responsibility of the occupation powers to develop a balanced economy within a unified Germany.[10] Dismissive of the State Department's
misgivings about Soviet actions, Clay chose to downplay (or failed to grasp fully)
the full repercussions of the zonal alternative built into Byrnes's Potsdam "package
deal" on reparations. Unified treatment of Germany required continued Allied, including Soviet, cooperation. Questioned about the future of Allied relations at his
first press conference in mid-May 1945, Clay had slammed his fist into his other
hand and declared: "It's got to work. If the four of us cannot get together now in
running Germany, how are we going to get together in an international organization to secure the peace of the world?"[11]

Single-mindedly focused on making Allied cooperation work, Clay was willing
to look past Red Army "excesses in the Russian area." The "rather primitive way
the war is conducted by the Russians" impressed him as self-defeating rather than
effective.[12] His August trip to the Soviet Union alongside Eisenhower reinforced
his sense of Soviet backwardness. Given the immense destruction of Soviet lands by
the Germans, the Soviet government would in Clay's estimation want to cooperate
to retain access to reparations from the western occupation zones. Clay's approach
to the Soviets would in time also derive from his new vantage point in Berlin: from
there the situation in the eastern zone looked far more complex and fluid than it
did from Washington.

Clay had an ally in the State Department's top man in Berlin, Robert Murphy, whose Office of the Political Adviser (with a staff of 100) paralleled the military government's major functions, leading some to see it as an "OMGUS within
OMGUS." A man "with definite and very positive opinions" but "very mild in their
assertion," Murphy brought to his job equanimity and quickly developed a sense for
the complexity of occupation politics in Germany. Like Clay, he had little patience
for communism and, more importantly, thought that communism held little attraction for Germans. In Murphy's view, Soviet policies were quickly dissipating any
remaining goodwill among the German population. According to the testimony of
Joseph Davies, who visited with Murphy on his way to the Potsdam Conference,
the diplomat was convinced that the Soviet long game envisioned nothing less than
the "complete Eurasian domination of Europe."[13] Even so, Murphy believed—once

again in the words of Davies—that "there was a good chance of Allied control working out cooperatively." The "top Russians were obviously cordial and trying to work it out."[14] Murphy, too, considered the Soviet occupation zone, along with the Allied Control Council in Berlin, a "laboratory" for probing Soviet intentions and capabilities. The metaphor, favored by Eisenhower and Clay as well, suggested that the success of joint occupation was by no means preordained: but they would try to make it work if they could.[15]

Fully cognizant of the anti-communist bias among many administration officials, Clay was sensitive to Soviet suspiciousness: He thought that any hesitation on the part of the United States about its withdrawal from the territories in central Germany that were slated for Red Army occupation per the European Advisory Commission agreements was "certain to be misunderstood by Russia."[16] (American withdrawal from these territories started in July.) Conscious of domestic pressure on Byrnes and the administration to address the dire economic situation in the U.S. occupation zone and western Europe, Clay felt "just as apprehensive over possible impatience and lack of understanding at home of our failure to obtain rapid progress" as he did about "our ability in the long run to work out many mutual problems in the Allied Control Council."[17]

Like Murphy, Clay was heartened by the personal relationships that he developed with his Soviet counterparts as the Allied Control Council began its work in mid-1945. Clay saw the Soviet deputy military governor, Vasily Sokolovsky, socially and genuinely respected the former schoolteacher who loved Jane Austen novels and had risen to the highest ranks within the Soviet military. "I am much encouraged by the general attitude of cooperation and the apparent desire, especially on the part of the Russians, to work with us in solving various problems," he wrote to McCloy in September 1945. "I believe we are making real headway in breaking down their feelings of suspicion and distrust."[18] Critical of what he saw as little-disguised British tendencies to apply balance-of-power considerations to German policy, principally in an anti-Soviet direction, Clay and his staff at times favored Soviet proposals over British ones. Perplexed by this "quite odd" behavior, Soviet officials noted that it created the impression that the Americans wanted to play the "role of a friendly mediator" in the Allied Control Council.[19]

Clay may have in fact shared Byrnes's skepticism (and that of many of his State Department colleagues) about the possibilities for longer-term cooperation with the Russians. There was a chance that the Control Council might "become only a negotiating agency," not an "overall government for Germany," he noted in a remark curiously reflective of his vision for the Control Council's mandate.[20] If the four powers could not run Germany as a unit, the Western allies had to consider running western Germany on a tripartite basis, "with full realization of all the implications involved."[21] He was apprehensive when a Soviet general stated in the early phase of the occupation that "Russian gauge" was being placed on railroad tracks in eastern Germany. That indicated to him that "German economy is being thought of as a [four-]unit economy," not a single entity.[22]

Clay combined the top military brass's brother-in-arms empathy for Soviet hardships and security interests with ebullient confidence in the superiority of the American political-economic (and military) system.[23] Whereas Byrnes and many Washington officials emphasized unbridgeable ideological differences with the Soviets as impediments to longer-term cooperation, Clay was inclined to believe that the ideological competition would work out to the advantage of the West, if such competition could take place throughout all of Germany. Whereas many within the administration fretted over the USSR's ulterior motives, Clay and his political adviser, Murphy, came to see Soviet policy in Germany as largely defensive, contradictory, and ultimately self-defeating. While State Department officials viewed the promise of reparations as liabilities, Clay looked at them as levers built into the Potsdam system to force Moscow's hand and extend western influence to the east. Unconvinced by the need for zonal retrenchment implicit in the reparations deal, Clay saw a chance to use the Potsdam agreements to break down zonal boundaries to the West's advantage.

Clay did not naively believe that quadripartite solutions would come easily and quickly. He expected that they would be reached "gradually through long drawn out negotiations" and that the zones would have to be governed "on an almost independent basis for many months."[24] He thought that controversial issues would have to be set aside until less-difficult problems could be solved, and that there would have to be some give-and-take on all sides. In the course of solving these problems, "we may develop a mutual understanding which will later make the difficult ones easier to solve." The lack of delegation of authority to lower-level officials within the Soviet system was bound to make negotiations "extremely slow." The language barriers alone impressed Clay as formidable and likely to slow any progress: free and full discussion would be most difficult and time-consuming. Even more time—"many, many months"—would pass, he assumed, before the Soviets would be willing to allow Allied investigation teams into the Soviet occupation zone.[25]

But *if* solutions could be reached across the four occupation zones; *if* quadripartite agencies could be established throughout Germany; *if*, therefore, the Soviet-controlled zone retained a degree of openness and ties with the western parts, then, Clay believed, the zone would eventually gravitate "West"—and so might other parts of Soviet-controlled Central Europe. Cooperation with the Soviets was for Clay a way to an eventual "rollback" of Soviet power in Germany.

Clay was hopeful that the Soviets would join Allied control mechanisms and that "we will be able to forge a national administration over those things which should be administered nationally."[26] Next to the reparations deal, the most important stipulation agreed to at Potsdam had been the establishment of German central administrations for communications, finance, industry, trade, and transport. Headed and staffed by German officials and acting under Allied Control Council supervision, these agencies would function across the zonal borders as lower-level precursors of a central German government. Both Clay and Murphy argued that these "central agencies," though for now largely limited to economic tasks, would, more than any other Potsdam provision, assure unified treatment of Germany. In opening up channels of exchange among the different parts of the country, they were establishing a prerequisite for stabilizing the western zones economically and for maintaining some measure of influence in the eastern part.

Clay viewed reparations from the western zones, in which, he presumed, the Soviets had a keen interest, as a tool to demonstrate good faith and to incentivize the creation of all-German agencies. In September, the Soviets requested advances on their reparations allocations from the western zones promised to them in Potsdam and submitted a detailed list of some forty industrial plants, nine of which were located in the U.S. occupation zone. Clay advised McCloy that he was "anxious to make available those which will clearly not be needed for the German peace economy." But Clay also insisted that any advance deliveries required a Germany-wide level of industry plan, based on what the Allies considered a "minimum livable German economy." That, in turn, involved knowing what resources were left in the Soviet zone. Hence Clay proposed a "mixed commission" that would investigate the removals that had taken place in eastern Germany. Conceptually Clay's argument cut against the Byrnes-Molotov agreement that left the USSR to its own devices in taking what it wanted from its zone.[27]

Not surprisingly, in response Moscow reaffirmed the Soviet interpretation that the "Berlin Conference" had "established one procedure of reparations collection in the Eastern Zone and another in the Western Zones," thus obviating the need to draw up a single reparations plan. But by mid-September, the Soviet Foreign Ministry signaled its willingness to provide information on removals and to allow inspections by a mixed commission, even consenting to move the Allied Reparations Commission from Moscow to Berlin. This Soviet accommodation seemed to confirm to Clay that the Soviets could be engaged in a cooperative quid pro quo.[28]

On the pivotal question of German central administrations, Russian archival documents suggest, the Soviet position had been rather ambivalent. Before Potsdam, officials in the Soviet People's Commissariat for Foreign Affairs had advised against any central agencies: Central administrations headed by German officials could be seen as precursors for a German government that would signify the end of the occupation period. The specter of reduced occupation control and an end to occupation—just a few weeks after the end of the war with Germany—evoked deepseated anxieties among Soviet officials. Restoring any central governmental powers to the Germans, even at a functional agency level, so soon after war's end seemed as much anathema to the Soviets as it did to the French. From the Soviet perspective, large-scale industrial disarmament, thorough denazification, and the strengthening of a Communist-party-led "democratic bloc" within a new German party system, were prerequisites for the creation of any all-German institutions—processes that would take years to complete. The Soviet occupation chief, Marshal Georgy Zhukov, had reacted with shock on July 10 when Clay suggested that such all-German agencies, established under the Allied Control Council's supervision, might develop into government ministries. The exchange reflected the grave reservations among Soviet officials about any early revival of central German power; it also betrayed the potential envisioned by Clay well before Potsdam that these administrative agencies might become precursors of a future central German government.[29]

Once the zonal reparation solution had been agreed upon "in principle" at Potsdam, it was the Soviet foreign minister who had raised the issue of "whether we still intended to have some central German administration, not a government, but some central organization through which the Control Council could operate in matters affecting finance, transport, foreign trade etc. on which it had been agreed to treat Germany as an economic whole." According to the Russian document of the conversation, Molotov suggested giving such a central administration the responsibility of implementing the Allied reparations agreement, including authority over the Rhein-Ruhr area. Pointing to the emerging zonal reparations scheme, Byrnes rebuffed Molotov's advance but professed agreement once his Soviet counterpart had clarified that he did not imply creating a German government but merely "a central administration for the centralized supervision of such departments as transport, foreign trade, finance, industry, and traffic." Only then did the Soviet delegation formally request the establishment of central administrations in Germany. Rather than an attempt to gain influence on the western coal and steel industrial hub, or even to achieve a dramatic reversal of the Soviet attitude toward any kind of central administrative agencies, Molotov's overture was probably meant to reassure himself of Western intentions in light of the zonal reparations scheme and to forestall potential Western reach into the Soviet occupation zone via such agencies.[30] For Clay's purposes, however, the Soviet government was on record in support of central German administrations.

Instead of the Soviets, it was the French government that emerged in Clay's eyes as the immediate obstacle to his drive for central German agencies. When a proposal for the creation of a central German administration for transport was tabled in the Allied Control Council's Transport Directorate on September 12, the French military governor, General Marie Louis Koeltz, invoked the French veto the next day. In a memorandum to the Council of Foreign Ministers, which was meeting in London September 11 to October 2, Foreign Minister Georges Bidault made French agreement to central administrations contingent on the separation of the Rhineland and Westphalia from Germany. Five days later, the Allied Control Council's Directorate for Internal Affairs proposed a central German postal administration. Following the Control Council session on September 20, Eisenhower queried Soviet deputy military governor Vasily Sokolovsky about his position on central administrations and emphasized that such a step should not be delayed. According to the Soviet memorandum of the conversation, Eisenhower suggested that, should the creation of such agencies and thus joint Allied policies fail to develop, the question arose as to the purpose of a continued U.S. troop presence in Europe. Koeltz confirmed to Eisenhower that France rejected the creation of all-German administrations: they impeded, he argued, the destruction of German military potential and offered the Germans an opportunity to sabotage Allied efforts.[31]

France had been a latecomer as an occupation power: its zone was carved out of the initially projected American and British zones after Yalta. Not invited to participate in the Potsdam Conference, the French government had learned of the Allied agreements only two days before they were signed and objected strongly to the establishment of central German administrative departments led by German state secretaries. Part of a tough-toned public discourse that appealed to the French populist demands for revenge, security, and economic rehabilitation, the French government objected in principle to any kind of German-led central institutions that could be seen as prejudicing a future German central government and a final territorial settlement. Paris hence withheld authority from its representatives in the Allied Control Council in Berlin to negotiate or agree to any decisions on central German agencies.

Recent scholarship has emphasized that this maximalist position was only one dimension of an evolving French approach to the German question that combined harsh rhetoric with security policy priorities focused on decentralization, economic supremacy, democratization and long-term rapprochement. Charged to administer an occupation zone that was incapable of subsisting on its own, the French government had in fact a vital interest in treating Germany as an economic unit and thus creating central economic agencies. France was thus not opposed to the uniform treatment of occupied Germany, nor to central agencies as such (it proposed "Allied offices" in 1946), only to *German-headed* central administrations. Offensively projected, the French "obstruction" on such agencies was also rooted in growing concerns that the Soviets would gain control over them and thus expand their influence into western Germany. For domestic political reasons—the Communists were part of the government coalition until 1946—French leaders could not openly admit to such motivation. Foreign Minister Georges Bidault, the most important figure in French foreign policy in the immediate postwar period, referred to the German danger as a "convenient myth" that provided political cover for a policy that was directed against the Soviet threat.[32]

British government officials in London shared French skepticism about German central administrations: such agencies would afford Moscow opportunities to exert influence across Germany while, as William Strang, political adviser to the British military governor, perceptively noted, "the Russian oppose any proposal that is likely to open a window into their zone." While the British deputy military governor, Sir Brian Robertson, backed the insistence on such agencies by his counterpart Clay, British Foreign Office officials made it clear that they would "not regard the French proposals with an unsympathetic eye." British foreign minister Ernest Bevin in fact asked Byrnes "not to press the French too hard" and immediately relayed his intervention to Bidault. In a remarkable transatlantic alignment, reservations about Clay's approach to German central agencies (and sympathy for the French position) were also widely shared within the State Department.[33]

The lackluster nature of British (and Soviet) official support for the rapid establishment of German central administrations was entirely overshadowed by the French stance against such agencies. Fully aware of the French position, Sokolovsky expressed agreement with Eisenhower when pressed by the U.S. occupation chief after the September 20 Control Council session, arguing that German central agencies were intended after all only to execute Allied orders. He formally agreed to the establishment of a German transport and postal administration at the September 22 meeting of the Control Council's coordinating committee. Two days later, Clay, outraged by what he perceived as unreasonable and rigid French obstructionism on one of the core Potsdam decisions, asked the U.S. War Department for permission to propose establishing German central administrations on a tri-zonal (American-British-Soviet) basis. Three days after Clay proposed in the Control Council that zonal commanders might be authorized to negotiate bilaterally if the French vetoed central administrations, the British government effectively rejected such a proposal. But the British rejection was eclipsed by France's decision, announced by Koeltz on October 1, to withdraw its representatives from all Control Council deliberations on German central administrations.[34]

If recent scholarship has "exonerated" France as the great obstructionist in the Allied Control Council, Clay has emerged as the new bogeyman. In the face of the Soviet imposition of police-state party dictatorships in eastern Europe, Clay's "simplicité brutale" in pursuing his occupation goals, especially German central administrations, retrospectively is seen as naive, futile, and shortsighted. Yet these views fail to appreciate the seriousness with which Clay hoped to engage his Soviet counterparts to exert a measure of restraint on their actions in the East and possibly roll back Soviet influence. Exasperated by the French and British positions, Clay in fact considered proceeding unilaterally with the Soviets, as the Soviet archival documents that have only recently become available reveal: In a one-on-one with Sokolovsky the day after the French veto, Clay intimated that he would propose to Washington an agreement with the Soviet government to establish central German administrations for their two zones: "Then the others," Sokolovsky reported Clay's saying, "would willy-nilly have to follow." He apparently also told his Soviet counterpart that he regretted that the French had been given authority over a part of German territory that had once belonged to the U.S. zone. Now they would not withdraw, for example, from the Saar territory for anything in the world, which apparently explained why they did not want to see central German agencies established. Queried by Sokolovsky about the various efforts evident in France to establish a "Western bloc," something that Soviet observers had suspected for months, Clay emphatically declared that the U.S. government unequivocally rejected any kind of bloc formation; he claimed that ideas of a Western bloc had no support in the United States.[35]

Clay proceeded to outline his essential Rooseveltian vision for the postwar world: According to Sokolovsky's report, Clay maintained that there were currently only two great powers left, the USSR and the United States, and the fate of the world, at least for the next fifty years, depended on friendly relations between them. It was therefore necessary that both countries determine the principles of governing Germany and the policy of the Control Council. At the end of the "relaxed and friendly" conversation, Sokolovsky was left to agree with Clay that both countries pursued the same goals, as evidenced by the friendly interactions of their delegations.[36]

Clay's overture was all the more striking since Washington did not sign off on his proposal for a bilateral or trilateral surge on central administrations until almost three weeks later. Worried over the rise of the French Communists and the stability of the fragile Gaullist government and sharing the latter's concerns about Soviet intentions, State Department officials hesitated to put pressure on Paris, cautioning Clay on October 20 that they sanctioned his initiative "for administrative purposes only," not prejudging the final disposition of the territories.[37]

Despite Clay's assurances to the contrary, Soviet perceptions of a rising "Western bloc" heightened their suspicions about their former allies. While they viewed Eisenhower and Clay personally as genuinely committed to the Potsdam agreements, they repeatedly complained that lower-ranking officials in the Control Council directorates were sabotaging cooperation.[38] Worse, from Moscow's perspective, the West increasingly seemed to be calling the Yalta and Potsdam agreements into question altogether. A U.S. proposal for a 25-year Soviet-American demilitarization pact, pitched by Byrnes to Molotov during the London Council of Foreign Ministers conference in September 1945, was interpreted by Stalin to aim at upending the postwar settlement. Molotov characterized the London CFM as was the "first postwar diplomatic attack of pertinent American and English circles on the foreign policy positions of the USSR accomplished during the war." While the French delegation, according to the Soviet foreign minister, had played a special role in the effort to undermine the decisions of the Potsdam Conference, they had in fact "been indirectly supported by the English and the Americans." On the side of "our [Allied] partners," the Council of Foreign Ministers meeting had demonstrated, the Americans "set the marching tone."[39] In a rare explicit "analysis" two months later, Stalin told Molotov that defending Soviet accomplishments in the wake of the London Council depended on Soviet strength. It was clear, Stalin ventured, that "especially with partners such as the USA and England we cannot accomplish anything if we begin to give in to such intimidation attempts, if we present ourselves as fickle. To get anywhere with such partners we have to arm ourselves with a policy of strength and endurance."[40]

In early November, Clay and Murphy headed to Washington to prod the State Department to change French behavior. Clay noted that the Soviets suspected that "French obstinacy was receiving tacit support from the British and the United States."[41] Pressed by Clay, State Department officials at the meeting many of whom were sympathetic to the French position, had to admit that no steps had been taken to "bring pressure to bear upon the French to cooperate with the other members of the Control Council in carrying out the Berlin protocol with respect to the treatment of Germany as an economic unit." State Department representations to the French officials, such as Foreign Minister Couve de Murville, who visited Washington in mid-November, remained "perfunctory."[42]

Frustrated by the evident absence of pressure on the French government, Clay reacted vehemently when James Riddleberger questioned Moscow's commitment to the Potsdam agreements. Clay "took sharp issue with the point of view that it was the USSR which was failing to carry out the Berlin Protocol," he saw "some merit" in the Soviet refusal to lower zonal barriers in the face of the lack of progress on all-German agencies, and he argued that "the USSR had gone further than the French in the introduction of democratic procedure in their zone" and, in such matters as the land reform (which it had launched in the fall of 1945), was "acting unilaterally in the absence of quadripartite agreement." The "entire record" of the Control Council showed that the USSR was "willing to cooperate with the other powers in operating Germany as a single political and economic unit."[43]

The archival "record," however, suggests that the reality was more complex than either Clay or his critics in Washington and Paris made it out to be. To be sure, deputy SMA chief Sokolovsky seemed open to Clay's overtures, clearly a key cause for the deputy U.S. military governor's optimism. Soviet Foreign Ministry officials now generally supported the establishment of central agencies. Maxim Litvinov felt that it was in Soviet interests to create such administrative mechanisms that would be accountable to the Control Council.[44] Andrey A. Smirnov, head of the Foreign Ministry's Third European Department, which was responsible for Germany, found the proposals for central transportation and postal administrations drafted within the Control Council in line with the Potsdam decisions to be "satisfactory" and "acceptable," and urged Molotov to instruct Marshal Zhukov to raise the issue again within the Control Council or to pursue it by diplomatic means.[45]

But when it came to granting German central agencies working under the Allied Control Council competencies in such crucial areas as finance or economic policy, Soviet officials suspiciously sought to contain any infringement on full control of their zone: Within days after meeting with Clay in early October, Sokolovsky himself, for example, had attempted to limit the authority of a proposed German central administration for finance for the sake of preserving the fiscal autonomy of the Soviet zone. And in mid-October, faced with American insistence in the Control Council's Economic Directorate on establishing central agencies as quickly as possible, the SMA's economic administration had advised the Soviet Foreign Ministry bluntly that it was "currently not in fact interested in accelerating the organization of these departments."[46] Most importantly, Stalin and his foreign minister remained silent on the issue.

Once he was back in Berlin in mid-November, Clay, according to the Russian documents now accessible, reiterated to Sokolovsky his offer of establishing joint (U.S.-British-Soviet) central administrations, explicitly underlining his authorization from Washington to do so. In response, Sokolovsky stated evasively that proceeding in such a way would "pose problems for our governments as the French could interpret this to mean their zone was entirely excluded from Germany and left to their devices." Clay dismissed such concerns, optimistic that the French would join a central administration for all zones sooner or later. According to the Soviet minutes of the November 15 meeting, he even—remarkably—thought it possible to begin with the creation of an American-Soviet central administration, which could also be seen as a signal that the United States had no intention of joining any Western bloc projects and that "effective cooperation between our two countries was possible." Clay seemed particularly "insistent" on a joint U.S.-Soviet central administration for telecommunications. Sokolovsky assured Clay that he would "rethink the issue once more" and consult with his leadership in the matter. Clay's proposals were relayed to Moscow the same day.[47]

A week later, Deputy People's Commissar for Foreign Affairs Andrei Vyshinsky confirmed to Zhukov that Clay's ambitious proposal had to be rejected: it was not expedient to agree to the American proposals, as that would create a precedent for circumventing the principle of unanimity in Control Council decisions.[48] Fearful that such a precedent might justify Allied interventions in the Soviet zone, the Soviet government was more than happy to let the matter rest where the French veto had left it.[49]

The ambiguity of the Soviet attitude toward Clay's aggressive push for central administrations was not just a result of the hypersensitivity about any encroachments on the control of their zone. At the beginning of December 1945 the head of the Third European Department in the Soviet Foreign Ministry, Andrey A. Smirnov, reminded Molotov of the fundamental concern about these agencies: the creation of central departments was a first step in the formation of a central German government and in the unshackling of the occupation regime, which, given the presumed lack of demilitarization and denazification in the western zones could have grave consequences. Smirnov also insisted that the USSR make its approval of such agencies contingent on the prior implementation of those aspects of the Potsdam agreements that were "of particular interest to us"—reparations, disbanding the German fleet, and the implementation of certain political and economic principles in the treatment of Germany. Central administrations apparently were not.[50]

At a more practical level, much of the ambivalent reception of Clay's push for such administrations was owed to the fact that the Soviet Military Administration lagged behind its Western counterparts in organization and was not fully functional until late 1945. By the end of the year, the deputy head of the SMA's Political Department, Vladimir Semenov, complained that Soviet officials in various occupation capacities had spoken "without having a specifically formulated and coordinated point of view," which at times had led to disputes with the Allies over trivia. "Instances took place when our representatives in committees, for one reason or another, spoke from one point of view but in the directorate, from another, directly contradictory [point of view]."[51]

Contrasting with worries in the West that Moscow would seize the all-German administrations to extend its influence into the western zones, bureaucratic disconnects and inertia within the Soviet government continued to plague its approach to these agencies: "All the specific proposals" with regard to central administrative structures, Semenov alerted Zhukov in December, so far "had come from the [Western] Allies."[52] Internal deliberations showed that Soviet officials felt very much on the defensive. They were far behind Western preparations for all-German agencies. Smirnov warned Molotov in early December 1945 that "at this time we do not yet have the necessary [German] cadres capable of taking on the leadership of central administrations."[53]

Convinced that the Soviet Military Administration was entirely unprepared should central German administrations come about in the near future, Semenov argued two weeks later that the personnel choices for these administrations would be critical: Problematic relations with future German administrations could have damaging effects on relations with the Allies. He urged Moscow to counterbalance what he called Western Allied "centers for the selection of German officials" to have "a solid reserve of German organizers at our disposal who are known throughout Germany and who satisfy us with their political characteristics." As far as he could tell, there was "presently no clarity in SMA departments on the issue of whom we will propose as candidates for major and minor posts from the Soviet Zone."[54]

Semenov implored Zhukov to have the SMA outline its views on the central agencies to the American and British in greater detail, "select our candidates for the positions of greatest interest to us, develop them beforehand, and, if possible, also be instructed by the "special [intelligence] agencies."[55] Semenov warned internally that under no circumstances "can we [or] should we leave the national German administrative departments to the Americans and British."[56]

As a result, Zhukov put Semenov in charge of developing cadres and plans for the day when central administrations would be established.[57] By the end of February 1946, Semenov could finally report that SMA's postal, transport, finance, and foreign trade administrations had developed regulations and organizational charts for respective national agencies, though neither Soviet nor Western candidate lists had apparently been examined for their political viability.[58] But even at that point, Moscow's approval to proceed with the preparations for central administrations was still not forthcoming.

In Moscow and in the Soviet Military Administration headquarters in Karlshorst, suspicions heightened over presumed Western intrusions into the Soviet occupation zone.[59] From discussions with Communist youth leaders in the Soviet zone Heinz Kessler (who later became East Germany's defense minister) and Erich Honecker (who later came to lead East Germany's party-state), Soviet occupation officials learned that Protestant churches in their zone were allegedly receiving support from U.S. authorities to establish youth organizations. The churches were actively seeking to gain influence over the youth, particularly in those parts of the Soviet zone formerly under U.S. occupation.[60] Soviet officials noted that the Americans were reportedly "doing everything to gain influence over the churches in the Soviet zone."[61]

British efforts, in Soviet eyes aimed at paralyzing the growing Communist influence in Germany by driving a wedge into the antifascist party bloc that had been formed in the eastern zone in the summer of 1945, began to show their first results. Statements by leading Social Democrats in the Soviet zone signaled to Soviet observers their increased "Western orientation in thinking."[62]

The Soviets viewed Eisenhower's and Clay's push to open the Soviet zone to Western media with particular suspicion. In November, Eisenhower personally pressed Zhukov to allow American journalist to travel in the Soviet zone. Vyshinsky had warned Zhukov already of an increased anti-Soviet campaign on the part of some British, American, and French correspondents in Berlin to circulate and amplify the allegedly fake news (Lügenmärchen) of international press agencies such as Reuters. Even among the news media controlled by the Western Allies, anti-Soviet reporting had supposedly increased.[63] In response to Eisenhower's proposal, Zhukov insisted that the Soviet Military Administration pre-select the journalists who would be permitted to enter the zone.[64] In a similar effort to pull back the curtain that was increasingly being lowered along the eastern zone's border, U.S. delegates to the Allied Control Council demanded in December that travel restrictions between the zones be lifted.[65]

What little evidence we have suggests that Stalin, during the fall of 1945, was more intent on consolidating exclusive control in the territories occupied by the Red Army. Confronted with the possibility of being shut out of a peace treaty with Italy over Western opposition to the undemocratic regimes being propped up in Eastern Europe, he had cabled Molotov: "So what? Then we would have a precedent.

We will then have the possibility to conclude peace treaties with our satellites without the Allies." He would favor this even at the price of a breakdown in relations with the Allies.[66] It was thus not surprising that he was unwilling to go down the slippery slope of opening up the possibility of Western interference in the zone through central administrations.

With negotiations over central administrations at a standstill by the end of 1945, the Potsdam mandate to agree on a quadripartite level-of-industry plan for Germany within six months offered Clay an opportunity to prove that four-power governance could be made to work. Not only did he consider such a plan essential for the stabilization of the U.S. zone's economy, but an agreement on industry levels across the zonal dividing lines could bring a measure of restraint on Soviet exploitation of the eastern zone. Clay saw leverage in Soviet interest in reparation deliveries from the western zones: after all, the volume of excess capacities available for reparations was linked to the level of industry to be maintained.

But despite Clay's eagerness to incentivize Soviet cooperation by making good on some advance deliveries, negotiations among the occupation powers had been dragged out, not in the least due to reticence in Washington to prioritize reparation deliveries to the USSR over those demanded by West European countries. Moreover, Clay saw his efforts undercut by efforts within and outside of the administration to begin conditioning advance deliveries of dismantled factories and equipment from the western zones to Soviet commitment to a minimum living standard for Germany potentially higher than anticipated in Potsdam. Implicit in the production capacity and exports required to achieve it were sharp limits on capital equipment available for reparations.[67]

The U.S. approach clashed with Moscow's more ambitious dismantling goals, which led the Soviets to favor severe limits on German industrial output—well below what Washington and London considered necessary to keep their zones economically self-sufficient. Zhukov and other Soviet officials complained to Eisenhower that while the Americans "were concerning [themselves] with the economy and living standards of France, Belgium, Holland, and even in Germany, no one had spoken up to talk about living standards in Russia." Soviet living conditions were "deplorably low" and the present German standard "at least as high" as it was in Russia." Once reparations started to flow from the western zones to the Soviet zone, Zhukov told the U.S. occupation chief, "You will find that a lot of the difficulties that you are experiencing will probably disappear." Impressed, Eisenhower advised Clay to keep negotiating with Sokolovsky and be prepared to meet the Soviet side "always at least half way." Thanks to Eisenhower's intervention, Clay could finally announce on November 16, 1945, that the United States supported the Soviet proposal for dismantling a portion of the request for advance deliveries.[68]

In what Carolyn Eisenberg aptly termed "a stunning assault on Potsdam,"[69] the State Department in mid-December essentially reversed its position on the original Potsdam formula that the German industrial standard was not to exceed the average European peacetime economy (excepting the Soviet Union and the UK). The State Department's reinterpretation of the August agreement now held that the minimum German industry standard was to be on a par with the European average by 1948, transforming "what had been offered as a ceiling on German production into a floor." That minimum production had to allow for exports to pay for "essential imports," thus dramatically reducing was available for dismantling or reparations from current production for Western Europe and the Soviet Union.[70]

The problem was that as late as December 1945, Soviet dismantling goals still amounted to turning Germany by and large into an agrarian nation. Soviet draft plans called for a reduction of Germany's industrial output to 40 percent of the prewar level. Allied disagreement turned on the level of steel production, central in the Soviet view to Germany's economic disarmament and the reparations capacity of the western zones. By the end of the year, Soviet officials at the Control Council in Berlin developed a number of compromise proposals—but these failed to win Stalin's approval.[71] Faced with declining economic conditions, in particular food shortages, in the western zones as winter conditions set in, Clay pressed on. In February 1946, Clay's chief economic adviser, William Draper, was able to obtain Soviet agreement to stop the dismantling of capital equipment for German light industry critical to exports that could pay for food imports. More importantly, the SMA agreed that as part of a level-of-industry agreement, Germany would be allowed to export three billion Reichsmarks' worth of goods to pay for part of the food imports program. Murphy hailed the decision as "a significant Russian compromise."[72]

Soviet concessions seemed to pave the way for a compromise on the level-of-industry plan: Within weeks further problems were ironed out, and at the end of March an agreement was reached. To Clay, the industry plan was evidence, at long last, that quadripartite government could work, especially if backed up by the lure of reparations. As a step closer to unified economic treatment of Germany ostensibly postulated by Potsdam, Allied agreement on the nationwide industry level forced a measure of quadripartite restraint on Soviet exploitation of its zone. The episode proved, Clay wrote to Eisenhower, "conclusively . . . that cooperation and understanding are still possible between our country and the Soviets, if we are willing to have patience and . . . a little more understanding of the tremendous problems which the Soviets face internally."[73]

Eisenhower's and Clay's earnest efforts at a compromise on the level of industry that took Soviet concerns into account may have caused SMA officials in Berlin to respond in kind. Sokolovsky, for example, intimated to Clay "privately" that the American proposals on steel production quotas would be acceptable, apparently ahead of official confirmation from Moscow.[74] But what—unbeknownst to U.S. officials at the time—was likely far more decisive in spurring the first significant quadripartite compromise was the rapid decline of the Soviet zone economy and the ensuing major shift in Soviet reparations policy. Only after Moscow— spurred by pressure from the SMA—changed course on reparations policy in January 1946 by moving from removals to reparations from current production, and the transfer of two hundred of the largest industrial plants into Soviet stock companies (SAGs), was Sokolovsky authorized to agree to the higher industry levels acceptable to Clay and the British. On March 23, Stalin signaled his agreement, freeing a way for the adoption of the "Plan for Reparations and the Level of the Postwar German Economy" three days later. Rather than American pressure and the lure of reparations, internal Soviet dynamics opened up the possibility for agreement. In the course of the negotiations, it had not been lost on Soviet officials that Clay had sought to exploit their keen interest in reparations: "We should, it seems," Semenov noted, "exhibit a certain restraint on this issue."[75]

Though the change in Soviet reparations policy pointed to an ever tighter hold on the Soviet zone, the Soviet military government saw advantages in reviving trade within Germany. Local occupation authorities and state governments sought state-to-state agreements to expand trade and to rein in unregulated barter deals between companies that had sprung up after the end of the war. In November 1945 the Soviet zone's central administration for trade and supplies signed a trade agreement with the state of Bavaria in the U.S. zone, followed by trade agreements in March 1946 between Soviet zone Thuringia and western Länder Hessia, Lower Saxony, and Bremen. "Develop trade with the West and other countries," the Soviets instructed the German Communist Party leadership in their zone in early 1946.[76]

For their part, U.S. officials pressed for further liberalization of interzonal trade with the Soviet zone, both in quadripartite fora as well as in bilateral trade discussions with Soviet military government officials in the spring of 1946. In May, German state representatives of the U.S. zone signed a framework agreement with Soviet zone representatives, after such a deal had been approved by American and Soviet occupation authorities. Trade talks in the summer of 1946 across the zonal borders developed so dynamically that it seemed that such interzonal deals might pave the way to the kind of all-German economic administration that had been envisioned in Potsdam.[77]

For Clay, establishing the German central administrative machinery and the fall of the zonal barriers remained the "acid test" of American ability to work effectively with the USSR.[78] In February 1946, Clay and Murphy launched a major push for the establishment of quadripartite central administrations. It was past time, they argued, to take a "firmer and more aggressive stand" for what they considered one of the basic elements of the Potsdam decisions. A recent speech by German Communist Party strongman Walter Ulbricht represented the "opening salvo" in a campaign to rally German public opinion behind the Communist movement in favor of a united Germany. U.S. occupation leaders hoped that the Soviet position on German central administrations would force the Soviet government to show its true colors.[79]

To Murphy and Clay, French intransigence had played into Soviet hands: Moscow had taken full advantage of French obstructionism "to consolidate the Soviet position in eastern Germany." The operation of central agencies would have "militated against zonal boundaries and served to break down the exclusive Soviet control of one of the largest and most important German areas." If necessary, the United States had to put pressure on the French, possibly by withholding cooperation in other fields. Clay once again appealed to Byrnes and Secretary of War Robert Patterson to weigh in with French foreign minister Bidault. Thanks to the French refusal, Moscow and the German Communists now were able to pose before the German people as "the hope of a restored Germany." Embryonic at this stage, the situation appeared to have "more future political significance than any other development up to this time."[80] Things seemed to improve when, in March, the new socialist premier, Leon Blum, agreed to establish German administrative "departments."[81]

At the heart of Clay and Murphy's argument was their conviction that any externally imposed partition of the country along the Elbe—which, as Murphy put it, was "a river . . . not very wide or deep"—would not prove a lasting solution: such an artificial division "will only lead to dangerous conspiracy."[82] Division might be the necessary result if a cold war could not be avoided. But, as Murphy put it, whether "the gentlemen in the Politburo in Moscow plan to cooperate with the US and UK or to fight them—not necessarily with weapons but by psychological, political and economic means" remained very much a question. It was "not proven that the specialists of the Politburo are planning such a hostile campaign." If they were not, Murphy maintained in the spring of 1946, "cooperation on the German problem is possible." In that case, "we should cooperate with them on one German problem, not two." But even if he and Clay were wrong in their basic assumption, Murphy argued, "it would be defeatist to yield to them [the Russians] suzerainty over all of eastern Germany without using the present agreements to organize a German state embracing that territory."[83] Delays in establishing these mechanisms had meant that the West had to watch "from across the line without opportunity to bring broader democratic influence to bear" as selected Germans—"the vast majority of them Communists"—were installed in provincial and local governments, trade unions, and cooperatives. "Central German agencies, I am convinced," Murphy cabled Washington, would have effected the "gradual relaxation of zonal barriers" and facilitated greater American influence.[84]

The renewed push by the American military government for central administrations in early 1946 intersected with a heated debate within the Truman administration about policy toward the Soviet Union and Germany, crystallizing around the February 1946 "Long Telegram" from the Moscow Embassy's chargé d'affaires, George F. Kennan. The telegram, analyzing "the sources of Soviet conduct," had been circulated widely among top administration officials, even sent to top military commanders and many U.S. missions abroad. In Washington, it was "received in the highest quarters" as a "basic outline of future Soviet policy."[85] Concerns about Soviet intentions—reinforced by growing misgivings over Soviet troop movements in northern Iran—led Washington to take "an extremely serious view of the present situation."[86]

The reception of the "Long Telegram" in Germany was quite different. Eisenhower's successor as supreme commander of U.S. forces in Europe, General Joseph McNarney, reportedly commented on the cable "with a shrug of his shoulders that after all the telegram did not offer anything new." Clay's reaction was apparently "pretty violent," as he interpreted the State Department's sending the telegram to army commanders as "a sort of Pearl Harbor warning."[87] In addition, Clay believed that the cable represented the more anti-Soviet "British line," remarking that "it is evident that the British technique of needling our people over a period of months is bearing fruit." By contrast to "some Americans . . . prone and eager to blame the Soviet representatives for everything that is unhappy in the situation," he and Murphy found the record of quadripartite accomplishments in Germany "not too discouraging." On the contrary, the Soviets could not be accused of having violated the Potsdam agreement: "Whatever secret cynicisms they may maintain, it has not been manifest in their negotiation or official action." Instead, they had "gone out of their way repeatedly and throughout the months to be friendly with the Americans." Though "disparaged" by Kennan, personal relationships between Soviets and Americans, beginning with Eisenhower and Zhukov, had left a "very definite local imprint here which has influenced in a marked degree the Soviet-American relationship in Berlin."[88]

In the shadow of the "Long Telegram," Kennan developed a powerful counter-argument to Clay's approach on Germany.[89] In early March 1946, he had warned from Moscow that Soviets' demands for a harsh reparations regime for Germany pursued two objectives: maximum reduction of Germany's economic-military potential *and* undermining the social classes that were not readily susceptible to penetration of Soviet-controlled political groups. Central administrations were a similarly dangerous tool: though the Soviets "were happy to have several months in which to exercise a completely free hand in their own zone" they nevertheless saw in central administrations "a possibly indispensable device for entering at an appropriate moment into [the] other three zones and facilitating there [the] accomplishment of [the] Soviet political program."[90]

Recognizing that central administrations were a "plainly two-edged sword" for the Soviets, "depending on realities of underlying political control," Kennan maintained that the success of their authoritarian methods in the Soviet zone persuaded them that "in the end they cannot lose." He warned of "undue optimism about central agencies serving to break down exclusive Soviet control in their own zone." Rather, the Soviet authorities would hold back until the time "that they are fairly sure that within this new framework they can contrive not only to preserve in effect their exclusive control in their own zone but also to advance materially their possibilities for influencing [the] course of events elsewhere in Germany." With Germany territorially crippled, economically unbalanced, and psychologically dependent on the food resources controlled by the USSR, the United States, in Kennan's view, was left with only two alternatives:

> (1) to leave the remainder of Germany nominally united but extensively vulnerable to Soviet political penetration and influence or (2) to carry to its logical conclusion the process of partition which was begun in the east and to endeavor to rescue [the] western zones of Germany by walling them off against eastern penetration and integrating them into [the] international pattern of western Europe rather than into a united Germany.[91]

Kennan was certainly not alone in his call for "walling off" the Soviet zone. Perry Laukhuff, a political officer on Robert Murphy's staff, similarly questioned the priority Clay had ascribed to the establishment of central German agencies. Echoing Kennan, Laukhuff argued that the deadlock on the Allied Control Council was much to the liking of the Soviets who were allowed to pose as proponents of quadripartite cooperation while at the same time carrying out in their own zone "a sweeping social, economic and political revolution, now practically past recall" and using the French as "a very convenient whipping boy." To counter Soviet policy effectively, Laukhuff argued in favor of a frank admission that quadripartite control of Germany had failed and American withdrawal from the Allied Control Council. While maintaining the American position in Berlin, Laukhuff proposed to concentrate on developing the unity of the three western zones and to reconstruct interzonal and international trade "so clearly necessary in Western Europe." Such a decision, he admitted, "would mean writing off for the time being the Soviet Zone of Germany as a completely separate entity, entirely outside our control and influence," but it only recognizes "what is today a fact." An acknowledgment that "Eastern Germany is *wholly* in Russian hands," Laukhuff predicted, would allow the United States not only to pursue more-constructive policies in Germany but also to win influence in Eastern Europe by "penetrat[ing] to the utmost into Austria, Czechoslovakia and Poland." Referencing Winston Churchill's invocation of the term in his famous speech in Fulton, MO, just weeks earlier, to Laukhuff it seemed "evident that we must seek by every means to outflank the 'iron curtain', meanwhile temporarily lowering an iron curtain of our own in the center of the stage."[92]

Equally skeptical of Soviet intentions, James Riddleberger, the chief of the State Department's Central European Division, argued that Russia would "only permit the functioning of such [central] agencies in the Soviet zone and cooperate in their operation throughout Germany to the extent that it believes these agencies can be used for Soviet purposes." Hence central agencies were to be construed in ways that, in the case of a complete breakdown of quadripartite government, they could be "utilized in the western zones alone."[93] From Paris U.S. ambassador Jefferson Caffery echoed the French government's view that central agencies would only benefit "Soviet penetration in the French, British and American zones" with the goal of a "Communist-dominated central German government which would control the Ruhr and Rhineland." Even if they agreed to establish such institutions, Caffery argued, the Soviets would refuse to cooperate loyally.[94]

Ironically, Clay's offensive on central administrations did not only engender criticism among his detractors in the State Department and his own staff, but also set off alarm bells with his Soviet counterparts who viewed the U.S. deputy military governor's initiative not as an opportunity but a threat: Semenov, now the acting political adviser to the Soviet military governor, cautioned against Clay's initiative which he characterized as the "Allied campaign *against* the walling-off" of the zones (author's emphasis).[95] Initial western calls for a currency reform throughout Germany led the Soviet Finance Ministry in March to demand that the "independence of our zone" be secured in the face of a potential new joint currency.[96] In early April, the American military government —"ostentatiously," in the opinion of one Soviet observer—moved its headquarters from Frankfurt to Berlin; an increased American presence in the city in the heart of the Soviet zone carried ominous forebodings in Soviet eyes as U.S. commandant in Berlin Frank L. Howley called for a reorganization of the Communist-dominated city government and its police department and intervened more heavy-handedly in the political affairs of the city.[97] From the Soviet military's perspective, the United States intended to separate all of Berlin from the Soviet zone and increase its influence there.[98]

The American military government's activism against the "walling-off" of the zones showed itself in other ways as well. The U.S. delegate on the Allied Control Council's Central German Administrative Committee in May 1946 proposed a quadripartite commission that would tour the four zones to study the functioning of zonal and provincial/state economic administrations in preparation for nationwide agencies. Reacting defensively, the Soviet delegate professed at first to be unable to find time for such a tour, then argued that the Americans were "trying to do too much and trying to secure too detailed information." He finally argued that he had no problem with an effort to "approach the problem abstractly," but that as a matter of fact, economic organization among the zones differed "only in minor details." In the initial phase, it should be left to the zone commanders to assure economic unity; any quadripartite commission would be limited to formulating a program for central agencies.[99]

In the Control Council's Economic Directorate discussions about a central German administrative department for industry and agriculture, Soviet officials explicitly rejected any interference in the authority of the zonal commander: Confronted with the U.S. member's assertion that central administrations were "cardinal provisions" of the Potsdam protocol, the creation of which needed to be "begun immediately" to avoid the danger of setting up "separate economies for the different Zones," Soviet officials emphatically rejoined that the final decision in implementing any directives from central agencies should be made by the zone commander, similar to the reparations regime. When the American official asked incredulously whether this would mean that the zone commander could "for example, set aside coal allocations or taxes ordered by the Allied Control Council, the Soviet Member replied in the affirmative."[100] Soviet representatives remained sharply opposed to any infringements on their control of the zone.

Given Soviet opposition to all-German agencies, Clay sought to build on the momentum spurred by the quadripartite agreement on industry levels by negotiating a joint export-import plan for Germany. Such a plan was critical to facilitating the imports necessary to relieve the declining economic conditions in the western zones.

By March 1946, the food situation in the U.S. zone had become dire: reduced food rations in the western zones (1,275 calories per day, as compared to 1,500 in the Soviet zone), Clay believed, would "pave the road to a Communist Germany." After all, there was "no choice between becoming a Communist on 1500 calories and a believer in democracy on 1000 calories."[101] A joint export-import plan also required lowering trade barriers between the occupation zones, furthering the breakdown of the zonal division pursued by Clay. In contrast to Byrnes's position at Potsdam to control trade on a zonal basis, Clay demanded that the first charge on proceeds for imports be applied to *all* of Germany's exports, including those from the Soviet zone, thus dramatically reducing the amount of short-term German deliveries to the USSR. Even German plants that had been turned into Soviet stock companies (SAGs) would have initially produced to pay for imports into Germany.

Soviet officials were well aware of the Americans' concerns. Semenov learned that Murphy had expressed "during a private conversation within closest circles" his dissatisfaction with the industrial development of the U.S. zone. He quoted Murphy as acknowledging that "in this regard the Soviet zone had leaped ahead greatly." The Soviet political adviser relayed to Moscow Clay's view that the U.S. zone did not receive any raw materials from eastern Germany and that, by contrast with the dismal economic picture in the West, of the four zones the Soviet zone was "the richest, as it had coal, factories and an abundance of foodstuffs." Semenov called Clay's claims an "exorbitant exaggeration," and instead pointed to the growing shortages in metals and other raw materials that would in due course put pressure on the Soviet zone's economy.[102]

The Soviet government was unwilling to forgo one of its most effective tools of economic extraction. Even more disconcerting to Soviet officials, the unified foreign trade program held out the specter of a far greater voice of the Western powers in Soviet zone affairs, to which Soviet officials from top down remained adamantly opposed. At the April 5 meeting of the Control Council's Economic Committee, Konstantin I. Koval, the SMA chief's deputy who was responsible for economic matters, emotionally declared that "primary responsibility" for maintenance of life and order in the zones rested with zonal commanders. Quite in line with what Byrnes had suggested at Potsdam, Koval argued that the zonal principle applied to foreign trade just as much as to reparations, with each occupation power being responsible for the results of its occupation regime. Three weeks later, Sokolovsky countered the U.S. proposal in the Control Council by invoking a clause in the Potsdam agreement that provided for foreign trade for Germany to be conducted on a zonal basis "within the net balance of each zone."[103]

Confronted with these dead ends in the Allied Control Council negotiations,

Clay issued a "stop order" on April 26, halting all dismantling and reparation deliveries from the American zone. The rationale behind Clay's renewed play for all-German solutions was rooted in his continued belief that he could leverage Soviet interest in reparations from the western zones for progress on economic unification. Soviet interest in reparations, Clay remained convinced, would make them amenable to a negotiated settlement, and his reparations stop order sought to rachet up the pressure on Moscow.[104]

Soviet observers noted a "definite change" that spring, observing that American policy in Germany was marked by greater "single-mindedness and aggressiveness." Against the background of shifting U.S. interests from Asia to Europe, Semenov portrayed the Truman administration as pursuing a "policy of the open door" throughout Germany that would give the United States the opportunity to undermine Soviet influence. Interpreting the Potsdam principle for treating Germany as a single economic unity "very broadly to their advantage," Moscow's top diplomat in Berlin admitted, was a "quite effective propagandistic slogan." Clay was ostensibly intent on "disentangling the zonal structure," abolishing the sovereign rights of the individual occupation powers in their respective zones and transferring them to a quadripartite organ such as the Allied Control Council. This would result, Semenov suggested, in the Control Council assuming "real power" and the zonal commanders being relegated to its representatives in the zones.[105]

By late May, Molotov was told that American officials, in their campaign against zonal separation, made no secret of their desire "to put the Soviet zone economy under their own control."[106] To Soviet officials, this broader strategy explained the American attitude in opposing zonal balances on foreign trade and reparations from current production. SMA official Georgy Arkadeev cabled Moscow that the cessation of the dismantling showed that the United States and the UK "were juggling with the reparations issue to use it as a means of pressure against us."[107] Referring to the Soviet-American crisis over Iran in early 1946, when Washington had mobilized intense international pressure to coerce Soviet withdrawal from northern Iran, another SMA official put it more pointedly: against the backdrop of the broader U.S. offensive, "this is the Iranian question in Germany."[108]

Clay wanted the reparations issue to be addressed at the Paris sessions of the Council of Foreign Ministers, slated to take place from April 25 to May 16, 1946. Before leaving for Paris, the deputy U.S. occupation chief forcefully impressed upon Sokolovsky that there would be no resolution to the reparations question unless the main decisions made at Potsdam were implemented: German central administrations, and unified economic treatment of Germany, including the acknowledgment that zonal boundaries should only serve to delineate territory administratively and should not prevent free interzonal trade and a unified export-import plan.[109] But in the view of Foreign Ministry officials in Moscow, Clay's pressure tactics aimed at the exact opposite—a revision of the Potsdam agreements. Pointing to the Byrnes-Pauley formula, they argued that the zone commanders were masters of their zones, both administratively and economically.[110]

The Paris Council of Foreign Ministers meeting, extended after an unproductive first round to mid-July (with a month-long break in-between), was an important transition moment in the East-West negotiations over Germany. With economic conditions in the Western zones declining, Clay remained hopeful for greater economic integration of the zones as a solution to the economic difficulties, yet he was also prepared to proceed with zonal mergers—at least temporarily—without the Soviets, should the reparations fail to produce an opening up of the Soviet zone. Clay's optimism contrasted with the skepticism with which much of the State Department by now viewed the prospects for agreement with the Soviets. Though there were those, like William Clayton, who shared Clay's hopes that the Soviets would come around to cooperate, many State Department officials seemed increasingly resigned to push forward with an economic and political merger of the western zones.[111] George F. Kennan, returning to the department from his counselor assignment in Moscow, warned that the "Russians want in Germany [to be] the dominant power over the life of the country."[112] In early May, Acting Secretary of State Dean Acheson conveyed the agency's prevailing view to Byrnes in Paris: The Soviets regarded the split of Europe into Eastern- and Western-oriented blocs as inevitable, they deemed it necessary to consolidate firm political and economic control over their zone, and they feared that common economic policies would interfere with their reparations practices. Employing Clay's idea of a close interrelationship between reparations plan and treatment of Germany as an economic unit, Acheson proposed that the reparations program be resumed for sixty to ninety days on the condition that the Allied Control Council develop a joint export-import program centered around the pooling of German economic resources to support recovery in all zones. Contrary to Clay's rationale, however, the proposal rested on the expectation of Soviet rejection. Abandoning the Potsdam zonal principle, Acheson was helping Byrnes set the stage for a clash with the Soviets: The proposal would allow the United States to "confront Russians with a plan which will really put their protestations of loyalty to Potsdam to a test and place [the] onus for failure of Potsdam on them in event they do not meet the test."[113]

For Soviet officials, it was the United States that was abandoning Potsdam. In May, after extensive consultation, Stalin's advisers had agreed that Byrnes's proposal for a demilitarization pact, put forward in draft form in February, aimed at terminating reparations, loosening occupation controls, and pushing back Soviet influence.

In a speech in Paris on July 10 scripted by Stalin, Molotov assailed American policies and portrayed the USSR as the champion of German recovery and unity.[114] In response, Byrnes offered the fusion of the American zone with any of the other zones in preparation for economic unity. While Molotov refused, the British government agreed on July 30, and though the French government hedged, it moved closer to such a solution. At Clay's request, Byrnes also addressed the Germans in a speech in Stuttgart on September 6, seeking to buoy German spirits by declaring that they should become economically self-sustaining and enjoy an average European standard of living. Though not forsaking the goal of German unity, the speech provided Germans a perspective for a democratic future within a Western European context. Breaking with the punitive thrust of earlier U.S. policy, the speech thus signaled a broader change in U.S. occupation policy.[115]

Faced with the prospect of a bizonal arrangement between Americans and British that would have precluded any Soviet influence in western Germany, Moscow took a more conciliatory attitude. Even before the Paris negotiations concluded, Molotov advocated an increased level of industry that would allow increased German exports, as well as a larger amount of reparations. He even signaled readiness to establish central administrations as a transitional step, if the USSR would be assured a voice in the Ruhr. The price for such a role, a senior State Department official sympathetic to Clay's line of thinking argued, would have to be "real quadripartite control over the whole of Germany" unless the Soviets "grab[bed] off the East entirely for themselves and then horn[ed] in on a western arrangement."[116] Two days after the Byrnes offer, Soviet occupation chief Sokolovsky echoed Molotov's statement, demanding in the Allied Control Council improved cooperation among the occupation zones "as a preparatory first step towards the establishment of a central administration."[117]

In informal talks between U.S. and Soviet officials in the following days and weeks, the outlines of a compromise that would allow for reparations from current production were sketched out: The level of industry would be increased; a reparations plan would be based on the treatment of Germany as an economic unit; export proceeds from plants not slated for dismantling would be used to pay for imports first; and the recipient countries would provide Germany with raw materials. On October 11, the head of the U.S. military government's economic administration, General William Draper, handed to his Soviet counterpart in the Allied Control Council's Economic Directorate an "informal" document, which called for the creation of central administrations as soon as a reparations plan had been agreed upon, a balanced export-import program, and even the elimination of economic zonal borders.[118]

The informal conversations confirmed Clay's belief that the reparations issue would force Moscow to open up its occupation zone. By mid-October 1946, Murphy felt so encouraged by the prospects for a mutually agreeable reparations plan that he ventured, "We would be well advised to use the opportunity regarding the introduction of democratic methods in the Soviet zone."[119] Well aware that by 1946 the Soviets enjoyed little support among the German population, Clay expected that a unified German state would be a "gain for Western democracy," enabling it "to contest for its philosophy throughout Germany" and "to extend its frontiers to the borders of Poland and Czechoslovakia, thus encouraging any will for democracy in the peoples of these countries." For Clay, the United States had "much at stake in gaining the opportunity to fight for democratic ideals in Eastern Germany and in Eastern Europe" . . . an opportunity that would "result from the true political unification of Germany under quadripartite control." A failure to explore these possibilities would allow the Soviets "to mine the industry of Eastern Germany" and create "ultimate political and economic competition between Western Germany under Allied controls and Eastern Germany under Soviet controls. Obviously, this establishes the frontier of Western democracy along the Elbe."[120]

Clay's visions of a peaceful rollback of Soviet power in eastern Germany and beyond coincided with a mounting economic crisis in the Soviet zone and evident uncertainty among Soviet officials over the future course in Germany in the fall of 1946. But while Clay and Murphy saw the Soviets as coming around, to Soviet officials, it was the Americans in Berlin, "apparently with agreement from Washington," who were putting out feelers for a potential agreement before the next Council of Foreign Ministers meeting in New York. They remained skeptical. After all, the American feelers were still noncommittal toward the overall amount and length of the reparations program even while implying the dismantling of Soviet control over their zone in critical areas. Well aware that Clay was far more ready for a compromise than others in the administration, as well as his British and French allies, Soviet officials surmised internally that the logic of Byrnes's Stuttgart speech had in fact argued against reparations from current production. Sokolovsky thus preferred that discussions be limited to informal contacts, postponing the "resolution of principled questions" until the November meeting of the Foreign Ministers.[121]

Pragmatic informal contacts had brought Clay tantalizingly close to a deal on economic unity by the fall of 1946, yet they ran into the ideologically grounded "principles" that increasingly pulled both sides in opposite directions. As we shall see in Chapter 3, Clay's approach, for one, had to contend with the transformation of the Soviet zone—and the growing skepticism among Truman administration officials that it generated.

The United States and the Political Transformation of the Soviet Zone, 1946–1947

The Soviet Zone Comes into Focus

Soon after the end of the war, the Soviet occupation zone (SBZ) in Germany became, according to former Berlin CIA station chief David E. Murphy, terra incognita to Western military commanders and their intelligence officers. Information on developments in the former German territories to the east was "meager," as deputy military governor Clay cautioned well into the occupation. During the war, the U.S. government's fledgling civilian foreign intelligence service, the Office of Strategic Services (OSS), led by the charismatic William ("Wild Bill") Donovan, as well as the military intelligence services, had been focused on supporting the war effort against the Third Reich. To this end, OSS had even agreed to share intelligence information on Germany with the Soviet People's Commissariat for State Security (NKGB). At the same time, the NKGB had extensively penetrated the OSS. The OSS had recruited only a few sources inside Germany, and on Victory in Europe Day "American intelligence had no significant networks and few reliable contacts inside the country."[1]

With the Allied occupation of Germany, the country, and especially Berlin, turned from terra incognita into an espionage jungle. Donovan appointed the energetic OSS station chief in Bern, Allen Dulles, to head a new mission in Germany in June. Even before July 4, when American forces finally entered Berlin, the head of the secret intelligence branch, Frank Wisner, had sent OSS officers through Soviet lines to Berlin to seek agent recruits. The mission produced the first OSS report on life in Soviet-occupied Berlin. But with Donovan engrossed in protracted bureaucratic struggles with the U.S. military's intelligence services, low morale resulting from demobilization, lack of professionalism, and mission uncertainty, the initial reporting was low in quality. Briefed by Dulles personally, Clay and Murphy were unimpressed.[2]

Briefly attached to the War Department as part of the Strategic Services Unit (SSU) before it moved to the newly established U.S. Central Intelligence Group (which would transform in 1947 into the Central intelligence Agency (CIA) as the central foreign intelligence service of the United States), the Berlin Operations Base (BOB) was fixated on the potential threat posed by fugitive Nazi officials and underground groups of fanatic Hitler loyalists, the top intelligence priorities for the U.S occupation authorities. "Hard-pressed to collect any intelligence at all," Allen Dulles's Berlin station was squarely focused on political, economic, and social developments in the U.S. occupation zone. Intelligence gathering on Soviet-occupied territory was initially beyond the unit's mission and limited capabilities.[3]

The SSU/CIG/CIA unit competed with a massive presence of War Department intelligence organizations operating in occupied Germany, in particular the Military Intelligence Division (MID), the Army Security Agency (ASA), the Counter-Intelligence Corps (CIC), and the Army's "G-2" departments attached to armies and divisions. While the CIC, at the end of the war, was actively engaged in espionage well beyond the countering of enemy intelligence operations in the U.S. occupation zone, MID and G-2 were largely focused on collecting information on Red Army strength and deployments, which by 1946 were estimated to involve some 700,000 troops in eastern Germany alone. The Army's need for intelligence on the USSR led it to recruit in late 1945 former members of the Wehrmacht's "Foreign Armies East" intelligence organization led by General Reinhard Gehlen.[4]

A war scare over Soviet troop movements in southeastern Europe in mid-1946 led to an "urgent shift to military targets." In the course of "Operation Grail," SSU Berlin built up "large agent chains reaching out and covering the Soviet Zone throughout its length and breadth." BOB chief Dana Duran recalled with some pride in 1948 how he was "able to pinpoint a target anywhere in the Russian zone and dispatch an agent to cover it almost at a moment's notice." With its interest largely focused on the Soviet order of battle and early warning of a potential Soviet attack, however, the United States initially lacked even the most basic information to judge the political and economic situation in eastern Germany.[5]

Clay had personally contributed to the problem in two ways: He had laid down at the beginning of the occupation his "goldfish bowl policy," which had forced the military government to be transparent about its policies, hampering the work of the U.S. Military Government's Office of the Director of Intelligence and the OSS/SSU Berlin. Much to the frustration of U.S. intelligence agencies, Clay had also refused to permit the use of OMGUS cover for clandestine operations, for the sake of (as Duran put it) his "lofty concept of the integrity of Military Government function." Decidedly unimpressed by early reporting, Clay was skeptical of the burgeoning American "cloak and dagger" efforts. More importantly, he had let it be made known to everyone within the American military government in Germany that he did not want espionage activities directed against the Soviets to heighten their suspicions and undercut his efforts to establish a cooperative relationship.[6]

But not everyone agreed. Sobered in his views about Soviet policy by his experience at the OSS mission in Romania, Wisner pushed for greater coverage of the Soviet zone. Harry Rositzke, chief of the OSS Wiesbaden mission's steering division, began to add eastern Germany to the collection program. In September 1945, Wisner strongly advocated priority coverage for the political, military, and socioeconomic situation in the Soviet zone. That same month, Wisner resigned out of frustration over the lack of support in Washington for Soviet coverage, but his successors, Richard Helms and Peter Sichel, slowly managed to build up operations in the Soviet zone, soon resulting in a steady flow of reporting. In the course of 1946, the Berlin Base increasingly made the Soviet zone its "target of primary interest" and began to penetrate deeply into its central administrations. Statistical reports based on confidential documents purloined from the zone's Railways Directorate and other administrations soon constituted the "bread-and-butter output" of the Berlin base. In Political Adviser Murphy, BOB found a receptive customer and supporter at the highest level of the U.S. military government.[7]

Among the early sources on conditions in the Soviet zone were Allied interrogations of refugees and prisoners of war released from captivity by the Soviets. The civil censorship division of the U.S. military government's intelligence staff monitored and intercepted postal, telegraphic, and telephone communications from the Soviet zone on a massive scale.[8] On the basis of unwritten rights validated by Western Allied practice and Soviet acquiescence, American military officials had access to the whole of Greater Berlin to observe conditions in the Soviet sector of Berlin firsthand. Starting in 1947, officers of the U.S. Military Liaison Mission in Potsdam, who were authorized to travel freely throughout the Soviet zone, were able to gather important information on Soviet zone military and other developments.[9]

The difficulty of making definitive generalizations about Soviet behavior and German reactions quickly became clear. If anything, the letters and reports were striking for their cacophony of opinion and for apparent contradictions: Some of them described conditions in the Soviet zone in the rosiest hues, some in the bleakest colors; others painted a more neutral picture. Much seemed to depend on what segments of the Soviet military the informants had encountered—whether, as one U.S. intelligence report stated with Orientalist overtones, they had come into contact with the frontline "'Asiatic' troops or with the more 'civilized' troops who usually relieve the shock troops."[10] One impression stood out: Soviet military officers did not "appear to act under uniform instructions." Conditions and policies differed widely across the zone.[11]

In the early months of the occupation, U.S. intelligence agencies were generally skeptical about their German sources. Nonfraternization policies prohibited close contact with the German population. American soldiers had been exhorted to distrust Germans attempting to elicit their sympathy or favors. American officials therefore suspected that much of what they were hearing was aimed at "playing the Russians off against the Americans and the British."[12] They fully expected German nationalists to make every effort to stir up conflict between the Anglo-American Allies and the USSR. One intelligence report from mid-May 1945 noted that German leaders were already at work "to gain for Germany the status of a co-belligerent against Russia." Forwarded by Murphy to Washington, the reports suggested that senior German officers were only too eager to offer their knowledge and services for the coming confrontation with the USSR. One former SS-Obergruppenführer apparently advised his interrogators that if the West was planning "to start anything against the Russians . . . now would be a good time to go ahead."[13]

Clay himself had heard reports of "excesses in the Russian area."[14] Germans described the situation in the wake of the Red Army's advance into East Prussia, Silesia, Pomerania, and the Soviet occupation zone as one of "utter hopelessness and near-extermination."[15] But many American military officials were not inclined to put much stock in such reports. Word of atrocities and the barbaric behavior of Red Army troops often struck Americans as exaggerations by Germans eager to exonerate themselves from the terrible pains and horrors inflicted by the Nazi regime. Subjected to scrutiny, Murphy noted, evidence of Soviet misbehavior "usually becomes less breathtaking."[16] German soldiers and occupiers had ravaged Soviet lands, and Americans understood that many Red Army soldiers harbored profound feelings of hate and revenge. Fanaticized by anti-German propaganda such as Ilya Ehrenburg's tirades of hatred, Red Army soldiers occupied the German Reich's eastern provinces, looting, threatening, raping, and killing the local German population. Such acts, American officials noted, "should be considered as accidents of war—similar in many ways to the shelling and bombing of residential areas."[17] One American observer commented, "All war is rough. People who dislike being treated rough should not commence wars of aggression."[18]

Perhaps no single dimension of Soviet military actions would sear the memory of the German population as much as the rape of women and children undertaken on a massive scale in the wake of the Red Army's East Prussian campaign.[19] Berlin suffered the brunt of the rape and abuse. The taking of the city, in prolonged and fierce battle, as historian Norman Naimark has shown, was accompanied by "an unrestrained explosion of sexual violence by Soviet soldiers."[20] Innumerable cases of indiscriminate rape (often gang rape) occurred on a daily basis, first in the bunkers, then in apartments and houses.[21] American occupation officials initially tended to take reports on rape with a grain of salt. True, rape and "its less violent sister acts" were "common," one military intelligence official noted dismissively, but German reports were prone to emphasize the rape issue "because of its erotic appeal to some Americans and British."[22]

How deeply ingrained the issue had become in German memory and how much it would thus complicate Soviet-German relations were not lost on American observers: "Most Germans," one report in late 1945 noted, "still associate all Russians with rape and looting."[23] The rape issue reinforced the darker stereotypes of the Soviet forces that the Germans held. While Germans at times referred to Soviet troops individually as generous, good-natured, and childishly amazed at the most ordinary gadgets or household fixtures, "somewhere in the German estimate, it is almost always mentioned that the Russians are 'barbaric' and 'enslaved by a system worse than ours was.'"[24] Many Germans reportedly considered the establishment of Communist rule in the Soviet-occupied areas as "the end of everything" and were "inclined to write off the Russian zone as lost to Germany." As American observers noted, in the minds of many Germans, the Soviet Union "begins at the border of the Russian zone."[25]

American observers, however, also noted that liberal Soviet cultural and information policies—in particular Radio Berlin's broadcasts—proved increasingly effective in "tending to modify the original attitude of fear and hostility toward everything Russian."[26] In setting the pace for cultural and political renewal, the Soviets were "first in every respect."[27] During the two months of undivided sovereignty over Berlin prior to the arrival of Western Allied troops, they had laid the foundation for cultural renewal with liberalism and pragmatism. Their strategy of opening up instead of restricting "roused the soul," as British press officer Peter de Mendelsohn aptly observed.[28] Many of the Soviet cultural officers were highly educated and often fluent in German, and they easily collaborated with German intellectuals, many of whom were inclined toward communism.[29]

As initial masters of the city, the Soviets had taken over the still largely intact Reichsfunk building in the Masurenallee in the Charlottenburg district. Broadcasting of German-produced programming resumed within a few days of the end of the Third Reich, tightly controlled in advance by Soviet censors and trusted German Communists. But the Soviets did not take a heavy-handed propagandistic approach; instead they put in charge two of the more liberal members of the National Committee for a Free Germany, Matthäus Klein and Hans Mahle, to pursue a "middle path between the previous broadcasting patterns and established audience habits and political and programmatic reforms." The Soviet policy was "Reeducate but Don't Intimidate," in Wolfgang Schivelbusch's apt words.[30]

Even before the Western Allies entered Berlin, officials with the Anglo-American Psychological Warfare Division, based in Bad Homburg, quickly noticed the effects of Radio Berlin's attempts at "on-air fraternization": programming represented the Soviet Union "as a friend, and almost a defender, of all good Germans."[31] Internally, officials warned of a potential "sharp change in German attitude toward the Russians": the population in the American zone took Soviet propaganda at face value, and some wished to be under Soviet control.[32] "I thought that the people would wish that the Americans or English were here [in Thuringia] instead of the Russians," one U.S. zone resident, whose correspondence was intercepted by U.S. agencies, wrote to a friend about his recent trip to the Soviet zone: "But what I heard was very much the opposite. They seem very content with the Russians."[33] By the end of 1945, American officials in fact noted a decided decrease in emphasis on hardships and unpleasantness of life in the Soviet zone.

To be sure, requisitioning and dismantling remained a sore subject with many Germans, but a noticeable number of sources now pointed to the rapidity of reconstruction and reorganization of life in the Soviet zone. Complaints from Soviet zone businessmen about shortages in materials and tense relationships with the occupation authorities mixed with frequent praise for the help extended by the Soviets to German industry and commerce; one writer from Leuna in the Province of Saxony described that the workers at the Leuna Works, the former IG Farben oil and chemical plants, which had been heavily bombarded during World War II, were reportedly "enthusiastic about the Russian occupation and dread the day when the Russians might withdraw."[34] Comparing conditions under Soviet occupation favorably with those in the West, numerous letters intercepted by U.S. occupation authorities spoke to the "rapid return to normalcy in the Russian zone."[35]

U.S. political adviser Murphy and his staff were aware that the resurgence of political activities in the Soviet zone in particular had outpaced those in western Germany. In late April and early May 1945, the Soviet government had sent Moscow-trained Communist cadres to Germany in three "initiative groups" under Communist leaders Walter Ulbricht, Anton Ackermann, and Gustav Sobottka. Their mission was to cooperate with the occupation power, reestablish local administrations, and take over key administrative positions in Berlin and elsewhere in the Soviet-controlled areas. On Moscow's orders, the Kommunistische Partei Deutschlands (KPD), outlawed by Hitler in 1933, formally reconstituted itself on June 11. In the following months, the KPD would play a cardinal role in the development of Soviet rule in the Soviet occupation zone. Soon after the relaunch of the KPD, the Social Democratic Party (SPD), the Liberal Democratic Party (LDP), and the Christian Democratic Union (CDU) (growing out of the Catholic Zentrum Party) followed and joined forces with the KPD in an antifascist "unity front."[36]

It had not escaped Murphy that the Communists had taken over the "command posts" in the emerging political structures. But while there was some concern that this early admission of parties in the Soviet zone could give the Soviets a lead once party activities could be resumed on a nationwide scale, he was confident that this would be "slowly rectified with the passage of time" as local elections would "reveal that the Communist Party lacks majority support."[37] Clay did not seem concerned either: he told Stimson in mid-August 1945 that it was "too early to judge their relative strength, popular support and ultimate goals."[38]

Brewster Morris, a staunchly anti-communist adviser to Murphy who served as POLAD's liaison to U.S. intelligence agencies, established himself as the State Department's authority on Communist activities in Germany and avidly tracked Soviet and Communist activities in the eastern zone, reassured the U.S. occupation leaders that social revolution was not immediately on the agenda of the Soviets and the German Communists. Moscow's ultimate goals remained uncertain, and for now, emphasizing moderation proved exceptionally advantageous for the KPD's broader popular appeal. Many local Communist functionaries continued to display diligence and fairness in their official dealings and, in the eyes of American officials, seemed to be sensitive to the reservations and skepticism among broad segments of the population.[39]

To be sure, the Soviet military government had quickly sought to bring its influence to bear on the new non-communist parties. Murphy reported that in July the CDU "gave in to the Russian invitation to move party headquarters into the Russian sector of Berlin." It quickly became apparent that the CDU and the LDP were dependent on the Soviet authorities for the printing of their daily newspapers, "bringing them under the unpleasant control of the Russian censor."[40] But while such worries were in the back of American officials' minds, they soon realized that Soviet efforts were faltering. The enthusiasm with which many party members had greeted the arrival of Soviet troops evaporated within days as a result of pervasive violence and fear. "It is the same people for whom the Russian army couldn't appear soon enough who now wish to see them far away," Murphy reported based on a "highly-reliable" source.[41]

Murphy and his staff also noted growing tensions within the antifascist bloc over an ill-conceived land reform implemented in the Soviet zone in the summer of 1945 that undermined the KPD's relationship with the other parties in the Soviet zone. Thanks to their direct contacts with the CDU leadership in the Soviet zone—in particular former German State Party Reichstag-member-turned-Christian-Democrat Ernst Lemmer—American officials were fully aware that the CDU and the LDP opposed Soviet sequestering policies and criticized the expropriation of personal property and the expulsion of former landowners from their districts.[42]

The United States and the SPD-KPD Merger

No event brought American views of Soviet zone developments into sharper focus than the coerced fusion of the SPD and the KPD into a united socialist party. Intersecting with the American debate over all-German institutions and reparations, the merger signified to some Truman administration officials the consolidation of Communist control in eastern Germany. Clay and Murphy, by contrast, did not view the merger as an irreversible step toward the sovietization of the zone.

In the late fall of 1945, the KPD leadership began to reverse its earlier protestations against a fusion of the parties of the Left. It now called for a "new offensive" of the party's political-ideological work aimed at the unity of the SPD and the KPD. Despite a rapid rise in membership numbers and generous material support by the Soviets, the KPD had found itself outrun by the SPD in popularity nationwide. Many Germans continued to view the KPD as an extension of Soviet policy and blamed "the Russian party" for food shortages, looting and removals, the loss of the eastern territories and Red Army depredations. Communist defeats at the polls in Hungary and Austria that autumn did not bode well for Soviet plans to turn the KPD into a party of mass appeal. Not only did this trend call into question the utility of the KPD as a tool to strengthen Soviet influence throughout all of

Germany, but Soviet intelligence picked up on indications that the British government was supporting the SPD in the western zones in its strident opposition to a merger. More alarmingly, the British seemed increasingly intent on gaining control over the Berlin-based SPD leadership in the Soviet zone by encouraging its more conservative, anti-communist factions and turning it into a "weapon of English policy."[43] This raised the ever-sensitive specter of Western intrusions into the Soviet zone via the SPD.

By late fall, Soviet officials and German communist leaders had become convinced that the only way to assure communist control and to crush the SPD as an active force in Soviet zone politics would be a merger of the two parties. Soviet leader Stalin approved the unity campaign during a visit by KPD strongman Walter Ulbricht in Moscow from January 28 to February 6, 1946, setting May 1 as a target date for the establishment of the "Socialist Unity Party of Germany."[44] With the zonal SPD leadership unwilling to commit to fusion pending hopes for a national party convention, regional Soviet military commanders started to support a KPD campaign for a merger "from below." They began to pressure SPD members with a combination of courting and coercion to unite with the communists on the local, county, and state (Länder) levels. In the West, the SPD leadership under the staunchly anti-Soviet and competitive Kurt Schumacher refused to schedule a national convention that SPD leaders in the Soviet zone under Otto Grotewohl had called for. Without support from the West, a majority of the SPD Länder representatives in the Soviet zone voted in favor of holding a party convention at the zonal level at a Soviet zone SPD leadership meeting on February 10–11, 1946. At an SPD-KPD leadership meeting five days later, the date for the merger was set for April 20–21, 1946.[45]

The American occupation officials were well aware of the "powerful Communist campaign" for a merger.[46] "Inside reports from all areas of the Soviet Zone" furnished the Americans with insights into the sophisticated tactics the Soviets and KPD had employed to create a groundswell of support for fusion among the party rank and file. The chief of the Berlin Command's intelligence section, Lieutenant Colonel William F. Heimlich, had friendly relations with Grotewohl and Max Fechner, another leading Social Democrat who would join the SED.[47] Reports of these conversations, passed by Murphy to Washington, reflect an undercurrent of empathy, almost admiration for the besieged party leader Otto Grotewohl.[48] U.S. officials knew that Grotewohl and the other top SPD leaders had been repeatedly called to Soviet headquarters in Karlshorst and urged by Zhukov and other Soviet occupation officials to join with the communists; that he was confronted with the genuine support of some SPD members for the fusion, especially in Saxony and Thuringia, and with the persecution of others who strongly opposed it; and that tensions between Grotewohl on the one hand and the KPD and the Soviets on the other were growing.[49]

The SPD leader remained forthcoming with the Americans, acknowledging after a trip to the western zones in early 1946 that people there "feel no compulsion exercised over them" and suggesting that elections in the Soviet zone were still a matter of the distant future, as the Communists were still suffering from Red Army behavior. The Soviet leaders, Grotewohl informed his American interlocutors, were well "aware of this and taking no chances." They saw in a single labor party the "surest guarantee against the re-emergence of such forces in Germany as might again attack Russia." Asked whether he believed that the communists had become sincere advocates of democracy, the SPD leader wryly stated, "They are doing their best, by their actions from day to day, to prove the contrary."[50]

Despite the "entirely un-neutral attitude" of the Soviets, Clay and Murphy adopted what they called a "policy of political neutrality" throughout much of the merger crisis.[51] Clay pointedly refrained from criticizing Soviet pressure tactics and refused to engage in tit-for-tat actions vis-à-vis the communists. He did intercede with Sokolovsky in several instances during the fusion process in which KPD leader Wilhelm Pieck and his deputy Walter Ulbricht openly criticized the Western occupation powers.[52] His Soviet counterpart apparently promised that "he would see to it that such performances [by the German Communists] would not again be repeated and expressed the strongest kind of disapproval." The Soviet general seemingly distanced himself from the KPD leaders, intimating that "the German communists trade in the name of the Soviet Military Government and do not hesitate to indicate that the Soviet Military Government supports actions on which, at times, it has not been consulted."[53] To Clay and Murphy, Sokolovsky's reaction confirmed that it was important to keep the merger from sowing Allied discord and undermining quadripartite government.

Nonetheless, the struggle of the growing number of those within the eastern SPD who opposed the merger confronted U.S. occupation leaders with democratic principles on which the occupation effort was premised. Clay addressed the issue, but he did so in characteristic fashion, using it to push for all-German solutions that ultimately required Soviet cooperation. In early February, the American representative in the Political Directorate of the Allied Control Council proposed that political parties should not be able to merge without the democratically legitimated decision of a national (!) party congress.[54] Echoing warnings in late February by the

British occupation chief about the detrimental effects of the zonal fragmentation on the political parties, Clay declared on February 25 that the United States would not recognize forced mergers in its zone or elsewhere in Germany. As the top Soviet diplomat in Berlin noted, Clay went on to bemoan that "every day the zonal system created ever new problems for the unity of Germany as the occupation powers seek to implement with ever more lasting effect their own policies in their own zones." Reflective of Soviet sensitivities against any Western interference in the Soviet zone, Semenov viewed Clay's arguments as yet another example of what he termed the "Allied campaign against the 'walling off' of the zones."[55]

Meeting at the State Opera House in the Soviet sector on March 1, 1946, more than a thousand SPD functionaries from all over Berlin revolted against the Central Executive Committee's merger decision. When Grotewohl observed that the KPD was independent because the Communist International had been dissolved, "the whole audience roared with laughter," according to a U.S. official.[56] The meeting resolved to hold a referendum in Berlin and the Soviet zone on the merger, "a first serious setback to KPD and Soviet plans for rapid amalgamation," as Murphy reported to Washington.[57] On March 23, Clay restated publicly, this time more forcefully, that the U.S. administration would not recognize the proposed merger "unless it is done by appropriate expression of the majority of members of the parties." Referring to the Social Democratic leadership in Berlin, he asserted that these "old leaders" had been permitted to "act as leaders" but had never received instructions from party members. Therefore, "[a]s far as we are concerned we don't accept the leaders as representing the will of the party until and unless they have received instruction on merger policy matters either by referendum or by vote of party."[58] Clay's statement galvanized the anti-merger forces: on March 27 their leaders decided to hold a referendum on the fusion in Berlin and the Soviet zone on March 31.[59]

Clay's more forceful tone had come in part in reaction to growing criticism of his hands-off attitude and internal demands for a more aggressive U.S. action: In late March, the American military government's labor relations official, Louis Wiesner, had pleaded that the United States "undertake more vigorous action to combat Soviet and Communist influence."[60] Barely a week later, Brewster Morris of Murphy's staff insisted, "We must put an end to the new KPD line of openly criticizing the Western occupation powers," actively promote "our concept of democracy," and bring the American public up to speed on the German situation; "otherwise there may be a rude and unpleasant awakening."[61] U.S. intelligence sources reported that an "air resembling desperation over the lack of open American support" had beset the anti-merger group, which felt cut off from its fellow opposition in the west.[62] Rationalizing his decision to yield to the merger, Grotewohl blamed the Western powers for not giving him "what he regarded as sufficient political support."[63] In conversations with U.S. officials he claimed that the independence of the SPD in the Soviet zone had "been lost through the unwillingness of the Western powers to give any but verbal assistance."[64]

Clay, however, had done more than verbal assistance. Bolstering the public voice of the anti-merger forces, the U.S. military government's Information Control Division put supplies of paper at the disposal of the SPD opposition and allocated additional newsprint to raise the daily circulation of the U.S.-licensed *Der Tagesspiegel*—the leading public outlet for those opposed to the fusion—from 325,000 copies to 500,000.[65] In addition to what Semenov called a "provocative media campaign," Soviet sources reported that some Social Democrats campaigning for unification had been called to the U.S. headquarters in Berlin and told to end their activities. Western Allied authorities were said to have arrested about a dozen KPD members in the Schöneberg district and even two Soviet officers who had tried to attend a meeting by the merger opposition.[66]

While the Soviet Military Administration managed to quell preparations for a referendum throughout the Soviet zone and Berlin's Soviet sector, the March 31, 1946, vote in the western sectors produced an overwhelming (82 percent) majority among SPD members against an immediate merger.[67] Though Soviet officials mainly faulted the KPD's haphazard work with the SPD's rank and file, Semenov told Moscow that the "undisguised and direct material and political support" of the merger opposition by the Western Allies had played a role in outmaneuvering the communists.[68] Clay signaled his readiness to recognize the new anti-merger SPD leaders who broke away from the SPD central leadership to form a new Berlin SPD Executive Committee on April 7.[69] By contrast, three days after the KPD/SPD merger in the Soviet sector of Berlin, Clay declared that the newly established "Socialist Unity Party" (SED) could be recognized in the western sectors and zones only by a referendum or after application as a new party, effectively barring the SED from legally carrying out activities outside the Soviet-controlled areas. Once again Clay used the occasion to emphasize his desire to see the zonal boundaries eliminated soon.[70]

The SPD-KPD merger, ceremoniously staged at the Admiralspalast theater on April 22, 1946, reinforced the increasingly "grim" outlook among many Truman administration officials in Washington. The State Department noted the "undemocratic methods" employed by the Soviet government and in a rare note of concern emphasized to Murphy that the issues involved were considered "very important" in Washington.[71] The administration viewed the events in Berlin through a much wider lens. At least to some, the fusion now appeared to be part of "a broad pattern of events occurring in all eastern and central European countries." They considered it "the most significant political event in Germany since the overthrow of the Nazi regime."[72] Key officials within the State Department were increasingly convinced that the Soviet zone should be "written off," and more and more western German political leaders reinforced their views, particularly within the western CDU.[73] With the merger viewed as a textbook example of the kind of Soviet conduct that he had described in his "Long Telegram" just a few weeks earlier, George Kennan saw the efforts of the German communists in "penetrating, paralyzing and bending to their will the German Social-Democrats" as an attempt "to prepare that zone as a spring-board for a Communist political offensive elsewhere in the Reich."[74]

Clay and Murphy had been upset by the fusion forced upon the SPD. The Americans, in particular Murphy, the ever-perceptive Semenov told Moscow, had been "extremely irritated" by the recent developments.[75] Yet both were keen to preserve a modicum of cooperation with their Soviet counterparts in order that over the long run, jointly arrived at all-German solutions would allow for Western influence to reverse Soviet transformations. They viewed the merger as being in line with Soviet strong-arm methods since the takeover of Berlin a year earlier. It had been "obvious" that Moscow would place its chosen people in key public offices. "I cannot," Murphy argued near the height of the unification drama, "work myself up into a lather about it." It had all along been more important to him and Clay to avoid "falling into the pitfall of Allied discord if we ever wanted to achieve a definitive solution to the German problem."[76]

As pro- and anti-merger forces battled each other, the Soviet city commandant in fact gave in to Western calls to oust one communist member of the Berlin city government and reprimand another because they had publicly spoken in favor of fusion.[77] Reassurances from Sokolovsky served to reinforce Murphy's impression that Germans—Communist or not—were eager to play the occupation powers off against one another.[78] Murphy suspected, in particular, that the German communists at times traded in the name of the Soviet military government: "In fact I feel that the thinking of some German Communists may well be in advance of that of their Soviet associates."[79] Taking issue with those who argued in favor of abandoning official policy that still classified communist parties as democratic parties and instead "go[ing] all out" for the SPD, Murphy wondered how "our policy would differ from any other totalitarian methods. In other words, I feel that we cannot continue to talk about democracy as we understand it and practice some other form."[80]

Underlying the different approaches between U.S. officials in Washington and Berlin were expectations of the success and irreversibility of Soviet policies in the Soviet zone—and the potential to project American influence beyond the zonal boundaries. In Washington's view (and, to be sure, that of some military government staffers), the zone was irreversibly being transformed along the Soviet model into a people's republic: "a revolution has been accomplished in the Eastern Zone which has been brought so far that the status quo ante can hardly be restored."[81] Murphy, by contrast, remained skeptical that the merger would be successful: "The Soviet technique in all these things seems to me exceedingly primitive, and in their obvious determination to impose a single party structure I think they will meet with failure . . . [T]heir efforts delude but few." The United States stood to gain little from "cheap imitation of their methods."[82]

To local American observers, difficulties for the Soviets abounded in their zone. In conversations with American military government officials, Grotewohl had been frank about the serious problems plaguing the Soviet zone economy. And even as he steered his party into fusion, he had held out hope that the SPD would "be able to absorb the KPD" if the merger were replicated on a nationwide scale.[83] Clay and Murphy were also attuned to the persisting rifts within the socialist "unity" party, in particular between former KPD and SPD members, many of whom remained very skeptical about the sudden conversion of communists to democratic principles. Instead of unity, the SED was plagued by ideological and personal schisms, inner-party repression, and power struggles. Doubts lingered even at the top level of the new party: After conversations in mid-April with Grotewohl, who was about to become SED co-chairman, U.S. observers reported that he was "far from being pleased over the merger-path" and might even break away from the SED.[84] In May, Grotewohl reestablished contact with the Americans, seeming tense and "not entirely happy about the new situation, though determined to make the best of it."[85] During the conversation, Grotewohl referred several times to the "experiment of the SEPD [SED]," implying that the merger might not hold. The party leader "seemed particularly glad of this opportunity to renew contact with the Americans, suggesting very definitely that he does not want to become isolated from the Western occupation powers and dependent on his Soviet contacts."[86]

Clay's focus on maintaining quadripartite and especially Soviet-American cooperation seemed to be borne out by progress in the Allied Control Council. In the midst of the highly charged political atmosphere, quadripartite interactions in the

Control Council remained "businesslike and cordial."[87] When the four Berlin city commandants failed to reach agreement on recognizing the new city committees of both the SPD and the SED on a citywide basis, the matter was quickly resolved in the Allied Control Council. So too was the question of elections to replace the appointed magistrate with an elected body. Though all four commandants agreed on the need for early elections as mandated by the Potsdam agreements, discussions in the Berlin Allied Kommandatura broke down over appropriate timing. Likely worried about the impact of elections on the surrounding Soviet zone, the Soviet city commandant Aleksandr Kotikov hedged on a decision. Once referred to the Allied Control Council, however, the four deputy military governors found a compromise solution quickly, on June 3: the Berlin elections would be held in October. Soviet zone elections were scheduled for the same time. As William Stivers and Donald Carter have noted, "A tone of friendship and mutual respect governed personal relationships and this clearly affected the work of the council."[88] Clay had developed genuine friendships with Zhukov and Sokolovsky. Murphy told Washington his counterpart, SMA Political Adviser Arkady A. Sobolev, had told him "in different times and different ways" of the Soviet desire for the "friendship of the Americans."[89]

Washington officials cautioned against drawing broader conclusions from these local experiences. Doing so, the State Department's European bureau chief, John "Doc" Matthews, had told Murphy, would lead to an "entirely distorted picture."[90] The differences between Washington and Berlin perspectives found apt expression in the report by one State Department German hand who had been dispatched to Berlin as the merger crisis unfolded. Writing home, he argued that from the vantage point of Washington "we are all inclined, I think, to be a bit pessimistic, to think that Germany is inevitably lost to the great push from the East or that at any rate the Eastern Zone of Germany is already lost as a result of the social and economic reorganization put through under Soviet auspices." From Berlin, he noted, "the situation does not look so bad, and I must say that my short stay here has already made me feel much more optimistic about the general situation and its prospects in relation to fundamental American interests. No matter what decisions may be made with regard to a closer organization of the Western Zones, I am convinced that we should in no sense write off Eastern Germany or Berlin."[91]

The United States and the Non-Communist
Opposition in the Eastern Zone

Following the SPD-KPD merger in April 1946, the three Western powers moved quickly to preempt similar pressures on the non-communist Left in the West by preventing the SED from forming in their zones. The forced-fusion process had raised the specter of the SED spilling over to the western sectors and zones: Allied officials worried that party members at lower levels of the SPD beyond the control of Kurt Schumacher, the anti-communist party leader of the SPD in the western zones, would follow the Soviet zone model for party unification from below: joining with the lower KPD ranks to form a Socialist Unity Party in the western zones. With Schumacher dead-set against joining his party with the western KPD headed by Max Reimann, American military government authorities announced that it would permit parties to merge at the state or Länder level only. Until that had occurred, no meetings could be held in the U.S. zone under the name of the SED. Those Social Democrats eager to support the SED had to join the KPD.[92]

Clay's reaction also followed his basic approach of challenging communist power in the East by demanding Germany-wide solutions: he made it clear that the SED would not be licensed in the western zones until the SPD and other parties in the Soviet zone had those very same rights. In the ensuing weeks, Clay pressed for simultaneous quadripartite recognition of a reorganized SPD (composed largely of the anti-merger forces) and the SED throughout all of Berlin. Not only would such action counter the growing division between the eastern and western sectors in Berlin, but the attraction of the SPD was certain to aggravate the problems within the SED, whose popular appeal continued to evaporate as Soviet tutelage and micromanagement tainted the party's public image.

Clay's efforts bore fruit in May 1946 when, to the surprise of many in the West, Soviet officials agreed to recognize an independent SPD in their Berlin sector, denying that they stood for a single-party system in Germany.[93] Responsible for the Soviet about-face on recognizing the SPD were apparently concerns that a continued stalemate that prevented the communists from competing in the western sectors might lead to "further disintegration" of the newly founded SED.[94] Internally, Soviet occupation officials had acknowledged that the non-recognition of the two workers' parties by the Western and Soviet governments, respectively, created an "unusual and unhealthy political climate," which the West was using to solidify the position of "Schumacher's men" by undercutting those Social Democrats who were willing to join the SED. Clay had launched, Moscow was told, a "virtual terror campaign" against the unity proponents.[95] The Soviet Military Administration also announced that local government elections would be held in the Soviet zone in September.

Within weeks, Stalin also agreed to schedule county and state elections in the zone for October 1946. U.S. officials correctly suspected that this owed less to Soviet commitment to free elections than to a desire to influence and overshadow the Berlin municipal elections scheduled shortly after the zonal elections.[96] Impressing Berliners with an overwhelming victory for the SED in the zone would counter

any fallout from a sizable vote for the CDU and reconstituted SPD in Berlin.[97]
Scheduling state elections soon after local elections, Moscow policymakers believed,
would allow the USSR to "exploit" the favorable conditions presumably created by
Communist success in the local elections and prevent the non-Communist parties
from building on their campaign experience and strengthening their organizational
networks.[98] Soviet intentions notwithstanding, Clay believed that the Berlin and
Soviet zone elections provided the kind of opportunity he had sought for democratic
forces to compete in the Soviets' territory.

In the run-up to the elections in the Soviet zone, Russian documents show,
Sokolovsky authorized a number of "measures of an agitation and propagandistic
[agit-prop] nature" to "raise the mood of the German population" and secure support
for the SED candidates.[99] By contrast, the non-Communist parties—the Christian
Democratic Union (CDU) and the Liberal Democratic Party (LDP)—suffered from
massive discriminatory interference by the Soviet authorities.[100] While actual voting
in the communal elections might be technically free, almost all Western observers
agreed that heavy pressure was exerted on the population during the months before the elections in order to influence the outcome.[101] The SED received detailed
direction and massive assistance from the Soviet military authorities; its opponents
were greatly disadvantaged, "drowned in the overwhelming propaganda facilities"
available to the SED, as CDU leader Ernst Lemmer told U.S. officials. A particular
handicap was the inability of the CDU and the LDP to register local party groups
to set up a list of candidates. Altogether, U.S. military government officials estimated that in some 9,000 communities in eastern Germany, the SED was the only
party on the ballot.

American observers got the impression that general directives from the Soviet
occupation headquarters in Karlshorst prescribed when and where the LDP and
CDU had to be curbed. In one case, a Soviet officer reportedly displayed anxiety
because he had registered more groups than his orders permitted.[102] Soviet officials
accused CDU and LDP speakers of having furnished information on the Soviet
zone to the Americans.[103] The CDU leader in the Soviet zone, Jakob Kaiser, as
well as LDP leader Arthur Lieutenant, were reproached by the SMA for having
invoked the Byrnes speech in Stuttgart "but not mentioning that of Molotov."[104]
Taken together with other measures to intimidate CDU and LDP sympathizers
and sabotage the parties' campaigns (as well as to tap into the reservoir of former
Nazis), the election presented itself to some within the American military government as "a contest between the totalitarian occupying power and two unsponsored
political groups."[105]

The question facing the Truman administration was to what degree it should intervene on behalf of the remaining non-Communist parties in the Soviet zone. As early as March 1946, CDU leaders asked for U.S. support of a party convention in Berlin—the first of growing demands for greater backing of the non-Communist parties.[106] The issue sparked an intense debate between Clay and Washington. Reflecting the growing Cold War consensus in Washington that the Soviet zone was following the road taken by the Communist Party–led "people's democracies" to its east, State Department officials argued for greater support of the anti-SED opposition: "We cannot afford the luxury of political neutrality towards German political parties."[107] State Department counselor Charles Bohlen advised Murphy in August 1946—somewhat obliquely—that he would soon see "indications of a more active and dynamic encouragement" to non-Communist forces than had previously been the case.[108] State Department officials urged the U.S. military government to assure "in every feasible way" that the non-Communist parties in the Soviet zone could maintain their organizations.[109] Some within the department favored providing "a certain amount of quiet, discreet unofficial assistance" for the SED's opponents,[110] others advocated "hinting at the possibility of forbidding the SED in the U.S. sector" should there be no "marked relaxation in repressive practices." There were those in Washington who wondered whether the political situation in the zone had developed so far that CDU participation in the elections would not make sense at all.[111]

U.S. military government proponents of a tougher policy vis-à-vis the Soviets were growing impatient, as "time is so rapidly slipping by." Perry Laukhuff of Murphy's staff bemoaned "our present passivity" and came close to accusing Clay of acting against the State Department's decision "to actively assist the non-Communist, democratic forces in Germany."[112] While the CDU continued "to wage as gallant a fight as it can in the Soviet zone under present circumstances, it is hindered and discriminated at every turn and it seems impossible that it will be able to stand against the SED with any success." Laukhuff argued that there were a number of actions that might alleviate the situation: American officials could formally protest Soviet violations of the Potsdam Conference provision to allow and encourage political parties, and could draw public attention to the suppression of democratic parties in the Soviet zone through press conferences. Taunting his superiors, Laukhuff proposed "tell[ing] the truth" about the situation in the Military Governor's public "Monthly Report." The American officials could also ask the Kaiser and the CDU to withdraw openly from political activity in the Soviet zone and request permission from the Soviet occupation authorities to send election observers. In Berlin, the Americans could assist the SPD with additional cars, gasoline, food, furniture, meeting halls, and paper. The CDU could be supported in a similar fashion—"to whatever extent is necessary." Though doubtful that such steps would "bring about free democratic political life in the Soviet Zone," the time had come, Laukhuff argued, "to put up an active fight in our own interest here."[113]

Clay and Murphy, however, would have none of it. They remained vehemently opposed to the United States throwing its full weight behind the CDU and LPD in the Soviet zone (and the SPD in Berlin). In fact, at the very time the non-communist parties were struggling in the zone, Clay gave official permission to Ulbricht, Pieck, and Grotewohl to engage in a speaking tour throughout the U.S. zone, allowing the SED leaders to proselytize for Socialist unity, provided that the meetings were publicly sponsored by the KPD. To the chagrin of Washington, Ulbricht, Max Fechner, and other SED Politburo members used their appearances to promote SPD-KPD unity and draw unflattering comparisons between life in the U.S. zone and the conditions in the Soviet zone. When Murphy's staff demanded that the SED speakers be reprimanded, Clay personally intervened, telling his subordinates that they had to uphold the right of Communists to make strong speeches "at all costs."[114]

Clay did agree to set up a new afternoon paper in Berlin that while not a CDU Party paper, would be staffed by "people sympathetic to the CDU stand" and would bolster the CDU reach throughout Berlin. But he denied an SPD request to start a paper there ("they hardly need another daily").[115] U.S. occupation leaders were confident that the parties had a fair chance in the Berlin elections. Top American occupation officials were convinced that semi-overt sponsorship of a political party by any of the occupation powers would "put the 'kiss of death' on said party."[116]

More importantly, Clay and Murphy believed that far more was to be gained by extending Western influence to the east through quadripartite solutions, rather than launching into a futile "active fight" with the Soviets. Instead of open interference on behalf of individual political parties in the Soviet zone, Clay pushed a policy guideline on political parties through the quadripartite control machinery that provided all licensed parties with authority to present candidates in the voting districts of that zone.[117]

In addition to trying to engage the Soviets cooperatively, Clay authorized a series of military government–inspired articles in the American press that focused on the discriminatory pre-election practices in order to increase public pressure on his Soviet counterparts. It is difficult to assess the efficacy of these efforts: U.S. occupation officials later credited American and British media coverage, "which turned the spotlight on Soviet and German communist methods and aims in the elections" with the fact that the elections were not a complete travesty.[118] American intelligence sources confirmed that the Soviet leaders' concerns about foreign reactions led them to moderate Soviet pressure methods. Perhaps the most tangible result of Clay's efforts might have been Soviet permission for a group of eight American journalists to travel around the zone in the summer of 1946.[119] General Clay "may have done 'something' to cause the Russians to permit more freedom," one intelligence source surmised.[120]

Against the backdrop of the zonal elections, Byrnes's September 6 speech in Stuttgart also appears in a new light. Beyond heralding a change in American occupation policy, the speech seemed to have had a powerful effect on the election politics in the Soviet zone. Soviet officials carefully watched as it became a reference point for non-communist party candidates. Internally, U.S. officials credited the Byrnes speech as having had a "great effect" on the communal elections that occurred within a few days of the event. According to U.S. estimates, the speech "increased the CDU and LDP vote in Mecklenburg and Vorpommern by about 25 percent."[121]

The volatility of the SED's strength became evident when, despite massive Soviet support, the party achieved only meager success in a string of local and state elections that fall. To the embarrassment and shock of SMA and SED alike, the disadvantaged non-Communist parties nearly outflanked the SED at the polls. In heavily Protestant Saxony, combined votes for the CDU and the LDP nearly matched those cast for the SED in local elections on September 1, 1946.[122] In communal elections in Thuringia and Sachsen-Anhalt on September 8, the SED actually trailed the LDP in the towns of Apolda, Eisenach, Erfurt, Gotha, Jena, and Weimar, with the CDU coming in third. Altogether, the SED was outvoted in 90 percent of Saxon cities.[123] By contrast, the SED dominated in the remaining, far more rural areas of Mecklenburg-Vorpommern and Brandenburg in elections on September 15. There, land reform had won over many traditionally conservative farmers, but according to U.S. estimates, the CDU and the LDP had also been prevented from reaching some 50–60 percent of the voters. While the CDU had been bolstered by recent election victories in the western zones, the SED's focus on the CDU as the main adversary had evidently allowed the LDP to gain strength.[124]

Most important, both parties apparently attracted the votes of former SPD supporters, many of whom used their votes to signal dissatisfaction with the forced merger. While the SED narrowly prevailed in the total vote due to its monopoly position on the ballots in the rural areas, Murphy could report to Washington that the Soviets and the SED had "suffered a moral and strategic defeat of considerable magnitude." Where another option existed, voters had "flocked to that alternative in large numbers."[125] The elections showed that the "communism of Soviet State Party [*sic*] has not captured the minds of the voters in the Soviet zone."[126] The electoral setback for the SED in the local elections was compounded in the zonal and Berlin elections held on October 20, in which the party—despite increased efforts to frighten voters—failed to obtain any majority at the zonal level, outmatched by the combined votes of the non-Communist parties. In Berlin, the SED suffered a resounding defeat to the SPD.[127]

Truman administration officials debated the longer-term effects of the fall elections in Berlin and the Soviet zone, which had presumably made Soviet leaders "disappointed and quite angry."[128] Some argued that the results might lead the SED, backed by the Soviets, to increase pressure tactics vis-à-vis the non-Communist parties. By contrast, the U.S. Central Intelligence Group suggested that the Kremlin was intent on working "through non-communist parties."[129] Impressed by the blow to the SED, Murphy ventured that the "moral bankruptcy" of the policy of creating and supporting the SED "might even lead to some complete change of attitude, such as the dissolution of the SED, rapprochement with the Social Democrats and greater cooperation with the bourgeois parties."[130] Soviet uncertainty about the SED added to Clay's and Murphy's plea to Washington to use concessions in the reparations question to produce a political opening in eastern Germany.[131]

U.S. military government intelligence even suggested (on the basis of conversations with the CDU's Jakob Kaiser) that the Soviets were preparing for a readmission of the SPD in the zone and that "a rather drastic change in Soviet policy in Germany"[132] was imminent.[133] This information was based in part on the expectation that the March 1947 Moscow Council of Foreign Ministers meeting might "result in the unification of Germany." The reappearance of the SPD in the Soviet zone—"a bitter pill for the present leaders of the SED to swallow," U.S. officials speculated—might come as early as mid-February, allowing the Soviets "to get credit for having done so at their own initiative."[134] By February, "fairly reliable sources" reported that the SED Central Committee had been informed that the Soviet authorities "are reconsidering readmitting the SPD in their zone."[135]

At the same time, U.S. observers speculated about "a highly important change in the leadership of German communism." For several weeks, rumors had it that Walter Ulbricht, recognized since the beginning of occupation as "more Russian than the Russians" and the real leader of the KPD/SED, had fallen into disfavor with the Soviets because German communism failed to develop mass political support. The Soviets had allegedly instructed Ulbricht to "remain more in the background," presumably since they had realized that his methods and mentality had "in fact irritated many of the Germans he had to contact, and also served to identify the KPD and SED too closely in the popular mind with the SMA."[136] SED leader Pieck indicated that after the election debacle, the Soviets had instructed the SED to take a more independent line and to cooperate more with the other parties.[137] On the basis of sources within the SED, U.S. intelligence had reported in late December that the SED leadership had been informed by the Soviets that they had decided to agree to the unification of Germany, which "allegedly took the party completely by surprise, as its propaganda had been busy denouncing the bizonal agreement."[138] Several other intelligence reports around this same time suggested that Karlshorst was making similar statements to other Germans.[139]

New Russian and German evidence shows that Stalin indeed floated the idea of readmitting the SPD in the Soviet zone. Meeting with top SED leaders in January 1947, he brought up the idea of "licensing the SPD in the Soviet Occupation Zone," asking the Germans, according to Wilhelm Pieck's notes, whether the "SED feared the SPD," and suggesting that "it had to be fought politically."[140] Chosen as a former SPD leader to present the SED's case, Grotewohl evasively countered that the Western Allies were demanding the readmission of the SPD despite the "fusion" of the party with the KPD. Stalin again stated with determination: "One had to license it [the SPD]." The shaken SED leaders tried to convince Stalin that this move was impractical. But Stalin himself seems not to have seriously pushed his "advice" on the German comrades: despite the SED's repeated attempts to prepare for the day when the SPD would be readmitted in the zone, as late as July 1947 neither the SED nor the SMA could obtain a final word on the issue from Moscow.[141]

Despite his musings about the SPD, Stalin, as well as the SMA, was in fact far from abandoning the SED. Internally Soviet officials blamed the disappointing election results on the lack of unity of Communists and former Social Democrats within the SED, which had almost broken up over the even distribution of candidates on the ballot. SMA propaganda chief Sergey I. Tiulpanov emphasized the need to strengthen the SED organizationally and counter the "chauvinist" and "nationalistic" propaganda of the bourgeois parties. He suggested intensifying the confrontation against the divisive activities of the Berlin SPD, recognizing the impact that the city's free politics—the SPD in particular—had on the surrounding zone.[142] Fedor Bokov, who was responsible for SMA's political work, demanded creating "conditions for the SED's greater maneuverability in domestic and foreign affairs of Germany" that would undercut the non-Communist parties' claims that the SED was a "Russian party." Back at the Kremlin a few weeks later, the SED leaders received Stalin's endorsement of the party's moderated program. "The position of the SED in favor of unity," the Germans were told, "is correct." The Communist Party in the western zones, Pieck jotted down, "was burdened by the old KPD program," by the fact that people "feared dictatorship—revolution." Hence the KPD was to adopt the "new SED program for the coming period." The Soviet leader wondered "whether leftist elements within the SPD" would join the Communists in "unity front committees" that would work "against the Reaction in the West."[143] Far from giving up on the SED, Stalin sought to strengthen its influence throughout Germany and stabilize the situation in the Soviet zone.[144]

The United States and the 1947 Moscow Council of Foreign Ministers

Clay's and Murphy's "neutral" attitude toward the transformation of the Soviet zone, especially the SPD-KPD merger and the zonal elections, were part of a strategy that sought to keep the door open for Germany-wide solutions with the potential of extending Western influence to the East. This strategy sought to engage Moscow in quadripartite agreements rather than oppose the Soviets in Germany head-on, while simultaneously increasing the pressure through reparation stop and the Byrnes offer. The results of the elections in the Soviet zone were a blow to Soviet aspirations. Despite massive privileging of the SED, the party's dismal election performance called into question the viability of the very instrument on which the success of the Soviet occupation in Germany hinged. Over the summer, to Clay the possibility of a deal on economic unity reparations seemed within reach.

Perhaps sensing an opportunity, top U.S. occupation officials pressed further for a grand bargain of economic unity through reparations. When McNarney had repeated Byrnes's fusion offer in the Control Council on July 30, Sokolovsky had emphasized Soviet desire for "an intensification of interzonal trade" and proposed the "creation of a special organ for interzonal trade," a position that had struck Murphy as a potential advance even as they hedged on zonal fusion. Following informal feelers in the fall, in early November, Clay personally pitched the idea to Sokolovsky and Semenov of a 10 percent raise in the level of industry to allow for reparations from current production in the amount of $7.5 billion. Clay's proposal did initially require raw-material imports into Germany (estimated at up to $2.5 billion), with major reparation deliveries to start only after five years. The possibility that reparations from current production could be "accepted as a basis for economic unity" was serious enough to "disturb" British occupation officials: in their view, the Soviets would "simply milk the cow which the US and British are feeding," as a British official reportedly put it.[145]

Sokolovsky and Semenov told Clay his proposal "seemed solid," and apparently considered the "Clay plan" so important that they cabled both Stalin and Molotov, arguing that it represented "a measure of progress" from the earlier, principled refusal to reparations from current production to attempts to find agreement on overall figures and ways to cover them. Much as Clay had surmised, Sokolovsky and Semenov advised the Kremlin leaders that a solution to the reparations problem *had* in fact to be found in a Germany-wide formula. The USSR, they wrote to Moscow, would not be able to secure all required reparations payments from its zone due to the "tremendous difficulties" and "insufficient industrial capacity." Since there was no agreement, deliveries from the western zones were not forthcoming, and industrial plants there were corroding away. "We cannot see a different basis for the solution of the economic problems associated with Germany."[146]

Clay thus agreed with Sokolovsky on a number of important points. Most significantly, they shared a belief that the approach to solving the thorny reparations issue required a unified approach across zonal boundaries. Both believed that the other was making a genuine effort to work toward such a compromise. Both seemed inclined to think that if left to the Allied Control Council, the issue could be worked out. And both were willing to advocate the basic concept with their leaders. As far as "political questions" were concerned, as Clay had put it to Sokolovsky, "Americans and Russians had for all intents and purposes the same positions."[147]

A few weeks later, the special representative of the USSR foreign trade ministry in Germany, Boris Kolpakov, reinforced Sokolovsky's warnings: he argued that a further autonomous existence of the Soviet zone, a number of advantageous aspects notwithstanding, would lead to extraordinary difficulties since raw material supplies were nearly exhausted and remaining hardware and transport systems required renovation. "The question as to whether the autonomous existence of the Soviet Zone is expedient has to be decided as quickly as possible." In his report, which he had coordinated with Sokolovsky and Konstantin Koval, Kolpakov advised his government to distance itself from the SED, to strengthen the provincial governments of zones, and to prevent the political independence of the zone. While it is not clear whether the report was in fact communicated to the USSR Council of Ministers in Moscow, for which it had been written, it is further indication that senior Soviet officials in Germany had grave doubts about the thrust of Soviet occupation policy.[148]

To be sure, American and Soviet positions were still far apart. When Sokolovsky pressed Clay personally in November to raise the level of industry beyond the proposed 10 percent to shorten the time period for reparations, the latter reportedly demurred, supposedly professing that the United States would not tolerate an

economically vibrant Germany. France, Clay argued according to Sokolovsky's report, would oppose even a 10 percent raise, aspiring to become the leading economic
power in Western Europe. From the Soviet perspective, the need to wait five years
for substantial reparations payments was a major drawback of the Clay plan—and
perhaps a deal breaker. Though the plan seemed to have the backing of "influential
American economic experts," Clay himself, Sokolovsky noted, apparently admitted to skepticism as to whether the Council of Foreign Ministers would be able to
resolve the German question.[149]

Eager to seize the opportunity that he sensed, Clay decided to take his argument
for a U.S.-Soviet deal personally to Washington. In November 1946, he advised
Byrnes that reparations were the key to obtaining economic *and* political unity at
the next Council of Foreign Ministers meeting in Moscow. In preparation, Clay
outlined the quid pro quo: reparations for economic and political unity.[150] While
Clay sought to persuade the Truman administration that a grand bargain on German unity could still be struck, Soviet officials tried to raise the issue with Moscow:
"Should we continue such talks with the Americans and how far can we go?"[151]

Though Clay's arguments had clearly resonated with Sokolovsky, Semenov, and
the SMA's economic specialists, Stalin and the Moscow bureaucracy, as far as the
record shows, remained unresponsive. In failing to develop official proposals based
on the rudiments of a deal that had developed in Berlin, the Soviet Foreign Ministry
effectively buried the flickers of a compromise on Germany. While Soviet officials
in Moscow and Berlin internally voiced support for the establishment of central
administrations and continued work on a reparations plan that accepted "in principle" the idea of abolishing economic barriers between the zones, the voice that
mattered—Stalin's—remained silent.[152]

In Washington, too, the air required to keep an all-German approach alive was
rapidly thinning. By the time the Council of Foreign Ministers convened in the
Soviet capital in the spring of 1947 for a meeting on Germany, top American policy
makers, in sync with British and French official thinking, had also come to view
German unity as more a risk than a gain. They feared that the Soviets were bound
to dominate a unified Germany. In September 1946, a State Department policy
committee on Germany led by James Riddleberger had recommended that in the
case of "continued stalling" of the Soviets on unification, "we should pursue our
unification of western Germany with the British and if possible the French and with
the revival of the economy of that area" even if that meant "the splitting of Germany
into an eastern and a western state."[153] In November, George Kennan had warned
Byrnes that "time is running short on us in the German question." With prospects

for progressing to a peaceful, united Germany "slender indeed," he cautioned Byrnes that the United States could reach an understanding with the Russians only from a position of strength, and that "the only way in which we can create that strength in our bargaining position vis-à-vis the Russians in Germany is to undertake immediately an energetic and incisive program of economic development and of restoration of public hope and confidence in our own zone."[154]

From Moscow, U.S. ambassador Walter Bedell Smith reinforced the skepticism about Soviet intentions that was gripping Washington: Intent on dominating a unified Germany, the USSR would inevitably tighten control of the eastern zone as it sought to exploit opportunities to destabilize the west. Having "once gotten their teeth into Germany," the Kremlin would pursue "power-political and ideological considerations" at the Moscow meeting. To Smith it seemed inevitable "that we must be prepared if necessary to accept further separation of eastern and western zones of Germany." The United States had to "promote and support in word and deed all true democratic and progressive forces in our zone and at the same time we must defend them from infiltration and subversion by totalitarian machinations from the east."[155]

Many of the key policy makers in Washington, as Carolyn Eisenberg has shown, were now tilting toward the "Kennan-Smith line," including those charged with formulating the administration's approach to the Moscow conference.[156] Concerns about Soviet intentions mixed with growing anxiety about the economic stagnation in the western zones. A Council of Foreign Relations task force headed by Allen Duller and staffed with leading Germany experts from politics and business recommended scrapping the Potsdam apparatus and turning the Ruhr into a powerhouse for rehabilitating Western Europe. Similar recommendations resulted from a mission by former president Herbert Hoover, who declared that "the world was involved in the most dangerous economic crisis in all history." Allen Dulles's brother, John Foster Dulles, emerging as a top Republican foreign policy expert, similarly argued for the need for Western European integration and abandonment of the Potsdam dictum that Germany was to be treated as a single economic unit. What was needed was a free hand in combating Western Germany's economic stagnation. Important voices in the Washington policy debate were now willing to risk tensions with the USSR and partition of Germany along the central zonal line.[157]

By the spring of 1947, spiraling confrontation between the Soviet Union and the Western Allies had thus sucked the air out of any trial balloons for a compromise in Germany. As the Moscow Council of Foreign Ministers meeting was about to convene, Truman went before Congress to announce U.S. emergency aid for the

Greek and Turkish governments, declaring that the United States had to be prepared to "support free peoples who are resisting subjugation by armed minorities or by outside pressures." The "Truman Doctrine" pledged American assistance to countries around the world threatened by Soviet aggression or indigenous Communist insurgency backed by Moscow and led to preparations for the European Recovery Program (ERP), to be announced by General George C. Marshall in early June. The "Marshall Plan" prioritized the economic rehabilitation in Western Europe—including the western zones of Germany—over the recovery of Germany as an economic unit, further stimulating the buildup of bizonal administrations.[158]

To be sure, at the Moscow meeting, George C. Marshall, Truman's new secretary of state, was wary of an open break with the Soviet Union, his initial argument called for the immediate implementation of central economic agencies. And not just that. Marshall also demanded the creation of a provisional German government composed of the heads of democratically elected state governments. The provisional government would act as a constituent assembly, writing a new constitution. Even greater was its proposed authority in economic matters, drastically curtailing the autonomy of zonal commanders. But unlike General Clay, Marshall and his advisers were unwilling to agree to a quid pro quo in the form of an agreement on reparations from current production for opening up the Soviet zone: reparations would have to wait until the German economy was in balance.[159]

It quickly became clear to Clay that the Western conditions for cooperation with the Soviets were almost prohibitive, without any chance for agreement by the Kremlin leadership.[160] In Moscow, Clay saw his more expansive vision of American influence throughout Germany and Eastern Europe undercut by Stalin's reticence to relinquish control of his zone, as well as mounting anxieties within the Truman administration over Soviet intentions and economic disintegration in Western Europe.

With the growing Cold War confrontation, crises from Iran to Eastern Europe reverberated into Allied relations and local politics in Germany, shaping and reinforcing confrontational attitudes in Moscow, Washington, and Berlin, and pulling the rug out from under the tentative feelers for a compromise solution on reparations and German unity. As both sides grew concerned about the economic sustainability of their zones, they also became increasingly averse to the risk of losing control. Frustrated by his inability to sway a reparations deal that would open up the Soviet zone, Clay—the only fervent proponent of a last-minute compromise on Germany—departed early from the Soviet capital.

4

"Springboard for Penetration"
1947–1949

"Trojan Horse" or "Dead Duck"? Containing
the People's Congress Movement

In the aftermath of the Council of Foreign Ministers meeting in Moscow, American occupation officials noted that Soviet goodwill, moderation, and flexibility seemed to dissipate. The American military government's intelligence staff suggested that "regular visitors in Karlshorst" reported a sudden somberness on the part of Soviet officials. Soviet zone propaganda administration chief Sergei Tiulpanov, regarded by many as a hard-line ideologue, became more prominent in zonal affairs, and his speeches and instructions, U.S. intelligence officials pointed out, were more "demonstratively communist and aggressive than ever." During a zonal conference of the SED held in September in Berlin, Tiulpanov spoke as a passionate Sovietizer—in the words of American observers, "as communist to communists."[1]

The chilling atmosphere in Berlin reflected that the quadripartite chemistry on Germany was quickly evaporating. Stalin had assured Secretary of State George Marshall in Moscow in April 1947 that the discussions there had been only "the first skirmishes and brushes of reconnaissance forces" on the German question. In retrospect it is clear that Stalin was referring not to the theater of four-power negotiations but to a battle for German national unity that would play out on the field of public opinion.[2]

The lines had been redrawn since spring of the previous year. American occupation officials noticed how Soviets and East Germans began to heighten their appeals to German nationalistic proclivities. Early indications had come in June 1946, when Soviet zone Christian Democratic Union (CDU) leaders Jakob Kaiser and Ernst Lemmer reported to American occupation officials that Tiulpanov had conveyed to a gathering of CDU officials "with great earnestness" the thesis that "Russia's prime policy" was to "build a strong Germany and a united Germany." Though the presentation, Kaiser admitted, might have been a tactical ploy, it "made a deep impression on the assembled delegates."[3]

Soviet playing to German national aspirations was particularly evident on the sore question of the German eastern territories, assigned to Polish administration. In late March 1946, Grotewohl had reminded the Germans that Moscow might consider a revision of the unpopular German-Polish borderline along the Rivers Oder and Neisse; that, after all, the decision on the issue rested with Moscow. Ulbricht similarly hinted at the possibility that not all of the eastern territories might be lost. Later that month, the Soviets assured Kaiser and Lemmer, the Americans learned, that a definitive border settlement depended entirely on the Germans.[4]

The Truman administration was well aware of Soviet appeals to German nationalism. In the lead-up to the June 1946 meeting of the Council of Foreign Ministers in Paris, Dean Acheson, the acting secretary of state, emphasized repeatedly the "danger that Soviets might put [the] onus of breaking with Potsdam on US." In a sharp departure from his original zonal approach in 1945, Byrnes had called in Paris for a unified economic treatment of Germany that in Acheson's view avoided "any imputation that US is abandoning Potsdam." If it turned out to be impossible to put the Potsdam arrangements into effect, Byrnes had announced on July 9, the United States would have no choice but to merge the U.S. zone with any other zone where the occupying power was willing to implement a multizonal policy along the lines that the United States desired. Molotov had responded to Byrnes the next day. In a speech carefully scripted by Stalin, "On the Fate of Germany and on the Peace Treaty with Germany," the Soviet foreign minister emphasized in turn Soviet support for German unity. Blaming the other side for the failure of Potsdam was central to the long-term legitimacy of each side's German project.[5]

While condoning appeals to the Germans' desire for unity in a general way, Moscow had not yet been ready to give in to repeated SED calls for a nationwide plebiscite on the nature of a future German state and other all-German initiatives. During the Kremlin discussions with the German Communist leaders in January 1947, Stalin still evaded an endorsement of the plebiscite idea, despite assurances from the SED leadership that a vast majority of Germans would favor a centralized and presumably Communist-dominated state. This changed, subtly at first, in the following months. U.S. officials noted, for example, frequent references to former German Reich chancellor Otto von Bismarck by high-ranking Soviet officers, in allusion to Russian-German cooperation in the era of the first German nation-state. In July 1947, U.S. occupation authorities reported that former Wehrmacht field marshal Friedrich Wilhelm Ernst Paulus, who had surrendered to the Red Army in Stalingrad in 1943 and became one of the leaders of the National Committee for a Free Germany supporting Soviet propaganda efforts during the war, was slated for a prominent position in a new "central government."[6]

Stalin's hesitation in giving the German Communists free rein to pursue national populism became evident when the head of the Bavarian state government invited state leaders from all zones to Munich in May 1947. It was the first major initiative for a nationwide gathering of leading German politicians and immediately elicited widespread support. That support reached deep into the SED, where many former Social Democrats and Communists were eager to pursue national unity. Suspecting a Western trap, Molotov, at Stalin's behest, instructed the Soviet occupation authorities to let Soviet zone state leaders know that "it would under no circumstances permit the participation of the Soviet zone in the meeting planned by the Americans," only to reverse himself the same day, arguing that absence might "damage our interests" in Germany. In advance of the meeting, SED leader Walter Ulbricht committed the representatives of the Soviet zone's state governments to demanding revisions in the agenda for the meeting upon arrival in Munich, a ploy certain to sabotage the conference even before it began.[7]

Moscow reacted even more strongly to a far less significant initiative by Ferdinand Friedensburg, a CDU district mayor in the Soviet sector of Berlin, who in November 1947, just before the London Council of Foreign Ministers meeting, called for the creation of a "Forum of National Representation." In a November 17 telegram, worded in stark and principled terms and reflecting Stalin's imprimatur, Molotov reminded the SED that it had to be in decisive control of all-German initiatives. Molotov's cable suggested a turning point in Soviet policy: abandoning its reservations, Stalin now made the SED seek front and center in all-German initiatives, even if that, as Kaiser anticipated, would weaken support by the western zones' parties.[8]

By summer 1947, it was widely expected throughout Germany that the next Council of Foreign Ministers meeting, scheduled for November–December in London, would fail to reach an accord on Germany. Without objections from the other capitals, Washington had called for a postponement of the critical preparatory meeting of the deputy foreign ministers just before its scheduled gathering in early

October 1947. The postponement virtually eliminated any remaining practical possibilities for agreements at the Council of Foreign Ministers meeting the next month on such issues as reparations and currency reform, then still under negotiation at the Allied Control Council in Berlin.[9]

For Washington, the paramount goal was now to make the Soviets appear responsible for the failure, thus clearing the way for a separate West German government. "The difficulty under which we labor," Ambassador Walter Bedell Smith wrote to Eisenhower during the London discussions, is "that in spite of our announced position, we really do not want nor intend to accept German unification in any terms that the Russians might agree to, even though they seemed to meet most of our requirements." The negotiations in London would require "delicate maneuvering to avoid the appearance of inconsistency if not hypocrisy."[10]

That task was made more difficult as the Soviet zone became a staging ground for Communist-led popular appeals for German unity. Moscow, too, readied for a failure of the London Council meeting. Weeks before the meeting, Molotov's deputy, Fedor Gusev, surmised internally that "the ruling reactionary circles of the USA have entered the path of active propaganda and the preparation of a new war against the Soviet Union and the countries of the new democracy in Europe." As expectations of cooperation dwindled, he recommended that Moscow not await the final outcome but prepare for measures after the inevitable quadripartite meltdown. That was precisely what the Soviet Politburo decided to do, putting proposals for a German peace treaty and the formation of a German government at the center of its conference strategy.[11]

Instead of quadripartite solutions, Stalin seems to have placed his hopes in popular opposition to Western Allied policies. Having been restrained since the summer, the SED suddenly received the green light for its plebiscite initiative and rushed to convene the "German People's Congress for Unity and a Just Peace," on December 6–7, 1947. In the Soviet perspective, the people's congress movement served two ends: solidifying the leading role of the SED in the eastern zone, and broadening its influence to all of Germany.[12]

American officials watched warily as the Soviet-sanctioned SED initiative led to the final break with the CDU leaders Kaiser and Lemmer, the last non-Communist leaders in the zone with a national stature. For Kaiser, the national question was inextricably linked to the survival and independence of his party in the Soviet zone: without an all-German perspective, his party could not stand in the way of SED domination. Following Byrnes's September 1946 Stuttgart speech, Kaiser had pinned his hopes on convening a "national representation." The proposal had met with widespread approval across all of Germany; even Soviet occupation authorities had refrained from voicing opposition publicly.[13]

By summer 1947, Kaiser's open support of the Marshall Plan and overt criticism of the Soviet military government brought relations with SMA officials to the brink. In a heated exchange with Tiulpanov at Karshorst on August 18, related by Murphy to Washington, Kaiser complained about Soviet actions and stated that measures such as the U.S.-sponsored European Recovery Program were necessary for the reconstruction of the country. Sharp verbal exchanges on the issues of borders, reparations, and the Soviet-owned companies in Germany followed. When Kaiser warned in November that a Communist-dominated people's congress would be dead on arrival in western Germany and withheld his support, Tiulpanov engineered his ouster from the party leadership. With Kaiser's departure, Moscow had rid the zone of its last major political figure passionately fighting against its growing separation from the West.[14]

Two weeks before the December 1947 London Council of Foreign Ministers meeting, the SED party leadership published its "Manifesto to the German People on the Occasion of the London Conference," denouncing the Marshall Plan and demanding a democratic and united Germany based on denazification and expropriation modeled after the Soviet zone. In an SED-run "people's referendum" in mid-November 93.8 percent of those polled affirmed that "the desire for national unity is a desire of the entire German people." In spite of the Western powers' refusal to recognize the SED petition to the Council of Foreign Ministers, the SED called on all parties, mass organizations, and leading individuals on November 24, 1947, to convene an all-German "People's Congress for Unity and a Just Peace" on December 6–7.[15]

Assembling an impressive 2,215 delegates from eastern and western Germany, the first people's congress took place in Berlin, highlighting the symbolic importance of the former Reich capital. The congress set up a national weekly, the *German Voice*, designed for interzonal circulation on a large scale. Western observers fretted that the congress had "tremendous potential propaganda value" and quickly suspected that Moscow intended to try to turn it into a de facto parliament for all of Germany, "a coup [that] if successful, could have untold possibilities for influencing votes and direct action in the Western zones."[16]

In the wake of the Communist-led Putsch in Prague in February 1948 and reports of Soviet troop concentrations and maneuver activities along the zonal demarcation line that would escalate into a full-blown war scare in Washington by the end of March, the SED's machinations were not taken lightly by the Truman administration. On the eve of the Second People's Congress, convened on March 17–18, 1948, ranking German Communists talked openly about armed sabotage, resistance, and even a "war of independence" against the Western occupation powers, drawing parallels to the tactics employed by General Markos Vafiades, the leader of the Communist insurgents in the Greek Civil War.[17]

Timed for explicit appeal to the historical traditions of 1848, the people's congress blamed the Western Allies for Germany's deepening division and passed a motion to "dethrone" the Allied Control Council. Aside from demanding all-German central administrations in Berlin and dissolution of the bizonal Economic Council, the congress created a 400-delegate-strong "German People's Council" (and a smaller presidium), charged with drafting a constitution for Germany and conducting a massive drive for a people's initiative petitioning the Allied commanders to hold a "people's referendum" on a law that declared Germany an "indivisible republic." Throughout the country, some 11,000 "People's Committees for Unity and a Just Peace" sprang up in plants, residential areas, universities, and local governments. Between May 23 and June 13, 1948, the People's Council collected 13 million signatures in favor of the referendum, 1 million of which came from the British zone. At its third session, on July 2, the People's Council appealed to the Allied Control Council to order a referendum on the people's initiative resolution as a basic law for all of Germany.[18]

American officials watched the people's initiative and people's congress movement with growing apprehension. U.S. intelligence sources reached deep into the movement. They included Wilhelm Külz, a former Reichstag Deputy for the Weimar-era Democratic People's Party who headed the Soviet-zone Liberal Democratic Party. Külz ostensibly collaborated with the SED but actually served as a source for the U.S. Army's Counter Intelligence Corps, "instructed to play along," even being nominated to the People's Council presidium.[19]

Despite the clumsy beginnings, SED officials left no doubt about the significance they ascribed to the people's congress movement: U.S. military government officials learned that at a March 22 meeting with top SED officials Pieck had emphasized that the nationwide referendum was the "decisive task" for the party. In what American observers termed a "war of nerves which the communists have been carrying on throughout Germany," numerous reports told of SED pressure methods to spur a large turnout. In Berlin, the Soviets apparently went so far as to use their exclusive control of the city's subway system to equip stations in all four sectors with voting booths, overruling the non-Communist municipal government's decision not to make public facilities available for the people's initiative. Throughout the Soviet zone, voting was recorded by local residential and occupational people's initiative committees who publicly listed those who failed to vote and calling them "saboteurs of democracy." With "totalitarian control already established in the Soviet zone," Brewster Morris noted, "countless people" had signed the petition. U.S. intelligence expected 100 percent approval.[20]

Reports from the western zones indicated that by April 1948 the signature collection was well under way there, too, and American officials emphasized "the natural appeal of such propaganda to the German public today." While it quickly became evident that the people's referendum initiative failed to attract any real attention in the western zones, U.S. occupation officials expected "many ignorant and naïve Germans" to be taken in by the "nationalist appeal" of the referendum. Just how effective the campaign might be was illustrated by an open-air meeting in Berlin-Wilmersdorf in the British sector: Though the crowd of five hundred to six hundred people—U.S. observers noted—must have come as a disappointment to the organizers, the SED speakers managed to turn "an initially rather unresponsive audience into an enthusiastic demonstration against the United States," and the meeting occasioned "heated group discussions in the streets for a full hour after [it] had ended." As U.S. officials admitted, the initiative was "one of [the] cleverest Soviet-Communist propaganda moves to date."[21]

Even before the people's congress movement got under way, Clay had announced, much to the surprise of many on his staff, "Operation Talkback," a public anti-communist campaign in the western zones. At a press conference in October 1947, Clay ordered American-controlled media outlets to "abandon any former policies of neutrality and engage in an open propaganda war with the Soviet Zone media." Though the U.S. military governor tried to downplay the change, it was for Clay an astonishing turnabout that in the words of CBS's Edward R. Murrow amounted to a declaration of "psychological war" between the United States and the USSR "for possession of the German mind." Soon after the first people's congress, Clay decided to prohibit any meetings of the movement at the state or zonal level. One such meeting had taken place in Vegesack near Bremen, featuring speeches by Grotewohl and the new Soviet zone CDU leader Otto Nuschke. The SED had considered it an instant success. But other such events planned for North Rhine–Westphalia, Schleswig-Holstein, Hamburg, Hessia, Bavaria, and Rhineland-Palatine had to be canceled in light of the U.S. and British prohibition.[22]

The people's referendum in the spring of 1948 presented American occupation officials with a somewhat more difficult dilemma—after all, the drive for signatures was a basic democratic practice. Ousted CDU leader Jakob Kaiser proposed a competitive referendum, but Washington was uneasy about linking the procedure with the one planned by the SED. Once the referendum went into full swing, Clay decided to allow the circulation of petitions while both ridiculing and banning the collection of signatures on behalf of the people's congress, forcing the SED to carry out the count largely on an "underground basis."[23]

Internal records from the SED archives show that the East German Communist leadership viewed American actions as a measure of its success. Meeting with Stalin in Moscow at the end of March 1948, SED leaders hailed the success of the people's congress movement. Pieck told Stalin that the SED was winning the confidence of the masses in its fight against the reactionary forces and for German unity, citing the people's congress movement as evidence. The SED managed, the Soviet leader learned, to include broad segments of the bourgeoisie in the movement, "to uncover Schumacher's policies and to counter the reactionary efforts within the bourgeois parties." The second people's congress in particular, Pieck noted, had made a "strong impression on the masses, in the West too." The congress needed to be more "impulsive" and better organized, but its "success was confirmed by the countermeasures and propaganda of the Western powers."[24]

Back in Berlin, the SED leaders drew a more sober assessment. The people's congress movement, one leading official conceded, was making only meager progress, and to some extent none at all, "thanks to the malicious propaganda of the Western press." According to one source, Franz Dahlem, the SED's top official charged with the campaign in western Germany, told a friend that the SED "had lost all hope for the success of the referendum in western Germany," adding that the prohibition by the Western powers was perhaps a "blessing in disguise," affording an excuse for the expected failure of the campaign and an opportunity for propaganda in the form of protests. Yet Stalin seemed to have been convinced of the success of the all-German project: in June 1948 he decided to broaden the appeal of the people's congress movement, signaling the Germans to create a new nationwide organization, the "National Front."[25]

"Action Point Berlin"

The failure of the London Council of Foreign Ministers meeting in December 1947 spurred efforts by both the Western Allies and the Soviets to "organize" their zones further. In January 1948, Clay and British occupation chief Sir Brian Robertson reconfigured the bizone, giving its structures greater resemblance to governmental organs. In the "Frankfurt Documents," handed to the assembled Western German minister-presidents and bizonal Economic Council leaders, the occupation chiefs recommended the expansion of the council, the creation of a Länder council, the formation of an executive committee, and a central bank. In February, the three Western Allies, meeting in London with representatives from the Netherlands, Belgium, and Luxembourg, agreed on key aspects of the further development of the western occupation zones in Germany and their inclusion in the Marshall Plan. They asked a West German constituent assembly (Parlamentarischer Rat) to create a constitution by September 1. The West now pressed ahead with preparations for a currency reform in the western zones, which was deemed vital for their struggle for economic recovery: the State Department instructed Clay that it was no longer the policy of the U.S. government to reach an agreement on a quadripartite currency reform. Clay was to bring about an end to the negotiations by June 1.[26]

In the Soviet zone, the Soviet Military Administration and the SED leaders had been working toward more-centralized zonal administration since the spring of 1946. Insisting on increased German participation in economic decisions, Ulbricht had suggested in late September 1946 the creation of a central German office for economic planning in the Soviet zone. Semenov endorsed Ulbricht's proposal, arguing that it was "imperative" to establish "some kind of German zonal government" in the Soviet zone. Semenov reasoned that the SED leadership had to learn how to run a country, and that it was necessary to create a state apparatus that could serve as "the core and basis of future German government agencies." In January 1947, German communist leaders told Stalin—who seemed to agree—that a "zonal council" made up of German representatives was absolutely essential, paving the way to the creation of the German Economic Commission (Deutsche Wirtschaftskommission, DWK) in June. Six months later, the commission was elevated to the status of a provisional government for the Soviet zone. Its charge, as historian Jochen Laufer noted, no longer included cooperation with the Western powers in the Control Council.[27]

With neither side any longer committed to quadripartite governance in Germany, the conventional historical narrative has Western Allies-Soviet relations unraveling in a series of events in the spring of 1948, driven largely by Stalin's desire to prevent the formation of a West German state. At the end of March, Sokolovsky staged a dramatic exit from the Control Council, followed weeks later by the Soviet withdrawal from the Allied Kommandatura in Berlin. In April the Soviets instituted restrictions on transport between Berlin and the western zones. When the Western powers announced that they would proceed with plans for currency reform in the western zones on June 18, the Soviet Military Administration reacted by closing the zonal borders to the West, still allowing, however, for passenger trains to move out of Berlin. On June 22 Sokolovsky ordered the introduction of a new Soviet zone mark that would also be the legal tender in all of Berlin, making, for a time, both the Westmark B mark and the Soviet zone mark parallel currencies in West Berlin. Two days later, the Soviet Military Government blocked the train connection between Berlin and the western zones, an action that was followed shortly thereafter by interruptions to West Berlin's electricity supplies and barge traffic.[28]

In the eyes of Western observers at the time, and historians since, Stalin's maneuvers amounted to a showdown over Berlin designed to deliver a blow to the prestige of the Western powers and further his efforts to prevent a West German state. The introduction of the Soviet zone mark in all of Berlin violated Western occupation rights in Berlin, and the zonal closures were widely seen as an aggressive act that took West Berlin's population hostage. Convinced that American credibility was at stake, Truman and his advisers believed that the West's withdrawal from Berlin under Soviet pressure would constitute a "political defeat of the first magnitude," with repercussions not just in Germany but throughout the world. Reports from the city suggested that in "Soviet-Communist circles" Berlin was referred to as the West's "political Stalingrad." Top SED officials were reportedly convinced that the Western powers would leave Berlin in the spring of 1948, with the Soviets moving into all sectors of the city. The Western evacuation of the city, Washington was told, was considered by the communists to be "the first phase in the liberation of Germany."[29]

Russian archival documentation on Stalin's decision making in the spring of 1948 remains fragmentary. Russian historian Mikhail Narinsky has argued, on the basis of privileged access to Russian documents, that the Soviet military government—presumably with Stalin's consent—was indeed intent on smoking out the Western powers from Berlin. Russian notes of a meeting between the East German Communist leaders and Stalin at the end of March seem to corroborate this interpretation. To Pieck's statement that the SED leaders "would be happy if the Allies were out of Berlin," Stalin apparently responded: "Let's try with [our] common efforts; maybe we'll force [them] out."[30]

But newly available Russian archival sources also suggest that Stalin's decision to institute the currency reform and trade restrictions might have been more than an offensive effort to force the Western Allies' hand. In the spring of 1948, barely three years after the end of World War II, Soviet officials harbored serious concerns about Germany's role in Western "preparations of a new war" against the USSR and its new allies. Such concerns combined with a growing sense that the Soviet zone was on the brink of collapse—and with it, the USSR's main stake in central Europe. Contrary to Western perceptions of the eastern zone's growing isolation from the West, Soviet officials felt that exactly the opposite was true: Well before the currency reform in the western zones threatened to flood the Soviet zone with now devalued old Reichsmarks in what Soviet officials referred to as a "currency war," they blamed the zone's decline on destabilizing Western influence, emanating in particular from Berlin.

Alarming reports from the Soviet zone were mounting in early 1948. In January, the head of the Soviet Foreign Ministry's Third European Department, Andrej Smirnov, according to conversations with leading SED officials, told Vyshinsky that "the current situation in the country was very tense." In most major cities there were great difficulties in providing the population with potatoes, which had, in turn, strongly affected the prestige of the SED. "Would elections be held today, the SED could lose up to one third of the votes it received in the last elections." There was a sense of "indetermination" of the economic situation, of a "lack of any economic prospect" for the zone, widespread resentment over the loss of the eastern territories to Poland, and "unequivocally negative" attitudes toward the Soviet stock companies. Even within the party many were unsure how the eastern zone could compete with the country's western half. One frequently heard the opinion, Moscow was told, that "the West would have everything, but what would happen to the Soviet zone[?]"[31]

With their zone failing, Soviet officials believed that anti-communist groups, harbored and supported by the West, were engaged in machinations vis-à-vis their zone: The "fascist underground," Molotov learned in early March 1948, was considerably expanding its activities against the backdrop of "contradictions" among the occupation powers. Two weeks later, "reactionary propaganda" was still on the rise. The Western press was increasingly reaching the zone, "while our print runs were low." Proposals within the top ranks of the Soviet Foreign Ministry for "countermeasures" against the formation of an anti-Soviet Western bloc in Germany included efforts to seal off the Soviet zone further: The USSR would see itself forced, Smirnov told Molotov, "to eliminate the disparity of our zone in Germany which [in contrast to the other zones] is de facto open." In mid-March Smirnov recommended that Moscow "close its zone" to put it in the same situation as that of the western zones.[32]

By the time the German Communist leaders arrived in Moscow in late March 1948 for briefings with Stalin, the Soviet government had decided on an action plan aimed at shutting off Western influence into the zone. Pieck's and Grotewohl's suggestions merely reinforced what Stalin had already concluded. In a late-night session at the Kremlin, they warned Stalin that "the Western powers are trying to influence the population and direct it against the USSR, arousing hostility against communism." SED counter-agitation against Western Marshall Plan propaganda had not been as successful as on the issue of German unity, Pieck posited to the Soviet leader. Sharp differences had arisen with the Western powers, which had taken "terrorist measures" against the SED. Finally, there was "the powerful propaganda apparatus which the western occupation authorities have in Berlin which the SED cannot even match." Viewed from Moscow, the Western airlift for Berlin launched that summer looked as if the the Allies were doubling down on its beachhead deep inside the Soviet zone.[33]

Declassified U.S. documents, in turn, suggest that concerns for the strategic advantages that Berlin afforded the United States were uppermost on the minds of Truman administration officials as the Berlin crisis unfolded: the Western outpost disrupted the unqualified control that Moscow sought for its zone at the very moment when the Western Allies sought to shore up their zones' viability by launching the formation of a Western German state. Contrary to public perceptions, the CIA informed Truman in June 1948, the main detrimental effect of Soviet access restrictions was *not* the interference with transport and supply. Instead, the tightened Soviet security measures that had accompanied the closing of the zonal borders had "impaired Berlin's usefulness as a center of a U.S. intelligence network" spanning the city, the Soviet zone, and Eastern Europe. Increased police controls in and around Berlin had also made "access to Soviet deserters and anti-communist Germans more difficult." Restrictions on the free movement by West Germans in the Soviet zone threatened, the CIA advised the president, American "support [for] anti-Communism within the Soviet Zone" and dissemination of "pro-West" publication. As America's top diplomat in Germany, Robert Murphy, put it, Berlin was an "action point far inside Soviet-held territory from which to observe developments and to support and influence resistance to Communism in a vital area."[34]

American-sponsored "rollback" activities, in fact, expanded during the 1948–49 period. This was, most obviously, the case in the growing American dominance of the airwaves. The U.S.-controlled and German-staffed Radio in the American Sector (RIAS) had launched in February 1946 (initially as a wired broadcast station) to offer an alternative to the Soviet-controlled and widely-listened-to Radio Berlin as hopes in the immediate postwar period for a quadripartite radio operation for all of Berlin dissipated. Under the leadership of its station chief from 1946 to 1948, liberal émigré and Office of War Information veteran Ruth Norden, RIAS adhered to Clay's conciliatory policy toward the Soviet Union, avoided criticism of other occupation powers, and established itself as doggedly objective, balanced, and nonpartisan. Committed to remaining impartial during the KPD-SPD fusion crisis in the spring of 1946 and the Berlin municipal elections that October, the station had continued to give airtime to SED leaders Pieck, Ulbricht, and Grotewohl, frustrating anti-communist German politicians and in November causing Berlin SPD leader Ernst Reuter to label it "the second Communist station" in Berlin.[35]

But as Clay had shifted from accommodation to counteroffensive and launched Operation Talkback in the fall of 1947, the station had taken an increasingly anti-Communist stance. Still under the liberal Norden, RIAS had begun preparations for a counter-propaganda campaign against Radio Berlin. After a "Captain America style take-over" of the RIAS leadership by former OMGUS intelligence director William Heimlich in February 1948, the station adopted a strategy of propaganda by entertainment and shifted from elite to mass programming with anti-communist overtones. Transformed into a dedicated anti-communist propaganda station with improved equipment and expanded personnel, by late 1948 RIAS, until then second in popularity to Radio Berlin, had become the most-listened-to radio station in Berlin, with a deep reach into the Soviet zone. According to opinion surveys, by 1949 some 90 percent of Berliners identified RIAS as their favorite station.[36]

In the shadow of the Berlin Blockade, the western sectors also became a hotbed of individuals and clandestine groups engaged in espionage and anti-communist activities in the Soviet occupation zone. Since the forced SED merger, the SPD's East Bureau had utilized its links with former party members in the zone, to engage in espionage and black propaganda, claiming, according to CIA documents, some 2,000 agents or informants in the East. In the summer of 1948, the first waves of releases from the secretive "special camps" in the Soviet zone, where tens of thousands of Germans had been held (on the basis of often scanty evidence of their involvement with the Nazis) highlighted the tightening police-state practices in the East. With government services paralyzed by the emergence of rival administrations in Berlin, private citizens groups in the city stepped in to track down missing persons who had vanished into one of the special camps of the Soviet Ministry of Internal Affairs. The activities of these citizens groups frequently were not limited to combined charitable missions; searching for missing persons led to efforts to identify perpetrators and inform Western Allied intelligence services and the public about conditions in the Soviet zone.[37]

The most prominent among these groups was the Kampfgruppe gegen Unmenschlichkeit (Fighting Group against Inhumanity, known by its German acronym, KGU). The Kampfgruppe grew out of a public rally organized by several youth groups in early August 1948 under the banner "Silence Is Murder." The rally featured former detainees from Soviet zone camps and prisons and was broadcast by RIAS into the eastern zone. A little over two months later, on October 17, 1948, Rainer Hildebrandt, who had participated as a courier in the anti-Hitler opposition group led by Albrecht Haushofer, announced the establishment of the KGU at a public "Rally against Tyranny." Following harrowing eyewitness accounts by victims of incarceration, rape, death, and mistreatment at the hands of Soviet camp or prison guards, Hildebrandt decried the Soviet zone as "one big concentration camp" and called Nazi methods "children's play" compared to the Stalinist practices of the Soviet secret police. The Kampfgruppe, he promised, would systematically investigate such crimes by Soviet zone authorities. Espousing radical anti-communism combined with criticism of Western complacency in the face of developments across the zonal border, Hildebrandt effectively called for a cold war against the Soviet zone.[38]

Provisionally headquartered in a villa in the Grunewald forest in the British sector, the KGU initially focused on organizing film screenings, data collection, and humanitarian work. In November 1948, Gerhard Finn, one of the early members of the group, started to build a registry for missing persons who had been arrested in the Soviet zone. Soon the idea emerged to start a second registry for informers and Communist officials. The resonance of these efforts nearly overwhelmed the group's capacity: by June 1949, the registry comprised some 12,000 search requests. The small KGU staff was able to identify the whereabouts of 8,500 detainees.[39]

Well before the Berlin crisis, American intelligence agencies began to tap the information gathered by German organizations with extensive networks in the Soviet zone, involving them in an expanding network that penetrated Soviet zone political, economic, and (para-)police and other institutions. In late 1948 the head of the U.S. Army's Counter Intelligence Corps (CIC)'s Berlin office, Severin F. Wallach, began to draw on the KGU for intelligence purposes and to support it financially. After it was licensed by the Allied Kommandatura as a political organization in April 1949, the KGU moved its headquarters to two well-guarded buildings in the U.S. sector. The group quickly developed multiple links to the U.S. intelligence community in Berlin, including the Military Intelligence Division and, later, the CIA's Office for Policy Coordination. To be sure, the Allied condominium of Berlin also placed constraints on the group's activities. Many years later, Hildebrandt recalled being told by British Kommandatura officials in 1948 to refrain from organizing anti-Soviet events in the British sector ("This is the law").[40]

Under American tutelage, by contrast, the KGU turned increasingly toward active opposition to the Soviet zone authorities from its Berlin base, beginning with the "F campaign" in July 1949. The KGU asked the Soviet zone population to draw the letter "F" on houses and walls around the zone as a sign of resistance, "F" symbolizing "freedom for the terrorized people" and hostility (Feindschaft) against the "terror regime." Soon "F" signs appeared all over the zone. The measure apparently proved so successful that the Soviet zone police found themselves forced to contain the damage by turning the letter into "FDJ" (the German acronym for the Communist "Free

German Youth"). In addition, the KGU printed and covertly disseminated the widely popular satirical magazine *Tarantel*, as well as other flyers and publications.[41]

As a "sanctuary" for non-Communist politics, Western Berlin also undercut Soviet efforts to stabilize its zone by subduing the non-communist political forces and to use the capital vantage point for all-German appeals, especially with a view to winning over "recalcitrant bourgeois elements." A newly cooperative approach by the Soviet Military Administration toward the CDU and LDP in early 1948, the U.S. mission in Berlin suspected, was driven by the desire to "lull" the non-communist forces within the population into a sense of security. It rewarded compliant CDU and LDP leaders, but also reflected the realization that "real support for the SED and the people's congress was less widespread than was hoped." Operating from West Berlin since they had been ousted by the Soviets, Kaiser and Lemmer remained powerful voices in the Soviet zone's political discourse.[42]

The Truman administration continued to wrestle with the question of to what extent the non-communist parties represented resistance potential within the SBZ and how far they should be supported to that effect. While many Germans in the western zones felt that the eastern zone CDU was by now "completely under Tiulpanov's thumb," incapable of resisting the communization of the zone, Lemmer tried to counter the inclination among Murphy's staff to write off the Soviet zone CDU. In repeated conversations he sought to persuade the U.S. officials that the party's rank and file (as opposed to its leadership under Otto Nuschke) "still represented a considerable opposition and would do so as long as they believed that they were not totally cut-off from the West." That opposition, Murphy noted, did indeed occasionally rise to the surface, as in the case of the tumultuous protest against the party's new "strongman," Georg Dertinger, at a CDU meeting in Brandenburg.[43]

But many within the administration remained skeptical about whether this opposition could have "substantially any more effect on the progress of the communization of the zone" than did the protests of the former opposition parties in Eastern European countries." The CIA, in fact, concluded as early as the spring of 1948 that Moscow had virtually completed its "campaign to eliminate all overt opposition in the Soviet Zone."[44]

Truman administration officials carefully monitored Soviet efforts to set up what they termed "Quisling political parties" in Berlin to undermine the powerful Western-oriented Berlin LDP Land organizations. Following the death of the Liberal Democratic Party leader Wilhelm Külz in early April 1948, the Soviets engineered the split of the LDP Land organization in Berlin, led by the anti-Soviet Carl-Hubert Schwennicke (who went on to co-found the Free Democratic Party's east bureau).

They set up an LDP working group (Arbeitsgemeinschaft) (the "real aim" of which, American observers estimated, was "a new Sovietized Land organization" in Berlin that could align itself with the zonal LDP), and they groomed Professor Hermann Kastner as "potential head of an Eastern German government." In July 1948, Alfons Gaertner, the president of the Landesbank of Thuringia and second chairman of the LDP Land organization, who was slated by the Soviets to head the LDP in the Soviet zone, fled to the West. The defection was seen as a "heavy blow to the Soviet Zone LDP" precisely at a moment when the party "had gathered its courage to attack the SED in a surprisingly uninhibited manner."[45]

Yet much of the party leadership throughout the zone remained intact at the local level, American officials learned, and under pressure had resolved many of their differences with the CDU leaders. People throughout the zone, one defected LDP leader reported, were "only waiting" in the hope that the eastern zone would decline to such a "wretched state" that it would no longer be of use to the Russians, and were expecting the Western Allies not to make any compromises with Moscow.[46]

The Truman administration also sought to heighten dissension within the SED, which was suffering from poor morale as well as widespread lethargy and dissatisfaction. The SED's performance had created increasing concern on the part of the Soviets as to the effectiveness of the party. By mid-1948, the party started to undergo a series of changes and purges designed to strengthen it as a Marxist-Leninist strike force. In May, U.S. intelligence reported the creation of an SED Parteiaktiv at a secret meeting. Former Social Democrats in particular now came under more intense pressure. Defections from the SED rank and file increased. Ulbricht's call at the thirteenth meeting of the SED executive committee, on September 15–16, 1948, to abandon the notion of a "peculiar German way to socialism" had to be considered, according to Murphy, as "the funeral ovation over any nationalistic deviations in SED policy."[47] The SED's internal assessments picked up by OMGUS offered a "remarkable confession of failure." SED leaders postured aggressively: Saxony's prime minister, Max Seydewitz, stating, "All we need when the time comes are sufficient weapons and ammunition. We have the fanatics to fight when the occasion arises." Such statements exemplified to Americans the "desperation" that the SED had fallen into "in the face of the hostility of all except a small minority in the Soviet Zone." To U.S. observers, the SED's "even more slavish acceptance of the Marxist-Leninist line" pitted it against the great majority of German public opinion, which was presumed to be "intensely anti-Soviet and anti-Communist."[48]

The defection of the prominent former SPD functionary Erich Gniffke from the ranks of the SED leadership underlined the difficulties. Truman administration officials held out hope that they could induce other prominent SED leaders from the party's Central Committee to bolt from their positions in the Soviet zone, particularly Max Fechner, Friedrich Ebert (son of the Weimar era Reich president), and (most prized of all) Otto Grotewohl, co-chairman of the party and former SPD leader. At the end of 1948, Friedrich Ebert reportedly contacted Western intelligence officers, apparently expressing his desire "to quit and flee Berlin," prompting OMGUS officials to advocate that he be given sanctuary in the U.S. zone. Western intelligence sources included Heinrich Graf von Einsiedel, a member of the Von Seidlitz Group of the National Committee for a Free Germany, who was taken into custody by the Army's Counter Intelligence Corps on May 25, 1948, while visiting Wiesbaden. Achieving the goal of inducing defections was made more difficult by the unremitting position of western SPD leader Kurt Schumacher, who argued that potential high-ranking SED deserters had "burned their bridges" and deserved "absolutely no commitment" to be brought back into the SPD. In the view of one U.S. diplomat, Grotewohl's more recent statements and actions left "little reason to doubt that he has been completely won over to the Communist viewpoint."[49]

The Soviet Zone as a "Springboard for Penetration"?

The Berlin crisis produced the opposite of what Stalin had hoped for: in the short run a Western "counterblockade" that dramatically curtailed Western trade aggravated the economic hardships in the Soviet zone, and the airlift turned former enemies, Western Allies and Berliners (and West Germans) into partners. In the embattled western sectors of the city, anti-communist activists saw their support growing. Yet the longing for national unity had not lost its powerful grip to Germans across all zones. By the spring of 1949, when Western Allied–German relations had fallen to a new low over Allied criticism of the draft constitution developed by the Parliamentary Council in Bonn, Communist efforts couched as all-German initiatives underscored the continued risks to the Western state project.[50]

Soviet zone leaders played to the political malaise by turning to renewed emphasis on German unity, and hard-line "Sovietizers," such as Colonel Tiulpanov, receded into the background of zonal politics. At the SED Party Conference in January 1949, Pieck and Ulbricht renounced any suggestion that the Soviet zone was identical to the "people's democracies" to its east. A new SED Politburo directive placed renewed emphasis on the people's congress movement, which, Americans noted, "had been dormant until quite recently." Reversing earlier claims that Berlin was an integral part of the zone, Ulbricht now declared it to be the capital of all Germany. U.S. officials in Berlin warned that it would be "extremely unwise to dismiss the present Soviet line lightly on the ground that the Germans are basically anti-Soviet."[51]

American officials watched warily as Western Allied measures, such as the Ruhr agreement, the installment of the Military Security Board, and western boundary changes, were enacted amid growing nationalist attitudes and general dissatisfaction in western Germany. East-CDU leader Otto Nuschke, who had succeeded Kaiser and was regarded by U.S. officials as a "handy tool of the Soviet Military Administration," visited the western zones for talks with his western counterparts in early March 1949. Although he seemed to have only limited success at first, U.S. observers noted that "he may have sowed his seeds in miracle soil." Nuschke met with Konrad Adenauer, the president of the constituent Parliamentary Council, who was rapidly emerging as the leading political figure in the western zones, to convince him and other West German leaders that "the bourgeois parties have a real part to play in Germany's future." According to U.S. reporting, Nuschke expected the CDU to come off as the strongest party in Soviet zone elections in the "near future." Former CDU leader Andreas Hermes, who had been ousted by the Soviets in 1945 (over the land reform issue), and former German diplomat Rudolf Nadolny organized a meeting in Bad Godesberg, near Bonn, which included leading German personalities such as Adenauer and former diplomat Friedrich Wilhelm von Prittwitz und Gaffron, who "did not wish to close [the] door [to the East] completely." Much to the dismay of American observers, even the generally pro-Western von Prittwitz und Gaffron reportedly attacked the emerging "Bonn State" as "leading to nationalism and totalitarianism."[52]

Adding to the pressures from the East, the Volksrat, at its sixth session, in March 1949, initiated what it called "the hand-stretched-out-to-the-west." In a letter to the Parliamentary Council in Bonn and the Economic Council in Frankfurt, it invited both bodies to select a delegation to meet in the British zone city of Braunschweig with members of the People's Council for a discussion of Germany's future. A meeting between representatives of the People's Council and some West Germans took place on May 20 in Hanover, but was broken up soon after it opened by the British Military Government. While any meeting with a Volksrat delegation was unacceptable to many "responsible" West German leaders, the idea of a rapprochement between both parts of Germany, American observers surmised, would be welcomed by various elements in the western zones. Germans there seemed increasingly responsive to overtures from the East—"more than could have been imagined a few months ago"—and in growing numbers, appeared eager to revive relations with the SED-controlled authorities in the Soviet occupation zone. In Murphy's view, the situation was "sufficiently serious to warrant a careful re-evaluation of our present course in Germany."[53]

That reevaluation took place in the spring of 1949, triggered by George Kennan, the driving force behind the new covert action program and head of the Policy Planning Staff. As early as August 1948, Kennan had begun to outline a "Program A" for Germany that envisioned Allied troop withdrawals to limited enclaves on the fringes of the country, opening up the possibility for free elections and a German administration in charge across the four occupation zones. In sharp contrast to his own views in 1946–47 but in striking similarity to Clay's views at the time, Kennan now argued that "time is on our side," and that the Berlin Crisis had improved the U.S. position to the extent that "we could go much further in risking the immediate establishment of a German authority than would have been the case six months or a year ago." The state of the Soviet zone figured prominently in Kennan's reasoning: central to this view was that the airlift and counterblockade had weakened the Soviet hold on eastern Germany, bringing it nearly to economic collapse.[54]

The opposition to the organization of a western German state, Kennan argued, stemmed from their realization that in the long run a Communist regime in eastern Germany would not be able to compete successfully with the non-Communist regime in western Germany, "particularly if the political development of the eastern zone along communist lines continues to be disrupted by the presence of western forces in Berlin." Moscow was acting less from strength than from insecurity, Kennan surmised, and the blockade was turning into a decisive failure. The western option for a unified Germany, said Kennan, provided a unique, perhaps final chance to roll back Soviet influence throughout the entire country. CIA estimates seemed to support his view: the blockade had resulted in "growing anti-Soviet sentiments" among eastern Germans, and presented "the basis of a political problem" for Moscow. U.S. intelligence agencies had also picked up on SED uneasiness about the prospect of an end to the blockade that might lead to the elimination of the zonal borders.[55]

Kennan's proposals, in particular his call for partial military withdrawal by the occupation powers to marginal enclaves, were met with strong criticism from many within the administration who felt that "it was too late for the U.S. to change its position regarding the establishment of a West German government." Officials in the War and State Departments feared that without a strong U.S. military presence in the country, Soviet interference in German internal affairs might bring a pro-Soviet government in Germany to power, which would make it impossible to maintain Western-oriented governments in France and Italy. Others felt that it was unrealistic to expect the USSR to tolerate a free, united, and likely Western-oriented Germany. They expected that the Soviets would likely try "by every device of sabotage and terror to over throw it." Recent tightening of control in the Soviet zone suggested to some that free institutions could be restored in the eastern part of the country only "at cost of a civil war." Still others pointed to the economic degradation of eastern Germany, which would "make it difficult to achieve an integrated sound economy."[56]

Kennan's critics pressed for continued efforts toward a separate West German state in the belief that the Western powers first needed to build a position of strength by recognizing France's and Britain's security interests and securing Germany within a Western European framework, if necessary at the expense of German unity. Rather than pursuing an "ideal" program for German unity such as Program A, they favored, in any future discussions with the USSR, a modus vivendi with regard to Germany that would be limited to the resumption of normal trade, allowing the Soviets "at least to stabilize the deteriorating economic conditions in their zone."[57]

Clay, who since 1948 had become the main proponent of the London decisions, now reacted sharply to Kennan's proposals, warning that any all-German solution had to include continued U.S. economic assistance and that the U.S. security screen had to remain in place, since its withdrawal would "discourage the resistance movements" in the satellite countries. True to his earlier convictions, however, Clay shared Kennan's belief that Western support for German unity offered an opportunity he had sensed since first taking charge in Germany: "Obviously," he argued, a unified Germany could be an advantage to the West, and could be used as a "spring board for penetration into the Satellite countries." Other key foreign policy figures, such as Philip C. Jessup and Republican foreign policy expert John Foster Dulles, supported the longer-term rollback potential of a unified Germany. Contrary to the "hypercautious" attitudes of the French and British, they agreed that U.S. policy should "not rest on our laurels but exert unremitting pressure to reduce Soviet influence in Eastern Europe." In this view, "the Soviets and their German stooges have far more to fear from the partial opening of Eastern Germany to Western influences than we have from a slightly increased exposure of free Germany to Communist associations." Germany and Austria might "offer the most favorable fields in which to press forward now."[58]

Truman's new secretary of state, Dean Acheson, resolved the debate within the administration in March 1949 by setting American policy on dual tracks that placed emphasis on consolidating the West German arrangements, while leaving open the possibility for quadripartite agreement. After a trip to Germany by Kennan that convinced him to throw U.S. support behind pro-Western German leaders, Acheson signed off on NSC recommendations for the creation of a West German state. On March 31, he suggested to Truman that the United States push for a simplified occupation statute, a stronger central government in western Germany, and the transfer of authority from a military governor to a civilian high commissioner. At the Washington talks in April that established NATO, Acheson reassured the British and French foreign ministers of the U.S. commitment to Western European security. At the same time, the Truman administration began to negotiate secretly for an end to the blockade. Discussions at the UN in early May resulted in agreement to lift the blockade and convene another Council of Foreign Ministers meeting on Germany.[59]

Some within the Truman administration expected that the USSR, faced with the imminent prospect of complete exclusion from the heart of Germany and with the "Soviet zone milked dry," would make a "drastic and dramatic shift" at the forthcoming Council of Foreign Ministers meeting in Paris. Signs of such a shift could be seen in indications by SED leaders that in order to achieve an all-German solution, they would be willing to give up the "anti-Fascist democratic order" and reach an understanding with "big industrialists and former Nazis." Suspecting that the Council of Foreign Ministers session in Paris and the rapid progress in Bonn had caused the SED to accept "strange bedfellows," James Riddleberger, Murphy's successor as political adviser, argued that the statements might imply a "radical change in SED policy."[60]

But the foreign ministers' meeting failed to produce a breakthrough. Soviet foreign minister Vyshinsky advocated a return to the system of four-power control, which was a non-starter the Western ministers. Instead of an all-German government, he limited his demand to a council composed of representatives of the economic councils in the eastern and western zones. The Soviet leaders, Truman was told, "feel that their political position in Germany, and the position of their German friends and partisans, [is] so weak that they do not dare take a chance at this time on the establishment of a real all-German government." Could it be, Kennan wondered, that "the fortunes in the cold war have shifted so fundamentally in the past two years that it is now the Russians who are trying to follow with regard to us, a policy of firmness and patience and unprovocative containment?"

But Washington shied away from exploiting the "fortunes in the cold war" by a bold offer on German unity as Kennan had advocated. All that the foreign ministers could agree on, in the end, was the resumption of interzonal trade, to be negotiated by German authorities. Following their agreement to the Basic Law for a Federal Republic, the Western Allies proceeded with elections to a "Deutscher Bundestag" throughout the western zones in August. In September, a West German federal government under Adenauer took office, restrained by the reserve powers held by the Three Powers as represented in their newly installed high commissioners. Within weeks, Stalin followed suit.[61]

Moscow's "Major Satellite"? The United States and the Establishment of the German Democratic Republic

The establishment of the German Democratic Republic (GDR) shortly after the founding of the Federal Republic of Germany did not take the Truman administration by surprise. Since the SPD-KPD merger in April 1946, U.S. officials had expected—and to a certain degree even hoped—that Moscow would move ahead with the creation of a separate government in the Soviet occupation zone. The questions for American policy makers were not *whether* the USSR would launch its "own" government in Germany, but *when, how*, and—most importantly—*why* this would be done. The answers to these questions had significant implications for the status and security of Berlin and the western zones as they were being merged into a separate government in the West. The developments in the Soviet zone, the Truman administration continued to assume, would thus allow for a further "reading" of Soviet intentions on the German problem. Would Moscow forgo its all-German aspirations and turn the Soviet zone into a people's democracy modeled after its East European neighbors? Or would the new government in the Soviet zone simply offer new, possibly more-dangerous opportunities for expanding Soviet influence throughout the country, peacefully or militarily?[62]

Initially the impetus behind setting up a centralized German administration in the Soviet zone had, in the eyes of U.S. Military Government observers, been an effort to offset the "particularist" tendencies in the Länder and provinces in the Soviet zone and the administrative difficulties created by overlapping responsibilities of local and Länder governments. The creation of zone-wide administrative bodies would not only resolve administrative confusion; it would also allow the SED to assert its authority more effectively over local opposition forces. Since the launch of the people's congress movement just before the inconclusive London Council of Foreign Ministers meeting in December 1947, however, Americans suspected that Stalin would use the congress "as the basis for a possible eventual Communist-dominated German government." Given the SED-dominated composition of the

People's Council, the movement's executive committee, Truman administration officials figured that such a Soviet creation would be easily "recognized as a patent fraud." U.S. intelligence reports noted that "certain top SED-KPD leaders expect the *Volksrat* and/or its successor with governmental pretensions may eventually be given complete authority in Northeastern Germany."[63]

To others within OMGUS, however, the German Economic Commission, set up in mid-1947, was a far more likely option as a precursor for a full-fledged government. In March 1948, U.S. intelligence noted that the Soviet zone administration was stepping up controls at the zonal border, purportedly to clamp down on illegal border crossings, and building up paramilitary units, and in May, DWK decisions were announced as quasi-governmental ordinances. A few months later, following changes in the western zones, Sokolovsky expanded the DWK from 36 to 101 members, leading American officials to wonder whether the Soviet Military Government would promote "the oft-rumored East Zone government through the instrumentality of the DWK rather than through the *Volkskongress*."[64]

But it was the People's Council's Constitutional Committee that the SMA authorized in May 1948 to draft a constitution for a German Democratic Republic. How soon the people's congress movement would develop into a government remained even to OMGUS specialists "as much of a riddle as ever." In July 1948, the People's Council's Constitutional Committee published a draft of basic principles for a German constitution, then was instructed by the People's Council at its August 3 session to have a final formulation ready by mid-September. Despite public denials by leading People's Council members that the body was planning an East German government as answer to a West German government, the fifth session of the People's Council, in late October 1948, adopted a "German constitution." To many U.S. observers, the activities of the committees of the People's Council already gave that body "all aspects of [an] embryo parliament."[65]

What was the reason for these confusing assessments? To Stalin, there was no question that there would have to be a government in the zone if the West proceeded with its plans. "If a separate West German government is created in the west then a government will have to be created in Berlin," the Soviet leader told SED leaders, who were ordered to Moscow in December 1948. If American analysts were getting conflicting signals, it resulted from the lack of resolution between the Kremlin and the SED about *how* and *when* to establish such a government in the zone. The Soviet government tended to favor the people's congress with its all-German appeal; Walter Ulbricht argued for an expansion of the DWK, where SED-dominated parties and mass organizations held a slim majority. The discussions culminated during the secret summit in Moscow in December 1948. Countering the Germans' arguments for a zonal parliament (people's chamber) based on an expanded DWK, Soviet foreign minister Molotov pointed to the German People's Council, "which for some reason the SED leaders never talk about in their proposals." When Pieck replied that the People's Council was an all-German body, Molotov asked whether it was "possible to tie the government to the People's Council so that the zonal nature was not stressed"—something that Stalin himself confirmed was very important: "Why couldn't it be done so that the People's Council elects the government[?]"[66]

Uncertainty about the procedure notwithstanding, to American observers it was clear that any eastern government would be set up in Berlin "in view of its great psychological implications" as the former Reich capital. They suspected that such a government would "definitely have national pretensions," rather than being limited to the zone alone. Such an assumption reflected the near consensus among Western observers that Soviet and German Communist objectives still encompassed all of Germany. Vying for popular support throughout Germany, neither Moscow and the SED nor the Truman administration was eager to take the blame for openly dividing the country. As the Truman administration sought British and French agreement to a West German state in early 1948, U.S. officials would have considered an early Soviet announcement of the establishment of a German republic an "advantage," inasmuch as it would force the "Soviets [to] take [the] onus of [a] split and destruction [of the] ACC [Allied Control Council]." A Soviet move prior to a final Western decision was regarded as an action that would "clearly shift responsibility to Soviets for splitting Germany." American officials were careful to avoid allowing the decision for a Western solution to be viewed as writing off German unity and the Soviet zone altogether, even if some of those involved internally acknowledged that such was, for now, the case.[67]

Stalin was eager not to take the blame either: "You don't want to be the initiators of the division of Germany," Stalin told the SED leadership in late 1948. In fact, the Soviet leadership held out hopes for appealing to the concerns by Germans on both sides of the demarcation line: as early as June 1948 Semenov had urged the SED leaders to think about such a manifesto for a "National Front" that would appeal to all Germans—even, as SED leader Pieck noted, to "for[mer] Nazi" and "for[mer] military" in order to serve as a "combat formation" for the "strengthening of the nat[ional] liberation struggle." Shortly before the Third People's Congress, Semenov sought to impress upon the German comrades that Stalin wished for more than the kind of rhetoric that was typically on display at unity and peace events. The SED leaders were asked to go "a step further than the People's Congress"—but they were unsure where this would lead: "Creation of a Nat[ional] Front," Pieck noted, but "what is this supposed to be?" It had not been "prepared," and the suggested propaganda slogans seemed "precarious: Nazi slogans to the outside—poss[ibly] nat[ional] unity front—in inward direction." The Third People's Congress convened in Berlin on May 29, 1949. The following day, the congress ratified the draft constitution and adopted the "Manifesto to the German People," calling for a "National Front for Unity and a Just Peace."[68]

Nonetheless, further Soviet actions would be, the Truman administration acknowledged, "to a great extent . . . determined by the further measures which the occupation powers take in western Germany." Stalin, in fact, seems not to have made the final decision to set up the GDR until after the September 15 election of Konrad Adenauer as federal chancellor. The following day, an SED leadership delegation—Pieck, Ulbricht, Grotewohl, and Oelssner—arrived in Moscow for yet another meeting to receive instructions on the establishment of a government in the East. In their meetings with Soviet officials, Pieck argued that the establishment of the GDR had become unavoidable since the "Western occupation powers under American leadership [were working] towards a colonization of the West" and were—"by integration into the North Atlantic Pact [NATO, founded in April 1949] and by the occupation statute"—imposing "their absolute rule over the Western population." In this situation, it was necessary to "proceed now in the Soviet occupation zone with the creation of a German government." The new government would be "based on the Potsdam Accords and call for the German unity, a peace treaty and national independence." According to Pieck, the new regime would receive additional legitimacy through a "campaign for the uncovering of the Western government as an organ of the Western powers," which would prompt a "call by the people for a German government."[69]

Yet it took another eight days before Stalin gave the green light on the foundation of the GDR. Stalin agreed to the postponement of an election until the fall of 1950, and advised the SED to facilitate its transformation to a "party of a new type" through a purge of its membership. After the establishment of the West German republic, a joint meeting of the Volksrat presidium and the Democratic bloc on October 5 demanded unanimously that the Volksrat, in an "act of national self-defense," reconstitute itself as the Provisional GDR Parliament (Volkskammer) and elect a "constitutional" government—which it did in an October 7 session. Three days later, Moscow endorsed the action, reconstituting the Soviet military government as the Soviet Control Commission (SCC) and overtly ceding authority to the new government in Berlin. On October 11, the Volkskammer and the Länderkammer elected Pieck president, and the following day Grotewohl presented his cabinet, with SED functionaries occupying key ministries. With the new regime installed, Stalin cabled his blessings, hailing the GDR as the "foundation for a united, democratic and peace-loving Germany" and a "turning point in European history."[70]

5

"Preventing Roll-up"

Diplomatic Blockade, Free Elections, and the "Battle of Berlin"

Retooling for Rollback: Getting the West Germans on the Offensive

For the United States, the establishment of the GDR in the fall of 1949 did not relieve the Cold War confrontation in Germany but in fact heightened the problem. Choreographed by Stalin to blame the country's division on the West, the launch of the GDR appeared to give the USSR new momentum and new opportunity in Germany. It "jolt[ed] the smugness which has surrounded both Allies and Germans at Bonn" since the founding of the Federal Republic, the *New York Times*'s Germany bureau chief, Drew Middleton, commented. Rather than making the best of what they had in Germany, the Soviets, Middleton asserted, "were opening a new political offensive toward their primary objective—Germany."[1] The emergence of two rival German states was a "monstrous offspring" of the Soviet-American confrontation, Pulitzer Prize–winning American journalist Anne O'Hare McCormick commented. Coming on top of the "shattering defeat of Western policy in China" with the founding of the People's Republic and the Soviet Union's first successful atomic test, the formation of a communist state in Germany helped "shake the optimism that grows so easily in the American soil and climate."[2] The Cold War in Europe, it seemed, had reached a new inflection point.

This dim view of the situation in Germany was shared by officials within the Truman administration. The setup of the East German regime did not give American officials the sense of "advantage" or even "settlement" that they had hoped for in the wake of the Paris four-power foreign ministers' meeting that ended the Berlin blockade. Instead it brought on a new sensation of uncertainty, threat, and vulnerability vis-à-vis the East. From Moscow, U.S. Ambassador Alan G. Kirk predicted in a message laced with martial language that the GDR would serve the Kremlin primarily as a strategic base for conquest, "not only of Berlin, but also [of the] far-more important western zones, including [the] key Ruhr area" and the "eventual domination of all of Europe." Stalin's blessing the GDR as the cornerstone of a united Germany revealed to Kirk the manner in which the Kremlin had endeavored "to ride two horses at once: the rapid communization of the Soviet zone; and the capture of all Germany."[3]

No less evocative in his language was the man who would be responsible for leading American policy in Germany: John J. McCloy, the newly minted U.S. high commissioner, intoned that the United States was facing the next phase in the "struggle for the soul of Faust." The creation of the GDR, said McCloy, had injected a "new threat" into postwar German politics, and at a minimum, the Soviets had acquired important new propaganda tools. They could exploit the appeal of Berlin as the capital of the new Germany in the East, and the potential for trade with Germany's eastern neighbors, the country's traditional trade outlet, compared favorably with the problems the Federal Republic was facing in regaining markets in the West. East Germany would not be just another Soviet "vassal state": the Soviets, McCloy surmised, might "be planning to make East Germany their major satellite."[4]

Within weeks of its establishment, the new East German government went on the offensive and renewed earlier all-German unity campaigns with added vigor. On February 22, 1950, the new GDR foreign minister, Georg Dertinger, publicly demanded the immediate conclusion of a peace treaty with a united Germany and described the German Democratic Republic (GDR) as the "trustee of the entire German people." The same month, the people's congress movement formally re-constituted itself as the National Front and geared up for a major convention in August. Appealing to key audiences in West Germany, nationally minded citizens, export industries and youth, it demanded the reunification of Germany through a "national plebiscite," the termination of the occupation statute in West Germany, and the expansion of trade with the Soviet Union and Eastern Europe.

The East German government also announced that the SED-led Free German Youth (FDJ) would stage an "international" youth rally, the Deutschlandtreffen, in Berlin on the last weekend of May. East German government spokesman Gerhart Eisler announced the rally at a press conference on January 30. He previewed plans for some 20,000 youth selected from the anticipated 500,000 participants to enter the three Western sectors as "propaganda agitation groups" that sought support from West Berliners to "fight against remilitarization and war."[5]

What made these statements all the more threatening was that they were not just formal declarations, not simply echoes of Soviet policy directions; the frenzied activism with which the new communist state appeared on the international stage reflected the East German Communists' sincere hopes of expanding the "antifascist-democratic order" of the Soviet zone to the west. SED leaders were deeply committed to achieving German unification in short order, on socialist terms. For the members of the Politburo, historian Michael Lemke has demonstrated, there was no contradiction between socialism and German unity; indeed, they saw themselves as much as German patriots as their counterparts in Bonn.

Even so, the SED's efforts in these early months fell short of Stalin's expectations, and the Soviet leader demanded even greater focus on all-German unity. In early May 1950, he chided a delegation of German Communist leaders (Wilhelm Pieck, Otto Grotewohl, Walter Ulbricht, and Fred Oelßner) visiting Moscow for lacking offensive on all-German activities. The central purpose of the SED leaders' Moscow trip was to align expectations for the SED's Third Party Congress, planned for July 1950. The Soviet leadership ordered the SED to strengthen its activities in West Germany. On its return to Berlin, the SED Politburo, in best Stalinist practice, adopted a self-critical resolution, admitting that the party was "insufficiently oriented towards resolution of all-German tasks." Given that "the main task is the development of an all-German policy, the leading organs of the party must not confine themselves to their tasks in the GDR alone."[6]

Not surprisingly, then, the GDR's activist stance in the first half of 1950 impressed Truman administration officials as a serious challenge. Not only had the economic disparities between the two German states yet to fully emerge. While the Soviets seemed to have gained in the GDR a platform for consolidating SED control unimpeded by constraints that the quadripartite co-dominium had imposed under the Allied Control Council, the Truman administration's relationship with "its" Germans was rapidly deteriorating. By early 1950 the successful founding of the Federal Republic the preceding September was fast losing its luster in the eyes of many Germans. To be sure, the November 1949 "Petersburg agreement" between the three Western high commissioners and Chancellor Konrad Adenauer had brought about a turning point on the contentious issue of industrial dismantling, and FRG's accession to the International Ruhr Agency later that year offered West Germans a voice in the control of this important industrial hub. But it also highlighted the

FRG's continued treatment as a defeated and occupied country—one with which the United States and its wartime allies remained formally at war.

While the Soviets had been building up centralized regular police forces in the Soviet zone since March 1948 and in May began forming paramilitary "barricaded" police, officially referred to as "alert squads" to avoid complications with the Western Allies in view of the Potsdam agreement on Germany's disarmament, an Allied Military Security Office continued to oversee the Federal Republic's strict demilitarization. Western Allied officials initially ruled out developing West German military or federal police forces, limiting police functions to the local and state authorities. Anxious over its exposure vis-à-vis the east and internal "fifth column," the federal government had begun demanding Allied security reassurances soon after it came into being. As early as November 1949, Adenauer had warned Secretary of State Acheson that the Soviets expected the SED and the People's Police forces to take over the rest of Germany and overwhelm the weak communal police forces if the Allies withdrew their troops. Time and again the chancellor warned about the "very lively subversive activities from the Eastern Zone" that could cause centers of unrest at any moment. In December 1949 Adenauer had requested a declaration by the Western Allies that they would protect the Federal Republic, and McCloy complained about the "continual pressure" from the German leader on the issue. Adenauer's advisers also developed ideas for a mobile West German federal police, some 25,000 men strong and "modeled after the East German people's police," only to encounter firm Allied opposition in the early months of 1950.[7]

Most egregious from the perspective of many West Germans in the spring of 1950 was the unresolved final status of the industrially and strategically important Saar territory, which, despite being considered a part of Germany under the Potsdam agreement, had effectively come under French control. GDR foreign minister Dertinger played to widespread national dismay over the contentious issue by "appealing" to the federal government on January 18 not to agree to the separation of the Saar territory. In early March, the French government sought to formalize its hold on the territory through a set of secretly negotiated conventions presented to the Germans as a fait accompli. Worse, France, with backing by the United States, insisted that the Federal Republic join the Council of Europe, viewed by many Germans as an anti-Soviet "coalition" that served only to deepen the rift with the East, at the same time as the Saar government—a stark reminder of the FRG's less than sovereign status. So were "vetoes" with which the Allied High Commission intervened against new federal civil service and tax reform laws in April 1950.[8]

With Western Allied–West German relations at a low point, McCloy worried about the West Germans' will to resist the unity temptations emanating from the East. To be true, the Soviets faced an uphill battle in their effort to use the new Communist-run state in East Germany in the guise of the "National Front" as a platform for attracting western Germans to a socialist vision of Germany's future. Most of the Federal Republic's political class viewed the Grotewohl government with utter contempt. Chancellor Adenauer had thoroughly anti-Communist credentials, had even been decried by the SPD opposition as "Chancellor of the Allies" (after he signed the Petersburg agreements). U.S. opinion polls indicated that a vast majority of Germans in the U.S. zone who had actually heard of the GDR discounted it as a Soviet puppet regime. Its extended arm in West Germany, Communist Party (KPD), remained a marginal force politically.[9]

Yet U.S. officials were not without reason to be wary of potential future shifts in German popular opinion. Barely two-thirds of U.S. zone residents polled were informed enough to have even heard of the GDR. Disillusioned by war and Nazism, large swaths of German society remained disengaged from politics and thus could potentially become fertile ground for GDR propaganda efforts. In Washington, President Truman was told by the intelligence community that frustrated national aspirations, powerful forces favoring the country's neutrality between East and West, or a resurgence of the extreme Right outspoken in their support of rapprochement with the USSR might undermine German support for pro-Western policies.[10]

Adenauer, moreover, was personally difficult to deal with, viewed as increasingly authoritarian in style and given to bouts of gloom over the West's strength and reliability. Berating an irritated McCloy in a late-night session in mid-April 1950, Adenauer testily excoriated the "major deterioration" of the West European situation, especially compared to the "awesome bloc of Russia and his satellites." His dilatory attitude on the FRG's joining the Council of Europe did little to quiet lingering doubts on the part of the Allied officials about the West Germans' commitment to the West. (The Federal Republic would join the Council as an associate member in July 1950.)[11]

Adenauer, in fact, fed American worries about popular sentiment in Germany, certainly in part to enhance his own essential role, though his fears seemed to have been genuine. In his very first conversation with Acheson, the chancellor had told the U.S. secretary of state that "the German nation was in a state of mental instability," that eastern Germany had always looked to Russia, and that many Germans, including some SPD leaders, believed that Russia "may one day extend her influence into Western Germany if and when American troops should leave." McCloy he told that there were "wide circles, especially among the industrialists" in the Federal Republic which were inclined "to see advantage in looking for a link to the East." At other times, the chancellor drew a grave picture of "growing degradation of public life" resulting from the "spiritual infiltration infected by the East."[12]

The Truman administration's response to the Soviet–East German challenge therefore evolved along two tracks. First, it sought to reassure the West Germans that a Soviet attack was unlikely in the short run: The Soviet Union, Adenauer was informed, was not yet prepared economically for World War III. Yes, Western Europe's military capacity, especially that of France, was "entirely insufficient," McCloy acknowledged on another occasion that spring, but a Soviet invasion would come at the terrible price of atomic attacks on "all Russian centers." American troops, moreover, McCloy imparted to Adenauer on yet another occasion, were being equipped with newly developed anti-tank weapons. The Allies, the Germans were told, had placed about 10,000 troops in the Western sectors of Berlin and were rushing heavy arms in to guard against a Volkspolizei takeover. No signs had thus far been detected that the Soviet military was mobilizing. Even if, as Allied officials generally seemed to agree, a Soviet attack was quite likely, it would not come for another year or two. The West could use this window of time to prepare, which, military experts expected, would involve a German defense contribution, persistent French objections notwithstanding. Finally, in May, the Allies sanctioned a small federal police force in West Germany, a "Republican Guard" some 5,000 men strong.[13]

Rather than military, however, the threat was—for now—viewed by the Americans to be first and foremost psychological in nature: Moscow and its East German ally were on the offensive. Among the U.S. High Commission staff (HICOG), some officials fretted about a Soviet "master plan" for using the GDR as a base and instrument to "dislodge the Western Allies and their sponsored German governments from Western Germany and Berlin." They suspected that the Soviets were operating according to a specific timetable. One particularly alarmist scenario argued that 1950 would be the decisive year—all events in the GDR and Berlin, such as the planned youth rally in May, the party congress in July, the National Front convention in August, and parliamentary elections set for October would be "exploited, designed and adapted" to serve National Front objectives. If the opportunity was "ever judged ripe, organized mobs will be directed against Western Allied installations."[14]

In the GDR, Moscow had gained a pliable proxy in the German Cold War. The Truman administration realized that reassurances of support for the Federal Republic against a potential Soviet invasion were thus not sufficient to secure the Germans' allegiance. In addition to inoculating Western Germany against Communist subversion, U.S. officials in Germany were convinced that it would take nothing short of a Western counteroffensive that would seek to undermine Moscow's hold on its "base" in Germany. An "essential" condition "for securing the adhesion of Germany to the West," the CIA told Truman in late April was to minimize the internal effectiveness and external appeal of the Communist-dominated East German regime.[15]

The U.S. high commissioner's office had in fact deliberated elements of a more active policy toward the East since late 1949. A first plan, aptly named "Touchback," had called for a variety of measures that would impede sovietization efforts in the GDR by "maintaining the morale and will to passive resistance among the great majority of anti-Soviet East Germans." Through radio and "coordinated clandestine printed material distribution," Western information media were to aim at keeping the East German population informed of conditions in the West, "hammering at Soviet propaganda myths," and repeating the West's desire for German unification through free elections. In addition to ensuring Berlin's role as a "model and prosperous Western pocket deep within the Soviet Zone," the U.S. presence in Berlin would "facilitate all Western Allied operations behind the Iron Curtain."[16]

Much to the frustration of the Truman administration, Adenauer's new government seemed far less interested in actively opposing the threat from the East than recovering German sovereignty. To be sure, Adenauer himself had declared in a March interview that "the Cold War is based on psychological warfare." With his widely anticipated first speech in Berlin on April 18, he had intended above all to "strengthen the East Zone population in its fight against the East," he told British High Commissioner Sir Brian H. Robertson afterwards, claiming that his speech had left a deep impression in the East.But on the whole the Federal Republic appeared to HICOG officials to be "too much on the defensive" against the Eastern unity propaganda. The State Department tried to impress upon West German officials the need for a more active policy on the unification issue. McCloy himself repeatedly insisted that "we must get the western Germans more on the offensive against the eastern Germans," but had to admit that Adenauer was "not interested in this question."[17]

Adenauer did create a "Department of All-German Affairs" under former Soviet zone CDU chief Jakob Kaiser that was to deal with unification and eastern zone matters. Central to the department's mission was keeping alive the idea of the one German people, first and foremost by systematically studying the social, legal, economic, and political development of the "Eastern zone" and the territories beyond its eastern border along the Oder and Neiße rivers (now under Polish administration), and by disseminating its research to other government departments and the West German public at large. The "Kaiser ministry" (or BMG) would also pursue "every possible avenue," internal planning documents postulated, to give the "Germans in the East" a "sense of the nature and development" of the Federal Republic, "the core territory of a future unified Germany." With his background as a Christian union-ist, member of the anti-Hitler resistance and leader of the Soviet zone CDU whose insistent efforts in favor of all-German unity had brought him into conflict with the Soviets, Kaiser certainly enjoyed broad respect among Germans east and west.[18]

But his fledgling ministry—a "political agency" rather than a full department—lacked administrative authority, funding, and ambition. Limiting the ministry's purview was Adenauer's unchallenged prerogative in foreign policy, which was, to the chancellor, the key arena for any efforts toward future unification. Kaiser was left with a largely domestic agenda of documentation, research, and public outreach. He was forced to depend on other departments for resources and implementation. Lacking the interest or skills to manage even a small bureaucracy, he left much of the day-to-day operation to his small professional staff, many of them refugees from the Soviet zone.

Complicating relations with Adenauer and the running of the BMG was the chancellor's personal animosity toward Franz Thedieck, Kaiser's confidant, whom the latter had chosen as state secretary, effectively his deputy. The two had clashed decades earlier when Thedieck, then heading the Prussian state agency fighting sepa-ratism in the Rhineland, had opposed Adenauer's cooperation with the "Rhineland Movement." Not until July was Thedieck able to take over managing the department. Much of the initial operation—one of the ministry's stalwarts later revealed—looked like "inept attempts at political dilettantism."[19]

Nor were the Americans impressed by the other side of West Germany's political class: Kurt Schumacher, a concentration camp survivor, acerbic anti-Communist, and vehemently national-minded SPD leader, enjoyed the "greatest dislike imagin-able" among Western Allied officials. The opposition chief was profoundly skepti-cal that any European union would be adequate protection against the East and ventured that the 18 million Germans in the eastern zone would view the Federal Republic's accession to the Council of Europe as directed against them. Though the SPD retained a formidable intelligence and aid network in the GDR through its Eastern bureau, in the eyes of U.S. officials Schumacher seemed to have had little concrete to suggest except that policy toward the GDR had to be planned on a long-term basis. Schumacher told American officials that it was essential to keep up the courage of the masses in East Germany and "make them feel that they had something to hope for." But they found it difficult to "keep him [Schumacher] on p[oin]t, esp[ecially] as to what actually might be done re[garding the] E[astern] Zone." Internally, they had to admit that in the months following the founding of the GDR, American efforts had themselves been "almost exclusively of a defensive character."[20]

Reflecting his sense of urgency about mounting an effective countereffort to Soviet and East German activities, McCloy set up an innovative bureaucratic node that could coordinate such efforts across the High Commission. In doing so, he drew on his deep involvement in the creation of the U.S. national security bureaucracy in the late war and early postwar years. One of his principal contributions had been the creation in 1944 of the State-War-Navy Coordinating Committee (SWNCC), which helped coordinate the government's psychological warfare efforts. The committee became a forerunner of the National Security Council (NSC), a high-level decision-making body within the administration for national security policy, with the purview of coordinating and integrating activities among the various national security departments, including the newly created Department of Defense and the Central Intelligence Agency. The SWNCC also served as a precursor to the Psychological Strategy Board (PSB), launched in 1951, which in addition to its coordination role, conducted planning for psychological operations undertaken by various U.S government agencies.[21]

While much has been written about the NSC and the PSB, the high commissioner's Political and Economic Projects Committee (PEPCO) has been overlooked in the scholarly literature. Many of its proceedings and activities were classified. Composed of the chiefs of the political, economic, public affairs, and intelligence branches of HICOG, the committee met weekly and oversaw the coordination of HICOG operations. The fact that the U.S. Berlin commandant, General Maxwell Taylor, frequently joined the PEPCO meetings indicated a measure of its importance.

In particular, PEPCO was to advise McCloy on Soviet and East German activities with the aim of anticipating, countering, and frustrating moves by the East. In a rare allusion to the committee in the press, *New York Times* reporter Jack Raymond, who as a former editor and reporter for the Armed Forces' *Stars and Stripes* maintained excellent connections within HICOG, noted later that spring that McCloy had "a group of advisers who concern themselves especially with the East-West problem and who hold regular meetings." With regard to East German initiatives, HICOG sources told Raymond that "from now on we will stick pins in their balloons before they can hoist them." In a generally critical review of HICOG's operations in this area later that year, RAND social scientist Hans Speier was impressed with PEPCO

as an "administrative novelty," calling it in a secret report a "testimony to the progress in organized political thinking." In effect, PEPCO became the operational and
intelligence headquarters for a more concerted approach toward the GDR, McCloy's
kitchen cabinet for the Cold War in Germany.[22]

A few weeks later, moreover, HICOG set up the Soviet zone Reporting and Programming Office in Berlin. Headed by Foreign Service officer George Morgan and
drawing its personnel from the HICOG Berlin Office's Political Affairs Division and
the economic and intelligence offices of HICOG in Frankfurt, the Eastern Affairs
Division—or Eastern Element, as it was eventually called—bore primary responsibility for political and economic reporting on the Soviet zone and the preparation of
policy and programs vis-à-vis the USSR in Germany designed by PEPCO.[23] Within
a few months of taking the helm of American effort in Germany, McCloy had created an institutional infrastructure for an American counteroffensive in Germany.

"Ideological Rollback": Defining the Cold War
Discourse in Germany

Stalin had deliberately staged the establishment of the GDR in September-October
as a reaction to the founding of the "west state." The choreography, fine-tuned
by the Soviet leader personally, placed the blame for the division of the country
squarely on the West. The new SED-led government decried the Federal Republic
as a "separatist" puppet regime at the hands of the Western Allies. It considered itself to be "the first independent all-German government" and claimed to speak not
just for eastern Germans but for the German people as a whole. To lend credibility
to such claims, both within Germany and abroad, Stalin had provided the newly
fashioned GDR government trappings of sovereignty, such as a foreign ministry
and diplomatic recognition by Soviet-sphere governments. As we have seen, the
Grotewohl government quickly seized the offensive in the national unity discourse.
Soviet and GDR officials also hoped that growing international acceptance of their
German state would enhance its legitimacy and internal consolidation in the face
of democratic and economic shortcomings.[24]

The Adenauer government did not dismiss such theatrics lightly, even if few
Germans appeared to be deceived by semblances of the GDR's independence. East
German claims gnawed at the legitimacy and identity of the Federal Republic, whose
sovereignty defects were all too obvious in heavy-handed Allied interventions in
domestic affairs and Allied representation on the international stage. No one was
more attuned to the importance of symbolic language on the international stage
(and their domestic repercussions) than the federal chancellor.[25]

Little surprise then that Adenauer swiftly rejected the East German government's claims to represent all of Germany. Pointing to "what was now happening" in the Soviet zone as lacking the support of the population, Adenauer declared in the Bundestag on October 21, 1949, that the Federal Republic was "the sole legitimate state organization of the German people." Five days later he formally notified the Western high commissioners of his view, urging them in turn to communicate the matter to other countries they had relations with. In his letter, Adenauer also laid claim to all external German assets once released by the Allies.[26]

The importance of dispelling the official narrative promulgated by the Grotewohl government was not lost on the Western Allies. On the contrary, even before Adenauer's declaration, on October 10, 1949, the Allied High Commission had dismissed the "so-called government of the People's Republic of Germany" as an "artificial creation." Pointing to the postponement of elections for a constituent assembly as evidence that the process unfolding in East Germany was following "the undemocratic patterns of other satellite states," the commission declared that "this so-called government" was devoid of any legal basis and had no right to represent Eastern Germany. It had an "even smaller claim to speak in the name of Germany as a whole."[27] Meeting in Paris the next month, the Western foreign ministers firmed up the common line toward the GDR: They would neither recognize the GDR diplomatically, nor take any actions that would imply recognition. They would be "opposed, in present circumstances, to *de jure* or *de facto* recognition of 'The German Democratic Republic,'" and they called on other governments to follow suit. In effect, the Allies instituted what William G. Gray has called a "diplomatic blockade" of the rival German government.[28]

The Western endorsement of Adenauer's stance stopped short of a full embrace of his government's claim to be the sole legal successor to the German Reich. Nor were the Allied high commissioners disposed for now to advocate such a claim with other governments. They also resisted West German entreaties to create a state secretary for foreign affairs in the weeks after the GDR's foreign ministry had leaped into action. The West Germans, the French deputy high commissioner advised Adenauer's liaison to the AHC, should not let themselves "get irritated by the events in the Soviet Zone, in particular the zealousness of Mr. Dertinger."[29]

Nonetheless, the coordinated Western response in isolating the GDR on a global scale was a remarkable achievement. After all, despite grandiose declarations about the "liberated" Europe, in particular the fate of Poland, only a few years earlier, Washington had quickly resigned itself to Communist-led governments in Warsaw and other Central European capitals. While scaling back diplomatic representation, the Truman administration had not denied the other emerging Soviet "satellites" their basic legitimacy as actors in the international arena, inviting them, for example, to the Paris Marshall Plan conference in July 1947. The joint diplomatic blockade of East Germany also contrasted with the divided Western response toward the other Communist state established in 1949: the People's Republic of China (PRC). The Truman administration had chosen to back the claim by Jiang Jieshi's Nationalists—banished to the island of Formosa following their defeat at the hands of Mao Zedong's Communist forces—that the Guomindang represented the only legal government of China. Unwilling to disavow the political reality of the "new China" and forgo a major market—and concerned about the fate of its adjacent Hong Kong colony—the British government, by contrast, recognized the PRC on January 5, 1950.

When it came to East German recognition, however, Washington and its European allies demonstrated a common front. While Washington alerted Western Hemisphere and Marshall Plan recipient governments to U.S. interests in this matter, Prime Minister Clement Attlee's government pressed Commonwealth governments to adopt a similar attitude. U.S. diplomats assiduously sought to undercut an East German trade mission headed for Latin America in December 1949. They actively shored up support for non-recognition among the European neutrals, all of whom had stakes in East Germany: Some 5,000 Swiss citizens resided in the GDR, Sweden depended on East German rail lines, and Finland had close trade ties to the Baltic coast. American efforts were helped by the often clumsy and truculent steps of the new East German government, which in categorical terms demanded recognition as a prerequisite to doing business. Within a few weeks, an effective "diplomatic blockade" was in effect: countries outside the Soviet bloc "heeded the Western standpoint and refrained from establishing political relations with the regime in East Berlin."[30]

While the "diplomatic blockade" denied the GDR legitimacy at the international level, McCloy came to understand that critical to regaining the political initiative in Germany was the West's ability to shape the public discourse on the issue of German unity. Unification of the country was no longer feasible as a practical short-term outcome, though many Germans continued to hope and believe that it was. The Paris four-power negotiations in the summer of 1949 had demonstrated the incompatibility of Western and Soviet designs for reunifying the country, and the setup of two rival regimes had grown out of this basic incongruity.

Rather, McCloy came to recognize, the country's division was for most West Germans a festering sore on their political conscience. That sore bred a low-grade infection throughout the German body politic, despite outward signs of recovery, and the United States had to appear credibly committed to fighting it, at least in the long term. At the same time, the danger persisted that Soviet offers, genuine or not, could suddenly and perhaps uncontrollably rip the wound of division wide open. The United States needed an antidote that would counter Soviet unity propaganda and seize the initiative.

The idea for a winning formula might have been prompted by two press conferences, on January 3 and February 10, 1950, during which McCloy was asked about the chances for free elections to overcome German division. Within days McCloy sought State Department approval to push free elections as a way to regain the initiative on German unity. Carefully crafted by PEPCO, a press statement by McCloy on February 28, barely a week after Dertinger's call for a peace treaty and Allied troop withdrawal, declared that German unification based on free all-German elections was a "principal objective" of American policy, and a day later, he specified October 15—the presumptive day of the Volkskammer elections—as the date for the elections to be held.[31]

McCloy's idea was ingenious for its simplicity—and yet, as we shall see, also disingenuous for its complications. Not only was the call for free elections firmly grounded in German historical tradition, it was consistent with American policy since the end of World War II. The basic assumption was that free all-German elections would assure the defeat of communism at the polls, and hence be central to achieving unification on Western terms. Calling for such elections would place the United States clearly on record as being in favor of German unification and—presuming Soviet opposition to the idea—would "expose" the insincerity of the National Front program for German unity.

More than any other measure, free elections, HICOG planners calculated, would also capture the imagination of the East German population—the West Germans had, after all, gone through a series of democratic elections—expose the "travesty" of the GDR Volkskammer elections anticipated for later that fall, and put the SED on the defensive. McCloy had acknowledged the pressures on the East German population when asked about the potential for anti-Communist resistance in the Soviet zone. Eager to ensure that the project appealed to the Germans in the GDR, PEPCO insisted that the proposal indicate that the all-German elections would pave the way for an all-German constituent assembly in which the East Germans could participate in the framing of a new German constitution.[32]

Within the American establishment in Germany, the initiative was deemed a major success. Much of West German public opinion, carefully watched by High Commission staff, reacted enthusiastically to McCloy's announcement. On March

22, 1950, the Bundestag seconded McCloy's initiative by adopting a resolution that called for all-German elections to a national constitutional assembly under the control of the four occupation powers or, alternatively, the United Nations (UN). The GDR government's vicious reaction was one indication of the proposal's impact on East Germany: GDR president Pieck attacked the McCloy proposal as an "attempt to extend his colonial rule to the East Republic," and Albert Norden, head of the press office of the GDR information department, characterized it as "gigantic impudence." But among the East German population, McCloy's proposal likely garnered widespread support. HICOG analysts felt that it had "tapped a mainspring of German feeling," which, "if properly directed," could "delay and possibly disrupt Soviet plans and timetable for East Germany."[33]

Disrupt, or at least complicate, SED plans in fact it did. The very day McCloy issued his proposal, declassified GDR records reveal, the SED was involved in difficult internal negotiations with the increasingly docile non-Communist parties over agreeing to a united slate of candidates for the October Volkskammer elections, an event deemed critical to the further consolidation of the regime by Soviet and East German officials alike. Dismissed as a "confusion maneuver" by SED officials at the outset of the secret discussions in East Berlin, McCloy's well-timed free-election initiative highlighted the undemocratic nature of the proposed unity list. It almost certainly complicated the SED's task by encouraging or prolonging resistance by Liberal Democratic Party (LDP) leaders Hermann Kastner and Karl Hamann to the proposed scheme. An informant for the precursor of the West German foreign intelligence service, the Gehlen Organization, since 1948, Kastner, who was also deputy GDR premier, might have alerted Western intelligence to the SED plans. Much to the frustration of GDR officials, the U.S.-sponsored *Neue Zeitung* highlighted the LDP opposition to the unity list on April 7.[34]

In the following weeks HICOG planned for an all-out campaign for free all-German elections directed at East Germany. Two days after the Bundestag proposal, PEPCO began to consider the "systematic barrage via all U.S. media of propaganda at the Soviet Zone." In early April, moreover, officials within HICOG's Eastern Element drafted an ambitious "all-inclusive propaganda outline for the next six months." In contrast to the sporadic play given to the "free elections" theme during the preceding months by West German and Berlin media, HICOG officials now argued that "this line must be hammered until it comes as naturally to every German's mind as eating." At least one five-minute daily radio broadcast on RIAS and other West German broadcast stations was to feature "a new angle of this subject," in addition to "spot announcements of suitable slogans during the station breaks throughout the broadcasting period." Similarly, with the *Neue Zeitung* taking the lead, all West Berlin and some West German newspapers "must at least print some election, unification, or anti-Communist slogan near the masthead" on a daily basis. Topping off this all-out propaganda scheme, David Mark of Eastern Element recommended that billboards—some of them flashing neon signs—with election and unification slogans be set up along the inner-German demarcation line, highway exits, and Berlin sector entries. They suggested other slogans as well, such as "You can relax now; you are in an area of freedom and democracy." PEPCO approved most of the proposals in mid-April.[35]

Yet the campaign had raised fundamental concerns about the basic goals of American policy: Most fundamentally, did the initiative imply that the United States would give priority to German unity over West European recovery and integration? And how far would the United States go to solicit support from the East German population against the SED government? Surprised by McCloy's initiative, Federal Chancellor Adenauer, for one, was keenly sensitive to any unilateral actions on unification on the part of the Allies, ever fearful that a deal might be struck over the heads of the Germans and undermine his pro-Western course. In Washington, Secretary of State Dean Acheson warned McCloy that it might be dangerous to proceed "too far along [the] road of Ger[man] unity based on free elections alone." State Department officials were worried that other conditions, such as the elimination of the GDR police forces, would have to be attached to the reunification procedure to ensure an outcome compatible with broader Western security interests, above all a united Germany's adherence to the West. Even some of McCloy's close advisers were apparently uncertain about the ultimate rationale of American policy and wondered: "Is it firm U.S. policy to favor and now press for a unified Germany? Is it now time to arouse the hopes of the East Germans? Should we take steps to encourage East Germans to resist Sovietization?"[36]

McCloy faced yet another dilemma with his free-elections initiative: If the United States failed to follow up on his statement with a concrete plan for unification, German opinion in the East and West would likely conclude that the move had lacked sincerity. Yet the U.S. proposals were unlikely to force any change in Soviet policy in Germany, and would hence, as his advisers put it, be "essentially a propaganda move on our part." The predicament of any further move on German unification was that "to be successful it must not appear as such." British officials, for one, assumed that Allied proposals on German unity "were primarily intended for propaganda purposes."[37]

HICOG did endorse a practical follow-up measure that did not smack entirely of propaganda: the Western high commissioners should negotiate a nationwide electoral law with the Soviet Control Commission. This proposal, however, elicited little enthusiasm from either London or Paris. Suspecting that particularly the French would drag their heels on any issue that would raise the specter of early unification, HICOG officials were prepared to engage in "a unilateral propaganda campaign which would keep the issue alive." In fact, even a joint propaganda campaign with the British seemed to American officials out of the question for now—any "joint program might handicap our freedom of action without according substantial reward."[38]

In the end, the Western foreign ministers did endorse McCloy's initiative at a meeting in late May, and they also supported the Bundestag's call for holding elections to a national assembly, though not without important stipulations: German unity was to be based on the principles of free elections and freedom of movement and parties, as well as economic unity. The foreign ministers agreed that the elimination of all paramilitary troops had to be a precondition for free elections. On May 25, 1950, the three Western high commissioners proposed to their Soviet counterpart to begin preparations of an election law that would conform to the foreign ministers' proposal. But the Western bar for unification had been set so high that Soviet rejection was virtually guaranteed.[39]

The United States and the 1950 Free German Youth Deutschlandtreffen in Berlin

The timing of the Western notes to Chiukov, as much of the American effort in the spring of 1950 to develop an effective strategy vis-a-vis East German moves, was geared toward a brewing storm on the Cold War front—"the great test of 1950," as the *New York Times* called it: the Deutschlandtreffen, a large international youth rally in Berlin planned by the SED-controlled Free German Youth (Freie Deutsche Jugend—FDJ) for the Whitsuntide holiday at the end of May. The rally has received little attention in the scholarly literature, which has instead focused on the negotiation of the Schuman plan to pool the French and West German coal and steel industry. The Schuman plan marked an important turning point in the deteriorating Western European situation in the spring of 1950—and in the longer-term process of integrating the Federal Republic into the West. Yet for weeks that spring it was the impending FDJ plans to "storm Berlin" that preoccupied U.S., Allied, and West German officials at the highest levels. Its portents for the future of the Cold War in Germany seemed to many Truman administration officials ominous, and it energized American efforts to develop a more effective and offensive policy toward the GDR.[40]

The decision to hold the rally reflected the importance that German communist leaders assigned to mobilizing the next generation in its political strategy, reaching back to the party's wartime planning in Moscow. In the early days of the occupation, Pieck, Ulbricht, and other communist leaders had purposefully forgone the revival of the prewar Communist Youth League in favor of establishing a "broad anti-imperialist democratic youth organization" that played on long-standing traditions of the German youth movement and widespread disillusionment and hopelessness among young people in the wake of the war.[41]

Sanctioned by Stalin himself in his discussion with the German communists in June 1945, the idea to create a unified youth organization formally independent from the Communist Party had owed much to the lack of Communist youth cadres and the spontaneous emergence of local "youth committees" throughout occupied Germany, which began the task of re-educating and re-engaging the next generation. The supra-partisan façade of the movement in which the communists in fact outnumbered their political rivals in the leadership committee (later Central Council) also aligned with the early KPD line that emphasized parliamentary-democratic methods and forswore revolutionary rhetoric.[42]

Formally founded in February 1946, the FDJ had grown within months to an impressive 500,000 members throughout Germany, far outnumbering other youth organizations; by 1950 its membership was estimated at more than 2,000,000. Initially, many of its rank-and-file members did not belong to the Communist Party. But with the Stalinist transformation of the SED in 1948–49, the FDJ lost any vestiges of non-partisanship. After the exodus of any remaining non-Communist leaders in January 1948, the FDJ apparat had come under the exclusive control of the SED; its activities drew increasingly on Communist Youth League traditions, Soviet Komsomol models, and from the summer of 1949 on, the Stalin cult. By 1949, Free German Youth had effectively become an SED mass organization—an instrument of one-party rule. Among its declared top priorities was the fight for German unity; it also served as recruiting grounds for the paramilitary police forces.[43]

Authorized by the SED Central Committee in September 1949, the staging of the Deutschlandtreffen in the frontline city of Berlin promised to be the largest event of its kind in postwar Germany thus far. The Soviet-licensed press had given the rally considerable prominence since December 1949, and by early 1950 a major propaganda buildup was under way: To the SED, the Deutschlandtreffen would provide an impressive sounding board for SED propaganda, showcase the GDR's "superiority" and standing in the international arena, and dramatically underscore its putative all-German appeal. In February, the SED Politburo charged the National Front with the task of preparing the Deutschlandtreffen nationwide. The FDJ's ambitious young leader, the future SED general secretary Erich Honecker, was eager to demonstrate the fighting force his organization could bring to bear in the East-West confrontation. Honecker envisioned thousands of FDJ members—dressed in the widely recognized blue uniforms—crossing the sector border under the slogan "The Free German Youth storm Berlin" and marching in several columns into the West.[44]

Within weeks, Allied officials grew suspicious that the GDR planned to use the Deutschlandtreffen for an invasion of the city's Western sectors—"to roll up the Western imperialist bridgehead in Berlin."[45] Western intelligence agencies confirmed that the rally might escalate into a serious military crisis: in January, the U.S. European Command (EUCOM) reported that the FDJ rally was specifically directed against the Western sectors, a tactic that was "consistent with the Communist practice [of] provoking riots for political advantage." The planned demonstrations, according to a further EUCOM report, would include the Western sectors of Berlin, "with or without the permission of the Western Sector authorities." The FDJ rally seem to build on what media reports called a Communist "campaign of direct action and incitement to violence" that had resulted in smaller incidents from Hamburg to Munich during March.[46]

Alarming reports about the rally reaching the administration abounded. "Reliable" sources confirmed East German public declarations that the FDJ Central Council was planning to send contingents of 10,000 to 12,000 well-trained FDJ members to the West as "blitz groups" for agitation and demonstration purposes. The agitation supposedly included the "throwing of stones at shop windows containing American goods." One member at a Central Council meeting allegedly remarked that a "certain number of dead must be expected." Other sources indicated that the Whitsuntide rally would be used to "instruct and train the youth in East Germany and Berlin in the art of cold revolution," which would produce "what the blockade failed to achieve, namely a unified Berlin under a communist hegemony." By early March Western intelligence officials reportedly had no doubt that the rally would be "the most serious attempt since the blockade to win greater Berlin."[47]

As part of an intelligence offensive, the CIA initiated "Operation Baldur," an effort by the agency-sponsored Gehlen Organization to clarify the potential involvement of GDR police units and Soviet troops in any future actions. Reports from well-placed U.S. sources within the FDJ's leadership in late February led the Truman administration to believe initially that the GDR's People's Police and paramilitary alert squads would participate in the Whitsun rally. While the ostensible purpose of the militarily organized alert squads was to reinforce traditional police functions, SED leaders also considered them to be an "operative reserve should the case arise" in a situation of "civil war and escalating Cold War."

The reported participation of the People's Police units and alert squads in the rally reinforced the militant overtones that the event took on in FDJ pronouncements. In early March, U.S. intelligence passed on the transcript of the proceedings of the January 31 FDJ Central Council meeting, which suggested that Honecker had received instructions from Moscow that the Deutschlandtreffen would be carried out in a military manner. According to the report, Honecker had declared that the time for pacifism was over and stated, "We are prepared to bear arms." Western media envisioned two million members of Free German Youth, "modeled after the Hitler youth" and trained in paramilitary skills, standing behind the police formations. The GDR was reportedly "ready to become a military power as soon as the Russians give 'the word.'"[48]

Rather than giving the East German threats greater credence, the Western Berlin commandants initially had resolved to play down the subject for as long as possible in order to avoid further deterioration of morale in Berlin. They stated publicly that they would take all necessary means to defend the Western sectors and ignored for weeks a request made by the FDJ in early January for permission to hold the event in the iconic Olympic Stadium in the western part of the city.[49]

To some the silence suggested complacency, and press reports soon called out "the higher levels of Western authorities" for not taking the impending crisis seriously. Journalist Anne O'Hare McCormick was not alone in blaming emboldened FDJ claims to "storm Berlin" at least in part on the Truman administration's "tragicomic" decision in late January to return to Soviet control the operating headquarters of the GDR railway system, located in the U.S. (!) sector. Two U.S. army officers and fifty West Berlin police had seized the building on January 17. Faced with Soviet reprisals in interzonal trade, U.S. commandant Maxwell Taylor had yielded to Soviet protests, resulting in "the first American retreat in the Cold War," as the *Washington Post* put it. British officials agreed that the U.S. reaction had "undoubtedly been interpreted as a sign of weakness and may correspondingly encourage the belief that violent action might not be met with firmness." If the aforementioned FDJ Council transcript is to be believed, this was not far off the truth: according to the document, the head of the Deutschlandtreffen organizing committee, Gerhard Sredzki, predicted that the Americans would back out of Berlin "just like they retreated from the Reichsbahn headquarters building."[50]

Offering a glimpse of what might be expected on a much larger scale on the climactic May weekend, 3,000 FDJ functionaries met in East Berlin on March 1 under the slogan "Berlin must be ours." On the night of March 2, three torchlight parades took place in the Soviet sector, and the following night, about 500 FDJ youth—accompanied by People's Police and loudspeakers—made speeches along the border of the U.S. sector, without, however, crossing the line. Worried that the FDJ meeting would further undercut West Berlin morale, McCloy now became "very keen on the propaganda side being properly organized" and contemplated setting up a "fairly substantial Deutschmark fund for use in this way."[51]

McCloy was not the only one in the Truman administration who was growing more alarmed by the prospect of the FDJ rally. During McCloy's visit to Washington later that month, Secretary of State Acheson expressed his own deep misgivings about the Deutschlandtreffen. Perhaps he recalled what Adenauer had told him a few months earlier: that People's Police was made up largely of German youth who had already been "strongly infected by the Russian propaganda and were thus completely dependent on Russia." Acheson's concerns prompted a HICOG–State Department planning meeting to agree on further military and propaganda measures that would demonstrate to the West Berlin public that the West was determined to withstand the blue-shirt onslaught. McCloy also held meetings with Pentagon officials about the Berlin situation.[52]

Concerns about the implications of the rally for Berlin's security spilled into the public discussions in the United States the following weeks. The *New York Times* warned on its front page in mid-March that the descent of "more than 500,000" FDJ members upon Berlin "to invade and overrun Berlin" was the "touchstone of Russian ambitions in Germany." Reports emerged that McCloy, during his March trip to Washington, had conferred with the Pentagon on the increasingly tense situation underlined the seriousness of it. Veteran American war reporter and Germany bureau chief Drew Middleton saw Soviet ambassador Georgy Pushkin and Ulbricht plotting "the boldest Russian bid for power" since the Berlin Blockade and predicted it would probably lead to "rioting and bloodshed involving not only German but possibly Western Allied lives." Echoing media reports, Senator Millard E. Tydings (D-MD), the chairman of the Armed Services Committee, speculated publicly that "there may be some shooting" at the planned rally.[53]

Internally, HICOG officials cautioned that reports on Communist strong-arm tactics were "often conflicting," and they suspected that such information "may well [have been] intentional." But even if the GDR was not planning organized, large-scale violence during the rally, visions of thousands of FDJ blue shirts streaming into the Western sectors were sure to take their toll on the morale of West Berliners. Reflecting the palpable unease gripping West Berlin's political class, SPD leader Kurt Schumacher demanded that U.S. tanks be made ready to defend the city against a potential mass invasion. Another leading SPD official, the chairman of the Bundestag's Committee for All-German Questions, Herbert Wehner, characterized the FDJ rally as the "Russians' war project in Berlin."[54]

In fact, the Berlin commandants had begun to prepare for the Deutschlandtreffen. They had appointed a nine-member Standing Action Committee that took charge of coordinating information and developing countermeasures. On March 2, the commandants had decided to turn down the FDJ request and prohibit all organized FDJ marches in the Western sectors. Individual FDJ members would still be allowed to enter the Western sectors; "no Chinese wall" would be set up along the Western sector boundaries. Eager to avoid escalating the siege mentality spreading in Berlin, HICOG also decided early on that the first line of defense in the Western sectors would be the West Berlin police and that life there should be kept "as normal as possible during Whitsuntide."[55]

Behind the façade of studied normalcy, Allied officials engaged in extensive planning for a violent confrontation. In mid-March, the Western city commandants agreed to increase the West Berlin police force permanently by 2,000 men (to 12,000 men overall), a remarkable decision given initial Allied resistance to Adenauer's demands for a federal police force. They also authorized the use of tear gas, smoke bombs, gas masks and water throwers. Auxiliary units made up of deputized and uniformed members of the anti-communist Independent Union Organization (UGO) would reinforce regular West Berlin police in sensitive spots. Occupation troops were readied as the "second line of law and order," in case the German police would be overwhelmed. The 6,000–7,000 Allied military troops expected to be available in Berlin could, according to Allied planning, be reinforced by three battalions by air. Joint Allied maneuvers in the Hanover area close to the East-West German border would allow for a "road march over the autobahn to Berlin." The western zones would have 75,000 rounds of canister available for use in Berlin.[56]

The State Department, moreover, instructed the Allied Combined Travel Board—in charge of authorizing Western travel to East Germany—to "make [a] special effort" to deny entry permits to some 20,000 West German youths expected to attend the Deutschlandtreffen. It also took "all possible steps to prevent American youths from participating" in the meeting. Truman administration officials also considered a number of counter-attractions: The Economic Cooperation Administration (ECA) would provide support of up to Deutsche Mark (DM) 1 million for sports events, air displays, an automobile show, and musical attractions that would divert attention from the FDJ gathering.[57]

Beyond defensive measures, McCloy pushed his new Cold War apparatus to undercut the East Germans' momentum more effectively. In mid-March, the *New York Times* cited unnamed American officials, presumably on McCloy's staff, that had advocated a "full-fledged propaganda campaign against Eastern Germany." High on the list of countermeasures were warnings to East Germans "not to allow their sons to be sent to Berlin to fight for Russian imperialism" in the city's streets, facing well-armed Western soldiers. Declassified documents suggest that the Truman administration began to actively seek to undermine FDJ morale by playing on the fears of parents of the Young Pioneers, the youngest group of participants, who ranged in age from ten to fifteen.[58]

Reporting in late March from Frankfort, the headquarters of the U.S. High Commission, journalist Drew Middleton reflected the shift there towards a more aggressive posture by pointing to the "real potential for rebellion" in East Germany and advocated a "solid integrated propaganda policy for Eastern Germany" to halt the GDR program. The FDJ rally, Middleton went on, was a threat but "also an opportunity for the West." In early April, the Western commandants in Berlin bolstered their budget for Allied propaganda efforts, which involved the distribution of some 60,000 letters and 400,000 leaflets in the Soviet sector and the GDR but also some DM 5,000 to West Berlin organizations "for secret intelligence work" in obtaining information on GDR preparations for the rally. The State Department, moreover, authorized covert "confusion broadcasts" via RIAS and other outlets which would announce that the rally had been called off.[59]

With media reports warning that the situation in Berlin was one "in which an ill-chosen order, an unreliable subaltern or a trigger-happy soldier" might involve East and West in a full-fledged military conflagration, by mid-April key officials within the Truman administration were wondering whether they had an international crisis of major proportions on their hands. Ambassador-at-large Philip C. Jessup, who had played a central role in resolving the Berlin Blockade crisis the previous year, now argued in favor of alerting the UN Security Council regarding the situation in Berlin. A few days later, the influential journalist Walter Lippmann called on the administration to appeal to the Soviets to cooperate with the United States in preventing violence and bloodshed; and if such an appeal proved unsuccessful, to place the UN Security Council on formal notice that there was a threat to the peace in Berlin. On April 28, Secretary of the Army Frank Pace raised the Berlin rally and the projected courses of action for discussion at the National Security Council, "pointing up the possibilities of international difficulties that might result from this action, seeking approval of the progressive application of military measures as planned."[60]

Truman administration officials now went public in their efforts to demonstrate to Soviet and East German officials and Western Berliners alike that the West was resolved to fight in the face of belligerent FDJ pronouncements. Most dramatic among these signaling efforts were the special anti-riot drills that U.S. troops conducted that month. In April, Berlin residents gazed in amazement as U.S. infantry men with fixed bayonets drove back a fictitious mob of thousands of communists impersonated by 800 jeering U.S. constabulary troopers in a smoke-wreathed exercise in the Grunewald, the city's central public park. The papers hailed the simulation as "realistic show of anti-riot strength." U.S. officials also announced that they would use machine guns and cannons to stay in Berlin and had brought in light tanks and other weapons.[61]

While the Truman administration's preparations were increasingly military in nature, Honecker's ambitious plans deflated in the face of Soviet objections to the militant overtones of the event. On April 6, the head of the Soviet Control Commission, General Vasily Chuikov, instructed SED party leader Wilhelm Pieck to tone down the "exaggerated propaganda." Allied intelligence apparently picked up on the change of course immediately; on the basis of intelligence sources, the *Washington Post* reported that the Soviet Control Commission had stepped in and ordered the emphasis to shift from fight to words. The march on Berlin would now be a "propaganda invasion" instead of a "putsch."[62]

Later that month, Honecker found himself in the line of fire as Moscow officials "at the highest levels" expressed their annoyance over the crisis created by the aggressive plans for the Deutschlandtreffen. Soviet youth officers participating in the FDJ Central Council chastised Honecker and harshly criticized the invasion project as a "circus" and the East German propaganda as "primitive": It had only bolstered the cause of the "warmongers" in the West. Plans for marches to the Western sectors were canceled: not a single FDJ member was to go west. Consequently, Honecker proclaimed in the FDJ journal *Junge Welt* in mid-April that the youth organization had "no intention of forcing [its] way into the Western sectors as the high commissioners and their German lackeys wish." The goal, Honecker argued, was "to win the hearts of the Berliners over to [the] new German youth and the National Front of [the] democratic Germany."[63]

It is not clear whether Stalin raised similar concerns with Ulbricht when the SED leader led an SED delegation to Moscow in early May. According to Wilhelm Pieck's notes of the meeting, plans for the Deutschlandtreffen were not on the agenda for the Germans' nightly session with the Soviet leader. With memories of the Berlin Blockade debacle still fresh, it is unlikely that Stalin was intent on stumbling into a full-blown crisis over Berlin. Had the Allied troop reinforcements "cowed the Red strategists," as the *Washington Post* editorialized? Certainly Stalin would have been cognizant of the Western military buildup. More important, however, was likely the fact that the FDJ's militant approach was out of sync with his broader priorities in Germany. Stalin still harbored hopes that the new German state had the potential to hold considerable sway over large segments of West German society, including neutralist, pacifist, and progressive "bourgeois" segments. It was precisely these groups that Honecker's provocative theatrics would deter from seeking cooperation with the GDR.[64]

Although, according to media reports, "the majority of observers in West Berlin" regarded Honecker's volte-face as an effort to "lull the Western forces into complacency," by early May U.S. intelligence and diplomatic channels had confirmed the turn of events in Berlin to Washington. HICOG now informed the administration that the mass rally would amount to no more than a propaganda effort: "Barring some major change in the situation, the Commies will not attempt major, organized parades and demonstrations in [West] Berlin during Whitsun." Rather than trying to "take over the West Sectors," the GDR aimed to mount the "most impressive possible mass demonstration and spectacle in the East Sector." The U.S. Army leadership agreed: the threat posed by the rally was now "primarily a political one." Reassured and relieved, Truman was able to tell the NSC on May 4, 1950, that he "felt the necessary precautions were being taken."[65]

But in the zero-sum thinking increasingly prevalent in the Truman administration's foreign policy approach at the time, the sudden change of course in East Berlin was regarded as holding the potential for new and unexpected risks. U.S. officials now worried that with the threat of violence considerably diminished, West Berliners might be attracted to the rally activities in East Berlin and venture in massive numbers into the Soviet sector, possibly providing the East Germans with a spectacular propaganda victory in turn. Any such exodus to the East was therefore regarded as undesirable in the eyes of the administration.

Consequently, PEPCO considered staging a number of counter-attractions, including hastily arranging a football match in the Olympic Stadium, a bicycle race along the Avis autobahn, or a regatta on Lake Wannsee as ways to prevent the "draining off of West Berliners to the East sector." Others, however, feared that staging counter-attractions of similar entertainment value in West Berlin would "reflect adversely upon the West by permitting disparaging comparisons capable of political exploitation." PEPCO also worried that the Soviets might score a propaganda coup by permitting Whitsuntide to pass peaceably, and some within the State Department argued that any additional public warnings to the Soviets might "leave us looking unduly alarmed" and "frightened by a peaceful gathering of mere children." If the demonstration developed in an essentially peaceful manner, "we do run the real risk of looking somewhat over-excited if not foolish."[66]

Such concerns notwithstanding, Allied propaganda efforts moved into full swing in April. On April 19, the Standing Action Committee agreed on a comprehensive propaganda program directed at various parts of the GDR population, focusing on refugees (April 26), parents (May 3), sportsmen and sports leaders (May 10), and churches (May 17). Other measures called for the covert distribution of an abridged version of the George Orwell novel *1984*—"through an American agency" (probably the CIA), further distribution of propaganda letters to FDJ functionaries and Soviet zone residents, and the display of 500,000 anti-rally adhesive propaganda stickers. Allied efforts were complemented by the Federal Department for All-German Affairs campaigns, which included the dissemination of some 400,000 flyers through various German organizations it supported, including the SPD and CDU East offices. The West Berlin Landesjugendring (state youth association) fired numerous small rockets carrying hundreds of leaflets into the city's suburbs on GDR territory. A month before the Deutschlandtreffen, the top U.S commander in Europe, General Thomas Handy, could inform the Department of the Army that psychological warfare was "being pushed aggressively by all means" and that "extensive undercover operations are being conducted in the East Zone to undermine support."[67]

Western efforts to counter the climactic weekend at the end of May crescendoed in two major public events earlier that month designed to upstage the SED's Deutschlandtreffen. On a warm May 1 Labor Day, an estimated half a million people from all Berlin sectors jammed into the city's Tiergarten Park and the "Place of the Republic" in front of the burned-out Reichstag building near the sector border and "roared defiance to the Soviet Union and German communism," as one American observer captured the moment. Under the watchful eyes of the Allied officials and the world press, they listened to speeches by Kaiser, Irving Brown of the American Federation of Labor and Berlin Governing Mayor Ernst Reuter who earned thunderous applause for demanding free all-Berlin elections. In what the *Washington Post* called the "battle of the loudspeakers," the outpouring of demonstrators in the British sector dwarfed number of participants at a May Day rally sponsored by the SED barely two miles away at the Soviet-sector Lustgarten. Aside from a flurry of stone-throwing at Potsdamer Platz, where the two crowds merged to catch the subway, and some fistfights at the Brandenburg Gate, the day of rival rallies passed quietly. Enduring a barrage of stones and a shower of insults with restraint, the People's Police seemed to Western observers to be under instructions not to provoke.[68]

A week before Pentecost, moreover, the United States put on public displays of military might in Frankfurt and Berlin in celebration of "Armed Forces Day." On May 20, 1,000 U.S. soldiers paraded in front of some 20,000 Berliners on Tempelhof Airfield in an unmistaken message to the East. An airshow included helicopters, which would circle the airspace over Berlin during the FDJ rally, and a public demonstration of the loading and unloading of the C54s, the "work horses" of the Berlin airlift, a thinly veiled reminder of the last East-West crisis over the divided city. For the first time, all three military branches (now unified in the new Department of Defense) joined to observe the holiday in what was announced as a "spectacular show of power." Finally, as mentioned above, the Western foreign ministers issued letters to their Soviet counterpart, timed to coincide with the eve of Deutschlandtreffen, calling for all-German elections based on a catalog of eight principles that would ensure that the elections be free and fair.[69]

The impact of Western efforts to undermine the success of the Deutschland-treffen can be gleaned from declassified East German records. Internal FDJ reports in the aftermath of the rally noted that "the systematic spread of the false news by RIAS" had created "certain unrest" among the East Berlin population, which at first evinced "a negative attitude" toward the rally and greeted the youth in a "slightly reserved" manner. In its report to the NSC, the U.S. State Department noted as early as May 3 that particular efforts to "instill fear in Soviet Zone parents so that they may prevent their children from participating in the rally" had been "fairly success-ful." McCloy cabled to Washington that the Soviets were encountering "difficulty in creating the desired enthusiasm for the rally," and intelligence reports confirmed that RIAS broadcasts were "causing drops in FDJ and *Junge Pioniere* applications" for participation in the rally. Yet all in all, about 440,000 youth participated in the meeting, according to American intelligence sources.[70]

Despite the calm confidence they exhibited, Truman administration officials sighed in relief when the "monster youth rally" that had become front-page news even in the United States came and went without major incidents. "We have de-flected another blow at Berlin," McCloy cabled Acheson. Just before the four-day event began with a gathering of several thousand Young Pioneers in the Wuhlheide Stadium some eight miles southeast of the city center, the East German organizers introduced slight changes in the plans for the major demonstration on May 28,

FIGURE 6. Demonstration during the FDJ Deutschlandtreffen in Berlin, May 28, 1950. © Pressebild-Verlag Schirner/Deutsches Historisches Museum, Berlin.

moving the route of the march still farther from the Western sector boundaries. The majority of the participants camped out in a tent city set up on the outskirts of Berlin. People's Police units lined solidly shoulder to shoulder on the far sides of barricades erected along the Brandenburg Gate and heavily guarded all sector borders. East German authorities appeared keen to prevent rally participants from entering Western sectors at all, by force if necessary.[71]

Despite these efforts, hundreds of young East Germans sifted through the police cordons into the Western sectors, shopping for bicycle tires and flashlights and other items hard to come by in the GDR, visiting RIAS, and supplanting their skimpy food rations with free meals offered by Western Berlin establishments. According to U.S. authorities, at least forty-two FDJ members and thirty-six Volkspolizei (People's Police) members defected to the West. The only major disturbance took place not in Berlin, but New York, where General Lucius Clay, the hero of the airlift, was interrupted by demonstrators during a "Hold Berlin" speech.[72]

Publicly and privately, the Truman administration reveled in the bloodless outcome of what had been dubbed in the media as "the battle of Berlin." In the aftermath of the Deutschlandtreffen, Drew Middleton commented acerbically, Allied officials engaged in a "spate of self-congratulation rivaling that observed at a higher military headquarters after a successful and distant battle." McCloy asserted that the West had "foiled Communist plans for overrunning Berlin." Referring to the day of the main FDJ march, U.S. commandant General Maxwell Taylor insisted that "Sunday was the day that Berlin was to fall but the challenge was met" and declared that "victory was ours." The entire episode, as the U.S. ambassador in Moscow, Alan Kirk, put it, was an "impressive example that firmness and determination [result] in rolling back Soviet encroachment attempts."[73]

Yet it was not lost on Truman administration officials that the GDR leaders were equally jubilant about the organizational feat and psychological impact of the Deutschlandtreffen, especially on the youth. Ulbricht, too, claimed victory. Not only had the event involved well over 20,000 West German youth and participants from abroad, including from the USSR, China, Eastern Europe, and most West European countries and neutrals. American officials internally agreed that the event represented a major accomplishment in the organization and indoctrination of German youth in the GDR. A week later, McCloy confessed to Adenauer privately that the Whitsuntide rally had impressed him deeply and he considered it a demonstration that gave him pause. It had no equal on the Western side. U.S. officials considered it "remarkable" that in East Germany a "foreign imposed totalitarian order" was successfully taking hold "despite negative antagonisms."

FIGURE 7. FDJ march during the Deutschlandtreffen, Berlin, May 28, 1950. Courtesy of
Edmund Thiele/Deutsches Historisches Museum, Berlin.

Much as Ulbricht had announced, the rally had to be seen, they agreed, as an
"impressive demonstration of strength." British High Commissioner Robertson
agreed: to him the rally had been "the biggest success the Soviets have had during
the past five years."[74]

It was disconcerting to the Truman administration that the FDJ was "patently
reactivating many Nazi psycho[logical] and social patterns, utilizing the still potent residues of the Hitler era." East German youth seemed to be "in the hands of
remorseless and experienced molders," though in their majority still "plastic." An
internal after-action report by HICOG judged that "pending [a] major change in
the world picture, [the] Commie steamroller in East Germany [was] unlikely [to
be] halted by any local tactics." All one could hope for was some delaying action
"keeping alive some elements of plasticity until the strategic context was more favorable." Though time was perceived as working against the West, the East Germans
were not yet considered entirely lost to Communist indoctrination. Even the FDJ
rally had shown that the "Commie digestion process" in East Germany was far from
complete. But the passing of time seemed to favor the SED authorities, and HICOG
warned Washington in early June that the "time for action is now."[75]

McCloy was disturbed by the "fundamental handicap" of not being able "to exert full measure of influence on the east Germans." Given increased shutting off of East Germany to the West, the Soviets were in a far more advantageous position to "to frustrate our objectives in West Germany than we are in relation to East Germany." Nevertheless, the Soviets had not yet won the battle for German minds, and McCloy argued that the "ultimate tipping of scales in Germany" would largely depend on each side's deploying power "in sharper focus than either antagonist has thus far brought to bear on [the] German scene."[76]

Planning for Rollback in Germany, 1950–1951

"Living on a Volcano"? Managing the East German Threat

On June 25, 1950, North Korean troops crossed the Thirty-Eighth Parallel and invaded South Korea. Kim Il-sung, the leader of the People's Democratic Republic of Korea (DPRK), sought to reunify his country, divided since 1945, by force. After receiving a "green light" from Stalin, he launched a massive armored assault on the Republic of Korea. DPRK forces overran the South Korean capital, Seoul, on June 28 and pressed forward deep into the southern half of the peninsula.[1]

Caught by surprise, the Truman administration announced on June 27 it would intervene to repel the invading force, rushed in American troops stationed in Japan, and mobilized an international "police action" under the auspices of the United Nations, taking advantage of the absence of the Soviet representative in the Security Council. Under the impression of the early military retreats by American and South Korea troops, the United States went into full-scale mobilization mode, not seen since World War II. Truman now authorized a massive expansion of the defense budget to $48.2 billion, a 257 percent increase over the administration's original budget request. Calls for "preventive war" against the USSR reflected the depth of the crisis mood that gripped the country. Historian Thomas Schwartz has characterized the "atmosphere of sustained crisis" over these months as unique in the history of the Cold War.[2]

The outbreak of the Korean War in June 1950 also reverberated powerfully into Cold War tensions in Europe. Across Western Europe, news of the North

Korean invasion prompted fears of Soviet aggression, fears that lurked never far below the political surface. Throughout the spring, as U.S. and West European government officials had discussed ways to bolster Western Europe's poor defenses against the massive Soviet military presence to the east, they had voiced their anticipation in internal discussions that a Soviet attack on Western Europe would occur within a span of a few years, perhaps months. Even so, most had firmly discounted the possibility that an attack was imminent. Inside the Truman administration, a reassessment by the National Security Council in the spring of 1950 held fast to the belief that the USSR was not yet prepared to initiate a war with the United States.

The unexpected outbreak of war on the Korean peninsula tested these assumptions. It certainly suggested that the USSR, widely believed to be responsible for the North Korea attack, was willing to resort to "limited" military conflict even in the face of existing U.S. nuclear superiority. Eager to avoid the intelligence failure it had suffered in Korea, the CIA sought to detect "any signs of worsening situation in Europe." The crisis heightened fears among American allies in Europe that the USSR might engage in a Korean-style "proxy" war on the continent. British Foreign Secretary Ernest Bevin was not alone in seeing parallels between divided Germany and divided Korea. He confided to his cabinet that he feared that "next year the Soviet Government will seek to repeat in Germany what they have done in Korea."[3]

Germans, still preoccupied with the reconstruction of their daily lives in a divided country, were jolted by the developments taking place more than 5,000 miles away. Perhaps news of the fighting in Korea struck a deeper chord with Germans than with others in Europe because of their prevailing sense of disempowerment and defeatism—and the potential prospect that Germans might face Germans in battle. Though many in West Germany took heart in the determined and forceful U.S. response in the face of Communist aggression, the apparent U.S. failure to foresee the North Korean assault and early South Korean and U.S. reversals on the Korean peninsula shook their confidence badly.

West German media "fanned the fires of alarm," spreading anxiety that the conflict on the Korean peninsula was a precursor to a Soviet or East German attack on the Federal Republic, especially if U.S. military units, as some speculated, might be diverted to the Far East. Along major westward routes from the GDR, Adenauer told the Allied high commissioners on June 29, residents were anxious that Soviet tanks might suddenly start rolling through their villages. There was no panic yet. But two days later, he penned a letter to the Allied High Commission warning that even without any Russian moves, panic might break out, unleashing massive population flows to the West. Could not the high commissioners do something to calm the population?[4]

Widespread fear of what the conflict in Korea implied for central Europe was not limited to the German street and media. The shock to West Germany's new political class was profound. Bonn officials' reaction "verged on the hysterical," Mc-Cloy's staff reported. In the days after the outbreak of war in Korea, the U.S. High Commission was besieged by German requests for air tickets to the United States. German federal government employees demanded to be equipped with weapons to shoot invading Communists.

Adenauer, it seems, initially expected the "incident" in Korea to be over in a matter of days, but early North Korean military successes shattered that hope. The events in Korea exacerbated his sense of danger from the East, in particular the GDR. Not only did the conflict in the Far East reinforce his long-standing fears about a "fifth column" inside the Federal Republic that worked in cahoots with the regime in East Berlin. As the North Korean army overpowered the poorly trained, poorly equipped, and poorly motivated ROK forces, his worries heightened about the "Eastern Army" he saw rising in the Soviet zone. Harking back to his decade-old anti-Prussian sentiments, he believed this "army" to be particularly dangerous since its recruits came from the part of Germany that had produced the best soldiers for the Prussian and German armies because they were the most "hardheaded." Reflective of his momentary loss of equilibrium, Adenauer requested from the high commission two hundred automatic pistols to defend the Palais Schaumburg, the government seat, against a potential communist uprising and renewed his plea for an American security guarantee. His sense of threat was deadly serious.[5]

McCloy was as surprised as anyone by the outbreak of war in Korea, but he dismissed the frenzied arguments that it offered an ominous analogy to the German situation. In the early days he repeatedly sought to reassure the West German public: "I do not believe there is going to be any attack." In fact, the high commissioner argued, the events in the Far East had lessened the danger of Soviet aggression in central Europe. Allied troops would stay in Germany until peace and freedom were secured, he stated in an interview on the U.S. independence holiday (July 4). The Federal Republic did not need a formal security guarantee, "as an attack on the federal territory would automatically be seen as an attack on the Western powers." A key difference from the Korean situation, he argued, was the presence of Western Allied troops in Germany. While insufficient to halt a Soviet invasion, a Soviet attack on Germany would likely face Western troops. To drive home the point that there was no imminent danger of war, he told the

German press that he had invited his eighty-six-year-old mother to visit him in Frankfurt that summer.[6]

Across the inner-German demarcation line, the hostilities in Korea also weighed heavily on people and regime. Heeding the official Soviet line, the SED portrayed, and may have in fact genuinely believed, the war to be a U.S.-engineered South Korean attack on the North. Much like their West German brethren, the GDR leaders were quick to compare the Korean conflict to the situation in divided Germany, and to see themselves at likely targets of "American imperialism's" next move. On June 27, the SED party mouthpiece *Neues Deutschland* declared that the Korean War was nothing less than a practice run for an American attack on central Europe.

For East Germany's (and the Soviet Union's) Communist leaders, the U.S. military intervention in Korea fit seamlessly into a narrative of Western preparations for World War III in which a remilitarized Federal Republic would play a key role. At the SED's Third Party Congress in late July, GDR president Pieck decried "American imperialism" as pursuing "world domination," building on the creation of "aggressive blocks and alliances," by which he meant the Council of Europe, NATO, and most recently the Schuman Plan. In Korea, American imperialism had moved from war propaganda and preparation to direct military intervention, said Pieck, to the "most brutal acts of aggression." The German leader warned of a third world war, which would bring "only death and destruction to Germany."[7]

Such statements served not only to rationalize the militarization of the People's Police and, splashed across the front pages of *Neues Deutschland*, to whip the party rank-and-file and the population into a war scare that would help counter widespread defeatist attitudes. They also betrayed deep anxieties on the part of the SED leaders that the Western powers would use the Korean conflict as an opportunity to accomplish regime change in the GDR by force through an "inner-German police action." As late as early June 1950, Pieck had stated in front of the senior SED party leaders that he expected that "the imperialist occupation powers will after all finally strike a blow against peace and against the East." Evidence from the GDR archives suggests that during these tense summer days the Communist leadership considered such a possibility a "real threat."[8]

Mirroring Adenauer's concerns over the lack of any meaningful defense forces at his disposal (at the end of July the Allied High Commission finally granted an expansion of the police by 10,000 men but at the state level only), SED leaders were keenly aware of the inadequate state of GDR security forces, which only enhanced their sense of vulnerability. Internal inspections of the barracked police units in July and August detected "grave deficiencies in the know-how and capabilities."

Handicapped by the lack of manpower, inadequate equipment, and tight Soviet control, the GDR "alert squads" remained entirely unprepared for military action, a situation that precluded any thought of their offensive use for a "liberation" of the Federal Republic at this stage.[9]

The latter, however, was what Adenauer was worried about most. Scholars have disagreed over the extent to which he played up these fears, exploiting the Korean crisis to promote West German rearmament and regain sovereignty. After all, he seemed to have regained his footing within a little more than a week of the beginning of hostilities in the Far East, when it looked as if the conflict would not widen beyond the Korean peninsula. His reassurance was partly a matter of simply gaining more information on the situation from McCloy or his own aides (interacting with Allied officials as they negotiated the Schuman Plan in Paris), given that his government lacked its own foreign ministry apparatus. Reports from his fledgling intelligence service, the Friedrich-Wilhelm-Heinz-Dienst, overdrew the combat strength of the GDR alert squads but advised Adenauer that they were not yet capable of offensive operations against the Federal Republic. Echoing initial CIA assessments, Gehlen's service, too, had dismissed the likelihood of major actions from the East.[10]

Other scholars, however, have emphasized Adenauer's near hysteric concerns about Soviet or East German aggression. His nervousness shone through his conversation with the British high commissioner, Sir Ivonne Kirkpatrick, on July 11: how much could they rely on U.S. intelligence reports that Moscow was not planning a coup in Western Germany, the chancellor had asked rhetorically, "after the conspicuous failure of American intelligence in Korea." In Bonn, Adenauer aide Herbert Blankenhorn, accompanied by two former Wehrmacht generals, secretly sought out General George P. Hays, the deputy U.S. high commissioner, to discuss, at the chancellor's behest, "measures required in case of a sudden attack of Russian troops on the territory of the Federal Republic." French high commissioner André Francois-Poncet did little to reassure the Germans when he made the startling proposition that the federal government consider relocating to Canada in case of an invasion.[11]

More likely than a Soviet invasion, in Adenauer's view, was renewed pressure in Berlin of the kind initially anticipated for the FDJ Deutschlandtreffen a month earlier: Had the West considered what we should do "if the Russians played the Korean game in Berlin and employed the Volkspolizei to attack the western garrisons in the Western Sectors"? Kept largely in the dark about Allied defense plans, Adenauer suspected that the United States would not be willing to escalate to a general war with the USSR in case an attack was limited to East German forces, leaving the disarmed Federal Republic exposed. Reflecting his deep nervousness about the situation, he characterized the moment as "living on a volcano."[12]

McCloy was not convinced that the volcano was about to erupt. Though worried about troop concentrations at the Yugoslav border and movements by the Czechoslovak army, he did not believe that a Soviet attack in Europe was imminent. Soviet forces would not march this summer, he reassured Adenauer (again) on July 12. McCloy, too, considered the Volkspolizei a "real danger," but he dismissed the idea that a Korea-style attack in Europe was imminent. He discounted Adenauer's concerns over a revival of pro-Russian sentiment among Germans as a "gambit" by the chancellor to strengthen his government by finally obtaining approval for the creation of a federal police force. Deeply mistrustful of the German military, McCloy remained wary of the chancellor's quest to leverage an offer of German manpower and resources in support of Western defenses to gain a greater measure of political authority.[13]

Yet within days, McCloy edged closer toward and then embraced a policy reversal on German rearmament. On July 18 he cabled Acheson urging that the Germans be permitted to enlist in the American army and to train and fight in larger groups "in the event of an emergency," measures that would require a "radical change in our present European defense plans." Driving McCloy's reversal was not a change of mind on the likelihood of a Soviet attack in Europe. By late July, the consensus among intelligence and policy communities was still that such an attack was not imminent. Instead, a combination of short- and long-term factors led McCloy to advocate German rearmament: the widespread belief that using German resources and manpower for European defenses was indeed essential in the long run; its importance to the stability of the Adenauer government, as well as the potential impact of the military setbacks in Korea on the "general stability of the population" in West Germany; and the massive erosion of confidence that had federal government officials scrambling to plan for worst-case scenarios. If the Germans were given no means to fight in an emergency, the high commissioner argued, "we should probably lose Germany politically as well as militarily without hope of regain." McCloy's dramatic escalation of the stakes set the stage for a decisive policy reversal on German rearmament by the Truman administration.[14]

Enter the SED. In the midst of the massive erosion of confidence in the Federal Republic, the SED held its long-planned Third Party Congress on July 20–24, in Berlin. As the archival record shows, the event was tightly scripted by Stalin. There SED leaders held forth on grandiose schemes for the communization of East Germany and the takeover of West Germany. The party convention adopted a fighting program and called for mobilizing "in the Bonn separatist state . . . national resistance against the separatist, colonial and warmongering policies of Anglo-American imperialism and its German stooges." SED strongman Walter Ulbricht even proclaimed that the GDR would not need to build a new seaport because soon "democratic Germany" would have Hamburg or Lübeck. In a telegram from the convention to the Soviet leader, the SED promised to "develop even more strongly than heretofore an all-German policy of struggle for the preservation and support of peace, for the united, and independent democratic German Republic." Party co-chairman and GDR prime minister Grotewohl confidently proclaimed that "we cannot be content with the successes of the German Democratic Republic alone: it has to be all of Germany."[15]

The thrust of the party convention, a greater emphasis on all-German policies, had been determined during the SED leader's visit to Moscow in early May, well before the outbreak of war in Korea. Against the backdrop of the fighting in the Far East, and debate over the rearmament of West Germany, however, these pronouncements took on a more militant, threatening tone. Declassified East German records show that they in fact camouflaged considerable uncertainty within the SED over whether the new unity and peace drive prodded by Moscow should involve more than just heightened rhetoric. After all, a united Germany on Soviet terms would require nothing less than Allied withdrawal from Germany, as GDR president Pieck reminded Semenov, now the chairman of the Soviet Control Commission in Germany. Clearing his speech in advance of the convention with the top Soviet representative in Germany, Pieck, for one, remained perplexed just days before the party congress as to whether the fight for unity was "just a matter of consistent agitation among the working masses in all of Germany" against "the policy of the Americans and the English" or "what else could be done [to] implement this task." Even to the SED leadership, a takeover of the Federal Republic in any form seemed far from a realistic possibility.[16]

To McCloy, however, the SED congress's challenge to Western Allied authority was "apparent and unequivocal." Not only did the militant tone of the convention demoralize the West German public further and emphasize the urgency of stemming the erosion of confidence in the Federal Republic. Against the foil of unexpected military successes of North Korean forces, the long-anticipated announcement of GDR "independence" after the October elections took on new and ominous meaning as a critical moment for a potential East German move.[17]

On July 22, a few days after his clarion call for a course reversal on German rearmament, McCloy gave Acheson an alarming estimate of the GDR's role in Soviet moves in Germany that echoed Adenauer's. McCloy predicted that the USSR was "prepared to go very close to precipitating world war in order to win the whole of Germany within the next five years." Soviet strategy would be "somewhat analogous to that employed in Korea," a combination of consolidating power in East Germany, integrating East Germany within the Soviet orbit, heightening pressure vis-à-vis West Germany, and subverting the FRG from within, and preparing for the "ultimate attack by GDR with East German troops." McCloy expected stepped-up subversive activities and increased efforts to "maneuver [the] GDR into fuller diplomatic recognition." He expected that the "danger period" for Berlin as the first point of attack would begin when the USSR granted the GDR some form of peace settlement and restored the GDR to full sovereignty. An elevation of the GDR to full sovereignty seemed "relatively certain" in connection with the October Volks-kammer elections, though the "timing, [and] extent of pressure acceleration of [the] Soviet timetable" would depend closely on "Korean developments."[18]

McCloy's focus was shifting subtly as concerns over an imminent Soviet attack on West Germany waned. He was not alone within the administration in appreciating instead the SED regime's growing capacity as an actor in the German Cold War. Arguing that the Korean events demonstrated that the Soviets had "openly moved into the use of force through puppets," the U.S. secretaries of the navy, army, and air force on August 1 singled out Berlin as one of a few global soft spots where a "satellite thrust" in particular was possible. In their view, Berlin was also among the likely possibilities for "internal Communistic *coups d'états.*" A secret CIA memorandum for Truman later that month indicated that the East German alert forces were probably capable of undertaking "a surprise movement against Berlin with considerable prospects for rapid success," even if there was consensus that the Soviets were not yet prepared to risk general war. The Supreme Commander of U.S. troops in Europe, General Thomas T. Handy, thought that "an attack on West Sectors of Berlin by maximum Bereitschaften strength probably would succeed now," and, days later, together with the high commissioner, warned that the "temper" of the party convention suggested that the "Communists' schedule against Berlin may move faster and more aggressively than we have estimated in the past." HICOG's GDR watchers, for their part, assessed that "the SED has never been in such satisfactory condition" as then, constituting "an adequate Soviet tool for the attempted execution of current Soviet plans in Germany."[19]

In the course of the summer of 1950, anti-Allied propaganda swept the Federal Republic "like an artillery barrage that precedes the general attack," as one journalist described the militarized atmosphere. West German officials detected "increased influence attempts of the East zonal government" in Berlin and the FRG territory since the beginning of the "Korean action." Communist-sponsored rallies took place throughout West Germany, triggering weeks of nervous speculation. In the southwestern city of Esslingen, Communist groups even conducted paramilitary exercises. In Berlin, American officials noted a "revived 'cold war'" in a series of moves restricting traffic between the city and West Germany. On July 27 the CIA reported relocation of Soviet airborne units to the GDR, and media reported that eight Soviet divisions stationed in the GDR had begun extensive maneuvers near Grafenwöhr on the Czech border, exacerbating the tense atmosphere in Germany. At the end of the month, the first congress of the National Front escalated talk of the Communist liberation of the Federal Republic.[20]

Illustrative of the impact of what American observers termed the "Communist softening-up process" was an incident in a small West German town in Lower Saxony near the GDR border. A man in Soviet uniform reportedly appeared at the local town hall and informed the mayor that Soviet troops would come the next day to straighten out the zonal boundary to include the town's slate factory in the Soviet zone. Only the appearance of a British officer the next day saved the situation, as the townspeople had prepared to evacuate by noon and had already dismantled the switchboard from the central telephone station.[21]

Pieck and Ulbricht were also on Adenauer's mind in mid-August as he returned from his summer vacation in Switzerland. The SED leaders had gotten under the chancellor's skin with their repeatedly declared intent to try West German "collaborators" before a people's court. Put together with the military training of the Eastern police, there was "no doubt" as to their purposes, Adenauer told the assembled high commissioners on August 17. Despite "offensive" troop concentrations of the Soviet army, he assumed that "the Russian would not march," because if that was the case there was "no point in talking further." Adenauer's gaze was instead squarely focused on the People's Police, which he expected to reach 150,000 men by 1951 and 200,000 the following year, forming the core of a future East German "Wehrmacht." While it was not yet ready for real military operations, it was "obviously heading straight towards the building of an East German army." Lacking a formal security guarantee, the chancellor professed doubts that the Western Allies would be willing to launch a third world war if the People's Police initiated operations to "liberate" the West German territory.[22]

To be sure, there was an instrumental character to Adenauer's threat scenario. He professed himself shocked by the "erosion of the population's will to resist" to back up his demand that the Western powers demonstrate their military might in

West Germany. He held out West German industrial potential as decisive in the next world war, implying that its loss to Stalin would tip the scales toward the East. He raised the "the option" of establishing by the spring of 1951 a West German "defense force" manned by volunteers as an alternative to his "preferred" solution of the Western Allies protecting West German territory at the border to the GDR. Such a volunteer force could eventually, in understanding with France and with the assistance of the United States, "develop into something else," as he put it. He added public pressure on the Allied High Commission by reiterating his ideas in an interview with the *New York Times* published the next day.[23]

Yet Adenauer's concern over the East German threat was real—a "nightmare," as one of his biographers put it. Certainly the SED challenge framed the problem for him. Thus he envisioned the anticipated West German volunteer force to encompass some 150,000 men, the very force level he anticipated the GDR People's Police to reach the next year. The degree to which the East German People's Police drove Adenauer's thinking reflected a secret "security memorandum" drafted by his aide Herbert Blankenhorn after the chancellor's proposal for a German defense force had fallen flat with the high commissioners. Adenauer now scaled back his "offer" to a demand for a federal protective police force. Though that implied a responsibility limited to dealing with internal security threats, such as a Communist "fifth column" that he had warned about, the People's Police remained the main concern of Adenauer and his advisers: an August 21 draft of the memo called for a volunteer police force manned and trained by Germans but armed by the Allies "corresponding in the strength, armament and training to the people's police."[24]

Given to McCloy on August 30 to inform the Western foreign ministers meeting slated to take place in New York on September 12–18, the final (August 29) version of the security memorandum omitted this reference to the People's Police. But it reiterated the estimate that the People's Police would swell to 150,000 men in the near future, with an anticipated total of 300,000. It had to be expected, the memorandum spelled out, that, once fully consolidated after the October elections, the GDR could begin its unification work with a liberation of Berlin and later People's Police actions against the Federal Republic. Such liberation actions would be occasioned and supported by marches of the tightly organized FDJ and an active fifth column. Into early September Adenauer, while acknowledging the need for "democratic control," refused to be pinned down on the precise nature of the "protective police force" (Schutzpolizei) in order "not to diminish its fighting capacity against the people's police of the eastern zone."[25]

How much the SED regime weighed on the chancellor's mind was reflected in his focus on the October elections in the GDR as a key turning point. Along with a renewed request for a formal Western security guarantee in case of an East German invasion, Adenauer also demanded a revision of the occupation statute. In a second top secret memorandum sent along with the security memorandum, he proposed to put the Federal Republic's relationship with the Western powers on a contractual basis. Historians have long emphasized the quid-pro-quo nature of his diplomatic strategy. But the dismantling of much of the occupation controls also made sense in light of the "greater autonomy" both Allies and Adenauer expected the GDR would be given after the October elections, even if this was largely a matter of appearance than fact. The focus in Western Allied-German discussions that summer on the October elections in the GDR as a turning-point is striking: The French high commissioner bluntly stated on August 17 that it was likely the point at which an East German attack would occur.[26]

Finally, Adenauer's strategy vis-à-vis the East remained defensive, at least in McCloy's view. At his discussion with the Allied High Commission on August 17, it was the issue of a propaganda offensive that evoked the sharpest exchange between Adenauer and McCloy: confronted by the latter's laments that the West Germans had remained passive in the face of propaganda drumbeats from the East, Adenauer countered that a propaganda campaign against the East, against Communism was presently "entirely mistaken," given the apathy among the population. It was, however, precisely a more robust approach to the GDR with which McCloy sought to complement the long-term project of integrating West Germany's potential into a common West European defense.[27]

Visions of Rollback in Germany: Psychological Warfare Planning against the GDR

The Korean War "decisively shifted" opinions within the Truman administration in favor of German rearmament. But a West German military contribution to the Western European defense would, as discussions within the Western alliance showed that fall, be a longer-term proposition. Meeting in New York in mid-September, the three Western foreign ministers agreed to move several Allied divisions to Germany in a demonstration of strength, offered the Federal Republic a formal security guarantee, even conceded a modest expansion of the German police, though only at the state level. They failed, however, to agree on German rearmament. Finding a solution would be a protracted process.[28]

From the perspective of the Truman administration, that very prospect lent even greater urgency to dealing with an emerging threat in Germany that was brought into sharper relief by the North Korean invasion: the growing political and military capabilities of the German Democratic Republic. Western observers largely agreed that the GDR would claim greater "legitimacy" as a result of the October Volkskammer elections, a claim that might possibly be bolstered by being granted "autonomy" by the USSR soon after. The SED regime's new "agency" posed not only the "practical problem" of dealing with GDR representatives on traffic and trade controls along the West German and Berlin borderlines, calling into question non-recognition and foreshadowing the dilemmas that would haunt the West during the second Berlin Crisis of 1958–62. It also raised the specter that Soviet leaders might come to believe they could keep a conflagration over Berlin "localized" as they employed East German forces rather than Soviet manpower. The GDR's growing capacity "to attempt a coup in the Korean pattern," had been, McCloy recognized, the "most significant change" in the Berlin situation. McCloy therefore recommended "that immediate steps" be taken to intensify psychological warfare vis-a-vis the Soviet and the East German Communists.[29]

McCloy had in fact pushed for a more concerted effort by the administration well before the North Korean invasion. In the wake of the FDJ Deutschlandtreffen in late May, McCloy approved a new comprehensive psychological warfare program. Drafted and discussed within the Political-Economic Projects Committee since mid-April, "A Program for PEPCO" sought to provide a "general blueprint for action," and was designed to "contain the USSR momentum and to advance U.S. policies by denial of those of the Soviets." According to the program signed off by McCloy, U.S. policy sought to "contain the Soviets more firmly in their own zone" and to stimulate passive resistance to Communist ideology, Soviet propaganda, and the consolidation of "totalitarian rule." Echoing the lessons learned from the SED's successful staging of the FDJ mass rally, HICOG's program focused on helping East Germans to overcome "a feeling of defeatism and of the inevitability of a Soviet triumph in Germany." The program sought to "retard the Sovietization of East Germany." PEPCO strove to place the Soviets on the defensive, allowing the United States to "extricate ourselves permanently from a position of merely seeking ways and means of parrying Soviet initiatives and moves."[30]

Yet in many ways the PEPCO program reflected itself a certain degree of defeatism about future prospects for the East Germans and seemed as much geared to strengthening anti-Communist sentiments in the Federal Republic as undermining Communist control in the East: Thus PEPCO called for maintaining the policy of nonrecognition of the GDR and keeping the political and psychological initiative on German unification, and argued for a campaign to convince Germans that the National Front was a "façade for Russian expansionism." To counter the effect of National Front propaganda, the PEPCO program proposed to create a mass movement – one that could promote unification in line with Western interests in the Federal Republic![31]

To be sure, the PEPCO program also hinted at more active measures such as mobilizing West German and West Berlin organizations to support anti-Communist resistance in the GDR. That would entail "liaising" with the Eastern offices of the West German parties and covertly extending financial and other assistance to groups operating in the GDR underground. But such operations were clearly a secondary order, reflecting the tight limitations McCloy saw in his ability to influence developments in the East.

HICOG officials were particularly eager to press ahead on the issue of free elections on which they believed they had gained the initiative since McCloy's pronouncements in February. The lack of any response from Soviet high commissioner Vasily Chuikov to the Western High Commissioners' May 25 initiative to draft an election law seemed to corroborate the idea that this was a winning proposition. Since early April, PEPCO had been developing a "systematic propaganda campaign" against the October 15 "elections" which limited voters' choices to one (unity) list. American officials felt strongly that intensified propaganda in favor of German unity would provide a positive alternative to the unity-list elections in the Soviet zone and suggested to East Germans that in voting "no," they would be voting "yes" for the concept of free elections. Moreover, it would counter the "psychological adjustments" East Germans were expected to make in reaction to West Germany's accession to the Council of Europe in July 1950, widely seen as deepening partition and writing off the East.[32]

The American found their push to counter GDR and Soviet propaganda and policies circumscribed by British and French reservations against any efforts to "hot-up the Cold War." The European allies had been skeptical about what they termed "Cold War" policies. The outbreak of hostilities in Korea only deepened these reservations. French officials resisted efforts that might provoke the Soviets to more drastic actions in Europe. British officials struck their American counterparts by an "attitude of calmness and no anxiety to the immediate future." In the spring, London and Paris had considered a propaganda campaign against the October 15 elections as "somewhat premature," and even by late June were worried that "if started now, we might run out of propaganda material before the event."[33]

HICOG's cold warriors were therefore prepared to go it alone. HICOG embarked on a unilateral campaign for all-German unity and against the Soviet zone elections. At the end of June, PEPCO approved a massive propaganda effort in support of free all-German elections. The PEPCO program, moreover, called for

efforts to induce East German leaders to resist and denounce the Soviet intention
to proceed with the unity-list elections, even to organize a large-scale letter-writing
campaign from West Germans to their eastern compatriots, and to encourage the
GDR population to invalidate their ballots at the polls or to vote against the unity
list.[34] HICOG also considered ways and means to discourage and curtail collaboration by East Germans with the Communist authorities. One idea was to state
publicly that political asylum for East German defectors was not an "unconditional
right" and to compile a list of prominent East German collaborators that would be
ineligible for political asylum, thus reversing a policy under which, as late as June
1950, key GDR officials—such as East-CDU leader Otto Nuschke—had apparently been invited by U.S. agencies to defect.[35]

Much like in the summer of 1946, Washington policymakers favored an even
bolder approach. Responding to the proposed "Program for PEPCO," the State
Department took issue with the key assumption that the Soviet intention to extend
control over Western Germany "is not—and presumably cannot be—matched by
equally firm aggressive intention on our side regarding Eastern Germany." Contrary
to McCloy's frustrations over the West's limited influence in the East, in the State
Department's view the Soviet zone was "exceedingly vulnerable to Western-type
propaganda to an extent that our chances of interfering with Soviet policies inside
the Soviet zone and influencing their course . . . may be assumed to be considerably
better than vice versa." The State Department recommended intensifying internal
difficulties within the Soviet zone regime through a higher degree of coordination
and planning, including the coordination of intelligence activities. Foreshadowing
later debates within the U.S. government over the efficacy of rollback, the department admitted that the question "as to how far we should go in stimulating the East
Germans openly to resist Soviet policies" was "a delicate one." Careful consideration
should be given, the department argued, to the potential effectiveness of resistance
and to the possibility that a violent Soviet reaction might render such resistance
"too costly in terms of the advantages to be gained."[36]

The State Department favored engineering "total anti-Soviet Zone propaganda"
in a way that would let the Soviets know that "we are stepping up this type of
propaganda" as a response to Moscow's intensified anti-Western drive. Western
propaganda should constantly strive to maintain the image of Communist expansion before the German people. Administration officials also suggested blacklisting
GDR officials for entry into the Federal Republic and delaying, confiscating, or
"losing" mail from the SED to the West German KPD organizations in retaliation
for Soviet interference with interzonal mail. Washington also expressed support

for HICOG's plans to encourage the East Germans to protest the unity-list voting procedure and to demonstrate their opposition to invalidate their ballots or voting against the unity-list candidates.[37]

Over the summer, HICOG ramped up its anti-GDR campaign but continued to be hampered by both a lack of resources and Allied considerations. HICOG needed additional "money, slots and experienced personnel."[38] Moreover, the British and French remained unenthusiastic about much of the American effort, though by mid-September they were at least ready to step up propaganda against the Soviet zone elections. Even more difficult was attaining the "active and wholehearted cooperation" of the West Germans that the State Department had demanded. The West Germans resisted the idea of following up on the Western High Commissioners' letters to Chuikov, and despite continued efforts, HICOG officials admitted that "great success is not expected."[39] In the end, the Western High Commissioners sent a letter to Chuikov on October 10, on the eve of the elections, reminding the Soviet high commissioner of his failure to respond to the May 25 letter and pointing to the fraudulent character of the East German elections.

Kurt Schumacher, the staunchly anti-Communist leader of the SPD, emerged as an unlikely obstacle to American plans to instruct the East Germans to stage a secret vote against the Volkskammer elections by mailing their expired ration cards to West Germany. Despite the fact that PEPCO continued to consider the plans "excellent," Schumacher argued that SED agents would go from house to house demanding old ration cards, outing those whose had participated in the protest. Schumacher apparently felt certain that the West Germans had too little interest in the matter to ensure that ballots received in the West were forwarded to some central tally office. Minister for All-German Affairs Kaiser proved hardly more enthusiastic: the Soviet zone population, Kaiser suspected, was already intimidated to such an extent that it would not participate in sufficient numbers. In the end, McCloy had to abandon the plan. RIAS refrained from encouraging oppositional East Germans to invalidate their ballots or otherwise expose themselves, arguing that to cast one's ballot *for* the regime list would "deceive the deceivers" on October 15.[40]

The results of the October 15 elections, an overwhelming 99 percent vote for the SED-dominated unity list, had in the eyes of U.S. officials a depressing effect on the East German population. To be sure, there were those who argued that the elections had only intensified the determination of the Soviet zone population to oppose the regime. There were some indications that East Germans had reported enthusiastically to the RIAS line of "deceiving the deceivers." But others suggested that the slogan had discouraged "resistance elements" in the GDR who wished "to keep alive and strengthen the thesis that the individual must assume personal responsibility . . . and be encouraged and sustained in this by advice from respected leaders and institutions, like RIAS." On the whole, American officials concluded that the October election results—following on the success of the Deutschlandtreffen—had further consolidated Communist control in East Germany.[41]

The outcome of the October elections reinforced a sense among U.S. officials that more had to be done to mount an effective counteroffensive against the GDR. That fall, Shepard Stone, McCloy's public affairs director, hired two external consultants, Wallace Carroll and Hans Speier, to review and develop HICOG's strategy vis-à-vis the GDR. Carroll (1906–2002) was the executive news editor of the *Winston-Salem Journal-Sentinel.* A veteran journalist who had managed the United Press International (UPI) bureau in London and reported from the USSR in 1941, he had headed the overseas branch of the Office of War Information during World War II and recently published his experience in *Persuade or Perish* (1948). Speier, a German émigré who had worked under Carroll during the war, was a veteran of OMGUS's Information Control Division, a founder of RAND, and a leading psychological warfare expert. Underlining the urgency of the need to counter the SED, Speier was pulled out of the administration's secret "Project Troy" exercise then taking place at MIT to review U.S. propaganda vis-à-vis the GDR.[42]

The two consultants took a comprehensive approach to their task, reflecting the "total" approach Washington favored. For several weeks, they had access to everyone at HICOG and immersed themselves in high commission affairs: they talked to McCloy, his deputy, and all division chiefs. Speier attended one of McCloy's weekly staff conferences and two PEPCO meetings. The top U.S. representative in Bonn and liaison with the German government, Charles Thayer, a Foreign Service officer who had headed the Voice of America (VOA) radio network, hosted a dinner that included many leading German politicians. In Berlin, Speier talked to a range of key personalities, including the U.S. military commander, General Maxwell Taylor; the Americans who were running RIAS; American editors of German-language publications; Ernst Lemmer; the KGU's Ernst Tillich and *Der Tagesspiegel* editor Ernst Reger; four or five leading officials in "the department mainly concerned with the Soviet Zone" (presumably the All-German Affairs Ministry), as well as "top operators" in West Germany's fledgling intelligence apparatus.

In another round of information gathering, Carroll, who did not speak German, saw Lieutenant General Manton Sprague Eddy, commander of the Seventh Army in Heidelberg; M. Armand Bérard, deputy French high commissioner; and Sir Ivone Kirkpatrick, British high commissioner; and Speier met with Peter Tenant, the British chief of Berlin operations; Lindley Frazer, of the BBC; and Sir Frederick Stacey, the UK Foreign Office's expert on Soviet information policy. The two consultants also interviewed a number of Germans living in the Soviet zone who were visiting West Berlin.[43]

By December 1, Carroll and Speier produced an outline for a new U.S. strategy in Germany that was strident in tone and sweeping in assumptions. Their thirty-eight-page "top secret" report, "Psychological Warfare in Germany," first released to this author in response to a Freedom of Information Act request, argued that the objective of U.S. policy was to integrate the whole of Germany into Western Europe and thus turn it into a partner in the building of a "healthy international community." They assumed that East Germany was the "springboard for Soviet ambitions in the much more attractive areas to the West," but, as was a commonplace assumption among experts inside and outside the U.S. government, that the Soviet government would shrink from initiating a general war in pursuing its goals in the near future. To achieve a united Germany tied to the West politically, militarily, economically, and culturally, the United States had to "destroy Soviet power in Germany." For this purpose, aggressive psychological warfare "waged with a fixed purpose" would be required.[44]

Echoing McCloy, they urged the administration to "shed the vestiges of our defensive mentality" and launch a great psychological warfare offensive, directed toward making the GDR a liability to the Soviets. The goal was to force the Kremlin to withdraw its forces from East Germany, an effort that they aptly named "Operation Exit." Though the offensive and defensive military value of the Soviet zone to the USSR was possibly so great that the USSR might accept considerable economic losses and deal ruthlessly with political difficulties rather than abandon the GDR, Carroll and Speier argued, these considerations should not lead the West to lower its sights. They proposed a catalog of measures, ranging from economic warfare to the display of military might (i.e., military parades) and political initiatives on such controversial issues as the Oder-Neisse line. The—orientalist—concept of the East's "return to Europe" was to frame American efforts in the GDR and Eastern Europe in ideological terms.

What set Carroll and Speier's recommendations apart from ideas that had been germinating within HICOG was their focus on the German resistance in the Soviet zone. Much of the "resistance" work had, in their view, been confined to disseminating forbidden news and propaganda and providing intelligence to the West. Clearly impressed by the large number of anti-Communist operators they had encountered during their trip, they argued that the resistance work suffered from a lack of coordination and cooperation, which in part was attributable to jealousy and distrust among the organizations engaged in opposition work. According to the report, opposition in the GDR lacked "strategic direction." As yet, there was neither "an American long-range plan" that stated the goals and phases of the operation nor a "timetable" for coordinating resistance work in the GDR with overall U.S. strategy. Given that the Soviet hold on the East German youth and Soviet-inspired East German military power was bound to gain strength, Carroll and Speier emphasized an urgent need for long-range planning of "a vigorous Resistance" in East Germany.

Carroll and Speier advocated that anti-Communist activities in the GDR move from intelligence and propaganda work to "resistance proper." This would include the infiltration of selected Soviet zone organizations, such as the paramilitary alert squads and the Volkspolizei, sabotage, abduction, direct action against selected, highly placed functionaries, etc." The two consultants recommended providing "unified direction" to the opposition movement within the GDR. The East German resistance movement would be part of an overall U.S. strategy, and for that reason it would be necessary "to reserve in fact, if not in law, certain planning and directive powers to U.S. agencies" and to establish more effective liaison with the "special activist groups which engage in the most advanced type of Resistance work." Far from harming its prestige, American steering of the resistance would be "proof of the U.S. intention to unify Germany."

Carroll and Speier cautioned that before the active phase of "intensive subversive work" began it would be necessary to develop a "specific action plan" to keep the hopes of the East Germans alive. This goal was to be met by fostering a belief in the existence of a "unified, strong, and growing resistance movement within the Soviet zone, one that had a name, was secure and disciplined, acted according to plan, and bided its time." East Germans had to be convinced that American and West German interests in their liberation remained intense. In an effort to impress upon East Germans that sacrifices might be necessary, Carroll and Speier suggested raising "one or the other German victim of Soviet persecution" to the level of "legendary martyrdom." Since the spirit of resistance could not be evoked by propaganda alone, the report recommended measures to increase defections and strengthen loyalty to the West among East German leaders, along with making "controlled efforts to compromise influential Germans . . . whom we cannot hope to win over." Finally, "direct actions"—i.e., assassinations—would help to dramatize the opposition move-ment: "It may be advisable to abduct or execute the one or the other notorious Ger-man Communist who is widely hated in the Soviet zone." German Communists would not be the only targets: "Operation Exit" also proposed concerted efforts to increase defection among the Soviet forces in Germany, sensitive nerve endings of the Kremlin's position in East Germany. A clandestine campaign would magnify the effects of defection and demoralization in the minds of the Soviet leaders.

With its aggressive tone and ambitious approach to a coordinated psychological warfare program, the Carroll-Speier Report struck like a thunderbolt in Washington and the HICOG orbit. Against the backdrop of an escalated Cold War tensions, the report apparently evoked an "enthusiastic" response among the "cold warriors" within the administration and was hailed as a "distinct contribution." Assistant Secretary of State Edward W. Barrett, chairman of the Truman administration's newly created interagency Psychological Strategy Board (PSB) in Washington, cabled from Washington that he was especially interested in HICOG's reaction to the program toward East Germany.[45]

To American officials in Germany, much of the report rang true, such as the complaint about the lack of effective propaganda coordination among Allies and Germans. That task was made difficult by the sheer "multitude of Allied and German organizations operating in this field"; by internal political squabbles within and rivalry among the German organizations; and by the poor relationship between intelligence and propaganda units on the American side. Propagandistically useful information from the intelligence agencies, HICOG officials argued, had amounted to "little more than a trickle." Carroll and Speier's emphasis on East German youth as the audience most susceptible to Soviet propaganda engendered wide support. Reinforcing the points made by the report, HICOG officials strongly advocated "an all-out offensive against the FDJ and the Soviet-Zone educational system."[46]

To the extent that the report by two external consultants could be read as a critique of the high commission's activities, HICOG, not surprisingly, reacted defensively: many of the measures proposed in the report, officials argued, mirrored existing U.S. efforts. HICOG assured Washington that it was developing a plan for "effective and coordinated Resistance in the Soviet Zone," including a more widespread infiltration of the Volkspolizei. The high commission was "preparing the mood for resistance," drafting long-range plans to increase the strength of clandestine networks operating behind the "Iron Curtain" from West German bases and to train "partisan warfare cadres."[47]

In fact, the Carroll-Speier Report, in the view of HICOG officials, understated East Germany's economic dependence on the Federal Republic. HICOG officials were more bullish on the range of economic-warfare targets: they should be expanded to include technicians and skilled labor. GDR personnel shortages in those areas could be "aggravated by carefully planned and executed measures." HICOG's Intelligence Division was reportedly considering a plan that would deny key industries in East German critical materials; key economic figures were to be included in a defection program aimed at "East German and orbit personnel and military figures."[48]

Over the following weeks and months, the Carroll-Speier Report framed much of the discussion on American policy vis-à-vis East Germany. At the very moment when Western plans for the military integration of the Federal Republic were taking shape, the report implied that German unification, and the integration of *all* of Germany into Western Europe, was an overriding goal in American policy. As HICOG officials noted, a "mass of empirical evidence" suggested otherwise. With much of German public opinion doubtful about the sincerity and determination of both the Allies and the Federal Republic with respect to German unity, Western statements on the issue were "susceptible to being interpreted primarily as propaganda moves." Making it "crystal-clear" that U.S. policy was not limited to the integration of West Germany into Western Europe would go a long way "in stimulating resistance to Sovietization, in inspiring the will to resist, in dispelling present doubts in respect to American aims in Europe."[49]

In suggesting a catalog of tactical measures, Carroll and Speier also assumed that the Soviet government would continue to shrink from general war with the United States. Some HICOG officials argued that the report was based "on a too-rosy estimate of the balance of forces" in favor of the West. Reflecting the dire expectations by Allied officials in Europe, HICOG officials saw evidence that the USSR would "make a determined effort to take Eurasia within the next few years, even if such entails World War III." With the Soviets possibly "prepared to seek certain objectives even at the risk of war," the problem for psychological warfare was how to seize the offensive without provoking Soviet aggression. Some of the more militant measures in the report, such as military demonstrations, sabotage, abductions, and assassinations, might prompt the USSR to unleash a world war, and hence required "extreme caution from the standpoint of timing and execution." Geared toward making the GDR a liability to the Soviet Union and increasing Soviet insecurity, the Carroll-Speier Report ignored the possibility—some within HICOG felt—that it might actually be in America's interest to "instill the Soviets with a false sense of security." And it was by no means certain that the program would dislodge the Soviets from East Germany. After all, even Carroll and Speier had pointed out that the Soviets had never withdrawn militarily from an occupied country without establishing a reliable satellite.[50]

To what extent were the East Germans willing to actively resist? HICOG officials thought that here, too, Carroll and Speier had been "somewhat over-optimistic." Opposition to the Soviets and the regime was considered to be "almost entirely devoted to the dissemination of forbidden news and propaganda." Efforts to coordinate resistance activities had thus far failed. In the spring of 1951, HICOG's Reactions Analysis Staff carried out a number of surveys on the "state of mind" among East Germans and the resistance potential behind the Iron Curtain. The great bulk of respondents characterized the post-election mood of GDR residents as "very depressed," with three out of four East Germans feeling that they could do nothing toward improving their political situation. Only 18 percent of eastern zone residents could be counted as a "core resistance potential." Contrary to what Carroll and Speier had claimed, however, the feeling of helplessness was least widespread among the East German youth, suggesting to HICOG that despite the special measures taken by the SED "to coddle and win over the East German youth, they are still the group that the West can count on most heavily for resistance to the East Zone regime."[51]

Finally, to what extent should American psychological warfare efforts privilege anti-Communist work in the Federal Republic over supporting resistance in the GDR? In July 1951, HICOG consultant Edmond Taylor made the case that the former had priority: he developed an outline for a counteroffensive that aimed at defeating Communist psychological warfare in Western Germany, acknowledging "the impossibility at this time of achieving any major positive psychological warfare objectives behind the Iron Curtain." His "Interim Plan for Intensified Psychological Warfare in Germany" called for a "heightened emotional tone in propaganda on constructive themes," "more vigorous use of mass-participation and mass-action techniques to generate enthusiasm" by greater reliance on more militant pro-Western groups in Germany, by "more aggressive and hard-hitting counter-propaganda," and by "introducing a more dramatic and spectacular flavor" to all American -sponsored or -stimulated propaganda activities: "We must be prepared on a 24-hour basis seven days a week to exploit instantly any propaganda opportunity created by spot news development."[52]

Even with its focus on West Germany, the plan prescribed intensified psychological warfare efforts aimed at Eastern Germany, particularly continued vigorous attacks on Communist police-state methods and slave-labor practices behind the Iron Curtain. Propaganda toward the GDR was also to "play" the German unity theme "hard," tied in with a special campaign in West Germany "to remember their East Zone brothers."

Taylor had warned that in the intensified propaganda efforts, "we should be careful to avoid sounding like Goebbels." The methods proposed by Taylor, some within HICOG's Eastern Element commented, "smack entirely too much of totalitarian propaganda methods" that would "merely dull the senses" and demanded that the

West be sensitive "to the Easterner's probable aversion against having only spam [directed at them]." HICOG Eastern Element chief George A. Morgan told Taylor that the "high voltage propaganda" advocated by Taylor's plan would likely arouse old European prejudices against American "super-salesmanship" and Americans as "Russen mit Bügelfalten" (Russians in pinstripes).[53]

In an effort to provide a more positive framework for propaganda toward the GDR, HICOG staff further developed the "return to Europe" concept proposed by Carroll and Speier. The idea, PEPCO officials felt, would counter the increasing "psychological fatigue" among the Soviet-orbit population: "Hope and a mood of resistance, especially among the youth, will not persevere indefinitely in the absence of a clearer enunciation of U.S. and Western policy objectives vis-à-vis Eastern Europe."[54]

By fall, HICOG approved merging Taylor's plan with the "return to Europe" concept. In its final form, Taylor's plan preserved much of the tone and many of the themes of the original draft, but, significantly, highlighted as the leading objective the strengthening resistance to the East German Communist regime, "in preparation for more active and organized forms of resistance after June 1952." The section of Taylor's plan titled "Five-Year Plan for Liberation" was to convey to GDR residents that "the liberation of East Germans is confidently expected within a period from three to five years hence." Taylor also called for a "substantial shift from overt to covert and gray activities," a result, in part, of the limits that the anticipated contractual agreement with the Federal Republic would place on U.S. overt propaganda.[55]

In seven still largely classified appendixes, Taylor's plan outlined specific programs to implement its general approach. Appendix E, "Special and Semi-Covert Activities," envisioned, among other things, the "creation of permanent German agencies" to pursue psychological warfare activities as stipulated by the contractual agreements. Appendix E also provided clandestine support for a permanent European youth camp, a strong and militant youth organization, an inter-European radio agency, speakers' bureaus, study centers, and research institutes of various kinds, available to produce films, pamphlets, posters, and stage rallies, sports festivals and plebiscites, as well as large-scale polls. The projected youth organization, for example, would agitate militantly for a united Europe that is "within the broad letter of the law," engaged in "the crashing of borders, the publishing of 'black books,' 'raids,' and 'invasions,'" as well as "orthodox activities" such as parades and wall-writing.

In November 1951, the State Department approved the plan generally, especially the "return to Europe" component, even as it questioned European psychology, especially French attitudes toward a European union encompassing "anything resembling a strong Germany." Cautioning that the "tempo of propaganda" should not run too far ahead of "political realities," Washington authorized the U.S. high commissioner in Germany to proceed with those projects that fell directly under his jurisdiction. A special committee headed by Alfred "Mickey" Boerner was set up at HICOG to coordinate execution of the Interim Plan in Germany with "the activities of other agencies."[56]

Though most of the "covert" activities carried out under the Taylor Plan remain classified, "special" or "grey" projects executed by non-U.S. agencies and organizations provide a sense of the range of the informational activities that were to keep East Germans connected with the West. These included, above all, financial and logistical support for anti-Communist books, pamphlets, and posters for distribution to both West German institutions and, via "special channels," East Germans. HICOG, for example, produced 40,000 copies of pocket editions of five books written by defected GDR officials, a former German POW, and a former Spanish general who had fought in the Spanish Civil War but had since turned against the USSR, for distribution at the World Youth Festival with a view to "penetration into the Soviet Zone." With U.S. support, a Berlin publisher produced a flip-pad designed for young boys and girls that told the adventures of "Michel," who was given a specially conducted tour through East Germany, only to come back to the West "disillusioned and a firm opponent of communism." Five hundred thousand pamphlets "exposing" the Soviet peace campaign and 180,000 fake editions of the FDJ organ *Junge Welt*, too, were distributed at the August youth festival.

The following year, HICOG authorized DM 222,260 to underwrite a book-publishing program with the Cologne-based publishing house Kiepenheuer and Witsch, which over the following six months would produce such titles as *Nationalismus und Kommunismus* (by Lothar von Ballusek, 20,000 copies), *Die Satellisierung der Sowjetzone* (by Gerd Frieddenrich, 20,000 copies), and *Sibirien* (by French author Anton Ciliga, 5,000 copies), all to be distributed at no charge through "special channels" to the GDR.[57]

The United States and the Cold Civil War in Germany

Eastern Initiatives and West German "Rollback" Efforts

Countering the Grotewohl Initiatives

The Volkskammer elections turned out not to be the watershed moment that some in the West had feared in the tense summer of 1950. They did not occasion more aggressive military actions on the part of the GDR. Nor did the Soviet government formally confer full sovereignty on the GDR in its aftermath. But prodded and aided by Moscow, German communist leaders lost little time to leverage new claims to electoral legitimacy (however hollow and questionable they may have seemed) into new momentum on the all-German political front. The ensuing moves, centered around offers for an all-German constituent council, effectively came to constitute the Soviet-GDR response to the Western calls for free all-German elections, which initially had caught Moscow off guard. They also fit the logic underpinning Soviet strategy since forming the GDR: strengthening East German agency in this pivotal Cold War theater, one in which Germans in East and West would increasingly take center stage.

The idea of an all-German national assembly had in fact surfaced in Western proposals as recently as the September 14, 1950, Bundestag resolution to the tripartite foreign ministers then meeting in New York. Convening in late October in Prague in what amounted to a response to the New York conference, the foreign ministers of the USSR and its European allies, including the GDR, made the idea their own, stipulating, however, that the constituent assembly would be composed on the basis of parity between East and West Germany.[1]

Soviet archival evidence suggests that the Prague meeting owed its impetus to East German foreign minister Georg Dertinger's idea to hold such a conference to counter the push for West German rearmament. The meeting would also demonstrate East German agency on the international stage, upstaging the Adenauer government which had not participated in the New York sessions. Relishing this diplomatic debut, coming on the heels of the GDR's inclusion in the Council for Mutual Economic Cooperation the previous month, the GDR foreign minister could tell GDR deputy premier and SED strongman Walter Ulbricht that the Prague conference was "the first time that a legitimately elected German government, confirmed and supported by the people, could take a seat at an international negotiating table."[2]

Dertinger's triple emphasis on the popular legitimacy of the GDR government may have betrayed considerable doubts even in the minds of East German leaders that such was in fact the case. But barely six weeks later the GDR government followed up the Prague Declaration with another missive at Bonn: in a letter written at Soviet instruction, drafted by Ulbricht and dispatched by Grotewohl to Adenauer on November 30, the GDR again called for the establishment of an "All-German Constituent Council" of an equal number of West and East German representatives that would pave the way to a provisional all-German government, advise the occupation powers on a peace treaty and prepare all-German elections.[3]

Only more recently have historians credited Grotewohl's letter for the ingenious intervention it was. With its call on Germans to take their national fate more firmly into their own hands, the proposal resonated deeply within the population of the Federal Republic and tapped into yearnings for national unity across the political spectrum. It also played on the unease among many Germans over the prospects for West German rearmament, which was seen as further deepening the country's division. For the GDR, talks at the governmental level would also help undermine the federal government's claim to be the sole representative of the German people, to which the Western powers had given their formal *placet* in New York.[4]

The timing of the Grotewohl letter could have not been more auspicious. It arrived in a situation when the Western setbacks in Korea in the wake of the Chinese entry into the war days earlier appeared to many Germans, as Adenauer was quick to warn the Western high commissioners, "even more menacing and dangerous" than the past summer. To his mind, the developments in Korea dramatically heightened the stakes in the Western discussions over a West German rearmament. McCloy, too, professed to forebodings of a grand Soviet offensive that conjured in his mind recollections of the beginning of the Berlin blockade. According to internal HICOG polls, some 60 percent of Germans favored the talks as proposed by Grotewohl, in principle. Moscow would seek to lure Germany away from the West with the bait of unity. The U.S. high commissioner remained deeply impressed and worried by the "great magnet effect" exercised by the East on Germany.[5]

Thanks to its sources within the West German parties, the SED Politburo was well informed about the political soul-searching the letter stirred up in the West German political establishment. Minister for All-German Affairs Jakob Kaiser, politically scarred by his experiences in the Soviet zone and reflecting the anticommunist predilections deeply ingrained in his ministry's staff, opposed the Grotewohl offer outright, but, as the SED leaders learned, others, including Federal Economics Minister Ludwig Erhard, considered it possible to put out secret informal feelers to the East, possibly through the business community.[6]

To soften up the Adenauer government, the SED politburo unleashed a massive public relations campaign in both parts of Germany to promote the Grotewohl offer. U.S. intelligence soon learned from a "fairly reliable source" about a lengthy catalog of measures to exploit the Grotewohl letter that had been adopted at an SED Central Committee meeting on January 9, 1951. The extensive program directed various mass organizations in the GDR to engage specific propaganda targets in Western Germany. East German cities and organizations sent thousands of letters and telegrams to their West German counterparts. Framed in a conciliatory tone, such propaganda mailings were often directed at intellectual circles, lawyers, architects and physicians. West German businessmen were told that the People's Republic of China was ready to place orders for industrial products in the FRG at the magnitude of $5 billion. Intimations to West German politicians hinted at the potential for more reasonable terms in that the envisioned all-German assembly might be constituted proportionally to actual population numbers, giving the larger Federal Republic a majority of the votes. It "must be conceded," McCloy told Acheson, that "the Grotewohl letter, aided by an unprecedented propaganda campaign of great variety and flexibility, [had] made a definite impact on West Germans and proved again that blood is thicker than ideology" with regard to German unity.[7]

Even Adenauer was impressed by the "well-thought-out" GDR propaganda campaign that accompanied Grotewohl's letter. He doubted that the East German offer was real, was initially inclined to rebuff the letter sharply, and in a special cabinet session on December 10 sought to close ranks among his cabinet and the leaders of the democratic parties. Even he had been approached by the East, he told the high commissioners on December 14, with the idea to start converging West German and "East zone" legislation. It had been intimated to him that the East would not expect West German laws to be adapted to GDR laws but rather the reverse. All in all, Adenauer concluded, the Grotewohl letter "lock, stock and barrel" had to be taken more seriously that initially assumed. Adenauer also did not preclude that the letter signaled a serious intention on the part of the Soviets in the lead-up to the four-power meeting they had proposed on November 3.[8]

To demonstrate the seriousness with which he took the East German initiative, Adenauer instructed the federal government's Berlin representative, Heinrich Vockel, to meet with GDR Foreign Minister Dertinger, who had told a Dutch journalist days earlier that Grotewohl's initiative was aimed at improving inner-German trade which had collapsed by the end of the year. (See Chapter 8.) Chastized internally by Grotewohl for speaking to Western media representatives, Dertinger was quick to back off of his "generous interpretation" of the letter in his meeting with Vockel. Yet the East Germans "contact offensive" did not let up. In early January 1951, top SED officials Hermann Axen and Franz Dahlem, for example, conferred with former Federal Interior Minister Gustav Heinemann, who had recently resigned from the Adenauer cabinet over his objections to the chancellor's rearmament initiative, and cleric Heinrich Grüber, the Protestant Church's representative with the GDR government. Still organized nationally, the Protestant Church was particularly interested in exploring to what length the SED was willing to take the inner-German dialogue. The head of the Berlin-Brandenburg diocese, Bishop Otto Dibelius, offered to serve as a go-between the two German governments.[9]

With a delay of several weeks, Adenauer's reply to the Grotewohl letter took the form of a declaration at a press conference on January 15, avoiding any semblance of recognition of the GDR authorities that a direct response to Grotewohl might have implied. Without referencing the idea of an all-German constituent council, Adenauer demanded free elections and improvement of conditions in the GDR. Sharp in tone, the declaration, which had reportedly undergone twenty-nine drafts, struck McCloy as "not entirely satisfactory from the psychological point of view," particularly in view of the groundswell of public sentiment in favor of the Germans' talking among themselves.[10]

Suspecting (correctly) that the Grotewohl letter was Soviet-inspired, HICOG officials very much doubted that the Grotewohl initiative was a genuinely conciliatory move on the part of the East Germans, given "general Soviet history, dogma, inferred strategy, rational self-interest and present actions." The continued trend toward communization of the GDR seemed to prove, some argued, that the Soviets had no hope of bringing about early unification; free elections in the GDR would destroy the SED regime, undermine Soviet prestige within the satellites, and constitute the loss of a "forward base" that would preclude any future "Korea-type action in Germany." There was broad agreement that acceptance of the Grotewohl offer would in effect "hand control of Germany's future to [the]) Soviets." U.S. officials agreed that the Soviets would be "masterminding [the] GDR delegation behind the scenes" and would prolong East-West German talks as long as possible to stall West German rearmament. The Grotewohl initiative thus appeared to U.S. officials as an integral part of Soviet strategy since the "legitimization" of the GDR at the October elections, aimed at neutralizing Germany under a demilitarization pact and isolating the Western Allies by fostering neutralist, defeatist, and nationalistic sentiments.[11]

But the Eastern initiative could not be dismissed out of hand, and Adenauer had not put the issue to rest. Grotewohl himself, internal SED documents suggest, was apparently unsure as to whether Adenauer's response had actually been affirmative or negative, and showed himself unwilling to draw a final conclusion. Pieck was convinced that it would still be possible to aggravate the differences between the parties in the Bundestag further. At the end of January, the SED intensified its "policy of contact" under the slogan "Germans to one table." "We are not," the U.S. high commissioner warned, "through [the] woods on this issue."[12]

At a special session of the GDR Volkskammer on January 30, 1951, Grotewohl replied to Adenauer's January 15 statement with a point-by-point rebuttal, reiterating that the ongoing need was for East and West Germans to sit down together for talks on German unity. At the end of the session, the Volkskammer appealed to the Bundestag and the federal government with a renewed call for an all-German constituent council. In discussions with Semenov and the commander of the Soviet occupation forces in Germany, Vasily Chuikov, Pieck seemed to have been confident that "the Bundestag will not say no" to the Volkskammer appeal, even as one had to reckon with "trickery on the part of the federal government." The SED chief also suspected that "the Am[ericans] won't allow" the West Germans to engage with the Volkskammer arguments.[13]

Once more the GDR had stunned the West. Adenauer seemed to have considered Grotewohl's speech very dangerous, and Vice Chancellor Franz Blücher acknowledged that the government's responses to the Grotewohl letters and speeches had been wanting: "The Grotewohl side is psychologically on the offensive." PEPCO officials, too, were quick to conclude that Adenauer's initial riposte had failed to counter the East Germans' call for "Germans at one table!" effectively. Designed to exploit the growing neutralist sentiment in Western Germany and the Germans' restiveness to take matters in their own hands, the Volkskammer resolution—with its conciliatory and non-polemical tone—was, as McCloy put it, a "singularly adroit document" and left the impression of a genuine diplomatic move. It should hence "not be regarded solely as a propaganda move and is not so considered by a wide segment of West German opinion."[14]

With Adenauer's failure to effectively stymie Grotewohl's initiatives, thus complicating (and threatening to unravel) the delicate negotiations in Paris and Bonn over a West German defense contribution, the Americans took matters into their own hand. To "extricate" the United States from its "present defensive position," the Truman administration now reasserted four-power competence over matters relating to German unification, thus taking the pressure off of the Adenauer government. A few days earlier, the Western powers had agreed to exploratory talks for a new Council of Foreign Ministers meeting in response to a Soviet proposal made on November 3. The Truman administration intended to cast the discussions in broader terms than just the German issue. McCloy argued that the Western approach to the anticipated meeting should emphasize that the German problem could not be solved within the German context alone, but only within a European framework. The exploratory talks, held at the Palais Rose in Paris starting March 15, quickly stalemated in mutual accusations.[15]

To the relief of the Truman administration, the West German parliament on March 9, 1951, sanctioned another proposal, submitted by Adenauer, for free elections. Much as he welcomed the new Adenauer initiative, McCloy failed to convince his fellow Western high commissioners to endorse the proposal; they deemed it too risky if the Soviets would accept the free election proposal in conjunction with a potential Soviet proposal for the neutralization of Germany at the anticipated Council of Foreign Ministers meeting. Yet the Bundestag rejoinder did have the desired effect: Grotewohl flatly rejected the West German proposal five days later, considerably undercutting his earlier initiative. West German political leaders and the press widely interpreted Grotewohl's rejection as evidence of the "real" Soviet-SED intentions.[16]

Grotewohl's negative reply may have reflected the fact that the SED had moved on in its efforts to engage pacifist and neutralist segments of West German society in a broad "National Front" coalition: by mid-March 1951, Soviet officials and East German leaders were preparing to launch a plebiscite against West German rearmament. They continued to see, as Pieck's notes of his April 4 conversation with Chuikov seem to suggest, "the general mood favoring all-German talks." But the referendum had moved "to the forefront" and would effect "the failure of Adenauer's plans, the only way in which war could be prevented." Rather than embracing the Adenauer government, which had underpinned the Grotewohl letter campaign, the referendum sought to amplify popular reservations to halt the momentum toward rearmament. It also served as a "plebiscitary means of pressure" to affect the nego-tiations at the four-powers preparatory conference in Paris.[17]

In close coordination with the Soviet Control Commission (down to the phrasing of the ballot), a "Main Committee for the Plebiscite" in West Germany launched the campaign for the referendum in Essen on April 14. Soviet officials envisioned some 10,000 local plebiscite committees springing up across the Federal Republic in a campaign carried largely by the SED-controlled KPD. The East German com-munist leadership also mounted what Western Allied observers called a "terrific barrage of propaganda," which was reportedly even more intense, if somewhat less overt, than in the fall of 1950.[18]

As in the case of the Grotewohl initiative, PEPCO made the plebiscite a U.S. "intelligence target." With discussions for Western defense plans still unsettled, HICOG officials decided to give the referendum the "silent treatment." Much to the surprise of PEPCO, the West Germans themselves—"without prodding"—initiated a nationwide "exposure campaign," designed to discredit the plebiscite. U.S. officials had initially questioned whether there was a legal basis for prohib-iting the plebiscite as such. But on April 25, the federal government banned the plebiscite on constitutional grounds. Washington grew concerned that the ensuing arrests and trials of plebiscite proponents would be used by the SED as a platform to propagate neutralism and undermine the Western defense program. The State Department urged a line for the prosecution that might turn the trials to the psy-chological advantage: "Identify and expose [the] real sponsors, agents and victims of the plebiscite." Much to HICOG's relief, the West German interior ministry indicated that police action against the plebiscite would be "primarily preventive in nature" and foresaw few arrests.[19]

Much more controversial was the question of how the West would seek to influ-ence the plebiscite in the GDR—scheduled for June 3–5, 1951. What guidelines should HICOG-controlled media outlets, principally RIAS, would give to the East Germans? Given the divisive experience of the October elections, HICOG's Berlin Element decided that Western media outlets should not advise the East Germans how to vote—whether "no" or "yes"—on a ballot that asked: "Are you against the remilitarization of Germany and for the conclusion of a peace treaty with Germany in 1951?" Instead, Western media would express their sympathy with the East Ger-mans' predicament over what choice to make.[20]

This solution reflected both the limits that U.S. officials saw in influencing events in East Germany and the hope of maintaining resistance potential across the border. HICOG officials argued that while urging a "no" vote could not prevent an overwhelming proportion of East Germans from voting "yes," it might cause conscientious "resisters" to expose themselves to persecution and ultimately reduce the potential for resistance within the GDR. Endorsement of a "yes" vote, however, as in October 1950, had come under considerable criticism by church circles and youth leaders for absolving the individual from personal responsibility and for constituting a "blow at their will to resist."[21]

By June 1, however, it became evident that no "united front" existed among the Americans, the Kaiser Ministry, and the SPD. In the last days preceding the plebiscite, three different courses of action were apparently broadcast to the East Germans. Exasperated by the intra-German dissensions, HICOG officials chided party leaders that "a united front on the Eastern question is too important to U.S. propaganda media to permit clashing personalities and thin skins to disrupt it."[22]

The Soviets, too, were dissatisfied with "their Germans." The plebiscite movement in the West had been off to a slow start. By mid-May, Soviet control commission officials complained to Pieck that the campaign was "still weak." Of the 10,000 committees that had been envisioned, barely 1,000 had been set up, and the KPD, the main instrument of operation in the Federal Republic, was plagued by "sectarianism" (likely a reference to the resistance among many KPD members to embrace Social Democrats and even right-wing circles) and remained "separated from the masses" and "disconnected from strikes." The KPD, Pieck penned in his notebook, was seen as the "Russian party" and was losing authority. It had "never been so weak." But the SED chief also noted the "pressure of the occupation powers." In the GDR, the SED, perhaps worried about a lackluster performance, mobilized some 150,000 agitators, and SED strongman Ulbricht undertook a last-minute "stomping tour."[23]

Once the results of the referendum were announced, the U.S. high commission was quick to declare victory. From HICOG's point of view, the plebiscite "clearly proved a failure." Officials pointed to limited participation in the referendum in West Germany due to the government's ban: U.S. officials doubted that more than 700,000 votes had been cast in the western zones—many of them, they suspected, obtained "under false pretenses." The actual number in fact turned out to be larger: of more than 6 million people who had been questioned, more than 5.9 million had voted "yes." Historian Wolfgang Benz has thus called the referendum, in pure statistical terms, an "undeniable success of the first extra-parliamentary opposition in the Federal Republic."[24]

In East Germany, the government announced an affirmative vote of more than 95 percent, not an unexpected result given the massive repressive and indoctrination effort on the part of the Soviet Control Commission and the SED. As they pored over the official results, American officials noticed with some satisfaction that the number of "no" votes had been higher in areas bordering West Berlin, West Germany, Poland, and Czechoslovakia. But what struck U.S. observers most was the percentage of official "no" votes in the youth demographic—youths between the ages of sixteen and eighteen were allowed to cast a special vote. Considerably lower than the no-vote among the rest of the population, the youth vote demonstrated that young people constituted the most vulnerable targets for indoctrination. Even in the absence of an immediate dramatic impact of the plebiscite for East Germans as a whole, American officials feared that events such as the referendum contributed to "chipping away at the core of the anti-regime resistance."[25]

Despite the statistical success of the referendum, in its aftermath the East German Communists fell largely silent. The referendum had failed to shift the political momentum decisively against West German rearmament. In late June, the quadripartite exploratory discussions for a Council of Foreign Ministers meeting ended without agreement. Not until late July do the archival traces pick back up. "Fight against remilitarization— what is to be done?" Pieck jotted down in his notebook after a discussion at the Soviet occupation headquarters in Berlin-Karlshorst on July 30. McCloy might contemplate ending the state of war with Germany, Pieck apparently observed, and the opposition was "very weak." Ulbricht seemed at a loss as well: "What can be done against it? So far their [the SED's] efforts had emphasized demasking Western efforts." "How can the masses be made to understand that the SU wanted peace and the USA war?" Grotewohl too seemed perplexed: "The initiative used to be with us, until the [referendum] vote. Now it was resting with the adversary."[26]

This was not lost on the Truman administration: By summer, administration officials felt that the West had succeeded in keeping the unity issue alive and turning it into "one of our most useful propaganda themes." As a result, the State Department noted, Germany unity "virtually dropped out of Commie propaganda"—at least for the time being.[27]

American Support for German Rollback Groups

In the late fall of 1950, John B. Holt, the acting director of HICOG's Berlin Element and longtime head of its "Soviet Sector branch," set out to survey "the future resistance potential" in the GDR. While he quickly concluded that there had been no "slackening" of hostility among the great majority of East Germans though the "fading prospects of liberation" were taking their toll, he soon found his effort hamstrung by the unwillingness of "the chief agencies directing resistance"—most of which were Allied entities—to share even some general insights (not to mention operational details).[28] To this day, the U.S. government withholds a great deal of information on its "cold war" against the GDR from public review. Thanks to the Freedom of Information Act, I have been able to pry loose documents, and historians have exploited the windfall in the former Communist world archives after 1989–91 and, more recently, the archives of the West German foreign intelligence service, to fill in some of the gaps.

Back in 1950–51 Holt found the Germans more communicative than his own government and Allied governments. Based on interviews with leaders of several anti-communist organizations operating out of Berlin, Holt argued that, on the whole, resistance groups favored actions that encouraged East Germans but did not worsen their conditions. Thus they welcomed Western broadcasts, especially RIAS, and the clandestine distribution of printed material, and "merely maintaining" active resistance groups. They did not, Holt underlined, condone industrial or economic sabotage. One of Holt's interlocutors, the editor of the SPD organ *Das Berliner Stadtblatt*, Willy Brandt, for example, spoke out against organizing partisan or guerrilla movements in the GDR but thought that a "black station" that claimed to be transmitting from within the GDR but in reality was based in the Federal Republic, along with the formation of a united front of resistance groups, a "Free German Resistance Movement," would help to improve the East Germans' deteriorating morale.[29]

In Holt's view (echoing the Carroll-Speier report), two fundamental actions were therefore required if Soviet power in East Germany was to be eliminated without war: First, East Germans had to be encouraged to accept sabotage, partisan activity, foul play to communist collaborators, and "constant tension": they must become a populace in which the great majority was willing to collaborate with the resistance. Second, a "cold war of liberation," supported by U.S. money, operating agencies and "man-hours," required a "high command" in which American agencies "must have the predominant voice." The need was for an "American chief."[30]

Certainly the Truman administration welcomed signs of increased commitment to psychological warfare activities among West German leaders. Even Adenauer, ever wary of the volatility of German public opinion, had recognized the well-thought-out nature of the Grotewohl letter campaign, and in his discussions with the Allied high commissioners in December 1950 he professed his enthusiasm for a "great propaganda crusade among the German people" in favor of rearmament. With its focus on the Federal Republic, however, Adenauer's statement was emblematic of the West German government's much more narrow priority: solidifying support for the government's west integration policy.[31]

Within the West German government, anti-communist activism developed especially in the Federal Ministry of All-German Affairs (BMG), which had played a critical role in coordinating the propaganda approach to the October 15 election in the GDR. In the days after Grotewohl's proposal, officials there promised to counteract the initiative with a "stepped-up propaganda campaign." Meeting with HICOG public affairs chief Shepard Stone in early January 1951, Kaiser, his state secretary Franz Thedieck, and SPD leader Herbert Wehner, a former communist who had become the SPD chairman of the Bundestag's All-German Affairs Committee, emphasized the desirability of cooperating and consulting "on as many anti-communist projects as possible." The Kaiser Ministry had just completed distributing some 30,000 pamphlets during the October 1950 GDR elections throughout East Germany. The West Germans, the Americans noted with some degree of satisfaction, were "becoming more conscious of the danger of infiltration from the East and more uneasy about the fact that little [was] being done to prevent it."[32]

By the second half of 1950, the Federal Ministry for All-German Affairs had come into its own as the German "rollback agency" under Thedieck, who, as a forceful administrator, increasingly came to run the agency in the shadow of Jakob Kaiser. The first generation of BMG's staff, recruited to a considerable extent from expellees from the former eastern Reich territories or Soviet zone dissidents, shared a staunchly anti-communist esprit de corps and saw the agency as a "politically powerful Cold War instrument." With Deutschlandpolitik diplomacy the nearly exclusive domain of the chancellor, the BMG increasingly focused on both overt and covert psychological warfare operations designed to undermine the SED regime and stymie its influence on the Federal Republic. It collected information on developments in the "Soviet zone," aided in pamphlet production, and maintained direct contacts to some East Germans as well as overt and covert agencies. American rollback ideas served as an inspiration, and Kaiser Ministry officials understood themselves as engaged in a broad international anti-communist coalition.[33]

For no one was this truer than for Ewert Freiherr von Dellingshausen, who joined the agency in October 1950. A refugee from the East who was deeply conservative in political outlook, von Dellingshausen rose to head the powerful political department (Abteilung I–1) and became one of the most influential "cold warriors" within the BMG. Five years of working under the SED regime in Magdeburg and Halle had given him, he felt, privileged insight into the "inner logic" of the events unfolding in the GDR. He quickly grew skeptical of the Kaiser Ministry's initially limited priorities in funding the printing and dissemination of selected academic publications. Deeply influenced by radical American rollback thinkers such as James Burnham, author of *The Coming Defeat of Communism* (1950), he argued for designing a broad anti-communist public-outreach program that would mobilize large segments of West German society against the political-ideological challenge of communism in Germany. For him, it was imperative to make a concerted effort to undercut the SED's machinations and those of its agents in the Federal Republic, the KPD, and a host of Communist front organizations.[34]

Von Dellingshausen's unpublished autobiography, which was classified by the German government until 1994 and is now accessible in the Federal Archives in Koblenz, suggests that with his direct access to Thedieck, he saw himself as a trusted partner for U.S. officials and a key liaison for the Americans and private anti-communist groups operating in West Germany and Berlin. In the early 1950s von Dellingshausen and his colleagues were, however, mostly on the receiving end of the relationship, often little more than a conduit for covert financial transactions. In their largely covert support for West German rollback groups, which often doubled as intelligence sources, CIA officials played their cards close to their chests, even as recruitment and operations cut across activities by the German government and its fledgling intelligence community. Often German officials were kept in the dark about Allied efforts and would discover only by accident that a certain operation or individual was receiving help from Allied sources.[35]

Even the crafty von Dellingshausen apparently did not always know whether the name of his American or British counterpart was a cover. Allied officials, he recounted years later, would appear on his doorstep and hand him "a large envelope containing considerable amounts of money to be passed to some organization for a certain anti-communist activity"—without a receipt (which must have unnerved the German bureaucrat). Not until Allied relations with West Germany were about to be put on a new "contractual" basis in 1952 did the CIA and other U.S. officials become more forthcoming with their German counterparts, in particular on their support for private rollback groups operating in both parts of Germany.[36]

Organizationally, too, the BMG's anti-communist hard-liners sought to emulate U.S. psywar efforts. Impressed by the central coordinating role played by the NSC and, as of April 1951, the Psychological Strategy Board (PSB), they sought to bring administrative coherence to the federal government's anticommunist activities. Coordination initially rested largely on the personal relations between Thedieck and Heinrich Krone, a close adviser to Adenauer; Hans Globke, the chancellor's chief of staff (a former Nazi-era lawyer who had written the legal commentary of the Nuremberg race laws); and the state secretary in the Ministry of Interior, Ritter von Lex. Von Dellingshausen came to champion a PSB-like administrative body that would centrally coordinate anti-communist activities within the federal government. Prompted by repeated queries from the CIA's Office of Policy Coordination (OPC) in 1951 and 1952, which was eager to develop "joint operations" with the Germans, Adenauer finally tapped Globke as the chancellery official responsible for clandestine Cold War activities in the summer of 1952.[37]

From the vantage point of the U.S. High Commission, the anti-communist consensus among West German political leaders offered a rare opportunity to bridge the deep political divides within the young republic. Kaiser Ministry officials coordinated activities with key Social Democrats, especially Herbert Wehner. McCloy encouraged such inter-party coordination, but it was a fragile alliance at best. A case in point was Kaiser's pet project, conceived in late 1950, of establishing informal anti-communist "self-defense" groups in cities and townships throughout the Federal Republic—so-called Ortskartelle—led by what von Dellingshausen called "solid personalities" and composed of militant youth. The Ortskartelle were to help protect against expected KPD sabotage in West German industrial plants at a local level. McCloy thought the effort was "encouraging," particularly as he assumed it had a broad political basis. As it turned out, the project proved abortive: Social Democrats were allergic to organizations reminiscent of Nazi-era block guards and abhorred the prospect of a new citizens' militia that resembled Nazi Sturmabteilung (SA) units. Deeply suspicions of any machinations by a CDU-led government, moreover, the SPD insisted on carrying out its own activities at the local level.[38]

Though Kaiser's idea failed, it reflected the BMG's broader efforts "to have a lasting effect on the political culture of the nascent Federal Republic." Against the backdrop of heightened Cold War tensions, the BMG's activities, in the apt words of historian Stefan Creuzberger, took on "facets and scope of a cold civil war." As early as 1950, the BMG thus started advocating loyalty tests for public servants. A year later it successfully promoted harsher state protection laws that criminalized the import and distribution of anti-constitutional publications. Ministry officials even briefly considered such radical measures as censoring mail and prohibiting the printing of Communist propaganda literature, measures fundamentally at odds with democratic practice.[39]

Von Dellingshausen and his fellow BMG hard-liners, moreover, engaged in a virtual "domestic rollback policy" by defaming, often covertly, the Adenauer government's domestic political opponents: communists, left-wing social democrats and proponents of neutralism or dialogue with the GDR. In this they showed few qualms about supporting extreme right-wing groups, such as the Volksbund für Frieden und Freiheit (People's Federation for Peace and Freedom, VFF), set up in August 1950. The founder and *spiritus rector* of the organization was a "Dr. Kohl," alias Dr. Eberhard Taubert, who had served as a midlevel official in the Nazi propaganda ministry under Joseph Goebbels, with responsibility for anti-communist propaganda. Shortly after Christmas 1950, von Dellingshausen and the short but agile Taubert quickly came to a meeting of minds: Taubert saw in von Dellingshausen a "pragmatically minded *Gegenwartsmensch* [man of the time] who was interested in all suggestions for fighting communism by democratic means." Von Dellingshausen, in turn, was fascinated by the VFF's plans.[40]

Von Dellingshausen encouraged new leadership at the organization but relented, perhaps because he learned from Taubert that Wehner had supposedly approved of the VFF plans. Reassured, von Dellingshausen arranged for Ministry (and industrial-corporate) support for the VFF. In the late fall of 1950, the BMG began to support a VFF poster campaign calling for greater alertness against Communist subversion and sabotage in industrial plants in West Germany. By 1951, the organization had established a network throughout all the West German Länder, had moved from a dingy basement apartment into a more representative villa in Bonn, and had launched a major public campaign as a "non-partisan *Sammlungsbewegung* for the defense against Bolshevism." Another VFF campaign, apparently scripted in the BMG, targeted Dr. Günter Gereke, a Weimar-era Reichstag member and CDU minister of agriculture in Lower Saxony. Critical of Adenauer's Deutschlandpolitik, Gereke advocated closer ties with the East and even met with Walter Ulbricht. To the cold warriors in the BMG, Gereke seemed to belittle the danger of Communist infiltration.[41]

In his autobiography, von Dellingshausen claims he realized only belatedly that the VFF also enjoyed covert CIA support. One of the VFF projects that the agency supposedly funded was deploying a float in the annual Cologne carnival parade, the popular Rosenmontagszug. At a time when floats with hard-charging political content were rare, the plan involved a tractor disguised as a "Trojan horse" that, steered by Stalin and led by a peace dove, represented the danger of Communist infiltration through the profiles of three well-known pacifist or neutralist personalities: the former Center Party leader (and future federal president) Gustav Heinemann, who had resigned his position as interior minister after clashing with Adenauer over rearmament; Helene Wessel (also from the Center Party); and renowned theologian Martin Niemöller, a fervent rearmament opponent. After the Cologne carnival organizers failed to see any humor in the idea, the VFF, with support from the agency and the

BMG, attempted to "infiltrate" the parade. The Trojan horse float also penetrated the carnival parade in Bonn, traditionally held the day after the Cologne festivities. Though the CIA float's appearances in both cities were short-lived and triggered outrage on the part of the Zentrum Party for maligning some of its standard-bearers, the event generated considerable publicity and was thus considered a win in von Dellingshausen's, and likely the CIA's, book.[42]

Though, by democratic standards, the gloves came off in dealing with domestic political opponents, when it came to dealing with the GDR, West German officials generally eschewed extreme violent measures such as sabotage and assassination plots employed by the more radical, U.S.-sponsored private rollback groups that often caused "collateral damage" by endangering East Germans. Globke outlined a German psychological warfare program that aimed at the "decomposition of the spiritual, mental, intellectual and psychological strength of Bolshevism in the So- viet Zone." In marked contrast to the American approach, the German program explicitly excluded sabotage, resistance, and paramilitary activities. Controversial among the Germans, too, was the notion of meshing "Cold War" activities with intelligence collection work. West German officials generally drew the line when it came to putting dissidents or average East Germans, who, after all, were fellow countrymen, at risk. A case in point was Kaiser's seemingly innocuous idea in the fall of 1950 to organize a centrally coordinated letter-writing campaign directed at the East, perhaps borrowing a leaf from Grotewohl's book. The project was quickly abandoned when the SPD opposition argued that the East German recipients of the letters would be put in danger.[43]

From the U.S. perspective, the BMG, with its limited mission and funds, could not fulfill the need for a central coordinating agency: "The Kaiser Ministry can- not be the high command" of the anti-communist resistance movement, judged HICOG's Holt in January 1951. Neither, as both sides realized, could the Gehlen Organization, as much as its incipient intelligence network came to intersect that of the OPC. Vying to develop the Federal Republic's foreign intelligence agency, which would also own covert operations, Reinhard Gehlen hedged his bets. Pressed by the OPC, the Gehlen Organization finally devised a psychological warfare plan in December 1952, but it was deemed by the CIA as too general and at best "a rough blueprint for intended future work."[44]

As the Truman administration amplified its psychological warfare efforts in volume and ambition in 1950–52, it found willing partners in a complex network of private anti-communist groups that had sprung up in the shadow of the Allied occupation, especially in postwar Berlin. The OPC "took command," supporting a variety of individuals and organizations that included, most prominently, the east bureaus of the non-communist parties that maintained extensive contacts in the GDR, as well as the Investigating Committee of Free Lawyers (Untersuchungsaus-schuss freiheitlicher Juristen, UFJ) and the Kampfgruppe gegen Unmenschlichkeit (KGU). American officials found that "a great deal" could be accomplished by "stimulating" these German private organizations to increase their independent propaganda activities and sponsor American-inspired projects. HICOG's public affairs chief, Alfred "Mickey" Boerner, who in 1951–53 coordinated many of the overt and "grey" activities in Berlin, felt that such an approach scored "successes all out of proportion to our investment in time and money." It can be assumed that the same was true for the CIA's work with German organizations.[45]

The UFJ was founded in October 1949 by Horst Erdmann. Known by his alias, Dr. Theo Friedenau, Erdmann, who had practiced law in the Soviet zone but found himself in conflict with the Soviet authorities there, had published three articles in the Berlin journal *Sie* in October 1948, critically assessing the justice system in the zone as well as the NKVD's methods. Within a year he had established a small office in Berlin to launch a committee that would track illegal acts by the SED regime and collect evidence that could lead to criminal indictments in a reunited and democratic Germany.

Erdmann sought to mobilize the East German population to expose those who committed injustice in the name of the SED regime, and thus to put moral and political pressure on the GDR's ruling class. In addition, the UFJ provided counseling in West Berlin for East Germans seeking legal advice (taking advantage of the large corpus of basic rights proclaimed by the first GDR constitution of 1949) and produced informational and propaganda materials with a particular focus on legal issues. Within months, the group had established a network among jurists throughout the GDR and was superbly informed of developments within the GDR, virtually creating a "shadow justice ministry." Its focus on the legality of the Soviets' and East German Communists' actions struck at the very heart of the regime's legitimacy. Voluminous files in the archive of the GDR Ministry of State Security document the notoriety that the UFJ soon enjoyed in the eyes of the SED apparatus. None less than the CIA's deputy director of plans, Frank Wisner, credited the Free Lawyers for a "very effective campaign" against Soviet and East German authorities.[46]

Early in 1950 Erdmann sought and obtained support from the Federal Justice Ministry (which was particularly keen on the UFJ's aid in screening East German jurists seeking employment in the West) and the BMG (which later that year pulled Erdmann, among others, into a committee planning for the October Volkskammer elections). But it was the CIA's Berlin station that became the UFJ's main sponsor. Perhaps Erdmann's early articles caught the eye of the agency's Berlin team; he later recalled that in 1948 a "Mr. Henry" of the U.S. military government arranged for funding by an "American foundation" and provided him with regular stashes of cash. Confirmation of whether Erdmann was in fact "recruited" by Henry Hecksher of the CIA's Office of Special Operations, as former Berlin Operating Base (BOB) chief David Murphy and his coauthor Sergei Kondrashev claim in *Battleground Berlin* (1997), will have to await the declassification of further CIA documentation.[47]

Murphy's claim that the UFJ was simply Hecksher's brainchild may reflect CIA lore, but there can be little doubt that American intelligence agencies instrumentalized the UFJ for espionage purposes as the organization's reach into East Germany expanded rapidly. By the end of 1950, it had been visited by 20,000 people from all over the GDR. Soon some 200 people a day knocked on the UFJ's doors. The CIA's interest went beyond "hand[ing] Erdmann an occasional assignment or debrie[fing] him along lines of interest to [the CIA]:" the agency also decided to involve the UFJ in its planning of clandestine paramilitary "stay-behind operations" that would be activated behind the lines in case of "Day X"—a Soviet invasion—to maintain contact and keep radio equipment, arms, and explosives.[48]

Declassified documents suggest that Truman administration officials considered the Free Lawyers to be loyal and effective partners in its psychological warfare campaign against the GDR: "Doubtless," the UFJ, along with RIAS, had "been more effective in retarding communization in the East" than any Soviet "harassment" of West Berlin, claimed HICOG officials in 1952. No less important was the Free Lawyers' support for exposing illegal East-West trade, a pet peeve for the Americans, especially since these activities elicited "severe opposition" from the West German business groups. When Erdmann's second-in-command and head of the group's Economics Department, Walter Linse, was kidnapped by GDR state security in July 1952 (see below), CIA deputy director Wisner pressed the State Department to unleash full reprisal measures that went well beyond what Allied officials in Berlin thought feasible at the time, given the divided city's precarious security. U.S. officials continued to consider the group a major problem for the "Commies": GDR trials of alleged UFG agents were in fact leading to new collaborators for the group, HICOG staff in Berlin reported, as the "trials indicated to them where to go!"[49]

At the height of its influence in 1953–54, the UFJ launched a campaign for a "Deutsche Selbsthilfe" (German self-defense) that projected, much as Carroll and Speier had envisioned some years earlier, the idea of a homegrown movement by East Germans to express their rejection of the regime without endangering themselves.

The campaign, as CIA officials told von Dellingshausen with approval, was important psychologically, especially after the 1953 uprising (see Chapter 9), for it instilled in East Germans a sense that they belonged to a larger resistance front against the SED government.[50]

Yet the UFJ never condoned violent acts of resistance. In that respect it differed from the Kampfgruppe gegen Unmenschlichkeit (KGU), which, as we have seen (Chapter 4), was founded by Rainer Hildebrandt in the shadow of Allied occupation in West Berlin in 1948. With its initial focus on more charitable tasks (including support of refugees from the Soviet zone), the KGU, too, had enjoyed financial support from a number of German sources, including the West Berlin Senate (city government) and later the BMG. But under Hildebrandt's deputy and successor (in 1951), Ernst Tillich, the KGU's activities across the Iron Curtain grew increasingly more militant. A nephew of the theologian Paul Tillich who, as an émigré in the United States, had led the Council for a Democratic Germany, Ernst Tillich had been a member of the anti-Hitler resistance and had spent three years in a concentration camp. Judged by U.S. personnel to be "capable, balanced aggressive," he developed close contacts to U.S. agencies. The CIA's Berlin Operations Base (BOB) in particular regarded the group as an asset in its espionage and psychological warfare efforts.[51]

Though Tillich had spoken out against industrial sabotage as too dangerous and pointless unless it contributed to a "well-organized, general and decisive effort," the KGU engaged in increasingly hard-hitting "rollback" operations against the Communist regime in the East. These ranged from removing or disfiguring Communist posters and exploding handbill rockets to sabotage projects involving arson, explosions, and assassinations. KGU agents launched balloons carrying propaganda material across the zonal border, blackmailed SED officials, exposed Soviet and Soviet zone security personnel, and carried out acts of sabotage against East German government structures and vehicles. Materials for sabotage acts, however, Tillich intimated, were lacking, supplies were badly needed, and the production of counterfeit documents went wanting. Enter the CIA's Office of Policy Coordination (OPC), led by Frank Wisner. The CIA's arm for covert operations took over funding the group indirectly in 1949. By 1950 the KGU had become a "principal project" for OPC Berlin, with the CIA covering about half of the organization's budget.[52]

Under OPC tutelage the KGU's covert activities in the GDR grew more professional and conspiratorial, but also ever more militant and expansive. Covertly, Henry Heckscher, the deputy chief of the CIA's Berlin Operations Base, provided hands-on direction. In the fall of 1950, about the same time that the Carroll-Speier report demanded more aggressive actions against the GDR, the KGU stepped up its operations in East Germany, including terror attacks and assassination plots. Clearly believing it had the Americans' license to do so, the Kampfgruppe's activities grew more radical and riskier. For the CIA, the KGU constituted a "flexible instrument for conducting a full range of covert operations against the East German regime."[53]

With OPC support of the group, not disclosed to the Bundesregierung till 1952, the KGU increasingly eluded control by West German agencies. Owing in part to growing penetration by Soviet and East German agents, in part to continued recklessness and flawed preparations, a good number of operations resulted in failures, collateral damage, and massive waves of arrests in the GDR, drawing increasing criticism by West German government agencies and the public. In 1951–52 alone, Soviet and GDR authorities arrested hundreds of people in the GDR in (alleged) connection with KGU operations, and many of those arrests resulted in death sentences and long labor camp penalties. Soviet services carried out more than 130 death sentences against people accused of collaborating with the KGU. West German officials complained to U.S. agencies that the group's "senseless sabotage operations and propaganda activities in the Eastern Zone had sen[t] many people to their doom at the hands of the East-zonal security service." While such complaints mostly fell on deaf ears, some U.S. diplomats in Berlin were increasingly concerned that that extreme rollback operations such as those practiced by the KGU were self-defeating: "Western-oriented people in both East and West were beginning to feel that the West, after all, may be willing to sacrifice human beings in the East for its ends—sacrifice them when it cannot protect them, sacrifice them without hope of immediate change of conditions."[54]

Target: East German Youth

Viewed as a most vulnerable but also critical part of East German society, youth remained a central target of American psychological warfare efforts in Germany. In January 1951, the SED announced that Berlin would host the World Youth Festival (WYF) that August. The decision by the Communist-controlled World Federation of Democratic Youth (WFDY) in November 1950 to hold its third convention in Berlin—following meetings in Prague in 1947 and Budapest in 1949—emphasized the continued importance of Berlin as a central staging ground for the globalizing Cold War: With nearly one and a half million participants from all over the world expected to come to Berlin for a fourteen-day display of international solidarity, the festival was designed to make a powerful statement on behalf of the world's youth for the new socialist German state and against West German rearmament. Plans for the program included mass singing of fighting songs for peace, performances of national dances, and international sports contests.[55]

The decision in favor of Berlin was also a validation of East Germany's successful orchestration of the May 1950 Deutschlandtreffen and the FDJ's growing importance in the socialist world's youth movement. Having survived the debacle over the militant posturing prior to the Whitsuntide rally, FDJ chairman Erich Honecker led the prestigious preparatory committee alongside WFDY president and Italian Communist Enrico Berlinguer, as well as International Union of Students chairman Joza Grohman.[56]

Given the sheer difference in size, Communist-world preparations for the World Youth Festival quickly outdid those for the Deutschlandtreffen. No efforts seemed to have been spared to provide the more than one million young people with transport, food, and lodging in a city still reeling from the devastation of the war. At the beginning of February 1951, the site of the old Hohenzollern Palace in the center of Berlin was leveled to create a vast assembly area, which on May Day that year was given the name "Marx-Engels-Platz." To lend the city a prosperous air, monuments in the downtown area—such as the Arsenal Museum and the Brandenburg Gate—underwent renovation, and several new "luxury" stores opened on the main streets. "Socialist Sundays" saw FDJ members constructing and renovating stadiums, pools, and campsites. Foreign participants were to be accommodated in hotels, boardinghouses, and private rooms; most of the East German visitors would sleep in huge group tents. The organizers set up some 542 kitchens to feed the delegates and recruited some 6,000 doctors, 20,000 nurses, and 50,000 medical assistants to provide free care for the rally participants. All in all, the costs of hosting the festival amounted, according to official GDR sources, to some 160 million East German marks ($48 million at the official exchange rate), a significant burden on the struggling GDR economy.[57]

American officials quickly realized that the World Youth Festival would differ from the May 1950 Deutschlandtreffen in its larger international appeal, and, more importantly, its lack of overt threats for an invasion of West Berlin. To be sure, GDR authorities beefed up the East Berlin police force and a 920-strong "youth battalion" was to support the Volkspolizei. Some Western officials did fret over the potential for a violent crisis. Yet the festival preparations bore none of the militancy that had beset the run-up to the Deutschlandtreffen; threats to West Berlin ran counter to the stated purpose of the gathering as a peace demonstration against the anticipated rearming of the Federal Republic. East German measures that aimed at keeping the assembled youth from visiting the West seemed to confirm that an "invasion" of West Berlin was not on the agenda.[58]

Instead, the Truman administration came to view the event as an opportunity to strengthen anti-regime attitudes among the Communist-world youth. Contrary to British nervousness over the unprecedented influx of youth into the city, Washington now saw the event as an opportunity for a massive political-cultural counteroffensive. In striking contrast to Deutschlandtreffen, the emphasis within HICOG planning focused almost exclusively on exploiting this chance for a rare encounter with youth who were increasingly secluded behind the Iron Curtain. In February, the Western Berlin commandants formed the "August Committee," which would coordinate Western preparations. (A corresponding West Berlin preparatory committee included, notably, the KGU's Ernst Tillich.) At first, HICOG planners agreed that they should avoid "trying to beat the Communists at their own game" by staging a Western youth rally. Last-minute counter-attractions might also play into the hands of the Communists by showing undue concern and defensiveness, on top of further highlighting the festival. The West would do best by displaying "normalcy" in Berlin.[59]

That things were not left to "being normal" was evident in the systematic efforts that the Allies and the West German government undertook to limit the participation of Western youth in the perceived Communist-front event: Throughout the spring, Allied authorities in Germany tightened border controls along the inner-German borderline to prevent illegal departures of Western German youth to Berlin. Transit permits were screened closely to deny potential foreign participants access to Berlin via West Germany. Key Communist leaders, such as the World Peace Council's Frédéric Joliot-Curie, were blacklisted for visa refusal.[60]

Other measures were intended to actively undermine the youth gathering. U.S. counterintelligence officials, for example, suggested deterrence by "dealing out a number of exemplary sentences" to FDJ agitators apprehended in West Berlin. With the experience of the Deutschlandtreffen in mind, HICOG launched a campaign to scare parents of FDJ members into keeping their kids at home. American officials in West Germany even encouraged the militantly right-wing Bund Deutscher Jugend (Federation of German Youth, BDJ) to conduct "harassing operations" against the FDJ, despite the fact that the BDJ's extremist principles were "not considered completely compatible with U.S. interests." The State Department put the sixty-five American citizens slated to join the WYF under surveillance; lists of purported "subversives" headed for Berlin, including eight southern Australians and five Ceylonese, poured in from embassies and consulates around the world.[61]

As the World Youth Festival (WYF) drew closer, intelligence reports confirmed that the SED was discouraging any thought of violence. With a sense of vulnerability waning further, the Americans in Berlin increasingly favored the kind of counter-measures they had initially abstained from. As early as February, Deputy High Commissioner Samuel Reber and HICOG Public Affairs Director Shepard Stone had argued in favor of staging "political and psychological demonstrations on the part of the West European countries . . . to offset the effect of the Communist festival." West Berlin was to be "in a very normal way, full of very desirable attractions such as good films, music programs etc. at the time of the Communist festival."[62]

In March, Stone and his colleagues suggested holding a European Youth Festival—with the U.S. role in the program to be kept secret. American authorities in Berlin requested four mobile motion-picture units, complete with projection facilities, to broaden East-West sector border showings "to facilitate contacts with and influence upon Communist youth brought to Berlin for political purposes." They would provide an "invaluable border attraction," especially "since we're not attempting competitive sideshows per se." No longer worried about militant Communist incursions into the West, the Americans were the ones who sought to induce the Eastern youth to transgress the sector borders. HICOG officials, moreover, advanced the idea of holding a plebiscite on the subject of European union as a major counter-attraction. Apparently undeterred by the East German Communists' overuse of such mobilizing efforts, they discussed the idea with West Berlin mayor Ernst Reuter, who responded enthusiastically. Given, however, that other German leaders reacted more cautiously and that the British and French were "dragging their heels" in using Allied funds for the project, the idea was eventually shelved.[63]

Nonetheless, compared to the efforts in May 1950 to contain the East Germans within the Soviet sector, by the spring of 1951 U.S. policy had come full circle. By the end of May, the State Department cabled McCloy that plans were on the way for a "coordinated global campaign to counteract and discredit [the] Communist World Youth Congress." Earlier that month, the August Committee had finalized various counter-attractions such as a Marshall Plan exhibit, a Europazug display and a television exhibit in the Western Berlin sectors. Some two million pamphlets and satirical booklets were to be distributed to the visiting youth. Radio Free Europe would feature broadcasts by prominent Iron Curtain refugees on the World Youth Festival.[64]

Soviet intelligence quickly picked up on the new approach in Western preparations for the festival. In July, Politburo member Mikhail A. Suslov received a seven-page report that suggested—correctly—that the Western authorities expected some 200,000 festival participants to visit the Western sectors, some of whom might seek permanent refuge there. U.S. intelligence reports that month indicated that, in turn, the Soviets were intent on imposing stricter bans against visits to West Berlin than had been the case during the Deutschlandtreffen. Reflecting the more aggressive stance outlined in the Carroll-Speier report and the Taylor Plan, High Commission officials now abandoned the normalcy concept in their approach to the World Youth Festival altogether, discarding the "ostrich attitude." U.S. policy was to be "more positive and aggressive than heretofore contemplated" and take full advantage of "an unusual opportunity to propagandize Eastern youth." HICOG now appropriated an additional $200,000 in funding for counter-attractions, a dramatic increase that needed to "be handled very delicately" vis-à-vis the British, French, and West Germans.[65]

PEPCO now favored issuing a public invitation to East German youth to come visit West Berlin; a targeted hospitality program at some fifty youth centers would be awaiting the 200,000 WYC participants who were expected to visit the Western sectors. Leaving nothing to chance, the Western youth officials would receive preparatory courses in history, politics, and international relations, "enabling them to converse intelligently with the visitors to the West." Arguing that the risk of a mass defection was minimal, the Americans rather expected that an open invitation would cause the Soviets to tighten the ban against visits to the West. This in turn would allow a "prison psychology" to develop among many of the East German youth, a result that was considered one of the more tangible propaganda advantages that the West could obtain from the World Youth Festival.[66]

The fourteen-day World Youth Festival of August 1951, which culminated in what one impressed American observer called a "monster parade" by the FDJ through the Soviet sector, did provide Americans with the unprecedented opportunity to influence "the largest group of East German youth ever to come into contact with the West." Of the approximately 1.4 million East Germans and 35,000 youth from abroad participating in the festival, more than half a million—according to some estimates, more than 680,000—turned their backs on sports, cultural events, and speeches in the Eastern sector and visited West Berlin "to taste the forbidden fruits of capitalism." (The Americans counted 1,004,206 crossings into West Berlin, though this number probably included repeat visitors.) So crowded were the Zoo Rail Station area and the Kurfürstendamm in the heart of West Berlin with blue-shirted and blue-skirted youth that, as one American observer noted, one could gain the impression that the festival was being held in the Western sectors.[67]

Among the chief attractions was RIAS; by August 16, nearly 7,000 crowded into the station's facilities. SPD leader Kurt Schumacher and Federal Minister for All-German Affairs Jakob Kaiser were on hand to assure the visitors that "under Soviet domination they could never hope to become free and equal." Eleven teenage World

Youth Festival delegates even found themselves surprise luncheon guests of High Commissioner McCloy, though it remained an open question whether they were more awed by their proximity to the top-ranking U.S. official in Germany or by the quantity of the food served to them. McCloy, who apparently got so wrapped up in the discussion that he fell behind two hours in his schedule, pledged to the young visitors that "we will do everything we can to help you," and sent them on their way with the assurance that "the Lady of Liberty still holds aloft her torch in New York harbor, and one day freedom and peace will come not only for Western but also for Eastern Germany."[68]

Free meals, free theater tickets, and free sightseeing were particularly enticing in light of the festival's massive organizational shortcomings: "We get worse food than at home, and that is pretty bad, and sleep like pigs in straw in cellars," one young participant was quoted as saying. East German participants were especially outraged by the far larger food rations and better accommodations received by the few West German and international festival participants. Numerous participants "defected," including young Traude Eisenkold, who East German propaganda had reportedly built up as the "ideal progressive woman" and as such was to be the "queen" of the proceedings. "I'd rather pound a typewriter, even scrub floors, in the West than be a Communist glamour girl in the east," she reportedly told the Associated Press. In a dramatic last-ditch effort to halt the flow of East German youth to the West by exposing the alleged brutality of West Berlin police—and perhaps to reestablish his credibility in the wake of severe criticism for some of the logistical deficiencies at the World Youth Festival—FDJ leader Erich Honecker led some 8,000 FDJ members, organized in fifty-person groups, in an "invasion" of the Western sectors on August 15. The "disturbance mission," however, proved ineffective, and by the next day, West Berlin police reported "all quiet on the eastern front."[69]

The World Youth Festival therefore turned out to be, in HICOG's opinion, "a gain for the West." American officials expected the East German youth who had "tasted a non-communist atmosphere" to be long affected by the experience. The rally was considered to have contributed to the strengthening of East German anti-regime and pro-Western sentiment, "a factor which should not be underestimated for its effect upon future attitudes in East Germany." According to some accounts, a million pieces of literature had been distributed, and "many youngsters planned to smuggle them back."[70]

But while the West had sought to assure the young East Germans that it was determined not to "write them off," many of them, officials suspected, would likely be disappointed that no "immediate radical alleviation" of their situation was in store. Overly optimistic assumptions about the resistance potential of young East Germans were therefore misplaced. Aside from the "generally submissive nature of the East German population," HICOG officials argued, it had to be recognized that the motives of many festival attendees had been nonpolitical.

Rather, left to their own devices, many had been impelled to go West by curiosity, free snacks, and the desire to buy Western goods. Many were not necessarily pro-West in attitude, and revealed a lack of information and a misunderstanding and skepticism about Western policies. Though they might not subscribe to the Communist program, the HICOG analysts noted, "many East German youth reflected in their reactions to certain ideas, in their modes of expression, and in their mental images the effects of communist propaganda." Once again, the large mass demonstration had illustrated, thus the pessimistic postscript by U.S. officials, the "ability of a totalitarian regime to carry along the masses via a small proportion of hardcore fanatics."[71]

Mobilizing East German Resistance Spirit

By summer 1951, the divisive debate within the Western alliance over how to rearm Germany had reached a tentative conclusion. Negotiations on the Petersberg seat of the Allied High Commission in Bonn for a "NATO track" to bring German soldiers quickly and directly into the alliance—favored by Acheson, the Pentagon, and the Adenauer government—were subsumed under the Paris negotiations for a "European army track," favored by the French and British governments, McCloy, and eventually the newly appointed NATO Supreme Commander, Dwight D. Eisenhower. French premier Rene Pleven's idea of having smaller units of German soldiers integrated into a European army led to a compromise between Americans and their European counterparts in July 1951 for a European Defense Community (EDC) that offered Germany substantial equality within the Western alliance while avoiding the creation of an independent German Wehrmacht. At the same time, the Western allies set about negotiating a "General Agreement" with the Germans that would restore German sovereignty, excepting Allied reserve rights, particularly with regard to Allied troops and matters relating to Berlin and Germany as a whole. After protracted negotiations during the winter of 1951–52, Acheson was pressing for a rapid conclusion of both the EDC and contractual agreements by the following spring.[72]

Undeterred by the failure of the anti-remilitarization plebiscite earlier that year, the Soviet and East German governments continued in their attempts to derail the rearming of West Germany. Their efforts came in the form of ever-bolder proposals for German unification, tapping into the continued longing among many Germans both East and West for unity of their country. In a hastily arranged speech to the GDR Volkskammer on September 15, 1951, Grotewohl called for an all-German consultation and free and secret elections to a German National Assembly. Unlike earlier proposals, this one did not demand the equal representation of both German states to the consultation, and it emphasized free elections. With Allied support, Adenauer responded on September 27 with a proposal for United Nations supervision of the elections, momentarily blocking the East's initiative. A month later the SED Politburo launched a new campaign aimed at West Germany, in particular the SPD and unions. The issue faded temporarily, though Truman administration officials expected it would reappear before the treaties were signed.[73]

Timed to play on the debates evoked by the parliamentary sanction of the agreements on the EDC and the large-scale restoration of German sovereignty in the spring of 1952, the "Stalin note," delivered on March 25, 1952, by Soviet deputy foreign minister Andrei Gromyko, raised the stakes by going well beyond earlier Soviet proposals. The Soviet government proposed to conclude a peace treaty with a unified but neutral German state, which—most significantly—would be permitted to have national armed forces for its defense.[74]

After initial hesitation, Washington and its allies concluded that the note had to be taken seriously. The Soviet offer implied profound advantages for Moscow—at best creating a German state that could be drawn into Moscow's orbit, at worst impeding the imminent conclusion of the "general treaty" and the EDC. The note had, as Acheson's advisers admitted, the "ring of considered policy," which omitted demands for continued four-power control, long dismissed by the Western allies, and reversed the previous Soviet position on German armed forces. State Department officials sought reassurance in the assumption that only an actual relaxation of controls in East Germany would sway West German and Western European opinion enough to delay or block the conclusion on the EDC. U.S. intelligence agencies estimated that Moscow would not pay such a price. Administration officials were far more concerned that actual Soviet measures, such as speaking invitations by the GDR to prominent West Germans, relicensing of the SPD in the GDR, or a proposal for all-Berlin elections under quadripartite supervision, might in fact succeed in undermining West German support for the EDC while not really endangering the Soviet position in the GDR. In a protracted exchange, the West rejected the Stalin offer.[75]

The American response to the Stalin note has to be viewed in the context of a larger American offensive strategy to counter Soviet moves in Germany. Since December

1951, the Psychological Strategy Board had set out—at the suggestion of CIA director Walter Bedell Smith—to develop a national psychological strategy plan to strengthen pro-integration sentiment in West Germany and to make East Germany a "strategic liability" to Moscow. The interdepartmental effort reflected lingering doubts about the West Germans' allegiance to the West, and continued concerns that they might give in to Soviet and East German appeals to unity just as the negotiations over the Federal Republic's defense contribution entered its decisive phase. To some, the East had regained the initiative in the discourse over unification: Moscow's shift to a "direct indigenous approach" that fronted the GDR authorities and individuals had "fallen on fertile ground." Adenauer "may take matters into his own hands," thus the speculative scenario some saw unfolding, and enter into direct discussions with East Germany. Others within the Truman administration warned that the Kremlin's view of the period from late 1951 to mid-1952 or even 1953 as decisive in determining "whether the future leads to preventive revolution or war" might impose a "quicker tempo on Communist plans." Yet others continued to be frustrated by the Adenauer government's lackluster ambition in its approach to the East.[76]

Over a period of seven months, the PSB's "Panel F," which included officials from four government agencies—besides the PSB, the Department of State, the Department of Defense, and the CIA—and employed several outside consultants such as Speier, Philip Davidson, Walt Rostow, and Henry Kissinger, developed a plan that was code-named "Plutonic" (renamed, in August 1952, "Pocketbook"). The new plan built on the Carroll-Speier report and Taylor's "Interim Plan for Intensified Psychological Warfare in Germany," which despite State Department approval, strong CIA interest, and ongoing implementation had failed to crystalize a sense of administration-wide cohesion. In their discussions of a comprehensive psychological warfare strategy vis-à-vis West and East Germany, panel members envisioned "blasting the [West] Germans out of their political apathy," advocated a propaganda focus on "European unity," and underscored the need for "the most definite, vigorous, ambitious, psychological offensive against the Soviet position in Eastern Europe."[77]

Nowhere did Soviet vulnerabilities seem more pronounced than in East Germany, where, PSB staff explained in an introductory statement designed as a "starter" for the panel's discussion, "extensive, sharply offensive and effective psychological operations, both overt and covert" were already under way, supported by German resistance organizations "in growing strength" and by a "widespread spirit of resistance." With U.S capabilities for effective psychological operations "probably higher than anywhere else in the world," East Germany offered a "particularly favorable and perhaps decisive terrain." Early in the process, CIA representatives on the panel, per-haps worried that the new PSB plan would more tightly circumscribe its activities in Germany, made clear that they considered the "stimulation of controlled resistance to the Soviet regime" to be one of "the most important objectives" of the Germany plan. Comments on the early draft of the Germany plan by the chief of the CIA's Eastern Europe Division, John A. Bross, suggest that and that the agency wanted a "clear and unambiguous charter to *continue* its efforts" to "strengthen and increase psychological resistance" [emphasis added]. East Germans had to be encouraged to look forward to "an undetermined but nevertheless certain day of liberation."[78]

No one captured the "hell-for-leather spirit" of some of the discussions sur-rounding the strategy document better than Wallace Carroll, coauthor of the first comprehensive psychological warfare plan who had joined the PSB's Office of Plans and Policy. In late September 1951 he urged the PSB to "fire the rocket to signal the opening of a major offensive." Fed up that "we have fussed too long" over plans for such an offensive (a reference to the debates over his and Hans Speier's plan and the Taylor Plan), Carroll bemoaned that the offensive side of the U.S. effort, "to roll back Soviet power," had been largely neglected. With the struggle in Germany key to winning the Cold War, the administration's fixed objective for the next eighteen months should be "to liberate Eastern Germany." Carroll professed to be unwilling to reconcile himself to the "unproved" and "defeatist" assumption that only superior military force would make the Soviets leave Germany. With a "healthy, growing resistance movement in East Germany," and Berlin as a base from which "we can direct the Eastern resistance, gather intelligence and wage economic warfare," the German battleground was "highly favorable to psychological operations. Liberat-ing East Germany, said Wallace, was a "less difficult and ambitious project than the Marshall Plan."[79]

Proponents of a stepped-up support for resistance activities could point to indi-cations that the East German populace seemed to favor West Germany's inclusion in Western defense arrangements. Letters and visitors received by RIAS in early 1952 suggested that many of its East German listeners believed that only a (West) European army could put enough pressure on Moscow to retract Communist power from East Germany. Further research by HICOG into popular attitudes behind the Iron Curtain revealed that the defense debate in the Bundestag in February 1952, in particular, contributed to crystallizing East German opinions, convincing many that only through a militarily strong Western Europe would it be possible to force Moscow to negotiate a peaceful and lasting solution to the German problem. After the World Youth Festival and the 1951 Kirchentag (a large Protestant lay convention that drew large number of East Germans) in Berlin, attended by Germans in East and West, the Bundestag defense debate had become the "third miracle for the West." On March 10, 1952, the very day Stalin sent his note on German unification, West Berlin officials informed Washington that the Western policy of integration was regarded by the majority of East Germans not as precluding, but rather as furthering, unification.[80]

But U.S. officials in Berlin also cautioned that the remarkable degree of "immunity" maintained by the East Germans vis-à-vis their government's unity campaign depended to a large extent on the actions of the Western powers to project a convincing alternative: East Germans, HICOG staff argued, viewed free, internationally supervised all-German elections as a corollary to integration and wanted constant and concrete reassurances to that effect. The Stalin note offered an opportunity to do just that. Throughout the note exchange, the State Department continued to emphasize the importance of free elections as central to any Western response. Increasingly convinced that the West had more to gain by a careful proposal for negotiations, at the end of March Acheson even signaled his willingness to enter into negotiations with the Soviets. Unwilling to run the risk of such a counterstrategy, the British and French governments, with Adenauer's support, added conditions to the Western counterproposal, such as settling the issue of Germany's eastern border (the Oder-Neisse line). Most importantly, the Western notes sent to Moscow on March 25 insisted that a unified Germany would be free to enter any alliance it saw fit to choose, a demand that Moscow was expected to resist at all costs.[81]

Psychological warfare efforts toward East Germany centering on a "return to Europe" concept underpinned this strategy. In the short run, Western efforts to foster liberation hopes in the East could not but reinforce doubts in Moscow about the allegiance of the vast majority of East Germans and ensure that the Soviet offers precluded any real choice of alliance in the future. In the long run, maintaining the resistance spirit of the East Germans was essential to turning the GDR into a liability for the USSR that, Truman administration officials believed, would create conditions under which Moscow would accept the rollback of communist control and the unification of Germany. Creating a sense of insecurity on the part of the Soviets and the Grotewohl regime also took on a more immediate purpose in the spring of 1952: countering what American officials perceived as the SED regime's mounting scare campaign against West Berlin and Western Germany and slowing its efforts to consolidate its grip on power in the eastern zone.

With negotiations for the agreements anchoring the Federal Republic in the West in their final stage, High Commissioner McCloy in particular harbored "deep concern" about new Soviet and East German threats to drive home to the West Germans the perils of rejecting the Kremlin offers. Berlin was the "obvious point of exploitation." Moscow and East Berlin would attempt to unsettle West German confidence by launching a "creeping blockade" of the city, creating East German armed forces, staging border incidents, and setting off "rumblings" of Soviet military power. Following the Western rejection of Stalin's March note, McCloy expected a "scare campaign" to parallel the fizzling diplomatic exchange, possibly climaxing in a full-fledged war scare as the signing of the Bonn and Paris agreements drew closer. Border incidents, plane incidents, and troop concentrations or maneuvers could all be "part of the game," as could be the closing of the GDR border and a proclamation of GDR sovereignty. The Kremlin, McCloy argued, might insist that the West take its troubles to the German communist authorities: "The GDR may be increasingly thrust into a front position against us."[82]

Among the ways in which the Kremlin's "new tough line" toward the Federal Republic played out were incidents of obstructing Western Allied military police movements between West Berlin and West Germany, as well as a new level of militancy among SED leaders toward the West. In early May, Ulbricht threatened West Berlin security in "shrill tones," while Communist riots in Essen underlined the potential for disturbances in West Germany. While the Germans had come to regard threats from the GDR as "cries of wolf," the "crust of West German courage," McCloy warned, was "understandably thin." The high commissioner suggested using police and military measures on a global scale ("in areas where we have the upper hand") to deter the Soviets from actions that might trigger a real war scare, and considered even a "probing action" or "sending a column through the Soviet Zone" to assert Allied access rights. Meeting with Acheson later that month, he called for a "propaganda offensive" to counter possible Soviet moves in Berlin that should particularly stress German unity as a goal basic to tripartite policy on Germany.[83]

Approving McCloy's request for a propaganda offensive, Acheson also asked for speedier buildup of the Berlin stockpile to increase Western "staying power" in the city in case of a blockade. In Washington, the NSC set up a steering group to explore potential courses of action to counter Soviet measures, quickly dismissing McCloy's proposals for "probing actions" and more forceful measures that risked early escalation of any conflict over Berlin. Instead, at a press conference on May 14, Acheson reaffirmed the intention of the United States to protect its position in Berlin and pushed for the preparation of an all-weather airlift to the city. Concurrently, a "Day X" plan was developed for the coordination of psychological warfare between civilian and military agencies in time of war, including strategies for more-active resistance and sabotage. Following the signing of the EDC agreement in Paris in late May, the three Western foreign ministers restated their commitment to the security of West Berlin.[84]

Few events underlined the volatility of Berlin's security and its exposure as the sharp edge of American-supported psychological warfare efforts as clearly as did the subsequent kidnapping of Walter Linse, the head of the Free Lawyers' economic department, who had joined the UFJ in 1951 and was currently involved in planning for the upcoming International Congress of Jurists in Berlin. On July 8, outside his home in the U.S. sector of Berlin, Linse was dragged into a car by security agents, who sped off across the sector border. For HICOG officials, the audacious kidnapping, which, as recent archival research indicates, had been planned for some months by Soviet intelligence and executed by the GDR State Security, was part of a "creeping campaign of harassments" designed to "affect adversely the morale of West Berlin."[85]

But the Linse kidnapping, even more than earlier Soviet measures, had "stirred Berliners." Days after the event some 25,000 people protested against the Eastern actions in front of City Hall in the Berlin district of Schöneberg, demanding retaliation and defensive measures. To retaliate and prevent such incidents in the future, the West Berlin city government issued a press release announcing police checks for all vehicles traveling from West to East Berlin, the arming of border police with machine pistols, and mobilization of the emergency "Force B" of the Berlin police for duty on the sector borders.[86]

Dismayed that the city government had taken such steps without the prior approval of the Western Allied commandants, Allied officials rejected many of the countermeasures requested by the Berlin Senate (government) and agreed to a more restrained response: the erection of barriers on all roads leading into the Soviet sector and roving armed police patrols along the boundary. But the damage was done: The impression that American authorities had been reluctant to react vigorously, HICOG reported, had already hurt U.S. standing. Adding to the "psychological gravity" of the situation was that GDR government spokesman Gerhard Eisler had for some time intimated that they would take actions of this type, stressing West Berlin's use as a base for espionage.[87]

To HICOG officials in Berlin, any local reprisals could only draw on an "almost empty arsenal" in the city. By contrast, the CIA's Frank Wisner argued that "considerable local capabilities" included actions against the 10,000 known SED members working or living in West Berlin, a "sudden search and arrest" of SED functionaries in West Berlin, and raids of SED offices, or a protest by the Catholic bishop for Berlin and Brandenburg, Bishop Wilhelm Weskamm. Wisner also proposed using the United Nations to develop international interest in the case, and advocated setting up a "liberation fund" that could expose the perpetrators of such acts as the Linse kidnapping.[88]

The Truman administration soon realized that the most significant thrust of Soviet and SED policy was no longer to dislodge the Western Allies from Berlin politically or even militarily, but instead was directed at further isolating the East German population from the West with expanding repressive measures. In early April 1952, Stalin had in fact told the East German leaders, in an apparent reaction to the Western rejection of his March offer, to "organize an independent state." The Soviet leader demanded that they turn the relatively open demarcation line between East and West Germany into a "border," and that they do everything necessary to "strengthen the defense of this border." As early as May, HICOG's GDR watchers alerted Washington to the "pattern of isolation and militarization" taking shape in East Germany for the purpose of scaring Germans into thinking that their country would be indefinitely split and the East turned into a full-fledged satellite unless the West acceded to the Kremlin's unity offers.[89]

Within weeks, HICOG Berlin noted GDR efforts to reorganize the East German border police and the construction shacks being erected near the Elbe autobahn bridge. U.S. intelligence detailed alleged Soviet plans discussed in Chuikov's office in late March to establish a thirty-kilometer restricted zone around greater Berlin, thus cutting off GDR residents from easy access to the city. The construction of a bypass rail and bypass canal that would have obviated the need to cross the Western sectors reinforced the increasing conviction on the part of many in HICOG that, short of risking war by forcing an end to the Western Allied presence in Berlin, Soviet and SED leaders sought "to insulate the East zone population from it." The latest turn in Soviet policy, the new U.S. high commissioner, Walter J. Donnelly, cautioned from Bonn "might even imply a decision to live with us rather than eliminate us."[90]

The decision of the Second SED Party Conference, in July 1952, to proceed with the accelerated construction of socialism in the GDR and the establishment of national armed forces appeared to American officials to confirm a new Soviet commitment to consolidate the SED's position in East Germany and to frighten the West Germans and the Western Allies into abandoning their integration plans. American intelligence sources that reached deep into the halls of the SED Politburo cited Ulbricht at leadership meetings in early June anticipating a long period prior to any British and French ratification of the contractual agreements "affording the greatest possibility for effective resistance" against the Western schemes.[91]

The turn in Soviet policy underlined the importance of the "Western outpost" of Berlin for Allied operations in the GDR. By May of 1952, the PSB's Plutonic panel had overcome the initial bureaucratic turf war between the PSB and the State Department, and by August a draft plan was in hand, as was a proposal to set up a coordinating committee to "vigorously stimulate operational planning." Approved by the PSB on October 9, the final version of the plan, PSB D-21, had in fact been drafted largely by a working group within the Department of State and, "over the objections of the PSB staff," had been considerably "watered down from earlier drafts" that had apparently also called for substantial economic and military measures to support the psychological warfare strategy.[92]

What was left was, in the regretful words of one PSB staff member, "essentially a propaganda plan." Nonetheless, PSB D-21 enlisted "all elements of the U.S. government and appropriate private U.S. organizations," to work toward maintaining contact with the East Germans to "stiffen their spirit of resistance to Soviet-communist rule" and thus to weaken the system in the GDR and lay the groundwork for eventual incorporation in the free Western Community. HICOG's Alfred "Mickey" Boerner would chair a field coordinating panel that oversaw the operational planning in Germany.[93]

While extensive parts of PSB D-21 relating to East Germany, especially its "Annex B," on covert actions, remain classified, collating several partially declassified versions of the paper as well as supportive documentation suggests that it authorized (1) efforts to keep East Germans informed of world events via RIAS and other "overt" media, (2) measures to "encourage disaffection towards the regime and defection of East German military and para-military forces," and (3) nonattributable psychological, political, and economic "harassment activities" against the GDR, as well as (4) the preparation "under controlled conditions for such more active forms of resistance as may later be authorized." RIAS, Voice of America, and other official information media were to "create a climate conducive to disaffection," and publications disseminated covertly in the GDR were to discredit Communist personalities and "stimulate resistance attitudes." It also called for efforts to convince West Germans of the need to weaken Soviet capabilities by impeding the flow of strategic materials to East Germany and intimidating West German traders who engaged in transactions with the East.[94]

As the CIA had demanded at the outset, the agency received its "charter" to prepare for more active resistance in East Germany: it would develop "controlled resistance nuclei capable of expansion and deployment for the purpose, when authorized, of conducting sabotage and other activities" and encourage East Germans to work with "controlled resistance networks" in passive harassment measures such as work slowdowns, faulty workmanship, and misrouting of shipments to reduce the GDR's economic contribution to the Soviet military-industrial complex. Similarly, U.S. media and U.S.-controlled "resistance networks" would inspire East Germans to cause administrative inefficiency and weaken the reliability of GDR government organs through noncompliance with governmental regulations. PSB D-21 also authorized support of defections of selected officials, especially from the GDR military and paramilitary forces (but apparently not "large-scale defection among East German military personnel," as called for in earlier drafts).[95]

Not everyone agreed with the PSB's blueprint for pursuing an intensified Cold War vis-à-vis East Germany. State Department officials were critical of the notion of "increasing our potential aggressiveness," and questioned whether pushing the propagandistic pursuit of European unity (and a "return to Europe") went beyond the existing U.S. commitment to West European integration. Some within HICOG, such as its Eastern Affairs Division, "heartily" supported the more offensive tone, while others wondered aloud whether further encouragement of resistance groups would not imply support of violent sabotage that would raise the very "same objections which are the West's most justified complaint against communism." Less controversial at the time, but no less significant in the long run, was the questionable notion that a groundswell of resistance in the GDR could be inspired and "controlled" by the United States. Internally, top HICOG officials acknowledged that "some of the means used, particularly by [the] Kampfgruppe," were "questionable" and needed to be coordinated more effectively "in the future to ensure activities are confined within [the] generally approved framework."[96]

PSB D-21's call for stimulating defection came under similar criticism. Indiscriminate defection as advocated in earlier PSB drafts, HICOG officials argued, might lead to a breakdown of the "structure and morale of resistant Soviet Zone society." In the summer of 1952 such concerns crystallized in a prolonged debate within the Truman administration over whether it should encourage mass defection among East German youth. In March 1952 Truman had announced a new program designed to assist *selected* refugees from "iron curtain countries" and aid their emigration. The administration, however, considered support of "political persecutes" from the GDR the responsibility of the Federal Republic, given its liberal asylum policy enshrined in the West German "Basic Law" constitution. In Germany, the U.S. escapee program was therefore limited to non-German refugees who had fled the Soviet orbit more recently. Even after the refugee stream swelled after the East German government's accelerated drive for socialization, collectivization, and militarization in the summer of 1952 the Truman administration denied Adenauer's request that refugees from the GDR be included in the program.[97]

HICOG had generally followed the Adenauer government's policy to discourage flight and urge East Germans to remain in the GDR unless doing so became impossible on political grounds. RIAS had "long and consciously leaned over backward in avoiding any implication that we encourage defection." To be sure, PEPCO had considered defections by key East German officials to be part of its psychological warfare repertoire since 1950. As early as April 1950 McCloy's cold warriors had considered that as many as fourteen East German political leaders "might be lured into defection." The Carroll-Speier report in December 1950 had in fact called for actively soliciting "defection" among East Germans and Soviet forces in the GDR as part of an aggressive rollback program. In early 1951, HICOG also prepared a program to solicit the defection of key East German technical experts in an effort to denigrate the GDR's plans for achieving economic autonomy from the Federal Republic (see Chapter 8). But on the whole, the Truman administration had eschewed calls for mass emigration of Germans from behind the Iron Curtain.[98]

The GDR's turn to an open buildup of armed forces and its "voluntary enlistment" to the People's Police and paramilitary "Dienst für Deutschland" [Service for Germany] organization in the summer of 1952 begged the question of a policy reversal. RIAS "and other U.S. activities" faced the pressing problem of taking a stand on the mass defection of military-age male East Germans likely to be conscripted. The urgency of the issue was compounded by growing suspicions on the part of U.S. officials in Berlin that the open border in the city, the last escape valve, might be sealed off after the ratification of the Bonn and Paris treaties. The opportunity to "drain off large numbers of GDR youth" might be limited. The SPD East bureau representatives told HICOG that it was unwise to do so now, "as much could be done on the spot to impede the rearmament effort." HICOG officials, too, wondered whether in the long run it might not be advantageous to the West "if the East German satellite army retained a maximum number of defectors." Worried that any encouragement of mass flight to the West by East German youth would be more than West Berlin and the Federal Republic could absorb at a time when refugees already pouring into the city were creating acute problems, the State Department in August instructed its field offices in Germany that U.S.-controlled "covert media" should ask youth to abstain from defection.[99]

Amid the efforts by the PSB to step up rollback vis-à-vis the GDR through an ambitious new psychological warfare plan, however, the project caught the eye of Edmond Taylor, HICOG's former psychological warfare consultant who had joined

PSB and, along with PSB director Raymond B. Allen, became a fierce champion of the project. To the proponents of the project, it had a compelling logic: each youth "that comes over adds one man to our side and subtracts one from the communist." While the Federal Republic had "no urgent need" for these individuals, East Germany, given its chronic manpower shortage, "could ill-afford to lose them." PSB calculations figured that some 50,000-100,000 youth could be persuaded to defect. The project's significance would go well beyond its impact on the GDR's military potential, for the SED leaders were "pinning their hopes and basic program" on the youth. CIA director Walter Bedell Smith, too, stressed the "important strategic nature" of mass defection from East Germany.[100]

Dissenting from his superiors, HICOG's top GDR watcher, Spencer Barnes, endorsed the idea, arguing that the East German youth had reached the "peak of anti-regime and pro-West sentiment" and put Americans in position to win the allegiance of a large segment of GDR youth for the west. Once in uniform, according to Barnes, the East German youth would "lose resistance potential and become incapable of individual action." Barnes suggested reexamining a possible expansion of the West German border police or the introduction of a "voluntary youth labor service" as a way to cope with the additional influx. But by late September the State Department, pointing to the West Germans' difficulties in handling the refugees already pouring into West Berlin, still showed "little inclination to reverse present policy."[101]

Fresh from an election campaign in which Republicans had advocated "liberation" of Eastern Europe's captive peoples, key members of the new Eisenhower administration threw their weight behind the project in early 1953. Defection programs were high on the agenda for the Eisenhower's new CIA director, Allen Dulles, and the president's new special adviser for psychological warfare strategy, C. D. Jackson, under whom the PSB started to advocate a more offensive stance vis-à-vis the Soviet bloc. Despite criticism by some within the State Department that encouragement of mass flight of East German youth was "morally irresponsible" and "indefensible under prevailing conditions" in Berlin, the German desk, led by James Riddleberger, also came around to support the idea, though conditionally: encouragement would be primarily effected through covert channels, and the policy reversal would have to get German cooperation.[102]

The latter proved difficult in the face of widespread skepticism in the Federal Republic. Amid rising numbers of refugees streaming into Berlin—some 10,000 per month since August 1952—Adenauer had called on East Germans to stay in the GDR and Kaiser's Ministry for All-German Affairs was adamant in its position that no one should leave the GDR unless they were exposed to immediate danger. A large influx of young East Germans, West German officials feared, would compound difficulties in the West German labor market and possibly stoke resentment among millions of expellees from former German territories in Poland, Czechoslovakia, and Russia, and other East German refugees, many of whom still lived in camps.[103]

American officials even raised the issue with the office that coordinated West German rearmament efforts, in the hope that "the fleeing youth" might be absorbed in future West German army contingents. But Blank and other officials, too, were apparently unsympathetic to the idea. German officials warned that inducing mass defection could "backfire" if larger numbers of East German youth would arrive in the Federal Republic only to face unemployment an ill-housed in refugee camps. More generally, in late 1952 Americans found West German leaders "distressed about the present exodus from Eastern Germany."[104]

HICOG officials wondered whether the damage the project would inflict would be commensurate with its costs. After all, the Truman administration had refused to provide support for German escapees under its new program (in part for budgetary reasons) but would have to shoulder the cost for this project. With reception and transportation costs of German refugees received in Berlin by West German authorities amounting to $50 per refugee, the overall budget for the program ran at about $2.5 million for an estimated 50,000 youth, though others suggested that the real figure for "integration" costs per person was closer to $3,000. Material costs aside, an active mass defection program could, some feared, hasten further measures by the SED to isolate the East German population from the West by closing the sole remaining open door in Berlin. All said, HICOG opposed the project.[105]

Even though "quite a large number of people" in Washington had become interested in the issue, the unprecedented and staggering spike in refugees from the GDR effectively pulled the rug out from under any American efforts to stimulate mass defection. By early 1953 the enormous exodus generated by Ulbricht's hard-line policies threatened to overwhelm the reception capacity of Berlin and the Federal Republic (and the capacity of Allied intelligence agencies involved in screening for GDR spies). The "dramatic character of the Berlin influx," the new U.S. high commissioner, former Harvard University president James B. Conant told Dulles, could have negative fallout for Adenauer's election prospects later that fall. The refugee emergency led Adenauer to renew his demands for additional U.S. aid during his Washington visit in April. Keen not to create additional problems for Adenauer, whose political survival he viewed as critical to the European policy of the administration, Secretary of State John Foster Dulles instructed his diplomats in Germany in early May that no further burdens should be put on the Federal Republic, "at least until after the Bundestag elections" that fall.[106]

In addition, in early 1953 American intelligence agencies came under criticism by Germans over the preferential treatment they had afforded to prominent GDR defectors. RIAS had annoyed the German political class by giving the wife of the former GDR minister of trade and supply a broadcast opportunity to appeal to the GDR Justice Ministry for mercy on behalf of her husband. Even more outrage had accompanied the treatment of Leo Zuckermann, the onetime chief of GDR president Wilhelm Pieck's chancellory, who had been pulled out of the "refugee pipeline," housed under American auspices since his defection six weeks earlier, and apparently would be allowed to go to France or Mexico. Public outcry over the case led to a unanimously adopted resolution by the Berlin House of Representatives on January 22, directing the Berlin city government to prevail on the Allies not to accord special favors to prominent political refugees. The cases highlighted German sensitivity to American interference in the "refugee-defector question."[107]

By the spring of 1953, then, Washington was stepping up its efforts to destabilize the GDR and to maintain and increase the resistance potential among East Germans. A corollary to the West's negotiations over a German contribution to Western Europe's defenses, these efforts sought to undercut Soviet-GDR initiatives on German unity that threatened to derail West German rearmament. Given the Adenauer government's preoccupation with "domestic rollback" efforts directed at anti-democratic as well as democratic opponents of its Western policy, American officials helped create, co-opted, and instrumentalized a complex network of private German anti-Communist organizations with deep reach into the GDR. Largely operating out of West Berlin, these private groups were inspired by American rollback visions, acted with political, operational, and financial support from U.S. and Allied intelligence agencies, and pursued more-radical rollback agendas, never submitting to full control by the United States. The alliance of hard-liners in the Truman and incoming Eisenhower administrations with anti-Communist groups engaged in a host of activities ranging from overt information programs to largely covert intelligence, disinformation, sabotage, and defection efforts that helped foster and increase a climate of resistance inside East Germany at the very moment when the forced socialization and militarization drive brought the GDR to the brink of explosion.

8

Economic Cold War?

The United States and Inter-German Trade, 1950–1952

IN THEIR EFFORTS TO CONFRONT Communist power in East Germany, in particular Soviet pressure on West Berlin, Truman administration officials believed they had a powerful weapon in West German trade with the GDR. The underlying rationale stretched back to the early occupation period, during which Soviet needs for reparations from the western occupation zones were widely considered leverage to contain and even roll back Communist influence in the east. It also fit seamlessly with the prevailing narrative of the "Berlin Blockade": U.S. officials credited the "counterblockade" of western shipments to the Soviet zone with helping to bring the Soviets to the negotiating table.

The Truman administration's attempts to control West German trade with the East also reflected the growing understanding of the Cold War as a "total war" that, like World War II, required the mobilization of all resources, especially economic ones—and the denial of strategically important goods to the adversary. As it supplied American economic aid for the rehabilitation of Western Europe, the Truman administration also sought to restrict Western European exports to the emerging East bloc countries in order to deny the Soviet Union strategic technologies, material and manpower that could strengthen its military potential. Yet in the German case, American objectives went farther. After the establishment of the two German states, the American officials believed they could leverage East Germany's structural economic imbalance and its dependence on trade with West Germany to counter Soviet and East German pressure on West Berlin and to destabilize the Communist regime.

Cold Economic Warfare

At the end of World War II, American policymakers became convinced that rebuilding Western Europe was an essential part of assuring the survival of the liberal-capitalist international order and the American way of life. Against the specter of communism, Western European economic recovery, including the western occupation zones, became a central element in the U.S. strategy to contain the rise of communist parties and Soviet influence and expansion. In launching the European Recovery Program (ERP), a four-year, $12 billion aid program, the United States harnessed its economic prowess to support the socio-economic rehabilitation of Western European countries after years of war-induced physical destruction and political-moral disillusionment.[1]

Preventing trade from augmenting the war potential of the USSR and its European satellites became the other side of the coin. To be sure, to a certain degree the Marshall Plan was premised on the resumption of prewar trade between eastern and western Europe as a way to accelerate economic rehabilitation and reduce costs to the U.S. Yet the European Cooperation Act, which set up the European Cooperation Administration (ECA) charged with implementing the massive aid program, also provided the basis for a new export control program: The Mundt Amendment (Section 117(d)) to the act barred any country from receiving U.S. aid if it exported U.S.-supplied commodities to a European country that was not a participant in the Marshall Plan. In 1948-1949, the United States began to institute a wide-ranging catalog of export controls vis-à-vis the Soviet bloc.[2]

The Truman administration also considered its economic might as a means to exacerbate burgeoning political and economic tensions behind the Iron Curtain, which had become openly manifest in the Soviet-Yugoslav split of 1948. It was "in the economic realm," declared the Truman administration's policy guideline on Eastern Europe of December 8, 1949, "that we can most concretely make our influence felt." The United States should "fully bring to bear on the Soviet-satellite relationship the economic forces we control or influence."[3]

Since U.S. trade with the Soviet Union and Eastern Europe was minimal, the main focus of the American economic denial strategy became Western Europe's trade with the eastern part of the Continent. In the spring of 1948, the Truman administration developed inventories of goods that would be subject to export controls. Most importantly, List 1A included military and semi-military items, which would be denied to Soviet bloc countries entirely; List 1B included items that would be limited in quantity for export with a view to reducing trade volumes to "the smallest quantities consistent with existing agreements and necessary in order to obtain essential import (grain, potash, cola and timber) from Eastern European countries on a quid pro quo basis." In August 1948, Truman instructed ECA administrator Paul Hoffman and his deputy, former U.S. ambassador to the Soviet Union Averell Harriman, to persuade Western European Marshall Plan recipients to adopt these lists. The Export Control Act of February 1949 reinforced efforts to involve European nations in American embargo policies.[4]

Western European governments, however, considered this approach extreme and counterproductive and sought to renew trade relations with the Soviet-orbit countries through a series of trade agreements.[5] The UK, France and other Marshall Plan aid recipients asserted that the success of their recovery efforts depended on the resumption of trade with their traditional commercial partners in the East. They also considered exports to non-U.S. currency countries critical for reducing the "dollar gap" created by American imports. They objected to Washington's expansive notion of "strategic" items, which encompassed virtually all goods serving the basic economy of Communist countries and would lead in the eyes of many Europeans to severing all economic relations with the East, thus be tantamount to all-out industrial warfare. Europe, British officials told their American counterparts, did not wish export controls to be regarded by "the iron curtain countries as a declaration of warfare." In January 1949 Britain and France agreed on their own ("international") lists of commodities to be embargoed for exports to the East, which, however, fell significantly short of the American versions. Even after the export control accords of January 1950, which created a joint Coordinating Committee (COCOM), the issue remained a sore point in U.S.-Western European relations.[6]

The Truman administration's export control policy toward the Soviet bloc in 1948–49 also clashed with the interests of the Western German political and business communities in trade with the East. Many business leaders believed that Germany, due to its history, geography and industrial strength, could expect to reclaim the leadership the country had had in *Osthandel* (trade with the East) before the war. Even stronger was the interest among Germans in the western zones in reviving the commercial exchange with the Soviet occupation zone: not only was the zone a traditional outlet for western German production; to many it also took on significance as a last remaining bond with the brethren east of the deepening zonal divide. How powerful this desire was had been manifest in the fact that German representatives from East and West had managed to negotiate a first comprehensive interzonal trade agreement in the Westphalian town of Minden in early 1947. They had managed to win approval by American, British, and Soviet occupation officials, even amidst rising Cold War tensions. The Minden trade framework agreement envisioned a trade volume over one year of some RM 206 million. It was built around the traditional exchange structure: two-thirds of the Soviet occupation zone's imports were iron and steel, and deliveries to the western zones were made up largely of grains, sugar, potatoes, and textiles.[7]

U.S. officials were sensitive to the possibility that the agreement would result in American subventions for their zone being transferred to the Soviet zone, concerns that underpinned the first-charge principle and the zonal reparations solution in 1945 and the early prohibition of barter transactions with other zones. Similar worries caused American officials in 1947 to force the Central Economic Office in Minden to require permits (Warenbegleitscheine, henceforth WBS) for all exports from the Anglo-American bizone to the Soviet zone, foreshadowing the post–1949 licensing system. As East-West relations deteriorated, trade across the interzonal border came under increasing Allied scrutiny and pressure to reorient to the West. In November 1947 western German trade representatives were forced to turn down Soviet zone deliveries of synthetic rubber, sugar, wheat, and textiles in favor of imports of such goods from the United States and Cuba. In the words of the Soviet zone trade negotiator Josef Orlopp, it was "the first shadow of the Cold War."[8]

Yet amidst further segregation of the western and eastern occupation zones, German political leaders on both sides of the growing divide advocated trade across zonal boundaries as paving the way to unification of the country. At the Munich Conference of German state minister-presidents in June 1947, leaders from the western and Soviet zones supported interzonal trade as a way to diminish the economic dislocations stemming from the growing division of the country. The Second SED Party Congress in September 1947 postulated the SED's commitment to double the volume of trade between the eastern and western zones of Germany. Internally, the DWK's Main Administration for Interzonal and Foreign Trade emphasized in April 1948 that "from the perspective of the fight for the political and economic unity of Germany," interzonal trade was of "greatest significance." The SED's Two-Year Plan for 1949–50 called for the "largest-possible expansion" of interzonal exchange. Consequently, the second interzonal trade agreement (for 1948), negotiated in November 1947 against the backdrop of the contentious London Council of Foreign Minsters session, envisioned an increase in interzonal trade by more than 50 percent.[9]

The agreement, however, never came to pass. Beginning in 1948, the European Recovery Program and the London decisions for the formation of a West German state accelerated the integration of the western zones into Western European economic and political structures. The Soviet "blockade" of Berlin and the Western "counterblockade" caused interzonal trade to collapse by more than a third. To be sure, economic exchange between the Western sectors of Berlin and their Soviet zone hinterland remained strong through the spring of 1949. Smuggling from the bizone into the Soviet zone during the counterblockade, estimated by Clay in January 1949 to amount to some $200,000, was extensive. The Jessup-Malik agreement at the United Nations in New York in May and the results of the Paris foreign ministers' meeting in May/June 1949 that ended the conflict over Berlin envisioned a resumption of interzonal exchanges in goods, capital, and communications at pre-March 1948 levels. But preparations for the imminent establishment of a separate West German state and Washington's new export control offensive in the spring of 1949 overtook efforts to reestablish closer economic ties.[10]

Since late 1948, the growing economic disparity between the eastern and western zones had become increasingly evident. Separate currency regimes and stark price differences resulted in a massive drain of Soviet zone goods to the West, further aggravating existing shortages in the East. Typewriters, cameras, textiles, and raw materials flowed to the West, particularly via Berlin, further depleting the zone before the Soviets' eyes. Sokolovsky had, the CIA reported, expressed "great consternation" at the devastating impact of the counterblockade, having been "led to believe the East could be independent of the West." Much as the perceived threat of another Berlin blockade became a recurrent nightmare of American officials, overcoming the Soviet zone's dependence on West Germany for vital commodities became an obsession for Moscow and its SED allies. Addressing the need to reduce economic weakness put shifting trade flows to the East uppermost on the minds of East German Communist authorities: "Our only resort is a radical import from the East."[11]

Pressures for a fundamental reorientation of the economies in the divided country notwithstanding, in the months after the end of the Berlin Blockade, Germans in East and West continued to attach enormous political and economic value to inter-German trade. Western German businesses remained keen on the Soviet zone market; inter-German trade diminished inflationary pressures in Western Germany by providing access to cheaper goods from the Soviet zone, and it took on ever greater importance as a symbolic precursor to a process of reunification that many Germans still expected in the not-too-distant future. In the face of growing shortages in raw materials and consumption goods and weighed down by Soviet dismantling, East German Communists were, if anything, even more keen to resume trade with the West. The months of the blockade had left whatever industrial production remained in the Soviet zone dramatically under capacity. Critical to fulfilling Soviet reparation demands, interzonal trade also offered a chance to close the opening gap in living standards vis-à-vis Western Germany.[12]

Though the basic mechanism for a resumption of interzonal trade had been worked out by late May 1949, it took German negotiators meeting in Frankfurt until early October to complete a new agreement. One important problem from a Western perspective was how to facilitate economic exchange while avoiding a diplomatic upgrading of the Soviet zone authorities, which on October 7 constituted the German Democratic Republic. Neither side in fact considered trade with the other part of Germany to be "foreign" trade, though the new East German government quickly seized trade as a way to force Bonn's hand at diplomatic recognition.[13]

The prolonged negotiations resulted in a number of ingenious diplomatic and technical innovations as part of the Frankfurt Agreement: To avoid fixing exchange rates between the two new German currencies, the West German Bank of German States (later the Federal Reserve Bank, or Bundesbank) and the GDR central bank, the Deutsche Notenbank, set up clearing accounts for essential and non-essential goods, with "clearing units"—and a "swing" credit that allowed either side to overdraw accounts to a certain extent. To preclude diplomatic recognition, the agreement was signed by representatives on behalf of the two "supreme economic authorities of the economic area of the German Mark [DM]" (adding DM-West and DM-East, respectively). In the Federal Republic, the Adenauer government created the Treuhandstelle für Interzonenhandel (TSI), an agency manned by Economic Ministry officials but nominally attached to the nongovernmental industry and trade chamber (Deutscher Industrie- und Handelstag). In the GDR, a newly created Ministry of Foreign Trade, Inter-German Trade and Procurement, took charge of interzonal trade dealings.

Significantly, neither the Western powers nor the USSR relinquished the right to control trade between the two German states: "interzonal" trade, in the West's parlance that eschewed any implication of acknowledging the GDR as a separate "state," remained, until German unification in 1990, one of the few areas for which the three Western Allies reserved a right to intervene on the basis of their original occupation powers. The new Adenauer government contended that the Allied prerogative was limited to continued Allied control over "foreign trade and exchange" since the Occupation Statute (in paragraph 2(g)) did not explicitly reference German-German trade as within Allied reserve fields. But the Allied High Commission (AHC) would not budge; it considered trade with the East to be a branch of the Federal Republic's foreign trade. All along, that trade had been, according to Military Government Law No. 53, in principle prohibited; any transactions thus required Allied approval. In September 1949 the Western Allies did delegate the authority

to grant permits for trade with the East (Warenbegleitscheine, WBS) to the new
Federal Ministry for Economics. But the AHC reserved the right to approve such
permits in the last instance, to sanction any inter-German trade agreements and
involve themselves in the Federal Republic's economic dealings with the East. The
Soviets, for their part, remained intimately involved in all aspects of East German
trade policy vis-à-vis the Federal Republic, as Pieck's notes of his discussions with
Soviet officials demonstrate.[14]

The Frankfurt Agreement projected trade between the two German states
through June 1950 at a total volume of DM 312 million. But the accomplishment
that was remarkable was not so much volume projected in the agreement but its
conclusion: it went into effect at the very moment when the establishment of the
two rival German governments deepened the country's division and Washington
sought to severely limit West-East trade. On October 4, two hours before the agreement was to be signed, U.S. officials in the AHC insisted on a final review, trumping
the West German government's argument that German-German trade was within
its competence. Infuriated, German officials told the AHC—in vain—to sign the
agreement in their place. Coming on the heels of Allied intervention into the setting of German coal prices, the delay of several days caused by the AHC's scrutiny
highlighted the limited sovereignty the Federal Republic enjoyed at the time and
tended to undermine its authority. In approving the agreement on October 6, Allied
officials, moreover, insisted that it would not constitute a precedent for future West
German deals with the East. Most poignantly, the Allied-West German squabble
effectively forced the West Germans to sign the trade deal with the SED-led government the day after the official founding of the GDR on October 7 whose very
existence they sought to deny, causing, in the words of one U.S. official, "the Germans to question whether the East-Zone government had been sanctioned by the
West even before its official proclamation."[15]

Even more insulting to the Adenauer government were the U.S. embargo lists
it received in late November 1949. Unlike most other Marshall Plan recipients, the
Federal Republic alone was to abide by the strict American 1A and 1B standards,
not the more liberal Anglo-French "international" lists. While admitting that "under
the given circumstances" it could not "evade the necessity of such measures," the
Adenauer government objected to such flagrant "discrimination" in trade practices.
Economics Ministry calculations suggested that by 1948 Western European countries' trade with the East had risen to about 150 percent of 1938 figures. By compari-
son, West German trade stood at one-fifth of the 1938 level. "Cautious estimates"
of the impact of the new embargo lists, Adenauer told McCloy in early February

1950, put the loss in trade to the Federal Republic at $200–$250 million. Playing on all registers of American strategic sensitivities, the chancellor warned that the new export controls would widen the dollar gap, undercut Berlin's economic vitality, and increase unemployment—and hence "social difficulties." The new measures also meant, Adenauer pointed out, that the Frankfurt interzonal trade "pact," concluded just weeks earlier, could to a large extent not be implemented.[16]

In the course of the spring, German federal government officials, spurred by increasingly vocal West German industrialists, expressed their growing dissatisfaction with the curtailment of trade with the East due to the tough export control standards. "Ancient traditional links with great potential for expansion" were being lost, Economic Minister Ludwig Erhard held forth; there could be no denying that West Germany occupied a "special economic position vis-à-vis the countries behind the Iron Curtain." After overcoming the discrimination that the Federal Republic faced, the head of the Economics Ministry's export control office, Ambassador Hans Kroll, announced in phrasing infused with nationalistic exceptionalism, "We have to use every appropriate occasion to cement our claim to supremacy in trade with the East." He pointed to geographic location, traditional bonds of the past, and the "*natural* economic gap between the German market and the countries of the East."[17]

The Americans looked at East-West trade "from a political perspective," Erhard told Adenauer quite perceptively. The closer the economic and personal ties between Western and Soviet bloc countries, said Erhard, the warier the Americans were of communist infiltration and sudden unilateral trade cut-offs by the USSR. By contrast, the Adenauer government saw itself following the entirely pragmatic principle "maximum strategic security through a minimum of economic sacrifice," as Kroll put it. Ignoring their own political-ideological blinders, Adenauer's advisers confidently predicted that "surely" the Americans would not object to an increase in trade with the East in the face of "compelling economic circumstances." Kroll, whom Adenauer sent to Paris as West German representative to the Coordinating Committee, even called for a rather loose implementation of COCOM controls: given the "generous" approval policy exercised by other countries when it came to granting export licenses, "we should not shy away from applying a not-too-strict standard in our approval practice."[18]

One reason for such an aggressive stance on trade was the perception that the GDR might emerge as a competitor in facilitating trade between the West and the East. In early 1950 Ulbricht and several GDR ministers had advocated involving West German companies in their trade program; during a visit to West Germany's industrial heartland in late May, Josef Orlopp, a former Social Democrat, union leader, and veteran Soviet zone trade official who had become the GDR's chief interzonal trade negotiator, and Willi Stoph, head of the SED Economics Department in the SED leadership, even proposed to have West German companies join in a planned GDR trade deal with the newly established People's Republic of China with which the East Germans, unlike their West German counterparts, had promptly established diplomatic relations.[19]

The Iron and Steel Embargo

German efforts to insulate inter-German trade from "political" considerations did not survive even the first trade cycle set in motion by the Frankfurt Agreement. In early 1950 the Soviet authorities began to interfere again with trade between West Berlin and the Federal Republic. On January 13, the Soviets impounded eleven German trucks loaded with non-ferrous metal scrap leaving Berlin. Six days later, they prohibited any furniture from being moved out of Berlin. By January 20, perhaps in reaction to the Federal Republic's joining COCOM the previous day, all trucks carrying metal scrap, furniture, or any items on the Western restricted lists were apparently held up on the Soviet side of the Helmstedt checkpoint on the zonal border. On January 22, numerous trucks coming from Berlin were turned back at Helmstedt. Moreover, the Soviets now extended the restrictions to trains running between East and West Germany.[20]

For all of the city's corrosive effects on the East as a show window of the West, Soviet actions underlined above all the continued volatility of the Western position in Berlin. For the West, the city was both a political-cultural beachhead deep inside the GDR and, militarily indefensible, an obvious Achilles heel open to pressures from the East. U.S. officials worried about the possibility of another blockade. The crescendo of blows to West German–Berlin trade, the U.S. Army's European Command headquarters warned, was a "deliberate Soviet plan to sabotage the economic rehabilitation of Berlin." Other incidents would certainly follow, "leading up to major demonstrations next spring." Moscow's ultimate motive was presumably "complete control in Berlin." Eight months after the end of the Berlin Blockade crisis, American officials pondered the prospects of a "little blockade" and the need for a reimposition of the Western counterblockade.[21]

In dealing with new Soviet "harassment" of Berlin's supply lines, the Truman administration soon focused on inter-German trade as a lever to assure continued access. After all, the Jessup-Malik Agreement and the Paris foreign ministers' meeting had explicitly tied the resumption of inter-German trade to Western communications with the Western Berlin sectors. Worries about Berlin meshed with concerns in Washington that West German trade with the GDR prolonged the Federal Republic's dependence on foreign aid, exposed Bonn and the West German economy to pressures from the East and benefited the Soviet economic and military buildup through reparation payments. By January, West German steel deliveries to the GDR threatened to over-obligate that clearing account by about 8 million clearing units. Four-fifths of all East German imports fell into the iron and steel sector—far exceeding the quota of one-third originally agreed to in the Frankfurt Agreement. Moreover, East German promises of potato and grain deliveries had not been carried out. Much to the consternation of the Americans, the GDR trade ministry had instead successfully lured West German businesses to facilitate a questionable barter deal outside of the Frankfurt agreement that involved the import of some 40,000 tons of overpriced GDR sugar in return for 100,000 tons in steel deliveries to the East. Declaring that it was "imperative" to take action to "protect the West German economy," the three Western deputy high commissioners resolved on February 2 to impose an embargo on all West German iron and steel shipments that were on order from the GDR.[22]

The decision had papered over severe disagreements between Americans and their European allies over instrumentalizing East-West German trade to preserve Western access to Berlin, strengthen the strategic embargo, and put pressure on the GDR. Washington favored a more forceful reaction to the Soviet access restrictions, including an increase in military convoys between West Germany and Berlin. The State Department suggested that the West German government establish control points along the GDR and Berlin sector border prohibiting movement of commercial supplies by highway except through those designated points. Nominally justified under the Frankfurt Agreement, this would "in reality set up control machinery along Soviet zone border which will enable countermeasures that we may agree upon later." The Truman administration thus contemplated creating an inter-German border regime that could be "weaponized" well beyond mere defensive trade considerations. Time and again the administration would push for building up the border regime over the ensuing months.[23]

British and French officials objected to a formal junction between Berlin access and "interzonal trade" and only agreed to justify the embargo under the provisions of the interzonal trade agreement "and not necessarily connected with the interruption of traffic by [the] Soviets." A few days later, the U.S. Embassy in London reported that British foreign minister Bevin was "considerably upset" by the widespread press reports that the embargo was a first step in the direction of a counterblockade in retaliation for Soviet harassment of Berlin communications: "He . . . pointed out that he had only agreed to [the] embargo on condition that it would not be linked to Soviet restrictions on transportation and that every effort would be made to keep publicity to [a] minimum."Less inclined toward drastic steps, British and French officials argued for a gradual application of countermeasures "under [the] guise of protection of the West German economy." All of it should be done with "minimum publicity."[24]

Professing to be "increasingly disturbed" at the persistent inter-German trade imbalance, the Allied high commissioners followed their deputies' recommendation and ordered an immediate suspension of Western deliveries of steel until the accounts between the Federal Republic and the GDR had evened out. Otherwise, they noted, West Germany "would be financing the economic recovery of the eastern zone at the expense of its own earnings in foreign exchange." It could "not be justified to use ERP aid in this way to extend credits to the Soviet Zone," the high commissioners told Adenauer. On February 8, Federal Economics Minister Ludwig Erhard instructed the Länder economic administrations to immediately cease issuing new licensing papers (WBS) for iron and steel deliveries to the GDR until March 15.[25]

The embargo could not have hit the GDR at a worse time. The day after it was put into effect, the GDR government adopted an ambitious 1950 plan for reparations to the USSR. A large part of the reparations payments came from those areas in which the GDR was dependent on imports from West Germany: 75 percent of the East German reparations in 1949 had consisted of machine and heavy machine deliveries. The 1950 plan charged the Ministry for Foreign and Inner-German Trade with obtaining critical metals and ball bearings—a task now made much more difficult. Internally, GDR officials conceded that the embargo had effectively upset the new reparations plan, aggravating Soviet dissatisfaction with East German reparation payments. Soviet Control Commission officials frequently interfered, modifying the plan, lamenting the lag in GDR deliveries, and urging East German officials to fulfill the Frankfurt Agreement according to schedule "at all costs."[26]

The aggravating effects of the embargo extended far beyond reparations. Imports from the FRG were also crucial to the success of the SED's Five-Year Economic Plan, which had been in the works since September 1949 and was scheduled to be announced at the SED's Third Party Congress in late July 1950. Postwar dismantling had wrought havoc in the iron and steel industry in the Soviet zone, which failed to meet production requirements, in fact forcing the USSR to return rolling mills and other capital equipment. Now the deliveries from West Germany in this critically important sector fell dramatically short of the anticipated totals: only 28,500 tons of the projected 90,000 tons of iron and just 77,725 tons of a projected 195,500 tons of rolling mill products had reached East Germany by June. The GDR remained painfully dependent on inter-German trade, particularly for West German rolling mill products. The economic dislocations and potential plan failure threatened by the embargo gnawed at the political legitimacy of the SED regime.

Internally, the leadership blamed the technocrats of the Main Administration for Interzonal and Foreign Trade (MAI) for political miscalculations. Alternative sources, such as imports from other capitalist countries, like Belgium or the Netherlands, were hampered by the lack of trade agreements and foreign currency reserves. "Resolving this difficult shortage caused by the steel embargo" had thus far not been possible, GDR premier Otto Grotewohl had to admit to SCC chief Vasily Chuikov in late August 1950.[27]

The East German government therefore tried its utmost to undercut the steel embargo and have it revoked. In mid-February, East German trade negotiator Josef Orlopp secretly met with his West German counterpart, Dr. Gottfried Kaumann, a former official with the Reich Association of the German aircraft industry. Working for the Frankfurt Economic Office after the war, Kaumann had conducted the negotiations with the Soviet zone economic authorities to revive trade in the wake of the blockade. A proponent of inter-German trade, Kaumann was imbued with the Economics Ministry's reticence regarding the Americans' strong predilections for far-reaching embargo measures and Allied interference in inter-German trade relations. He may also have come to see himself as the Federal Republic's unofficial ambassador to the GDR: in April 1950, the Bundesregierung resolved to channel all West German government communications with East Germany through the TSI, significantly elevating Kaumann's role. Orlopp, who had been promoted to the position of GDR official trade representative in a little-disguised effort by the SED to nudge the Adenauer government ever closer to recognizing GDR authorities, promised that the GDR would fully carry out the terms of the Frankfurt Agreement until its expiration on June 30 if the West issued WBS for GDR orders placed since February 8. Unbeknownst to Allied officials, Kaumann quickly assured his East German counterpart that the embargo would be brought to an end.[28]

Moreover, GDR Trade Ministry officials lobbied West German iron and steel producers at a meeting in Düsseldorf to intervene with the Bonn government to repeal the embargo. Earlier in the year, in what Ulbricht considered an "important test run" for instrumentalizing the West German industries' sway over the Bundesregierung, the East Germans had successfully circumvented the Frankfurt Agreement by offering to buy 100,000 tons of steel from Gute-Hoffnungs-Hütte, one of the largest West German steel producers in the Ruhr, in return for the corporation's effort to facilitate Western purchase of 40,000 tons of overpriced GDR sugar. Now GDR officials asserted that the trade imbalance that had occasioned the embargo had been largely rectified. West German industrialists, many of whom had been opposed to the steel embargo from the outset, assured the East Germans quick fulfillment of outstanding steel deliveries and committed to work "with all means towards eliminating the problems for the further fulfillment of the Frankfurt Agreement." But the embargo remained in force.[29]

East Berlin also began to take even more proactive and repressive measures. On April 21, the GDR adopted the "Law on the Protection of Inner-German Trade," in turn making trade permits compulsory for trade between the GDR and West Berlin and threatening draconian sanctions for any transgressions. In May, the SED government threatened to cancel existing contracts with West German companies unless the embargo was lifted. More disconcertingly to the Truman administration, the GDR froze deliveries of potatoes and lignite (brown coal) briquettes and reduced electricity and water provisions to West Berlin (which relied almost entirely on East German brown coal resources). The SED government also stopped wood deliveries to West Germany, which affected the important construction and mining sectors. Finally, it continued its confiscation of metal scrap deliveries from West Berlin.[30]

Hand in hand with threats to cut off trade with the Federal Republic went renewed East German efforts to circumvent the embargo by importing rolling mill products from Austria, Belgium, France, Britain, and Finland through three-way agreements and barter deals. At the end of July, the Grotewohl government resolved to make greater efforts to obtain critical materials through imports from Eastern Europe in order to avoid the "dangers of blockades and embargos." In the short run, these efforts to diversify steel imports proved futile, but in the long run they pushed the GDR to expand its own industrial base. Later that summer the East German government launched the ambitious construction of a massive new industrial combine with ten-blast-furnices for the production of iron and steel, the Eisenhüttenkombinat Josef Stalin near Fürstenberg/Oder.[31]

While the embargo had aggravated the tensions between the Soviets and the East German leaders, it also brought into sharp relief differences in approach to inter-German trade between the Americans and "their" Germans. Eager to counter Soviet and East German pressure on Berlin, U.S. officials viewed inter-German trade as the "pivot on which to swing our entire plan of action." But echoing their frustrations with getting the West Germans on the political offensive against the East, Truman administration officials believed that West German actions in the trade field had failed to bring "pressure on the Soviets which might force them to give up their present harassing tactics" around Berlin. The halfhearted steel embargo was emblematic of West German reticence to curtail trade with the East. To American observers, the Germans' attitude was likely to recall German efforts during the 1948–49 Berlin crisis to revive East-West German trade, as one U.S. official put it then, "without any indication of a feeling of responsibility for helping to make the counter-blockade thoroughly effective." German businessmen on both sides had regarded the Western counterblockade as something that could be "circumvented with good conscience."[32]

In fact, Kaumann's secret negotiations with Orlopp in mid-February had led to a tentative understanding between East and West Germans to lift the embargo. Outraged by the agreement that Kaumann had initialed behind its back, the Truman administration leaned on the Allied High Commission to formally overrule the Bonn Government in its decision to lift the embargo. Reflecting American frustrations with Bonn's perceived obstinacy, the AHC also decreed two new laws that explicitly applied prohibitions in supplying military equipment, as well as nuclear energy production facilities and equipment, to the East bloc to inter-German trade, underlining Allied authority in this field.[33]

With a selective embargo seemingly ineffective, the State Department now called for an immediate general embargo: West German authorities were to cease issuing WBS permits completely. To further avoid future trade imbalances, the State Department also suggested a new procedure once trade resumed: in addition to the WBS, Western shipments were to show proof that adequate GDR funds had been earmarked by the western Bank Deutscher Länder before actually letting the merchandise cross the inter-German border. Moreover, administration officials proposed once again that the Allied High Commission and the Bundesregierung assure the physical control of the movement of goods to the GDR by setting up border checkpoints. Given the likely British and French opposition to any tit-for-tat over Berlin, HICOG was to "concentrate purely on the trade agreement and [the] necessity of living up to its terms."[34]

McCloy had hesitated to repudiate the agreement clandestinely negotiated by Kaumann outright. Instead he suggested that the Allies should intervene promptly if trade did not come into reasonable balance soon. He also urged the "sacking" of Kaumann, whom he characterized as a "rather notorious bad actor." Kaumann, HICOG officials claimed, had kept not just the Allies but even Adenauer and Erhard "ill-informed" about his negotiations with the Eastern authorities. U.S. officials called on the Adenauer government to "clean house" and replace Kaumann immediately "with [a] person of ministerial caliber and Western-oriented political viewpoint." Adenauer denied that he had sanctioned the deal and professed outrage over Kaumann's actions, even suspected, with recourse to his favorite metaphor for the ideological danger from the East, that the TSI head was "infected by the Russians." But the West German trade negotiator had in fact obtained authorization from Erhard before agreeing to lift the embargo. In the end, the embargo remained in place—but so did Kaumann.[35]

By mid-March, the GDR had in fact made up most of the trade deficit, yet the Bundesregierung instructed the state governments to continue the WBS suspension indefinitely. By the end of the month, pressure from West German and West Berlin industrialists for a resumption of Western deliveries became increasingly vocal. Kaumann warned that the East might cancel existing contracts, and Economics Minister Erhard demanded that Adenauer intervene with the Allies to allow the resumption of trade negotiations. Adenauer finally requested that the Allies allow a "far-reaching relaxation" of the embargo on May 22.[36]

U.S. officials, however, continued to see the embargo as a potent tool not just to ensure trade balance, but also to enforce export controls and put pressure on the GDR, especially vis-à-vis Berlin. The payments imbalance on the "A" account (of most important goods) under the Frankfurt Agreement, which had been the official reason for the iron and steel embargo, had changed to the credit of the Eastern side, but largely as the result of the delivery of what U.S. officials considered overpriced quantities of sugar. Most of the West German deliveries had been in iron, steel, and other metals, machines, ball bearings, calcinated soda, and textile raw materials—not in the highly manufactured commodities for which West German industries were supposedly seeking new markets. The GDR, American intelligence officials advised, had lived up to its commitment only with regard to sugar and potatoes.[37]

Rather than relaxing the embargo as the West Germans favored, the Truman administration continued to advocate tightening inter-German border controls. Stricter trade controls would "put us in readiness to take counter measures as reply to Soviet restrictions on Berlin transport," the State Department told the high commissioners in May. With Soviets and East Germans increasing pressure on Berlin access ever more "thoroughly and impudently," the State Department considered restricting "critical Western [German] deliveries to [the] East as [a] direct retaliatory measure." This included the maintenance and real enforcement of the steel embargo until Soviet and German restrictions were lifted.[38]

The U.S.-West German crisis over the inter-German trade embargo fed into the malaise enveloping Allied-West German relations in the spring of 1950 over

what FRG officials considered overbearing Allied interference into German politics. After U.S. officials pointedly reminded Kaumann on May 24 that interzonal
trade was within their reserve authority and that negotiations with the GDR "over
implementation, modification, expansion, extension of the Frankfurt Agreement
were only to be conducted with permission," Kaumann queried the Economics
Ministry as to whether such was in fact the case. No doubt egged on by Erhard, who
had questioned the embargo from the start, Adenauer fired off a letter to the AHC
claiming that inter-German trade was domestic commerce and as such fell outside
of Allied competence. Despite the tart response by French High Commissioner
Andre Francois-Poncet that interzonal trade was not to be considered domestic, as
it involved different currency regimes, Adenauer dug in, taking exception to the
AHC position but agreeing to seek Allied permission, even if it was "not formally
required."[39]

Authority over the control of trade and payments across the zonal border remained firmly in Allied hands. In fact, the Allied officials seemed keen to expand
their authority in this area: In late April, the Allied High Commission's Tripartite
Trade and Transport Committee recommended that the German border controls be
supervised by Allied authorities to "provide a flexible means of exerting retaliatory
measures." The committee also urged the Germans to draft new customs procedures
that would apply to the German-German border and provide greater control over
postal consignments. In mid-June the AHC instructed the Western Commandants
to establish checkpoints in Berlin at its western approaches as well as along the sector
border, and to set up "roving controls." Joint planning by HICOG and the Army's
European Command for full-scale counterblockade envisioned regulating, curtailing,
or terminating all traffic crossing the U.S. zonal border with East Germany, McCloy
told Acheson, if necessary, by taking "full military control over [the] border and
German border officials." As late as spring 1951, the U.S. High Commission was
prepared to impose military control over the West German border and even close
that border to enforce potential countermeasures against the GDR.[40]

Reflecting U.S. policy priorities, any new trade agreement was now to be contingent on new guarantees of unimpeded Berlin communications. At least 25 percent of the orders covered by the agreement were to be placed in Berlin, stipulated
within a special Berlin East-West trade agreement. In the American vision, the city
would effectively become the center for the East-West trade machinery, and the
Treuhandstelle would move from Frankfurt to Berlin. To demonstrate its seriousness,
the United States also refused to grant the West Germans authority to negotiate a
new inter-German trade agreement. On June 30, 1950, the Frankfurt Agreement
therefore lapsed without extension.[41]

The sudden breakdown of the inter-German trade mechanism (that is, of any legal basis for FRG-GDR trade), however, did not have the impact the Truman administration had hoped for. Rather than negotiating new terms to accommodate the West, the East Germans returned to the practice of trade negotiations with individual West German state governments. Lower Saxony's minister of agriculture, Günther Gereke, a neutralist critic of Adenauer, eagerly seized the opportunity. Moreover, illegal trade across the inter-German border spiked dramatically. An increasingly sophisticated contraband system was making a virtual mockery out of the steel embargo. Soviet zone firms dispatched large-quantity but low-value consignments of goods to West Germany in return for high-value commodities. Besides outright smuggling through West Berlin or over the permeable "green border" between East and West Germany, deliveries were justified as being carried out under old, pre-embargo contracts; others were documented under false descriptions or had outright forged documentation. According to some accounts, some $3 million worth of steel was smuggled from West Germany into the Soviet zone in the six months following the beginning of the embargo. Keen on avoiding a complete break in the legal flow of goods, West German officials, apparently once again without consulting the Western Allies, issued interim regulations that provided for a limited continuation of trade on a barter basis.[42]

Worried over new "harassing action" around Berlin after the outbreak of the Korean War, over the summer the Allied High Commission relented to West German interest in resuming preliminary trade negotiations with the GDR government on a month-by-month extension of the Frankfurt Agreement until September 30. Once again the talks quickly deadlocked over Western demands to tie Berlin security to inter-German trade: At the behest of the SED Politburo, Orlopp refused to guarantee in writing that the GDR would not interfere with Berlin communications and transport and cease its interruption of the power and water supplies for West Berlin. For two weeks the talks stalled; then Washington blinked. Shaken by North Korean military successes in the early weeks of the war, the Truman administration sought to avoid a complete breakdown of the negotiations. With German industries, various Länder governments, the TSI, and the Federal Cabinet rather understanding of the GDR's efforts to see the embargo repealed, Bonn readily dropped its demand for Berlin guarantees. On July 20, the Allied High Commissioners agreed to extend the Frankfurt Agreement retroactively by three months, until September 30.[43]

The extension permitted steel and iron shipments to the East to resume, though the West Germans were secretly instructed to limit deliveries of the critical steel rolling mill products to 10,000 tons per month. At Washington's behest, West German representatives informed the GDR representatives that any agreement would be "null and void" if the East did not remove existing or re-imposed restrictions on access to Berlin. Despite such threats, East Berlin refused to formally recognize a link between trade and Berlin access; Orlopp was ready to commit only to granting that no special conditions be applied to trade between West Berlin and the Federal Republic. But it was enough of a face-saving gesture on the part of the GDR government to achieve Western approval of an interim agreement that lifted the trade embargo on August 11.[44]

As negotiations for a new IZT agreement that would take effect on October 1 started on September 6, both sides declared victory in the trade struggle. East Germans officials confidently asserted that their most urgent steel requirements would soon be satisfied by shipments from other Western European countries and that the GDR was therefore immune to any pressure from West Germany. U.S. officials read the experience with the steel embargo as putting the West in a strong negotiating position for the next trade agreement and urged the West German negotiators to exploit the GDR's dependence upon West German commodities to their best advantage. Reversing the earlier logic, Truman administration officials now were hopeful that "recent events"—the North Korean invasion and ensuing widespread fears in the Federal Republic over the possibility of an East German attack—would force the West Germans into cooperating. The State Department told HICOG that it was "extremely reluctant to see present agreement extended"; any new agreement was to achieve the "most advantageous economic exchange," guarantee the participation of West Berlin, and minimize the export of "strategic commodities." Nevertheless, the administration was "not now willing [to] precipitate a breakdown of the negotiations" if it would result in a renewed Berlin blockade. Mindful of the uptick in "black trade" when legal flows had stopped, Washington thought it would be equally disastrous if all controls of inter-German trade were lost.[45]

Initially, new East-West German agreements in early September that assured West Berlin's supply with some 2.6 million tons of brown coal briquettes and electricity (the GDR supplied an average of 850,000 kilowatt-hours daily of the 2,000,000-kilowatt-hour consumption of the Western sectors) seemed to augur well for the new round of trade negotiations. But at midnight on September 20, Cold War skirmishes, perhaps echoes of the tense military situation in the Far East, once again overtook the delicate trade issue. Following an intense face-off between Soviet and British soldiers near Gatow Airfield in which about a hundred British troops, supported by armored cars and machine guns, forcibly retook an area of 150 yards of British sector territory seized earlier that day by more than a dozen Soviet soldiers, the East cut the power supply for the Western sectors of the city. When West German efforts to obtain a resumption of power proved in vain, the Bundesregierung broke off the trade negotiations.[46]

One week later, armed British "Tommies" occupied West Berlin canal locks and detained forty-five Soviet zone barges in retaliation for Western barges held up by the Soviets since February in what was soon termed the "canal lock war." Within days, the Allied High Commission decided that the Frankfurt Agreement would not be extended again; however, Warenbegleitscheine (permits) would be issued for unfulfilled contracts placed prior to October 1—in a sense extending trade in a limited way through the end of the year. To sharpen the impact of the non-extension, the AHC forbade barter transactions between East and West in October. Once again, Washington officials hoped that a lapse of the trade agreement would coerce the GDR to lift its pressure on West Berlin, and to accommodate Western conditions for a trade deal.[47]

Another factor played into the American decision to tighten the inter-German trade screws: Moscow's designs for Berlin after the October 15 elections in the GDR. Western officials expected the Soviet Union to upgrade the GDR diplomatically in some fashion, perhaps relinquishing some or all of its occupation rights to the SED authorities. How would this affect Western access to Berlin? HICOG discussions over potential countermeasures "clearly brought out" that the only effective countermeasure to potential Soviet or East German restrictions on traffic and communications between West Berlin and the Federal territory were the commodity deliveries from West Germany to the GDR. Assuming that East Germany continued to be "dependent to a considerable extent" on the Federal Republic for the successful fulfillment of its new Five-Year Plan (1951–1955), the denial of critical items was considered the most effective weapon against any interference with Berlin communications.[48]

The specter of the GDR's assuming greater agency after October 15 added urgency and ambition to American planning. Reflecting McCloy's growing desire for an offensive posture, HICOG officials sought to go beyond a game of tit-for-tat reprisals in which the Soviets' capacity for interference with Berlin's communications outweighed the retaliatory possibilities of the West. The West had to "place [its] house in order," U.S. officials argued, not just to effectively control the flow of goods but to keep the industrialization program in the GDR "off balance." HICOG's Eastern Element even suggested encouraging the Bundesregierung to initiate legislation "similar" to the GDR's Law on the Protection of Inner-German

Trade. French and British government officials, by contrast, cautioned that such extreme countermeasures risked provoking a complete blockade.[49]

Once the October elections had passed without signs of any new Soviet moves toward Berlin, an emboldened State Department advocated "increased pressure" to use the "present breathing spell" to improve the Western position in Berlin and to obtain a more satisfactory trade agreement. Washington wanted to seize the initiative from the Soviets in the trade field: "the time may now be more ripe than at any time recently for such moves." An end had to be put to trade "leaks" across the border, custom controls had to be tightened to stop the illegal "black trade," and once again Washington wondered whether "pressure to remove Kaumann as too conciliatory" would have any effect on the West German attitude in the negotiations." Eager to effect a tighter guarantee for Berlin's participation in any future trade agreement, Washington officials considered making West German deliveries contingent upon Berlin trade. If negotiations resumed, HICOG assured Washington that it would maintain a "tight rein" on inter-German trade negotiations by daily and weekly conferences with the West German team.[50]

Yet in the absence of a trade agreement, Western controls over the flow of trade were practically nonexistent, resulting in, according to one HICOG official, "smuggling on a grand scale" between the two Germanies. Iron, steel, and other metals—in particular fine metal sheets, high-quality seamless tubes, and ball bearings—were smuggled from West Germany and West Berlin into East Germany, from where sugar, spirits, fuel, and lubricating oil were illegally brought into the Federal Republic and West Berlin. U.S. army intelligence had received information as early as August that the Soviet Control Commission had instructed the SED to tap the unutilized capacities in the GDR's textile industry for illegal sales to West Germany (directly or through Switzerland) to obtain West Marks. Emblematic of the lax West German controls, that same month—two months after the beginning of the Korean War—custom unit troopers were stunned to see railroad flatcars rolling up to the Schirnding border crossing with Czechoslovakia loaded with 105 U.S. Army two-and-a-half-ton and six-by-six trucks consigned to the East, the first batch of 1,050 shipped by the Frankfurt firm "Trucks and Spares." Though the vehicles were reportedly in perfect condition, the export license described them as "spare parts" from U.S. army surplus stocks that had been turned over to the Germans.[51]

Contrary to the American schemes to turn Berlin into the heart of inter-German trade control machinery, the city became the central node for the flourishing illegal exchange. Information obtained by HICOG set the overall amount of illegal trade through Berlin alone at some DM 800 million. While Federal Economics Minister

Erhard maintained that illegal trade was "hardly measurable," some German estimates ran as high as DM 1 billion ($238 million) for the annual total of West Germany's illegal trade with the GDR, with an estimated 40 percent of it going directly from the GDR to the Soviet Union and other bloc countries. Despite the embargo, U.S. officials estimated, Moscow had received some 300,000 tons of steel in 1950 through Germany.[52]

In the fall of 1950, U.S. and Western Allied intelligence agencies also uncovered several large illegal trade organizations cooperating with the Soviets. Based in Berlin and Vienna, the complex and far-flung smuggling ring extended to Switzerland, Belgium, Sweden, French North Africa, and the Netherlands and involved some of Germany's oldest and most respected business concerns, including the Rheinische Röhrenwerke in Mühlheim/Ruhr and the Berlin Iron and Steel Stock Company, with the Berlin company Haselgruber thought to be the primary operator. West German Föderalismus, or decentralization of authority to Länder governments, impeded efforts to effect greater central supervision and control over trade. Länder economic offices were reportedly more or less ignoring the implementation of federal controls because of the pressure of local business and industry, and American officials found the physical setup for the issuance of Warenbegleitscheine "appalling," especially in Nordrhein-Westphalia, the Federal Republic's most significant industrial area.[53]

Washington regarded the Federal Republic as the "greatest single source of strategic commodities for the Soviet area." Yet West Germans, in the eyes of Truman administration officials, were sorely lacking in their efforts to clamp down on illegal trade and to enforce trade controls. Increasingly confident that their manpower contribution to Western defenses could be leveraged for greater sovereignty, West German officials instead objected ever more strongly to being held to stricter U.S. export controls than other West European countries. Kroll, the German COCOM delegate, excoriated the Western powers over discrimination against West Germany and argued that controls should be uniform and voluntary.[54]

The Adenauer government even made known its intention to include some commodities prohibited under the stricter U.S. 1-A and 1-B lists in a new inter-German trade agreement. Confronted with West German reticence, the State Department pointed to "very unfortunate repercussions" should the Federal Republic in fact allow deliveries of prohibited commodities, at the very moment when the Western powers were relaxing occupation controls further. With West German actions endangering the success of U.S. efforts to increase multilateral trade controls, Washington informed HICOG that it would likely have to "veto" any inter-German trade agreement that did not abide by the stricter American controls. Such threats notwithstanding, in November the West German trade delegation initialed a protocol that extended the liquidation of the lapsed Frankfurt Agreement through the end of March, despite explicit American demands to the contrary. When Orlopp warned that without signing of the extension the GDR would be unable to deliver electricity and brown coal briquettes to Berlin, McCloy consented to a formal extension.[55]

For McCloy, West Germans' resistance to enforcing strict export controls and embargo policies vis-à-vis the GDR reflected a deeper dynamic within Germany. Their attitude was rooted in a "basic reluctance . . . to separate themselves psychologically or economically from eastern Germany." Any measures that appeared to split Germany wider were bound to encounter "reluctant acceptance if not covert sabotage." Most West Germans had the "instinctive feeling," another U.S. official noted, that "Eastern Germany is really a part of Germany." Even the removal of Kaumann as chief West German negotiator would not really affect this basic attitude toward interzonal trade.[56]

Toward Economic Warfare?

On January 1, 1951, elaborate ceremonies took place in Fürstenberg on the Oder, near the border with Poland, to dedicate a new steel mill and formally launch an ambitious GDR Five-Year Plan. Under the plan, first outlined by Walter Ulbricht a few months earlier, industrial production was to be increased 190 percent, accelerating production in particular strategic materials, such as iron and steel as well as selected key industrial branches (*Schwerpunktindustrien*—heavy machines, machine tools, and electric engineering). With its focus on materials of which East Germany faced critical shortages, the plan underscored the SED's efforts to relieve its dependence on West German imports. For the Truman administration, the GDR's "drive for economic autarchy" had far-reaching political consequences: if successful, it would weaken what was believed to be the most important Western tool for deterring future Soviet moves against West Berlin.[57]

Observing the GDR's drive for self-sufficiency, U.S. officials in Berlin were impressed with the "rapid headway" that the GDR was in their view making. Despite the GDR's overall lagging behind the Federal Republic, "the Soviet Zone authorities and their Russian masters are eminently successful in achieving their economic aims." The SED's 1949–50 economic plan, ridiculed earlier in the West as "utterly fantastic," had, in the judgment of HICOG officials in February 1951, "by and large been fulfilled," particularly in the metallurgical and mechanical engineering industries—a noteworthy achievement, as the GDR had to reconstruct most of its production capacities, which had by and large been dismantled in 1945 and 1946.

Seven months later, HICOG's GDR watchers viewed the turn of 1950–51 as having been a "milestone" in East Germany's economic development: 1951 marked the start of a "strenuous reorientation" of the economy toward basic and heavy industries and a rapid economic drive toward economic independence from the West. Yet the GDR's dependence on raw materials and semi-finished products and its shortage of technical skill had also led to increasing strains and tensions.[58]

Critical of McCloy's inclination in the wake of the Berlin crisis to encourage West German trade with the East (or, more recently, not to discourage it), PEPCO officials in early 1950 had advocated treating East-West trade as a "species of economic warfare." By late 1950, officials in HICOG's Eastern Element in Berlin demanded a "much more aggressive economic policy" vis-à-vis the East. Their proposals certainly reflected broader concerns within the administration about East-West trade. Against the backdrop of Chinese entry into the Korean War, President Truman emphasized the importance of the strategic embargo (COCOM) and asked the State Department in late December 1950 to recommend new measures to prevent the flow of critical goods "to countries supporting Communist imperialist aggression." Barely two weeks later, the State Department pointedly called for "prompt action" to enforce customs regulations on the Federal Republic's "eastern border." Military policy customs units began to supervise and direct German customs at U.S. zone airports, as well as at crossing points to the GDR, Austria, Czechoslovakia, and East Berlin. HICOG officials also recognized that strengthening border controls was not enough: it would be essential to centralize the licensing and other administrative procedures, many of which were prerogatives of the Länder governments, prior to the actual shipping of the goods.[59]

In the tense atmosphere of the 1950–51 winter, some officials within HICOG went as far as proposing a "rollback" of East-West trade in Germany to retard the GDR's drive to self-sufficiency. They recalled that in 1950 the East had received an estimated DM 300 million in legal and illegal metal and machine deliveries (as opposed to DM 100 million in essential goods on the part of the West), deliveries that amounted to half of the GDR government's net investment in its people's-owned industries. The East Germans had been allowed "to pick out the raisins from the cake." These HICOG officials, centered around PEPCO, advocated that the West abandon its approach to inter-German negotiations "based on the idea of maximizing trade" altogether. A basic decision for a "virtual embargo on East-West trade," of course, would clash with the "softer" German negotiating approach.

What was needed, they argued, was a more adequate Allied organization "to implement a 'Cold War' in the economic field," to use the economic potential of

Western Germany as a "lever against the Soviet Zone," and to launch a campaign in West Germany to "dispel the fallacies of their irrational approach to German unity," which would help overcome "German resistance and inertia" in the trade field. Reversing the prevailing priority on the security of Berlin, they argued that if the West continued to buy Berlin's survival by making concessions to the East, "we may win the battle of Berlin [only] to lose the war against the East."[60]

Congressional and Bundestag investigations in the spring of 1951 added to the sense of urgency in efforts to choke off at least the illegal flow of strategic war materials. A fact-finding mission by the U.S. Senate Subcommittee on Export Controls toured border points and ports in Germany in April, driving south from Hamburg for thirty-six hours without sleep, stopping at five customs points along the four-hundred-mile border. Contrary to official HICOG reports that some 20 percent of cargoes were being inspected, "this was nowhere in evidence except in the case of the Helmstedt" border crossing, where the "sudden efficiency may have been staged." The congressional investigators criticized the lax customs operations and faulted HICOG's political leadership for showing "not nearly enough interest or effort, and very little results in solving the problem of strategic shipments eastwards." A congressional subcommittee under Representative Laurie C. Battle, Democrat of Alabama, prepared legislation that would cut off aid to countries "trading with the enemy."[61]

In May 1951, McCloy was forced to admit that West Germany had sent $103,748,000 worth of iron and steel products, machinery, and chemicals eastward—with the blessing of the Allies. The admission followed a scathing fifty-three-page report published in April 1951 by the oppositional Social Democratic Party. Herbert Wehner, the fiercely anti-communist SPD chairman of the Bundestag's All-German Affairs Committee, estimated illegal transfers at DM 1.2 billion per year—four times the volume of the legal trade agreement, decried illegal trade as an instrument to undermine West Germany morally and politically, and proposed the establishment of a central control office.[62]

Under fire from within and without HICOG, McCloy established an "East/West Trade Working Party" under PEPCO that brought HICOG's political, intelligence, and economic expertise and capacity to bear on the issue. With congressional and public pressures mounting, McCloy also turned from behind-the-scenes cajoling to more public performative pressure. Howard Jones, one of his top lieutenants in Berlin, publicly threatened to withhold Marshall Plan aid if the Adenauer government did not get serious about curbing the illicit trade with the East. In May, in a demonstrative move, McCloy deployed the 7751st Military Police (MP) Customs Unit to the 350-mile German-German frontier line "to plug the holes in the iron curtain." When a Chinese Communist Party delegation appeared in East Berlin later that month to negotiate for materials needed for its Korean War operations, Jones announced a series of measures to prevent the Chinese from purchasing strategic goods produced in West Germany, including roving military police controls along the sector's border, stricter documentation requirements for goods moving east, and the transfer of an MP customs unit to bolster the anti-smuggling forces in West Berlin.[63]

More ambitious planning for economic warfare against the GDR was not limited to clamping down on illegal inter-German trade in strategic materials but envisaged denying East Germany critically important materials to "retard the self-sufficiency drive," a "counter-*Schwerpunkt*" program. In late 1950, HICOG's Eastern Element identified fifty-three "primary Soviet Zone industries" that would play a crucial role in the fulfillment of the SED's Five-Year Plan as targets for—unspecified—Western "actions." By December, PEPCO endorsed the plan and authorized espionage operations involving "all US intelligence collection agencies" in Berlin to establish what supply sources were open to these industries.[64]

East Germany's manpower shortage seemed to be even more promising for exploitation. Since 1948, the Truman administration had sought to deny Germans deemed sufficiently important to U.S. national security, especially scientists, access to the East. Moving from containment to rollback thinking, the Carroll-Speier report in December 1950 called for actively encouraging the defection of crucial segments of East German society, such as technical intelligentsia and youth. HICOG's GDR watchers predicted that the GDR's manpower problem would become dangerously critical "after 1961," anticipating an argument that Walter Ulbricht would make that year for building the Berlin Wall. The exodus of young men from the GDR was "very harmful to the normal development of a healthy society." HICOG soon focused on the shortage of technical intelligentsia, technical auxiliary personnel, and skilled workers as major "bottlenecks" for economic expansion in East Germany and the "hard core" of an estimated 100,000 persons "on which the industrial progress of the GDR depends." In February 1951, HICOG's Eastern Element proposed a covert defection program aimed at some 200 top scientific and technical personnel and, in a second phase, some 25,000 key technical specialists, whose defection would have a "serious disruptive effect" on the GDR. At its March 13 meeting, PEPCO approved the first phase of the project for implementation by HICOG's Office of Intelligence.[65]

Within weeks, this program "was under way." The more ambitious second part of the program, the defection of 25,000 highly skilled personnel and their families, however, quickly ran into difficulties. HICOG's Displaced Populations Division, the Office of Economic Affairs, and the Office of Labor Affairs argued that the

Federal Republic would be unable to absorb the additional 100,000 persons or unwilling to finance the program, and the program might discriminate against the Soviet zone refugees now in West Germany. Though HICOG's Eastern Element continued to favor the second phase as well, maintaining that "the obstacles aren't insuperable," the Offices of Economic Affairs and Labor Affairs won out. The program was launched selectively and based on the principle that defections should not be encouraged until positions could be obtained for the defectors involved. By early May 1951, a "small and discreet investigation" by the Office of Labor Affairs in the Ruhr for the purpose of estimating the capacity of the coal and steel industries to absorb key technicians from the GDR proved to be "discouraging."

In June 1951, PEPCO therefore agreed to a reduced program, limited to five or six crucial industries designed to attract personnel from the GDR who would be hard to replace. Yet interest in the project among HICOG officials in Berlin remained strong: when key officials in the new Eisenhower administration sought to expand U.S. defector programs in early 1953, HICOG's top East Germany watcher renewed his calls for fostering the "deliberate denial" of critical manpower to interfere with the planned economic development of the GDR. In the midst of the refugee crisis that engulfed the GDR that spring, Spencer Barnes argued for a defection program that would use covert channels, including the Free Jurists and the East Bureau, to encourage some 25,000 highly skilled workers to flee to the West. Apparently some type of targeted defection program was carried on without the explicit approval of the federal government. Well into the mid-1950s U.S, officials held onto hopes for an even larger-scale defection program to deprive the GDR of scarce scientists and technicians, only to run into West German opposition to the idea of encouraging mass refugee flows from across the "Iron Curtain."[66]

The Second Embargo

As HICOG began to plan and at least partially implement more aggressive economic rollback measures against the GDR, Moscow introduced a new bureaucratic procedure that had the potential to strangle Berlin's economic lifelines. In May 1951, Soviet authorities started requiring West Berlin–based firms to supply "certificates of origin" to accompany the WBS licenses submitted to the Soviet Control Commission in order to have the Soviets stamp and approve shipments of goods from West Berlin to the Federal Republic. In the Soviet view, the proof–of–origin certificates served to protect the GDR against the illegal flow of materials via the open border in Berlin to the West. It certainly provided the Soviet authorities with new pressure points on Berlin. The Soviet Control Commission refused to stamp Warenbegleitscheine for westbound goods from Berlin in seventeen critical commodity groups without detailed "proof of origin" of the raw materials used in various components of manufactured goods. By the end of May 1951, approximately 1,500 WBS had accumulated at Soviet headquarters in Berlin-Karlshorst. The West Berlin Senate (city government) was holding an additional 4,000 WBS pending clarification of the situation.[67]

For the Truman administration, the proof-of-origin requirements cut to the heart of Allied rights in Berlin: it was yet another Soviet tactic in the long-term strategy to undermine the Western position in the city. By demonstrating the West's vulnerability in Berlin, the new measure could serve Moscow as a lever to force a relaxation of the inflexible East-West trade approach advocated in the United States. Finally, the measure, U.S. officials surmised, would help build opposition to the Adenauer government and thus impede decisive legislative steps toward a West German defense contribution. Washington therefore firmly opposed recognizing the validity of the demand for proof-of-origin certificates. On May 31, the Allied High Commission decided that West Berlin companies should not yield to the new Soviet requirement. Playing what they believed to be the key countermeasure, on June 11, the West Berlin Commandants suspended the negotiations for a new inter-German trade agreement which had been carried on since the previous September.[68]

While the Truman administration favored a forceful response, West Berliners were less inclined to make an issue of the proof of origin. Berlin city leaders told the Western Allied Commandants on June 10 that in their view the situation was satisfactory since in fact only 40 percent of Berlin's shipments were affected, and that the certificates of origin were an acceptable demand. It turned out that the Berlin Senate had in fact returned the 4,000 WBS to the West Berlin firms, informally suggesting that they provide proof of origin to accompany the WBS and thus comply with the Soviet demand. Governing Mayor Ernst Reuter, who one week earlier had called on the Allied Commandants to express his concern, now told them that "the time was not ripe" for opposing the Soviets. Displaying a caution that sharply contrasted with his usual demand for firm reactions to Soviet encroachments, he argued that it might be better to "muddle along" five or six months longer until Berlin would be in a stronger position. Was this the time, Reuter asked, "to rock the boat if arrangements could in fact be made to keep trade flowing"?[69]

Allied officials warned against the West accepting such a "clear-cut violation" of the 1949 New York and Paris Agreements that had ended the blockade. The Allied Kommandatura instructed Reuter to start denying the new documentation. When the Soviet authorities returned more than 700 WBS forms unstamped two days later, McCloy and the State Department insisted that countermeasures were "essential."[70]

But even within Allied ranks consensus failed to materialize: The French High

Commissioner saw some merit in the Soviet claims to forestall the drain of scarce resources, and cautioned that the West might appear "as if they were protecting 'some sort of black market.'" The French government had little interest in provoking a fresh crisis over Berlin with national elections approaching on June 17. French officials were skeptical that the Allies could assert a clear violation of the Paris Agreement and suggested that the West had "already imposed a semi-blockade" upon itself. On his own, the French commandant sought out his Soviet counterpart to sound out the possibility of quadripartite discussions of the trade crisis. Privately, French officials questioned whether the Americans really wanted to resolve the current crisis. Adept at exploiting fissures in the Western Allied position, Moscow signaled that the French proposals could be the basis for a solution. Grudgingly, McCloy agreed for negotiations for a new inter-German trade agreement to resume in mid-June.[71]

McCloy's weakened hand was evident in the conditions he attached to a successful outcome of these negotiations. First, prior to any agreement the Bundesregierung had to institute a new "interzonal trade ordinance" that would finally give it complete control of practically all inter-German commodity movements and prevent the export of strategic and short-supply goods. Without it, HICOG officials internally admitted, any new agreement would be "essentially meaningless." No less important was, secondly, for the new agreement to stipulate free access to Berlin, but the administration was now willing to settle for an exchange of letters to that effect if a clause in the agreement was not obtainable. Third, the State Department insisted that an escape clause would be necessary to provide for the possibility of voiding the agreement if the Soviets or East Germans resumed trade restrictions. Under pressure from Congress and other parts of the administration to tighten East-West trade, the State Department threatened that it would not permit HICOG to approve a commodity exchange that did not comply with COCOM policies and provide at least as great an economic benefit to the Federal Republic and West Berlin as it did to East Germany. The latter indicated how much the administration had walked back its earlier, more ambitious goals.[72]

The negotiations soon deadlocked over the East Germans' outright refusal—as in the past—to combine the trade agreement with discussion on the Berlin traffic restrictions, as the West demanded. Orlopp, the East German negotiator, informed Kaumann that if agreement were not reached by July 3, "everything would collapse." With almost 8,000 WBS forms (valued at some DM 60–70 million and tied to some 50,000 jobs) awaiting approval by the Soviet Control Commission by the end of June, Washington in turn was inclined to bring the negotiations to a halt. As neither side was willing to budge, the existing temporary advance arrangement (totaling about 170 million clearing units each way) in place since January lapsed on July 3. After a flurry of meetings, a new draft agreement was on the table within days, notably without, as Washington had demanded, a resolution of the WBS matter. The draft trade agreement called for a commodity exchange of 482 million clearing units with a total swing of 30 million clearing units, covering the period from February to December 1951. Arguing that the deal was "probably the best that can be obtained," McCloy allowed the West German negotiators to "initial" the agreement on July 6. Allied approval and final signature of the trade deal would depend on prior clearing of the WBS backlog. Four days later, the SED Politburo consented to the new trade deal.[73]

McCloy's decision did not sit well with Washington. Over Secretary of State Dean Acheson's signature, a State Department cable informed HICOG that the administration was concerned that in their discussion with the Soviets, the Western Allies were giving a "cumulative false impression [of] weakness and over-eagerness." Rather than giving in, the State Department wanted to increase pressure on the East through new countermeasures, extending the embargo to "hard goods of high value," which was particularly crucial to fulfilling the GDR's Five-Year Plan. On July 12, Washington even suggested warning that a "total embargo," including all soft goods, would be imposed if the certificate-of-origin requirement were not rescinded. The next day, the Western Berlin commandants in fact threatened that an extended embargo would be instituted within days unless their Soviet counterpart removed the trade restrictions.[74]

Unfazed by the possibility of retaliation, however, the Soviets remained as reluctant as ever to stamping WBS, returning some 1,400 WBS unstamped on July 13, and 1,500 on July 15. By late July, some 12,000 tons of goods were held up for shipment to the Federal Republic, and by early August more than 10,000 WBS had been retained by the Soviet authorities. Carloads of parcel post were being prevented from entering or leaving West Berlin. In addition, the Rothensee shiplift along the Mittelland Canal, part of the main inland water route between Berlin and Western Germany, remained closed "for repairs." Soviet interference, the commandants warned, was creating an "increasingly serious economic and political situation in this city."[75]

Neither the French nor the West Germans were prepared to implement tougher countermeasures. The French government did not want "to close the door to negotiations" and raised doubts that any trade stoppage would be effective: time was not "yet ripe for any sanction to be imposed." To U.S. officials, Paris continued to appear "most anxious" to sign a new German-German trade agreement. Asked what his government would have done if it had been free to act independently of other allies, the French economic adviser gave the "unhesitating reply that they would, of course, have agreed to submit certificates of origin." To U.S. officials, the "apparent defeatist attitude" of the French government left the "inescapable" impression that the Soviets had succeeded in "working on Fr[ench], and with some success" to divide the Western Allies. American officials in Berlin warned that should the "united western front here" be broken by the French, "we may well be faced with [a] disastrous situation." At Washington's urging, the Allied High Commission in mid-July publicly demanded a return to the status quo prior to the requirement for certificates of origin, triggering a new round of GDR electricity interruptions in response.[76]

West German support for a tougher policy was similarly tenuous. HICOG officials credited a "massive Soviet propaganda campaign" that sought to persuade German public opinion that U.S. policy to curtail trade with the Soviet orbit was to blame for the impasse in trade negotiations. The Adenauer cabinet finally, after being pressed by Washington for a "very long time," drafted and approved a new government ordinance to allow for more-effective control of inter-German trade. But even after the trade agreement had been initialed on July 6, the ordinance had yet to be signed by Adenauer and published in the federal registry—a requirement for it to take effect.[77]

Rather than tightening the trade screws on East Berlin, the Adenauer government had relaxed its trade restrictions within days of the initialing of the new trade agreement, approving new Warenbegleitscheine for West German "soft commodities" to the GDR—which included key commodities such as rubber, chemicals, and machinery. The Länder Economics Ministries, moreover, extended the validity of all WBS that had been issued prior to July 3, when the advance agreement had lapsed. British intelligence picked up information that suggested the West German Treuhandstelle was even facilitating "special barter contracts" with the East which had generally been prohibited. Kaumann, meanwhile, sought out Orlopp to obtain his agreement to a letter that outlined a new WBS procedure and would allow for the final signature of the trade deal. Objecting to the letter, the Americans forced Kaumann to cancel the meeting.[78]

The Truman administration's difficulties were compounded by its failure to understand what exactly was happening "on the ground." Since the spring, there had been complaints within HICOG about the "inadequacy of economic intelligence" to formulate policy. U.S. officials finally caught on that West Berlin firms were circumventing Allied orders not to voluntarily submit certificates of origin, which explained at least in part why the Soviet Control Commission approved a few WBS. (An Allied penalty ordinance that would punish such behavior was kept "on ice," as it was "bound to stir up widespread resentment" at a crucial time when the commandants were eager to create and preserve public approval for the Allied stance.) Similarly, Washington also learned that West Berlin firms were submitting multiple WBS applications to the Soviets, hopeful that at least some would be approved. Hence it was hard to assess with some confidence how severe the backlog actually was. American officials also professed "ignorance of the situation" as it existed on the GDR–West German border.[79]

In the face of these inter-Allied and Allied-German disagreements, the Truman administration sought to rekindle memories of the last time a united West had successfully overcome a Soviet challenge to Berlin. Despite its air cargo capacity being severely limited due to the conflict in Korea, Washington announced a commercial "airlift" starting July 27, flying 2,800 tons of goods that had been held up out of the city within the first month, and more than 6,600 tons by mid-October. Though relatively small and largely symbolic, the airlift, it was hoped, would have "beneficial psychological effect" on the West Berliners, serve as a "good propaganda weapon," and signal the Soviets that "we mean business."[80]

Undaunted by Allied and German cautions and misgivings, the administration continued to believe that the non-signature of the trade agreement represented an "extremely strong bargaining weapon." It also decided to sharpen the embargo's edge: extending the embargo to include spare parts and engineering products, and enforcing it more rigorously. Washington enthusiastically endorsed the proposals by HICOG's Eastern Element to extend the existing trade embargo to critical "soft" commodities, such as certain machinery, chemicals, and rubber products. Any escalation of the Soviet threat to West Berlin's "lifeline" just before the GDR-sponsored World Youth Festival, to take place in Berlin in August, would, U.S. officials argued, effectively undercut the latest Soviet peace offensive and induce another blow after the failure of the anti-remilitarization plebiscite. Under pressure from Washington, the Allied High Commission agreed and launched a new embargo on August 3, 1951.[81]

Western intelligence agencies soon confirmed that thanks to the cessation of trade and embargo East Germany was encountering production difficulties and delays in sensitive reparation and export orders. British intelligence suggested that the loss of critical imports from the West had hurt the GDR economy even more than the quantitative loss of trade would suggest. Particular shortages, it was reported, included screws, chains, magnets, spare parts and components for machine tools and compressors, rubber cables, cables for dredges, ball-bearing rods, boiler tubs, wheel tires and electrodes, sheets for motor vehicles and grinding agents. A measure of how badly the embargo stung the GDR economy, the intelligence reports suggested, was the uptick in East German efforts to evade the embargo through illegal imports and pressure on the West German government to ease the restrictions.[82]

Moreover, stricter control procedures inaugurated by the West German government based on Military Government Law 53, seemed to have made the embargo more effective, HICOG reported: a reorganized central licensing agency had been staffed up, its employees properly "indoctrinate[d]" by Allied officials, and a new "restricted list" was published in the official *Bundesanzeiger*. HICOG inspections of German border controls along the Eastern frontier indicated that the Germans were making genuine efforts to implement the new procedures. Reassured by the presumptive success of the embargo, the State Department asserted that the Western bargaining position was sufficiently strong "so that any solution which fails to achieve our minimum demands"—the return of outstanding Warenbegleitscheine by the time of signature of the trade agreement—was deemed "unacceptable."[83]

In Berlin, discussions between Kaumann and Orlopp had meanwhile focused on developing a mechanism for joint investigations into questionable WBS cases as a way to resolve the dispute. Washington strongly resisted any solution that implied the legitimacy of Soviet claims to be entitled to object to deliveries from West Berlin to the Federal Republic. Once accepted, State Department officials reasoned, the West would be at the whim of "any objections the Soviets might dream up" and thus give the Soviets a "veto" over West Berlin trade. By late August, however, the Allied High Commission had resigned itself to the fact that the East would not formally agree to make the continuation of trade contingent on unimpeded Berlin access. Not even in an exchange of letters: The most that could be achieved was a unilateral Western statement to the East Germans on the conditions under which inter-German trade would be carried out. Escalating the pressure on the negotiations, the GDR authorities instituted a heavy new tax on German highway traffic between Berlin and the Federal Republic on September 1. Frustrated by weeks spent "in vain haggling," the U.S. Commandant in Berlin was ready to "[cut] the Gordian knot" and sign the agreement, along with a transmittal letter to the GDR authorities that stated Western conditions. Washington, however, did not approve: "Western hesitation or vacillation has never gained anything from [the] Sov[iets] except more trouble."[84]

By September, the West Germans insisted on immediate signature of the draft agreement. Adenauer and Reuter, and even Federal President Theodor Heuss, personally impressed upon McCloy the need for prompt signature even without any additional oral or written conditions on Berlin access. With fall weather setting in, German officials worried about vital brown coal deliveries from the East to

Berlin. Once trade resumed, they argued, the Soviets would be less likely to risk its suspension through renewed harassment. The powerful Federal Association of German Industry publicly appealed to Erhard to reopen trade with the East. Bonn government officials also resisted Allied planning for retaliation against the new GDR highway tax, arguing that countermeasures, such as imposing taxes on East German–owned barges in the Western sectors of Berlin and levying a federal tax on GDR road transports in West German territory, would be "pointless" and possibly provoke "extremely dangerous countermeasures" by the East.[85]

After the Kaumann-Orlopp talks settled on creating a mixed committee composed of representatives of the Treuhandstelle and the Soviet Kommandatura that would jointly verify controversial WBS, the Western high commissioners agreed to the signing of the trade deal. As a face-saving gesture, it was also agreed that Adenauer would assure the AHC the next day in writing that GDR officials had verbally accepted Western conditions for the resumption of trade. The agreement that would constitute the basic framework for trade between the two parts of Germany until 1990 was finally signed on September 20, 1951.[86]

As East and West Germans were affixing their signatures to the Berlin agreement, administration officials in Washington objected to the course of action approved by HICOG: a merely oral declaration would put the Western powers in a weak position in case it became necessary to suspend the agreement. Hence they felt "strongly" that the agreement should not be signed unless the West German statement to Orlopp at the time of signing would be made in writing, and unless Orlopp's acceptance was clear. But it was too late. By the time the cable reached McCloy, the agreement had been signed. All that McCloy could do was to assure Washington that U.S. conditions had been put in writing to the East on July 6, had been repeated privately and publicly, and accepted "explicitly" by Orlopp, who, McCloy added, had been "frequently in touch with [GDR premier] Grotewohl." Confronted with McCloy's fait accompli, the State Department took until September 26 to formally agree to signature. With little faith in Soviet compliance, officials there added that the immediate future would probably be the best time to lodge protests effectively.[87]

Initially the trade agreement seemed to work: a new GDR highway tax was drastically reduced to a level "acceptable to the West," confiscations abated, and interference with parcel post shipments fell to a point where it was a "nuisance rather than a threat." East German newspaper reports hinted at the possibility that the Rothensee ship lift might be reopened before it had to close for winter. But within a month it became clear to the Americans that the signing of the trade agreement had not led to an improvement in the Berlin situation. By early October the Soviet Control Commission still held more than 8,000 WBS, half of which had been submitted since September 20. Rather than expediting the processing of the permits, the Soviets "actually have intensified their delaying tactics." In the third week of October some 5,356 WBS were returned unstamped by the Soviets without any reference to the procedure established when the Berlin Agreement was signed. The East German negotiators refused to discuss restrictions on Berlin trade and communications, arguing that these matters were "exclusively for consideration by the four powers."[88]

By mid-October the Truman administration was once again urging immediate suspension of the new trade agreement—and any movements of goods. British High Commissioner Kirkpatrick, speaking for the AHC, told Erhard that it was essential for the West German authorities to demonstrate their solidarity with the Allies in taking countermeasures: "Doing nothing" would lead to "continued Soviet encroachment, the paralysis of Berlin trade and the eventual acquisition by peaceful means of Berlin by the Russians." Even the West German negotiators agreed that fulfillment of the trade agreement was "less satisfactory than ever," but the Bundes-regierung still refused to suspend the agreement immediately. Bonn's position was in fact precisely one of "doing nothing": no efforts would be made to start trade under the new agreement. West German officials proclaimed that more-active measures would run the "considerable risk of retaliation, including the possibility of another blockade." Rather than making a "propaganda demonstration," most West German officials favored giving the East more time to demonstrate compliance with the Adenauer letter and simply letting trade "fade out."[89]

The AHC resolved to discuss the "unsatisfactory" situation with the chancel-lor, but not till November 7 was McCloy able to get Adenauer to agree to a set of "countermeasures" that amounted to a new embargo to take effect on November 12: no new WBS for pig iron, rolling mill products, iron and steel sheets, steel and iron machinery, and rubber would be issued, none revalidated, and a substantial amount of revalidated WBS would be revoked. But Adenauer seemed detached from the issue, leaving it to his Economics Ministry to implement the measures, the attitude of which U.S. officials characterized as one of "concession and accommo-dation" toward the East. Almost immediately circumventing the countermeasures, the Adenauer government exempted certain shipments from the embargo—such as DM 15 million worth of cast-iron pipe, which the GDR claimed was needed for water mains in the area of Halle and Bitterfeld to avoid an outbreak of typhus; and the sale of fish surplus, despite the known "record of the fishing firms as illegal East-West traders."[90]

Within days of the new embargo measures, Kroll and Stoph met secretly to find a way out of the impasse. U.S. officials were uncertain as to who Stoph was, as to who had initiated the discussions—or when exactly they took place—and, once informed, learned that the West Germans, rather than getting the Eastern side to abandon the trade restrictions, had held out additional Western concessions on "outstanding questions," such as some 108 blacklisted machinery shipments, a major increase of the cast-iron pipes, a speed-up of pig iron deliveries, and joint examination of transit trade through Federal Republic territory, all of which U.S. officials vigorously opposed.[91]

British and French officials, too, stymied the administration's efforts to assure an effective embargo. British officials did not want to "clamp down on" the ongoing interzonal shipments for fear of exacerbating Allied–West German differences at the very moment that Washington, London, and Paris were negotiating with Bonn about a German defense contribution. They preferred to let the Germans "stew in their own juice" and let the embargo issue "simmer" for a while. Similarly, the French government seemed to U.S. officials to favor leaving the initiative in German-German trade matters to the West Germans, whose "timidity . . . apparently suits them." McCloy could only report that at no time had there existed Allied-German or even real Allied unity: "This state of affairs must undoubtedly be known to [the] Sov[iet]s."[92]

By the turn of the year, there was a growing sense among Truman administration officials that the embargo had largely lost its effectiveness as a weapon against Soviet interference with Berlin's lifeline. The experience of the preceding six months, U.S. officials in Berlin surmised, had no doubt strengthened Soviet assumptions that any embargo would not be long-lived. "The trade embargo, the last remaining major weapon against Soviet harassment of Berlin communications, has been lost," HICOG officials pessimistically concluded. Time was running out, as the GDR seemed to gain economic independence and became less vulnerable to Western pressures.[93]

In the midst of delicate negotiations for German rearmament and new contractual arrangements to replace the occupation statute, maintaining Allied-German unity was uppermost on McCloy's mind: "I feel that we cannot . . . permit [the] present disturbing state of disunity to continue." Arguing that it would be better to initiate such a course rather than having his hand forced by the Allies, McCloy now proposed permitting the resumption of German-German trade—on the condition that the Allies and West Germans would agree to impose a complete embargo immediately in the case of substantial future harassment of access to Berlin. The U.S. initiative would demonstrate that the United States was not out to restrict East-West (German) trade beyond the point needed to assure free access to Berlin. Following McCloy's proposal, the Allied High Commission formally approved the resumption of inter-German trade within the framework of the Berlin agreement on February 1, 1952.[94]

The frustrating experience with the two inter-German trade embargoes had a profound effect on U.S. policy in Germany. The embargoes of 1950 and 1951 demonstrated that using West German economic leverage over the GDR was limited in its effect to counter Soviet efforts to make the Western Allied position in Berlin untenable, not to speak of destabilizing the GDR economically. Washington and its European allies had had great difficulties in restricting the flow of trade between the two Germanies, legal and illegal, effectively, and in carrying on even a limited embargo for an extended period of time. Compared to the "almost empty" West's arsenal of local countermeasures, Stalin had at his disposal a whole spectrum of "harassments" of Berlin communications that could destabilize the city economically and psychologically but fell short of a full blockade that might have evoked more extreme Western military reactions.

This became clear in the spring of 1952, when a number of incidents, including an attack on an Air France aircraft and Soviet stoppage of movements by Allied military police along the Berlin-Helmstedt autobahn, suggested to McCloy that the Soviets were planning "to terrorize the West Germans and embarrass the Allies" to prevent signing of the Bonn and Paris Treaties. "Heightened militancy" on the part of the SED regime underscored the high commissioner's concern: On May 8, GDR premier Otto Grotewohl warned the West Germans of a "fratricidal war of Germans against Germans" should the General Treaty be signed; GDR government spokesman Gerhard Eisler demanded riots and protest strikes in West Germany; and SED party boss Walter Ulbricht threatened "Volksrache" (people's revenge) against the West German leaders. McCloy even expected the East Germans to sabotage the Rhine bridge in Essen, a key link in the U.S. supply lines for Berlin. In light of the shrill statements from the East, West German courage, thought McCloy, was "understandably thin." (See chapter 7.)[95]

McCloy's request, "as a matter of extreme urgency," for instructions as to how to deal with the potential threats threat against Berlin spurred a hectic planning effort within the Truman administration to develop new contingency plans for Berlin. The result, NSC directive 132/1, adopted by the National Security Council on June 11, 1952, set out a fairly complex system of contingencies and countermeasures. To deter a "Soviet harassing measures or a full blockade, the NSC called for demonstrating Western commitment to the city by public reaffirmations as well as and black and gray propaganda, building up and maintaining a six-month stockpile (later changed into a staggered, phased twelve-month stockpile), and preparing for a massive airlift by improving airfields. Significantly, NSC 132/1 discarded the option of a military "probing action" to test Soviet intentions that had been advocated by Clay in 1948 and more recently by McCloy. Instead, the directive emphasized economic reprisals, complemented by diplomatic and covert actions. Reflecting the administration's experience with inter-German trade embargos, NSC 132/1 cautioned that these reprisals did not need to be local ones, "particularly since East Germany was becoming increasingly less vulnerable to the measures of economic retaliation employed up to now."[96]

Projecting firmness, the Truman administration followed much of the script: Visiting Berlin at the end of June, Acheson restated the tripartite guarantee and assured the Germans of the United States' "abiding interest in the protection of Berlin." To increase Western staying power, the administration checked and accelerated the stockpiling program in cooperation with the Adenauer government. By June, a six-month stockpile was complete, except for a shortage in coal, and the achievement of a twelve-month stockpile could be expected by April 1953. The Air Force confirmed that it was ready to lift 600–700 tons daily to Berlin in the first thirty days of a blockade, was capable of more than doubling these figures thereafter, and was undeterred by potential Soviet "jamming."[97]

Yet when it came to economic countermeasures, the Truman administration quickly realized that short of a full-fledged blockade, there existed few effective economic measures adequate to counteract Soviet harassments. The State Department believed that a "trade counterblockade" by the Federal Republic alone would be "ineffective and inadvisable" in light of growing trade possibilities through third countries, and HICOG Berlin officials discounted local countermeasures. Some thought was given at Foggy Bottom to economic countermeasures in West Germany, such as curtailing Soviet overflight rights or restricting the Kiel Canal or the lower Elbe River to "Bloc vessels." The administration eventually ruled out localized (i.e., solely West German or West Berlin) countermeasures against East Germany altogether. Interdepartmental explorations of economic reprisals on a global basis had also reached rather "pessimistic conclusions." Even the economic effect of a multilaterally construed set of countermeasures would not be "the major factor in determining the Kremlin's execution of a policy to harass or blockade Berlin."[98]

The American dilemma crystallized in July 1952, when, just weeks after the kidnapping of the Free Jurists' Walter Linse had unsettled Berliners, the Soviet Control Commission again closed the Rothensee ship in what U.S officials viewed as an escalating "creeping campaign of harassments" to demoralize Berliners. Unable to find any countermeasures that would not turn into a "war of reprisals" that was "almost sure to turn out worse for Berlin in the long run," the Western Berlin commandants fell back on the last remaining measure: "bottling up" East German barges within the Western sectors on the pretense of repair work that would involve blocking the passage. As long as East German construction of a canal bypass had not yet been completed, blocking the canal to GDR barges was the last remaining effective local countermeasure against East German pressures. But even this "most important" potential weapon was expected to be lost as the GDR canal bypass around the city would be completed in the following months. After yet another review of other countermeasures, the State Department was left to instruct its diplomats in Germany that "in fact our possibilities in this connection likely in practice prove not as great as has been generally supposed."[99]

The growing realization of how hollow the administration's countermeasure prowess vis-à-vis Soviet and East German actions actually was subtly began to influence the American approach to East Germany. West Berlin and, albeit to a lesser degree, West Germany seemed increasingly vulnerable to Soviet–East German pressure while the GDR's economy became increasingly immune to West German influence. Deprived of any effective response against "creeping" Soviet or East German restrictions on access, Truman administration officials came to realize that a long-term solution would have to involve "dealing" with East Germany. Notionally this ran counter to nonrecognition and certainly to any rollback efforts, yet in time Washington would come to realize that other players on this stage, particularly East German officials, had gained a greater degree of control of the access routes. Despite the 1953 eruption that would shake the GDR to its core, within little more than a year, secret Western Allied contingency plans called for recognizing the authority of GDR officials in access-route control as "Soviet agents."[100]

The transformation of the GDR into a socialist state, announced by Ulbricht at the July 1952 SED conference, persuaded the Truman administration to expect future problems from a further isolation of West Berlin from the Soviet sector and its GDR hinterland rather than direct interference with the city's communications with the West. The long-term repercussions for Berliners, and Germans in general, of shutting down contact and access to East Germany were no less dire than the immediate threats of access harassment and blockade, yet they required a very different response—one that transformed German-German trade from an economic weapon into a tool for contact and aid. The American experience with a food aid program launched on the heels of the June 1953 uprising—the subject of Chapter 9—became a catalyst for this shift in approach.

"Roll Them Out for Keeps"

The United States and the 1953 East German Uprising

ON JULY 9, 1952, SED leader Walter Ulbricht stepped in front of the Second SED Party Conference in Werner-Seelenbinder Hall in East Berlin and, in a seven-hour speech, announced the party leadership's decision to embark on the "planned construction of socialism." The Conference proclaimed that the decision necessitated a heightening of the "class struggle." To American observers at the time, the dramatic, book-length speech, and the congress's resolutions, seemed designed for shock effect in Western Germany, but even so also signified a "turning point" in Soviet policy in Germany, "heralding the transformation of the GDR into a people's democracy."[1]

In fact, the new policy continued the SED's course since the late 1940s, but did so with stepped-up pace and more aggressive methods. In early April 1952, Stalin had told the East German leaders to "organize an independent state." The Soviet leader demanded that they turn the relatively open demarcation line between East and West Germany into a "border" and that everything needed to be done to "strengthen the defense of this border." Stalin also decreed the creation of an East German army—"without making much noise"—announcing that the "pacifist period" was over. Finally, he also sanctioned the crash socialization of GDR agriculture and industry, but "even now they should not shout about socialism."[2]

Other east-central European countries had already adopted this course, above all seeking to promote rapid short-term economic growth. By late 1952, however, the devastating effects of these policies—in both human and economic terms—had gradually become evident, even to Moscow. Toward the end of that year, Moscow officials were receiving a growing number of reports about economic dislocations and popular unrest throughout east-central Europe. Soviet diplomatic and intelligence sources described a state of "near-total chaos" in the Czechoslovak economy, "severe deficiencies" in Hungary, and "extremely detrimental conditions and disruption" in Romania. Local Communist rulers maintained control only through massive expansion of the largely Soviet-run security apparatus, purges, and show trials.[3]

In East Germany, too, the forced socialization in industry and agriculture brought society and economy to the brink of collapse by early 1953. The regime had levied prohibitive taxes against remaining small and medium-size private enterprises in trade and industry, implemented massive confiscations of private properties, and coerced the remaining independent and wealthier farmers into collectivist "agricultural production cooperatives." Heavy industry was given unequivocal priority over consumer goods production. All of it led to food shortages and other hardships throughout the GDR, such as frequent electricity outages or heating cutoffs, that affected virtually the entire population. The regime also targeted the churches, especially the dominant Protestant Church. The FDJ organ *Junge Welt* defamed Protestant youth groups as "front organizations" for "warmongering, sabotage and espionage at the behest of the USA." The buildup of armed forces, now pursued openly, the closing of the border to West Germany, and the forceful relocation of population in the border area added to the brutal assault on society by the authorities.

The October 1952 GDR Law on the Protection of People's Property justified exorbitant penal sentences for minor wrongdoings or disobedience. As prisons were filling up with the victims of socialist criminal "justice," an unprecedented number of East Germans fled to West Germany. While some 166,000 people turned their backs on the regime in 1951, and 182,000 in 1952, in the first four months of 1953, according to internal GDR statistics, some 122,000 East Germans left. As the Soviet intelligence chief informed the Soviet Communist Party's Politburo, the GDR no longer held "any attraction to citizens of West Germany." Eager to close the last escape valve—the still open sector crossings in Berlin—and to put pressure on the Western powers, the SED leadership proposed to take the drastic measure of virtually closing off the border between the Eastern and Western sectors early in 1953, thus foreshadowing the construction of the Berlin Wall in 1961.[4]

The growing crisis in East Germany coincided with the epochal change of leadership in the USSR: on March 5, 1953, Stalin died. The new "collective leadership" that succeeded him, headed by Georgy Malenkov, Lavrenty Beria, Nikita Khrushchev, and Vyacheslav Molotov, seemed prepared to break with Stalin's hard-line and paranoid rule, which had placed the Soviet Union on the defensive worldwide, and moved to set Soviet foreign policy on a calmer and more flexible track. On March 15, Malenkov, chairman of the USSR Council of Ministers, announced before a session of the Supreme Soviet that there was "no litigious or unresolved question which could not be settled by peaceful means."

Caught unprepared by Stalin's death, officials within the newly inaugurated administration of President Dwight D. Eisenhower doubted that the speech or Moscow's other conciliatory gestures indicated a basic change in Soviet policies and long-range objectives. But in the following weeks, the USSR signaled readiness for a truce in Korea, waived its long-standing claim for control of Turkish territory, called off the "hate America campaign" in the Soviet media, and even hinted at its interest in a U.S.-Soviet summit on disarmament and other issues. The new Moscow leadership seemed to recognize the need for drastic changes in Soviet policies toward east-central Europe that would help stabilize the deteriorating situation in the region.[5]

In Germany, American observers noted steps to ease the contentious traffic problem around Berlin and calls for quadripartite negotiations on safety in the Berlin air corridors. The Soviets also reopened the Rothensee ship-lock, which had been closed since August. Suddenly the backlog of trucks on the Helmstedt/ Marienborn autobahn crossing point at the East-West German border was cleared, and the stamping of the *Warenbegleitscheine* necessary for interzonal trade transactions rapidly increased. The dramatic change of atmosphere in Moscow heralded by Malenkov's speech had the new U.S. ambassador in Moscow, Charles E. Bohlen, surmising that things seemed to be "building up towards a new offer on Germany,"— possibly even, "with Stalin gone . . . a really big one involving Soviet withdrawal from Eastern Germany."[6]

It is not clear when the East German leadership was informed of any changes in Kremlin policy toward the GDR. Unaware of the Kremlin's intentions—or perhaps in an effort to preempt any changes—Ulbricht, in an article in the main party paper, *Neues Deutschland*, published on March 8 (the day before Stalin's funeral), reasserted his fervent determination to proceed with the accelerated program of building socialism, including the creation of national armed forces, and he took pains to attribute these policies to Stalin directly. With the backing of General Vasily I. Chuikov, the commander in chief of the Soviet occupation forces in Germany, and Vladimir Semenov, political adviser to the Soviet Control Commission, Ulbricht also renewed an earlier request for Moscow's authorization to place border guards along the sector border between West and East Berlin, continuing his efforts to isolate the Western "outpost" in the heart of the GDR.[7]

But once back from Stalin's funeral, Ulbricht fell noticeably silent. Grotewohl had apparently received his first inklings of the new Soviet leadership's intentions in Moscow: for now the GDR would be left to its own devices to deal with its economic difficulties. A few days later, Moscow denied Ulbricht a "green light" on any further measures of "border protection" along the sector line in Berlin. The Soviet Control Commission was instructed to explain "tactfully" to the SED that the "grossly simplistic" measures they were proposing would interrupt the "established order of city life," would "create bitterness among the Berliners and produce economic dislocations, and, most importantly, place in doubt the sincerity of the policy of the Soviet government and the GDR government, which are actively and consistently supporting the unification of Germany and the conclusion of a peace treaty." Closing borders, Moscow declared, would present a "clear disadvantage" in the USSR's relations with the Western powers.[8]

Similarly, Moscow's propaganda directives for the month of April apparently admonished the East Berlin press to cease its vitriolic attacks against the Western powers and to focus their attention on Adenauer as an opponent to the peaceful solution of the German question. The Soviet Control Commission also forced a scaling back of the massive numbers of arrests and trials the SED regime had inaugurated under the pretext of enforcing a law for the protection of people's property.[9]

By mid-April Ulbricht had somehow managed to reassure himself of Moscow's support, possibly by soft-pedaling some of the harshest features of SED policy. On April 10, the USSR reduced the level of compulsory GDR shipments from Soviet enterprises in East Germany, and three days later granted East Berlin further economic support. In his first major policy pronouncements since the March 8 statement, Ulbricht reiterated in two *Neues Deutschland* articles, on April 15 and 16, that the construction of socialism in the GDR remained the most important contribution to peace and German unity, although he made no reference to the creation of armed forces or to any restrictive measures around Berlin. American observers detected "noticeably more restraint in tone than [the] usual Ulbricht style," including his reaffirmation of the voluntary nature of the production cooperatives and admission of mistakes by local courts and party officials in dealing with small and middle-class farmers. But the "de-dramatized" program, they noted, still stressed increases in productivity, especially in heavy industry. The "striking feature" of Ulbricht's pronouncements, U.S. officials noted, was how they fit "neatly into the changed tactical position currently being followed by Moscow."[10]

Despite the elimination of some of the "frightening features" of SED policy, the party continued to put pressure on large segments of the population. On the political level, the regime sharpened the battle against potential centers of opposition within East German society, such as the churches. In mid-May, after the January arrest of GDR foreign minister Georg Dertinger, the 13th SED Central Committee

Plenum ousted Ulbricht's main rival within the leadership, Franz Dahlem, whom the SED strongman accused of "Slánskýism," a reference to the purged Czechoslovak Communist leader who had been executed as an "Anglo-American spy" in December 1952. The SED also renewed its drive for austerity, "vigilance" against foreign enemies, and internal party discipline; reinforced efforts to increase industrial productivity and the viability of the existing agricultural production collectives and launched new measures to undermine the existence of small entrepreneurs. Ignoring the signs of growing dissatisfaction among the population, the Politburo had the SED Central Committee adopt a 10 percent compulsory raise in industrial work norms, effective June 1. The GDR Council of Ministers eventually decreed the norm increase "recommended" by the Central Committee, but changed the date for it to go into force to June 30, Ulbricht's birthday.[11]

In Washington, the shape of Eisenhower's response to the new Soviet leadership was the subject of a fierce debate between Secretary of State John Foster Dulles and the Special Assistant for Psychological Warfare, C. D. Jackson. The situation was further complicated by British Prime Minister Winston Churchill's proposal in mid-March for a diplomatic opening vis-à-vis the Soviets. Eisenhower settled on a major speech in mid-April, titled "A Chance for Peace," that demanded "deeds, not words" from Moscow. The administration followed events in the GDR closely to see whether they held any clue to the Soviets' real intentions.

Given how starkly Ulbricht's March 8 restatement of hard-line policies had contrasted with the Soviet peace campaign developed *after* Stalin's funeral, HICOG officials surmised that Ulbricht's emphasis on the necessity to develop national armed forces might have represented an "independent decision of Ulbricht not cleared with the new Kremlin leaders." German intelligence sources confirmed American suspicions that Ulbricht was "strictly a Stalin man," not liked by any of the other Kremlin leaders, and now facing one of the most serious trials of his career: establishing himself firmly with the new Moscow leadership. Rumors about his volatile position persisted; information from the SPD East Bureau in Berlin predicted that Ulbricht "might be sacrificed by [the] Soviets." Other signs suggested that Ulbricht "had his wings clipped somewhat by Moscow." But however much out of step with Moscow Ulbricht had been, by mid-April it appeared that coordination between East Berlin and Moscow had been fully realigned: U.S. officials had "every indication that Moscow [was] exercising complete control of SED policy and actions."[12]

In fact, American observers came to believe that the SED, led by Ulbricht, was firmly in control of developments in the GDR—but ironically, that occurred precisely at the moment when SED control in fact started to unravel. Symptomatic of the degree to which American analysts overestimated the stability of the GDR was the fact that they did not initially consider the rapidly increasing influx of refugees into West Germany from the East in early 1953 to be indicative of how quickly the situation in the GDR was deteriorating. In the eyes of U.S. officials, the growing flood of refugees pouring into Berlin was a sign of the East Germans' decreasing energy to resist. The government remained firmly in control: HICOG Berlin's Eastern Affairs Division had reported to Washington as early as February that it could not be expected "that even if called upon to do so, the East Germans would be willing and capable of carrying out a revolution unless such a call coincided with a declaration of war and/or assurance of Western military support."[13]

As the stream of East Germans seeking refuge in the West took on massive proportions that spring, the Eisenhower administration even considered the developments to be a deliberate measure by the SED regime rather than a reflection of the dire situation in the GDR. "It is my opinion that Commies have capabilities of cutting [the refugee] stream drastically," the newly appointed U.S. high commissioner in Germany, former Harvard president James B. Conant, pronounced. Panic therefore marked the initial American reaction to the flood of refugees. In February, Conant estimated that more than 300,000 East Germans would cross the border to the West (largely through Berlin) within the next hundred days. Despite a small airlift that flew about 1,000 refugees out of the city to West Germany every day, HICOG Berlin predicted that space in West Berlin was "bound to become tight" and that the "danger of epidemics" as well as the "possibility of riots and disturbances inspired either by general discontent or Communists" could not be discounted.[14]

HICOG therefore unilaterally considered plans for a "crash evacuation" of refugees utilizing military aircraft and recommended a $100 million loan to the Federal Republic. In addition, HICOG pressed for changes in the Federal Republic's liberal refugee recognition policy, which had resulted in an accumulation of a large number of unregistered refugees. Faced with the possibility that the influx of refugees might reach "staggering numbers," propelling the problem to "disaster proportions" and straining West German resources beyond their limits, Conant briefly considered abandoning the long-established American policy of treating the refugee problem as a German internal problem, the burden of which had to be carried by the West Germans themselves.[15]

By April, however, when Chancellor Adenauer arrived in Washington for his first visit to the United States (the first such visit by a top German leader since the war) and pleaded for economic assistance in the amount of $250 million for coping with the refugee crisis, U.S. apprehensions had been largely alleviated. West

Germany seemed able to manage the influx economically, and it had also become obvious that the refugees were causing serious embarrassment and problems for the SED. U.S. observers concluded that the Soviets had overestimated the effectiveness of propaganda and dissuasion in stemming the refugee flood but considered extreme and drastic measures politically unfeasible. If the Western Allies exercised ingenuity, imagination, and determination to prevent the refugee flow from becoming a security problem in West Berlin, they could "turn potential danger into [a] positive asset" and "embarrass seriously and hurt Soviet-SED strategy and tactics in Ger[many]." Consequently, the Eisenhower administration stuck to established policy and denied West Germany any extra aid for the refugees, discharging its special responsibilities for Berlin by earmarking a mere $15 million for refugee relief.[16]

Still, Ulbricht's removal from the scene and a radical change in the GDR's internal makeup seemed to American observers nearly unimaginable in view of his long-standing relationship with the Moscow leaders. Equally unimaginable was the change in Moscow's long-range objectives in Germany that Ulbricht's ouster would suggest. In March, HICOG's GDR watchers had warned that despite a "mellowing process" there were no signs that the basic tenets of Stalinist communism had been abandoned, and "a reversion of aggressive expansionism may be anticipated at a later date." Within a few weeks, American officials confirmed their earlier impressions: the SED apparatus was implementing "what amounts to basically the same internal SED program as before, with some slight outward modifications."[17]

In fact, East Germany's future course was under intense review within the Soviet leadership in Moscow in the spring of 1953. The available documentary record is still fragmentary but suggests that the discussions within the Soviet government initially aimed at boosting the prestige of the East German regime *and* renewing Soviet initiative on the question of German unity. Some senior Soviet foreign ministry officials proposed inviting a GDR government delegation to Moscow headed by Grotewohl, as such a visit would "increase the authority of the GDR." Semenov, who had been urgently recalled to Moscow, recommended the removal of the Soviet military authorities' control over the GDR as "clear, practical proof of the sincerity of the Soviet government's proposals on German unity." Most of the ideas put forth warmed up earlier proposals for the formation of an all-German government.[18]

In remarkable symmetry to the GDR watchers at HICOG, the Soviet government's foremost Germany expert, Semenov, also overestimated the extent to which the SED was in control of the situation in the GDR. He believed that the East German government had "by now grown and strengthened to a sufficient degree to govern the country independently." While the Eisenhower administration was worrying about Soviet–East German machinations behind the swelling refugee flow, Moscow apparently did not become aware of how dramatically the refugee crisis was unfolding in the GDR until May. That the Soviet government was blind-sided may have resulted partly from the efforts of KGB head Lavrenty Beria after Stalin's death to revamp the security apparatus, but part of it could also have been attributed to the reorganization and eventual dismantling of the Soviet Control Commission that spring.[19]

Alarming Soviet intelligence reports from East Germany finally spurred the Soviet Communist Party Presidium to act. In mid-May, it instructed the SCC to "tactfully" advise Ulbricht and Grotewohl that collectivization in East Germany should be halted "for at least the rest of the year." Another fortnight hence, the Soviet leaders decided to abandon the policy of "forced construction of socialism" in East Germany altogether in order to avert a full-blown crisis. Far less tactfully, they expressed their "grave concern about the situation in the GDR" to a delegation of SED leaders hastily summoned to Moscow and handed down a sharply critical order, "On Measures to Improve the Health of the Political Situation in the GDR," which rescinded many of the most repressive and brutal measures.

For their less-radical counterproposal, defensively drafted overnight, the East Germans took a verbal beating the next day: "Our document is [a] reversal, yours is [just] reform," an exasperated Lazar Kaganovich (a Presidium member) exclaimed, and Beria allegedly threw the documents at Ulbricht across the table with the remark "This is a bad rewrite of our document!" Demanding that the SED leaders should "not worry about [their] prestige," Malenkov warned that "if we don't correct [the political line] now, a catastrophe will happen." Upon returning to Berlin, the SED leaders drew up a statement on "the self-criticism of the work of the Politburo and the Secretariat," and publicly announced a "New Course" liberalization in *Neues Deutschland* on June 11.[20]

The New Course communiqué, in its wide-ranging policy shift and frank admission of past mistakes, came as a shock to many party members and the East German public. Reports from local party organizations, carefully monitored by SED headquarters in Berlin, candidly described the widespread disappointment, disbelief, and confusion within party ranks, as well as among the populace. To many, the communiqué signaled the SED's final bankruptcy and the beginning of its demise. Party members felt betrayed and "panicky"; some even called for Ulbricht's resignation. Many thought the SED retreat from crash socialization resulted from pressure by the West. In the small town of Seehausen, according to a local SED account, "the entire village is in the bar, drinking to the health of Adenauer." Another internal party report summarized the developments: "Broad segments of the population did . . . not understand the Party's New Course, viewed it as a sign of weakness or even as a victory by the Americans or the Church." To make matters worse, the only segment of the population that seemed to have been excluded from the New Course liberalization was the workers: the raised production norms—effectively wage cuts—that had been arbitrarily imposed in May remained in force and were confirmed on June 12.[21]

The Eisenhower administration failed to fully grasp the depth of the crisis in East Germany that had led the Soviet leaders to intervene and demand a course reversal. As late as June 2, the day Ulbricht was in Moscow listening to Malenkov's dire warnings about avoiding a "catastrophe," HICOG argued that the economic crisis brought on by collectivization and socialization was not critical: "There is currently no reason to believe the situation has reached the stage of catastrophe or that the GDR Government does not have the means at its disposal to prevent it from becoming such." Soviet moves in Germany, such as Semenov's promotion to high commissioner on May 27, seemed to show more than ever that Moscow would guarantee the existence of the Communist regime in the GDR. "Certainly no (rpt no) abandonment of East German Republic is indicated."[22]

If anything, U.S. officials emphasized the GDR's agency, viewed the Soviet moves as "prompted in part by pressure from East Germany," whose leaders recently appeared to be in an "assertive mood." As the storm of criticism engulfed Ulbricht within the Politburo in early June and within a month would bring him to the brink of ouster, American GDR specialists in Berlin reassured Washington that the SED leader's position looked "as strong or stronger than ever." The SED boss was, as one report put it, simply "in [a] class by himself among German communists as ideal and nearly irreplaceable East German representative for Moscow's purposes."[23]

Much as it had initially dismissed the Soviet peace campaign, the Eisenhower administration viewed the SED's "New Course" announcement as yet another tactical foreign policy maneuver by Moscow, rather than a desperate attempt to forestall an internal crisis. U.S. diplomats in Berlin emphasized its propaganda value for the East—the "dangerous extent" to which it would open "the flood-gates for widespread optimism in both East and West Germany" about a change in Soviet intentions. They concluded that the recent Soviet move in the GDR, coupled with negotiations for an armistice in Korea and "other Soviet moves on [the] world chess board," represented "a tactical and not . . . strategic shift in Germany." The CIA asserted that the Soviets' real intention was to "soften Western skepticism." Similarly, the State Department regarded the New Course measures as part of a buildup for a Soviet proposal for Four Power talks, as yet another attempt to forestall the rearmament of the Federal Republic following the anticipated ratification of the European Defense Community.[24]

The Revolt

With the SED in fact paralyzed and weakened, workers in East Berlin—joined soon by a growing number from other segments of East German society—decided to act on their grievances. After clashes with party officials at various worksites during the preceding days, a group from the Stalinallee construction site complex in East Berlin, a flagship building project of East Germany's reconstruction program that connected Friedrichshain with the city center, decided during a weekend cruise (June 13) on the popular Müggelsee to demand a retraction of the increased industrial production quota and go on strike. On June 15, the government ignored their demands, and they responded the next day, June 16, by marching from Friedrichshain down Stalinallee via Alexanderplatz toward the Haus der Ministerien, the government seat. Along the way other workers, residents, and passersby joined in, and the crowd's numbers soon swelled to some 10,000. Hoisting banners, the demonstrators soon broadened their demands beyond the socioeconomic issues that had first sparked the protests to include political changes. Stunned, the SED leaders hastily retracted the norm increase but remained out of the public eye. At a nightly party cadre meeting, Ulbricht admitted mistakes but blamed Western provocateurs for the unrest and called for a propaganda offensive. Emboldened by the regime's retreat, the protestors called for a general strike and a demonstration at the central Strausberger Platz the next day, June 17.

Throughout the night of June 16 and the early morning of June 17, news of the events in East Berlin spread quickly throughout the GDR—by word of mouth as well as by Western radio broadcasts. On the morning of June 17, some 25,000 people gathered in front of the House of Ministries, and tens of thousands more were en route via Leipziger Strasse or across Potsdamer Platz. By midday an estimated 150,000 protestors from across East Berlin and surrounding suburbs had swarmed into the city center with no apparent reaction from the regime. Some 80 to 100 demonstrators apparently managed to storm the government seat, and only the sudden appearance of Soviet military vehicles, and then tanks, seemed to prevent a complete collapse of the regime. Within an hour, Soviet troops had cleared and isolated the area around the government headquarters. Skirmishes between Soviet forces (and later GDR police) and the demonstrators, however, continued well into the afternoon and night.[25]

Developments throughout the GDR mirrored the events in East Berlin. Pent-up frustrations exploded loudly and at times violently across the country. News

of the worker demonstrations in Berlin and impending strike actions filtered out
to the rest of East Germany, in part through long-distance commuters. RIAS's
afternoon broadcasts on June 16 and 17 reported on the demonstrations in the
capital and the demands for a rescission of the norm increase, the resignation of
the government, and free elections. Strikes and demonstrations were particularly
widespread in rural areas, villages and smaller towns, but attracted most attention
in industrial population centers in the southern part of East Germany. More than
1 million people in more than seven hundred East German cities and communities are now estimated to have participated in the first wave of protests, between
June 16 and June 21.[26]

The Soviets, too, were completely surprised by the widespread protests: the unrest had been "totally unexpected for the German Democratic Government as well
as for our organs," Moscow was told by Soviet officials in Germany. Neither Soviet
military commanders in the GDR nor the Soviet high commission had taken the
events starting on June 16 seriously, charged Marshal Vasily D. Sokolovsky, the military's foremost Germany hand, who had headed the Soviet military administration
after the war, had since risen to the position of deputy defense minister and chief
of staff, and had been dispatched to Berlin at the height of the crisis.

With the SED leaders rapidly losing control, Semenov had evacuated the SED
Politburo to the Soviet headquarters in Karlshorst on the morning of June 17. At
noon, the Soviet authorities terminated all tram and metro traffic into the Eastern
sector and essentially closed the sector borders to West Berlin to prevent further
demonstrators from reaching the city center; one hour later, they declared martial
law in East Berlin (and later in 167 of 217 districts of the GDR), decreeing curfew
between 9:00 p.m. and 5:00 a.m. Only the forceful "active intervention" of Soviet
tanks and troops on the afternoon of June 17, hastily deployed to Berlin and major
city centers throughout the GDR, began to quell the popular outburst and prevented the total collapse of the SED government. At least fourteen people died in
the skirmishes in Berlin alone; executions and mass arrests followed.[27]

From the beginning of the East German uprising, Soviet officials viewed it as
more of a Cold War crisis than an internal matter. Reports reaching Moscow that the
British had declared martial law in their city sector, that NATO forces had been put
on alert, that "big crowds" moved from West into East Berlin probably reinforced
such perceptions. While KGB agents, some "with trepidation and hesitation," fanned
out to mingle clandestinely among the protestors to understand their demands, top
Soviet officials in Berlin assumed from the very first moment that the demonstrations
were a "major planned provocation" by the West. Citing the simultaneous outbreak

of unrest across the GDR, the similarity of "rebel demands," and the prevalence of anti-Soviet slogans as "proof," the commander of the Soviet forces in Germany, Andrei Grechko, informed the Politburo in Moscow late on June 17 that "the provocation was prepared in advance, organized and directed from the Western sectors of Berlin." The simultaneous timing and the identical nature of tactics and slogans convinced Sokolovsky, too, that this could not have been anything but a "major planned uprising." In a first postmortem on the crisis a week later, Sokolovsky and Semenov claimed that June 17 had been the so-called "Day X," "the day of open action" against the GDR "by fascist and other underground organizations working primarily under the leadership of American intelligence."

The SED would soon turn this distorted version of the events into the official Communist narrative of June 17, yet Soviet officials, it should be noted, voiced their assessment that the unrest had been planned and instigated by Western organizations under U.S. leadership at first internally and alongside accusations blaming the SED leaders for grave mistakes before and during the uprising. This suggests that the Soviet officials firmly believed that the unrest had been stirred up by the West. Although they fundamentally misread the genesis of the homegrown protests, their almost reflexive recourse to blaming American-led underground organizations demonstrated the extent to which U.S. psychological warfare efforts, however covert and limited, had in fact succeeded in fostering the idea of a "Day X" in the Soviets' (and presumably the East Germans') minds. Ironically, even the Americans were not entirely sure as to any Western role. As late as July 1, HICOG's top GDR watcher confessed that the degree and nature of Western encouragement was "not completely known." Circumstantial evidence prompted him to think it possible that the KGU "took an active hand in affairs in East Berlin on June 17."[28]

Paradoxically, at the very moment that popular resentment and political opposition to the SED finally erupted into open defiance, key American officials in Berlin actually found themselves out of pocket. High Commissioner Conant and his public affairs chief Alfred Boerner were on visits in the United States. The small staff of the CIA's Berlin Operations Base (BOB), was caught off guard by the news of the demonstrations in the Soviet sector, unable to fathom the idea that East Germans would revolt against the authorities. Still reeling from the Linse kidnapping, BOB staff and HICOG officials—much like their Soviet counterparts—scrambled to get a better picture of the protests by mingling with the crowds in the Soviet sector. But since they were cut off from agents and sources in the East by the unrest and increased Soviet sector border controls, the early U.S. intelligence on the developments in East Berlin and the GDR that reached CIA headquarters and the White House seems to have been entirely improvised, anecdotal, and patchy. Much like the Kremlin, the uprising caught the Eisenhower administration by surprise and unprepared.[29]

The one U.S. government–sponsored (though partly German-staffed) agency that played an early and decisive role in the unrest was RIAS, with its reach deep into East Germany. Labor dissatisfaction had been a central theme in RIAS broadcasts throughout the spring of 1953. As an important dimension of the U.S. psychological warfare campaign against the GDR, the station had no doubt contributed to forging "an atmosphere of protest and dissatisfaction" in the GDR. Earlier than other Western stations, on the afternoon of June 15, RIAS announced, on the basis of information provided by workers from the Stalinallee construction site, that strikes were being staged in protest of the increase in work norms. Broadcast in the evening and then again in the early morning of June 16, when reception throughout the GDR peaked, these reports were at first met with disbelief within the American establishment in Berlin: "They had thought we'd gone off the deep end," the station's political director, Gordon Ewing, later recalled.[30]

RIAS's pioneering reports on the strike plans gave early visibility to the workers' demands beyond Berlin, which proved critical for transforming local actions into a country-wide uprising. By noon (June 16), the station confirmed, in part by monitoring the East Berlin police radio system, that demonstrations at the Stalinallee and Friedrichshain construction sites were indeed taking place. After a short announcement of the news at 1 p.m., RIAS broadcast a lengthy account of the day's events transpiring across the Soviet sector on the 4:30 p.m. news. The broadcast also provided vivid accounts of the shift in the demonstrators' demands from rescission of the higher work quotas to political change expressed in shouts of "We want free elections."[31]

While RIAS did not initially drive the "radicalization of the protests," its broadcasts echoed and increasingly championed the rapid escalation of the demonstrators' concerns beyond labor issues. Not surprisingly, then, it was RIAS to which a delegation of East Berlin workers turned on the afternoon of June 16 with requests to air their call for a general strike the next day. RIAS officials recognized that the rebelling workers expected the radio station to become their mouthpiece and central coordinating point, since only RIAS could effectively establish a link between strikers and the general population. Reflective of the workers' expectations, one of the delegates later recalled that they counted on RIAS's full support for their strike, followed by a Western Allied invasion to reestablish order.

Caught between objective reporting and taking on a direct role in stoking and steering the mass demonstrations, and apparently unable to consult effectively with

FIGURE 8. June 17, 1953, uprising: Strikers on Leipziger Strasse on the way to Potsdamer Platz. Courtesy of Gert Schütz/Landesarchiv Berlin.

Washington or HICOG Bonn, local RIAS staff decided on a cautious response. Mindful of the warning that night from HICOG's Eastern Affairs Element chief, Charles Hulick,—"I hope you know what you are doing. You could start a war this way"—Ewing decided that the station could not directly act as a mouthpiece for the workers. Instead it would factually and fully disseminate information about the demonstrations. But this policy decision, soon confirmed in Washington, was easier stated than carried out.[32]

RIAS evening broadcasts saw "factual reporting" of the day's news give way to unvarnished encouragement of the protests. In his nightly comment, Eberhard Schütz, RIAS's program director, called the regime's reversal on the norm question "a victory, which our Ostberliners share with the entire working population of the Soviet Zone." The regime would have never reacted as fast as it did, Schütz argued, if the workers had not manifested their opposition in discussions, passive resistance, and strikes throughout the zone. The East Berlin workers had not limited their demands to the question of work quotas, but had indeed called for the resignation of the SED regime and the introduction of Western-style liberties. "We would be unworldly and would not deserve the confidence of our listeners if we could not acknowledge the justification of the demands. . . . What the population of East Berlin and the Soviet Zone demands today and what it views as feasible is nothing less than the end to the totalitarian rule of the Kremlin's German satellites." Emphasizing that "everyone had to know himself how far he could go," Schütz encouraged his listeners to support the demonstrators. "It is your task today to show the Soviet and German rulers that we do not accept 'mistakes' anymore as mistakes, that we and you expect a change of mind which is not limited to a rescission of the 10 percent increase in work norms but which creates conditions for free decisions which go way beyond the so-called 'voluntary norm increases.' We," Schütz concluded, "would be happy to be able to report more such victories in the next days."[33]

Throughout the night, RIAS broadcasts regularly repeated the workers' demand to continue the strike the next day, calling specifically for all East Berliners to partici-pate in a demonstration at 7:00 a.m. on June 17 at the centrally located Strausberger Platz. In the early-morning hours, West Berlin labor leader Ernst Scharnowski (in a statement cleared with HICOG) reassured the demonstrators on air that West German unions stood behind their colleagues and called upon the population for support: "Don't leave them alone. They are fighting not only for the social rights of labor but for the human rights of everyone in the East Zone. Join the movement of East Berlin construction workers, of East Berlin tram and rail employees! Every town has its Strausberger Platz!"[34]

RIAS's increasingly supportive stance during the early hours of the uprising contrasted with the cautious response of Allied officials in Berlin. Meeting at 11 a.m. on June 17, even before the Soviet declaration of martial law shut down the Soviet sector, the Western Allied commandants agreed that their primary duty was "to maintain law and order in their sectors." West Berliners and GDR residents in the surrounding suburbs, they decided, "should if possible be dissuaded from mix-ing in East Berlin demonstrations where serious possibility of bloodshed existed." Western Allied authorities were also concerned that "many demonstrators in border areas have been under the influence of alcohol," and they pondered closing liquor stores and cafés in the border areas. Convinced that an SPD-sponsored solidarity demonstration scheduled for the evening of June 17 near the sector border would appear too provocative, the commandants ordered a change in venue, reminded city officials "that the status of Berlin is Allied responsibility," and warned of the "grave consequences" of circumventing Allied authority.[35]

U.S. and Allied officials in Berlin at first wondered whether the Soviets had delib-erately staged the demonstrations in order to create a convenient pretext to remove Ulbricht after all, or—of far greater concern—to move some 20,000-man military forces into East Berlin in preparation for the capture of the entire city. Concerned about an escalation of the crisis in the wake of the Soviet military intervention in the eastern half of the city, the U.S. commandant reportedly pulled U.S. forces back from the sector border; by 5:00 p.m. on June 17, all U.S. troops had been confined to their quarters. Moreover, he took the unprecedented step of "dissuading" Ernst Reger, editor of the popular Berlin daily *Der Tagesspiegel*, "from publishing inflammatory editorials." Not until June 18 did the Western commandants issue a formal letter to the Soviet commandant, Major-General Sergei Alexeyevich Dengin, protesting Soviet military actions in East Berlin. Allied concerns about militant speeches and possibly provocative actions on the part of the West Germans in support of their compatriots soon abated. Speaking before the Bundestag in Bonn later that day, Adenauer professed sympathy with the demonstrators but warned of further escalation of irresponsible violence and rioting, a line echoed in the following hours and days by many West German public representatives.[36]

By contrast, the cold warriors within the Truman administration, centered

FIGURE 9. Soviet tanks at Leipziger Platz in Berlin during the June 17, 1953, uprising. Courtesy of Gert Schütz/Landesarchiv Berlin.

around the Psychological Strategy Board (PSB), saw the crisis as a welcome opportunity to push a more offensive agenda. Eisenhower's special assistant for Cold
War matters, C. D. Jackson, thought the Soviet military's brutal suppression of the
uprising afforded Washington an "excellent propaganda opportunity." This was the
moment, PSB staff member Mallory Browne argued, "to hit hard through C.I.A. to
make all possible trouble covertly." Others thought it might be helpful to prevent
the Soviets from sealing off the Soviet sector if the East Germans could "be persuaded to 'blur' the border," or suggested that Soviet guards at the Rundfunkhaus
and Soviet memorials in the Western sectors might be made the target of Western
sympathy demonstrations. As they learned of the first casualties, PSB members
urged "immediately to martyrize" the victims.

"With very fundamental issues . . . involved," the PSB agreed on June 17 that all possible moral support should be given to the "East Berliners," both to help them achieve
improvements and "to stimulate further Soviet repression," which would provide "ammunition" for the future. Moreover, the administration should capitalize on the events
propagandistically in other parts of the Communist world, especially where resistance
"had shown its head," perhaps as far away as the Far East. The board also agreed to
"exploit the fluidity of the East-West travel situation" to step up defector operations.
Intent on avoiding identification of the United States with the "Berlin incident" (and
perhaps not quite sure what the U.S. role had been), Secretary of State Dulles advised
Eisenhower to evade media questions "about our stimulating this."[37]

In its offensive thinking, however, the PSB was considerably ahead of the rest of
the administration: the line given out by the deputy CIA director for plans, Frank
Wisner, was that "we should do nothing at this time to incite the East Germans to
further actions." The administration's initially cautious response stemmed in part
from a glaring failure by U.S. intelligence to provide precise and timely information
on the uprising even after it started. With the Soviet sector "hermetically sealed off"
by the Soviet military, American espionage agencies, including the U.S.-sponsored
Gehlen Organization that had some 1,000 informers in the GDR, experienced an
almost complete collapse of information flow from the east. Early CIA reports thus
speculated about the possibility of the unrest being a "controlled demonstration"
by the regime, which had "flared up into near revolt." Among the few remaining
sources were firsthand observations by the U.S. and British military liaison missions
in Potsdam. In Washington, officials initially relied heavily on Associated Press reports that spoke of 50,000 demonstrators. Meeting on June 17, the Psychological
Strategy Board members decided to launch a "special fact-finding operation" through
its own channels "to determine first exactly what transpired in East Berlin . . . what
its effects are likely to be, and what lay behind the whole affair."[38]

As late as June 18, the Western Berlin commandants apparently had "no precise information on hand" on the status of the strikes in East Berlin, let alone throughout the GDR. Later that day HICOG's Berlin office did pass on "unconfirmed reports [of] unrest and strikes" in major GDR cities, but the scarcity of intelligence made it "impossible [to] evaluate [the] extent" of the disturbances. Blaming "drastically reduced information" on events in East Berlin and the GDR under martial law conditions, HICOG was still "unable" on June 19 to "estimate degree of unrest and strikes." The CIA's Office of Current Intelligence by June 26 was still transmitting unsubstantiated information from German sources claiming that the demonstrations had been the subject of "elaborate prior planning." The agency did feel increasingly certain that the popular unrest and anti-regime activity were not limited to East Germany but also evident in neighboring countries such as Czechoslovakia, Romania, and Albania.[39]

Discussions at the National Security Council in Washington on June 18 therefore took a much more sober tone than the initial PSB discussions. The unrest in East Germany was a "sign of real promise," but it also "posed a very tough problem for the United States to know how to handle." This was particularly true since the events in the GDR coincided with unforeseen troubles in Korea. Only hours before the NSC meeting on June 18, South Korean president Syngman Rhee had freed some 25,000 North Korean prisoners of war in a bid to torpedo armistice negotiations with Pyongyang. Despite the administration's interest in extricating the United States from the Korean conflict, the NSC resolved to keep the pressure on the Soviet Union by continuing the armistice talks.

What Eisenhower called the "terrible situation" in Korea deepened the uncertainty about what to do about East Germany. A four-power conference, favored by British Prime Minister Winston Churchill since the spring, continued to be an option. According to Secretary of State John Foster Dulles, the State Department was giving the idea a great deal of thought, but Eisenhower sharply disagreed. Anxious not to lend any semblance of moral approval to bloody Soviet suppression, the president declared that "he had supposed he had made it crystal clear that if there were to be a four-power conference he himself would not be present." If anything, the uprising "certainly had provided us with the strongest possible argument to give to Mr. Churchill against a four-power meeting."[40]

The NSC discussions quickly revealed that the uprising in East Germany caught the Eisenhower administration entirely off guard: How far Washington was prepared to go "if this thing really gets cracking" was really the "64-dollar question," as presidential adviser C. D. Jackson put it during the NSC meeting. Following a report by CIA director Allen Dulles, Eisenhower, according to the now fully declassified NSC minutes, "inquired whether Mr. Jackson meant that we should intervene to prevent the slaughter by the Soviet forces." Jackson replied, "Not only that, but it is now quite possible that some of the satellite regimes are now prepared to follow the road Tito [has] taken." Indeed, he added, "this could be the bell pealing the disintegration of the Soviet empire. Do we stand idly by, or do we help the disintegration? And how much responsibility are we willing to take for the results of helping?"

With the question of intervening explicitly raised at the NSC meeting by Jackson, Eisenhower's reactions show a remarkable degree of exaggeration in his assessment of the East German protests—and suggest what it would have taken for him to risk direct U.S. involvement. The decision to intervene, he said, "depended on how wide-spread the uprising became. Would the riots spread to China, or even possibly to the USSR itself? If this should happen, we would probably never have a better chance to act, and we would be well-advised, for example to supply arms." As to whether "we should ship arms to the East Berliners," as Jackson seemed to advocate, Eisenhower reasoned that, "if to do so was just inviting a slaughter of these people, you certainly didn't supply the arms. If, on the contrary, there was a real chance of success, you might well do so. Our problem was to weigh the prospects of success."

In his opinion, the president added, the revolts had to be more serious and widespread than at this moment before they promised real success and indicated the desirability of U.S. intervention. Jackson pressed on, asking whether U.S. actions could "help [to] make this movement more serious and more widespread." But Eisenhower thought such ideas premature. To him, it was "very important that the unrest spread to China, because while the USSR would have no great difficulty in crushing uprisings in Europe alone, they would find it tough to deal with trouble both in Europe and in the Far East." For the moment, Eisenhower concluded that "the time to 'roll them out for keeps'" had not "quite" arrived. Uncertain what could be done, he finally asked the Psychological Strategy Board to devise a short-term plan on how to exploit the East German situation.

While the Eisenhower administration, prodded by Jackson, searched for options to support the protests, the British and French governments tried to prevent any active Western intervention. While the French government favored a "policy of watchful waiting," Churchill, fearing that the uprising would quash his hopes for a four-power summit, wanted to return to business as usual in Berlin as quickly as possible. The British prime minister hence reacted violently to the West Berlin commandants' June 18 statement that criticized the Soviet's "irresponsible recourse to military force." Citing diplomatic reports that characterized Soviet behavior as markedly restrained, he harshly reprimanded the British representative, arguing that the Soviet government, in the face of violent disorders, surely had the right to declare martial law in order to prevent anarchy. "We shall," Churchill concluded, "not find our way out of our many difficulties by making for purposes of local propaganda statements which are not in accordance with the facts."[41]

The Anglo-American strains over how to react to the unrest in East Germany resurfaced when the commandants agreed to issue another statement on June 22. Once again the Americans were inclined "to make it considerably stiffer" than the British wished; a sentence proposed by U.S. officials connecting the Berlin unrest to that throughout the zone "had to be dropped" at British insistence. The British high commissioner also showed concern about the role of anti-communist groups in the American sector, "where the propagandists do not always seem to be under control." Acting foreign minister Lord Salisbury warned of the "new and more dangerous American tendency . . . to interpret the situation behind the Iron Curtain as already very shaky and therefore to advocate new although unspecified measures to encourage and even promote an early liberation of the satellite countries."[42]

The American attitude—in Washington, Bonn, and Berlin—in fact soon grew tougher, for several reasons. First, U.S. intelligence was beginning to get a clearer picture of the scope of demonstrations and strikes as they spread throughout East Germany. The extent of the unrest gave the administration grounds for greater confidence, particularly as it became apparent that news of the protests was reaching to other satellite countries where they might have the potential to undermine Communist authority even further. A second reason was political in nature: Eisenhower and Dulles were sensitive to the gap between the markedly restrained actions of the United States during the first days of the uprising and the rhetoric of "liberation" on which they had campaigned and on which the expectations of many East Germans rested.

At the same time, the uprising threatened to upset the larger U.S. agenda for Germany. While Washington had hoped to keep attention focused on the Federal Republic's entry into the Western alliance, the New Course announcement and the ensuing unrest had thrust the issue of German reunification to the forefront, both on the international scene and in the West German election campaign, prompting a groundswell of calls for four-power talks. "In addition to bringing back in increased strength the feeling that something must be done to unify Germany," the U.S. high commissioner in Bonn reported, the riots had also "created the new feeling that something *can* be done." Thus, for example, the uprising led the influential bishop of Berlin-Brandenburg, Otto Dibelius, to lobby for a private meeting of the four high commissioners to restart quadripartite discussions on German unity.[43]

Sensing a broader shift in Cold War correlations of forces, many East Germans apparently expected the United States and the West Europeans to begin providing active support. In numerous discussions, local SED officials reported, the population believed that "the Soviet army, under pressure from the Western powers, was leaving the territories west of the Elbe, . . . the regime had fled to Russia, and American and British occupation forces would soon victoriously enter the area." Others felt that this was the beginning of a process of "slowly . . . acquiring Western conditions," while still others were expressing the view that "the SED has to go, it is time, they have run the country down. Soon we can start learning English." As late as August, rumors that the United States would intervene led farmers to refuse further deliveries: "When the American comes, we will get more money for our cattle and will be able to afford more with it." Internal SED estimates on the population's state of mind reflect that until late summer many East Germans believed that the West would not ignore their outcry.[44]

The Eisenhower administration was well aware of these expectations—and the dilemma they created for U.S. policy. Failing to meet widespread expectations of American support for the protests had the potential to upset the administration's larger goal of West Germany's integration with the West. After the initial surge of riots and demonstrations in East Germany, HICOG noted that "whether the SED suffers [a] further, perhaps crippling setback or substantially recovers [its] former power position (which could happen within the next six months) may depend largely on U.S. policy." Already public criticism of Western inaction, particularly of West German chancellor Adenauer's reserved response to the turmoil in East Germany, was on the rise. "Unless some sign is forthcoming very soon from the United States," presidential adviser C. D. Jackson pointed out to Eisenhower in early July, "there could be a terrible letdown in both East and West Germany, which would seriously affect the U.S. position and even more seriously affect Adenauer's position." Others argued that if the U.S. confined its response to press comments and statements, "we risk not only to lose the confidence of the Soviet Zone population, but may even cause considerable antagonism."[45]

Moreover, while Moscow's resort to force had in the view of some U.S. officials upset its "entire German gambit" and impaired the Soviet negotiating position, it was still unclear how much the unrest and its suppression might deflect the Kremlin's attempts to project an image of restraint—what the State Department called the "Soviet-GDR moderation pose." Washington was still concerned that the Soviets might capitalize on East and West German demands for unification by calling for a four-power conference." Therefore, the administration thought it was crucial to "keep [the] Soviets as much as possible on [the] defensive, with [the] aim of endeavoring [to] deflate any further gestures they may make at conciliation."[46]

U.S. officials also acknowledged that anti-Soviet sentiment among many East Germans was volatile: HICOG officials had detected signs of recognition among the strikers and demonstrators of the Soviet soldiers' "remarkable reserve," the apparent lack of any "wanton shooting into the crowds." Thus many demonstrators believed that it might not be impossible to negotiate with the Soviets. HICOG officials concluded that if such a feeling should gain credence, "it could have a significant effect upon East German attitudes vis-à-vis the Soviets and the Western Allies, shifting, perhaps, their bitterness somewhat away from the former and directing it toward the latter, particularly if the West does nothing positive to bring about unification." Indeed, as High Commissioner Conant warned from Bonn, unless some action was taken in the near future, the "Soviet[s] might regain control of the situation and recoup a major part of [their] lost prestige."[47]

That such fears were not entirely unwarranted is suggested by Soviet archival documents. As Jackson, in partnership with CIA director Allen Dulles, was putting the final touches on a new policy guideline, the three top Soviet officials in the Germany—Semenov, his political advisor, Pavel F. Yudin, and Sokolovsky—delivered to the Soviet leadership in Moscow a stinging fifty-page report that called for—in addition to relieving the GDR of its reparations, occupation, and other economic burdens and in extenuation of the June 2 decree—drastic structural and personnel changes within the GDR government. Ulbricht's position as general secretary would be liquidated, and the size and responsibilities of his "machine" within the party (the Central Committee secretariat) sharply reduced, and "more popular people ... with broader enlistment of representatives of other parties" were to be brought into the government, all amounting to a radical enhancement of the GDR's image "in the eyes of the German population." This was precisely what the Eisenhower administration sought to avoid.[48]

Charged by the NSC to develop a response to the uprising, the Psychological Strategy Board by the end of June, had drawn up the "Interim U.S. Plan for Exploitation of Unrest in Satellite Europe" (PSB D-45, adopted on June 24). Reflecting (and pushing) C. D. Jackson's larger geographic perspective, PSB D-45 placed the East German uprising in the context of signs of unrest in Czechoslovakia, Poland, Romania, and Albania. Czechoslovakia, where unrest had persisted since early June, "should be given major emphasis." While resentment over excessive production quotas, food shortages, and low living standards had triggered the revolt, these grievances were, in the narrative propelled by PSB D-45, "overshadowed by the clearly expressed political objectives of the German rebels." Highlighting the transformation of labor protests into large-scale political demonstrations, PSB D-45 cast the uprising as "a kind of spontaneous direct-action plebiscite in which the East German masses voted with their fists for free elections, the reunification of Germany and the withdrawal of Soviet occupation forces." With popular resentment of the Soviets "near the boiling point," the strategy document proposed "to start local strikes, demonstrations, or other manifestations of continuing resistance." Bearing the hallmark language of Jackson's expansive vision, PSB D-45 judged that the GDR uprising had created "the greatest opportunity for initiating effective policies to help roll back Soviet power that has yet come to light."[49]

Jackson's rollback ambitions, however, found themselves scaled back when PSB D-45 was discussed the next day at the National Security Council and subsequently adopted as NSC directive 158 on June 29. The NSC policy directive explicitly eschewed a call for mass rebellion; in approving PSB D-45, Eisenhower (and Secretary of State Dulles) asked specifically that, when it came to stimulating opposition to the regime, "more emphasis be placed on passive resistance." Any advocacy of free elections as called for in PSB D-45, he ventured in the NSC discussion on June 25, "had to be carefully calculated from the standpoint of Chancellor Adenauer." (By early July, Eisenhower and Adenauer had reversed their long-standing opposition to a high-level East-West conference, and on July 15 the three Western Allied foreign ministers, meeting in Washington called for a four-power foreign ministers' meeting on Germany for the coming fall.)[50]

Still, NSC 158 outlined a variety of short- and long-term overt, covert, and psychological warfare measures designed "to nourish resistance to Communist oppression throughout satellite Europe . . . without compromising its spontaneous nature, [and] to undermine satellite puppet authority." The proposed measures included a wide range of activities, from exploiting Soviet repressive tactics at the United Nations, to more extreme actions such as launching "black" radio intruder operations to induce defections, and encouraging the "elimination of key puppet officials." More ambitiously, and more long-term, NSC 158 called for organizing, training and launching "large-scale raids or sustained guerilla warfare," and for consideration of "new forms of covert organizations" and "large-scale systematic balloon propaganda operations" in Eastern Europe.

Beyond this list, the administration officials also considered a number of other propaganda measures, such as allocating $50 million for the reconstruction of West Berlin and urging Adenauer to announce the building of "a Bundestag" in West Berlin on the grounds of the destroyed Reichstag. After the September 1953 elections, it was proposed, "an all-out push" would be made for this "perpetual monument" featuring a "Hall of Heroes" in which the first to appear would be Willi Göttling, the West Berlin painter who had been executed by the Soviets during the riots.[51]

C. D. Jackson emphasized "the importance of vigorous implementation of PSB D-45 and its amended summary," but it is not clear what measures were actually carried out. For example, despite the fact that Senator Hubert H. Humphrey personally intervened with Eisenhower to lend support for the idea of an UN tribunal of those responsible in East Germany for "the murders of the anti-totalitarians," a proposal to resurrect the UN commission created in 1951 to investigate conditions for elections throughout Germany was aborted due to British, French and Canadian objections. As for a memorial to Göttling, characterized by Jackson as a "very handy martyr," UN Ambassador Henry Cabot Lodge intended to "make quite a to do about Willi" at the fall's UN General Assembly session. Yet West Berlin mayor Reuter reportedly "dragged his feet on the project," effectively dooming the idea. By far the most visible activity that did take place was a large-scale food program for East Germany, which the PSB approved on July 1.[52]

The Eisenhower Packages Program and the Dilemmas of Psychological Warfare

The Eisenhower administration's major response to the uprising also focused on the consumer-goods shortages in the GDR. U.S. officials thought a program to provide the East German population with food ideally combined humanitarian motives and political-psychological objectives. The distribution of food at no cost to the East Germans would help to alleviate the immediate crisis "but offer no long-range change in the deteriorating economic condition." The food relief would demonstrate Adenauer's sympathy for his East German brethren. High Commissioner James Conant emphasized that "our primary objective should be to put Adenauer in [a] position to take decisive action with respect to [the] East Zone crisis." By placing the food program officially under West German auspices, as Conant urged from Bonn, the United States could "provide [a] powerful stimulus to the Adenauer election victory" and to Western resolve on the EDC. The food program would also demonstrate continuing U.S. concern for the plight of the East Germans, yet keep the Soviets on the defensive and aggravate antagonisms between the SED regime and the populace.[53]

Debates within the administration over schemes for implementing the program reflected the multiple purposes the program served. Humanitarian considerations, it became clear quickly, were considered subsidiary to "psychological advantages" to be

FIGURE 10. An American plane carrying U.S. food packages is unloaded at Tempelhof Airport, July 1953. © Pressebild-Verlag Schirner/Deutsches Historisches Museum, Berlin.

gained. Another proposal called for Chancellor Adenauer to issue a formal request to Eisenhower, who would respond by making food available from the Allied Berlin stockpile and from agricultural surpluses in the United States, supplemented by Army C rations that "were about to spoil." The food would then be distributed through private channels, churches, and charitable organizations. This option, however, was soon discarded for fear of endangering these sensitive links across the Iron Curtain. The CIA, the Air Force, and the influential journalist Drew Pearson favored a riskier scheme, by which the Air Resupply and Communications Service, an arm of the U.S. Air Force, would send food to the East by way of balloons. This plan, however, that ran into strong opposition from High Commissioner Conant. Another proposal envisioned U.S. and Western food convoys arriving at selected Iron Curtain border crossings in East Germany, Poland, and Czechoslovakia on pre-announced days and demanding entrance. If, as expected, entry for the convoys would be denied, "it might be very effective to arrive at the border points anyway on the day and at the time announced, and permit the news cameras and reporters . . . to cover the event of Soviet denial."[54]

"From a psychological as well as political point of view," it was finally deemed most effective if the American offer of food for East Germany was made by a direct approach to the Soviet government. Thus, on July 10, the program was officially announced by the publication of an exchange of letters between Chancellor Adenauer and President Eisenhower. Simultaneously, Eisenhower's note to the Soviets, offering $15 million worth of food aid for the East Germans, was published. That very day, the CIA learned that GDR government officials expected a "new uprising" in East Germany: "the workers are planning another blowup there," Allen Dulles told his brother John Foster.

Planned as a fait accompli regardless of Soviet reaction, rejection by the Soviets on July 11 came as little surprise. An interdepartmental committee, chaired by Eleanor Dulles, then decided to support a plan that placed the food packages—labeled "Eisenhower packages"—at the disposal of the federal West German government and Berlin Senate for distribution to the East Germans. Modeled after a local Berlin "neighborly aid program," the parcels were made available on a "come-and-get-it" basis to East Berliners and East Zoners at various distribution centers in the Western sectors of Berlin easily accessible from the East. The distribution of the packages, each containing flour, lard, condensed or powdered milk, and dried vegetables from the Berlin stockpile and U.S. agricultural surpluses (canned horse meat available from the U.S. stockpile in Vienna were rejected "owing to potential adverse publicity"), commenced on July 27.[55]

Coinciding with the 15th SED Plenum, a crucial moment at which Ulbricht sought to reassert authority within the party leadership, the aid scheme received an "overwhelming" response from the East Germans. By the end of the first day, HICOG could report that the number of applicants for food packages—103,743 packages were issued—had exceeded all expectations, a success attributed mainly to the heavy play that RIAS gave to the operation. By the third day, more than 200,000 parcels were being issued daily. By the end of the program's first phase (August 15), 865,000 people had come from East Germany and East Berlin to get food. Since many East Germans carried identity cards belonging to friends and relatives, which allowed them to receive packages for those people as well as themselves, the average applicant collected about three packages. All in all, 2,598,202 parcels were distributed. By mid-August, an estimated 75 percent of East Berlin's population had received at least one parcel. Most importantly, however, two-thirds of the food went to people living in the Berlin periphery and to "deep zoners." A second program, lasting from August 28 to early October, evoked a similar response. In total, more than 5.5 million food packages were distributed.[56]

FIGURE 11. East Berliners and Soviet zone residents at the food program distribution centers, July 27, 1953 (covering their faces so as not to be identified). © Pressebild-Verlag Schirner/ Deutsches Historisches Museum, Berlin.

Within days of the food program's launch, its impact was becoming evident. The SED, underestimating the effectiveness of the American plan, initially reacted to the food distribution merely by increasing the propaganda effort. Upon noting the "relatively large number of inhabitants from all social strata" and the large influx of people from outside the capital area who were going to Berlin to receive their packages, the SED ordered a massive propaganda drive (Agitationseinsätze) at rail stations and other strategic points. In Potsdam alone, 150,000 leaflets denouncing the food program were printed. Loudspeaker systems were installed in key spots, and the National Front orchestrated concentrated actions by party agitators and at party meetings. Newspapers and radio broadcasts denounced the "Bettelpakete" (beggar's packages) and shamed those who were caught receiving packages. Contrary to the grand-scale propaganda drive, few punitive actions other than occasional package confiscations were thought necessary.[57]

By the end of the month, reports reaching the SED headquarters in Berlin sounded alarming. True, some East Germans believed the food relief to be "only propaganda for Adenauer," but many responded enthusiastically. Party officials sent to West Berlin noted the rapidly increasing numbers of people on their way to receive packages. By July 31, train ticket sales had multiplied, in some cases by a factor of seven. Two-thirds of the passengers on trains from Berlin, the SED was informed, were carrying food packages. Party observers were obviously impressed by the patience the food recipients showed in waiting, often for hours, to receive their packages. "It is remarkable," one report from Berlin noted, "that entire families and house communities were heading for the distribution points."[58]

Others similarly noted the "*starker Andrang,*" or throngs, at the distribution points. Pointing out that trains to Berlin had been occupied at 180–200 percent of normal ridership, one official observer noted the massive number of arriving and departing package recipients at one railway station, and commented that it "gave the impression of a demonstration." A report from the Cottbus party district noted "vigorous discussions" of the U.S. food program in factories and in the entire district. Many workers, according to these reports, went so far as to demand that food packages should be claimed for the entire factory by factory representatives. On July 31, 150 employees of an industrial plant in Wittenberg were reported to have organized a joint trip to West Berlin. But it was not only workers who deserted the party line again. Among the food recipients, the SED Central Committee learned, were growing numbers of train employees in uniform (taking advantage of their free train tickets), as well as mail and administrative personnel.[59]

Most disconcerting to the SED, numerous party members also made the trip to Berlin. Five hundred and seventy party members, sent to West Berlin to agitate against the food distribution, returned with only 150 packages, a remarkably small number, which was attributed to the fact that most of them had kept their packages for themselves. At a party meeting in Fürstenwalde, Berlin was informed, only eight of forty-eight SED members were consistently resisting the temptation. The fact that "even members and functionaries of the [SED] party were succumbing to the provocation and hence were becoming party enemies" was exemplified by the events in the town of Werder, where the local party secretary and his deputy, as well as the chairman of the farmers' association and local production cooperative, and even a member of the mayor's household, apparently went to Berlin to receive their packages: "Following this bad example all other residents one by one went to get the *Amipakete*."[60]

Furthermore, in order to make the trip worthwhile, many people were carrying several of the identity cards that were required for the pickup. In one incident, a farm employee was found to be carrying fifteen food packages. Even the number of people registering their children for ID cards increased. The police in the small town of Fürstenwalde reported to Berlin that on one of the first days of the food program, eighty people had requested registration, a startling number considering that despite encouragement on the part of the authorities, not a single registration had been requested since 1949![61]

It was clear that the East German government had—as it did during the initial phase of the uprising—underestimated the response that the disruptions would elicit among the population. In its August 1 meeting, the SED Politburo decided to launch a "shame" campaign against the food package program. To counter "provocative acts of the American and British warmongers," the Politburo also suspended the sale of train tickets to Berlin and declared it illegal to carry more than one's own personal identification papers. Security measures were to be put into effect at railway stations in order to prevent "enemy provocations." In addition, all freight and bus traffic to Berlin was halted. Party, the union, and other SED-dominated mass organizations were mobilized to carry out political agitation against the "imperialist" aid program. "It is necessary," the Politburo informed the local party organizations, "to take measures to ensure, in accordance with local conditions, the vigorous carrying out of the New Course. In doing so, the fight against agents of the American and West German warmongers should be the focus of our struggle for the workers' and peasants' power in the German Democratic Republic." In addition to propagandistic threats against those easterners who "succumbed" to the "Ami bait," food package recipients were registered, their names publicized, and, in increasing numbers, their personal identification papers and food parcels confiscated.[62]

The East German government also launched proactive countermeasures against the U.S. sponsored food program. GDR State Security, for example, mailed out forged invitations to West Berlin unemployed people to receive packages under the program in an effort to stir up discontent. This seems to have had some effect: in early August, Reuter pleaded with American officials to open the food program to jobless Berliners. Moreover, the regime sent hundreds of SED and FDJ agitators to West Berlin to spread fear and incite unrest among those waiting in line for their food packages in often miserable conditions. The SED even set up a rival program that distributed food from packages confiscated from those who had been to the Western sector issuing points. In the midst of the crisis, in what Eisenhower administration officials called a "stunt," the GDR offered to purchase food from the funds (more than $1.6 million) of the GDR Central Bank (Deutsche Notenbank), blocked since 1952 in the United States. When, however, Washington indicated that it would be willing to sell such food to the East German regime, the proposal was "dropped like a hot potato."[63]

While the crackdown considerably reduced their numbers, East Germans continued to reach the distribution centers in West Berlin by the thousands. The food program remained a focus of popular attention, thus preventing the SED from internal stabilization and keeping the regime on "a peevish defensive." Internal SED reports still indicated that "the enemy was increasingly succeeding in winning over large portions of the population, in particular retirees and housewives, but also workers." Leipzig reported "intense discussions over the food program in the plants." While the Politburo-ordered ticket-sale suspension was taking effect, the GDR Railways Ministry reported, "many [of its] employees were still carrying out their jobs without offensively exposing to the passengers the true character of the 'American aid.'" Others noted that the attitude of the railway officials "still varied a lot." Indeed, in some cases the Railways Ministry orders had been relayed only with considerable delay, enabling many East Germans still to acquire tickets.[64]

Furthermore, as the Americans intended, the imposition of restrictive measures served to heighten tensions in an already explosive situation in East Germany. Party officials recorded incidents of travelers to Berlin arguing "very aggressively," for example stating that "those in West Berlin are behind us. If we get in trouble, we just have to say so, then the matter will go before the UN." In discussions of the stoppage of all ticket sales to Berlin, some commented cynically, "This must be the freedom of the East Zone." Noting the "negative discussion" among those who were now precluded from going to Berlin—"This way the government cannot win the confidence of the people!"—the SED headquarters learned that "one can detect a general annoyance [with the countermeasures]." In some instances, disappointed East Germans resorted to what the authorities labeled "provocative" actions, coercing train rides to Berlin or simply going by car. In Groß-Schönebeck, north of Berlin, about 150 women forced the departure of a train by initially blocking the tracks. In Angermünde, located some 40 miles northwest of the capital, 2,000 people awaiting returnees from West Berlin assumed what local SED officials perceived to be a "threatening attitude against the VP [People's Police]." When the VP called in firefighters to turn hoses on the people, riots broke out, and it took three hours for order to be restored. Others tried to circumvent the regime's measures by buying train tickets for destinations close to Berlin, then completing their trip by other means. In other parts of the country, workers went on strike to protest the regime's measures. District SED officials repeatedly reported to Berlin threats of an imminent general strike and a "second June 17."[65]

RIAS continued to play an important role in the implementation of U.S. policy by publicizing the food program. Its broadcasts, to the agony of the SED, served as an effective means of propagandizing food distribution information deep into the Soviet zone. More importantly, many East Germans now openly listened to the American-sponsored radio program to show their defiance of the regime. Thus, in the small town of Germershausen, "the entire population was listening to RIAS or the NWDR [Nordwestdeutscher Rundfunk]," apparently turning their radios' volume up till they "could be heard in the streets."[66]

The food program sharply exacerbated tensions within the GDR and made it more difficult for the SED to regain its political footing through the reassertion of New Course policies at the 15th SED Central Committee Plenum. To the chagrin of the SED, internal party reports indicated that not only the population at large but party members at meetings were distracted by the ongoing Western aid deliveries. "The main issue in the discussions today," an internal party report of August 3 stated, "was again the food package program. On the other hand, any discussion of the proposals of our People's Chamber and the decision of the Fifteenth Plenum fell into the background." The party organizations were "still not able to influence the discussion in any decisive manner."[67]

During the next days, reports reached Berlin that "the population is hardly discussing the . . . decisions of the Fifteenth Plenum." The reason for this, it was pointed out, was that the party's propaganda drive was "almost exclusively concerned with the package program." Faced with train passengers outraged by the suspension of almost all traffic to Berlin, party officials were "still reacting defensively." The "fight for the enlightenment of the masses on the background of the food aid" was still not taken on effectively by the local party leadership. In one representative instance, an SED-sponsored effort to bring about a factory-wide "vote of condemnation" of the "Western package provocation" resulted in 60 out of 74 workers abstaining from the vote.[68]

The food program also undercut renewed Soviet efforts to regain the offensive in Germany and stabilize the GDR through economic support. In mid-August, Moscow sent diplomatic notes to the Western powers proposing the convocation of a peace conference, the formation of an all-German provisional government, and an easing of Germany's financial-economic burdens. At the same time, the Kremlin committed itself to supporting the weakened but unreconstructed Ulbricht regime as the "bulwark of the struggle of the German people for a united, peace-loving and democratic Germany."

On August 20–22, the Soviet leadership received Ulbricht, Grotewohl, and other GDR leaders to shore up the largely unreconstructed SED government. During the summit, the Soviets promised much of what had been discussed internally for months: the transfer of Soviet joint-stock companies, a sharp reduction in occupation expenses, and cessation of reparations payments by year's end, as well as substantial economic and financial aid—notwithstanding the lateness of the act, which a State Department cable characterized as "a literal example of locking [the] barn door after [the] horse [has been] stolen by Soviets." The Kremlin leadership also agreed to free additional prisoners of war and raise the status of its mission in Berlin to that of an embassy. Moscow's moves were viewed in Washington as a "serious effort to bolster the shaky GDR regime."[69]

But against the background of the food program, many East Germans questioned the "point of those food deliveries from the Soviet Union." Prices for the Soviet imports, thus the complaint, were too high, if they were available at all: "We would rather go to West Berlin to get our packages." The "bad Americans distribute free packages and the good friend makes us pay for them," East Germans observed, mocking the news of USSR credits and aid. Noting that the great majority of the population had still not recognized the "political and provocative background" of the package program, most people showed themselves "continually uninterested" in the Soviet aid program. When SED officials at one Berlin party meeting maintained that the Soviets' suspension of reparations benefited German interests, whereas Adenauer desired a fifty-year occupation of Germany, "the largest part of the participants broke into laughter." As late as mid-September, party officials acknowledged the "lasting influence of the enemy," the *Versöhnlertum* (conciliatory attitude) of local authorities toward food recipients, and the intensifying "discussions and demands at railway stations to reopen the ticket sales." As an internal SED public opinion survey stated ominously, the relationship of party and government to the population "has worsened recently."[70]

At first, the aid action was hailed in Washington, Bonn, and West Berlin as a "highly successful operation" fitting into a larger "overall psychological strategy." West Berlin's Lord Mayor, Ernst Reuter, emphasized how upsetting the program had been for the Eastern authorities: it had been "like an artillery attack." Indeed, to some the program's far-reaching effects seemed to be nothing less than "a continuation of June 17 by other means." It had provided a substantial amount of food to undernourished East Berliners and East Germans and had highlighted the shortages in the GDR, forcing the Soviets and the SED to increase rations for the population and further redirect industrial policy. The aid effort had squarely placed the Soviets and the SED on the defensive and undercut their unity propaganda.

While the need for food and the bargain value of packages were paramount to the recipients, as U.S. officials acknowledged, the operation had given the East German population another opportunity to demonstrate their defiance of the Communist regime—to "vote with their feet"—and once again showed the limits of the SED control. Furthermore, as a leading HICOG official cabled, the aid had "given East Germans contact with the West and . . . has made it once more a real, vital force in their lives. They know that the West exists, thinks about them and hopes someday that the east will be free." More disconcertingly, the program was widely interpreted among East Germans "as the first act of a new and more aggressive American policy" that presaged in in their minds further U.S. action "to liberate the Soviet Zone." Finally, it also was seen to have contributed to Adenauer's decisive victory at the polls on September 6, thereby assuring the continuation of his policy of integration with the West. "This important project has already bettered our position in the cold war," one American observer enthusiastically informed Washington.[71]

To the "cold warriors" within the administration the program demonstrated that there were means short of war to advance the liberation of Europe. On July 11 Eisenhower ordered the PSB—"while matters [were] still hot"—to develop food programs for all the other satellites. Inspired by their success in Berlin, U.S. officials contemplated various other schemes, such as deliveries of medical supplies and other commodities that were in great popular demand, a clothing drive for the East, hospitality programs, and setting up scattered "food depots along the interzonal border." On July 13, moreover, the CIA-funded National Committee for a

Free Europe launched a massive balloon propaganda program for Czechoslovakia ("Operation Prospero"). All in all, 6,512 balloons dropped some twelve million propaganda leaflets across the country, many of which cited slogans of the East German protests or showed images of burning SED posters. Attempting to preempt GDR plans to relax travel restriction to ease tensions reported by U.S, intelligence, the Western high commissioners considered proposing to the Soviets to abolish the Allied interzonal passes and restore free movement between the western zones and the Soviet zone—a measure intended to achieve "a sort of democratic infection" of the East German population.[72]

However, while the aid program, purposefully staged as a unilateral American action, kept East Berlin and Moscow on the defensive, it also exacerbated British and French resentment of American "Cold War" tactics. Instead of a new Cold War offensive after the uprising, the British government favored "get[ting] things back to normal as fast as possible" by "letting the Russians save face in East Germany." In addition, British and French officials worried that the program would endanger West Berlin's precarious security. In the view of Sir Ivone Kirkpatrick, the British high commissioner, the food program "might result in [the] city being cut and even Berlin communications being cut off." In the face of Communist demonstrations staged at the food centers in August, British officials again argued for the termination of the distribution operation and put pressure on Reuter to that effect. Like the French, they favored an early end to the operation and strongly opposed any further such schemes, which they considered "too blatant a type of political warfare against the East Zone regime and the Soviet occupation authorities." Their opposition to what had become a unilateral U.S. project left the British, as a Foreign Office official termed it, "in quite bad odour with the Americans on cold war matters."[73]

The cold warriors within the Eisenhower administration had indeed little patience for Allied concerns: said C.D. Jackson, "very little is going to be done in order to produce our kind of world if every single U.S. move has to be watered down to the lowest common denominator of French timidity and British reluctance to have American international leadership displayed outside the limits of the District of Columbia." Yet, Allied discord over post-uprising strategy vis-à-vis the East was quickly detected by the Soviet and East German side and tended to undercut the Eisenhower administration's effort to exploit the unrest in the GDR. As early as July 7, the GDR Foreign Ministry supplied Grotewohl with a report titled "Dissension within the Camp of the Western Powers over the Question of Four-Power Talks," which emphasized the efforts of British and French "imperialists" to withstand U.S. pressure for a more aggressive policy, to retain a "last bit of political independence and not to close the door on four-power negotiations." Similarly, a July 20 note to the Western high commissioners by Semenov suggested to U.S officials that that the Soviets were aware of the lack of unanimity in handling the food project and hoped "to drive a wedge between the allies through release of [a] note at this time." The Soviet government increasingly emphasized, Bohlen noted from Moscow, that the entire project demonstrated that the United States was only "interested in a revival [of the] cold war," a sentiment that found "a certain resonance" in Western Europe.[74]

Even in West Germany, where the food program had initially garnered widespread public support, signs of apprehension began to appear. The July 10 U.S. offer to the Soviets had already caused some "adverse reaction" among the press along the lines of "food yes, propaganda no." Arguing against increased "drum beating," Conant had warned early on that "East and West Germans would react against obvious propaganda to which they are hyper-sensitive." Wary of the possibility that the "smoldering fire [of] East German resistance may be prematurely fanned up and stamped out," Conant now pleaded for restraint.[75]

Federal Republic officials, too, grew more and more concerned about the pressures on food recipients, and in particular about the GDR's interference with the normal travel of East Germans to Berlin. West German charitable organizations, which had displayed a "highly negative" attitude all along toward involvement in the program, feared that the American action was jeopardizing their regular aid channels. If further action caused the Soviets to cut off the current flow of private parcels from West to East, this might have "serious repercussions for Adenauer," the U.S. high commissioner cautioned from Bonn. In addition, Reuter, initially among the most enthusiastic supporters of the program, became concerned about the negative impression made by denying food to West Berlin's unemployed and poor. Press reports with headlines such as "Don't Gamble with Hunger" reflected the increasingly critical reaction in West Germany. By the end of September, Thedick, speaking for the Bundesregierung, which had only belatedly been consulted in the actual implementation of the program, was urging a "visible stop" of the food distribution.[76]

Not surprisingly, when U.S. officials proposed at a meeting of the Western high commissioners on September 17 to establish an officially-sponsored private organization in Berlin as a central clearinghouse for long-range aid activities for the East German population, they ran into strong opposition among their allies. Admitting that the food program had been valuable "in breaching the iron curtain," Kirkpatrick termed the new American proposal "amateurish" and "inacceptable" and firmly vetoed the idea advanced as part of the American plan to have any new organization collaborate with "controversial" private anti-communist groups such as the KGU and UFJ. Initially not consulted, Reuter wanted to hold to an end of the food program by October 1. Conant agreed: any program of indefinite duration would run the risk of indefinitely extending the interruption of free traffic between East and West Berlin.[77]

Moreover, while the United States was still carrying out the food distribution, the entire concept of psychological warfare as codified in PSB D-45 began to face heavy criticism from within the Eisenhower administration, in particular from American diplomats in Europe. One gathering of senior American envoys in Luxembourg, in September 1953, declared that psychological warfare "should never be allowed to run ahead of carefully considered political objectives" because of the "danger" that it might "start to make policy rather than serve it." If a basic long-term objective of American policy was the withdrawal of the Soviet Army from the GDR and from the Eastern European countries, the senior U.S. diplomats declared, "stirring up resistance or incitements of revolts—'keeping the pot virtually at a boiling point'— might have the long-range effect of retarding a Soviet military withdrawal."

Rather than proposing intensified psychological warfare, U.S. diplomats tended to favor "the gradual liberation of the oppressed people through an evolutionary rather than revolutionary process." From HICOG Berlin came the warning that "aggressive US follow-up actions on food could conceivably produce another June 17." If the food action and repressive SED measures were to lead to uprisings on the same scale, HICOG Berlin officials believed that "[the] Soviets with KVP in forefront will put down such uprisings ruthlessly. End result could be severe blow to workers' morale, since there was little likelihood [that] such repression this time would be accompanied by economic concessions." High Commissioner Conant, too, cautioned that "we don't want to do anything that will cause any more blood-shed." The objective of American policy with regard to the Soviet zone, he wrote to Secretary of State Dulles, at least insofar as he understood it, was "to keep the pot simmering but not to bring it to a boil."[78]

Keeping the pot simmering, however, could not be achieved by psychological warfare alone: "Without under-emphasizing the significance of [the] food program [or] similar efforts," HICOG Berlin argued, maintaining a high degree of anti-regime attitude among East Germans required "clear-cut US and/or Allied political pressure on Soviets, exerted on high level and in simple terms, in order that East Germans can continue to believe there is real purpose in maintaining pressure on GDR Government and SED." Emphasizing the need for a more "positive policy," U.S. officials in Berlin thought that engaging in renewed negotiations with the

Soviets on German unification "would be a greater blow to their equilibrium than if we succeed in getting the entire Soviet Zone population into West Berlin for a turkey dinner."[79]

The administration's secret "Operation Solarium" policy reassessment of summer-fall 1953, while endorsing intensified reliance on covert action, concluded that rollback in Eastern Europe was not immediately feasible. At the end of September, the State Department outlined the U.S. position on unrest in the Soviet zone, reminding missions abroad that "it is possible to maintain a psychological climate of resistance" but that attempts to "reduce Soviet power in the GDR should always be examined for their impact on our efforts to integrate the Federal Republic with the West." Furthermore, the policy guideline warned that "we do not want to risk precipitating prematurely a mass, open rebellion" or "incur the blame for its consequences." Specifically, the department cautioned that American missions should not advise the East Germans "to engage in strikes and mass demonstrations," and that continued propaganda "should not be used to encourage a repetition of the events of June 17, 1953."[80]

This realization stemmed to some degree from the experience of the uprising and the food program itself. Indeed, because U.S. policy throughout the program retained limited objectives, it could not prevent—and might ultimately and inadvertently have aided—the consolidation of the Ulbricht regime. The initial announcement of the program, on July 10, had taken place at the very height of the struggle within the SED leadership, when Ulbricht's position was being challenged by Politburo member Rudolf Herrnstadt, Ministry for State Security chief Wilhelm Zaisser, and others. Only after the SED leader returned from a brief visit to Moscow (July 8–9, 1953) was Ulbricht able to overcome the rebellion within the leadership, as manifested in the accusations against both Herrnstadt and Zaisser before the Central Committee in mid-July. The U.S. initiative might well have added to the Soviets' sense that Ulbricht's demotion would be seen as a sign of weakness inviting further Western actions. Certainly the announcement of what Molotov called a "propaganda maneuver" provided Ulbricht with a powerful argument to assure his survival. By mid-September, U.S. observers had to admit that the operation "may in fact have increased somewhat the strength of the regime by furnishing it with an opportunity to prove for the first time after 17 June that it could still without the active intervention of Soviet troops maintain a degree of control over a hostile population."[81]

The development of the food program itself reflected its diminishing returns as an anti-regime measure. American observers noted that the stream of food recipients was slacking off during September, as GDR residents reported widespread confiscation of food parcels and "increased Communist harassment." The East Germans' early inclination to "thumb their noses" at their Communist rulers was thus decreasing; plebiscite-type demonstrations could not be maintained at a steady pitch over a protracted period of time. There were signs that East Germans, even within the Protestant Church (one of the strongest centers of resistance within the GDR), were getting wary of being used as tools of American propaganda. Diminishing in scope and becoming a minor sideshow in the Cold War, U.S. officials knew the food program "would lose its news value, its psychological effect and thereby no longer give any opportunity for encouraging manifestation of dissatisfaction or defiance among the East Zone population."[82]

More importantly, the alleviation of some of the economic grievances that had triggered the June uprising and the implementation of the New Course reforms helped diminish the program's effect. So did the heavy Soviet economic aid, which, U.S. observers estimated, "could result in [a] significant rise in living standard even by the end of this year." Despite the food program, Americans came to realize that the "regime [was] keeping [the] situation in hand without overtly greatly increasing police control." Commenting on the Communist reaction to the food program, HICOG pointed out that "two things stood out": GDR authorities neither closed off the sector border, thus keeping the East Berliners from getting packages, nor inflicted severe punishments on food recipients whom they apprehended.[83]

As the Ulbricht regime reestablished its grip on party and population, its repressive measures became more severe. In what Armin Mitter, Stefan Wolle, and Ilko-Sascha Kowalczuk have called "the internal founding of the GDR," the SED reinforced its efforts in the wake of the unrest to expand its repressive and disciplinary apparatus, resulting in a massive expansion of the state security system and barracked People's Police. The growing SED assertiveness reflected rising success in mobilizing party activists, especially in the resistant large plants, and in improving the discipline of police and state security to the degree that the latter were able without Soviet help to break up small-scale gatherings before they got out of hand. Given the liquidation of potential resistance and opposition, U.S. officials on the scene in Berlin predicted in November 1953 that a "June 17 repetition" was "at present unlikely."[84]

Later that fall, a series of political operations trials in the GDR found numerous people guilty of "nefarious activities" as "Western agents." In "Operation Fireworks" alone, a massive attack against the American-sponsored Gehlen Organization ("Org") starting on October 29, GDR state security rolled up a network of presumptive "Org" intelligence assets in East Germany, arresting 218 persons.

These "konzertierte Schläge" (concerted blows) by the GDR state security forces against real and presumptive Western agents sought not only to help "rehabilitate" the regime's, and in particular the state security's, unquestioned authority after its devastating intelligence and political failure in the June uprising, but to reinforce the narrative of June 17 as a Western-instigated coup attempt.

With a new, assertive strategy against the "American Fifth Column in the GDR," involving dramatic choreography of show trials, kidnappings, international press conferences featuring defectors, and media coverage, the East German government went on the offensive in the German-German propaganda war: by revealing the extent to which it had unmasked Western agents in the GDR and Berlin, infiltrated anticommunist groups and the Gehlen organization in the service of Western intelligence agencies, and demonstrated the retention of former Nazis ("fascists") particularly within the "Org," it sought to shock and unsettle the Federal Republic political establishment, undercut U.S. psychological warfare, and play on West European, in particular French reservations against West German rearmament. At least one of the show trials featured a GDR citizen, Helmut Schwenk, a 30-year old sport teacher from a village near Karl-Marx-Stadt who had begun to work for the Gehlen organization after obtaining an American food parcel.[85]

The reassertion of the SED government's authority in the face of American psychological warfare measures, and the dynamics of the East German uprising more generally, had a profound if ambiguous impact on U.S. roll-back efforts. Most succinctly it was reflected in National Security Council Directive No. 174 of December 1953. Previous policy directives, respectively, held out hopes for further Titoist, national-communist regimes in the wake of the Soviet-Yugoslav split, and in effect advocated actively exploiting the potential for "rollback." NSC 174 conceded that the "detachment of any major European satellite from the Soviet bloc does not now appear feasible except by Soviet acquiescence or by war." While the uprising had demonstrated that the Soviets failed fully to "subjugate" the Eastern Europeans or to destroy their desire for freedom, and had proved the unreliability of the satellite armed forces, the USSR's ability to "exercise effective control" over Eastern Europe had "not been appreciably reduced." East Germany posed "special and more difficult problems of control" than the other East European regimes, and hence could serve as a "focal point and example of disaffection for the rest of the Soviet satellites." But the aggressiveness of any U.S. policy toward East Germany had to be tempered by Washington's interest in integrating the Federal Republic with the West and ensuring continued access to West Berlin.[86]

The U.S. approach to Eastern Europe, as reflected in NSC 174, would continue to rely on a host of political, economic, and other measures, including covert operations, despite growing recognition of the mounting difficulties of conducting such operations. NSC 174 prescribed giving encouragement and assistance to the "satellite peoples" in "resistance to their Soviet-dominated regimes," but also warned against incitement to "premature action," which would only bring further terror and reprisals. In sum, U.S. policy makers needed to walk a "fine line, which is not stationary, between exhortations to keep up morale and to maintain passive resistance, and invitations to suicide." That tightrope would be difficult to tread for U.S. policy makers and operatives dealing with Eastern Europe; it would be even harder for the peoples of Eastern Europe to recognize, given the extent to which their geography, passions, and misperceptions influenced how they viewed the role of the United States.

CONCLUSION

THE UNITED STATES DID NOT INSTIGATE the June 1953 uprising. It took the West, in particular the U.S. government, by surprise, as it did the Kremlin and the East German leadership. So much so that American officials even wondered at first if the Communist government had staged the riots as a pretext for military action against West Berlin. But neither was the United States an innocent bystander. As a corollary to U.S. containment strategy, which prioritized the integration of West Germany with the West to bolster Western European prosperity and defenses, the Truman and Eisenhower administrations had launched a broad counteroffensive to keep the spirit of resistance alive behind the Iron Curtain, raising expectations among East Germans (and others in the Soviet orbit) that the West would come to their aid in opposing the SED government and other Moscow-imposed Communist regimes. The U.S. government, through its Radio in the American Sector (RIAS), through psychological warfare efforts geared toward destabilizing and possibly "rolling back" Communist power, and especially through support of German anti-communist groups, played a critical role in fostering a sense of—and at times acts of—opposition on the part of many East Germans and a sense of siege on the part of the regime. RIAS and other government media helped spread the word about the strikes and demonstrations and encouraged East Germans across the country to join them. Concerns that the crisis might escalate into a major military conflagration tempered the extent to which American officials in Germany actively intervened in the turmoil, such as providing arms to the rioters as they faced down Soviet tanks. Nor was Washington sure how far it wanted to push for German unity, the core political demand of the demonstrators, at the very moment when the European Defense Community, which itself had been created through painstaking negotiations of the United States and its European allies, offered a chance to have a West German contribution bolster West European defenses. But the Eisenhower administration, eager to keep the Communist government off balance, demonstrably sought to "keep the pot simmering" in East Germany after it had momentarily boiled over. The crisis revealed the very potential, as well as the limits of, a policy aimed at rolling back Soviet power in Germany (and Europe).

This strategy can be understood only in its larger context of American policy toward Germany since the early postwar years. As World War II drew to a close in Europe, the United States' approach to the defeated German Reich centered on abolishing the remnants of Nazism and transforming the country to demolish the basis for future German aggression. That focus quickly became constrained by the practical demands and exigencies of running the U.S. occupation zone and, increasingly, by shifting perceptions of the postwar ambitions of Stalin's Soviet Union, America's wartime ally with whom it shared supreme authority in occupied Germany through the Control Council. The thrust of American policy veered to the pursuit of a west state project in Germany.

The "American decision to divide Germany" was the result of a complex set of factors, including historical "lessons" about the utility of severe punitive reparations, hard-fought debates within the Truman administration between New Dealers and conservative "rebuilders" over the country's future (as Carolyn Eisenberg has shown), and growing concerns that social upheaval, moral debilitation, and economic desolation throughout much of war-torn Europe held the potential for exploitation by local Communist forces and the Soviet Union (as Melvyn Leffler has argued). Even before the end of the war, the lead American planners and policymakers came to favor resuscitating Germany's coal and steel industry in the Rhein-Ruhr area in the western part of the country as a critical catalyst to the rehabilitation and stabilization of western Europe and the survival there of free enterprise and market capitalism. But the narrative is incomplete without recognizing the dramatic impact developments in the Soviet occupation zone had on American policy. Early Soviet policy in Germany at its core aimed at emasculating German industrial-military might by a massive removal and reparations program. The massive and unilateral removals of German industrial capacities by Soviet agents in the early days of the occupation, experienced by President Truman and his advisers in the context of the Potsdam conference, had a profound effect on the Americans. It confirmed longstanding anti-Soviet sentiments and brought home the gap in expectations and difference in interests between Americans and Soviets. Shocked by massive Soviet plundering and extraction in the

Soviet-occupied territory, and playing to Soviet predilections to retain a free hand in their zone, President Truman's secretary of state, James F. Byrnes, put forward a zonal solution to handling the reparations and other economic problems at the Potsdam Conference in July 1945. Stalin agreed, over the objections of some of his advisers, setting the eastern zone on a very different track from the western zones.

It cannot but have been confusing and unsettling to the Soviets in Germany that American occupation policy under the aegis of General Eisenhower and his deputy military governor, Lucius Clay, did not abide by the Potsdam zonal solution to running Germany. From the summer of 1945 until mid-1947, Clay made persistent efforts to implement all-German solutions to the economic and political problems he faced in his zone, most importantly the establishment of central administrations in key areas. Declassified Russian documents suggest that Clay went further in his pursuit of an all-German solution that previously known. Convinced that he could work with his Soviet counterparts, Clay genuinely believed that his efforts to stabilize the U.S. zone economically depended on countrywide solutions. Convinced that reparations could incentivize Soviet cooperation, Clay had more far-reaching goals in mind as well: in what I call "rollback by cooperation," he was hopeful that implementing all-German solutions would extend American influence into the Soviet zone, eventually undercutting Soviet-backed Communist rule.

Clay's approach was evident in the policy of neutrality vis-à-vis the forced merger of the German Communist Party and the Social Democratic Party in the Soviet zone in the spring of 1946 and the plight of the non-Communist parties participating in the local and state elections in the fall of 1946. Much to the chagrin of many in Washington and within the U.S. military government who wanted him to oppose the merger and unfair elections actively, Clay insisted on a hands-off approach that limited his role to assuring fair political competition throughout Berlin and the U.S. zone. What looked from the perspective of Washington—just weeks after George Kennan's "Long Telegram"—as a textbook example of sovietization appeared much less irreversible from Berlin, where the weakness of the newly formed SED seemed evident and the Communist hold on the population rather shaky. If Western influence could make itself felt in the East, Clay's thinking went, these trends could be reversed. To accomplish that goal, he needed to avoid a break between the occupation powers; hence his proclaimed "neutral" attitude. In the summer and fall of 1946, his hopes seemed to be borne out: American and Soviet economic officials apparently came precipitously close to finding a compromise on reparations and levels of industrial production that, according to Robert Murphy, would have opened up the eastern zone.

Yet among the skeptics in Washington and even within Clay's military administration, the transformation of the Soviet zone was one more reason to forge ahead in building up the Western zones, to creating an "iron curtain of our own." By the spring of 1947, the spiraling confrontation between the Soviet Union and the Western Allies had sucked the air out of any trial balloons for a compromise in Germany. As the Moscow Council of Foreign Ministers was about to convene in March 1947, Truman went before Congress to pledge American assistance to countries around the world that were threatened by Soviet aggression or indigenous communist insurgency backed by Moscow, and set in motion preparations for a European recovery program, the "Marshall Plan," which placed priority on economic rehabilitation in Western Europe, including the western zones of Germany, over the recovery of Germany as one economic unit, in turn stimulating the political cohesion and integration of the Western zones.

The prevailing assumptions in Washington clashed with Clay's and Murphy's arguments that concessions to the Soviets on reparations from current production could be leveraged for extending Western-style democracy to East Germany and ultimately Eastern Europe. If the Truman Doctrine marked the support of governments threatened by Soviet aggression or Communist insurgencies in lands outside the Soviet sphere of influence in Eastern Europe, Clay believed that Soviet influence could eventually be rolled back from Eastern Europe itself by keeping the door open for American influence in East Germany and satisfying Soviet economic and security needs. Secretary of State George C. Marshall and his advisers were unwilling to agree to a quid pro quo in the form of an agreement on reparations from current production for opening up the Soviet zone: reparations would have to wait until the German economy, expected to be the engine of (West) European recovery, was in balance.

It quickly became clear to Clay that the conditions for cooperation with the Soviets were almost prohibitive, without any realistic chance for agreement by the Kremlin leadership. In Moscow, Clay saw his more expansive vision of American influence throughout Germany and Eastern Europe undercut by Stalin's reticence to relinquish control of his zone as well as the mounting anxieties within the Truman administration over Soviet intentions and economic disintegration in Western Europe. With the growing Cold War confrontation, crises from Iran to Eastern Europe reverberated into Allied relations and local politics in Germany, shaped and reinforced confrontational attitudes in Moscow, Washington, and Berlin, and pulled the rug out from under the tentative feelers for a compromise solution on reparations and German unity. As both sides grew concerned over the economic sustainability of their zones, they also became increasingly averse to risking loss of control.

With Stalin's approval, the SED launched a people's initiative for an all-German assembly just prior to the London Council of Foreign Ministers meeting in the fall of 1947. The "People's Congress" movement served to consolidate SED control within the Soviet zone, leading to the ouster of the last major non-Communist figures. But it also aimed (though largely unsuccessfully) at nationally-minded Germans in the western zones, thus highlighting the Soviet zone's potential as a springboard for Communist initiatives that could threaten Western plans for the formation of a West German government (announced at the Six-Power Conference in London in February 1948). In October 1947 Clay, too, had reversed course in his relationship with the Soviets and announced a propaganda counteroffensive against the Soviet Union in Germany.

Newly available Russian archival sources suggest that in the spring of 1948, barely three years after the end of World War II, Soviet worries (however mistaken) about Western "preparations of a new war" against the Soviet Union heightened Stalin's sense that the Soviet zone was on the brink of collapse and with it the USSR's main stake in Europe. Contrary to Western perceptions of the eastern zone's growing isolation from the West, many Soviet officials felt that exactly the opposite was true: they blamed the zone's alarming decline not on their own policies but on destabilizing Western influence, in particular from Berlin, located in the heart of the zone. These perceptions likely played a more influential role in Stalin's decision to institute the Berlin Blockade in the spring of 1948 than previously appreciated.

In fact, the Truman administration had come to appreciate that the jointly occupied former German capital was, for all its vulnerability to Soviet threats, also an "action point" for efforts to impede the sovietization of the eastern zone and destabilize Communist rule. Recently released CIA documents suggest that, with the growing conflict over Berlin brewing in the spring of 1948, U.S. officials were at least initially more concerned about risks and damage to Berlin's usefulness as a center of American intelligence and base of for anti-communist groups operating in the Soviet zone than the interruption of access to the city.

The formal establishment of the German Democratic Republic (GDR) in October 1949 suggested to Truman administration officials that the Soviets might be planning to make East Germany "their major satellite."[1] For the Truman administration, the establishment of two competing German states had not relieved but heightened the confrontation in Germany—and brought on a new sensation of vulnerability vis-à-vis the East. The way the founding of the GDR had been staged as a response to alleged Western "separatism" was only one reason for the profound sense of uncertainty besetting the U.S. High Commission in Germany. Fears that with the Communist-run state in Germany Stalin had acquired a new instrument for pursuing his larger goals in this most important of Cold War battlegrounds fed increasingly gloomy assessments of the "worldwide correlation of forces" that to many seemed to be shifting in favor of the USSR by 1950.

High Commissioner John McCloy therefore believed that beyond building a politically and economically vibrant West Germany that would exert a magnet effect on the GDR, the West needed to actively prevent being "rolled-up" by Eastern unity propaganda: by persistently denying the second German state international legitimacy through nonrecognition, by seizing the initiative in the unity discourse, and by developing psychological warfare apparatus and programs that could counter Communist propaganda. The massive Free German Youth rally held on Whitsuntide in the Soviet sector of Berlin and the October 1950 Volkskammer elections exemplified Western vulnerabilities—and opportunities—in the German Cold War.

In Germany, the American counteroffensive entailed a massive program of overt and covert measures that went well beyond inoculating the Federal Republic politically against similar measures from the East. Especially in the tense months after the outbreak of the Korean War, HICOG began to develop and implement psychological warfare plans that aimed to keep alive the spirit of resistance in the East and envisioned an active rollback of Communist control. As it sought to shore up support for a West German defense contribution within a European Defense Community, the Truman administration also worked with more hard-line elements in the West German government and supported a number of anti-communist (sometimes far-right-wing) groups operating out of West-Berlin and the Federal Republic to counter East German initiatives. Unlike the 1950 Deutschlandtreffen, American officials viewed the August 1951 World Youth Festival in Berlin as a major effort to influence East German youth. Only the outlines of this "psychological warfare" program are known even today, as much of the U.S. operational documentation remains classified. Nonetheless, hundreds of pages of materials declassified via the U.S. Freedom of Information Act for this project make clear that the program was not confined to planning papers in Washington and Berlin. Soviet and East German archival materials also help to demonstrate the extent to which this program affected the "hearts and minds" of the SED leadership and the East German population.

The extent to which rollback in Germany could be pursued was severely circumscribed by the overall American strategy in Europe. That strategy centered on the integration of the Federal Republic of Germany into Western European economic, political, and military structures, believed to be critical to prevent the resurgence of German nationalism and militarism *and* to boost the defense capabilities of Western Europe. The limits on an aggressive rollback approach to East Germany were defined largely by the American priorities in West Germany and requirements of building an increasingly sovereign and assertive Federal Republic. West German officials were reticent to push as far as some "cold warriors" in Washington advocated. Similarly, maintaining Western Allied unity in Germany in face of the threat from the East, particularly with regard to the exposed Allied position in Berlin, often, but not always, constrained American efforts toward East Germany. British and French officials were largely opposed to "hotting-up" the Cold War along the Iron Curtain.

Nowhere was this more evident than in the area of inter-German trade. U.S. economic warfare, in particular export control restrictions, clashed with West European, in particular West German interests in maintaining trade relationships with the East. Truman administration officials believed that exploiting the GDR's dependence on critical raw material deliveries from the West was a most effective measure to counter continued East German harassment of access to West Berlin. American officials, moreover, sought to impede the consolidation and strengthening of the GDR by exploiting East Germany's economic vulnerabilities. Persistent and increasingly frustrated American efforts notwithstanding, the West Germans stubbornly resisted cutting off interzonal trade and remained skeptical of more far-reaching economic warfare measures. Symbolic of this fact, West Germany renewed the "interzonal" trade agreement at the height of the June 1953 uprising.

Despite persistent efforts to keep alive the spirit of resistance behind the "Iron Curtain," American observers came to believe the SED led by Ulbricht to be in firm control of events—ironically precisely at the moment events spun out of control. Symptomatic of the degree to which American analysts overestimated the stability of the situation in the GDR in the months leading up to the June 1953 uprising was the fact that they initially considered the vastly increasing influx of refugees from the East into West Germany to be weakening the ferment of unrest in the GDR. Rather than a sign of bourgeoning unrest and deterioration, the growing numbers of refugees pouring into Berlin were interpreted to indicate the East Germans' decreasing energy to resist and flagging morale. HICOG reported to Washington in February 1953 that it could not be expected that even if called upon to do so, the East Germans would be willing and capable of carrying out a revolution unless such a call coincided with a declaration of war and/or assurance of Western military support. Four months later, political and labor unrest engulfed much of the GDR.

The June 17, 1953, uprising might have turned the regime crisis in the GDR into an international military conflict. Certainly many East Germans expected the West to intervene and support the uprising. Once the East German regime lay prostrated by its own people, the Eisenhower administration, much to the frustration of its more hardline "cold warriors" around C.D. Jackson, opted for caution—thankfully so, since U.S. military intervention might have quickly escalated into war. Lacking full understanding of the developments in East Berlin and the GDR, both Washington and Moscow were intent on avoiding a superpower conflagration over the Soviet military crackdown. Eisenhower administration officials did seek to exploit the opportunity to keep the East German regime off balance and to nourish the spirit of resistance among East Germans through a food aid program. These efforts, modestly successful as they were, as revealed by East German archival evidence, however, raised serious questions about the possibility of effective rollback so long as Moscow was willing to back its satellite regimes militarily.

In the aftermath of the June 1953 uprising, the Eisenhower administration continued to wrestle with the question of how the United States would respond should a repetition of the events of June 17, 1953, occur—and whether Washington should seek to stimulate comparable uprisings there or elsewhere in the Soviet bloc. In October 1953 a flurry of (unsubstantiated) press reports that suggested that some 5,000-10,000 anti-communist East Germans, Czechoslovak partisans, and Red Army deserters had banded together and were fighting their way to freedom in the West brought the issue to the fore. "What actions [could we] take if we were faced with a repetition of the June 17 incidents on a widespread scale, or an indigenous strike call, or the emergence of armed bands seeking either external safe haven or internal sanctuary in a guerilla-support area," an agitated C.D. Jackson queried the Operations Coordinating Board (which had replaced the PSB): "We might even be confronted with a premature 'Warsaw uprising' deliberately provoked by the Soviets," Jackson argued, in a distorted understanding of the summer 1944 effort by the Polish underground resistance to liberate Poland from German occupation. "I feel strongly that we must develop our capabilities for appropriate supporting, harassing and diversionary actions short of precipitating overt military action." A year and a half later, in the spring of 1955, indications of unrest in East Germany over food shortages led an unnamed "inter-Departmental agency" within the Eisenhower administration (likely the NSC) to devise suggested "courses of action for exploiting a second mass uprising in East Germany." The State Department alerted its missions in Germany that a "popular uprising similar to that which occurred on June 17, 1953," though not likely, could "not be entirely excluded."[2]

The options developed by the administration in June 1955 reflected how much the East German uprising had already affected the American reaction to a second June 17-type incident, and perhaps any revolt in Soviet-dominated East-Central Europe, even before the Hungarian Revolution finally called the policy of rollback into question. Reminding its missions that it was contrary to U.S. policy for U.S. troops and officials abroad "to instigate such an uprising or to seek to aid and abet it through participation therein," the guideline held out immediate Western demands for a high-level (heads-of-state or ambassadorial) meeting with the Soviets as the most effective way to dramatize the plight of the East Germans. The West, the guideline suggests, was also to indicate its willingness to lend technical assistance in overcoming agricultural and industrial difficulties in the GDR, though this aid would be conditioned on the relaxation of a series of repressive control measures. Anticipated Soviet refusals could be "turned to effective propaganda advantage" by the West. RIAS, finally, was to emphasize the "repetition of hard news and official statements" in the case of another uprising, but not lend its support to the rebels outright. No active intervention, even after an uprising was started, was apparently contemplated.[3]

Leveraging large-scale technical aid to improve political conditions in East Germany was controversial within the Eisenhower administration; after all, some U.S. officials asked, could it be in the American interest to stabilize the GDR economically given that economic dislocations fed popular resentment towards the regime? Yet the idea pointed to another lesson from the 1953 experience: Building on the Eisenhower packages program (July–October 1953), special and discreet U.S. relief efforts for the East German population, administrations officials came to believe, would not only serve to relieve human misery behind the Iron Curtain but achieve "the most powerful and long lasting psychological and political advantages." Above all, such programs would strengthen the Western orientation of the East Germans, maintain resistance potential among the GDR population, and demonstrate to West Germans genuine American interest in the plight of their compatriots.[4]

Thus, in the months after the food packages program, the Eisenhower administration provided funding for medical relief efforts in the GDR, helped fund free meals at zonal crossing points, and, during Christmas time, distribution of DM 20 cash to East Germans visiting the West. Up to mid-February 1954 alone, an estimated 280,000 East Germans received foodstuffs supplied at crossing points. U.S. funding also supported programs sponsored by West German charitable organizations that mailed packages containing food and clothing to East Germans, including political prisoners who often depended on such support for their subsistence. Similarly, U.S. aid furnished supplies and other assistance to church welfare activities in the Soviet Zone. In June 1954, Eisenhower authorized a $3 million allocation under the Mutual Security Act that encouraged "interzonal" travel as well as scholarships for East German students to attend the Free University of Berlin and other educational institutions in the Federal Republic. Early in 1955, American officials in Berlin even tried to interest the Protestant Church in arranging week-long vacations for young East Germans in the West, and approached the Adenauer government to support a greater number of bicycle trips by East German youth across West Germany. In the following years, U.S. financial support for what became known as "Soviet zone projects" increased steadily, anticipating "small step" improvements for East Germans that became the hallmark of West German *Ostpolitik* in the 1960s and 1970s. And in yet another regard, the administration learned lessons from the 1953 experience: American funding would be provided covertly and to a large degree channeled through the Ministry for All-German Affairs, which by the mid-1950s was reportedly supporting some 900 organizations involved in aid to East Germans.[5]

Maintaining contact with the people of East Germany and encouraging anti-communist elements in the GDR through such "Soviet zone projects" increasingly complemented, as part of a multipronged approach by the United States vis-à-vis the GDR, continued American efforts to place the Soviets and SED on the defensive on the issue of reunification, to stimulate conflicts within the communist regime, to exploit Berlin as an "island of resistance" and as a hub for intelligence and psychological warfare operations, and to oppose diplomatic recognition of the SED government by other countries and international organizations. Such efforts took on increasing importance as the 1954 foreign ministers conference in Berlin and the 1955 Geneva summit failed to make any appreciable progress towards German unity, and as the Soviet Union in March 1954 declared the GDR "free to decide on internal and external affairs," ostensibly bestowing sovereignty on the GDR and hardening the status quo of a divided Germany. The following year, West Germany's accession to NATO and the GDR's inclusion in the newly formed Warsaw Pact further cemented the country's division.[6]

But even as "any early prospect for liberation" increasingly dimmed, the head of the Eastern Affairs Division of the U.S. Mission in Berlin argued in the spring of 1956, East Germans "seem to be clinging to the notion of free elections as the means of freeing the Soviet Zone from the Communists and reuniting with West Germany." East Germans "looked toward the West and above all the United States for the future," their hopes "built around the idea that in some undefined way the United States will rescue the Soviet Zone from the Communists." Although the Eisenhower administration remained committed to the goal of German unification, U.S. possibilities to effect such an outcome, the NSC acknowledged in September 1956, were severely limited. Unprepared to resort to military conflict to roll back Soviet domination of East Germany (or any other Soviet satellite in East-Central Europe, for that matter), and increasingly dismissive of the likelihood of a successful internal revolution in the GDR in the face of an ever effective repressive system, American policymakers knew that reunification compatible with U.S. security interests ultimately depended on "a basic change in Soviet policy toward Germany." That basic change would not come until Mikhail Gorbachev.[7]

The contingency of another insurrection in East Germany would haunt American policy until the fall of 1989. More importantly, finally, it also consistently haunted the regime in East Germany, which never fully recovered from the crisis of legitimacy that it confronted in June 1953. Eisenhower was right when shortly after the uprising he professed to be "quite certain that future historians, in their analysis of the causes which will have brought about the disintegration of the Communist Empire, will single out those brave East Germans who dared to rise against the cannons of tyranny with nothing but their bare hands and their stout hearts, as a root cause."[8]

NOTES

PREFACE

1. President Bush to Federal Chancellor Helmut Kohl, 9 February 1990, in Hanns Jürgen Küsters und Daniel Hofmann, eds., *Deutsche Einheit: Sonderedition aus den Akten des Bundeskanzleramtes, 1989–90* (München: R. Oldenbourg, 1998), 784. Four days later, with a "highly satisfactory" Soviet agreement that Germany could unify internally in hand, Kohl told Bush during a phone conversation, "I do believe the letter you sent to me before I left for Moscow will one day be considered one of the great documents in German-American history." This was a great moment for the Germans, Kohl continued: "Without our American friends, this would not have been possible." Bush-Kohl telephone conversation on the situation in Germany, 13 February 1990, History and Public Policy Program Digital Archive, George H. W. Bush Presidential Library, http://digitalarchive.wilsoncenter.org/document/116232.

2. Jeffrey Engel, "Bush, Germany, and the Power of Time: How History Makes History," *Diplomatic History* 37, no. 4 (September 2013): 639–63, here 641. See also Jeffrey Engel, *When the World Seemed New: George H. W. Bush and the End of the Cold War* (New York, NY: Houghton Mifflin Harcourt, 2017).

3. Robert Michael Gates, *From the Shadows: The Ultimate Insider's Story of Five Presidents and How They Won the Cold War* (New York: Simon & Schuster, 1996), 484.

4. Philip Zelikow and Condoleezza Rice, *Germany Unified and Europe Transformed: A Study in Statecraft*, 1st Harvard University Press paperback ed. (Cambridge, MA: Harvard University Press, 1997), 28.

5. Robert L. Hutchings, *American Diplomacy and the End of the Cold War: An*

Insider's Account of U.S. Policy in Europe, 1989–1992 (Washington, DC: Woodrow Wilson Center Press, 1997), 97.

6. Thomas Alan Schwartz, *America's Germany: John J. McCloy and the Federal Republic of Germany* (Cambridge, MA: Harvard University Press, 1991), 307.

7. Burton C. Gaida, *USA–DDR: Politische, kulturelle, und wirtschaftliche Beziehungen seit 1974*, Beiträge zur Deutschlandforschung, Bd. 4 (Bochum, Germany: N. Brockmeyer, 1989). On non-recognition, see William G. Gray's superb *Germany's Cold War: The Global Campaign to Isolate East Germany 1949–1969* (Chapel Hill, NC: University of North Carolina Press, 2003).

8. Schwartz, *America's Germany*, 308.

9. Hutchings, *American Diplomacy and the End of the Cold War*, 43–44; Zelikow/Rice, *Germany Unified*, 31.

10. Melvyn P. Leffler, *A Preponderance of Power: National Security, the Truman Administration, and the Cold War* (Stanford: Stanford University Press, 1992); see also Melvyn P. Leffler, *The Specter of Communism: The United States and the Origins of the Cold War, 1917–1953* (New York: Hill and Wang, 1994). Gregory Mitrovich, *Undermining the Kremlin: America's Strategy to Subvert the Soviet Bloc, 1947–1956* (Ithaca, NY: Cornell University Press, 2000). See also Peter Grose, *Operation Rollback: America's Secret War behind the Iron Curtain* (Boston: Houghton Mifflin, 2000).

11. Bernd Stöver, *Die Befreiung vom Kommunismus: Amerikanische Liberation Policy im Kalten Krieg, 1947–1991* (Köln: Böhlau, 2002), 35–36. See also Michael Hochgeschwender, *Freiheit in der Offensive? Der Kongress fuer kulturelle Freiheit und die Deutschen* (Munich: R. Oldenbourg, 1998). On psychological warfare, see especially Kenneth Osgood, *Total Cold War: Eisenhower's Secret Propaganda Battle at Home and Abroad* (Lawrence, KS: University Press of Kansas, 2006). On the important new releases by the "Independent Commission for Research on the History of the Federal Intelligence Service," see www.uhk-bnd.de.

12. John Lewis Gaddis, "On Starting All Over Again: A Naïve Approach to the Study of the Cold War," in *Reviewing the Cold War: Approaches, Interpretations, and Theory*, ed. Odd Arne Westad (Portland, OR: F. Cass, 2000), 27–42; Melvyn P. Leffler, "New Approaches, Old Interpretations, and Prospective Reconfigurations," *Diplomatic History* 19, no. 2 (Spring 1995): 172–97.

13. Wolfram Hanrieder, *Deutschland, Europa, Amerika: Die Außenpolitik der Bundesrepublik Deutschland, 1949–1994*, 2nd ed. (Paderborn: Schöningh, 1995); Schwartz, *America's Germany*; see also Rolf Steininger, ed., *Die doppelte Eindämmung: Europäische Sicherheit und deutsche Frage in den Fünfzigern* (München: v. Hase & Koehler, 1993); John H. Backer, *Die deutschen Jahre des Generals Clay. Der Weg zur Bundesrepublik, 1945–1949* (München: C. H. Beck, 1983); Wolfgang Krieger, *General Lucius D. Clay und die amerikanische Deutschlandpolitik, 1945–1949* (Stuttgart: Klett-Cotta, 1987); Jean Edward Smith, *Lucius D. Clay: An American Life* (New York: Henry Holt, 1990).

14. For a good overview, see Jessica C. E. Gienow-Hecht and Frank Schumacher, eds., *Culture and International History* (New York: Berghahn Books, 2003); Jessica C. E. Gienow-Hecht, "Academics, Cultural Transfer, and the Cold War: A Critical Review," *Diplomatic History* 24, no. 3 (Summer 2000): 465–94; Frank Schumacher, *Kalter Krieg und Propaganda: Die USA, der Kampf um die Weltmeinung, und die ideelle Westbindung der Bundesrepublik Deutschland, 1945–1955* (Trier: WVT, 2000); Jessica C. E. Gienow-Hecht, *Transmission Impossible: American Journalism as Cultural Diplomacy in Postwar Germany, 1945–1955* (Baton Rouge: Louisiana State University Press, 1999).

15. Carolyn Woods Eisenberg, *Drawing the Line: The American Decision to Divide Germany, 1944–1949* (Cambridge: Cambridge University Press, 1996); March Trachtenberg, *A Constructed Peace: The Making of the European Settlement 1945–1963* (Princeton, NJ: Princeton University Press, 1999).

16. Geir Lundestad, *The American Non-Policy towards Eastern Europe, 1943–1947* (Tromsö: Universitetsforlaget, 1978).

17. John Lewis Gaddis, *The Long Peace: Inquiries into the History of the Cold War* (New York: Oxford University Press, 1989); Leffler, *A Preponderance of Power*, passim; John H. Backer, *The Decision to Divide Germany: American Foreign Policy in Transition* (Durham, NC: Duke University Press, 1978); Manfred Knapp, ed., *Die USA und Deutschland, 1918–1975: Deutsch-amerikanische Beziehungen zwischen Rivalität und Partnerschaft* (München: C. H. Beck, 1978); Frank Ninkovich, *Germany and the United States: The Transformation of the German Question since 1945* (Boston: Twayne, 1988).

18. Anjana Buckow, *Zwischen Propaganda und Realpolitik* (Stuttgart: Franz Steiner, 2003); Schanett Riller, *Funken für die Freiheit: Die U.S.-amerikanische Informationspolitik gegenüber der DDR* (Trier: WVT, 2004); Petra Galle, *RIAS Berlin und Berliner Rundfunk 1945–1949* (Hamburg: Lit, 2003); Gaida, *USA–DDR*; Stöver, *Befreiung vom Kommunismus*.

19. On the records of the former SED and GDR, see Hermann Weber, "Die aktuelle Situation in den Archiven für die Erforschung der DDR Geschichte," *Deutschland Archiv* 27, no. 7 (1994): 690–99; Lothar Dralle, "Das DSF–Archiv als Quelle zur Geschichte der DDR–Der Volksaufstand vom 17. Juni 1953," *Deutschland Archiv* 25, no. 8 (1992): 837–45; Hermann Weber, "Die Wissenschaft benötigt die Unterlagen der Archive. Einige Überlegungen zur Archivsituation in Berlin," *Deutschland Archiv* 24, no. 5 (1991): 452–57. Christian Ostermann, "New Research on the GDR," *Cold War International History Project Bulletin* 4 (Fall 1994): 34, 39–44; Ulrich Mählert, ed., *Vademekum DDR-Forschung: Ein Leitfaden zu Archiven, Forschungseinrichtungen, Bibliotheken, Einrichtungen der politischen Bildung, Vereinen, Museen, und Gedenkstätten* (Opladen: Leske & Buderich, 1999).

20. Hermann Weber, *DDR: Grundriß der Geschichte, 1945–1990* (Hannover: Fackelträger, 1991); Hermann Weber *Die DDR, 1945–1986* (München: Oldenbourg, 1988); Hermann Weber, ed., *Parteiensystem zwischen Demokratie und Volksdemokratie: Dokumente und Materialien zum Funktionswandel der Parteien und Massenorganisationen*

in der SBZ/DDR, 1945–1950. (Cologne: Wissenschaft und Politik, 1982); Hermann Weber, "Weiße Flecken," in der DDR-Geschichtsschreibung, *Aus Politik und Zeitgeschichte* 11 (1990): 3–15; Dietrich Staritz, ed., *Einheitsfront, Einheitspartei: Kommunisten und Sozialdemokraten in Ost- und Westeuropa, 1944–1948* (Köln: Wissenschaft und Politik, 1989); Dietrich Staritz, *Geschichte der DDR, 1945–1985* (Frankfurt/M.: Suhrkamp, 1985); Staritz, *Die Gründung der DDR: Von der sowjetischen Besatzungsherrschaft l zum sozialistischen Staat,* 2nd ed. (München: dtv, 1987); Karl Wilhelm Fricke, *Die DDR-Staatssicherheit,* 3rd ed. (Köln: Wissenschaft und Politik, 1989); Karl Wilhelm Fricke, *MfS intern: Macht, Strukturen, Auflösung der DDR-Staatssicherheit: Analyse und Dokumentation* (Köln: Wissenschaft und Politik, 1991); Karl Wilhelm Fricke, *Opposition und Widerstand in der DDR* (Köln: Wissenschaft und Politik, 1984); Gisela Helwig, "Die DDR in vergleichender Perspektive: Erste internationale Konferenz zur Innen- und Außenpolitik der DDR in den USA," *DeutschlandArchiv* (1983): 750–52; Gisela Helwig, *Rückblicke auf die DDR* (Köln: Wissenschaft und Politik, 1994); Peter Christian Ludz, *Die DDR zwischen Ost und West* (München: C. H. Beck, 1980); Ilse Spittmann, ed., *Die SED in Geschichte und Gegenwart* (Köln: Wissenschaft und Politik, 1987); Ilse Spittmann, ed., *DDR-Lesebuch: Stalinisierung, 1945–1955* (Köln: Wissenschaft und Politik, 1991); Carola Stern, *Ulbricht: Eine politische Biographie* (Köln: Kiepenheuer & Witsch, 1963).

21. Particularly noteworthy are the research and publications emanating from the Leibniz-Zentrum für zeithistorische Forschung in Potsdam led initially by Jürgen Kocka, Konrad Jarausch, and later Martin Sabrow and Frank Bösch. See especially the work by Jens Giesecke, Michael Lemke, and Thomas Lindenberger. For this study see especially Michael Lemke, *Einheit oder Sozialismus? Die Deutschlandpolitik der SED, 1949–1961* (Köln: Böhlau, 2001), and his edited volume *Sowjetisierung und Eigenständigkeit in der SBZ/DDR (1945–1953)* (Köln: Böhlau, 1999).

22. See Armin Mitter, "Die Ereignisse im Juni und Juli 1953 in der DDR," *Aus Politik und Zeitgeschichte* 5 (1991): 31–41; Armin Mitter, Stefan Wolle, and Ilko-Sascha Kowalczuk, eds., *Der Tag X: 17. Juni 1953: Die "Innere Staatsgründung" der DDR als Ergebnis der Krise 1952/54* (Berlin: Links, 1995); Andreas Malycha, *Partei von Stalins Gnaden? Die Entwicklung der SED zur Partei neuen Typs in den Jahren 1946 bis 1950* (Berlin: Dietz, 1996); Andreas Malycha, *Die SED, 1946–1953* (Paderborn: Schöningh, 2000); Ilko-Sascha Kowalczuk, *17. Juni 1953. Geschichte eines Aufstands* (München: Beck, 2013).

23. Timothy Garton Ash, *In Europe's Name: Germany and the Divided Continent* (New York, NY: Random House, 1993); Norman M. Naimark, *"To Know Everything and to Report Everything Worth Knowing": Building the East German Police State, 1945–1949,* Cold War International History Project Working Paper 10 (Washington, DC, August 1994); Naimark, *The Russians in Germany: A History of the Soviet Zone of Occupation, 1945–1949* (Cambridge, MA: Harvard University Press, 1995); Catherine

Epstein, *The Last Revolutionaries: German Communists and Their Century* (Cambridge, MA: Harvard University Press, 2003); Konrad Jarausch, ed., *Dictatorship as Experience: Toward a Socio-Cultural History of the GDR* (New York: Berghahn Books, 1999).

24. Notable exceptions are: Ingrid Muth, *Die DDR-Aussenpolitik 1949–1972: Inhalte, Strukturen, Mechanismen* (Berlin: Ch. Links, 2000); Hermann Wentker, *Aussenpolitik in engen Grenzen: Die DDR im internationalen System* (Munich: Oldenbourg, 2007); Joachim Scholtyseck, *Die Aussenpolitik der DDR* (München: Oldenbourg, 2003). On the events of 17 June 1953, see Roger Engelmann and Ilko-Sascha Kowalczuk, eds., *Volkserhebung gegen den SED-Staat: Eine Bestandsaufnahme zum 17. Juni 1953* (Göttingen: Vandenhoeck & Ruprecht, 2005); Ilko-Sascha Kowalczuk, Armin Mitter, and Stefan Wolle, eds., *Der Tag X*; Manfred Hagen, *DDR, Juni '53: Die erste Volkserhebung im Stalinismus* (Stuttgart: F. Steiner, 1992); Christian Ostermann, ed., *Uprising in East Germany 1953: The Cold War, the German Question, and the First Major Upheaval Behind the Iron Curtain* (Budapest: CEU Press, 2001).

25. Rolf Badstübner und Wilfried Loth, eds., *Wilhelm Pieck: Aufzeichnungen zur Deutschlandpolitik, 1945–1953* (Berlin: Akademie Verlag, 1994).

26. Important assessments are Stefan Creuzberger and Rainer Lindner, eds., *Russische Archive und Geschichtswissenschaft: Rechtsgrundlagen, Arbeitsbedingungen, Forschungsperspektiven* (Frankfurt/M.: Lang, 2003); Andrea Graziosi, "The New Soviet Archival Sources," *Cahiers du Monde russe* 40, nos. 1–2 (January–June 1999): 13–64; Silvio Pons, "The Papers on Foreign and International Policy in the Russian Archives: The Stalin Years," *Cahiers du monde russe* 40, nos. 1–2 (January–June 1999): 235–50; Norman Naimark, "Cold War Studies and New Materials on Stalin," *Russian Review* 61 (January 2002): 1–15; Patricia Grimsted, ed., *Archives of Russia: A Directory and Bibliographic Guide to Holdings in Moscow and St. Petersburg*, 2 vols. (Armonk, NY: M. E. Sharpe, 2000); Patricia Grimsted, *Archives of Russia Seven Years After: "Purveyors of Sensations" or "Shadows Cast to the Past,"* CWIHP Working Paper No. 20, 2 vols. (Washington, DC: Woodrow Wilson International Center for Scholars, 1999). See most recently Norman Naimark, "Post-Soviet Russian Historiography on the Emergence of the Soviet Bloc," *Kritika* 5, no. 3 (Summer 2004): 561–80; and Mark Kramer, "Archival Policies and Historical Memory in the Post-Soviet Era," *Demokratizatsiya* 20:3 (Summer 2012), 204–15.

27. Jochen P. Laufer and Georgij P. Kynin, with Viktor Knoll, eds., *Die UdSSR und die deutsche Frage, 1941–1948: Dokumente aus dem Archiv für Aussenpolitik der Russischen Föderation*, 4 vols. (Berlin: Duncker & Humblot, 2004) (hereafter cited as Laufer et al., *Die UdSSR*); Jan Foitzik, comp., *Inventar der Befehle des Obersten Chefs der Sowjetischen Militäradministration in Deutschland (SMAD), 1945–1949* (München/ New Providence: K. G. Saur, 1995); Bernd Bonwetsch, Gennadij Bordjugov, Norman M. Naimark (eds.), *Sowjetische Politik in der SBZ 1945–1949: Dokumente zur Tätigkeit der Propagandaverwaltung (Informationsverwaltung) der SMAD unter Sergej Tjul'panow*

(Bonn: J.H.W. Dietz Nachf., 1998); Gerhard Wettig, ed., *Der Tjul'panov-Bericht: Sowjetische Besatzungspolitik in Deutschland nach dem Zweiten Weltkrieg* (Göttingen: V&R Unipress, 2012).

CHAPTER I

1. Wolfgang Schivelbusch, *In a Cold Crater: Cultural and Intellectual Life in Berlin, 1945–1948* (Berkeley: University of California Press, 1998), 1–2.

2. Walter J. Brown, *James F. Byrnes of South Carolina* (Macon, GA: Mercer University Press, 1990), 268.

3. Joseph E. Davies Diary, 30 July 1945, Joseph E. Davies Papers, Library of Congress.

4. John J. McCloy Diary, 17 July 1945, McCloy Papers, ser. 2, DY1:18, Amherst College Archives.

5. Roosevelt to Secretary of State Hull, 29 September 1944, U.S. Department of State, ed., *Foreign Relations of the United States: Conferences at Malta and Yalta, 1945* (Washington, D.C.: U.S. Government Printing Office, 1955), 155 (hereafter cited as *FRUS, year*, followed by document title if any mentioned).

6. Ibid.

7. Roosevelt to Hull, 20 October 1944, ibid., 159.

8. Robert Dallek, *Franklin D. Roosevelt and American Foreign Policy, 1932–1945* (New York: Oxford University Press, 1979), 472; Thomas Alan Schwartz, *America's Germany: John J. McCloy and the Federal Republic of Germany* (Cambridge, MA: Harvard University Press, 1991), 19.

9. Special Assistant to the Secretary of State (Pasvolsky), "Treatment of Germany," memorandum, 15 November 1944, *FRUS, Conferences at Malta and Yalta, 1945*, 172.

10. John Morton Blum, ed., *From the Morgenthau Diaries: Years of War, 1941–1945* (Boston: Houghton Mifflin, 1967), 351. On Morgenthau's approach, see Bernd Greiner, *Die Morgenthau-Legende: Zur Geschichte eines umstrittenen Plans* (Hamburg: Hamburger Edition, 1995); Wilfried Mausbach, *Zwischen Morgenthau und Marshall: Das wirtschaftspolitische Deutschlandkonzept der USA, 1944–1947* (Düsseldorf: Droste, 1996); Warren Kimball, ed., *Swords or Ploughshares? The Morgenthau Plan for Defeated Germany, 1943–1946* (Philadelphia: Lippincott, 1976).

11. *FRUS, Conferences at Malta and Yalta, 1945*, 155.

12. S. M. Plokhy, *Yalta: The Price of Peace* (New York: Viking, 2010), 95–101. The Yalta Conference had tasked a committee to work out a solution, but its deliberations never really took off.

13. Maisky to Molotov, draft circular, 15 February 1945, in Laufer et al., *Die UdSSR*; Plokhy, *Yalta*, 110–11.

14. Marc Trachtenberg, *A Constructed Peace: The Making of the European Settlement, 1945–1963*, Princeton Studies in International History and Politics (Princeton, NJ: Princeton University Press, 1999), 4–10.

15. Cited in Geoffrey Roberts, "Sexing up the Cold War: New Evidence on the Molotov–Truman Talks of April 1945," *Cold War History*, 4:3 (2004), 105–25.

16. Melvyn P. Leffler, *The Struggle for Germany and the Origins of the Cold War*, Sixth Alois Mertes Memorial Lecture, no. 16 (Washington, D.C.: GHI, 1996), 15.

17. Ibid., 15–16.

18. Ibid., 20.

19. Carolyn Woods Eisenberg, *Drawing the Line: The American Decision to Divide Germany, 1944–1949* (Cambridge: Cambridge University Press, 1996), 26–31, 91; Mausbach, *Zwischen Morgenthau und Marshall*, 27; see also Ilse Dorothee Pautsch, *Die territoriale Deutschlandplanung des amerikanischen Aussenministeriums, 1941–1943* (New York: P. Lang, 1990).

20. John Lewis Gaddis, *George F. Kennan: An American Life* (New York: Penguin, 2011), 189.

21. Peter E. Fäßler, *Durch den "Eisernen Vorhang": Die Deutsch-Deutschen Wirtschaftsbeziehungen, 1949–1969*, Wirtschafts- und Sozialhistorische Studien, Bd. 14 (Köln: Böhlau, 2006), 19–27; Rainer Karlsch, *Allein Bezahlt? Die Reparationsleistungen der SBZ/DDR 1945–1953* (Berlin: Christian Links, 1993), 40–44.

22. Walter Brown Diary, 24 July 1945, quoted in Daniel Yergin, *Shattered Peace: The Origins of the Cold War* (New York: Penguin, 1990), 118; Trachtenberg, *A Constructed Peace*, 27.

23. Davies Diary, 21 July 1945, Davies Papers, box 19, Library of Congress.

24. McCloy Diary, 17 July 1945. At times such anti-Soviet feelings went hand in hand with compassion for the Germans' fate; McCloy, for one, thought the "future of these people is nothing less than terrible and one continually is sympathizing with them."

25. Davies Diary, 17 July 1945; ibid., 19 July 1945. On Davies's role, see Eisenberg, *Drawing the Line*, 91–93.

26. Davies Diary, 19 July 1945.

27. "Outline of a USSR Reparations Program," Maisky to Molotov, 28 July 1944; Jochen Laufer, "Politik und Bilanz: Der Sowjetischen Demontagen in der SBZ/DDR 1945–1950," in *Sowjetische Demontagen in Deutschland, 1944–1949: Hintergründe, Ziele, und Wirkungen*, ed. Rainer Karlsch and Jochen Laufer (Berlin: Duncker & Humblot, 2002), 31.

28. Emblematic of these anxieties, Stalin had told the Polish premier in exile, Stanisław Mikolajczyk, in August 1944 that "the Germans are a strong nation." The German military and economic cadres would outlast Hitler, and within twenty to twenty-five years the "German threat may rise again." Stanislaw Mikolajczyk Collection, box 49, folder 22, Hoover Institution Archives. By April 1945, he had revised his estimate downward; receiving a Yugoslav leadership delegation, he stated that the Germans "will recover, and very quickly. That is a highly developed industrial country with an extremely qualified and numerous working class and technical intelligentsia.

Give them twelve to fifteen years and they'll be on their feet again." Milovan Djilas, *Conversations with Stalin*, trans. from Serbo-Croatian by Michael Petrovich (New York: Harcourt Brace 1962), 97–117.

29. Maisky to Molotov, "Outline of a USSR Reparations Program," 28 July 1944, in Laufer et al., *Die UdSSR*, 1:425–36. Until 1946, the Soviet Foreign Ministry was called the People's Commissariat for Foreign Affairs, but I use the more generic term "foreign ministry" for ease of reading.

30. Maisky to Molotov, 9 October 1944, in Laufer et al., *Die UdSSR*, 1:477–82.

31. Gromyko to Molotov, 6 October 1944, in ibid., 1:472–76. On November 12 Gromyko reported on a dinner conversation with Morgenthau during which the U.S. Treasury secretary assured Gromyko that Germany would in fact be turned into an agrarian economy without any heavy or light industry. The Ruhr area would be separated, Germany would lose its shipbuilding industry, and 25 million Germans would be moved elsewhere, including to Africa, where there was enough space for them. Henry L. Stimson, who Morgenthau acknowledged opposed his plan, was "very advanced in years [and] did not live in the world of today." Secretary of State Cordell Hull, not enthusiastic about Morgenthau's plan either, was also "stricken with age" and sick and had not really fully grasped the proposal. Morgenthau professed to be mystified as to why Leo Pasvolsky, the top postwar planner at the State Department, whom he labeled a White Russian, was even involved in the matter. Morgenthau, as reported by Gromyko, continued to have the enthusiastic support of the president, and while he did not want to strengthen the German will to resist by publicizing his idea, would nonetheless continue to push it after war's end. He reportedly asked Gromyko not to share the nature of their conversation with the State Department. Gromyko to Molotov, 13 November 1944, in Laufer et al., *Die UdSSR*, 1:496–501.

32. Jochen Laufer, "Stalin und die deutschen Reparationen (1941–1953)" (unpublished paper presented at the Cold War International History Project Conference, Yale University, September 1999), 6–7; Laufer et al., *Die UdSSR*, 1:381–85.

33. From the Diary of the Armistice Commission, 30 April 1944, in Laufer et al., *Die UdSSR*, 1:383–84.

34. Voroshilov to Molotov, 12 May 1944, in Laufer et al., *Die UdSSR*, 1:395–98, quote 397; Voroshilov to Stalin, 12 June 1944, in ibid., 1:408–9.

35. "Proposed Control Mechanism," memorandum, 21 August 1944, in Laufer et al., *Die UdSSR*, 1:448–51; Molotov to Gusev, 25 August 1944, in ibid., 451–53. On the Soviet plans for zonal occupation, see Jochen Laufer, "Die UdSSR und die Zoneneinteilung Deutschlands (1943/44)," *Zeitschrift für Geschichtswissenschaft* 43, no. 4 (1995): 309–31.

36. Gunther Mai, *Der Alliierte Kontrollrat in Deutschland, 1945–1948: Alliierte Einheit-deutsche Teilung?* (München: Oldenbourg, 1995), 24–28.

37. Ibid.

38. Schivelbusch, *In a Cold Crater*, ix, 10.

39. Cited in Laufer, "Politik und Bilanz," 34.

40. Maisky to Stalin, 19 December 1944, in Laufer et al., *Die UdSSR*, 1:515–17; Maisky to Stalin, 20 December 1944, in ibid., 517–21.

41. Laufer, "Politik und Bilanz," 39.

42. Maisky to Molotov, draft circular, 15 February 1945, in Laufer et al., *Die UdSSR*, 1:534–36.

43. Pauley now backed away from discussing any number total for reparations, conceding at most a percentage key that would leave the USSR with half of the total, and suspended discussions on forced labor after Truman instructed him to avoid any impression of sanctioning "slave labor." Mausbach, *Zwischen Morgenthau und Marshall*, 130–34.

44. Maisky to Molotov, 2 July 1945, in Laufer et al., *Die UdSSR*, 2:36–40.

45. Ibid.

46. The Reparations Commission met twice more at the end of August, but without result. Stalin had weakened the Soviet participation by suspending Maisky as the Soviet delegate. In September the commission's mandate was effectively transferred to the Allied Control Council in Berlin. Laufer et al., *Die UdSSR*, 2:lxxix–lxxxi.

47. Maisky was not a member of the Special Committee responsible for dismantling. Laufer, "Politik und Bilanz," 45.

48. Ibid., 36, 38, 45–47; Karlsch, *Allein Bezahlt?*, 60–61.

49. Laufer, "Politik und Bilanz," 36, 48–50; Karlsch, *Allein Bezahlt?*, 60–61.

50. Laufer, "Stalin und die deutschen Reparationen," 14; Laufer et al., *Die UdSSR*, 2:xliii. The practice of arbitrary dismantling of war trophies continued until mid-October 1945, when, at Marshal Georgy Zhukov's initiative and with Molotov's support, it was finally abandoned.

51. Laufer, "Politik und Bilanz," 46.

52. Quoted in Eduard Mark, "Today Has Been a Historical One: Harry S Truman's Diary of the Potsdam Conference," *Diplomatic History* 4, no. 3 (Summer 1980): 320.

53. Ibid., 321.

54. McCloy Diary, 23–24 July 1945.

55. Averell Harriman and Elie Abel, *Special Envoy to Churchill and Stalin, 1941–1945*, 1st ed. (New York: Random House, 1975), 484.

56. Davies Diary, 21 July 1945, Davies Papers, box 19, Library of Congress.

57. According to Davies, the French were "carrying everything including the kitchen stove out of their territory," and even American soldiers as well as members of the U.S. delegation were "liberating things," but "the criticisms are leveled only against the Soviets." Davies Diary, 21 July 1945, Davies Papers, box 19, Library of Congress

58. Ibid., 29 July 1945.

59. Eugene Varga to Molotov, "Guiding Principles of Allied Economic Policy," memorandum, 12 July 1945, cited in Laufer et al., *Die UdSSR*, 2:lxxxi.

60. McCloy Diary, 23–24 July 1945.

61. Cited in Mausbach, *Zwischen Morgenthau und Marshall*, 137.

62. Trachtenberg, *A Constructed Peace*, 24.

63. McCloy Diary, 23–24 July 1945.

64. Ibid., 27 July 1945.

65. Ibid., 23–24 July 1945.

66. Trachtenberg, *A Constructed Peace*, 23.

67. Pauley to Maisky, 27 July 1945, U.S. Department of State, *FRUS, 1945: Diplomatic Papers, Conference of Berlin (the Potsdam Conference, 1945)* (Washington, DC: U.S. Government Printing Office, 1960), 2:894–96.

68. Trachtenberg, *A Constructed Peace*, 23; McCloy Diary, 23–24 July 1945.

69. Note by Litvinov, 5 July 1945, in Laufer et al., *Die UdSSR*, 2:44–48; ibid., 651.

70. Note by Arkadeev, 27 July 1945, in ibid., 2:59.

71. G. P. Arkadeev to V. M. Molotov, "Regarding the Issue of Our Arguments against the Current Proposed American Plan Imposing Reparations on Germany by Zones," 27 July 1945, in ibid., 2:58–61; Maisky suggested so in the Potsdam Conference economic committee; see ibid., 2:lxxxi–lxxxii.

72. Maisky to Molotov, 28 July 1945, in ibid., 2:62–63.

73. McCloy Diary, 25 July 1945.

74. The Allies had agreed at the 1943 Tehran Conference to move the Polish borders westward; at the Yalta Conference final determination was left to a peace treaty. As part of the Potsdam Conference accords, the German territories east of the Oder-Neiße line were provisionally put under Polish administration until a final settlement could be reached. On the history of the Oder-Neiße border line, see Michael A. Hartenstein, *Die Oder-Neiße-Linie: Geschichte der Aufrichtung; Anerkennung einer problematischen Grenze* (Egelsbach: Hänsel-Hohenhausen, 1997); Carsten Lilge, *Die Entstehung der Oder-Neiße-Linie als Nebenprodukt alliierter Großmachtpolitik während des 2. Weltkrieges* (Frankfurt/M.: Lang, 1995).

75. The agreement allowed the Western powers to determine the amount of reparations in view of occupation exigencies and western Europe's need for German coal. Since no overall sum for reparations had been fixed, it was essentially left to the Western occupation authorities to decide what constituted Moscow's 25 percent share in industrial excess capacities.

76. Molotov, circular, 5 August 1945, in Laufer et al., *Die UdSSR*, 2:79–91, here 81.

77. Trachtenberg, *A Constructed Peace*, 23–25.

78. Gen. Harry Vaughan, quoted in Brown, *James F. Byrnes of South Carolina*, 280.

79. McCloy Diary, 30 July 1945.

80. Ibid.

81. Eisenberg, *Drawing the Line*, 113.

82. Quoted in Trachtenberg, *A Constructed Peace*, 29.

83. Rolf Badstübner und Wilfried Loth, eds., *Wilhelm Pieck: Aufzeichnungen zur Deutschlandpolitik, 1945–1953* (Berlin: Akademie Verlag, 1994), 50.

84. McCloy Diary, 30 July 1945.

CHAPTER 2

1. Quoted in Harry C. Butcher, *My Three Years with Eisenhower: The Personal Diary of Captain Harry C. Butcher, USNR, Naval Aide to General Eisenhower, 1942 to 1945* (London: William Heinemann, 1946), 712.

2. "Conversation between Stalin and Hopkins," 28 May 1945, in Laufer et al., *Die UdSSR*, 2:11, 644; Sokolovsky and Semenov to Molotov, cable, 28 March 1946, in ibid., 2:335; Carolyn Woods Eisenberg, *Drawing the Line: The American Decision to Divide Germany, 1944–1949* (Cambridge: Cambridge University Press, 1996), 166–67.

3. On Clay's biography, see Jean Edward Smith, ed., *The Papers of General Lucius D. Clay: Germany, 1945–1949*, 2 vols. (Bloomington: Indiana University Press, 1974); Wolfgang Krieger, *General Lucius D. Clay und die amerikanische Deutschlandpolitik, 1945–1949* (Stuttgart: Klett-Cotta, 1987); John H. Backer, *Winds of History: The German Years of Lucius DuBignon Clay* (New York: Van Nostrand Reinhold, 1983); Jean Edward Smith, *Lucius D. Clay: An American Life* (New York: Henry Holt, 1990); Curtis F. Morgan, Jr., *James F. Byrnes, Lucius Clay, and American Policy in Germany, 1945–1947* (Lewiston, NY: E. Mellen Press, 2002). See also Donald R. Heath (USPO-LAD) to James Riddleberger (chief of the Central European Division, Department of State), 7 March 1946, NARA, RG 59, lot 55D371, box 2.

4. Apparently Roosevelt and Byrnes had preferred a civilian, such as McCloy, a former Wall Street lawyer who had seemed the logical choice to many. But Morgenthau had objected to anybody close to the business community. In a meeting with Roosevelt in late March 1945, Byrnes argued strongly for Clay, and Roosevelt "was ready to agree to anything at the last, being a tired man, and he acquiesced in Clay's appointment without much difficulty"; John J. McCloy Diary, 20 July 1945, McCloy Papers, ser. 2, DY1:18, Amherst College Archives; Backer, *Winds of History*, 4–5.

5. Robert H. Van Meter, "Secretary of State Marshall, General Clay, and the Moscow Council of Foreign Ministers Meeting of 1947: A Response to Philip Zelikow," *Diplomacy and Statecraft* 16, no. 1 (March 9, 2005): 143, https://doi.org/10.1080/09592290590916176.

6. Ibid.

7. Michael James Lacey, ed., *The Truman Presidency*, Woodrow Wilson Center Press. (Cambridge: Cambridge University Press, 1989), 29–30.

8. McCloy Diary, 18 July 1945, 20 July 1945, 30 July 1945.

9. Ibid., 20 July 1945.

10. Backer, *Winds of History*, 27.

11. Ibid., 16.

12. McCloy Diary, 17 July 1945.

13. "Transmittal of Report on Berlin Operations Base," Dana Durand (Chief, SSU Foreign Branch M) to Chief of SSU Station Karlsruhe, 8 April 1948, in Donald P. Steury, ed., *On the Front Lines of the Cold War: Documents on the Intelligence War in Berlin, 1946 to 1961* (Washington, DC: CIA, 1999), 42; Joseph E. Davies Diary, 13 July 1945, Joseph E. Davies Papers, box 19, Library of Congress.

14. Davies Diary, 13 July 1945.

15. The point is made most explicitly in Robert D. Murphy to "Doc" Matthews, 3 May 1946, NARA, RG 59, 740.00119 Control (Germany)/5-346. See Clay's use of the same image in "Résumé of Meeting at State Department," 3 November 1945, Smith, *Papers of General Lucius D. Clay*, 1:113. On Murphy's background, see Robert D. Murphy, *Diplomat among Warriors* (Garden City, NY: Doubleday, 1964).

16. Clay to George C. Marshall, 6 June 1945, Smith, *Papers of General Lucius D. Clay*, 1:21.

17. Clay to McCloy, 29 June 1945, ibid., 1:38.

18. Clay to McCloy, 3 September 1945, ibid., 1:63; Eisenberg, *Drawing the Line*, 169. The feeling seemed to have been mutual: see, for example, "Conversation between Sokolovsky and Clay," 2 October 1945, in Laufer et al., *Die UdSSR*, 2:130: "The conversation took place in a very relaxed and friendly atmosphere."

19. Semenov, "Report on the Activities of the Control Council in Germany (July 1945–March 1946)," 16 May 1946, in Laufer et al., *Die UdSSR*, 2:405–10, here 409.

20. Clay to Joint Chiefs of Staff, 6 June 1945, Smith, *Papers of General Lucius D. Clay*, 1:19.

21. Ibid., 1:20.

22. Clay to McCloy, 29 June 1945, ibid., 1:38.

23. To Byrnes intimate Walter J. Brown, he confided his "opinion that the Russian soldiers could not compare to the Americans or British in dress, physique or discipline." He said that, if need be, the Second Armored "Hell on Wheels" Division quartered in Berlin could move straight to Moscow with little effective resistance. Walter J. Brown, *James F. Byrnes of South Carolina* (Macon, GA: Mercer University Press, 1990), 278.

24. Clay to McCloy, 29 June 1945, Smith, *Papers of General Lucius D. Clay*, 1:37.

25. Ibid., 1:37, 39.

26. Clay to McCloy, 16 June 1945, ibid., 1:24.

27. Clay to McCloy, 3 September 1945, ibid., 1:65; Murphy to Secretary of State, 22 August 1945, NARA, RG 59, 740.00119 (8-2245); Eisenberg, *Drawing the Line*, 177–79.

28. Laufer et al., *Die UdSSR*, 2:lxxxiv; Eisenberg, *Drawing the Line*, 170.

29. Laufer et al., *Die UdSSR*, 2:lxvi.

30. Ibid. The very day Byrnes had tabled the zonal reparations proposal, the Soviet government began establishing administrative structures for its occupation zone; SMA order No. 17 (July 27) established central administrations responsible for traffic, communications, health, and education matters in the zone. Ibid., 2:lxv.

31. French Delegation to the Council of Foreign Ministers, memorandum, 13 September 1945, U.S. Department of State, *FRUS, 1945: Diplomatic Papers* (Washington: U.S. GPO, 1948), 3:869–71; memorandum of conversation between Sokolovsky, Eisenhower, and Koeltz, 20 September 1945, referenced in Laufer et al., *Die UdSSR*, 2:675.

32. Dietmar Hüser, *Frankreichs "Doppelte Deutschlandpolitik": Dynamik aus der Defensive—Planen, Entscheiden, Umsetzen in gesellschaftlichen und wirtschaftlichen, innen- und aussenpolitischen Krisenzeiten: 1944–1950*, Dokumente und Schriften der Europäischen Akademie Otzenhausen, Bd. 77 (Berlin: Duncker & Humblot, 1996); 518–19, 523–28; Rainer Hudemann, "France and the German Question, 1945–1949: On the Interdependence of Historiography, Methodology and Interpretations," in *France and the German Question, 1945–1990*, ed. Frédéric Bozo and Christian Wenkel (New York: Berghahn, 2019); Michael Creswell and Marc Trachtenberg, "France and the German Question, 1945–1955," *Journal of Cold War Studies* 5, no. 3 (August 1, 2003): 5–28, esp. 5–13.

33. Strang to Harvey, 21 September 1945, in *Documents on British Policy Overseas*, ser. 1, 5:144–45; Cooper to Dixon, 4 October 1945, ibid., 2:484–85; Hüser, *Frankreichs "Doppelte Deutschlandpolitik,"* 525–26; Eisenberg, *Drawing the Line*, 204–9.

34. Memorandum of conversation between Sokolovsky, Eisenhower, and Koeltz, 20 September 1945, referenced in Laufer et al., *Die UdSSR*, 2:675; Sololev to Vyshinsky, 24 September 1945, in ibid., 2:lxvii, 699.

35. For recent scholarship on France, see fn. 32. From the Journal of General of the Army V. D. Sokolovsky, "A Conversation with US Army Lieutenant General Clay," 2 October 1945, in Laufer et al., *Die UdSSR*, 2:126–30, here 129. Of course, Clay had acknowledged months earlier that "we are forming informal committees with the British to which we are also inviting the French liaison representation, to consider problems of mutual importance in western Germany." Smith, *Papers of General Lucius D. Clay*, 1:38.

36. Conversation between Sokolovsky and Clay, 2 October 1945, in Laufer et al., *Die UdSSR*, 2:129.

37. Hilldring to Clay, 20 October 1945, U.S. Department of State, *FRUS, 1945: Diplomatic Papers*, 3:885–86.

38. Memorandum for Stalin and Molotov, 7 November 1945, in Laufer et al., *Die UdSSR*, 2:166–68.

39. Molotov to Ambassadors and Ministers, 10 October 1945, in Laufer et al., *Die UdSSR*, 2:142–46; for Stalin's view, see Laufer et al., *Die UdSSR*, 2:671–72.

40. Stalin to Molotov for Cetverka, 9 December 1945, cited in Laufer et al., *Die UdSSR*, 2:680–81.

41. "Résuméof Meeting at State Department," 3 November 1945, Smith, *Papers of General Lucius D. Clay*, 1:112–13.

42. Ibid.; Eisenberg, *Drawing the Line*, 174.

43. Eisenberg, *Drawing the Line*, 174. McCloy echoed Clay's argument that blamed the French for the difficulties in quadripartite governance, as did an independent presidential commission headed by Byron Price. Eisenberg, *Drawing the Line*, 173–75.

44. Litvinov, "Differences with France with Respect to Germany," memorandum, 28 November 1945, in Laufer et al., *Die UdSSR*, 2:178.

45. Smirnov to Molotov, 27 October 1945, in Laufer et al., *Die UdSSR*, 2:163.

46. Laufer et al., *Die UdSSR*, 2:lxvii, 682; V. S. Semenov to A. A. Sobolev, cable, 16 October 1945, in Laufer et al., *Die UdSSR*, 2:148.

47. Laufer et al., *Die UdSSR*, 2:lxiii, 676; Smirnov to Dekanazov, 23 January 1946, in Laufer et al., *Die UdSSR*, 2:238–39; Semenov to Zhukov, "Regarding the Issue of the Need to Prepare for the Organization of National German Administrative Departments," memorandum, 18 December 1945, in Laufer et al., *Die UdSSR*, 2:199–200.

48. Smirnov to Dekanazov, 23 January 1946, in Laufer et al., *Die UdSSR*, 2:238–39.

49. Laufer et al., *Die UdSSR*, 2:699.

50. Smirnov to Molotov, 3 December 1945, in Laufer et al., *Die UdSSR*, 2:187–88.

51. Quoted in ibid., 2:676.

52. Semenov to Zhukov, "Regarding the Issue of the Need to Prepare for the Organization of National German Administrative Departments," memorandum, 18 December 1945, in Laufer et al., *Die UdSSR*, 2:199–200.

53. Smirnov to Molotov, 3 December 1945, in Laufer et al., *Die UdSSR*, 2:187–88.

54. Semenov to Zhukov, "Regarding the Issue of the Need to Prepare for the Organization of National German Administrative Departments," memorandum, 18 December 1945, in Laufer et al., *Die UdSSR*, 2:199–200.

55. Ibid.

56. Ibid.

57. Ibid., footnote a. Smirnov to Dekanozov, 23 January 1946, in Laufer et al., *Die UdSSR*, 2:199, 238–39.

58. Semenov to Zhukov, 22 February 1946, in Laufer et al., *Die UdSSR*, 2:261–62.

59. Novikov to Molotov and Vyshinsky, 21 November 1945, in Laufer et al., *Die UdSSR*, 2:174

60. Konstantin Tarchov, Heinz Kessler, and Erich Honecker, memorandum of conversation, 17 October 1945, in Laufer et al., *Die UdSSR*, 2:151.

61. Sobolev to Zhukov, 26 January 1946, in Laufer et al., *Die UdSSR*, 2:242.

62. I. Turgarinov, "On the New Course of British Policy in Germany," 17 October 1945, in Laufer et al., *Die UdSSR*, 2:158.

63. Vyshinksy to Zhukov and Sobolev, 24 September 1945, in Laufer et al., *Die UdSSR*, 2:116–17.

64. Zhukov and Eisenhower conversation, 7 November 1945, in Laufer et al., *Die UdSSR*, 2:167.

65. Semenov to Vyshinsky, 10 May 1946, in Laufer et al., *Die UdSSR*, 2:403–5. Sokolovsky opposed the request.

66. Stalin to Molotov for Cetverka, 9 December 1945, cited in Laufer et al., *Die UdSSR*, 2:680–81.

67. A German Standard of Industry Board under the chairmanship of economist Calvin Hoover reported by mid-September that in order to maintain a minimum standard of living, it was impossible to carry out a severe program of industrial disarmament spread over several key industries, given the loss of Germany's eastern food lands. Controversially, the report inverted the Potsdam clause that the German standard of living not exceed the European average, demanding that German production had to allow Germany to reach the European average. Though quickly disavowed by U.S. policy makers, the report foreshadowed American interest in increasing German production and dramatically reducing capacities available for reparations. See the excellent discussion in Eisenberg, *Drawing the Line*, 176–85.

68. Eisenhower to Clay, 8 November 1945, *Papers of Dwight D. Eisenhower*, 6:522–525, quoted in Eisenberg, *Drawing the Line*, 182–84.

69. Eisenberg, *Drawing the Line*, 184.

70. Ibid.,183–84.

71. Jochen Laufer, "Stalin und die deutschen Reparationen (1941–1953)" (unpublished paper presented at the Cold War International History Project Conference, Yale University, September 1999), 6–7; Wilfried Mausbach, *Zwischen Morgenthau und Marshall: Das wirtschaftspolitische Deutschlandkonzept der USA, 1944–1947* (Düsseldorf: Droste, 1996).

72. Eisenberg, *Drawing the Line*, 209.

73. Clay to Eisenhower, 21 March 1946, DDEL, Dwight D. Eisenhower Papers, Correspondence File, cited in Eisenberg, *Drawing the Line*, 210.

74. Murphy to Secretary of State, 31 December 1945, NARA, RG 59, 740.00119 Control (Germany)/12-3145.

75. Norman Naimark, *The Russians in Germany: A History of the Soviet Zone of Occupation 1945–1949* (Cambridge, MA: Harvard UP, 1995), 48–49; Vladislav M. Zubok, *A Failed Empire: The Soviet Union in the Cold War from Stalin to Gorbachev* (Chapel Hill: UNC Press, 2007), 69; Political Report by Semenov, 2 April 1946, in Laufer et al., *Die UdSSR*, 2:335–50, here 339.

76. "Note of a Conversation with Representatives of the Soviet Military Government in Germany" 23 January 1946, in Rolf Badstübner und Wilfried Loth, eds., *Wilhelm Pieck: Aufzeichnungen zur Deutschlandpolitik, 1945–1953* (Berlin: Akademie Verlag, 1994), 64.

77. See the discussion in the U.S. zone Länder Council in July 1946, Bundesarchiv Potsdam (BA), Z1/188, 43, cited in Peter E. Fäßler, *Durch den "Eisernen Vorhang": Die deutsch-deutschen Wirtschaftsbeziehungen, 1949–1969* (Köln: Böhlau, 2006), 35.

78. "Résumé of Meeting at State Department," 3 November 1945, in Smith, *Papers of General Lucius D. Clay*, 1:112.

79. Murphy to Secretary of State, 24 February 1946, NARA, RG 59, 740.00119 Control (Germany)/2-2446. See also David Harris to James Riddleberger and "Doc" Matthews, "Future Policy towards Germany," memorandum, 26 March 1946, NARA, RG 59, 740.00119 Control (Germany)/3-2646.

80. Byrnes to Bidault, 1 February 1946, U.S. Department of State, *FRUS, 1946: The British Commonwealth, Western and Central Europe* (Washington, DC: U.S. Government Printing Office, 1969), 5:496–98; Patterson to Byrnes, 25 February 1946, NARA, RG 59, 740.00119 Control (Germany)/2-2546; and Byrnes to Patterson, not dated, NARA, RG 59, 740.00119 Control (Germany)/2-2546.

81. Eisenberg, *Drawing the Line*, 207. To Blum's mind, however, these departments would be run by a committee of state secretaries from the four zones, likely to replicate the control council process rather than to break down zonal divisions.

82. Murphy to DeWitt C. Poole, 11 April 1946, box 59, Robert Murphy Papers, Hoover Institution Archives; Murphy to "Doc" Matthews, 3 May 1946, NARA, RG 59, 740.00119 Control (Germany)/5-346; see also Harris to Riddleberger and Matthews, "Future Policy towards Germany," memorandum, 26 March 1946, NARA, RG 59, 740.00119 Control (Germany)/3-2646; Allen W. Dulles to Murphy, 9 May 1946, box 57, Murphy Papers, Hoover Institution Archives; State Department economist Paul R. Porter to Norman Thomas, 30 June 1947, Paul R. Porter Papers, Harry S. Truman Library (hereafter cited as HSTL), Independence, MO.

83. Murphy to DeWitt C. Poole, 11 April 1946, box 59, Murphy Papers, Hoover Institution Archives.

84. Murphy to Secretary of State, 19 March 1946, NARA, RG 59, 740.00119 Control (Germany)/3-1946.

85. Matthews to Murphy, 12 March 1946, box 58, Murphy Papers, Hoover Institution Archives.

86. Ibid.

87. Murphy to Matthews, 3 April 1946, box 58, Murphy Papers, Hoover Institution Archives.

88. Ibid.

89. On Kennan , see David Mayers, *George Kennan and the Dilemmas of US Foreign Policy* (New York: Oxford University Press, 1988); Walter L. Hixson, *George F. Kennan: Cold War Iconoclast* (New York: Columbia University Press, 1989); Wilson D. Miscamble, *George F. Kennan and the Making of American Foreign Policy, 1947–1950*

(Princeton, NJ: Princeton University Press, 1992); John Lewis Gaddis, *George F. Kennan: An American Life* (New York: Penguin, 2011).

90. Kennan to Secretary of State, 6 March 1946, *FRUS, 1946*, 5:516–20.

91. Ibid, 519.

92. Perry Laukhuff, "Appraisal of Quadripartite Control and Soviet Policy," April 25, 1946, box 58, Murphy Papers, Hoover Institution Archives. Murphy passed Laukhuff's analysis on to Washington, with a rare editorial comment calling it "unsound" in its argument. Murphy to "Doc" Matthews, 3 May 1946, NARA, RG 59, 740.00119 Control (Germany)/5-346.

93. Riddleberger to Matthews, 26 March 1946, box 2, David Harris Papers, Hoover Institution Archives; and NARA, RG 59, FW 740.00119 Control (Germany)/3-2646. See also the assessment by the Joint Intelligence Staff, "Capabilities and Intentions of the U.S.S.R. in the Post-War Period," 8 February 1946, NARA, RG 218, Geographical File 1946–1947, box 53, compared to Joint Intelligence Staff, "Capabilities and Intentions of the U.S.S.R. in the Post-War Period," 15 January 1946, NARA, RG 218, Geographical File 1946–1947, box 52; see also Joint Intelligence Staff, "Capabilities and Intentions of the USSR in the Postwar Period," 9 July 1946, NARA, RG 218, Geographical File, 1946–1947, box 53.

94. Caffery to Secretary of State, 29 March 1946, NARA, RG 59, 740.00119 Control (Germany)/3-2946.

95. Political report by Semenov, 9 March 1946, in Laufer et al., *Die UdSSR*, 2:274–83, here 278.

96. Zverev to Molotov, 2 March 1946, in Laufer et al., *Die UdSSR*, 2:325.

97. Political report by Semenov, 22 April 1946, in Laufer et al., *Die UdSSR*, 2:363–75, here 372 and 374.

98. Political report by Semenov, 17 March 1946, in Laufer et al., *Die UdSSR*, 2:308.

99. Murphy to Secretary of State, 14 June 1946, NARA, RG 59, 740.00119 Control (Germany)/6-1446.

100. "Central German Administrative Departments," Murphy to Secretary of State, 13 July 1946, NARA, RG 59, 740.00119 Control (Germany)/7-3146.

101. Clay to Echols and Petersen, 27 March 1946, Smith, *Papers of General Lucius D. Clay*, 1:184.

102. Political Report by Semenov, 22 April 1946, in Laufer et al., *Die UdSSR*, 2:363–75, here 364.

103. Cited in Birgit Peterson, "Die amerikanische Reparationspolitik in Deutschland 1945–1949 im Spannungsfeld der deutschlandpolitischen Zielsetzungen der vier Mächte" (PhD diss., Julius-Maximilians-Universität Würzburg, 1993), 268.

104. See CORC/M(46)22, cited in Laufer et al., *Die UdSSR*, 2, n.382; Trachtenberg, *A Constructed Peace*, 45–47; allegedly "highly credible" intelligence sources seemed to confirm Clay's assumption. See the report of a secret meeting with Soviet

occupation chief Sokolovsky and Soviet zone Länder and province presidents and vice presidents on 28 May 1946, enclosed in Donald Heath to Secretary of State, 9 July 1946, NARA, RG 59, 740.00119 Control (Germany)/7-946.

105. Political Report by Semenov, 9 May 1946, in Laufer et al., *Die UdSSR*, 2:385–404, here 394–95.

106. Political Report by Semenov, 26 May 1946, in Laufer et al., *Die UdSSR*, 2:432–47, here 432.

107. Laufer et al., *Die UdSSR*, 2, n.382.

108. Skoryukov to Semenov, 29 May 1946, in Laufer et al., *Die UdSSR*, 2:464–66.

109. K. V. Novikov, Andrey A. Smirnov, and Georgy Zarubin to V. Vyshinsky, 1 June 1946, in Laufer et al., *Die UdSSR*, 2:469–70.

110. Ibid.

111. Melvyn P. Leffler, *The Struggle for Germany and the Origins of the Cold War*, Sixth Alois Mertes Memorial Lecture, no. 16 (Washington, DC: GHI, 1996), 29; Eisenberg, *Drawing the Line*, 233–41.

112. George F. Kennan to Carmel Offie, 10 May 1946, U.S. Department of State, *FRUS, 1946*, 5:555.

113. Acheson to Byrnes, 9 May 1946, U.S. Department of State, *FRUS, 1946*, 5:550–55; Marc Trachtenberg, *A Constructed Peace: The Making of the European Settlement, 1945–1963*, Princeton Studies in International History and Politics (Princeton, NJ: Princeton University Press, 1999), 47–53.

114. Zubok, *A Failed Empire*, 66. On Molotov's speech, see also Chapter 4.

115. Leffler, *Struggle for Germany*, 34; Eisenberg, *Drawing the Line*, 234–48.

116. David Harris (Division of Central European Affairs, Department of State) to Riddleberger, 17 July 1946, NARA, RG 59, 740.00119 Control (Germany)/7-1746.

117. Murphy to State Department, 30 July 1946, U.S. Department of State, *FRUS, 1946*, 5:585. In internal discussions, reported to Washington, Sokolovsky also espoused these views. See Donald Heath to Secretary of State, 9 July 1946, NARA, RG 59, 740.00119 Control (Germany)/7-946.

118. "On the Economic Unity of Germany," draft by Kostenko [after 11 October 1946], in Laufer et al., *Die UdSSR*, 3:23–25. Earlier negotiations on a draft constitution for Berlin that had stalled suddenly turned into "most conciliatory and cooperative discussions" and quickly resulted in an agreement, adding to the sense on the part of American officials of a "change . . . in the attitude and tactics of the Soviets towards the US." Heath to Secretary of State, 13 July 1946, NARA, RG 59, 862.00/7-1346.

119. Murphy to State Department, 16 October 1946, U.S. Department of State, *FRUS, 1946*, 5:622.

120. Clay to Byrnes, November 1946, Smith, *Papers of General Lucius D. Clay*, 1:279–84, here 282–83.

121. "On the Economic Unity of Germany," draft memorandum by Kostenko, [after 11 October 1946], in Laufer et al., *Die UdSSR*, 3:23–25.

CHAPTER 3

1. David E. Murphy, Sergei A. Kondrashev, and George Bailey, *Battleground Berlin: CIA vs. KGB in the Cold War* (New Haven, CT: Yale University Press, 1997), 3–4, 6; Clay to John McCloy, 3 October 1945, Jean Edward Smith, ed., *The Papers of General Lucius D. Clay: Germany, 1945–1949*, 2 vols. (Bloomington: Indiana University Press, 1974), 1:96; David J. Alvarez and Eduard M. Mark, *Spying through a Glass Darkly: American Espionage against the Soviet Union, 1945–1946* (Lawrence: University Press of Kansas, 2016), 87.

2. Alvarez and Mark, *Spying through a Glass Darkly*, 87–97; "Transmittal of Report on Berlin Operations Base," Dana Durand (Chief, SSU Foreign Branch M) to Chief of SSU Station Karlsruhe, 8 April 1948, Donald P. Steury, ed., *On the Front Lines of the Cold War: Documents on the Intelligence War in Berlin, 1946 to 1961* (Washington, DC: CIA, 1999).

3. Alvarez and Mark, *Spying through a Glass Darkly*, 96; Murphy, Kondrashev, and Bailey, *Battleground Berlin*, 11.

4. Thomas Boghardt, "America's Secret Vanguad: US Army Intelligence Operations in Germany, 1944–1947," *Studies in Intelligence* 57:2 (June 2013), 1–18; and Thomas Boghardt, *Covert Legions: U.S. Army Intelligence in Germany, 1944–1949* (forthcoming 2021). On the beginnings of the Gehlen Organization, see Thomas Wolf, *Die Entstehung des BND: Aufbau, Finanzierung, Kontrolle* (Berlin: Ch. Links, 2018) and most recently the excellent work by Ronny Heidenreich, *Die DDR-Spionage des BND: Von den Anfängen bis zum Mauerbau* (Berlin: Ch. Links, 2019), 47–65. By the end of 1946, only one of the "residencies" which "Operation Rusty" (as the fledgling German effort was codenamed) had established in the western zones, collected information on the Soviet zone. Heidenreich, *Die DDR-Spionage*, 60–61.

5. On the 1946 war scare, see Eduard Mark, "The War Scare of 1946 and its Consequences," *Diplomatic History* 21:3 (1997), 383–415; "Transmittal of Report on Berlin Operations Base," Dana Durand (Chief, SSU Foreign Branch M) to Chief of SSU Station Karlsruhe, 8 April 1948, in Steury, *On the Front Lines of the Cold War*, 13–14, 19.

6. "Transmittal of Report on Berlin Operations Base," Dana Durand (Chief, SSU Foreign Branch M) to Chief of SSU Station Karlsruhe, 8 April 1948, in Steury, *On the Front Lines of the Cold War*, 19; Murphy, Kondrashev, and Bailey, *Battleground Berlin*, 9; *Alvarez and Mark, Spying through a Glass Darkly*, 96.

7. *Alvarez and Mark, Spying through a Glass Darkly*, 96–101; Steury, *On the Front Lines of the Cold War*, 20, 27, 43; Heidenreich, *Die DDR-Spionage*, 59.

8. OMGUS [Office of Military Government, United States] Information Control Intelligence Summary No. 32, enclosed in Murphy to Department of State, 2 March 1946, NARA, RG 59, 740.00119 Control (Germany)/3-246. Firsthand observations remained hard to come by. Not until March 1947 were two officers from European Command's Intelligence Branch in Frankfurt allowed to attend the Leipzig Industrial

Fair. See "Intelligence Summary No 4," Dispatch 293, OMGUS to Department of State, 2 April 1947, NARA, RG 59, 740.00119 Control (Germany)/4-247. On the role of refugee interrogations, see Keith R. Allen, *Interrogation Nation: Refugees and Spies in Cold War Germany* (Lanham, MD: Rowman & Littlefield, 2017).

9. William Stivers and Donald A. Carter, *The City Becomes a Symbol: The U.S. Army in the Occupation in Berlin, 1945–1949* (Washington, DC: Center for Military History, 2017), 85; Anya Vodopyanov, *A Watchful Eye Behind the Iron Curtain: The U.S. Military Liaison Mission in East Germany, 1953–61* (MS, Stanford University, 2004).

10. Information Control Center Intelligence Report, 5 July 1945, enclosed in Murphy to Secretary of State, 23 July 1945, NARA, RG 59, 740.00119.

11. Ibid.

12. "Military Government Report on the Success of Russian propaganda in the Heidelberg Area," enclosed in Murphy to Secretary of State, 12 June 1945, NARA, RG 59, 740.00119 Control (Germany)/6-1245 (Freedom of Information Act [hereafter cited as FOIA] release to author).

13. Cited in Stivers and Carter, *The City Becomes a Symbol*, 100.

14. John J. McCloy Diary, 17 July 1945, McCloy Papers, ser. 2, DY1:18, Amherst College Archives.

15. Headquarters, USFET Military Intelligence Service Center, "The German View: A Report for Counter-Intelligence," 19 November 1945, NARA, RG 59, 740.00119 (Control (Germany)/11-1945.

16. Murphy to Secretary of State, 19 November 1945, NARA, RG 59, 740.00119 Control (Germany)/11-1945.

17. Ibid.

18. Ibid.

19. Norman M. Naimark, *The Russians in Germany: A History of the Soviet Zone of Occupation, 1945–1949* (Cambridge, MA: Belknap Press of Harvard University Press, 1995), 72.

20. Ibid., 80.

21. For much of the last year of the war, Stalin and the Soviet military leadership remained insensitive to the issue and indifferent to complaints about the behavior of Red Army soldiers by Communist leaders throughout Soviet-occupied Europe.

22. Murphy to Secretary of State, 19 November 1945, NARA, RG 59, 740.00119 Control (Germany)/11-1945.

23. Headquarters, USFET Military Intelligence Service Center, "The German View: A Report for Counter-Intelligence," 19 November 1953, NARA, RG 59, 740.00119 (Control (Germany)/11-1945.

24. Ibid.

25. Ibid.

26. G-5 Political Intelligence Letter No. 10, 19 June 1945, enclosed in

Murphy to Secretary of State, 23 June 1945, NARA, RG 59, 740.00119 Control (Germany)/6-2345.

27. Wolfgang Schivelbusch, *In a Cold Crater: Cultural and Intellectual Life in Berlin, 1945–1948* (Berkeley: University of California Press, 1998), 33.

28. Mendelsohn, "German Journal," cited in Schivelbusch.

29. Schivelbusch, *In a Cold Crater*, 33.

30. Ibid., 108–9.

31. Ibid., 107–8.

32. Ibid.

33. OMGUS Information Control Intelligence Summary No. 32, enclosed in Murphy to Department of State, 2 March 1946, NARA, RG 59, 740.00119 Control (Germany)/3-246.

34. Ibid.

35. Ibid.

36. "Certain Aspects of the Work of the Military Government in Berlin District," Murphy to Secretary of State, 10 September 1945, NARA, RG 59, 740.00119 Control Germany/9-1045; also Laufer et al., *Die UdSSR*, 2:xxxii–xxxiii. On the Muscovites within the German Communists, see Catherine Epstein, *The Last Revolutionaries: German Communists and Their Century* (Cambridge, MA: Harvard University Press, 2003), 83–85.

37. "Certain Aspects of the Work of the Military Government in Berlin District," Murphy to Secretary of State, 10 September 1945, NARA, RG 59, 740.00119 Control Germany/9-1045; Anjana Buckow, *Zwischen Propaganda und Realpolitik: Die USA und der Sowjetisch Besetzte Teil Deutschlands, 1945–1955* (Stuttgart: Franz Steiner Verlag, 2003), 109.

38. Clay to Stimson, 18 August 1945, Smith, *Papers of General Lucius D. Clay*, 1:60.

39. Brewster Morris, "Present Tactics and Position of German Communists," 22 January 1945, memorandum enclosed in Robert Murphy to H. Freeman Matthews (Department of State, Office of European Affairs), 25 January 1945; and Morris, "The Free Germany Movement and American Military Government," memorandum enclosed in Robert Murphy to H. Freeman Matthews, cited in William Stivers, "Amerikanische Sichten auf die Sowjetisierung Ostdeutschlands 1945 — 1949," in Michael Lemke, ed., *Sowjetisierung und Eigenständigkeit in der SBZ/DDR (1945–1953)* *(Cologne: Böhlau,* 1999), 273–361, here 276–77. On Morris, see "Transmittal of Report on Berlin Operations Base," Dana Durand (Chief, SSU Foreign Branch M) to Chief of SSU Station Karlsruhe, 8 April 1948, in Steury, *On the Front Lines of the Cold War*, 35, 45.

40. Murphy to Secretary of State, cable no. 464, 7 September 1945, NARA, RG 59, 862.00/9-745. The LDP initially resisted but eventually moved its headquarters

to the Soviet sector of Berlin. Murphy to Secretary of State, telegram no. 1344, 29 December 1945, NARA, RG 59, 862.00/12-2945.

41. Murphy to Secretary of State, 27 November 1945, cable, enclosed in memo from M. J. Dolbey/EE to Durbrow/EE, 4 January 1946, NARA, RG 59, 740.00119 Control (Germany)/11-2745.

42. A-804, OMGUS Berlin to Secretary of State, NARA, RG 59, 862.00/9-2746.

43. I. Tugarinov to Vyshinsky, 17 October 1945, in Laufer et al., *Die UdSSR*, 2:152–59.

44. Rolf Badstübner und Wilfried Loth, eds., *Wilhelm Pieck: Aufzeichnungen zur Deutschlandpolitik, 1945–1953* (Berlin: Akademie Verlag, 1994), 68.

45. The new party statutes for the SED had been published on February 27, leading U.S. officials to consider the merger "virtually completed." Murphy to Secretary of State, 5 March 1946, NARA, RG 59, 740.00119 Control (Germany)/3-546.

46. Murphy to Secretary of State, 19 January 1946, NARA, RG 59, 862.00/1-1946.

47. Stivers and Carter, *The City Becomes a Symbol*, 155.

48. See biographical appraisal of Grotewohl, OMGUS Berlin to Department of State, 22 April 1946, NARA, RG 59, 740.00119 Control (Germany)/4-2246.

49. "KPD anxious to avoid elections before merger with SPD," OMGUS Office of Political Affairs, enclosed in Murphy to Secretary of State, 29 January 1946, NARA, RG 59, 862.00/1-2946.

50. Murphy to Secretary of State, 27 February 1946, NARA, RG 59, 862.00/2-2746.

51. "The Current Campaign to Merge the Communist and Social Democratic Parties in Berlin," Murphy to Secretary of State, 8 April 1946, NARA, RG 59, 862.00/4-846; Murphy to Secretary of State, 8 March 1946, with enclosed OMGUS Intelligence Summary ICIS #33, dated 2 March 1946, NARA, RG 59, 862.00/3-846. See also British "Directive for Germany and Austria," which, with regard to the Soviet pressure tactics for the fusion, called on British officials to "content ourselves with drawing attention to our own methods of political administration and underlining the virtues of the party system." Copy in NARA, RG 59, 740.00119 Control (Germany)/2-246.

52. For example, see "Weekly Political Trend Summary, March 7, 1946," NARA, RG 59, 7400.00119 Control (Germany)/3-1346.

53. Murphy to H. Freeman Matthews, 26 March 1946, box 58, Murphy Papers, Hoover Institution Archives.

54. Political Report by Semenov, 9 March 1946, in Laufer et al., *Die UdSSR*, 2:274–83.

55. Ibid., 2

56. OMGUS to Secretary of State, 4 March 1946, NARA, RG 59, 862.00/3-446.

57. Ibid.

58. Quoted in Stivers and Carter, *The City Becomes a Symbol*, 157.

59. Ibid.

60. Memorandum by Louis Wiesner, 18 March 1946, as quoted in Murphy to

H. Freeman Matthews, 28 March 1946, NARA, RG 59, FW 740.00119 Control (Germany)/3-2546 [sic].

61. Brewster Morris, memorandum no. 121, 26 March 1946, enclosed in Murphy to H. Freeman Matthews, 26 March 1946, box 58, Murphy Papers, Hoover Institution Archives; E. A. Gross to General Hilldring, 6 April 1946, NARA, RG 59, lot 55D371, box 4.

62. Weekly Political Trend Summary #15, 18 April 1946, NARA, RG 59, 740.00119 Control (Germany)/4-1846.

63. Murphy to Secretary of State, 15 February 1946, NARA, RG 59 (FOIA release to author). By contrast, British intelligence successfully engineered the departure of Gustav Dahrendorf and his family to the British zone. Ibid.

64. Fusion opponents argued that Grotewohl's position was "mainly an attempt . . . to excuse the line he has taken in agreeing to the merger." Murphy to Secretary of State, 19 April 1946, NARA, RG 59, 862.00/4-1946.

65. Murphy to Secretary of State, 20 March 1946, NARA, RG 58, 862.00/3-2046; Murphy to H. Freeman Matthews, 26 March 1946, box 58, Murphy Papers, Hoover Institution Archives. See also "Interview with Erik Reger, Co-Licensee of 'Der Tagesspiegel,'" enclosed in POLAD Berlin, 19 March 1946, NARA, RG 59, 740.00119 Control (Germany)/3-1946; see also Baranov to Molotov, 25 March 1946, in Laufer et al., *Die UdSSR*, 2:328–31; Smith to Secretary of State, 25 May 1946, NARA, RG 59, 862.00/4-1946. Semenov reported that the merger opposition had published three leaflets with a print run of 620,000 copies as well as a large number of posters. See Political Report by Semenov, 2 April 1946, in Laufer et al, *Die UdSSR*, 2:335–50; Stivers and Carter, *The City Becomes a Symbol*, 156.

66. Political Report by Semenov, 17 March 1946, in Laufer et al., *Die UdSSR*, 2:305–13; Baranov to Molotov, 25 March 1946, in ibid., 2:328–31; Political Report by Semenov, 22 April 1946, in ibid., 2:363–75.

67. "Soviet Views toward Referendum," Lt. B. H. Brown to Mr. Wenner, 30 March 1946, enclosed in USPOLAD to Department of State, NARA, RG 59, 862.00/4-1546. Several U.S. observers, including POLAD staff member Louis Wiesner, were arrested in the Soviet sector during the day, but in each case they were released. Murphy to Secretary of State, 1 April 1946, NARA, RG 59, 862.00/4-146.

68. Political Report by Semenov, 2 April 1946, in Laufer et al., *Die UdSSR*, 2:335–50.

69. Murphy to Secretary of State, 6 April 1946, NARA, RG 59, 862.00/4-646; OMGUS Intelligence Summary No. 33, NARA, RG 59, 740.00119 Control Council (Germany)/4-1746.

70. Transcript of Clay press conference in Murphy to Department of State, 29 April 1946, NARA, RG 59, 740.00119 Control Council (Germany)/4-2946. Unlike the British government, Clay did not object to members of the American zone SPD becoming members of the newly formed SED Central Committee, as long as they

ceased to be active within the SPD or KPD in the U.S. zone. Murphy to Secretary of State, 6 May 1946, NARA, RG 59, 740.00119 Control (Germany)/5-646.

71. Department of State to Murphy, 9 April 1946, NARA, RG 59, 862.00/4-646.

72. OMGUS Special Report, 15 May 1946, NARA, RG 59, 862.00/6-1546.

73. Murphy to Secretary of State, 22 June 1946, NARA, RG 59, 862.00/6-2246.

74. George F. Kennan to Carmel Offie, 10 May 1946, NARA, RG 59, 740.00119 Control (Germany)/5-1046.

75. Political Report by Semenov, 2 April 1946, in Laufer et al., *Die UdSSR*, 2:335–50, here 344.

76. Robert Murphy to H. Freeman "Doc" Matthews, 26 March 1946, NARA, RG 59, FW 740.00119 Control (Germany)/3-2646

77. Political Report by Semenov, 17 March 1946, in Laufer et al., *Die UdSSR*, 2:303–13, here 310. In his report, Semenov criticized the Soviet Berlin commandant's weak political skills.

78. Murphy to H. Freeman "Doc" Matthews, 26 March 1946, NARA, RG 59, FW 740.00119 Control (Germany)/3-2646; Murphy to Riddleberger, 24 April 1946, NARA, RG 59, lot 55D371, box 2.

79. The reference is to an intelligence report of an Ulbricht speech before the April 1–2 FDGB conference in Berlin, in which Ulbricht called for rapid nationalization of enterprises before the establishment of central agencies. "And then," Ulbricht reportedly declared, "we shall devote ourselves to the other zones." Murphy to Riddleberger, 24 April 1946, NARA, RG 59, lot 55D371, box 2.

80. Murphy to H. Freeman Matthews, 26 March 1946, NARA, RG 59, FW 740.00119 Control (Germany)/3-2646; see also Brewster Morris, memorandum, enclosed in Murphy to Secretary of State, 8 April 1946, NARA, RG 59, 862.00/4-846.

81. E. A. Gross to General Hilldring, 6 April 1946, NARA, RG 59, 55D371, box 4.

82. Murphy to H. Freeman Matthews, 26 March 1946, NARA, RG 59, FW 740.00119 Control (Germany)/3-2546; see also Brewster Morris, memorandum, enclosed in Murphy to Secretary of State, 8 April 1946, NARA, RG 59, 862.00/4-846.

83. Murphy to Secretary of State, 19 April 1946, NARA, RG 59, 862.00/4-1946.

84. U.S. officials also noted that some of Grotewohl's associates believed that the "SPD leader gave in due to a combination of Russian pressure and flattery, and the fact that his character was not strong enough go stand up to this onslaught." Some suspected that "he may either have a nervous breakdown within the next year or break away from the SEPD [SED]." Ibid.

85. "Conversation with Otto Grotewohl," enclosed in Murphy to Secretary of State, 23 May 1946, NARA, RG 59, 862.00/5-2346.

86. Ibid. There is some evidence that Grotewohl maintained his contact with the Americans through the fall of 1946. See Murphy to Secretary of State, 20 September 1946, NARA, RG 59, 862.00/9-2046. For continuous reports on dissension within the SED, see also Riddleberger to Secretary of State, 27 June 1949, NARA, RG 59,

862.00/6-2449. OMGUS also maintained occasional contact with Pieck; see Murphy to Secretary of State, 13 June 1946, NARA, RG 59, 862.00/6-1346.

87. Stivers and Carter, *The City Becomes a Symbol*, 162.

88. Ibid., 161.

89. Ibid., 162.

90. H. Freeman Matthews to Murphy, 18 April 1946, box 58, Murphy Papers, Hoover Institution Archives. Murphy continued to warn Washington not to obsess over the Soviet threat. As late as summer 1947, Nicolas Nabokoff, head of the State Department's Soviet Unit, at Murphy's behest, tried to convince leading Soviet affairs specialists Charles E. Bohlen and George Kennan that "the constant preoccupation with 'that one problem' definitely condition[ed] one and [made] one see the world as if it were a large plain with only two volcanoes on it, Washington and Moscow." Nabokoff to Murphy, 18 August 1947, box 59, Murphy Papers, Hoover Institution Archives.

91. Howard Trivers to James Riddleberger, 27 June 1946, NARA, RG 59, lot 55D371, box 2. See also Donald R. Heath (USPOLAD) to James Riddleberger (Chief of the Central European Division, Department of State), 7 March 1946, NARA, RG 59, lot 55D371, box 2.

92. The British government adopted a slightly different procedure, which required Social Democrats and Communists to dissolve their parties and apply for a new license, practically precluding a new license for forming an SED organization in the British zone. Daniel E. Rogers, *Politics after Hitler: The Western Allies and the German Party System* (New York: New York University Press, 1995), 82–83.

93. Murphy to Secretary of State, 23 May 1946, NARA, RG 59, 740.00119 Control (Germany)/5-2346.

94. Political Report by Semenov, 29 May 1946, in Laufer et al., *Die UdSSR*, 2:466–69. Semenov ascribed the Western Allied decision to admit the SED in the western sectors to the proactive efforts of the SED on behalf of the Berlin population and the pressure from the SMA (Soviet Military Association) and Moscow. See Semenov, Information Letter No. 7 on the Political Situation in Germany, 22 June 1946, in Laufer et al., *Die UdSSR*, 2:516–35.

95. Political Report by Semenov, 9 May 1946, in Laufer et al., *Die UdSSR*, 2:385–404.

96. It is important, Soviet political adviser Semenov noted internally, that the results of a well-prepared communal election influence the Berlin elections in "positive ways." Semenov to Sokolovsky, [end of May 1946], in Laufer et al., *Die UdSSR*, 2:466–69.

97. Murphy to Secretary of State, 23 May 1946, NARA, RG 59, 740.00119 Control (Germany)/5-2346.

98. Dekanazov to Stalin, 24 August 1946, in Laufer et al., *Die UdSSR*, 2:608–9.

99. Semenov to Sokolovsky, [end of May 1946], in Laufer et al., *Die UdSSR*,

2:466–69; Information Report No. 8 on the Political Situation in Germany, 10 July 1946, in Laufer et al., *Die UdSSR*, 2:538–58.

100. Memorandum on evidence of Soviet discrimination in favor of the SED, enclosed in Donald Heath to Clay, 24 August 1946, NARA, RG 59, 740.00119 Control (Germany)/8-546; OMGUS Intelligence "Special Report: Pressure used to Influence Soviet Zone elections," 15 October 1946, NARA, RG 59, 862.00/10-2146.

101. POLAD to Department of State, 16 April 1946, NARA, RG 59, 740.00119 Control (Germany)/4-1646; Daily Information Summary No. 214, 23 April 1946, NARA, RG 59, 740.00119 Control (Germany)/4-2446.

102. OMGUS Intelligence "Special Report: Pressure Used to Influence Soviet Zone Elections," 15 October 1946, NARA, RG 59, 862.00/102146.

103. See ibid. For other instances of Soviet discrimination against the non-Communist parties, see Heath to Secretary of State, 22 August 1946, NARA, RG 59, 862.00/8-2246; Murphy to Riddleberger, 28 September 1946, NARA, RG 59, 740.00119 Control (Germany)/8-2846; Murphy to Secretary of State, 27 September 1946, NARA, RG 59, 862.00/9-2746.

104. Murphy to Riddleberger, 28 September 1946, NARA, RG 59, 740.00119 Control (Germany)/8-2846. On Jakob Kaiser's role, see Alexander Gallus, *Die Neutralisten: Verfechter eines vereinten Deutschland zwischen Ost und West, 1945–1990* (Düsseldorf: Droste, 2001), 57–61.

105. OMGUS to Department of State, 21 October 1946, NARA, RG 59, 862.00/10-2146; see also Murphy to Secretary of State, "Transmitting German Report on Pre-election Political Discrimination in Soviet Zone of Occupation," 25 September 1946, NARA, RG 59, 862.00/9-2546.

106. OMGUS to Department of State, 23 March 1946, NARA, RG 59, 740.00119 Control (Germany)/3-2346; Weekly Political Trend Summary, 28 February 1946, NARA, RG 740.00119 Control (Germany)/3-1336.

107. Heath to Howard Trivers, 30 September 1946, NARA, RG 59, 740.00119 Control (Germany)/9-3046.

108. Bohlen to Murphy, 23 August 1946, box 57, Murphy Papers, Hoover Institution Archives.

109. State Department to Murphy, 16 August 1946, NARA, RG 59, 740.00119 Control (Germany)/8-346 [*sic*].

110. Howard Trivers to James Riddleberger, 27 June 1946, NARA, RG 59, lot 55D371, box 2.

111. State Department to Murphy, 16 August 1946, NARA, RG 59, 740.00119 Control (Germany)/8-346 [*sic*].

112. Perry Laukhuff to Murphy and Heath, 12 August 1946, box 57, Murphy Papers, Hoover Institution Archives.

113. Furthermore, Laukhuff argued, "We could give the same kind of publicity in the world press in this case as suggested above in the case of the Soviet Zone. 4.

We should protest in the Kommandatura against the Russian order limiting the LDP in the Soviet Sector to speakers residing in that sector. 5. We should protest in the Kommandatura and refuse to recognize Soviet action in removing unilaterally the LDP City Executive Committee. This is a matter for the Kommandatura and not for any one of the Occupying Powers. 6. If necessary we could take certain retaliatory measures against the SED in our Sector if the Soviets persist in their suppression of the SPD." Ibid.

114. Roger H. Wells, Chief, Election Affairs Branch, OMGUS to Director, OMGUS Civil Affairs Division, 17 August 1946, OMGUS CAD 3/156-3/14; Heath to Wilkinson, 27 August 1946, POLAD/747/33, cited in Daniel E. Rogers, *Politics after Hitler: The Western Allies and the German Party System* (New York: New York University Press, 1995), 84–85.

115. The British military government agreed to the SPD request.

116. Heath to Howard Trivers, 30 September 1946, NARA, RG 59, 740.00119 Control (Germany)/9-3046.

117. Murphy to Secretary of State, 5 September 1946, NARA, RG 59, 740.00119 Control (Germany)/9-546; Murphy to Secretary of State, 28 September 1946, NARA, RG 59, 740.00119 Control (Germany)/9-2846; Heath to Howard Trivers, 30 September 1946, NARA, RG 59, 740.00119 Control (Germany)/9-3046.

118. Murphy to Secretary of State, 17 September 1946, NARA, RG 59, 862.00/9-1746.

119. "U.S. Correspondents' Observations about the Russian Zone," 10 July 1946, enclosed in Murphy to Riddleberger, 16 July 1946, NARA, RG 59, 740.00119 Control (Germany)/7-1646. The journalists' impressions were fairly positive: the "caliber of Soviet officials seemed to be superior"; "cooperation, not compulsion" was the thesis of Soviet officials. The journalists reported that feuding in Berlin and the western zones had "given us a somewhat distorted picture of the amount of cooperation being achieved between Germans and Soviets in the Russian Zone." According to the group, "In progress toward economic and industrial recovery, the Soviet Zone ranks first, the American Zone second, the British Zone third, and the French Zone fourth." The group's overall impression: "Pretty good; people are working hard; there is enough, if not plentiful amount of food. Smoke stacks are puffing. Factories are turning out goods. There is a certain confidence that the hump can be crossed."

120. Murphy to Riddleberger, 14 October 1946, RG 59, lot 55D371, box 2.

121. OMGUS to Department of State, 21 October 1946, NARA, RG 59, 862.00/10-2146. For U.S. efforts to "keep alive" the Byrnes speech in other than the U.S. zone, see instructions to OMGUS Intelligence, 17 September 1946, NARA, RG 59, F.W. 862.00/9-2446; for East German reactions, see Ulbricht editorial in *Neues Deutschland*, 12 September 1946; Murphy to Secretary of State, 12 September 1946, NARA, RG 59, 862.00/9-1246; Murphy to Secretary of State, 17 September 1946, NARA, RG 59, 862.00/9-1746; and CIA intelligence report, "Further Remarks by Dr.

Wilhelm Schroeder of the Central Administration of the Russian Zone, Germany," 5 September 1946, enclosed in Lester O. Houck (Dissemination Branch, Central Intelligence Group) to Llewellyn Thompson (Department of State), 25 November 1946, NARA, RG 59, 740.00119 Control (Germany)/11-2546 (FOIA release to author).

122. Murphy to Secretary of State, 5 September 1946, NARA, RG 59, FW 862.00/9-546.

123. OMGUS to Secretary of State, 20 September 1946, NARA, RG 59, 862.00/9-2046.

124. Murphy to Secretary of State, 22 June 1946, NARA, RG 59, 862.00/6-2246. On the elections, see Günter Braun, "Wahlen und Abstimmungen," in: Martin Brozart and Hermann Weber, *SBZ-Handbuch* (Munich: R. Oldenbourg, 1990), 381–432.

125. Murphy to Secretary of State, 11 September 1946, NARA, RG 59, 862.00/9-1146.

126. Ibid.

127. Murphy to Secretary of State, 24 October 1946, NARA, RG 59, 862.00/10-2446. U.S. intelligence indicated that the date of the zonal elections was moved from October 13 to October 20 in the wake of the local elections, as the SED "now fear[ed] zone elections will have [the] wrong effect on Berlin elections. Additionally, they may wish to cover up anti-SED results in Berlin by [the] flood of SED victories in [the] Soviet Zone." OMGUS Berlin to Secretary of State, 20 September 1946, NARA, RG 59, 862.00/9-2046.

128. Murphy to Riddleberger, 28 September 1946, NARA, RG 59, 740.00119 Control (Germany)/8-2846 [*sic*].

129. CIG Report, "Beria's Plans for Improvement of Russian-German Relations," December 1946 (FOIA release to author).

130. Murphy to Secretary of State, 24 October 1946, NARA, RG 59, 862.00/10-2446.

131. Murphy to State Department, 16 October 1946, U.S. Department of State, *FRUS, 1946*, 5:622–23.

132. Chase to Secretary of State, 20 January 1947, NARA, RG 59, 740.00119 Control (Germany)/1-2047.

133. American occupation officials noted "persistent reports" that the Soviet Military Administration was considering a "possible reauthorization of the SPD in the Soviet zone."

134. Warren M. Chase to Secretary of State, 30 January 1947, NARA, RG 59, 740.00110 Control (Germany)/1-3047; Maurice W. Altaffer (American Consul General Bremen) to Secretary of State, 10 June 1947, NARA, RG 59, 740.00110 Control (Germany)/10-647.

135. "ESD report No MGB-2307," as reported in Mucchio to Secretary of State, 24 February 1947, NARA, RG 862.00/2-447.

136. Warren M. Chase to Secretary of State, 30 January 1947, NARA, RG 59,

740.00110 Control (Germany)/1-3047; Mucchio to Secretary of State, 29 January 1947, NARA, RG 59, 740.00119 Control (Germany)/1-2947.

137. Chase to Secretary of State, 20 January 1947, NARA, RG 59, 740.00119 Control (Germany)/1-2047.

138. SSU report MGB-1351, 20 December 1946, cited in ibid.; POLAD Berlin to Secretary of State, 26 December 1946, NARA, RG 59, 740.00119 Control (Germany)/12-2646.

139. Chase to Secretary of State, 20 January 1947, NARA, RG 59, 740.00119 Control (Germany)/1-2047; see also Murphy to Secretary of State, "Reported Soviet Thinking on Central German Administrations," 1 March 1947, NARA, RG 59, 862.00/3-147; and the SED's declaration on March 2, reported in Murphy to Secretary of State, 5 March 1947, NARA, RG 59, 862.00/3-547.

140. Pieck notes, in Rolf Badstübner und Wilfried Loth, eds., *Wilhelm Pieck: Aufzeichnungen zur Deutschlandpolitik, 1945–1953* (Berlin: Akademie Verlag, 1994), 112.

141. Memorandum of conversation between Stalin and the SED leaders, 31 January 1947, in Laufer et al., *Die UdSSR*, 3:136–56, and xxvii.

142. Report, "On the Results of the County and State Elections in the Soviet Occupation Zone," by Tiulpanov, 18 November 1946, in Laufer et al., *Die UdSSR*, 3:52–60.

143. Badstübner und Loth, *Wilhelm Pieck*, 112.

144. As late as November 1948, U.S. intelligence was receiving many indications that the SPD might be revived in the eastern zone. A resuscitated party would be formed in a way that would avoid the impression of SED sponsorship, create the impression of an opposition party, and pro-Soviet in outlook, undermine the Allied position in Berlin. Robert F. Corrigan to Secretary of State, 9 November 1948, NARA, RG 59, 862.00/11-948.

145. Murphy to Byrnes, 30 July 1946, *FRUS*, 1946, 5:585–86. Sokolovsky and Semenov to Stalin and Molotov, 10 November 1946, in Laufer et al., *Die UdSSR*, 3:46–48; Donald Heath to Secretary of State, 11 December 1946, *FRUS, 1946*, 5:650–51.

146. Sokolovsky and Semenov to Stalin and Molotov, 10 November 1946, in Laufer et al., *Die UdSSR*, 3:46–48.

147. Ibid.

148. Ibid., xxxviii–xlix.

149. Sokolovsky and Semenov to Stalin and Molotov, 10 November 1946, in ibid., 3:46–48.

150. Clay to Byrnes, memorandum, November 1946, Smith, *Papers of General Lucius D. Clay*, 1:279–84.

151. Draft by Kostenko, [after 11 October 1946], in Laufer et al., *Die UdSSR*, 3:23–25.

152. Draft by Novikov and Smirnov, 27 January 1947, in Laufer et al., *Die UdSSR*, 3:126.

153. "Report of the Secretary's Policy Committee on Germany," 15 September 1946, NARA, RG 59, 740.00119 Control (Germany)/9-1546.

154. Kennan to Byrnes, 19 November 1946, NARA, RG 59, 740.00119 Control (Germany)/11-1946.

155. Smith to Secretary of State, 7 January 1947, *FRUS, 1947*, 2:139–42.

156. Carolyn Eisenberg, *Drawing the Line: The American Decision to Divide Germany, 1944–1949* (Cambridge: Cambridge University Press, 1996), 280. Not everybody agreed: In November 1946 J. H. Hilldring, assistant secretary of state, strongly disagreed with the central theses of a 21 October 1946 article by theologian Reinhold Niebuhr to "deliberately [build] Germany into an anti-Russian force." Hilldring to Benton, 7 November 1946, NARA, RG 59, 740.00119 Control (Germany)/11-746.

157. Hoover cited in Eisenberg, *Drawing the Line*, 285; on John F. Dulles, see ibid., 286–87.

158. Address of the President to Congress, 12 March 1947, *Congressional Record*, 80th Congress, Document 171.

159. Ibid., 292–93. Marshall also proposed a revised version of the twenty-five-year security treaty initially proposed by Byrnes, without expecting that Stalin would be any more ready to accept the proposal at that time than he had been fifteen months earlier.

160. See also Walt W. Rostow to Paul Porter, [March 1947], Porter Papers, HSTL.

CHAPTER 4

1. Office of the Military Government, United States, Office of the Director of Intelligence (ODI), Weekly Intelligence Review (WIR) No. 56, 7 June 1947, 2–3, OMGUS/3/429-3/5, BAK; ODI, WIR No. 61, 12 July 1947, 11–13, OMGUS/3/429-3/5, BAK; ODI, WIR No. 72, 27 September 1947, 2–3, OMGUS/3/429-3/7, BAK; ODI, WIR No. 73, 4 October 1947, 6–8, OMGUS/3/429-3/8, BAK; ODI Special Intelligence Summary, Political Developments in the British, French, and Russian zones, 22 October 1947, 230, OMGUS/2/429-3/9, BAK. All cited in William Stivers, "Was Sovietization Inevitable? U.S. Intelligence Perceptions of Internal Developments in the Soviet Zone of Occupation in Germany," *Journal of Intelligence History* 5, no. 1 (June 2005): 45–70.

2. Stalin's conversation with Secretary Marshall, Ambassador Walter Bedell Smith, Charles E. Bohlen, and Foreign Minister Molotov, 15 April 1947, U.S. Department of State, *FRUS, 1947*, 2:337–44.

3. "Conversations with Baron von Prittwitz-und-Gaffron, Jacob Kaiser, and Ernst Lemmer, Three Leaders of the CDU, on German Political Problems," Murphy to Secretary of State, 25 June 1946, NARA, RG 59, 862.00/6-2546.

4. A-265, Murphy to Secretary of State, 20 March 1946, NARA, RG 59, 862.00/3-2045; David Harris, memorandum, 26 March 1946, NARA, RG 59, lot 55D374, cited in Anjana Buckow, *Zwischen Propaganda und Realpolitik: Die USA und der*

sowjetisch besetzte Teil Deutschlands, 1945–1955 (Stuttgart: Franz Steiner Verlag, 2003), 134, 137.

5. Marc Trachtenberg, *A Constructed Peace: The Making of the European Settlement, 1945–1963*, Princeton Studies in International History and Politics (Princeton, NJ: Princeton University Press, 1999), 47.

6. Memorandum of conversation between Stalin and the SED leaders, 31 January 1947, in Laufer et al., *Die UdSSR*, 3:136–56; ODI, WIR No. 71, 20 September 1947, 11–13, OMGUS/3/429-3/7, BAK, cited in William Stivers and Donald A. Carter, *The City Becomes a Symbol: The U.S. Army in the Occupation in Berlin, 1945–1949* (Washington, DC: Center for Military History, 2017), 296; Carmel Offie to Secretary of State, 16 July 1947, NARA, RG 59, 740.00119 Control (Germany)/7-1647.

7. Rolf Steininger, *Deutsche Geschichte: Darstellung und Dokumente in vier Bänden* (Frankfurt/M.: Fischer Taschenbuchverlag, 2002), vol. 1, Document No. 72.

8. Molotov to Dratvin, Makarov, and Razin, 17 November 1947, in Laufer et al., *Die UdSSR*, 3:453–54; see also Murphy to Secretary of State, 21 November 1946, NARA, RG 59, 862.00/11-2146.

9. Smirnov to Semenov, 27 September 1947, in Laufer et al., *Die UdSSR*, 3:412–13.

10. Smith to Eisenhower, 10 December 1947, quoted in Carolyn Eisenberg, *Drawing the Line: The American Decision to Divide Germany, 1944–1949* (Cambridge: Cambridge University Press, 1996), 359.

11. Laufer et al., *Die UdSSR*, 3:lvii; Gusev to Molotov, 17 October 1947, in Laufer et al., *Die UdSSR*, 3:420–25.

12. Laufer et al, *Die UdSSR*, 3:lvii.

13. Murphy to Riddleberger, 31 August 1947, NARA, RG 59, 740.00119 Control (Germany)/8-3147.

14. Chase to U.S. Embassy in the United Kingdom, 12 December 1947, *FRUS, 1947*, 2:903–4.

15. *Dokumente der Sozialistischen Einheitspartei Deutschlands*, 1:241–43, quoted in Laufer et al., *Die UdSSR*, 703–4.

16. Murphy to Secretary of State, 7 August 1948, NARA, RG 59, 862.00/8-748; "Pan-German Coup Called Soviet Aim," *New York Times*, 1 January 1948; "Communist Front in Germany," *Wall Street Journal*, 19 January 1948; "Soviet Coup Hinted in Berlin March 18," *New York Times*, 4 February 1948. On the people's congress movement, see Klaus Bender, *Deutschland, einig Vaterland? Die Volkskongressbewegung für deutsche Einheit und einen gerechten Frieden in der Deutschlandpolitik der Sozialistischen Einheitspartei Deutschlands* (Frankfurt am Main: P. Lang, 1992), 99–106.

17. William A. Harris, "March Crisis 1948, Act I," *Studies in Intelligence* 10 (1966): 1–22; William Harris, "March Crisis 1948, Act II," *Studies in Intelligence* 11 (1967): 9–32. On the Greek Civil War, see André Gerolymatos, *Red Acropolis, Black Terror: The Greek Civil War and the Origins of Soviet-American Rivalry, 1943–1949* (New York: Basic Books, 2004).

18. Murphy to Secretary of State, 3 July 1948, NARA, RG 59, 862.00/7-348; Heike Amos, *Die Westpolitik der SED 1948/49–1961: Arbeit nach Westdeutschland durch die Nationale Front, das Ministerium für Auswärtige Angelegenheiten und das Ministerium für Staatssicherheit* (Berlin: Akademie Verlag, 1999), 16–17.

19. A. Dana Hodgden (American consul general in Stuttgart) to Secretary of State, 13 April 1948, NARA, RG 59, 862.00/4-1348; Hergard Robel, ed., *Wilhelm Külz: Ein Liberaler zwischen Ost und West: Aufzeichnungen, 1947–1948* (München: R. Oldenbourg, 1989), 76.

20. Murphy to Secretary of State, "Further Notes on the People's Congress Movement," 12 April 1948, NARA, RG 59, 862.00/4-1248; Murphy to Secretary of State, 16 April 1948, NARA, RG 59, 862.00/4-1648; Murphy to Secretary of State, "Further Notes"; Murphy to Secretary of State, "The People's Congress Movement's Popular Initiative (Volksbegehren)," 29 May 1948, NARA, RG 59, 862.00/5-2948; Consulate Bremen to Secretary of State, "Terrorist methods used by SED agents in Western zones in collecting signatures for Volksbegehren," 16 June 1948, NARA, RG 59, 862.00B/6-1648; Weekly Intelligence Report No. 108 by OMGUS Office of the Director of Intelligence, 5 June 1948, NARA, RG 59, 740.00119 Control (Germany).

21. Weekly Intelligence Report No. 108 by OMGUS Office of the Director of Intelligence, 5 June 1948, NARA, RG 59, 740.00119 Control (Germany); Murphy to Secretary of State, "Further Notes;" Murphy to Secretary of State, 15 June 1948, NARA, RG 59, 862.00/6-1548; Murphy to Secretary of State, 29 May 1948, NARA, RG 59, 862.00/5-3048.

22. Quoted in Nicholas J. Schlosser, *Cold War on the Airwaves: The Radio Propaganda War against East Germany* (Urbana: University of Illinois Press, 2015), 30; Bundesarchiv-Stiftung Archiv der Parteien und Massenorganisationen der DDR (hereafter cited as SAPMO-BA), NY 4036/656, 33; Amos, *Die Westpolitik,* 15.

23. State Department to Murphy, 19 April 1948, NARA, RG 59, 862.00/4-1648; Chase to Secretary of State, 21 April 1948, NARA, RG 59, 862.00/4-2148; Murphy to Secretary of State, "Popular Initiative (Volksbegehren)." The French government also banned the Volksbegehren petition, while the British government allowed the signature drive to take place. See Weekly Intelligence Report No. 108.

24. Rolf Badstübner und Wilfried Loth, eds., *Wilhelm Pieck: Aufzeichnungen zur Deutschlandpolitik, 1945–1953* (Berlin: Akademie Verlag, 1994), 192; Laufer et al., *Die UdSSR,* 3:541–42.

25. Ewald to Gniffke, 22 July 1948, SAPMO-BA, DY 6, vorl. 0494.

26. ESD Report MGB-6347, cited in Murphy to Secretary of State, "Popular Initiative (Volksbegehren)."

27. Semenov, memorandum, 6 October 1946, in Laufer et al., *Die UdSSR,* 3:3–5; memorandum of conversation between Stalin and the SED leaders, 31 January 1947, in Laufer et al., *Die UdSSR,* 3:136–56. Others within the Soviet Military

Administration saw the trends more critically. After consulting with Sokolovsky and the SMA's top economic official, a special envoy of the Soviet foreign trade ministry in Germany warned the leadership at the end of 1946 that the four occupation zones had acquired considerable economic autonomy. Despite some advantageous aspects, continued independent development of the Soviet zone would lead to "extraordinary difficulties," as the raw-material capacities had been exhausted and the remaining infrastructure required renovation and replacement. Recent German Communist efforts to "take the zone's economy into their hands completely" would involve a reduction in reparations deliveries for the USSR. "The question to what extent an autonomous existence of the Soviet zone is advantageous," he insisted, "should be decided as soon as possible." See Jan Foitzik, comp., *Inventar der Befehle des Obersten Chefs der Sowjetischen Militäradministration in Deutschland (SMAD), 1945–1949* (München/New Providence: K. G. Saur, 1995), 435–45.

    28. Laufer et al., *Die UdSSR*, 3:xlvi–xlviii.

    29. CIA, "Review of the World Situation," President's Secretary's File, NSC Files—Meetings, 8 April 1948, box 203, HSTL; W. Park Armstrong/R to Charles E. Saltzman/O, 30 June 1948, NARA, RG 59, 740.00119 Control (Germany)/6-3048; Murphy to Secretary of State, 8 April 1948, NARA, RG 59, 740.00119 Control (Germany)/4-848.

    30. "Record of a conversation between Cde. I. V. Stalin and the leaders of the Socialist Unity Party of Germany Wilhelm Pieck and Otto Grotewohl, 26 March 1948, at 1900 hours," AP RF, F. 45, Op. 1, D. 303, 53–79, Dimitri Volkogonov Collection, Library of Congress; Laufer et al., *Die UdSSR*, 4:xxxix–xl.

    31. Smirnov to Vyshinsky, 12 January 1948, in Laufer et al., *Die UdSSR*, 3:485–86; Orlov to Vyshinsky, 24 March 1948, ibid., 3:536–38; Tiulpanov to Semenov, 8 March 1948, ibid, 3:501–2.

    32. Tiulpanov to Semenov, 8 March 1948, in Laufer et al., *Die UdSSR*, 3:501–2; Smirnov to Vyshinsky, 12 January 1948, ibid., 3:485–86; Smirnov to Molotov, 10 March 1948, ibid., 3:520–21; Orlov to Molotov, 24 March 1948, ibid., 3:536–38; Smirnov to Molotov, 12 March 1948, ibid., 3:522–24. The unilateral extension of the Soviet zone currency to all of Berlin certainly violated Western Allied rights. Yet from the viewpoint of the Soviet leadership that saw the West waging a "currency war" against the Soviet zone mark, a common currency in Berlin was the logical consequence of Berlin's economic dependence on the surrounding Soviet zone. The alternative, to which in fact the Western powers had agreed, a new country-wide currency issued by the Soviet zone Notenbank, would have come at the price of granting some measure of Western Allied control over its policies. The problem was that by granting such authority, the Soviets would have also granted the Western powers a say in Soviet zone affairs, which was long-standing anathema to the Soviet leadership. Certainly the Soviet access restrictions interrupted Berlin's ground and water trade with the western zones, causing alarm and dislocation in Berlin, yet from a Soviet

perspective, sealing off the zonal borders aimed as much at protecting against the depletion of the Soviet zone in the wake of the currency reform in the western zones.

Other evidence corroborates this interpretation. No one in Moscow or Karlshorst had expected the massive public outcry in the West that accused the USSR of strangling the Western sectors economically. Contrary to public perceptions, the western Berlin sector borders remained open throughout the crisis, allowing for continued economic exchange with its zonal hinterland—in fact assuring West Berlin's economic survival. Moscow did not interfere with the massive Western airlift instituted to supply the "blockaded" city. In fact, the Soviet military administration made earnest efforts itself to supply West Berlin with food and materials. Choking the Western sectors would have run counter to Soviet efforts to broaden its all-German appeals, headlined by the people's congress. Adding insult to the surprise over the unprecedented public reaction in the West, Western accusations of a "blockade of Berlin" ridiculed in politically almost sacrilegious ways the memory of the far more devastating German blockade of Leningrad than had ended just four years earlier. See William Stivers, "The Incomplete Blockade: Soviet Zone Supply of West Berlin, 1948–49," *Diplomatic History* 21, no. 4 (October 1997): 569–602.

33. "Record of a conversation between Cde. I. V. Stalin and the leaders of the Socialist Unity Party of Germany Wilhelm Pieck and Otto Grotewohl, 26 March 1948, at 1900 hours."

34. CIA, "Effect of Soviet Restrictioons on the US Position in Berlin," ORE 11-48, 14 June 1948, in Donald P. Steury, ed., *On the Front Lines of the Cold War: Documents on the Intelligence War in Berlin, 1946 to 1961* (Washington, DC: CIA, 1999), 177–80; Murphy to Marshall, 26 June 1948, NARA, RG 59, 740.00119 Control (Germany)/6-2648.

35. Wolfgang Schivelbusch, *In a Cold Crater: Cultural and Intellectual Life in Berlin, 1945–1948* (Berkeley: University of California Press, 1998), 117, 119–25; Schlosser, *Cold War on the Airwaves,* 23–46; Nicholas J. Schlosser, "Creating an 'Atmosphere of Objectivity': Radio in the American Sector, Objectivity, and the United States Propaganda Campaign against the German Democratic Republic, 1945–1961," *German History* 29, no. 4 (December 2011): 610–27.

36. Schlosser, *Cold War on the Airwaves,* 31–33, 42.

37. "Transmittal of Report on Berlin Operations Base," Dana Durand (Chief, SSU Foreign Branch M) to Chief of SSU Station Karlsruhe, 8 April 1948, in Steury, *On the Front Lines of the Cold War,* 36; Sergej Mironenko, Lutz Niethammer, and Alexander von Plato, *Sowjetische Speziallager in Deutschland, 1945 bis 1950,* 2 vols. (Berlin: Akademie Verlag, 1998); Peter Reif-Spirek and Bodo Ritscher, *Speziallager in der SBZ: Gedenkstätten mit "doppelter Vergangenheit"* (Berlin: Ch. Links, 1999); Petra Haustein, Annette Kaminsky, and Volkhard Knigge, eds., *Instrumentalisierung, Verdrängung, Aufarbeitung: Die sowjetischen Speziallager in der gesellschaftlichen Wahrnehmung 1945 bis heute* (Göttingen: Wallstein, 2006), 44–62; Klaus-Dieter Müller, "Bürokratischer

Terror: Justizielle und außerjustizielle Verfolgungsmaßnahmen der sowjetischen Besatzungsmacht 1945–1956," in Roger Engelmann and Clemens Vollnhals, eds., *Justiz im Dienste der Parteiherrschaft: Rechtspraxis und Staatssicherheit in der DDR* (Berlin: Ch. Links, 1999), 59–92.

38. Enrico Heitzer, *Die Kampfgruppe gegen Unmenschlichkeit (KgU): Widerstand und Spionage im Kalten Krieg*, Zeithistorische Studien 53 (Köln Böhlau, 2015), 41–46; Kai-Uwe Merz, *Kalter Krieg als antikommunistischer Widerstand: Die Kampfgruppe gegen Unmenschlichkeit, 1948–1959*, Studien zur Zeitgeschichte 34 (München: R. Oldenbourg, 1987), 45–47; Gerhard Finn, *Nichtstun ist Mord: Die Kampfgruppe gegen Unmenschlichkeit—KgU* (Bad Münstereifel: Westkreuz Verlag, 2000), 11. See also Jochen Staadt, "Vergesst sie nicht! Freiheit war ihr Ziel. Die Kampfgruppe gegen Unmenschlichkeit," in *Zeitschrift des Forschungsverbundes SED-Staat* 24 (2008): 60–79; Jochen Staadt, "Ein Historikerreinfall: Die Kampfgruppe gegen Unmenschlichkeit—Desinformation macht Geschichte," in *Zeitschrift des Forschungsverbundes SED-Staat* 33 (2013): 94–111.

39. Heitzer, *Die Kampfgruppe gegen Unmenschlichkeit (KgU)*, 49–50.

40. Ibid., 57–58; Paul Maddrell, *Spying on Science: Western Intelligence in Divided Germany, 1945–1961* (Oxford: Oxford University Press, 2006), 134; Wolfgang Buschfort, *Das Ostbüro der SPD: Von der Gründung bis zur Berlin-Krise* (München: R. Oldenbourg, 1991), 74; Merz, *Kalter Krieg*, 74; Bernd Stöver, "Politik der Befreiung?" in *"Geistige Gefahr" und "Immunisierung der Gesellschaft": Antikommunismus und politische Kultur in der frühen Bundesrepublik*, ed. Stefan Creuzberger and Dierk Hoffmann (Munich: Oldenbourg, 2014), 223. British officials quoted in Rainer Hildebrandt, *Zur Geschichte der Kampfgruppe gegen Unmenschlichkeit, Manuskript zur Veranstaltung am 21.05.1997 im Haus am Checkpoint Charlie*, Privatarchiv Heitzer, cited in Heitzer, *Die Kampfgruppe gegen Unmenschlichkeit*, 45.

41. Heitzer, *Kampfgruppe gegen Unmenschlichkeit*, 50–55.

42. Murphy to Secretary of State, 4 June 1948, NARA, RG 59, 862.00/6-448; Murphy to Secretary of State, 13 June 1946, NARA, RG 59, 862.00/6-1346; Daily Information Summary No. 214, 23 April 1946, NARA, RG 59, 740.00119 Control (Germany)/4-2446.

43. Murphy to Riddleberger, 31 August 1947, NARA, RG 59, 740.00119 Control (Germany)/8-3147; Murphy to Secretary of State, 1 October 1948, NARA, RG 59, 862.00/10-148; Riddleberger to Secretary of State, 12 February 1949, NARA, RG 59, 862.00/2-1249; POLAD Heidelberg to Department of State, 6 June 1949, NARA, RG 59, 862.00/6-649.

44. Murphy to Secretary of State, 1 October 1948, NARA, RG 59, 862.00/10-148; see also Murphy to Secretary of State, 12 January 1949, NARA, RG 59, 862.00/1-1249;CIA memorandum, HSTL, President's Secretary's File, NSC Files—Meetings, 10 March 1948, box 203.

45. Riddleberger to Secretary of State, 19 October 1948, NARA, RG 59,

862.00/10-1949; Chase to Secretary of State, 30 April 1948, NARA, RG 59, 862.00/4-3048; Riddleberger to Secretary of State, 22 July 1948, NARA, RG 59, 862.00/7-2248.

46. USPOLAD Frankfurt to USPOLAD Berlin, memorandum, 25 January 1949, NARA, RG 59, 740.00119 Control (Germany)/1-2549, EUCOM Intelligence Report on LDP, enclosed in POLAD Heidelberg to Department of State, 12 August 1949, NARA, RG 59, 862.00/8-1249.

47. Murphy to Secretary of State, 8 June 1948, NARA, RG 59, 862.00/6-848; Robert F. Corrigan (POLAD Heidelberg) to Secretary of State, 21 December 1948, NARA, RG 59, 862.00/12-2148; "Eastern Germany," Douglas (American Embassy London) to Secretary of State, 13 July 1948, NARA, RG 59, 862.00B/7-1348; Corrigan (POLAD Heidelberg) to Secretary of State, 29 October 1948, NARA, RG 59, 862.00/102948; POLAD Berlin to Secretary of State, 11 December 1948, NARA, RG 59, 862.00/12-1148; "SMA Order Directing Screening of German Socialist Unity Party (SED)," Corrigan (POLAD Heidelberg) to Secretary of State, 21 December 1948, NARA, RG 59, 862.00/21-2148; EST Report No. MGB-6519, cited in Murphy to Secretary of State, 8 June 1948, NARA, RG 59, 862.00/6-848; Murphy to Secretary of State, 21 September 1948, NARA, RG 59, 9-2048.

48. Riddleberger to Secretary of State, 19 October 1948, NARA, RG 59, 862.00/10-1948; Corrigan (POLAD Heidelberg) to Secretary of State, 21 December 1948, NARA, RG 59, 862.00/12-2148; Riddleberger to Secretary of State, 19 October 1948, NARA, RG 59, 862.00/10-1948.

49. For some results of Gniffke's interrogation by U.S. Army Intelligence, see Corrigan to Secretary of State, 11 January 1949, NARA, RG 59, 862.00/1-1149; Murphy to Secretary of State, 9 December 1948, NARA, RG 59, 862.00/12-948; Corrigan to Secretary of State, 18 May 1949, with enclosed Intelligence Report No. RP-116-49, NARA, RG 59, 862.00/5-1849; "Renunciation of Communism by Heinrich Graf von Einsiedel," USPOLAD Frankfurt to Department of State, 26 April 1949, NARA, RG 58, 862.00B/4-2649; Murphy to Secretary of State, 8 June 1948, NARA, RG 59, 862.00/6-848; Murphy to Secretary of State, NARA, RG 59, 862.00/11-848.

50. American Consulate General Hamburg to Department of State, "Attitude of the German Public Opinion toward the Western Occupying Powers and the Reasons Therefor," 16 February 1949, NARA, RG 59, 740.00119 Control (Germany)/2-1649; Riddleberger to Secretary of State, 2 April 1949, NARA, RG 59, 740.00119 Control (Germany)/4-249.

51. Murphy to Secretary of State, NARA, RG 59, 862.00/1-2649; Kohler to Secretary of State, 18 January 1949, NARA, RG 862.00/1-1849; USPOLAD to Department of State, 15 February 1949, NARA, RG 59, 862.00/2-1549; Kohler to Secretary of State, 10 February 1949, NARA, RG 59, 862.00/2-1049 (FOIA release to author); Jacob D. Beam/CE to Thompson/EE, memorandum, 14 February 1949, NARA, RG 59, 2-1449; Riddleberger to Secretary of State, 27 March 1949, NARA, RG 59, 740.00119 Control (Germany)/3-2749.

52. Riddleberger to Secretary of State, 2 April 1949, NARA, RG 59, 740.00119 Control (Germany)/4-249; POLAD Heidelberg to Department of State, 6 June 1949, NARA, RG 59, 862.00/6-649; "Activities in the Bremen District of Oberkonsistorialrat Johannes Schroeder," enclosed in Maurice Altaffer, American Consul General in Bremen, to Secretary of State, 19 November 1947, RG 59, 862.00/11-1947; Riddleberger to Acheson, 2 April 1949, NARA, RG 59, 740.00119 Control (Germany)/3-249. Adenauer informed U.S. occupation officials that Nuschke's visit was designed to prevent or disturb the consolidating of a Western state, and that as a tool of the Soviets, Nuschke allowed himself to be frequently photographed with Adenauer. Altaffer to Secretary of State, 7 March 1949, NARA, RG 59, 862.00/3-749.

53. Altaffer to Secretary of State, 3 March 1949, NARA, RG 59, 740.00119 Control (Germany)/3-349; Riddleberger to Secretary of State, 5 March 1949, NARA, RG 59, 862.00/3-549; Riddleberger to Acheson, 2 April 1949, NARA, RG 59, 740.00119 Control (Germany)/3-249; Riddleberger to Secretary of State, 11 May 1949, NARA, RG 59, 740.00119 Control (Germany)/5-1149; Riddleberger to Secretary of State, 22 May 1949, 740.00119 Control (Germany)/5-2249. Murphy wondered whether "it might be useful if one of our people had a quiet and personal talk with Prittwitz. He used to be most cooperative. I wonder what is eating him?" Murphy to John J. McCloy, 6 September 1949, NARA, RG 59, 862.00/9-649. On Rudolf Nadolny's role, see his *Mein Beitrag: Erinnerungen eines Botschafters des Deutschen Reiches*, ed. Günter Wollstein (Cologne: DME, 1985); and Alexander Gallus, *Die Neutralisten: Verfechter eines vereinten Deutschland zwischen Ost und West, 1945–1990* (Düsseldorf: Droste, 2001), 146–48.

54. Kennan to Acheson, 14 February 1949, NARA, RG 59, 740.00119 Control (Germany)/2-1449; Henry A. Byroade to Murphy, 10 March 1949, NARA, RG 59, 740.00119 Control (Germany)/3-1049 TSF.

55. Kennan, draft memorandum, 4 October 1948, enclosed in George Butler to Bohlen, 5 October 1948, NARA, RG 59, 740.00119 Control (Germany)/10-548; George F. Kennan to Robert Murphy, 24 December 1948, NARA, lot 64D563, Policy Planning Staff Records, box 15; Kennan, memorandum, 8 March 1949, NARA, RG 59, 740.00119 Control (Germany)/3-849; CIA, "Review of the World Situation," HSTL, President's Secretary's File, NSC Files—Meetings, 20 October 1948, box 204; Riddleberger to Secretary of State, 27 June 1949, NARA, RG 59, 862.00/6-2449.

56. "Policy with Respect to Germany," memorandum of conversation, 9 March 1949, NARA, RG 59, 740.00119 Control (Germany)/3-949; Kennan to Acheson, 14 February 1949, NARA, RG 59, 740.00119 Control (Germany)/2-1449; "Military Implications Deriving from the Establishment of a Free and Sovereign German Government," enclosed in Ware Adams to Policy Planning Staff, 3 September 1948, NARA, RG 59, lot 55D371, box 8; "Plan for Germany," Jacob Beam, 27 September 1948, NARA, RG 59, 740.00119 Control (Germany)/9-2748; Hickerson to McWilliams, 23 November 1948, NARA, RG 59, 740.00119 Control (Germany)/11-2348;

Hickerson and Beam to McWilliams, 23 November 1948, NARA, RG 59, 740.00119 Control (Germany)/11-2348.

57. Hickerson and Beam to McWilliams, 23 November 1948, NARA, RG 59, 740.00119 Control (Germany)/11-2348; Jessup to Rusk, 21 February 1949, NARA, RG 59, 740.1100119 Control (Germany)/2-2149.

58. Clay to Vorhees, 6 May 1949, HSTL, Papers of Harry S. Truman, President's Secretary's Files, box 178; Charles W. Yost to Jessup, 21 May 1949, enclosed in Jessup to Kennan, 24 May 1949, NARA, RG 59, Policy Planning Staff Records, lot 64D563, box 15.

59. "Policy with Respect to Germany," memorandum of conversation, 9 March 1949, NARA, RG 59, 740.00119 Control (Germany)/3-949; memorandum, 17 March 1949, NARA, RG 59, 740.00119 Control (Germany)/3-1749; Dean Acheson, "German Policy Papers," memorandum for the president, 31 March 1949, NARA, RG 59, 740.00119 Control (Germany)/3-3149; Thomas Alan Schwartz, *America's Germany: John J. McCloy and the Federal Republic of Germany* (Cambridge, MA: Harvard University Press, 1991), 38; "Discussion of Malik-Jessup Conversation Concerning German Question," 17 March 1949, NARA, RG 59, 740.00119 Control (Germany)/3-1749; "Preparations for CFM on Germany—meeting in the Secretary's office May 12, 2:00 p.m.," NARA, RG 59, lot 64D563 (Policy Planning Staff), box 15.

60. Kohler to Acheson, 6 May 1949, NARA, RG 59, 740.00119 Control (Germany)/5-649; Riddleberger to Secretary of State, 11 May 1949, NARA, RG 59, Control (Germany)/5-1149.

61. Kennan, Draft Statement for Webb (for appointment with president), 26 May 1949, NARA, RG 59, lot 64D563, Policy Planning Staff Papers, box 15. The Basic Law held out the possibility of unification with the eastern zone if freely elected state parliaments chose to accede to the Federal Republic, extending the constitution to Eastern Germany.

62. See also Hermann-Josef Rupieper, "Die Reaktionen der USA auf die Gründung der DDR," in *"Provisorium für längstens ein Jahr": Die Gründung der DDR*, ed. Elke Scherstjanoi (Berlin: Akademie Verlag, 1993), 59–66, here: 63. OMGUS Political Research and Analysis Branch, "Centralization of Soviet Zone German Administration," 27 March 1946, NARA, RG 59, 740.00119 Control (Germany)/4-946; Murphy to Secretary of State, 12 April 1949, NARA, RG 59, 862.00/4-1248; Marshall to Douglas and Murphy, 3 April 1948, NARA, RG 59, 862.00/4-348.

64. Murphy to Secretary of State, 12 April 1949, NARA, RG 59, 862.00/4-1248; Murphy to Secretary of State, 8 April 1948, NARA, RG 59, 740.00119 Control (Germany)/4-848; Murphy to Secretary of State, 4 January 1949, NARA, RG 59, 862.00/1-449.

65. Brewster Morris, memorandum, 29 May 1948, enclosed in Murphy to Secretary of State, 29 May 1948, NARA, RG 59, 862.00/5-2948; Murphy to Secretary of State, 7 August 1948, NARA, RG 59, 862.00/8-748.

66. "Record of a Conversation between Cde. I. V. Stalin and the leaders of the Socialist Unity Party of Germany, W. Pieck, O. Grotewohl, and W. Ulbricht," 18 December 1948, APRF, f. 45, op. 1, f. 303, ll. 53–79.

67. Brewster Morris, memorandum, 29 May 1948, enclosed in Murphy to Secretary of State, 29 May 1948, NARA, RG 59, 862.00/5-2948; Marshall to Douglas and Murphy, 3 April 1948, NARA, RG 59, 862.00/4-348; Murphy to Saltzman and Hickerson, 16 July 1948, NARA, RG 59, 740.00119 Control (Germany)/7-1648; 37, Murphy to Secretary of State, 8 July 1948, NARA, RG 59, 862.00/7-448.

68. "Record of a Conversation between Cde. I. V. Stalin and the leaders of the Socialist Unity Party of Germany, W. Pieck, O. Grotewohl, and W. Ulbricht," 18 December 1948, APRF, F. 45, Op. 1, D. 303, 53–79; "Discussion with Semenov," 10 June 1948, in Rolf Badstübner und Wilfried Loth, eds., *Wilhelm Pieck: Aufzeichnungen zur Deutschlandpolitik, 1945–1953* (Berlin: Akademie Verlag, 1994), 233; Dietrich Staritz, *Geschichte der DDR, 1945–1985* (Frankfurt/M.: Suhrkamp, 1985), 32; ibid., 282; Riddleberger to Secretary of State, 20 May 1949, NARA, RG 59, 740.00119 Control (Germany)/5-2049; Riddleberger to Secretary of State, 30 May 1949, NARA, RG 59, 740.00119 Control (Germany)/5-3049.

69. Riddleberger to Secretary of State, 7 April 1949, NARA, RG 59, 862.00/3-3149. American officials understood this quite well, nearly universally sharing the belief that "much will presumably depend upon bizonal and/or trizonal developments." Brewster Morris, memorandum, 29 May 1948, enclosed in Murphy to Secretary of State, 29 May 1948, NARA, RG 59, 862.00/5-2948; Dietrich Staritz, "Die SED, Stalin, und der 'Aufbau des Sozialismus' in der DDR. Aus den Akten des Zentralen Parteiarchivs," *Deutschland Archiv* (1991), 685–700.

70. On October 15, the USSR established diplomatic relations with the GDR.

CHAPTER 5

1. *New York Times*, 9 October 1949.

2. *New York Times*, 10 October 1949.

3. Kirk to Secretary of State, 18 January 1950, RG 59, 762B.00/1-1850.

4. Quoted in Thomas A. Schwartz, *America's Germany: John J. McCloy and the Federal Republic of Germany* (Cambridge, MA: Harvard University Press, 1991), 67.

5. Dietrich Staritz, *Geschichte der DDR*, Erw. Neuausg, Neue Historische Bibliothek, Bd. 260 (Frankfurt am Main: Suhrkamp, 1996), 84; Drew Middleton, *New York Times*, 1 February 1950.

6. Michael Lemke, *Einheit oder Sozialismus? Die Deutschlandpolitik der SED* (Cologne: Böhlau, 2001), 48; Pieck notes, Pieck Papers, SAPMO-BA, NY36/556, Bl. 174, reprinted in Rolf Badstübner and Wilfried Loth, eds., *Wilhelm Pieck—Aufzeichnungen zur Deutschlandpolitik 1945–1953* (Berlin: Akademie Verlag, 1994), 343.

7. Torsten Diedrich and Rüdiger Wenzke, *Die getarnte Armee: Die Geschichte der Kasernierten Volkspolizei der DDR 1952 bis 1956* (Berlin: Ch. Links, 2001), 29;

conversation between Chancellor Adenauer and U.S. Secretary of State Acheson (German version), 13 November 1949, memorandum of conversation, *Dokumente zur Deutschlandpolitik*, ser. II (hereafter cited as *DzD* II), ed. Hanns Jürgen Küsters, with assistance by Daniel Hofmann (Munich: R. Oldenbourg, 1996), 784–86; Adenauer to Robertson, 28 April 1950, *Akten zur Auswärtigen Politik der Bundesrepublik Deutschland* (hereafter cited as *AAPD 1949/50*), ed. Auswärtigen Amts/Institut für Zeitgeschichte (Munich: R. Oldenbourg, 1997), 139, and *DzD* II/3, 716–17; *FRUS, 1950*, 4:591–96, here 595; Adenauer, memorandum, 15 January 1950, ibid. Herbert Blankenhorn Diary, 10 April 1950 (note 1), *DzD* II/3, 671; Blankenhorn, memorandum, 25 February 1950, *AAPD 1949/50*, 94–96; General Count von Schwerin, memorandum, 16 May 1950, *AAPD 1949/50*, 151–53.

8. Henning Köhler, *Adenauer: Eine politische Biographie* (Frankfurt am Main: Propyläen, 1994), 589–93; Diary entries by Herbert Blankenhorn, 10–14 April 1950, *DzD* II/3, 671–73, 674–80; "Memorandum on the Session of the Foreign Affairs Committee of the GDR Provisional Volkskammer," 22 March 1950, *DzD* II/3, 638–51.

9. Köhler, *Adenauer*, 566; William Glenn Gray, *Germany's Cold War: The Global Campaign to Isolate East Germany, 1949–1969* (Chapel Hill: University of North Carolina Press, 2003), 10–11.

10. Gray, *Germany's Cold War*, 10, 239; CIA, memorandum, "Political Orientation of the West German State," 25 April 1950, *DzD* II/3, 711–14.

11. Blankenhorn, note, 13 April 1950, *AAPD 1949/50*, 129–33; conversation between Adenauer and Robertson, memorandum, *ibid., 134–38;* CIA, "Political Orientation of the West German State," memorandum, 25 April 1950, *DzD* II/3, 711–14.

12. U.S. Department of State, *FRUS, 1949: Eastern Europe: The Soviet Union* (Washington, DC: GOP, 1974), 3:309–11 (hereafter cited as *FRUS, 1949*; Blankenhorn Diary, 12–13 April 1950, 675–76; General Count von Schwerin, memorandum, 25 May 1950, *AAPD 1949/50*, 159.

13. Blankenhorn Diary (Robertson), 6 June 1950, 165; Blankenhorn Diary (McCloy), 7 June 1950, 168; Blankenhorn, memorandum of conversation with Glain (Allied High Commission), 5 April 1950, *DzD* II/3, 669; Blankenhorn Diary, 8 June 1950, *AAPD 1949/50*, 174; Blankenhorn Diary, 4 May 1950, *DzD* II/3, 728; Recommendation by the Allied High Commissioners for the formation of a Federal Police Force, 11 May 1950, ibid., 761–63.

14. Memorandum, "Germany—Soviet Zone: Soviet and U.S. Objectives and Tactics," RG 466, HICOG Berlin, Eastern Affairs Division, box 1, folder 1.

15. Frank Schumacher, *Kalter Krieg und Propaganda: Die USA, der Kampf um die Weltmeinung, und die ideelle Westbindung der Bundesrepublik Deutschland, 1945–1955* (Trier: WVT, 2000); memorandum by the CIA, "Political Orientation of the West German State," 25 April 1950, in *DzD* II/3, 711–14.

16. Memorandum, "Germany—Soviet Zone: Soviet and U.S. Objectives and Tactics," NARA, RG 466, HICOG Berlin, Eastern Affairs Division, box 1, folder 1.

17. Cited in *AAPD 1949/50*, 105 (note 7); memorandum of conversation between Adenauer and Robertson, 21 April 1950, *DzD* II/3, 697–99; Schwartz, *America's Germany*, 89.

18. "Draft Proposal on the Responsibilities and Activities for the Ministry of All-German Affairs," 30 September 1949, cited in *Im Bogen der Zeit: Memoirs of Dr Ewert Freiherr von Dellingshausen*, part 2 (Bonn 1984–85), unpublished manuscript, BA Koblenz, N1515, vol. 2.

19. Ibid., 2:13; Köhler, *Adenauer*, 594–96. On the history of the Kaiser Ministry, see Stefan Creuzberger, *Kampf für die Einheit: Das gesamtdeutsche Ministerium und die politische Kultur des Kalten Krieges, 1949–1969* (Düsseldorf: Droste Verlag, 2008).

20. Köhler, *Adenauer*, 56; Blankenhorn Diary, 13 April 1950, *DzD* II/3, 678; "Record of Conversation with Dr. Schumacher," 12 January 1950, RG 466, HICOG/Eastern Element, box 3; memorandum, "Germany—Soviet Zone: Soviet and U.S. Objectives and Tactics," RG 466, HICOG Berlin, Eastern Affairs Division,, box 1, folder 1.

21. Schwartz, *America's Germany*, 12. On the PSB, see Bernd Stöver, Die Befreiung vom Kommunismus: Amerikanische Liberation Policy im Kalten Krieg, 1947–1991 (Köln: Böhlau, 2002), 221–22.

22. McCloy to Secretary of State, 20 April 1950, NARA, RG 59, 511.62B/4-2050; *New York Times*, 27 May 1950; Hans Speier, *From the Ashes of Disgrace: A Journal from Germany, 1945–1955* (Amherst: University of Massachusetts Press, 1981), 94. On Taylor, see Ingo Trauschweizer, *Maxwell Taylor's Cold War: From Berlin to Vietnam* (Lexington, KY: University Press of Kentucky, 2019).

23. See "Reprogramming Study," enclosed in Glen Wolfe to Arthur Kimball, 6 September 1950, NARA, RG 59, lot 55D371.

24. Gray, *Germany's Cold War*, 11.

25. See the famous carpet episode during Adenauer's first meeting with the three Western high commissioners on 29 September 1949, Köhler, *Adenauer*, 558–59.

26. Adenauer to McCloy, 26 October 1950, *AAPD 1949/50*, 4.

27. McCloy to Secretary of State, 10.10.1949, NARA, RG 59, 862.00/10-1049.

28. *FRUS, 1949*, 3:305. Trade with the GDR should be conducted solely through the intermediary of private organizations such as chambers of commerce. With regard to the negotiation of trade agreements, "the situation existing before the creation" of the GDR should be maintained: they would negotiate only through the intermediary of the Soviet authorities. The six countries also agreed to oppose the participation of the East German government in international organizations. Circular 1201, Department of State to American Diplomatic Officers, 10 February 1950, NARA, RG 59, 762B.02/2-1050; Gray, *Germany's Cold War*, 13.

29. *AAPD 1949/50*, 10; and Blankenhorn memorandum, 1 November 1949, ibid., 13; McCloy to Adenauer, *DzD* II/3, 596–97.

30. Gray, *Germany's Cold War*, 14–15.

31. Hermann-Josef Rupieper, *Der besetzte Verbündete: Die amerikanische*

Deutschlandpolitik 1949–1955 (Opladen: Westdeutscher Verlag, ca. 1991), 213; "Press Statement by the U.S. High Commissioner in Germany, McCloy," 28 February 1950, *DzD* II/3, 55–56; "From the Remarks by Federal Minister for All-German Questions, Kaiser, before the Federal Press Conference," 1 March 1950, *DzD* II/3, 56–59 (note 3).

32. Memorandum, E. A. Lightner and H. C. Ramsey, n.d., NARA, RG 59, HICOG Berlin, Political Affairs Division, box 3; *New York Times*, 3 February 1950.

33. *New York Times*, 10 March 1950; Rupieper, *Der besetzte Verbündete*, 213; Norden statement cited in *New York Times*, 3 March 1950; also: *DzD* II/3, 57; David E. Mark, HICOG Political Affairs Division, memorandum to PEPCO, 7 April 1950, RG 466, box 2.

34. On May 16, the Democratic bloc (of GDR parties) formally adopted a unity list for the October elections. "Short Report on the Discussions of the chairmen of the GDR Parties on March 28, 1950," 13 April 1950, *DzD* II/3, 663–65. On Kastner's role, see Johannes Zeller, *Prof. Dr. Hermann Kastner–Politiker, Lebemann, Agent: Eine Funktionärs-Biographie 1945 bis 1956* (Hamburg: Verlag Dr. Kovač, 2016), 173–80; Hermann Zolling/Heinz Höhne, *Pullach Intern: General Gehlen und die Geschichte des Bundesnachrichtendienstes* (Hamburg: Hoffmann und Campe, 1971), 159–61.

35. David E. Mark/HICOG Political Affairs Division to PEPCO, memorandum, 7 April 1950, RG 466, box 2; Page to PEPCO, 26 April 1950, NARA, RG 466, HICOG Berlin, Political Affairs Division, box 2.

36. Rupieper, *Der besetzte Verbündete*, 213; Acheson to HICOG, memorandum, 3 April 1950, U.S. Department of State, *Foreign Relations of the United States (FRUS, 1950)* (Washington, DC: GPO, 1980), 4:618; Lightner and Ramsey, memorandum, n.d., NARA, RG 59, HICOG Berlin, Political Affairs Division, box 3.

37. Lightner and Ramsey, memorandum, n.d., NARA, RG 59, HICOG Berlin, Political Affairs Division, box 3; "Minutes of the British Delegation on the Session of Working Group B of Subcommittee B in Preparation of the Conference of the Foreign Ministers of France, Great Britian and the United States in London," 5 May 1950, *DzD* II/3, 729–34, here 729.

38. Ramsey, "Minutes of the Tenth Meeting of PEPCO (3 April 50)," 3 April 1950, HICOG Berlin, Political Affairs Division, box 3.

39. McCloy to Taylor, 25 May 1950, *FRUS, 1950*, 4:641–43.

40. *New York Times*, 28 May 1950. On the Deutschlandtreffen, see Michael Lemke, "Die 'Gegenspiele:' Weltjugendfestival und FDJ-Deutschlandtreffen in der Systemkonkurrenz 1950–1954," in Heiner Timmermann, ed., Die *DDR in Europa: Zwischen Isolation und Öffnung* (Münster: Lit, 2006), 3–9. Peter Skyba, *Vom Hoffnungsträger zum Sicherheitsrisiko: Jugend in der DDR und Jugendpolitik der SED 1949–1961* (Cologne: Böhlau, 2000), 84–96.

41. "Overview over Tasks in Occupied Territories," 18 February 1945, in *"Gruppe Ulbricht" in Berlin, April bis Juni 1945: Von den Vorbereitungen im Sommer 1944 bis zur*

Wiedergründung der KPD im Juni 1945: Eine Dokumentation, ed. Gerhard Keiderling (Berlin: Berlin Verlag A. Spitz, 1993), 218.

42. Rolf Badstübner und Wilfried Loth, eds., *Wilhelm Pieck: Aufzeichnungen zur Deutschlandpolitik, 1945–1953* (Berlin: Akademie Verlag, 1994), 50; Ulrich Mählert and Gerd Rüdiger Stephan, *Blaue Hemden, Rote Fahnen: Die Geschichte der Freien Deutschen Jugend* (Opladen: Leske & Budrich, 1996), 13–51; Torsten Diedrich and Rüdiger Wenzke, *Die getarnte Armee: Geschichte der Kasernierten Volkspolizei der DDR 1952 bis 1956* (Berlin: Ch. Links Verlag, 2001), 44.

43. Mählert and Stephan, *Blaue Hemden, Rote Fahnen*, 52–65.

44. Minutes of 73rd Session of SED Politburo, 21 February 1950, *DzD* II/3, 597–601; Michael Herms, *Heinz Lippmann: Porträt eine Stellvertreters* (Berlin: Dietz, 1996), 87; Mählert and Stephan, *Blaue Hemden, Rote Fahnen*, 81.

45. Maj.-Gen. G. K. Bourne/Office of the G.O.C. Berlin, to the U.K. High Commissioner, Wannerheide, 23 February 1950, Public Record Office (PRO), Foreign Office (FO) 371/84981.

46. USPOLAD Heidelberg to Secretary of State, 30 January 1950, NARA, RG 59, 762A.00 (W)/1-3050; USPOLAD Heidelberg to Department of State, 8 February 1950, NARA, RG 59, 762B.00/2-850; *New York Times*, 26 March 1950.

47. Taylor to Secretary of State, 11 March 1950, NARA, RG 59, 762B.00/3-1150; Maj.-Gen. G. K. Bourne/Office of the G.O.C. Berlin to the U.K. High Commissioner, Wannerheide, 23 February 1950, PRO, FO 371/84981; *New York Times*, 12 March 1950. By early March 1950, HICOG Intelligence had gained access to the records of meetings of the FDJ's central organizing committee in November 1949. HICOG Frankfurt to Secretary of State, 2 March 1950, NARA, RG 59, 762A.00/3-250.

48. On "Operation Baldur," see Ronny Heidenreich, *Die DDR-Spionage des BND: Von den Anfängen bis zum Mauerbau* (Berlin: Ch. Links, 2019), 123–29; HICOG Heidelberg to Secretary of State, 20 February 1950, NARA, RG 59, 762A.00 (W)/2-2050; HICOG Frankfurt to Secretary of State, 18 March 1950, NARA, RG 59, 762B.00/3-1850; *New York Times*, 4 April 1950. Gehlen mobilized some 300 agents, yet seems to have provided few insights on the SED plans for the rally. Heidenreich, *Die DDR-Spionage des BND*, 127.

49. *New York Times*, 3 March 1950; British High Commission to Foreign Office, 11 February 1950, PRO, FO 371/84978; HICOG Berlin to Secretary of State, 4 February 1950, NARA, RG 59, 762A.00/2-450.

50. *New York Times*, 12 March 1950; *Washington Post*, 22 January 1950; Robertson to Bevin, 7 March 1950, PRO, FO 371/84981; USPOLAD Heidelberg to Department of State, 10 March 1950.

51. HICOG Berlin to Secretary of State, 3 March 1950, NARA, RG 59, 762B.00/3-350; British High Commission to Foreign Office, 11 February 1950, PRO, FO 371/84978.

52. Memorandum of conversation between Adenauer and Acheson, memorandum, 13 November 1950, *DzD* II, 18–21; H. C. Ramsey, "Minutes of the Ninth Meeting of PEPCO (16 March 50)," memorandum, 20 March 1950, NARA, RG 466, HICOG Berlin, Political Affairs Division, box 3.

53. *New York Times*, 15 March 1950, 16 March 1950, 1 May 1950.

54. Taylor to Secretary of State, 11 March 1950, NARA, RG 59, 762B.00/3-1150; Hays to Secretary of State, 10 March 1950, NARA, RG 59, 762B.00/3-1050; "From the Summary Minutes of the 7th Session of the Committee for aAll-German Questions of the German Bundestag," 17 May 1950, *DzD* II/3, 785–88, here 785.

55. Berlin to Secretary of State, 18 February 1950, NARA, RG 59, 762A.00/2-1850; *New York Times*, 8 February 1950.

56. Berlin to Secretary of State, 18 February 1950, NARA, RG 59, 762A.00/2-1850; H. C. Ramsey, "Minutes of the Ninth Meeting of PEPCO (16 March 50)," memorandum, 20 March 1950, NARA, RG 466, HICOG Berlin, Political Affairs Division, box 3; H. C. Ramsey, "Minutes of the Tenth Meeting of PEPCO (3 April 50)," 3 April 1950, HICOG Berlin, Political Affairs Division, NARA, RG 466, box 3; Taylor to Secretary of State, 10 April 1950, NARA, RG 59, 762B.00/4-850 (FOIA release to author).

57. Department of State to HICOG Frankfurt, 24 February 1950, NARA, RG 59, 762B.001/2-1250.

58. *New York Times*, 15 March 1950; HICOG Frankfurt to Secretary of State, 8 May 1950, NARA, RG 59, 762B.00/5-850; "Eighth Report of the Standing Action Committee," 24 April 1950, PRO, FO 371/84984.

59. *New York Times*, 19 March 1950. H. C. Ramsey, "Minutes of the Ninth Meeting of PEPCO (16 March 50)," memorandum, 20 March 1950, NARA, RG 466, HICOG Berlin, Political Affairs Division, box 3; H. C. Ramsey, "Minutes of the Tenth Meeting of PEPCO (3 April 50)," 3 April 1950, HICOG Berlin, Political Affairs Division, NARA, RG 466, box 3; Taylor to Secretary of State, 10 April 1950, NARA, RG 59, 762B.00/4-850 (FOIA release to author).

60. *New York Times*, 19 March 1950; Jessup to Hickerson, 17 April 1950, NARA, RG 59, 762A.00/4-1750; Byroade to Webb, 1 May 1950, NARA, RG 762B.00/5-150.

61. *New York Times*, 15 April 1950, 26 April 1950, 24 April 1950.

62. Badstübner und Loth, *Wilhelm Pieck*, 341; *Washington Post*, 3 April 1950.

63. Dieter Borkowski, *Für jeden kommt der Tag: Stationen einer Jugend in der DDR* (Berlin: Das Neue Berlin, 1990), 230–32; Berlin to Secretary of State, 19 April 1950, NARA, RG 59, 762B.00/4-1950.

64. Badstübner und Loth, *Wilhelm Pieck*, 345–47; *Washington Post*, 30 April 1950.

65. *New York Times*, 24 April 1950; E. C. Wendelin/HICOG Berlin Element to Perry Laukhuff, Political Affairs Division, Department of State, 6 April 1950, NARA, RG 59, 762A.0221/4-650 (FOIA release to author); Pace to Secretary of Defense,

enclosed in NSC 70, A Report to the NSC by the Secretary of Defense, 28 April 1950, NARA, RG 73; Shepard to Conger, 8 May 1950, NARA, RG 59, 762.00 MAY DAY/5-850 (FOIA release to author).

66. Frankfurt to Secretary of State, 8 May 1950, NARA, RG 59, 762B.00/5-850; H. C. Ramsey, "Minutes of the Fifteenth Meeting of PEPCO (8 May 50)," 11 May 1950, BICOG Berlin, Political Affairs Division, box 3; Byroade to Webb, 1 May 1950, NARA, RG 59, 762B.00/5-150; Perry Laukhuff, memorandum, 17 April 1950, enclosed in Hickerson to Jessup, 19 April 1950, NARA, RG 59, 762A.00/4-1750.

67. Allied Komandantura Berlin, Report of Sub-Committee "B" (Propaganda), 17 April 1950, PRO, FO 371/84984; memorandum, 19 June 1950, Bundesarchiv Koblenz, B 137/1145; CINCEUR Heidelberg to Department of the Army, 23 April 1950, Harry S. Truman Papers, President's Secretary File, HSTL.

68. The SED rally was attended by an estimated 250,000 people, though SED claims ran as high as 800,000. *New York Times*, 2 May 1950; *Washington Post*, 30 April 1950.

69. *New York Times*, 21 May 1950.

70. Report, 6 June 1950, SAPMO-BA, DY 24/1503; "Eighth Report of the Standing Action Committee," 24 April 1950, PRO, FO 371/84984.

71. *New York Times*, 27 May 1950; McCloy to Acheson, 29 May 1950, NARA, RG 59, 762B.00/5-2950; Herms, *Heinz Lippmann*, 88; HICOG Frankfurt to Secretary of State, 25 May 1950, NARA, RG 59, 662A.62B/5-2550; Heidelberg to Secretary of State, 27 May 1950, NARA, RG 59, 762A.00/5-2750; *New York Times*, 26 May 1950, 27 May 1950.

72. Berlin to Secretary of State, 31 May 1950, NARA, RG 59, 762A.00/5-3150; Berlin to Secretary of State, 31 May 1950, NARA, RG 59, 762A.00/5-3150; *New York Times*, 29 May 1950.

73. *New York Times*, 28 May 1950, 31 May 1950, 30 May 1950; Kirk to Secretary of State, 31 May 1950, NARA, RG 59, 762B.00/5-3150.

74. HICOG Berlin to Secretary of State, 30 May 1950, NARA, RG 59, 762B.00/5-3050; Blankenhorn Diary, 7 June 1950, *DzD* II/3, 808–9; *AAPD 1949/50*, 66; HICOG Berlin to Secretary of State, 2 June 1950, NARA, RG 59, 762B.00/6-250; Robertson to Bevin, 6 June 1950, *DzD* II/3, 806–7. *See also* Lothar Albertin, "Politische Jugendarbeit und nationale Frage im geteilten Deutschland, 1945–1961: Zu wenig Diskurse im Kalten Krieg," in *Doppelte Zeitgeschichte*, ed. Arnd Bauerkämper, Martin Sabrow, and Bernd Stöver (Bonn: Verlag J. H. W. Dietz Nachfolger, 1998), 37.

75. HICOG Berlin to Secretary of State, 2 June 1950, NARA, RG 59, 762B.00/6-250. For further information, see Karl-Heinz Füssl, *Die Umerziehung der Deutschen: Jugend und Schule unter den Siegernächten des Zweiten Weltkriegs 1945–1955* (Paderborn: Schöningh, 1994), 362–63.

76. McCloy to Acheson, 22 July 1950, NARA, RG 59, 762B.00/7-2250.

CHAPTER 6

1. On the history of the Korean War, Samuel F. Wells, *Fearing the Worst: How Korea Transformed the Cold War* (New York: Columbia University Press, 2019); Don Oberdorfer and Robert Carlin, *The Two Koreas: A Contemporary History*, 3rd ed. (New York: Basic Books, 2014), 6–7; William W. Stueck, *Rethinking the Korean War: A New Diplomatic and Strategic History* (Princeton, NJ: Princeton University Press, 2002).

2. Thomas Alan Schwartz, *America's Germany: John J. McCloy and the Federal Republic of Germany* (Cambridge, MA: Harvard University Press, 1991), 125.

3. CIA instruction dated 27 June 1950, quoted in Ronny Heidenreich, *Die DDR-Spionage des BND: Von den Anfängen bis zum Mauerbau* (Berlin: Ch. Links, 2019), 131; Bevin, quoted in Schwartz, *America's Germany*, 126.

4. David Clay Large, *Germans to the Front: West German Rearmament in the Adenauer Era* (Chapel Hill: University of North Carolina Press, 1996), 65; Adenauer to Kirkpatrick, 1 July 1950, in *AAPD 1949/50*, 217–18.

5. Large, *Germans to the Front*, 65; Henning Köhler, *Adenauer: Eine politische Biographie* (Frankfurt am Main: Propyläen, 1994), 621.

6. McCloy quoted in Kai Bird, *The Chairman: John J. McCloy and the Making of the American Establishment* (New York: Simon & Schuster, 1992), 338–39.

7. Torsten Diedrich und Rüdiger Wenzke, *Die getarnte Armee: Die Geschichte der Kasernierten Volkspolizei der DDR 1952–1956* (Berlin: Ch. Links Verlag, 2001), 50–51.

8. Ibid., 52–53.

9. Ibid., 54–55.

10. Large, *Germans to the Front*, 67; Heidenreich, *Die DDR-Spionage des BND*, 132–33.

11. Kirkpatrick to Gainer, 12 July 1950, *DzD* 11/3, 869; memorandum of conversation between Blankenhorn and Hays, 10 July 1950, *DzD* II/3, 864–67; memorandum of conversation between Blankenhorn and Francois-Poncet, 17 July 1950, *DzD* II/3, 879–83.

12. Kirkpatrick to Gainer, 12 July 1950, *DzD* II/3, 867–72; see also *FRUS, 1950*, 4:696–97.

13. Blankenhorn, Memorandum of 12 July 1950 conversation between Adenauer and McCloy, 15 July 1950, *AAPD 1949/50*, 246–59; Federal Government, memorandum on emergency measures in case of a Soviet invasion of West Germany, 15 July 1950, *DzD* II/3, 874–78; "Aide-memoire on Security Questions, 17 July 1950," *AAPD 1949/50*, 258–62; Large, *Germans to the Front*, 67.

14. Cited in Schwartz, *America's Germany*, 128.

15. *Protokoll der Verhandlungen des III. Parteitages der Sozialistischen Einheitspartei Deutschlands, 20–24. Juli 1950* (Dietz: Berlin, 1951); Dietrich Staritz, *Geschichte der DDR*, Erw. Neuausg, Neue Historische Bibliothek, 1260 = n.F., Bd. 260 (Frankfurt am Main: Suhrkamp, 1996), 84.

16. Pieck to Semenov, 11 July 1950, *DzD* II/3, 867–68.

17. John J. McCloy, Thomas T. Handy, and Maxwell D. Taylor, "A Review of the Berlin Situation," 29 August 1950, *DzD* II/3, 939–54, here 948.

18. McCloy to Acheson, 22 July 1950, NARA, RG 59, 762B.007-2250. The full memorandum was transmitted to the department on August 4. See Frankfurt to Department of State, 4 August 1950, NARA, RG 466, HICOG Berlin/Eastern Affairs Division, box 1, folder 1.

19. Finletter, Matthews, and Pace to Johnson, 1 August 1950, *FRUS, 1950*, 353–57; CIA to Truman, memorandum, 21 August 1950, *DzD* II/3, 921–22; Schwartz, *America's Germany*, 126; McCloy, Handy, and Taylor, "A Review of the Berlin Situation," 29 August 1950, *DzD* II/3, 939–49; HICOG Berlin/Eastern Element to Department of State, 31 August 1950, NARA, RG 59, 762B.00/8-3150. In mid-July, the CIA launched the "Jupiter program," a new early warning program for the Gehlen organization to obtaine "reliable and timely intelligence on hostile intentions" that resulted in the creation of a new "Sovzone intelligence collection apparatus" for the organization centered on major military, economic, transport and procurement targets in the GDR. Heidenreich, *Die DDR-Spionage des BND*, 136–41.

20. *New York Times*, 9 July 1950, 13 August 1950; Vockel to Adenauer, 11 August 1950, *AAPD 1949/50*, 311; HICOG Berlin/Eastern Element to Department of State, 31 August 1950, NARA, RG 59, 762B.00/8-3150; Heidenreich, *Die DDR-Spionage des BND*, 138.

21. *New York Times*, 13 August 1950.

22. Hans-Peter Schwarz and Reiner Pommerin, eds., *Adenauer und die Hohen Kommissare, 1949–1951* (Munich: R. Oldenbourg, 1989), 222–30.

23. Jack Raymond, "Bonn Chief Calls for Defense Force—Asks West German Unit Equal to East Zone Police—Urges U.S. to Send More Troops," *New York Times*, 18 August 1950.

24. Köhler, *Adenauer*, 622. The 21 August 1950 draft version of the 29 August memorandum by Adenauer is quoted in *AAPD 1949/50*, 326 (note 15).

25. Adenauer, memorandum, 29 August 1950, *AAPD 1949/50*, 322–27; Adenauer to Francois-Poncet, 2 September 1950, *AAPD 1949/50*, 337 (note 5).

26. *Adenauer und die Hohen Kommissare 1949–1951*, 222–30, here 227.

27. Ibid., 226.

28. Schwartz, *America's Germany*, 126.

29. McCloy, Handy, and Taylor, "A Review of the Berlin Situation," 29 August 1950, *DzD* II/3, 393–949, here 946.

30. McCloy to Acheson, 22 July 1950, NARA, RG 59, 762B.00/7-2250.

31. "A Program for the Political and Economic Projects Committee" (PEPCO), 19 July 1950, RG 466, HICOG Berlin, Political Affairs Committee/PEPCO, box 2.

32. Materials for the Nineteenth Meeting of PEPCO, 29 June 1950, RG 466, HICOG Berlin, Political Affairs Committee/PEPCO, box 2; see also H. C. Ramsey,

"Agenda for the Nineteenth Meeting of PEPCO," HICOG Berlin, Political Affairs Committee, box 2.

33. H. C. Ramsey, "Minutes of the Nineteenth Meeting of PEPCO" (20 June 50), HICOG Berlin, Political Affairs Committee, 28 [?-illegible] June 1950.

34. "Minutes of Tenth Meeting of PEPCO," 3 April 1950, NARA, RG 466, HICOG Berlin, Political Affairs Committee, box 3; "Minutes of the Eighteenth Meeting of PEPCO," 13 June 1950, ibid.; "Minutes of the Twentieth Meeting of PEPCO" (Annex II), 27 June 1950, ibid.; "A Program for the Political and Economic Projects Committee," 19 July 1950, NARA, RG 466, HICOG Berlin, Political Affairs Committee/PEPCO, box 2.

35. John B. Holt to George A. Morgan, memorandum, 27 June 1950, RG 466, HICOG Berlin, box 3, folder 1. Consideration of such ideas was, however, quickly abandoned, since the measures contradicted U.S. and West German defector policies and would—as a rigid formula—prove inexpedient "for tactical reasons [to] be adhered to in the 'cold war.'" "Minutes of the Twenty-First Meeting of PEPCO, 11 July 1950, NARA, RG 466, HICOG Berlin, Political Affairs Committee/PEPCO, box 3; HICOG Frankfurt to Department of State, 27 July 1950 (transmitting minutes of PEPCO meeting of 18 July 1950), NARA, RG 59, 762A.00/7·2750.

36. Department of State to HICOG, 25 August 1950, NARA, RG466, HICOG Berlin, Political Affairs Committee/PEPCO, box 3.

37. Ibid. See also Department of State to HICOG Frankfurt, 23 August 1950 (FOIA release to author). HICOG welcomed and implemented these suggested measures. See HICOG Frankfurt to Department of State, 31 August 1950, NARA, RG 59, 762A.00/8-3150.

38. McCloy to Byroade, 29 August 1950, NARA, RG 59, 762A.00/8-2950.

39. Ibid.; State Department to HICOG Frankfurt, 23 August 1950 (FOIA release to author).

40. "Minutes of the Twenty-Ninth Meeting of PEPCO held on September 12, 1950," 13 September 1950, NARA, RG 466, HICOG Berlin, Political Affairs Committee; "Conversations with Kaiser and Schumacher on 28 and 29 August 1950," in Gordon Ewing, "SOVZONE Secret Ballot Project," report, 25 September 1950, NARA, RG 59, HICOG Berlin, Political Affairs Committee, box 3; "Minutes of the Thirty-First Meeting of PEPCO, held on October 3, 1950," 17 October 1950, NARA, RG 466, HICOG Berlin, Political Affairs Committee, box 3.

41. John B. Holt, "Interview with [redacted] Concerning Resistance Potential in the Soviet Zone," 6 November 1950, memorandum (FOIA release to author).

42. Hans Speier, *From the Ashes of Disgrace: A Journal from Germany, 1945–1955* (Amherst: University of Massachusetts Press, 1981), 8; "Agenda for the Thirty-Fourth Meeting of PEPCO, to be held on Tuesday, November 21, 1950," 20 November 1950, NARA, RG 466, HICOG Berlin, box 3. On Carroll's background, see his *Persuade or*

Perish (Boston: Houghton Mifflin, 1948). On Speier's background, see Daniel Bessner's excellent biography, *Democracy in Exile: Hans Speier and the Rise of the Defense Intellectual* (Ithaca, NY: Cornell University Press, 2018). For background on Carroll and Speier's mission to Germany, see ibid., 163–68; Hans Speier, *From the Ashes of Disgrace*, 8, 68, 90–106; and generally Christopher Simpson, *Science of Coercion: Communication Research and Psychological Warfare, 1945–1960* (New York: Oxford University Press, 1994).

43. Speier, *From the Ashes of Disgrace*, 92–93; Bessner, *Democracy in Exile*, 168.

44. Wallace Carroll and Hans Speier, "Psychological Warfare in Germany: A Report to the United States High Commissioner for Germany and the Department of State," 1 December 1950 (FOIA release to author).

45. Edward Barrett to Henry Kellermann and Joseph Phillips, 9 January 1951, RG 59, 511.62A/1-2651; "Minutes of the Thirty-Eighth Meeting of PEPCO," 27 December 1950, HICOG Berlin, Political Affairs Division, box 3. See also Department of State to HICOG Frankfurt, 4 January 1951, NARA, RG 59, 511.62/127-50.

46. Richard W. Sterling to Ramsey, 18 January 1951, NARA, RG 466, HICOG Berlin, box 3, folder 1.

47. Henry Ramsey (PEPCO) to Walter Schwinn (Policy Planning Staff), 26 January 1951, NARA, RG 59, 511.62A/1-2651.

48. Ibid.

49. Ramsey to Department of State, 31 January 1951, NARA, RG 59, 511.62A/1-3151.

50. Henry Ramsey (PEPCO) to Walter Schwinn (Policy Planning Staff), 26 January 1951, NARA, RG 59, 511.62A/1-2651.

51. Richard W. Sterling to Ramsey, 18 January 1951, HICOG Berlin, box 3, folder 1; Henry Ramsey (PEPCO) to Walter Schwinn (Policy Planning Staff), 26 January 1951, NARA, RG 59, 511.62A/1-2651; Leo Crespi to Department of State, "Attitudes behind the Iron Curtain," 9 March 1951, NARA, RG 59, 762B.00/3-951; HICOG Berlin/Eastern Element to Department of State, "Pro- and Anti-Regime Attitudes: Technical Intelligentsia," 13 September 1951, NARA, RG 59, 762B.00/9-1451; HICOG/Eastern Element to Department of State, "Pro- and Anti-Regime Attitudes: Agricultural Population," 18 September 1951, NARA, RG 59, 762B.00/9-1851; HICOG/Eastern Element to Department of State, "Pro- and Anti-Regime Attitudes: Industrial Labor," 29 September 1951, NARA, RG 59, 762B.00/9-2951.

52. Edmond Taylor, "Interim Plan for Intensified Psychological Warfare in Germany," 18 July 1951 (FOIA release to author). Sections of the report—likely dealing with covert operations—are still classified.

53. Ibid., 21. MJS, memorandum, n.d., NARA, RG 466, RG 466, HICOG Berlin Element, box 3; typed notes, n.a., n.d., NARA, RG 466, HICOG Berlin Element, box 3; John B. Holt to George A. Morgan, "Comment on Taylor Paper," n.d., NARA,

RG 466, HICOG Berlin, box 3; George A. Morgan to Edmond Taylor, "Comments on first draft of 'Interim Plan for Intensified Psychological Warfare in Germany,'" 8 August 1951, NARA, RG 466, HICOG Berlin, box 3.

54. Henry C. Ramsey, "Exploitation of the 'Return of Europe' Concept," 24 July 1951, NARA, RG 466, HICOG Berlin, box 3.

55. HICOG Frankfurt to Secretary of State, 2 August 1951, NARA, RG 59, 762A.00/8-251; HICOG Frankfurt to Department of State, "Minutes of the Fifty-Third Meeting of PEPCO (July 31, 1951)," 3 August 1951, NARA, RG 59, 762A.00/8-351.

56. "Interim Plan for Intensified Psychological Warfare in Germany," HICOG Frankfurt to Department of State, 28 September 1951 (FOIA release to author); State Department Airgram A 1622, 23 November 1951 (FOIA release to author); Anspacher to Col. Davis, 7 January 1952, HSTL, President's Secretary's File, PSB, box 6 (MR release to author); Charles W. McCarthy (Executive Officer, PSB) to Henry Byroade, 7 February 1952, HSTL, PSF, PSB, box 6; John M. Anspacher to Edmond Taylor, 15 October 1952 (FOIA release to author).

57. "Highlights Review of PW Operations (PUB, Policy Staff)," Alfred V. Boerner to Pat Allen, memorandum, 19 March 1952, enclosed in: A.V. Boerner to G.G. Wolfe, 16 September 1952, NARA, RG 59, 511.62A/9-1652; Pat Allen to Al Sims, 27 March 1952, NARA, RG 59, 511.62A/9-2752.

CHAPTER 7

1. Michael Lemke, *Einheit oder Sozialismus? Die Deutschlandpolitik der SED, 1949–1961* (Cologne: Boehlau, 2001), 134.

2. Cited in Hermann Wentker, *Aussenpolitik in engen Grenzen: Die DDR im internationalen System, 1949–1989* (Munich: Oldenbourg, 2007), 90.

3. Lemke, *Einheit oder Sozialismus?*, 134.

4. Ibid.

5. Hans-Peter Schwarz and Reiner Pommerin, eds., *Adenauer und die Hohen Kommissare, 1949–1951* (Munich: R. Oldenbourg, 1989), 282, 305–6; McCloy to Secretary of State, 18 January 1951, *FRUS, 1951*, 3:1749–51.

6. Lemke, *Einheit oder Sozialismus?*, 135.

7. HICOG to Department of State, 8 February 1951, NARA, RG 59, 762B.00/2-851; McCloy to Secretary of State, 18 January 1951, *FRUS, 1951*, 3:1749–51; Schwarz and Pommerin, *Adenauer und die Hohen Kommissare*, 302.

8. Schwarz and Pommerin, *Adenauer und die Hohen Kommissare*, 302.

9. Lemke, *Einheit oder Sozialismus?*, 136.

10. McCloy to Secretary of State, 18 January 1951, *FRUS, 1951*, 3:1749–51; Schwarz and Pommerin, *Adenauer und die Hohen Kommissare,* 302.

11. John Holt to Secretary of State, 13 January 1951, NARA, RG 59, 762A.00/1-1351; HICOG Berlin to HICOG Frankfurt, 13 January 1951, RG 466, HICOG

Berlin, box 1; David E. Mark to John Holt, 26 January 1951, NARA, RG 466, HICOG Berlin, Eastern Affairs Division, box 3; Secretary of State to the Office of the High Commissioner for Germany, 12 February 1951, *FRUS, 1951,* 3:1757–58; McCloy to Secretary of State, 4 February 1951, *FRUS, 1951,* 3:1755–56; McCloy to Secretary of State, 6 February 1951, RG 59, 762A.5/2-251; Embassy Moscow to Department of State, 3 January 1951, NARA, RG 59, 762.00/1-351. HICOG Bonn had earlier reported the conjecture that the Grotewohl letter had been "written in the Kremlin." Bonn to Secretary of State, 1 February 1951, NARA, RG 59, 762A.00/1-3151.

12. Lemke, *Einheit oder Sozialismus,* 138; McCloy to Secretary of State, 18 January 1951, *FRUS, 1951,* 3:1749–51.

13. HICOG Berlin to Secretary of State, 31 January 1951, NARA, RG 59, 762A.00/1-3151; Rolf Badstübner und Wilfried Loth, eds., *Wilhelm Pieck: Aufzeichnungen zur Deutschlandpolitik, 1945–1953* (Berlin: Akademie Verlag, 1994), 361.

14. Blücher, quoted in Lemke, *Einheit oder Sozialismus,* 139; McCloy to Secretary of State, 4 February 1951, *FRUS, 1951,* 3:1755–56.

15. PEPCO to Secretary of State, 15 February 1951, *FRUS, 1951,* 3:1759–61; "Notes on Probable Soviet Approach to a CFM and Consequences for the Western Allied Position," HICOG Berlin, 26 January 1951, NARA, RG 466, HICOG Berlin, Eastern Affairs Division, box 3.

16. McCloy to Secretary of State, 14 February 1951 (FOIA release to author); McCloy to Secretary of State, 16 March 1951, NARA, RG 59, 762A.00/3-1651.

17. Badstübner und Loth, *Wilhelm Pieck,* 363; Lemke, *Einheit oder Sozialismus,* 143–44.

18. Badstübner und Loth, *Wilhelm Pieck,* 365; Maj.-Gen. G. K. Bourne/Office of the GOC to UK High Commissioner Ivone Kirkpatrick, 14 June 1951, NARA, RG 466, HICOG Berlin/EAD, box 1.

19. PEPCO to Secretary of State, 18 April 1951, *FRUS, 1951,* 3:1767–68; "PEPCO: Minutes of the Forty-fourth Meeting," HICOG Frankfurt to Department of State, 7 March 1951, NARA, RG 59, 762.00/3-751; Department of State to HICOG, 28 April 1951, NARA, RG 59, 762A.00/4-2651; HICOG Bonn to Department of State, 5 May 1951, 762A.00/5-551, *FRUS, 1951,* 3:1773. By early May, McCloy could report that the anti-plebiscite campaign was "developing satisfactorily." McCloy to Secretary of State, 1 May 1951, NARA, RG 59, 762A.00/5-151.

20. Eastern Element to PEPCO, 28 May 1951, NARA, RG 466, HICOG Berlin, Eastern Affairs Division, box 1.

21. Ibid.

22. McCloy to Secretary of State, 6 June 1951, NARA, RG 59, 762A.00/6-651.

23. Badstübner und Loth, *Wilhelm Pieck,* 363, 365–66; Maj.-Gen. G. K. Bourne/Office of the GOC to UK High Commissioner Ivone Kirkpatrick, 14 June 1951, NARA, RG 466, HICOG Berlin/EAD, box 1.

24. "PEPCO: Minutes of the Fifty-Second Meeting (Held July 9, 1951)," HICOG

Frankfurt to Department of State, 10 July 1951, NARA, RG 466, HICOG Berlin, box 3; Benz, quoted in Lemke, *Einheit oder Sozialismus*, 145.

25. George A. Morgan to Department of State, 18 July 1951, NARA, RG 59, 762B.00/7-1851; Maj.-Gen. G. K. Bourne/Office of the GOC to UK High Commissioner Ivone Kirkpatrick, 14 June 1951, NARA, RG 466, HICOG Berlin/EAD, box 1.

26. Badstübner und Loth, *Wilhelm Pieck*, 371–73. Pieck's notes are cryptic and open to interpretation. The United States terminated the state of war with Germany on October 24, 1951.

27. HICOG Frankfurt to Secretary of State, 20 August 1951, NARA, RG 59, 511.62A/8-1651.

28. "Resistance Potential in the Soviet Zone," 11 January 1951 NARA, RG 59, 662B.00/1-1151 (FOIA release to author).

29. Ibid.

30. Ibid.

31. *Adenauer und die Hohen Kommissare*, 292; HICOG Eastern Element to Department of State, "PEPCO: Minutes of the Forty-fourth Meeting," HICOG Frankfurt to Department of State, 7 March 1951, NARA, RG 59, 762.00/3-751; Carlo Schmidt's plea in HICOG Bonn to Secretary of State, 1 February 1951, RG 59, 662A.62B/1-3151. "Highlights Review of PW Operations (PUB, Policy Staff," Alfred Boerner to Pat Allen, memorandum, 19 March 1952, NARA, RG 59, 511.62A/3-1952.

32. McCloy to Secretary of State, 1 February 1951, NARA, RG 59, 762A.5/2-151; "Notes on Meeting with Kaiser, Thedieck, Wehner on January 4, 1951," memorandum, 5 January 1951, NARA, RG 466, HICOG EE, box 3.

33. Stefan Creuzberger, "Kampf gegen den inneren Feind," in *"Geistige Gefahr" und "Immunisierung der Gesellschaft": Antikommunismus und politische Kultur in der frühen Bundesrepublik*, ed. Stefan Creuzberger and Dierk Hoffmann (Munich: Oldenbourg, 2014), 88–89. Some of the Ministry's employees had evinced some affinity for Nazi ideology before and during the Third Reich.

34. "Im Bogen der Zeit: Memoirs of Dr Ewert Freiherr von Dellingshausen" (Bonn, 1984–85), unpublished manuscript, BA Koblenz, N1515, 2:26, 31–34. I thank Stephan Kieninger for help with accessing this document. On von Dellingshausen, see Stefan Creuzberger, "Ewert von Dellingshausen (1909–1996): Ein baltendeutscher Antikommunist im Dienste der Psychologischen Kriegführung," in Helmut Müller-Enbergs and Armin Wagner, eds., *Spione und Nachrichtenhändler: Geheimdienstkarrieren in Deutschland 1939–1989* (Berlin: Ch. Links, 2016), 208–28. On James Burnham, see Bernd Stöver, *Die Befreiung vom Kommunismus. Amerikanische Liberation Policy im Kalten Krieg, 1947–1991* (Köln: Böhlau, 2002), 102–20.

35. "Im Bogen der Zeit," 2:31–34. In April 1952 the CIA presented the U.S.-sponsored Gehlen Organization, which was vying to become West Germany's foreign intelligence service and had set up "planning staff" for psychological warfare in early 1952, with a plan for joint operations in the field of propaganda and psychological

warfare. "Close and critical obervers of American efforts," the Gehlen Organization submitted a "blueprint for an organization and program of activities in the Cold War field" in December 1952. "History of the Gehlen Intelligence Organization," September 1953," in *Forging an Intelligence Partnership: CIA and the Origins of the BND, 1949–1956*, ed. Kevin C. Ruffner (Washington, DC: CIA, 2006), 1:228–31.

36. "Im Bogen der Zeit," 2:49; "History of the Gehlen Intelligence Organization," September 1953, in Ruffner, *Forging an Intelligence Partnership*, 1:229–30; Bernd Stöver, "Politik der Befreiung?" in Creuzberger and Hoffmann, *"Geistige Gefahr" und "Immunisierung der Gesellschaft,"* 219.

37. Creuzberger, "Kampf gegen den inneren Feind," 91; "History of the Gehlen Intelligence Organization," September 1953, in Ruffner, *Forging an Intelligence Partnership*, 1:231–32.

38. McCloy to Secretary of State, 18 January 1951, NARA, RG 59, 762B.00/1-1851; "Im Bogen der Zeit," 2:29–30. Kaiser revived his favorite idea of creating local organizations above party lines as a way to foster all-German consciousness with his call for a people's movement for reunification, the so-called All-German Action, in 1954, which led to the creation of the "Kuratorium Unteilbares Deutschland."

39. Creuzberger, "Kampf gegen den inneren Feind," 93–94.

40. Ibid., 97. Von Dellingshausen claims not to have known initially about Taubert's activities in the Third Reich; "Im Bogen der Zeit," 2:41–42. On the VVN, see Mathias Friedel, *Der Volksbund für Frieden und Freiheit (VFF): Eine Teiluntersuchung über westdeutsche antikommunistische Propaganda im Kalten Krieg und deren Wurzeln im Nationalsozialismus* (St. Augustin: Gardez!, 2001).

41. Ibid., 2:34–43.

42. Ibid., 2:50–51.

43. "History of the Gehlen Intelligence Organization," September 1953, in Ruffner, *Forging an Intelligence Partnership*, 1:232; Creuzberger, "Kampf gegen den inneren Feind," 89.

44. "Resistance Potential in the Soviet Zone," 11 January 1951, NARA, RG 59, 662B.00/1-1151 (FOIA release to author); "History of the Gehlen Intelligence Organization," September 1953, in Ruffner, *Forging an Intelligence Partnership*, 1:231–32.

45. "Highlights Review of PW Operations (PUB, Policy Staff," Alfred Boerner to Mrs. Allen, memorandum, 19 March 1952, NARA, RG 59, 511.62A/3-1952.

46. Frank Hagemann, *Der Untersuchungsausschuss Freiheitlicher Juristen, 1949–1969* (Frankfurt/M.: Peter Lang, 1994); David E. Murphy, Sergei A. Kondrashev, and George Bailey, *Battleground Berlin: CIA vs. KGB in the Cold War* (New Haven, CT: Yale University Press, 1997), 113–26; Stöver, *Die Befreiung vom Kommunismus*, 250–83. For a collection of facsimile leaflets by the UFJ, see Friedrich-Wilhelm Schlomann, *Mit Flugblättern und Anklageschriften gegen das SED-System* (Schwerin: Der Landesbeauftragte for Mecklenburg-Vorpommern für die Unterlagen des Staatssicherheitsdienstes, 1998). Wisner quoted in "Notes of Fifth Meeting of Ad Hoc Berlin

Committee," by D. W. Montenegro, 15 July 1952, NARA, RG 59, 762A.5/7-1752 (FOIA release to author).

47. Hagemann, *Der Untersuchungsausschuss*, 81–92; Murphy et al., *Battleground Berlin*, 107–8.

48. Stöver, "Politik der Befreiung?" 223; Murphy et al., *Battleground Berlin*, 107–8.

49. HICOG Berlin to Department of State, 19 November 1952, NARA, RG 59, 662A.662B/11-1952; "Notes of Fifth Meeting of Ad Hoc Berlin Committee," by D. W. Montenegro, 15 July 1952, NARA, RG 59, 762A.5/7-1752 (FOIA release to author); HICOG Berlin to HICOG Bonn, 8 September 1952, National Security Archive, Soviet Flashpoints Collection.

50. Hagemann, *Der Untersuchungsausschuss*, 90–91.

51. Enrico Heitzer, *Die Kampfgruppe gegen Unmenschlichkeit (KgU): Widerstand und Spionage im Kalten Krieg*, Zeithistorische Studien 53 (Cologne: Böhlau, 2015), 42–60; Murphy et al., *Battleground Berlin*, 107–8; Stöver, "Politik der Befreiung?" 221–22.

52. "Resistance Potential in the Soviet Zone," 11 January 1951, NARA, RG 59, 662B.00/1-1151 (FOIA release to author; Stöver, "Politik der Befreiung?" 222–23.

53. Murphy et al., *Battleground Berlin*, 107–8.

54. Stöver, "Politik der Befreiung?" 222; Gregory Henderson (HICOG Berlin Element) to W. J. Convery Egan, HICOG memorandum, 3 September 1952, NARA, RG 59, 511.62a/9-352 (FOIA release to author). Though the CIA held on to its support for the group in the face of West German complaints, internal squabbles and growing pressure within West Germany led to the KGU's dissolution in 1959. Moreover, despite its sponsorship, even the CIA could at no time assert full control over the myriad propaganda and sabotage activities carried out by the KGU. HICOG officials in Berlin, for example, were not sure to what extent the KGU had been involved in the June 1953 uprising in East Germany. At what point could such activities run the risk of running counter to official U.S. policy goals? Despite the KGU's usefulness in American rollback efforts, its activities may have in fact unintentionally contributed to the consolidation of the GDR, adding credibility to the regime's rationale in expanding security apparatus on a massive scale. See also Stöver, "Politik der Befreiung?" 222.

55. HICOG Frankfurt to Department of State, 8 January 1951, NARA, RG 59, 762B.00/1-851. For background on the World Youth Festival, see Nick Rutter, "The Western Wall: The Iron Curtain Recast in Midsummer 1951," in *Cold War Crossings: International Travel and Exchange in the Soviet Bloc, 1940s–1960s*, ed. Patryk Babiracki et al. (Arlington, TX: Texas A&M University Press, 2014), 78–106.

56. Joel Kotek, *Students and the Cold War* (London: Macmillan, 1996), 189–91.

57. Ibid.

58. Jones to Department of State, 20 April 1951, NARA, RG 59, 800.4614/4-2051.

59. Marion Mitchell to Louis Wiesner, 7 February 1951, RG 59, 762B.00/2-751, and enclosures; Murphy et al., *Battleground Berlin*, 107

60. Kotek, *Students and the Cold War*, 192–93.

61. Headquarters, 66th Counter Intelligence Corps Detachment, European Command, to Director, Intelligence Division, Headquarters, European Command, "Recommended Action for Coming World Youth Festival," n.d. [3 January 1951]; and T. L. Squier (HICOG Office of Intelligence) to Col. Marshall, n.d.; R. W. Benton (PA/TC) to PEPCO, 29 June 1951, NARA, RG 466, HICOG Berlin, box 3.

62. "PEPCO: Minutes of the Forty-Third Meeting" (February 13, 1951), enclosed in HICOG Frankfurt to Department of State, 1 March 1951 (FOIA release to author).

63. "Minutes of the Forty-Fourth Meeting of PEPCO," Frankfort to Washington, 7 March 1951, RG 59, 762.00/3-751; Jones to HICOG Frankfurt, 6 March 1951, NARA, RG 59, 511.62A5/3-651; McCloy to Acheson, 28 May 1951, *FRUS, 1951*, 3:2005–6.

64. Secretary of State to McCloy, 23 May 1951, *FRUS, 1951*, 3:2004; McCloy to Acheson, 28 May 1951, *FRUS, 1951*, 3:2005–6.

65. Murphy et al., *Battleground Berlin*, 107; "PEPCO: Minutes of the Fifty-Second Meeting (Held July 9, 1951)," HICOG Frankfurt to Department of State, 10 July 1951, NARA, RG 466, HICOG Berlin, box 3.

66. Ibid.; Page to Shepard Stone, 17 July 1951, *FRUS, 1951*, 3:2008–10, here 2010; HICOG overrode the objections of Berlin city authorities, who cautioned against the invitation in light of the 20,000 youth who had used their West Berlin visit the previous year to "defect" permanently to the West and substantially added to the economic strains of the city. "PEPCO: Minutes of the Fifty-Second Meeting (Held July 9, 1951)," HICOG Frankfurt to Department of State, 10 July 1951, NARA, RG 466, HICOG Berlin, box 3.

67. *Christian Science Monitor*, 13 August 1951; George Morgan to Dean Acheson, 12 September 1951, *FRUS, 1951*, 3:2014–22; *New York Times*, 8 August 1951; *Christian Science Monitor*, 14 August 1951, 13 August 1951.

68. *New York Times*, 17 August 1951; Joel Kotek, "Youth Organizations as a Battlefield in the Cold War," in *The Cultural Cold War in Western Europe, 1945–1960*, ed. Giles Scott-Smith and Hans Krabbendam (London/Portland, OR: Frank Cass, 2003), 177; *New York Times*, 17 August 1951, 18 August 1951; *Washington Post*, 18 August 1951.

69. *New York Times*, 8 August 1951; *Washington Post*, 7 August 1951. Western authorities distributed more than one and a half million free meals. See Kotek, *Students and the Cold War*, 196.

70. Jones to McCloy, 16 August 1951, *FRUS, 1951*, 3:2012–14, here 2012; *New York Times*, 17 August 1951; *Christian Science Monitor*, 14 August 1951; Morgan to Acheson, 12 September 1951, *FRUS, 1951*, 3:2014–22.

71. Morgan to Acheson, 12 September 1951, *FRUS, 1951*, 3:2014–22.

72. Schwartz, *America's Germany*, 135–55.

73. Ibid.; Lemke, *Einheit oder Sozialismus*, 182–83.

74. On the Stalin note debate, see Jürgen Zarusky, *Die Stalinnote vom 10. März 1952. Neue Quellen und Analysen.* (Munich: Oldenbourg, 2002); Rolf Steiningerm, *Eine vertane Chance. Die Stalin-Note vom 10. März 1952 und die Wiedervereinigung: Eine Studie auf der Grundlage unveröffentlichter britischer und amerikanischer Akten* (Berlin: J. H. W. Dietz Nachf, 1985).

75. M. Scummon and R. W. Tufts to Nitze, 14 March 1952, NARA, RG 59, 762A.00/3-1452 TSF; John Ferguson to Acheson, memorandum, 27 March 1952, NARA, RG 59, 762A.00/3-2752 TSF.

76. Henry A. Byroade to Webb, 19 December 1951 (FOIA release to author); "Comments on HICOG Report," Warren S. Hawley to Craig, memorandum, 3 July 1952, NARA (FOIA release to author); "Psychological Strategy Plan prescribing Specific Course of Action with Respect to Germany (PSB D-21)," James W. Riddleberger to David K. Bruce, 6 August 1952 (FOIA release to author); "Problems of Propaganda Strategy vis-à-vis Lastest Soviet Notes," Henry Kellermann to James John M Anspacher to Edmund Taylor, memorandum, 23 January 1952, HSTL (mandatory review release to author); Riddleberger, memorandum, 13 October 1952, NARA, RG 59, 611.62A/10-1352.

77. Henry A. Byroade to Webb, 19 December 1951 (FOIA release to author); Col. Davis to Wallace Carroll, 28 December 1951, HSTL, President's Secretary's File, PSB, box 6; State Department Airgram A 1622, 23 November 1951 (FOIA release to author); Anspacher to Col. Davis, 7 January 1952, HSTL, President's Secretary's File, PSB, box 6 (MR release to author); Charles W. McCarthy (Executive Officer, PSB) to Henry Byroade, 7 February 1952, HSTL, PSF, PSB, box 6.

78. John M Anspacher to Edmund Taylor, memorandum, 23 January 1952, HSTL (mandatory review release to author); R. Hirsch to Taylor, memorandum, 4 February 1952, HSTL (mandatory review release to author); Charles W. McCarthy (Executive Officer, PSB) to Henry Byroade, 7 February 1952, HSTL, President's Secretary's File, PSB, box 6; "CIA Comments on German Panel Draft Paper Submitted by PSB Staff," [John A. Bross—name redacted in declassified copy] to Col. R. Hirsch," 29 May 1952, HSTL, President's Secretary File, PSB, box 6; James Riddleberger to Undersecretary of State David K. Bruce, 6 August 1952 (FOIA release to National Security Archive); Charles Johnson, memorandum, 12 August 1952, NARA, PSB 091 Germany/12 August 1952 (FOIA release to National Security Archive).

79. Palmer Putnam to Edmund Taylor, 4 February 1952, HSTL, PSF, PSB, box 6; "Taking the Offensive," Wallace Carroll to Gordon Gray, memorandum, 20 September 1951 (FOIA release to author).

80. Marion Mitchell to Charles Hulick, memorandum, 25 February 1951, NARA, RG 466, HICOG Berlin/EAD, box 1, folder 2; HICOG Berlin to Department of State, 30 July 1952, NARA, RG 466, box 11; HICOG Berlin to Department of State, "East German Opinion on German Unity and West German Defense," 30 July 1952,

NARA, RG 59, 762.00/7-3052; HICOG Berlin Eastern Affairs Division to Department of State, 10 March 1952, NARA, RG 59, 762.00/3-1052.

81. HICOG Berlin Eastern Affairs Division to Department of State, 10 March 1952, NARA, RG 59, 762.00/3-1052.

82. Perry Laukhuff to James Riddleberger, 15 May 1952, NARA, RG 59, 762A.5/5-1527 (FOIA release to author); McCloy to Secretary of State, 13 May 1952, NARA, RG 59, 762.0221/5-1352; McCloy to Secretary of State, 22 May 1952, NARA, RG 59, 762.0221/5-2252.

83. McCloy to Secretary of State, 22 May 1952, NARA, RG 59, 762.0221/5-2252; McCloy to Secretary of State, 13 May 1952, NARA, RG 59, 762.0221/5-1352; Perry Laukhuff to James Riddleberger, 15 May 1952, NARA, RG 59, 762A.5/5-1527 (FOIA release to author); McCloy to Secretary of State, 23 May 1952, NARA, RG 59, 762A.0221/5-2352; McCloy to Secretary of State, 11 July 1952, NARA, RG 59, 762A.00/7-1152.

84. "Action to Strengthen our Position in Berlin," Martin J. Hillenbrand to Perry Laukhuff, memorandum, 15 May 1952, NARA, RG 59, 762A.5/5-1552 (FOIA release to author); "Mr Bendetsen's Memo to Secretary of Defense re Berlin," Martin J. Hillenbrand to Perry Laukhuff, memorandum, 15 May 1952, NARA, RG 59, 762A.5/5-1552 (FOIA release to author); memorandum by Charles E. Bohlen, Counselor of the Department of State, 27 May 1952, *FRUS, 1952–1954*, 7:2, 1251–52; Walter K. Schwinn to Geoffrey Lewis, memorandum, 27 June 1952, NARA, RG 59, 511.62A/6-27.

85. HICOG Berlin to Secretary of State, 10 July 1952, NARA, RG 59, 762A.00/7-1052; "Notes of Fifth Meeting of Ad Hoc Berlin Committee," by D. W. Montenegro, 15 July 1952, NARA, RG 59, 762A.5/7-1752 (FOIA release to author); "The Allied Kommandatura during July," HICOG Berlin to Department of State, 21 August 1952, NARA, RG 59, 762A.0221/8-2152 (FOIA release to author). On the Linse kidnapping, see Susanne Muhle, *Auftrag Menschenraub: Entführungen von Westberliners and Bundesbürgern durch das Ministerium für Staatssicherheit der DDR* (Göttingen: Vandenhoeck and Ruprecht, 2015), 135–41.

86. "Notes of Fifth Meeting of Ad Hoc Berlin Committee," by D. W. Montenegro, 15 July 1952, NARA, RG 59, 762A.5/7-1752 (FOIA release to author).

87. Department of State to HICOG Bonn, 19 August 1952, NARA, RG 59, 762.0221/8-1352 [*sic*]; "The Allied Kommandatura during July," HICOG Berlin to Department of State, 21 August 1952, NARA, RG 59, 762A.0221/8-2152 (FOIA release to author).

88. "Notes of Fifth Meeting of Ad Hoc Berlin Committee," by D. W. Montenegro, 15 July 1952, NARA, RG 59, 762A.5/7-1752 (FOIA release to author).

89. HICOG Berlin to Department of State, 14 May 1950, NARA, RG 59, 762B.00/5-1452; memorandum of conversation between Joseph V. Stalin and SED

leadership, 7 April 1952, Library of Congress, Dmitri Volkogonov Collection, printed in translation in *Uprising in East Germany, 1953: The Cold War, the German Question, and the First Major Upheaval behind the Iron Curtain*, compiled, edited, and introduced by Christian Ostermann (Budapest: Central European University Press, 2001), 25–41 (hereafter cited as *Uprising in East Germany, 1953*). A copy can be found in Arkhiv Prezidenta Rossiisskoi Federatsii, Moscow (AP RF), f. 45, op. 1, d. 303, l. 179;

90. HICOG Berlin to Department of State, 14 May 1952, NARA, RG 59, 762B.00/5-1452; N. Spencer Barnes to Department of State, 21 April 1952, NARA, RG 59, 662A.662B/4-21; Donnelly to Acheson, 19 August 1952, NARA, RG 59, 762.0221/8-1952.

91. "Significance of the Second SED Party Conference With Regard to the Communist Unity Strategy," HICOG Berlin to Department of State, 26 July 1952 (FOIA release to author); see also John C. Ausland to Mr. Kidd, 26 August 1952, NARA, RG 59, 762A.00/82652.

92. "Chronology of German Plan," John M. Anspacher to Edmond Taylor, 2 July 1952, National Security Archive, Soviet Flashpoints Collection; Raymond B. Allen to David K. Bruce, William C. Porter, and Walter Bedell Smith, memorandum, 29 July 1952, National Security Archive, Soviet Flashpoints Collection; "PSB D-21—A National Psychological Strategy Plan for Germany," John H. Ferguson to David K. Bruce, 6 August 1952, ibid.; James Riddleberger to David K. Bruce, 6 August 1952, ibid.; William A. Korns to Mr. Sherman, 7 August 1952 (FOIA release to author); John M. Anspacher to Edmond Taylor, 15 October 1952 (FOIA release to author); George A. Morgan to PSB, 29 May 1953 (FOIA release to author).

93. Psychological Strategy Board, PSB D-21 Working Draft, 28 July 1952 (FOIA release to National Security Archive); William Korns (PSB Office of Coordination) to Mr. Sherman, "German plan (PSB D-21)," memorandum, 7 August 1952, NARA, PSB 091 Germany (FOIA release to author);

94. Psychological Strategy Board, PSB D-21, 9 October 1952 (FOIA release to National Security Archive).

95. Ibid. Dulles to HICOG Bonn, 6 March 1953, NARA, RG 59, 762B.00/3-953 (FOIA release to author).

96. "Working Group Meeting Panel 'F,' 7 April 1952, 10:00 A.M.," HSTL, PSB; PSB D-21 Working Draft, 13 May 1952 (FOIA release to author); Gregory Henderson (HICOG Berlin Element) to W. J. Convery Egan, HICOG memorandum, 3 September 1952, NARA, RG 59, 511.62a/9-352 (FOIA release to author); Psychological Strategy Board, PSB D-21 Working Draft, 28 July 1952 (FOIA release to National Security Archive); Howland H. Sherman to Alan G. Kirk, 30 September 1952 (FOIA release to author); Walter K. Schwinn to Geoffrey Lewis, memorandum, 27 June 1952, NARA, RG 59, 511.62A/6-27.

97. Gregory Henderson (HICOG/PUB) to W. J. Convery Eagan, "Comments

of Psychological Strategy Plan Prescribing Specific Courses of Action with Respect to Germany," memorandum, 3 September 1952, NARA, RG 59, 511.62A/9-352 (FOIA release to author); N. S. Barnes to the Director, "Brief Comments on PSB D-21 Document," memorandum, 5 September 1952, NARA, RG 59, 511.62A/9-552; HICOG Bonn to Department of State, 20 October 1952, NARA, RG 59, 762A.00/10-2052; HICOG Bonn to Department of State, 22 January 1953 NARA, RG 59, 662A.62B/1-2253.

98. "Minutes of the Eleventh Meeting of PEPCO (10 April 1950)," NARA, RG 466, HICOG Berlin/Political Affairs Division, box 3; Gregory Henderson (HICOG/PUB) to W. J. Convery Eagan, "Comments of Psychological Strategy Plan Prescribing Specific Courses of Action with Respect to Germany," memorandum, 3 September 1952, NARA, RG 59, 511.62A/9-352 (FOIA release to author).

99. HICOG Bonn to Secretary of State, 29 July 1952 (FOIA release to author); State Department to HICOG Bonn, 8 August 1952 (FOIA release to author); HICOG Berlin to HICOG Bonn, 15 August 1952 (FOIA release to author).

100. Joseph Phillips to David Bruce, "Defection fo German Youth," memorandum, 7 August 1952, NARA, RG 59, 662A.62B/7-2552 (FOIA release to author); "Memorandum for Record," Raymond B. Allen, 7 August 1952, HSTL, White House Office Files, PSB, box 28; Riddleberger to Phillips, "Should we Encourage Male German Youth to Defect from East Germany?" memorandum, 18 February 1953, NARA, RG 59, 662a.62b/1-2253 [*sic*] (FOIA release to author).

101. HICOG Berlin to HICOG Bonn, 15 August 1952 (FOIA release to author); HICOG Berlin to Secretary of State, 3 September 1952, 662A.62B/8-1552 (FOIA release to author); Dean Acheson to Certain American Diplomatic Officers, 19 September 1952, NARA, RG 59, 762B.00/9-1952.

102. "Encouraging German Youth to Defect from the Soviet Zone," Henry J. Kellermann to Brewster Morris, memorandum, 3 February 1953, NARA, RG 59, 762B.00/2-353; James Riddleberger to Phillips, "Should We Encourage Male German Youth to Defect from East Germany?" memorandum, 18 February 1953, NARA, RG 59, 662a.62b/1-2253 (FOIA release to author); Leonard Horwitz to Barbour, 27 March 1953 (FOIA release to author).

103. Bonn to Secretary of State, 25 July 1952 (FOIA release to author).

104. HICOG Bonn to Department of State, 19 March 1953, NARA, RG 59, 762B.00/3-1953.

105. L. Frechtling to Brewster Morris, 9 March 1953, NARA, RG 59, 762B.00/3-953 (FOIA release to author); HICOG Bonn to Department of State, 19 March 1953, NARA, RG 59, 762B.00/3-1953.

106. John C. Ausland to Spencer Barnes, 24 September 1952 (FOIA release to author); Dulles to HICOG Bonn, 8 May 1953, NARA, RG 59, 762B00/5-853; HICOG Bonn to Secretary of State, 12 March 1953, NARA, RG 59, 862A.411/3-1253.

107. HICOG Bonn to Department of State, 11 February 1953, NARA, RG 59, 762.00/2-1153 (FOIA release to author); HICOG Berlin to Department of State, 29 May 1953, NARA, RG 59, 762A.0221/5-2953.

CHAPTER 8

1. Melvyn P. Leffler, *A Preponderance of Power: National Security, the Truman Administration, and the Cold War* (Stanford: Stanford University Press, 1991), 199–200; Michael J. Hogan, *The Marshall Plan: America, Britain, and the Reconstruction of Western Europe, 1947–1952*, Studies in Economic History and Policy (New York: Cambridge University Press, 1987).

2. Frank Cain, *Economic Statecraft during the Cold War: European Responses to the US Trade Embargo*, Cass Series—Cold War History 13 (London and New York: Routledge, 2007), 4–5; Karl-Heinz Schlarp, *Zwischen Konfrontation und Cooperation: Die Anfangsjahre der deutsche-sowjetischen Wirtschaftsbeziehungen in der Ära Adenauer* (Hamburg: Lit, 2000), 26.

3. Report to the President by the National Security Council, NSC 58/2, "United States Policy towards the Satellite States in Eastern Europe," 8 December 1949, Department of State, ed., *FRUS, 1949*, 5:53; Policy Planning Staff Paper, PPS 59, 25 August 1949, *FRUS, 1949*, 5:21–26.

4. Cain, *Economic Statecraft*, 4–7.

5. In December 1947 the UK government had signed a new trade agreement with the USSR that included credits for the purchase of British goods. The UK depended on the USSR for 20 percent of its soft wood and 30 percent of its grains. Moscow in turn purchased rubber, coffee, wool, and tin from the British Commonwealth. Trade agreements with Yugoslavia (December 1948), Poland (January 1949), and Czechoslovakia (September 1949) followed. France, too, concluded a five-year trade agreement for imports of Polish coal.

6. Cited in Cain, *Economic Statecraft*, 23. Tor Egil Førland, *Cold Economic Warfare: CoCom and the Forging of Strategic Export Controls* (Dordrecht: Republic of Letters, 2009), 38–120; Michael Mastanduno, "Trade as a Strategic Weapon: American and Alliance Export Control Policy in the Early Postwar Period," *International Organization* 42 (Winter 1988): 121–50; Vibeke Sørensen, "Economic Recovery versus Containment: The Anglo-American Controversy over East-West Trade, 1947–51," *Cooperation and Conflict* 24 (June 1989): 69–97; Schlarp, *Zwischen Konfrontation und Kooperation*, 13–15.

7. Peter E. Fäßler, *Durch den "Eisernen Vorhang": Die deutsch-deutschen Wirtschafts-beziehungen 1949–1969*, Wirtschafts- und Sozialhistorische Studien, Bd. 14 (Cologne: Boehlau, 2006), 34–39. For a useful overview of the history of interzonal trade prior to the archival openings of the 1990s, see Hanns-Dieter Jacobsen, *Die Ost-West-Wirtschaftsbeziehungen als deutsch-amerikanisches Problem* (Baden-Baden: Nomos, 1986).

8. "U.S. Military Government Policy Regarding Interzonal Trade," U.S. POLAD to Secretary of State, 2 August 1946, NARA, RG 59, 740.00 Control (Germany)/8-246. Orlopp, quoted in Fäßler, *Durch den "Eisernen Vorhang,"* 40.

9. Quotes in Fäßler, *Durch den "Eisernen Vorhang,"* 39–40.

10. Robert Murphy to Secretary of State, 26 July 1948, NARA, RG 59, 740.00119 Control (Germany)/7-2648; "Control of Interzonal Trade between Bizone and Soviet Zone and Soviet Sector of Berlin," U.S. POLAD to Department of State, 14 October 1948, NARA, RG 59, 740.00119 Control (German)/10-1449; Hays to Department of the Army, 19 May 1949, NARA, RG 59, 740.00119 Control (Germany)/5-191949 TSF; "Trade with the Soviet Zone," POLAD Berlin to Department of State, 20 January 1949, NARA, RG 59, 740.00119 Control (Germany)/1-2049; Riddleberger to Secretary of State, 30 April 19949, NARA, RG 59, 740.00119 Control (Germany)/4-3049; see in particular William Stivers, "The Incomplete Blockade: Soviet Zone Supply of West Berlin, 1948–49," *Diplomatic History* 21, no. 4 (October 1997): 569–602.

11. U.S. POLAD to Department of State, 12 July 1949, NARA, RG 59, 740.00119 Control(Germany)/7-2149; "Current Situation in Berlin," CIA memorandum for the Secretary of Defense, 30 June 1948, in *On the Front Lines of the Cold War: Documents on the Intelligence War in Berlin, 1946 to 1961*, ed. Donald P. Steury (Washington, DC: CIA, 1999), 1845; Orlopp to SED Central Control Commission, 12 September 1949, cited in Fäßler, *Durch den "Eisernen Vorhang,"* 42; Gunter Mai, "Das Trojanische Pferd: Innerdeutsche Handelsbeziehungen zwischen Blockbildung und inter-systemarer Symbiose, 1945–1989," in *Ost-West-Beziehungen: Konfrontation und Détente, 1945–1989*, ed. Gustav Schmidt (Bochum: Universitätsverlag Dr. N. Bockmeyer, 1993), 2:437.

12. Report of conversation between von Schumann, head of the Berlin Liaison Office of Bizonal Economic Administration, and Heinrich Rau, president of the DWK, 8 March 1949, in US POLAD to Department of State, 16 March 1949, NARA, RG 59, 740.00119 Control Germany)/3-1649; Heinrich Rau to SED Party Leadership, n.d., SAPMO-BA, NY 4182/1194, 261.

13. Hays to Vorhees, 20 May 1949, NARA, RG 59, 740.00 Control (Germany)/5-2049. For the following sections I draw especially on Friedrich von Heyl, *Der innerdeutsche Handel mit Eisen und Stahl, 1945–1972: Deutsch-deutsche Beziehungen im Kalten Krieg* (Cologne: Boehlau, 1997), and Detlef Nakath, "Zur Bedeutung des Innerdeutschen Handels in der Nachkriegszeit (1948/49–1960)," in *Wirtschaftliche Folgelasten des Krieges in der SBZ/DDR*, ed. Christoph Buchheim (Baden-Baden: Nomos, 1995), 221–25. Thanks to Friedrich von Heyl for sharing his archival materials.

14. See the memorandum "Interzonal Trade under the Occupation Statute," by State Department legal adviser John M. Raymond, 23 August 1949, NARA, RG 59, lot 55D371, box 3; Fäßler, *Durch den "Eisernen Vorhang,"* 47–81; Rolf Badstübner und Wilfried Loth, eds., *Wilhelm Pieck: Aufzeichnungen zur Deutschlandpolitik,*

1945–1953 (Berlin: Akademie Verlag, 1994). Note that in April 1950, HICOG officials acknowledged that interzonal trade had not "heretofore been treated as falling within the field of reserve powers." "Minutes of the Eleventh Meeting of PEPCO," 10 April 1950, NARA, RG 466, HICOG Berlin, Political Affairs Division, box 3.

15. McCloy to Secretary of State, 7 October 1949, NARA, RG 59, 862.00/10-749; Fäßler, *Durch den "Eisernen Vorhang,"* 48–49.

16. Adenauer to McCloy, 2 February 1950, *DzD* II/3, 571–75.

17. Erhard to Adenauer, 13 June 1950, *DzD* II/3, 819–24, emphasis added; memorandum by Kroll, 15 June 1950, *DzD* II/3, 830–33.

18. Erhard to Adenauer, 13 June 1950, *DzD* II/3, 819–24; memorandum by Kroll, 15 June 1950, *DzD* II/3, 830–33.

19. Erhard to Adenauer, 13 June 1950, *DzD* II/3, 819–24.

20. Intelligence Summary No. 78, Headquarters European Command, 1 February 1950, enclosed in U.S. POLAD to Secretary of State, 7 February 1950, NARA, RG 59, 762A.00/2-750.

21. COMGEN-USAFE Wiesbaden to Secretary of State, cable, 10 February 1950, NARA, RG 59, 762A.00(W)/2-1050. See also Walter H. Dustman to Henry Byroade, "Memorandum: Berlin Blockade statement," 2 February 1950, NARA, RG 59, 962.50/2-250; L. A. Wiesner, memo, 23 January 1950, NARA, RG 59, 962A.50/1-2350.

22. Hays to Secretary of State, 2 February 1950, NARA, RG 59, 762A.0221/2-250; Heyl, *Der innderdeutsche Handel,* 54–57; Fäßler, *Durch den "Eisernen Vorhang,"* 111–14.

23. Hays to Secretary of State, 2 February 1950, NARA, RG 59, 762A.0221/2-250.

24. Ibid.; Holmes to Secretary of State, 7 February 1950, NARA, RG 59, 962.50/2-750.

25. Holmes to Secretary of State, 7 February 1950, NARA, RG 59, 962.50/2-750; Hays to Secretary of State, cable, 3 February 1950, NARA, RG 59, 762A.0221/2-350; memorandum [on a discussion in the Federal Economic Ministry on 8 February 1950] by Schmidhuber, 9 February 1950, BA Koblenz, B 102/108271.

26. Rainer Karlsch, *Allein bezahlt? Die Reparationsleistungen der SBZ/DDR 1945–1953* (Berlin: Ch. Links, 1993), 182–84; GDR Reparations plan, "Anlage 1 zum Protokoll der 15 Sitzung der Regierung vom 9. Februar 1950," BA Coswig, DC 20/I/3–12, 5–8, *DzD* II/3, 587–89; Orlopp to Minister for Inner-German Trade, Foreign Trade and Procurement, Handke, 17 April 1950, BArch, DL 2/7, 434–35, *DzD* II/3, 680–81.

27. Intelligence Summary No. 76, 3 January 1950, enclosed in US POLAD to Secretary of State, 12 January 1950, NARA, RG 59, 762A/1-1250; Wilhelm Pieck to Stalin, 28 February 1950, Pieck Papers, SAPMO-BA, NY 4036/736a, 62–63; *DzD* II/3, 602; Otto Grotewohl to Vasily Chuikov, 7 August 1950, Grotewohl Papers,

SAPMO-BA, NY 4090/338, 145–49; see also *DzD* II/3, 908–10; *Fäßler, Durch den "Eisernen Vorhang,"* 108–9.

28. Page to Secretary of State, 27 February 1950, NARA, RG 59, 862.00/2-2750; Hays to Department of the Army, 19 May 1949, NARA, RG 59, 740.00119 Control (Germany)/5-1949 TSF; Fäßler, *Durch den "Eisernen Vorhang,"* 114.

29. BA Potsdam DL 2, No. 1624, 182–83; *Fäßler, Durch den "Eisernen Vorhang,"* 111–12.

30. BA Potsdam, DL 2, No. 1379, 136, cited in von Heyl, *Innerdeutscher Handel,* 66–67; Fäßler, *Durch den "Eisernen Vorhang,"* 114–15.

31. Page to Secretary of State, 27 February 1950, NARA, RG 59, 862.00/2-2750; HEC-ID, "Intelligence Summary," 15 March 1950, enclosed in U.S. POLAD to Department of State, 18 March 1950, NARA, RG 59, 762A.00/3-1850; "Anlage: Beschlüsse zur Verbesserung der Erfüllung des Reparationsplanes vom 28. Juli 1950," *DzD* II/3, 900–901; Andre Steiner, *The Plans that Failed: An Economic History of the GDR* (New York: Berghahn, 2010), 70–71.

32. Department of State to HICOG Frankfurt, 23 February 1950 (FOIA release to author); John B. Holt to Gantenbein/Laukhuff and Riddleberger, 5 April 1949, NARA, RG 59, 740.00119 Control (Germany)/4-549; John B. Holt to Riddleberger, 12 April 1949, NARA, RG 59, 740.00119 Control (Germany)/4-1249.

33. Page to Secretary of State, 27 February 1950, NARA, RG 59, 862.00/2–2750; HEC-ID, "Intelligence Summary," 15 March 1950, enclosed in U.S. POLAD to Department of State, 18 March 1950, NARA, RG 59, 762A.00/3–1850; Fäßler, *Durch den "Eisernen Vorhang,"* 114–15.

34. Department of State to HICOG Frankfurt, 23 February 1950 (FOIA release to author).

35. McCloy to Byroade, 2 March 1950 (FOIA release to author); HICOG Frankfurt to Secretary of State, 6 April 1950, 462A.62B31/4-650; Berlin to Secretary of State, 24 March 1950 (FOIA release to author); Leopold to Federal Ministry for Economics, draft agreement, 22 February 1950, enclosed in Kaumann to Federal Ministry for Economics, cable, 1 March 1950, BA Koblenz B 102, No. 108251; memorandum of conversation between the Federal Chancellory Liaison and U.S. IZT representative Stroh on 4 March 1950, 6 March 1950, memorandum, BA Koblenz B 102, No. 108251. Thanks to Friedrich von Heyl for sharing these German documents.

36. Federal Ministry for Economics to the Länder governments and Berlin magistrate, cable, 16 March 1950, BA Koblenz B 102, No. 108251; Erhard to Adenauer, 15 March 1950, BA Koblenz B 102, No. 108251; memo by Schmidthuber (Federal Ministry for Economics), 22 May 1950, BA Koblenz B 102, No. 108251. I thank Friedrich von Heyl for sharing these German documents. On 28 May, Erhard told Taylor, the U.S. Commandant in Berlin, that "he feared further Soviet blockade measures unless [the] embargo was relaxed." Taylor to Secretary of State, 29 May 1950, NARA, RG 59, 862.00/5–2950.

37. "Review of Soviet Interference Berlin–West German Trade and Transport," undated memorandum [May 1950], NARA, RG 59, lot 55D371, box 3.

38. State Department cable to HICOG Frankfurt, top secret cable, 26 May 1950 (FOIA release to author).

39. Memorandum on Interzonal Trade by the Permanent Representative of the Federal Republic of Germany at the Consultative Group in Paris, Kroll, 20 June 1950, BA Koblenz, VS-B-102/1, *DzD* II/3, 837–38; Francois-Poncet to Adenauer, 28 June 1950, *DzD* II/3, 844–45.

40. Frankfurt to Secretary of State, 21 April 1950, NARA, RG 59, 962.50/4-2150; McCloy to Acheson, 27 July 1950, NARA, RG 59, 962.50/7-2750; McCloy to Secretary of State, 27 July 1950, *FRUS, 1950*, 4:865; Allied High Commission, Economic Committee ECON/P(51)14, 11 May 1951, NARA, RG 59, 462A.62B31/5-1151.

41. Berlin Joint Committee, "Study of Subjects Placed on the Draft Agenda for the First Meeting of the Berlin Joint Committee (BK/BJC(50)1)," 3 June 1950, NARA, RG 59, 762A.00/6-350 SP.

42. HICOG Eastern Element to Department of State, 5 September 1950, NARA, RG 59, 462A.62B31/9-550; HICOG Intelligence to Department of State, 11 September 1950, NARA, RG 59, 462A.62B/9-1150; "Examples of Illegal Export from Western Germany to the East," HICOG Frankfurt to Department of State, 15 November 1950 (FOIA release to author); "Berlin Smugglers to Face New Curbs," *New York Times*, 18 August 1950; "East-West Zones Ready Steel Accord," *Washington Post*, 12 August 1950; McCloy to Secretary of State, 17 July 1950, NARA, RG 59, 462A.62B/7-1750.

43. Morgan (HICOG Berlin) to Secretary of State, 8 July 1950 (FOIA release to author); McCloy to Secretary of State, 17 July 1950, NARA, RG 59, 462A.62B/7-1750; memorandum of conversation between the representative of the GDR Government for Interzonal Trade, Orlopp, and the head of the Treuhandstelle für Interzonenhandel, Kaumann, 6–7 July 1950, BA DL/2/7, 332–34; Kaumann to Kleiner, report on negotiations with Lefort and Stroh, 10 July 1050, BA, B 102/108246; Koelfens to Kaumann, cable, 11 July 1950, BA, B 102/108246.

44. Department of State to HICOG Frankfurt, 11 November 1950, NARA, RG 59, 462A.62B31/10-1950; McCloy to Secretary of State, 27 July 1950, *FRUS, 1950*, 4:864–65; Page/Berlin to Secretary of State, 27 July 1950, NARA, RG 59, 462A.62B31/7-2750; McCloy to Secretary of State, 27 July 1950 (FOIA release to author); Kaumann to Kleiner, Report on negotiations with Orlopp, 13 July 1950, BA, B 102/108246; memorandum of phone conversation by Kutscher, 20 Juli 1950, BA, B 102/108246; Report by Kaumann to Kleiner on negotiations with Orlopp, 27 July 1950, BA, B 102/108246; Agreement on the Extension of the Interzonal Trade Agreement, 11 August 1950, *DzD* II/3, 281; Page to Secretary of State, 11 August 1951, NARA, RG 59, 462A.62B31/8-1150.

45. "Soviet Zone Holds; West Sends Steel," *New York Times*, 17 August 1950;

Department of State to HICOG Frankfurt, 14 September 1950 (FOIA release to author).

46. "British in Berlin Check on Barge Traffic in Retaliation of Russian Interference," *New York Times*, 28 September 1950; McCloy to Secretary of State, 10 October 1950, NARA, RG 59, 462A.62B31/10-1050.

47. McCloy to Secretary of State, 10 October 1950, NARA, RG 59, 462A.62B31/10-1050; Allied Kommandatura Berlin, "Suspension of East/West Trade Negotiations," BK/Allied High Commission (50)60, 20 October 1950, enclosed in HICOG Berlin Element to Department of State, 24 October 1950, 462A.62B/10-2450 (FOIA release to author).

48. Allied High Commission/FOREX/IZTWP, "Countermeasures," 14 October 1950, enclosure to HICOG Berlin Element to Department of State, 24 October 1950 (FOIA release to author); see also Eastern Element to PEPCO, memorandum, 28 September 1950, NARA, RG 59, HICOG Berlin, Political Affairs Division, box 2.

49. Allied High Commission/FOREX/IZTWP, "Countermeasures," 14 October 1950, enclosure to HICOG Berlin Element to Department of State, 24 October 1950 (FOIA release to author); memorandum by H. C. Ramsey/PEPCO, undated, NARA, RG 59, HICOG Berlin, Political Affairs Division, box 3; George Morgan (Eastern Element) to PEPCO, memorandum, 24 October 1950, NARA, RG 466, HICOG Berlin, Political Affairs Division, box 2; Eastern Element to PEPCO, memorandum, 28 September 1950, NARA, RG 59, HICOG Berlin, Political Affairs Division, box 2.

50. Department of State to HICOG Frankfurt, 11 October 1950, NARA, RG 59, 462A.62B31/10–1950; Allied Kommandatura Berlin, "Suspension of East/West Trade Negotiations," BK/Allied High Commission(50)60, 20 October 1950, enclosed in HICOG Berlin Element to Department of State, 24 October 1950, 462A.62B/10–2450 (FOIA release to author); HICOG Frankfurt to Department of State, 29 November 1950 (FOIA release to author).

51. "German Goods Aid Soviets in Arming," *New York Times*, 14 April 1951; U.S. POLAD Heidelberg, "Illegal Interzonal Trade to Sustain the Soviet Zone Armament Potential," 18 August 1950 (FOIA release to author); see also "Examples of Illegal Export from Western Germany to the East," HICOG Frankfurt to Department of State, 15 November 1950, NARA, RG 59, 462A.62B9/11-1550 (FOIA release to author).

52. "German Goods Aid Soviets in Arming," *New York Times*, 14 April 1951.

53. HICOG-Eastern Element to Department of State, "Illegal Trade Activities of the Haselgruber Firm and Associates," memorandum, 24 October 1950 (FOIA release to author); "Germans Seek End to Smuggling Ring," *New York Times*, 9 April 1951; HICOG Berlin to Secretary of State, 18 November 1950, NARA, RG 59, 762A.00/11-1850.

54. "Background Papers for Byroade's Trip to Germany," 29 January 1951, NARA, RG 59, 762A.00/1-2951; Paris to Secretary of State, 19 September 1950, NARA, RG 59, 462A.509/9-1950.

55. Department of State to HICOG Frankfurt, 26 September 1950, NARA, RG 59, 662A.62b31/92650; HICOG Bonn to Secretary of State, 14 December 1950, NARA, RG 59, 762A.00/12-1450.

56. McCloy to Secretary of State, 27 July 1950, NARA, RG 59, 962.50/7-2750; HICOG Frankfurt to Department of State, 30 March 1951, NARA, RG 59, 462A.62B31/3-3051; HICOG Berlin to Secretary of State, 18 November 1950, NARA, RG 59, 762A.00/11-1850.

57. "Recommendations for Retarding the Rapid Economic Self-Sufficiency Drive of the GDR," HICOG Eastern Element to PEPCO, 30 November 1950, NARA, RG 466, HICOG Berlin, box 2.

58. Eastern Element to PEPCO, "Critique of Our Economic Warfare Position in Germany," memorandum, 2 February 1951, RG 466, HICOG Berlin Element, box 2; "The Soviet Zone Economy," HICOG Berlin to Department of State, 10 September 1951, NARA, RG 59, 862B.00/9-1051.

59. "Minutes of the Eleventh Meeting of PEPCO," NARA, RG 466, HICOG Berlin-Political Affairs, box 3; Eastern Element to PEPCO, "Critique of Our Economic Warfare Position in Germany," memorandum, 2 February 1951, RG 466, HICOG Berlin Element, box 2; "Minutes of the Fortieth Meeting of PEPCO (held in Frankfurt, January 16, 1951)," HICOG Frankfurt to Department of State, 6 February 1951, NARA, RG 59, 762A.00/2-651; HICOG Bonn to Secretary of State, 16 October 1952, NARA, RG 59, 462A.62B31/10-1652.

60. "Minutes of the Eleventh Meeting of PEPCO," 10 April 1950, NARA, RG 466, HICOG Berlin, Political Affairs Division, box 3; HICOG Eastern Element to PEPCO, "Critique of Our Economic Warfare Position in Germany," memorandum, 2 February 1951, NARA, RG 466, HICOG Berlin Element, box 2; J. T. Rogers/GEA to Mr. Lind/GEA, "Proposals under consideration in HICOG regarding interzonal trade," memorandum, 28 March 1951, NARA, RG 59, 462A.62B31/3-2851 (FOIA release to author); "Minutes of the Fortieth Meeting of PEPCO (held in Frankfurt, January 16, 1951)," HICOG Frankfurt to Department of State, 6 February 1951, NARA, RG 59, 762A.00/2-651.

61. "Interim Report on Trip to Accompany Kenneth Hansen, Staff Investigator for Senate Subcommittee on Export Controls," 17 April 1951 (FOIA release to author).

62. "German Goods Aid Soviets in Arming," *New York Times*, 14 April 1951; "West Acts to Check Illegal Trade to East," *Christian Science Monitor*, 27 April 1951; McCloy to Secretary of State, 17 April 1951, NARA, RG 59, 762A.00/4-1751.

63. McCloy to Secretary of State, 14 February 1951, NARA, RG 59, 762A.00/2-1451; "U.S. Acts to Bar Red China Buying from West Berlin," *Washington Post*, 22 May 1951.

64. "Recommendations for Retarding the Rapid Economic Self-Sufficiency Drive of the GDR," HICOG Eastern Element to PEPCO, 30 November 1950, NARA, RG

466, HICOG Berlin, box 2; HICOG Frankfurt to Department of State, 6 February 1951, NARA, RG 59, 762A.00/2-651.

65. "U.S. Science Programs in Germany," HICOG Bonn to Department of State, 5 December 1951, NARA, RG 59, 962.7014/12-551; "Psychological Warfare in Germany," report by Wallace Carroll and Hans Speier, 1 December 1950 (FOIA release to author); "Soviet Zone Manpower Situation," HICOG-Eastern Element to Department of State, 20 February 1951, NARA, RG 59, 862B.06/2-2051; HICOG-Eastern Element to PEPCO, memorandum, "Denial of Key Manpower to the Soviet Zone Economy," 23 February 1951, RG 466, HICOG Berlin, Political Affairs Division, box 2; McCloy to Secretary of State, 15 March 1951 (FOIA release to author).

66. "Minutes of the Forty-Seventh Meeting of PEPCO (10 April 1950)," 25 April 1951, NARA, RG59, 762A.00/4-2551 (FOIA release to author); George Morgan to H. C. Ramsey, "Sovzone Key Manpower," memorandum, 11 April 1951, NARA, RG 466, HICOG Berlin, Political Affairs Division, box 2; H. C. Ramsey, "Implementation of the Carroll-Speier-Paper: Denial of Key Manpower to Soviet Zone Economy," memorandum, NARA, RG 466, HICOG Berlin, Political Affairs Division, box 2; HICOG Frankfurt to Department of State, 10 May 1951 (FOIA release to author); PEPCO, Minutes of the Fifty-First Meeting of the Committee," 25 June 1951, NARA, RG 59, 762A.00/6-2551; Martin J. Hillenbrand (US Mission Berlin) to Department of State, 27 July 1945 (FOIA release to author); American Embassy Bonn to Department of State, 23 August 1956 (FOIA release to author).

67. HICOG Berlin to Bureau for German Affairs, Department of State, 28 June 1951, NARA, RG 52, 462A.26B31/6-2851.

68. HICOG Eastern Element to Department of State 26 July 1951, NARA, RG 59, 662A.62B/7-2651; AHC, "Addendum to AGSEC/Memo(51)37," 19 October 1951, NARA, RG 59, 462A.62B31/10-1951 (FOIA release to author).

69. Jones to Secretary of State, 10 June 1951, NARA, RG 59, 462A.62B9/6-1051 (FOIA release to author).

70. Ibid.; Department of State to HICOG Frankfurt, 13 June 1951, NARA, RG 59, 462A.62B9/6-1351 (FOIA release to author).

71. Slater to Secretary of State, 14 June 1951, NARA, RG 59, 462A.62B/6-1451; memorandum of conversation between M. de Juniac (French Embassy) and Perry Laukhuff, 15 June 1951, NARA, RG 59, lot 55D371, box 3; HICOG Berlin to HICOG Frankfurt, 18 June 1951, NARA, RG 466: HICOG, Allied High Commission/U.S.SEC, box 16.

72. HICOG Frankfurt to Secretary of State, 20 June 1951, NARA, RG 59, 462A.62B31/6-2051; Acheson to HICOG Frankfurt, 20 June 1951, NARA, RG 466: HICOG, Allied High Commission/U.S.SEC, box 16.

73. "Berlin Trade Talks Deadlocked," memorandum, 27 June 1951, NARA, RG 59, lot 55D371, box 3; Acheson to HICOG Frankfurt, 28 June 1951 (FOIA release to author); McCloy to Acheson, 4 July 1951, NARA, RG 59, 462A.62B31/7-451;

Acheson to HICOG Frankfurt, 6 July 1951, NARA, RG 466: HICOG, Allied High Commission/U.S.SEC, box 17; McCloy to Acheson, 6 July 1951, ibid.; Acheson to HICOG Frankfurt, 7 July 1951, NARA, RG 59, 462A.62B31/7-751; "Verbatim Transcript of Quadripartite Meeting of Experts on Berlin Trade," NARA, RG 59, 462A.62B/7-651 (FOIA release to author); on the 9 July meeting, see HICOG Berlin to Secretary of State, 11 July 1951, NARA, RG 59, 460.509/7-1151; HICOG Frankfurt to HICOG Bonn, 11 July 1951, RG 466: HICOG, Allied High Commission/U.S.SEC, box 17; "Berlin Trade Situation," memorandum [for Acheson], 12 July 1951, RG 59, lot 55D371, box 3; Fäßler, *Durch den "Eisernen Vorhang,"* 125.

74. Acheson to HICOG Frankfurt, 7 July 1951, NARA, RG 59, 462A.62B31/7-551; Acheson to HICOG Frankfurt, 12 July 1951, NARA, RG 466:HICOG, Allied High Commission/U.S.SEC, box 17; Allied High Commission decision contained in AGSEC(51)1182, 12 July 1951; see HICOG Bonn to HICOG Frankfurt, 16 July 1951, ibid.

75. HICOG Bonn to HICOG Frankfurt, 16 July 1951, NARA, RG 466:HICOG, Allied High Commission/U.S.SEC, box 17; HICOG Berlin to Secretary of State, 15 July 1951, NARA, RG 59 462A.62B31/7-1551; HICOG Berlin to Secretary of State, 16 July 1951 (FOIA release to author); "Monthly Report on East-West Trade," HICOG Frankfurt to Department of State, 20 October 1951, NARA, RG 59, 462A.62B31/10-2051.

76. HICOG Frankfurt to HICOG Bonn, 11 July 1951, NARA, RG 466: HICOG, Allied High Commission/U.S.SEC, box 17; McCloy to Secretary of State, NARA, RG 59, 462A.62B31/7-1451; HICOG Berlin to Secretary of State, 15 July 1951, NARA, RG 59, 462A.62B31/7-1551 (FOIA release to author); HICOG Bonn to HICOG Frankfurt, 16 July 1951, NARA, RG 466: HICOG, Allied High Commission/U.S.SEC, box 17; McCloy to Department of State, 20 July 1951, NARA, RG 466: HICOG, Allied High Commission/U.S.SEC, box 17; Page to Secretary of State, 24 July 1951, NARA, RG 59, 462A.62B31/7-2451. 77. "Minutes of the Fifty-Third Meeting of PEPCO," enclosed in HICOG Frankfurt to Department of State, 3 August 1951, NARA, RG 59, 762A.00/8-351; HICOG Frankfurt to Department of State, 1 August 1951, NARA, RG 466, HICOG, Berlin Political Affairs, box 3; HICOG Frankfurt to HICOG Bonn, 11 July 1951, RG 466: HICOG, Allied High Commission/U.S.SEC, box 17.

78. McCloy to Secretary of State, 14 July 1951, NARA, RG 59, 462A.62B31/7-1451; Jones to Secretary of State, 31 July 1951, NARA, RG 59, 462A.62B31/7-3151; memorandum of conversation, "East-West Trade Agreement," 15 August 1951, NARA, RG 59, 462A.62B31/8-1551; HICOG/Eastern Element to Department of State, "[British] Notes on the Present Position of Interzonal Trade," 29 August 1951 (FOIA release to author); Hays to Secretary of State, 8 September 1951, 462A.62B31/9-851.

79. PEPCO, "Summary 50th meeting (June 5)," HICOG Frankfurt to Department of State, 7 June 1951, NARA, RG 466, AHC-USSEC, box 16; HICOG Berlin

to Secretary of State, 16 July 1951 NARA, RG 59, 462A.62B9/7-1651 (FOIA release to author).

80. HICOG Berlin to Secretary of State, 16 July 1951, (FOIA release to author); McCloy to Department of State, 20 July 1951, NARA, RG 466: HICOG, Allied High Commission/U.S.SEC, box 17; HICOG Berlin to Secretary of State, 21 July 1951, NARA, RG 59, 462A.62B31/7-2151; CINC-USAFE Wiesbaden to COFS USAF Washington, 12 October 1951, NARA, RG 59, 762A.00(W)/10-1251.

81. Department of State to HICOG Frankfurt, 15 July 1951, NARA, RG 59, 462A.62B31/7-1451 [*sic!*]; Eastern Element to Department of State, 26 July 1951, NARA, RG 59, 662A.62B/7-2351; HICOG Berlin to Secretary of State, 1 August 1951, NARA, RG 59, 462A.62B31/8-151; Department of State to HICOG Frankfurt, 7 September 1951, NARA, RG 59, 662A.62B/7-2651.

82. "[British] Notes on the Present Position of Interzonal Trade," HICOG/Eastern Element to Department of State, 29 August 1951 (FOIA release to author). The two British reports remain classified, but the substance can be gathered from HICOG Berlin to Secretary of State, 30 August 1951, NARA, RG 59, 462A.62B31/8-3151; Department of State to HICOG Frankfurt, 30 August 1951, NARA, RG 59, 462A.62B31/8-3051.

83. "Monthly Report on East-West Trade," HICOG Frankfurt to Department of State, 20 October 1951, NARA, RG 59, 462A.62B31/10-2051; Department of State to HiCOG Franfurt, 13 July 1951, NARA, RG 466, HICOG, Allied High Commission/US SEC, box 17; Department of State to HICOG Frankfurt, 30 August 1951, NARA, RG 59, 462A.62B31/8-3051; see also Department of State to HICOG Frankfurt, 8 August 1951, NARA, RG 59, 462A.62B31/8-851.

84. HICOG Berlin to Secretary of State, 25 July 1951 (FOIA release to author); Jones to Secretary of State, 11 August 1951, NARA, RG 59, 462A.62B31/8-1151; "Decision by the Allied High Commission at Its Seventy-Fourth Meeting on 30 August 1951," Department of State, *FRUS, 1951,* 3:1860; Jones to HICOG Bonn, 1 September 1951, ibid., 1860–62; Jones to Acting Secretary of State, 7 September 1951, ibid., 1863–67; George F. Muller (DRW) to Office of Intelligence and Research (State Department), 1 September 1951, NARA, RG 59, 962A.7162B/9-151; Department of State to HICOG Frankfurt, 30 August 1951, NARA, RG 59, 462A.62B31/8-3051; Webb to HICOG Frankfurt, 15 September 1951, *FRUS, 1951,* 3:1871.

85. Jones to Secretary of State, 3 September 1951, NARA, RG 59, 462A.62B31/9-351 (FOIA release to author); Hays to Secretary of State, 17 September 1951 (FOIA release to author); McCloy to Webb, 22 September 1951, *FRUS, 1951,* 3:1874–75; Allied High Commission for Germany/Allied General Secretariat, AGSEC(51)1453, 18 September 1951 (FOIA release to author).

86. Allied High Commission for Germany: Economics Committee, ECON/Sec(51)155, 15 September 1951 (FOIA release to author); Jones to Secretary of State, 13 September 1951, NARA, RG 59, 462A.62B31/9-1351; Hays to Webb, 19

September 1951, *FRUS, 1951*, 3:1872–73; "Monthly Report on East-West Trade," HICOG Frankfurt to Department of State, 20 October 1951, NARA, RG 59, 462A.62B31/10-2051.

87. Webb to HICOG Frankfurt, 19 September 1951, NARA, RG 59, 462A.62B31/9-1951; McCloy to Webb, 22 September 1951, *FRUS, 1951*, 3:1874–76; Acheson to HICOG Frankfurt, 26 September 1951, NARA, RG 59, 462A.62B31/9-2251.

88. HICOG Frankfurt to Department of State, 10 October 1951, NARA, RG 59, 462A.62B31/10-1051; CINC-USAFE Wiesbaden to COFS USAF Washington, 12 October 1951, NARA, RG 59, 762A.00(W)/10-1251; Lyon to Secretary of State, 30 October 1951, NARA, RG 59, 462A.62B31/10-3051; HIGOG Frankfurt to Department of State, 5 November 1951, NARA, RG 59, 462A.62B/11-551; "Minutes of Special Meeting held between the Deputy High Commissioners and the Mayor of Berlin and Representatives of the Federal Ministry of Economics," 2 November 1951, NARA, RG 59, 462A.62B3/11-251.

89. HICOG Frankfurt to Department of State, 20 October 1951, NARA, RG 51 462A.62B31/10-2051; Department of State to HICOG Frankfurt, 6 November 1951, NARA, RG 59, 462A.62B31/11-251; Allied High Commission for Germany, memorandum, "Restrictions Imposed by the Soviet Authorities on Trade between Berlin and Western Germany," AGSEC(51)1610, 23 October 1951 (FOIA release to author); "Minutes of the Twenty-Ninth Meeting of the Council of the Allied High Commission," 24 October 1951 (FOIA release to author); HICOG Frankfurt to Department of State, 9 November 1951 (FOIA release to author); memorandum of meeting on 12 November 1951 of the Allied High Commission for Germany, Economics Committee, 14 November 1951, NARA, RG 59, 462A62B31/11-1451 (FOIA release to author); Taylor to Slater/AGSEC, 10 November 1951, NARA, RG 59, 462A.62B31/11-1051.

90. "Restrictions Imposed by the Soviet Authorities on Trade between Berlin and Western Germany," AGSEC(51)1610, 23 October 1951 (FOIA release to author); AGSEC(51)1667; and Allied High Commission Economics Committee, ECON/Memo(51)25, 14 November 1951, NARA, RG 59, 462A.62B31/11-1451 (FOIA release to author); McCloy to Byroade, 4 January 1952, NARA, RG 59, 462A.62B31/1-452; HICOG Frankfurt to Secretary of State, 13 November 1951 (FOIA release to author); Taylor to HICOG, 10 November 1951, NARA, RG 59, 462A.62B31/11-1051; HICOG Frankfurt to Secretary of State, 15 November 1951, NARA, RG 59, 462A.62B/11-1551 (FOIA release to author); CINCEUR Heidelberg to CSUSA, 17 November 1951, NARA, RG 59, 762a.00(w)/11-1751; Bonn to Secretary of State, 20 November 1951, NARA, RG 59, 462A.62B31/11-2051; HICOG Mehlem to Department of State, 26 November 1951, NARA, RG 59, 462A.62B/11-2651 (FOIA release to author); HICOG Berlin to Department of State, 4 February 1952, NARA, RG 59, 762A.0221/2-452.

91. HICOG Bonn to Department of State, 26 November 1951, NARA, RG 59, 462A.62B/11-2651 (FOIA release to author); HICOG Bonn to Secretary of State, 24 November 1951, NARA, RG 59, 462A.62B31/11-2451; McCloy to Secretary of State, 27 November 1951, NARA, RG 59, 462A.62B31/11-2751; McCloy to Secretary of State, 28 November 1951, NARA, RG 59, 462A.62B31/11-2851. A few weeks later, considerable confusion still existed as to the circumstances of the Kroll-Stoph talks. "The talks," HIGOG reported in mid-December, "are now believed to have been requested by the East through an intermediary who is nameless. (We feel it is at least possible that Kroll arranged the talks himself, but there is of course no proof of this.) Two meetings took place in East Berlin, the first about November 16, the second November 21. Dr. Kroll now reports that Herr Stoof [Stoph] is a Staatssekretar in the office of the GDR premier, president of the State Planning Commission and, most importantly, a member of the Soviet Zone politburo. Dr. Kroll emphasizes Stoof's high rank." HICOG Mehlem to Department of State, 10 December 1951, NARA, RG 59, 462A.62B/12-1051.

92. HICOG Bonn to Department of State, 10 December 1951, NARA, RG 59, 462A.62B/12-1051 (FOIA release to author); Penfield to Secretary of State, 3 January 1951, NARA, RG 59, 462A.62B31 (FOIA release to author); McCloy to Byroade, 4 January 1952, NARA, RG 59, 462A.62B31/1-452.

93. McCloy to Byroade, 4 January 1952, NARA, RG 59, 462A.62B31/1-452; "Appraisal of the Use of Trade Embargo as a Countermeasure against Soviet/GDR Interference with Free Access to Berlin," Charles E. Hulick (HICOG EE) to Mc-Cloy, memorandum, 30 December 1951, NARA, RG 59, 462A.62B31/12-3051; Hulick to Secretary of State, 12 January 1952, NARA, RG 59, 462A.62B31/1-1252; HICOG Berlin to Secretary of State, 12 March 1952, NARA, RG 59, 462A.62B31/3-1252; HICOG Bonn to Secretary of State, 6 January 1952, NARA, RG 59, 462A.62B31/1-552.

94. McCloy to Byroade, 4 January 1952, NARA, RG 59, 462A.62B31/1-452; McCloy to Byroade, 15 January 1951, NARA, RG 59, 462A.62B31/1-1552; AGSEC(52)102, HICOG Bonn to Secretary of State, 7 March 1952, NARA, RG 59, 462A.62B31/3-652; HICOG Bonn to Secretary of State, 8 March 1952, NARA, RG 59, 462A.62B31/3-852. The Allied High Commission approval was made contingent on written West German assurances that the Berlin agreement would again be suspended if access difficulties occurred. The Adenauer government provided such assurances in a letter dated 8 March 1952.

95. McCloy to Department of State, 13 May 1952, *FRUS, 1952–1954*, 7:1, 339–40; McCloy to Department of State, 16 May 1952, ibid., 341–45; memorandum by Karl Bendetsen, Undersecretary of the Army to Robert Lovett, Secretary of Defense, undated, *FRUS, 1952–1954*, 7:2, 1239–40. See also "Log of Recent Soviet Harassments in Germany," 24 July 1952, NARA, RG 59, 762.00/7-2452.

96. Memorandum by Karl Bendetsen, Undersecretary of the Army, to Robert

Lovett, Secretary of Defense, undated, *FRUS, 1952–1954*, 7:2, 1239–40; memorandum by Charles E. Bohlen, Counselor of the Department of State, 27 May 1952, ibid., 1251–52; "Memorandum of Discussion at the 118th Meeting of the National Security Council, Wednesday, June 11, 1952," *FRUS, 1952–1954*, 7:2, 1258–61; "NSC 132/1: United States Policy and Courses of Action to Counter Possible Soviet or Satellite Actions Against Berlin," 12 June 1952, ibid., 1261–69; see also Laukhuff to Riddleberger, 15 May 1951, NARA, RG 59, 762A.5/5-1552 (FOIA release to author); Department of State Policy Planning Staff paper, "Possible Soviet Action against Berlin," 29 April 1952 (FOIA release to author).

97. Laukhuff to Riddleberger, 15 May 1951, NARA, RG 59, 762A.5/5-1552 (FOIA release to author); "Notes on the Fifth Meeting of the Ad Hoc Berlin Committee," 11 July 1952, NARA, RG 59, 762A.5/7-1552.

98. "Notes on the Fifth Meeting of the Ad Hoc Berlin Committee," 11 July 1952, NARA, RG 59, 762A.5/7-1552; Acheson to McCloy, 19 June 1952, NARA, RG 59, 762A.0221/6-1952 (FOIA release to author); Isaiah Frank/EDT to Francis T. Williamson/EUR, memorandum, 25 July 1952, with enclosed draft "Report of the Economic Countermeasures Working Group, NARA, RG 59, 762A.00/7-2552 (FOIA release to author); see also Williamson to Frank, memorandum, 1 August 1952, 762A.00/8-152 (FOIA release to author).

99. HICOG Berlin to Secretary of State, 10 July 1952, NARA, RG 59, 762A.00/7-1052; HICOG Bonn to Secretary of State, 1 August 1952, NARA, RG 59, 762.0221/8-152; Department of State to HICOG Bonn, 22 August 1952, NARA, RG 59, 762A.0221/8-2252; "Berlin," memorandum, J. T.Rogers/GEA to Mr. Riley/GEA, 22 April 1952, NARA, RG 59, 762.00/4-2252; see also Cecil Lyon to James Riddleberger, 27 August 1952, NARA, RG 59, 762A.0221/8-2752 (FOIA release to author); HICOG Berlin to Department of State, 24 October 1952, NARA, RG 59, 762A.0221/10-2452 (FOIA release to author). In fact, U.S. officials even raised the possibility of sabotaging the completion or operation of the canal built to maintain it as leverage. See "[U.S. Policy] with Respect to Possible Soviet Action against Berlin," memorandum, 29 April 1952, NARA, RG 59, 762A,00/4-2952 TSF (FOIA release to author).

100. Hermann-Josef Rupieper hints at this in his "Die Reaktionen der USA auf die Gründung der DDR," *"Provisorium für längstens ein Jahr": Die Gründung der DDR*, ed. Elke Scherstjanoi (Berlin: Akademie Verlag, 1993), 59–66; see also William Burr, "Avoiding the Slippery Slope: The Eisenhower Administration and the Berlin Crisis, November 1958–January 1959," in *Diplomatic History* 18, no. 2 (April 1994): 177–205.

CHAPTER 9

1. The SED (Sozialistische Einheitspartei Deutschlands) approved the program at its Second Party Conference, held 9–12 July 1952. "Beschluss der 2. Parteikonferenz,"

Neues Deutschland, 13 July 1952; *Protokoll der Verhandlungen der 2. Parteikonferenz der SED, 9–12 July 1952* (Berlin: Staatsverlag der DDR, 1952); Lyon to Secretary of State, 12 July 1952, NARA, RG 59, 762A.00/7-1252.

2. Conversation between Joseph V. Stalin and SED leadership, 7 April 1952, Library of Congress, Dmitri Volkogonov Collection, printed in translation in *Uprising in East Germany, 1953*, 25–41. (A copy of the Russian document can be found in Arkhiv Prezidenta Rossiisskoi Federatsii, Moscow (AP RF), f. 45, op. 1, d. 303, l. 179); Jens Schöne, *Volksaufstand: Der 17. Juni 1953 in Berlin und der DDR* (Berlin: Berlin Story Verlag, 2013), 29; for the developments leading up to the Second Party Conference, see Heinz Heitzer, "Entscheidungen im Vorfeld der 2. Parteikonferenz der SED (Februar bis Juli 1952)," *Beträge zur Geschichte der Arbeiterbewegung* 34, no. 4 (1992): 18–32; Gerhard Wettig, ed., *Die sowjetische Deutschland-Politik in der Ära Adenauer*, Rhöndorder Gespräche 16 (Bonn: Bouvier, 1997); Elke Scherstjanoi, "Zwei deutsche Staaten?" *Tel Aviver Jahrbuch für deutsche Geschichte* 28 (1999): 257–302.

3. Cited in Mark Kramer, "The Early Post-Stalin Succession Struggle and Upheavals in Eastern Europe (Part 1)," *Journal of Cold War Studies* 1, no. 1 (Winter 1999): 3–55; see also the massive documentation in Galina Murashko et al., eds., *Vostochnaia Yevropa v dokumentakh rossiiskikh arkhivov*, vol. 2 (1949–53) (Moscow: Siberian Chronograph, 1998).

4. Schöne, *Volksaufstand*, 35; *Junge Welt*, special edition, April 1953, reprinted in ibid.; "Analyse der Republikflucht," 1954, Bundesarchiv Potsdam (BA-Potsdam), Ministerium des Innern, Hauptverwaltung der Deutschen Volkspolizei (MI/HDV), 11/962; S. Ignatiev, "TsK KPSS," top secret memorandum, 708/I, 19 February 1953, Arkhiv Sluzhby Veshnei Razvedki Rossiiskoi Federatsii (ASVR), f. 2589, tom. 7, d. 45513, ll. 97–99, quoted in David E. Murphy, Sergei A. Kondrashev, and George Bailey, *Battleground Berlin: CIA vs. KGB in the Cold War* (New Haven, CT: Yale University Press, 1997), 156; Hope M. Harrison, *Driving the Soviets Up the Wall: Soviet–East German Relations, 1953–1961* (Princeton, NJ: Princeton University Press, 2003), 19–21; *Uprising in East Germany, 1953*, 3.

5. *New York Times*, 17 March 1953; Vladislav M. Zubok and Constantine V. Pleshakov, *Inside the Kremlin's Cold War: From Stalin to Khrushchev* (Cambridge, MA: Harvard University Press, 1996); *Uprising in East Germany, 1953*, 3.

6. HICOG Berlin to Department of State, 27 March 1953, NARA, RG 59, 762.0221/3-2753; Bohlen quote from Robert to Strang, "Minute," PRO, FO 371/106 532/NS 10345/9, cited in Klaus Larres, "Eisenhower and the First Forty Days after Stalin's Death: The Incompatibility of Detente and Political Warfare," *Diplomacy and Statecraft* 6, no. 2 (July 1995): 431–69, here 449.

7. *Neues Deutschland*, 8 March 1953; *Uprising in East Germany, 1953*, 4.

8. Fritz Schenk, a personal assistant to GDR planning chief Bruno Leuschner, reported Grotewohl's reaction in his memoir, *Im Vorzimmer der Diktatur: 12 Jahre Pankow* (Cologne: Kiepenheuer and Witsch, 1962), 182; see also his "Wie die Regierung

den 17. Juni erlebte," *SBZ-Archiv* 13 (1962), 150. For the SCC instructions, see "Draft Instructions" to Vasily Chuikov and Semenov, 18 March 1953, Foreign Policy Archive of the Russian Federation, Moscow, F. 06, Op. 12, Papka 18, Port 283; document provided to author by Hope M. Harrison; *Uprising in East Germany, 1953*, 1953, 4.

9. HICOG Berlin to Department of State, 30 April 1953, NARA, RG 59, 762B.00/4-3053; Falco Werkentin, *Politische Strafjustiz in der Ära Ulbricht* (Berlin: Ch. Links Verlag, 1995), 70–71.

10. HICOG Berlin to HICOG Bonn, 20 April 1953, NARA, RG 762B.00/4-2053; *Uprising in East Germany, 1953*, 5.

11. Quoted in HICOG Berlin to HICOG Bonn, 20 April 1953, NARA, RG 762B.00/4-2053; Manfred Hagen, *DDR Juni '53: Die erste Volkserhebung im Stalinismus* (Stuttgart: Franz Steiner Verlag, 1992), 26. On Slánský, see Igor Lukes, "The Rudolf Slánský Affair: New Evidence," *Slavic Review* 58, no. 1 (Spring 1999): 160–87.

12. HICOG Berlin to Department of State, 13 March 1953, NARA, RG 59, 762B.00/3-3153; HICOG Berlin to Secretary of State, 16 March 1953, NARA, 762B.00/3-1253; HICOG Berlin to Secretary of State, 9 June 1953, NARA, RG 59, 762B.00/6-953; HICOG Berlin to Department of State, 30 April 1953, NARA, RG 59, 762B.00/4-3053. On the debate over the reaction to the Soviet peace offensive, see M. Steven Fish, "After Stalin's Death: The Ango-American Debate over a New Cold War," *Diplomatic History* 10, no. 4 (1986): 333–55.

13. HICOG Berlin to Department of State, 3 February 1953, NARA, RG 466, HICOG Berlin, box 3.

14. Conant to Secretary of State, 27 February 1953, NARA, RG 59, 862A.411/2-2753; HICOG Berlin to Secretary of State, 5 March 1953, NARA, RG 59, 862A.411/3-553. On Conant, see James G. Hershberg, *James B. Conant: Harvard to Hiroshima and the Making of the Nuclear Age* (NY: Knopf, 1993), esp. chap. 32–33.

15. HICOG Berlin to Secretary of State, 2 March 1953, NARA, RG 59, 862A.411/3-253; Conant to Secretary of State, 27 February 1953, NARA, RG 59, 862A.411/2-2753.

16. Conant began to change his views on the refugee crisis as early as mid-March. See Conant to Secretary of State, 12 March 1953, NA, RG 59, 862A.411/3-1253; HICOG Berlin to HICOG Bonn, 4 March 1953, NA, RG 59, 762B.00/3-453.

17. N. S. Barnes/HICOG Berlin to Department of State, 27 March 1953, NARA, RG 59, 762.0221/3-2753; HICOG Berlin to Secretary of State, 30 April 1953, NARA, RG 59, 762B.00/4-3053; HICOG Berlin to HICOG Bonn, 20 April 1953, NARA, RG 59, 762 B.00/4-2053.

18. *Uprising in East Germany, 1953*, 71–73. On the Moscow debate, see in particular Vladislav Zubok, "'Unverfrohren und grob in der Deutschlandfrage . . .' Beria, der Nachfolgestreit nach Stalins Tod und die Moskauer DDR-Debatte in April-Mai 1953," in *1953—Krisenjahr des Kalten Krieges in Europa*, ed. Christoph Klessmann and Bernd Stöver (Cologne: Böhlau, 1999), 29–48; Wettig, "Die beginnende

Umorientierung der sowjetischen Deutschland-Politik im Frühjahr und Sommer 1953," *Deutschland Archiv* 28, no. 5 (May 1995): 495–507; Elke Scherstjanoi, "Die sowjetische Deutschlandpolitik nach Stalins Tod 1953: Neue Dokumente aus dem Archiv des Moskauer Außenministeriums," *Vierteljahrshefte für Zeitgeschichte* 46, no. 3 (1998): 497–549.

19. Semenov to Molotov, "Memorandum on the German Question," 2 May 1953, *Uprising in East Germany, 1953*, 82–85; Murphy, Kondrashev, and Bailey, *Battleground Berlin*, 154–68; the quote is at 151–68, citing a report by Medvedev, 9 March 1953, SVRA, file 68881, 3:21–28, sec. 9.

20. AP RF, f.3, op.64, d. 802, ll. 153-161. The German version of the decree, "Über die Maßnahmen zur Gesundung der politischen Lage in der Deutschen De-mokratischen Republik," released in 1989, was first published in *Beiträge zur Geschichte der Arbeiterbewegung* 32 (1990), 651–54; *Uprising in East Germany, 1953*, 8–15, 18–21.

21. Cited in Christian Ostermann, "New Documents on the East German Upris-ing of 1953," *Cold War International History Project Bulletin* 5 (Spring 1995): 10–20; Schöne, *Volksaufstand*, 40.

22. See the first report on the New Course announcement in HICOG Berlin to Secretary of State, 11 June 1953, NARA, RG 59, 762B.00/6-1153; HICOG Berlin to Department of State, 2 June 1953, NARA, RG 59, 762.00/6-253; Bohlen to Secretary of State, 29 May 1953, NARA, RG 59, 762.0221/5-2953;Lyon to Secretary of State, 30 May 1953, NARA, RG 59, 762.0221/5-3053.

23. Berlin to Secretary of State, 9 June 1953, NARA, RG 59, 762B.00/6-953. Once the uprising had broken out, U.S. officials believed that in likely "significant changes in top East Zone government and party leadership" LDP leader Hermann Kastner might rise to greater prominence. Kastner had been an informant for the U.S.-controlled Gehlen Organization since 1948. HICOG Berlin to Secretary of State, 22 June 1953, NARA, RG 59,762.0221/6-2253.

24. Ibid.; HICOG Berlin to Secretary of State, 15 June 1953, NARA, RG 59, 762B.00/6-1553; CIA, Office of Current Intelligence, 11 June 1953, C. D. Jackson Records, box 3, Dwight David Eisenhower Library (hereafter cited as DDEL); Gen. Persons to President Eisenhower, 11 June 1953, Dwight D. Eisenhower Papers, Ann Whitman File, International Series, box 14, DDEL.

25. Armin Mitter and Stefan Wolle, *Untergang auf Raten Unbekannte Kapitel der DDR-Geschichte* (Munich: Bertelsmann, 1993), 76–77; Hagen, *DDR Juni '53*, 38; Schöne, *Volksaufstand*, 50. See also firsthand accounts published by Rainer Hildeb-randt, *The Explosion: The Uprising behind the Iron Curtain* (New York: Little, Brown, 1955); Hildebrandt, *Als die Fesseln fielen . . . die Geschichte einer Schicksalsverkettung in dem Aufstand des 17. Juni*, 3d ed. (Berlin: Arani Verlags-GMBH, 1966); Hildebrandt, *Der 17, Juni: Zehn Erlebnisgeschichten von Personen in verschiedenen Brennpunkten des Aufstandes* (Berlin: Verlag Haus am Checkpoint Charlie, 1983).

26. Ilko-Sascha Kowalczuk, Armin Mitter, and Stefan Wolle, eds., *Der Tag X: 17*

Juni 1953. Die "Innere Staatsgründung" der DDR als Ergebnis der Krise 1952/54 (Berlin: Ch. Links, 1995), 10; Schöne, Volksaufstand, 85, 98.

27. Vasily Sokolovsky and Leonid Gorov to Soviet defense minister Nikolai Bulganin, 18 June 1953, in *Uprising in East Germany, 1953*, 208–9; Hagen, *DDR*, 104–23; By some accounts, the Soviet Army eschewed violence against the protesters, seeking to calm the situation and deterring further escalation by a massive display of military might: atop a Soviet tank, the Soviet city commandant, Major General Pavel Dibrova, unarmed but fully clad in military regalia, appealed to the crowds to go home. Some Soviet officials later denied that their forces had been given firing orders; Semenov recalled being instructed from Moscow "to open fire on the insurgents, to establish military tribunals and to shoot twelve ring leaders" but supposedly decided to have the troops "fire over the heads." Yet violence did occur, some of the worst outside the East Berlin police headquarters, where Soviet tanks opened fire on what Soviet reports termed "the insurgents." Tanks drove into gathered protestors; Soviet soldiers opened fire on unarmed demonstrators. Semenov, *Von Stalin bis Gorbatschow*, 296; Schöne, Volksaufstand, 57; *Uprising in East Germany, 1953*, 168–69.

28. Vladimir Semenov and Andrei Grechko to Vyacheslav Molotov and Nikolai Bulganin, 17 June 1953, *Uprising in East Germany, 1953*, 181–82; Andrei Grechko and A. Tarasov to Nikolai Bulganin, 17 June 1953, ibid., 196–97; Valerij Masajew, "Zur Vorgeschichte der Berliner Mauer," in Heiner Timmermann, ed., *Juni 1953 in Deutschland* (Hamburg: Lit, 2003), 116<->18; Semenov and Sokolovsky to Molotov and Bulganin, 17 June 1953, in: Ostermann, *Uprising in East Germany, 1953*, 200–201, Sokolovsky and Leonid Govorov to Bulganin, 18 June 1953, ibid., 208–9; Sokolovsky, Semenov and Pavel Yudin, "On the Events of 17–19 June 1953 in Berlin and the GDR and Certain Conclusions from these Events," 24 June 1953, ibid., 257–85; HICOG Berlin to Department of State, 1 July 1953, NARA, RG 59, 762B.00/7-153.

29. CIA, "Comment on East Berlin Uprising," 17 June 1953, DDEL, C. D. Jackson Records, box 3; Nicholas J. Schlosser, *Cold War on the Airwaves: The Radio Propaganda War against East Germany* (Urbana, IL: University of Illinois Press, 2015), 81; David E. Murphy, "Der 17. Juni und die CIA-Operationsbasis Berlin," in: Timmermann, ed., *Juni 1953 in Deutschland*, 44–53; HICOG Berlin to HICOG Bonn, 16 June 1953, National Security Archive, Soviet Flashpoints Collection; Scott H. Krause, *Bringing Cold War Democracy to West Berlin. A Shared German-American Project, 1940-1972* (Routledge Studies in Modern European History 61), (London: Routledge, 2019), 146–47.

30. Ewing quoted in Schlosser, *Cold War on the Airwaves*, 80.

31. *Der Aufstand der Arbeiterschaft im Ostsektor von Berlin und in der sowjetischen Besatzungszone. Tätigkeitsbericht der Hauptabteilung Politik des Rundfunks im Amerikanischen Sektor in der Zeit vom 16. Juni bis zum 23. Juni 1953*, 3, copy in BA Koblenz, J. Kaiser Papers, NL 18/314; HICOG Berlin to HICOG Bonn, 17 June 1953, National Security Archive, Soviet Flashpoints Collection. — In the wake of the New Course

announcement, local party officials reported greater numbers of statements from the local population, such as, "All stations were lying, RIAS alone says the truth, our shackles are broken, we are free people again." An SED report on the situation on June 17 in Leipzig noted that "many RIAS listeners" could be found among the workers. Abt. Leitende Organe der Partei und der Massenorganisationen, "Analyse über die Vorbereitung, den Ausbruch, und die Niederschlagung des faschistischen Abenteuers vom 16.-22.6. 1953," 20 July 1953, SAPMO-BA, 2/5/546; "Durchsage der B[ezirks] L[eitung] Leipzig," 18 June 1953, SAPMO-BA, NY 90/437; M. C. Partridge, Major General, G-2, to Allen Dulles, 3 August 1953, C. D. Jackson Papers, box 74, DDEL; "Information über die Situation in Leipzig und Espenhain am 17.6.1953," 18 June 1953, SAPMO-BA, NY 90/437;

32. HICOG Berlin to Secretary of State, 16 June 1953, NARA, RG 59, 762B.00/6-1653; Hagen, *DDR Juni '53*, 97. The Hulick/Ewing quote is from Stewart Alsop, "Courage in Berlin and Its Reward," *New York Times*, 20 July 1953. The name and details are given in an interview by Ewing, printed in Ilse Spittmann and Karl Wilhelm Fricke, *17. Juni 1953: Arbeiteraufstand in der DDR*, 2nd ed. (Köln: Verlag Wissenschaft und Politik 1988), 234–37; Rainer Hildebrandt, *The Explosion: The Uprising behind the Iron Curtain* (New York: Little, Brown, 1955), 46–69; Diethelm Prowe, *Weltstadt in Krisen: Berlin, 1949–1958* (Berlin: Walter DeGryter, 1973), 113; HICOG Berlin to Secretary of State, 16 June 1953, NARA, RG 59, 762B.00/6-1653; "Bericht über die Geschehnisse am Mittwoch, dem 17. Juni 1953," n.d., SAPMO-BA, NL 90/437.

33. Stefan Brant and Klaus Bölling, *Der Aufstand: Vorgeschichte, Geschichte, und Deutung des 17. Juni 1953* (Stuttgart: Steingrüben, 1954), 5–6; see also the testimony of Wilhelm Grothaus, "Augenzeugenberichte von streikenden Arbeitern," in Spittman and Fricke, *17 Juni 1953*, 136.

34. Brant/Bölling, *Der Aufstand*, 6–8; Hildebrandt, *The Explosion*, 66; HICOG Berlin to Secretary of State, 17 June 1953, NARA, RG 59, 762B.00/6-1753.

35. HICOG Berlin to Secretary of State, 17 June 1953, NARA, RG 59, 762A.0221/6-1753; Prowe, *Weltstadt in Krisen*, 116.

36. French government officials were apparently particularly convinced that the uprising had started as an event staged by the Soviets. See Michael Gehler, "Von der Arbeiterrevolte zur spontanen politischen Volkserhebung: Der 17. Juni 1953 in der DDR im Urteil westlicher Diplomatie und Politik," *Militärgeschichtliche Mitteilungen* 54, no. 2 (1995): 363–416; C. D. Jackson to Operations Coordinating Board, 3 November 1953, DDEL (MMR release to author); Prowe, *Weltstadt in Krisen*, 116; USAREUR to SACEUR, 18 June 1953, National Security Archive, Soviet Flashpoints collection; HICOG Berlin to Secretary of State, 23 June 1953, NARA, RG 59, 762A.00/6-2353. The new Soviet military commander of Berlin, Maj.-Gen. Dibrova, replied to the commandants' letter on 20 June, arguing that the letter had described the events in the Soviet sector "in a distorted way" and "decisively" rejecting the Western protest. Lyon to HICOG Bonn and Department of State, telegram, 21 June

1953 (FOIA release to author). In a reply to Dibrova on 22 June, the Western Commandants rejected his "allegations that the disturbances of June 17 were the result of action by groups sent from [the] Western sectors of Berlin." Lyon to HICOG Bonn, telegram, 22 June 1953 (FOIA release to author). On Adenauer's reaction, see Hans Peter Schwarz, *Adenauer: Der Staatsmann, 1952–1967* (Stuttgart: DVA, 1991), 84.

37. "Memorandum of Informal PSB Meeting, June 17, 1953," 17 June 1953 (FOIA release to author); State Department to HICOG Bonn, 17 June 1953, NARA, RG 59, 762B.00/6-1753; John M. Anspacher to George A. Morgan, memorandum "East Berlin Riots," 17 June 1953, DDEL, C. D. Jackson Papers; George A. Morgan to C. D. Jackson, memorandum, "Berlin," 18 June 1953, ibid.; "Telephone Conversation between Dulles and Eisenhower, 17 June 1953, 10:10 a.m.," DDEL, John F. Dulles Paper, Telephone Calls Series, box 1; Richard Strauss/GER to Phillips/P, "East Berlin Demonstrations (briefing of the Under Secretary for PSB luncheon)," memorandum, 17 June 1953, DDEL, C. D. Jackson Papers, box 3; John M. Anspacher to Gorge A Morgan, "Working Group—Berlin," 17 June 1953 (FOIA release to author).

38. Frank G. Wisner to John Bross, 18 June 1953, CIA Records; Working Paper Prepared in the Eastern Affairs Division, HICOG Berlin Element, 25 June 1953, *FRUS, 1952–1954,* 7:1595; "Comment on East Berlin Uprising," 17 June 1953, in: Donald P. Steury, ed., *On the Front Lines of the Cold War: Documents on the Intelligence War in Berlin, 1946 to 1961* (Washington, DC: CIA, 1999), 245; "Comment on East Berlin Rioting," *CIA Current Intelligence Digest,* 18 June 1953 (CIA FOIA release to author); HICOG Berlin to HICOG Bonn, 19 June 1953, National Security Archive, Flashpoint Collection; Ronny Heidenreich, Daniela Münkel and Elke Stadelmann-Wenz, *Geheimdienstkrieg in Deutschland: Die Konfrontation von DDR-Staatssicherheit und Organization Gehlen 1953* (Unabhängige Historikerkommission zur Erforschung der Geschichte des Bundesnachrichtendienstes 1945–1968, vol. 3), (Berlin: Ch. Links, 2016), 43; Ronny Heidenreich, Die DDR-Spionage des BND: Von den Anfängen bis zum Mauerbau (Berlin: Ch. Links, 2019), 239–42; George A. Morgan to C. D. Jackson, "Berlin," memorandum, 18 June 1953, DDEL, C. D. Jackson Papers.

39. Richard Strauss/GER to Phillips/P, "East Berlin Demonstrations (briefing of the Under Secretary for PSB luncheon)," memorandum, 17 June 1953, C. D. Jackson Papers, box 3, DDEL; HICOG Berlin to Secretary of State, 18 June 1953, 6 p.m., NARA, RG 59, 762A.0221/6-1853; HICOG Berlin to HICOG Bonn, 19 June 1953, National Security Archive, Soviet Flashpoints Collection; "German Socialists Report Unrest prior to 16–17 June," *CIA Current Intelligence Digest,* 26 June 1953 (CIA FOIA release to author).

40. "Minutes of Discussion at the 150th Meeting of the National Security Council on 18 June 1953," 19 June 1953, DDEL (mandatory review release to author). For a brief biography of Jackson, see H. W. Brands, Jr., *Cold Warriors: Eisenhower's Generation and American Foreign Policy* (New York: Columbia University Press, 1988), 117–37.

41. Ward to Foreign Office, telegram, 20 June 1953, UK National Archives, FO/371/103840, CS 1016/85; Dillon/Paris to Secretary of State, 24 June 1953, NARA, RG 59, 762A.0221/6-2453; Prime Minister to Coleman, telegram 168, personal, 22.6.1953, PRO, FO/371/103840, CS1016/85. On British policy during the uprising, see Klaus Larres, "Neutralisierung oder Westintegration: Churchill, Adenauer, die USA, und der 17. Juni 1953," *Deutschland Archiv* 45, no. 6 (1993): 568–83; Michael Gehler, "Der 17. Juni 1953 aus der Sicht des Foreign Office," *Aus Politik und Zeitgeschichte* 25 (1993): 22–31; John W. Young, "Cold War and Detente with Moscow," in *The Foreign Policy of Churchill's Peacetime Government, 1951–55,* ed. John W. Young (Leicester: Leicester University Press, 1988), 55–80; Rolf Steininger, "Ein vereinigtes, unabhängiges Deutschland? Winston Churchill, der kalte Krieg, und die deutsche Frage im Jahre 1953," *Militärgeschichtliche Mitteilungen* 36 (1984): 105–44; Joseph Foschepoth, "Churchill, Adenauer, und die Neutralisierung Deutschlands," *Deutschland Archiv* 17, no. 12 (1984): 1286–1301.

42. FO Minute, Roberts to Strang, 23 June 1953, UK National Archives, FO/371/103841, CS 1016/116; Ward to Foreign Office, telegram 564, 22 June 1953, UK National Archives, FO/371/103840, CS 1016/90; Fish, "After Stalin's Death," 343. See also Lyon to HICOG Bonn, telegram, 22 June 1953 (FOIA release to author).

43. HICOG Bonn to Department of State, 6 July 1953, NARA, RG 59, 762B.00/7-653 (emphasis added); HICOG Berlin to HICOG Bonn, 26 June 1953, National Security Archive, Soviet Flashpoints Collection. As early as 26 June, the U.S. High Commissioner had notified Washington that since "the Berlin uprising there has been a groundswell of demand in press for initiative and immediate action on [the] part of [the] Adenauer Government toward achieving German reunification and reversing the previous order of priority: First strengthening the West (EDC) and then reunification." Conant to Secretary of State, cable, 26 June 1953, NARA, RG 59, 762A.00/6-2653.

44. "Information der Kreisleitung Oldenburg," 12 June 1953, SAPMO-BA, DY 30,IV 2/5/526; "Stimmungsbericht von Magdeburg," 12 June 1953, ibid.; FDGB-Bundesvorstand, "Vertrauliche Information," No. 21, 13 June 1953, SAPMO-BA, DY 30,IV 2/5/543; Lothar Dralle, "Das DSF–Archiv als Quelle zur Geschichte der DDR—Der Volksaufstand vom 17. Juni 1953," *Deutschland Archiv* 25, no. 8 (1992): 841.

45. C. D. Jackson to Eisenhower, memorandum, 3 July 1953, DDEL, C. D. Jackson Papers, box 41; John Albert to Ned Roberts/Brad Conners, memorandum, 18 June 1953, NARA, RG 59, 762B.00/6-1853.

46. C. D. Jackson to John F. Dulles, 8 August 1953, C. D. Jackson Papers, box 40, DDEL; Department of State to HICOG Bonn, 16 June 1953, NARA, RG 59, 762.0221/6-1653; HICOG Berlin to Secretary of State, 22 June 1953, NARA, RG 59, 762.0221/6-2253.

47. HICOG Berlin to HICOG Bonn, 30 June 1953, NARA, RG 59, 762B.00/6-3053; Conant to Secretary of State, 26 June 1953, NARA, RG 59, 762B.00/6-2653.

As early as 25 June, HICOG informed the State Department that West German officials also "privately recognized that—perhaps remembering fairly recent history when German troops had put down popular uprisings—Soviet countermeasures had not been as violent as could be expected and that actually much less blood had flowed than would normally have been anticipated under the circumstances" (HICOG Bonn to Department of State, 25 June 1953, NARA, RG 59, 762A.00/6-2553). On Conant, see James G. Hershberg, *James B. Conant: From Harvard to Hiroshima and the Making of the Nuclear Age* (New York: Knopf, 1993), 659–65.

48. "On the Events of 17–19 June 1953 in Berlin and the GDR and Certain Conclusions from these Events," report by Sokolovsky, Semyonov, and Yudin, 24 June 1953, in Ostermann, *Uprising in East Germany, 1953*, 257–85; Jackson Diary entry for 18 June 1953, DDEL, C. D. Jackson Papers, box 56.

49. "Interim U.S. Psychological Strategy Plan for Exploitation of Unrest in Satellite Europe (PSB D-45)," 1 July 1953, NARA, RG 273, NSC 158 Series; "Memorandum of Informal PSB Meeting, June 24, 1953," 24 June 1953 (FOIA release to author).

50. Hulick to Secretary of State, cable, 25 September 1953, NARA, RG 59, 762B.00/9-2553 (FOIA release to author); Conant to Dulles, 26 June 1953, NARA, RG 59, 762B.00/6-2653; Schwarz, *Adenauer*, 85; Hershberg, *James B. Conant*, 665.

51. Summary of PSB D-45, 22 June 1953, DDEL, White House Office Files, Office of the Special Assistant for National Security Affairs, Records 1952–1961, NSC Series, Policy Papers Subseries, box 4; S. Everett Gleason, "Discussion at the 151st Meeting of the National Security Council," memorandum, 26 June 1953 (Mandatory Review Release to author); "Soviet Repression of the Popular Demonstrations in East Germany," Sandifel and Merchant to John F. Dulles, memorandum, 25 June 1953, NARA, RG 59, 762B.00/6-2553; PSB, "Interim U.S. Psychological Strategy Plan for Exploitation of Unrest in Satellite Europe," 1 July 1953, NARA, RG 273, NSC 158 Series; NSC Executive Secretariat, "United States Objectives and Actions to Exploit the Unrest in Satellite States—A Report to the National Security Council," 29 June 1953, NARA, RG 273, NSC 158 Series; Report on the Implementation of PSB D-45, Strauss to Stevens, 23 September 1953, NARA, RG 59, 862B.03/9-2353 (FOIA release to author); State Department to HICOG Bonn, 3 July 1953, National Security Archive, Soviet Flashpoints Collection; Edward M. O'Connor to Abbott Washburn, memorandum, 18 August 1953, DDEL, C. D. Jackson Records, box 1; W. W. Rostow to C. D. Jackson, 22 June 1953, DDEL, C. D. Jackson Records, box 1. See also H. W. Brands, Jr., "The Eisenhower Administration and the Volunteer Freedom Corps," *Military Affairs* 52 (1988): 7–11.

52. "Memorandum of Informal PSB Meeting, July 1," 1 July 1953 (FOIA release to author); Hubert Humphrey to Eisenhower, 1 September 1953, DDEL, White House Central Files (Confidential File), 1953–1961, Subject series, box 68; William Bennett, memorandum for the President, n.d., ibid.; C. D. Jackson to Thomas Braden, 28 July 1953, ibid., box 61.

53. Riddleberger to Smith, memorandum, 6 July 1953, NARA, RG 59, 862B.49/7-653; Conant to Secretary of State, 3 July 1953, NARA, RG 59, 862B.49/7-353; Conant to Secretary of State, 26 June 1953, NARA, RG 59, 762B.00/6-2653.

54. Riddleberger to General Smith, 7 July 1953, NA, RG 59, 862B.49/7-753; *FRUS, 1952–1954*, 7:1611–14; W. K. Scott to General Smith, 27 July 1953, NA, RG 59, 862B.49/7-2753; Frederick Ayer, Jr., Special Assistant to the Secretary, Department of the Air Force, 29 July 1953, DDEL, C. D. Jackson Records, box 2; Frederick Ayer, Jr., Special Assistant to the Secretary, Department of the Air Force, 29 July 1953, DDEL, C. D. Jackson Records, box 2.

55. "Memorandum of Informal PSB Meeting, July 1," 1 July 1953 (FOIA release to author); Riddleberger to Smith, "Food to East Germany," memorandum, 6 July 1953, NARA, RG 59, 862B.49/7-653; HICOG Bonn to HICOG Berlin, 6 July 1953, DDEL, C. D.Jackson Records, box 3; *Department of State Bulletin* 29 (20 July 1953): 67–69. For Adenauer's 4 July 1953 letter to Eisenhower and Eisenhower's response of 10 July, see *FRUS, 1952–1954*, 7:1615–16, 1617. For the "fait accompli" element in the offer, see Edward M. O'Connor to C. D. Jackson, 8 July 1953, DDEL, C. D. Jackson Papers, box 3; Conant to Secretary of State, 11 July 1953, NA, RG 59, 862B.49/7-1153; Conant to Secretary of State, 13 July 1953, NARA, RG 59, 862B.49/7-1353; CIA Information Report, "Plans for the Renewal of Strikes in East Germany," 13 July 1953, in Ostermann, *Uprising in East Germany, 1953*, 351; "Telephone concersation with Allen W. Dulles," July 10, 1953, DDEL, John F. Dulles Papers, Telephone Calls Series, box 1; for the Russian reaction, see O'Shaughnessy to Secretary of State, 11 July 1953, DDEL, White House Central Files (Confidential File), 1953–61, Subject Series, box 37; *Neues Deutschland*, 12 June 1953; *Department of State Bulletin* 29:734 (20 July 1953), 68; Thompson (US Mission Vienna) to J. F. Dulles, 8 July 1953, NARA, RG 59, 862B03/7-853.

56. HICOG Berlin to Secretary of State, 28 July 1953, NARA, RG 59, 862B.49/7-2853; HICOG Berlin to Secretary of State, 27 July 1953, NARA, RG 59, 862B.49/7-2753; Edward M. O'Connor to C. D. Jackson, White House Central Files (Confidential File), Subject Series, box 37, DDEL; HICOG Berlin to Secretary of State, 17 August 1953, NARA, RG 59, 862B.49/8-1753; HICOG Berlin to Department of State, 17 September 1953, NARA, RG 59, 862B.49/9-1753. For more-detailed statistics on the first phase, see Conant to Secretary of State, 17 August 1953, NARA, RG 59, 862B.49/8-1753.

57. SED/Abteilung Agitation [Department of Agitation] to Grotewohl, 29 July 1953, SAPMO-BA, NL 90/437.

58. Kreisleitung der SED Rathenow [Local Party Headquarters in Rathenow] to Bezirksleitung der SED [SED District Leadership], 29 July 1953, SAPMO-BA IV 2/5/561; Abteilung Leitende Organe der Partei und Massenorganisationen, "1. Bericht über die Lage in Berlin—Ausgabe von Lebensmittelpaketen in den Westsektoren" [First Report on the Situation in Berlin—The Distribution of Food Packages in the

Western Sectors], 29 July 1953, SAPMO-BA, IV 2/5/561; Abteilung Leitende Organe der Partei und Massenorganisationen, "4. Bericht über die Ausgabe von Lebensmittelpaketen in den Westsektoren" [Fourth Report on the Distribution of Food Packages in the Western Sectors], 31 July 1953, SAPMO-BA, IV 2/5/561.

59. "1. Bericht über die Lage in Berlin—Ausgabe von Lebensmittelpaketen in den Westsektoren," 29 July 1953, SAPMO-BA, IV 2/5/561; "2. Bericht über die Ausgabe von Lebensmittelpaketen in den Westsektoren," 29 July 1953, SAPMO-BA, IV 2/5/561; Abteilung Leitende Organe der Partei und Massenorganisationen, "5. Bericht über die Ausgabe der USA-Lebensmittelpakete in Westberlin," 2 August 1953, SAPMO-BA, IV 2/5/564.

60. Abteilung Leitende Organe der Partei, "1. Bericht über die Lage in Berlin—Ausgabe von Lebensmittelpaketen in den Westsektoren," 29 July 1953, SAPMO-BA, IV 2/5/561; Abteilung Leitende Organe der Partei, "4. Bericht über die Ausgabe von Lebensmittelpaketen in den Westsektoren," 31 July 1953, SAPMO-BA, IV 2/5/561; Abteilung Leitende Organe der Partei und der Massenorganisationen, Informationsbericht, 12 September 1953, SAPMO-BA, IV 2/5/563.

61. Abteilung Leitende Organe der Partei und der Massenorganisationen, Informationsbericht, 12 September 1953, SAPMO-BA, IV 2/5/563; Abteilung Leitende Organe der Partei, "2. Bericht über die Ausgabe von Lebensmittelpaketen in den Westsektoren," 29 July 1953, SAPMO-BA, IV 2/5/561.

62. "Minutes of the Politburo Meeting," 1 August 1953, SAPMO-BA, DY 30, IV 2/2/311; R. Chwalek, Railways Ministry, to Grotewohl, 2 August 1953, SAPMO-BA, NY4090/437.

63. Abteilung Leitende Organe der Partei und Massenorganisationen, "Informationsnotiz 301," 4 August 1953, SAPMO-BA, IV 2/5/564; HICOG Berlin to Secretary of State, 10 August 1953, NA, RG 59, 862B.49/8-1053; Abteilung Leitende Organe der Partei und Massenorganisationen, "Informationsnotiz 302," 4 August 1953, SAPMO-BA, IV 2/5/564; HICOG Berlin to Secretary of State, 6 August 1953, NARA, RG 59, 862B.49/8-653; Richard Strauss to Stevens, memorandum, 23 September 1953, NARA, RG 59, 862B.03/9-2353 (FOIA release to author); "Kurzer Bericht über die Blockierung der Konten der Deutschen Notenbank in US-$ bei us-amerikanischen Banken," 25 July 1953, SAPMO-BA, NY 90/490; HICOG Berlin to Department of State, 17 September 1953, NARA, RG 59, 862B.49/9-1753.

64. Coburn Kidd to Geoffrey W. Lewis, 29 July 1953, NARA, RG 59, 862B.49/7-2953; Abteilung Leitende Organe der Partei und Massenorganisationen, "Zusammenfassung," 1 August 1953, SAPMO-BA, IV 2/5/563.BA; Ministerium für Eisenbahnwesen, Politische Verwaltung, "Situationsbericht," 2 August 1953, SAPMO-BA, NY 90/437; Ministerium für Eisenbahnwesen, Politische Verwaltung, "Situationsbericht," 3 August 1953, SAPMO-BA, IV 2/5/542.

65. SED/Abteilung Agitation to Grotewohl, 29 July 1953, SAPMO-BA, NY

4090/437; Ministerium für Eisenbahnwesen, Politische Verwaltung, "Situationsbericht," 3 August 1953, SAPMO-BA, IV 2/5/542; Ministerium für Eisenbahnwesen, Politische Verwaltung, "Situationsbericht," 2 August 1953, SAPMO-BA, NL 90/437; Abteilung Leitende Organe der Partei und Massenorganisationen, "Zusammenfassung der Berichte der Bezirksleitungen vom 5. 8. 53," 6 August 1953, SAPMO-BA, DY 30, IV 2/5/563. See also HICOG Berlin to Secretary of State, 6 August 1953, NARA, RG 59, 862B.00/8-653.

66. Ministerium für Eisenbahnwesen, "Anlage zur Zusammenfassung der Berichte vom 8.8.53 von den Bezirksleitungen," 7 August 1953, SAPMO-BA, IV 2/5/563; Abteilung Leitende Organe der Partei und Massenorganisationen, "Informationsbericht Nr. 2," 9 September 1953, SAPMO-BA, IV 2/5/563.

67. Abteilung Leitende Organe der Partei und Massenorganisationen, "Zusammenfassung," 3 August 1953, SAPMO-BA, IV 2/5/563.

68. Abteilung Leitende Organe der Partei und Massenorganisationen, "Zusammenfassung der Bericht der Bezirksleitungen vom 4. 8. 53 über die Auswertung des 15. Plenums und die Stimmung der Bevölkerung," 4 August 1953, SAPMO-BA, IV 2/5/563; Abteilung Leitende Organe der Partei und Massenorganisationen, "Zusammenfassung," 3 August 1953, SAPMO-BA, IV 2/5/563; Abteilung Leitende Organe der Partei und Massenorganisationen, "1. Bericht über die Lage in Berlin - Ausgabe von Lebensmittelpaketen in den Westsektoren," 29 July 1953, SAPMO-BA, IV 2/5/561; Abteilung Leitende Organe der Partei und Massenorganisationen, "Zusammenfassung der Berichte der Bezirksleitungen vom 5. 8. 53," 6 August 1953, SAPMO-BA, IV 2/5/563.

69. Harrison, *Driving the Soviets Up the Wall*, 44–45; Department of State to HICOG Bonn, 17 August 1953, DDEL, DDE Papers, Ann Whitman File, International Series, Box 14.

70. SED/Abteilung Agitation to Grotewohl, 29 July 1953, SAPMO-BA, NL 90/437; Abteilung Leitende Organe der Partei und Massenorganisationen, "Zusammenfassung," 3 August 1953, SAPMO-BA, IV 2/5/563; Abteilung Leitende Organe der Partei und Massenorganisationen, "Zusammenfassung der Berichte der Bezirksleitungen vom 7.8. 53," 8 August 1953, SAPMO-BA, IV 2/5/563; "Abteilung Leitende Organe der Partei und Massenorganisationen, Stimmung und Argumente zum sowjetisch-deutschen Kommuniqué über die Verhandlungen in Moskau," 28 August 1953, SAPMO-BA, IV 2/5/563; Abteilung Leitende Organe der Partei und Massenorganisationen, "Informationsbericht," 12 September 1953, SAPMO-BA, IV 2/5/563; Abteilung Leitende Organe der Partei und Massenorganisationen, "Zusammenfassung der Bericht der Bezirksleitungen vom 4. 8. 53 über die Auswertung des 15. Plenums und die Stimmung der Bevölkerung," 4 August 1953, SAPMO-BA, IV 2/5/563.

71. Conant to Secretary of State, 31 July 1953, NA, RG 59, 862B.49/7-3153; HICOG Berlin to Secretary of State, 4 August 1953, NARA, RG 59, 862B.49/8-453;

Prowe, *Weltstadt in Krisenzeiten*, 122; *FRUS, 1952–1954*, 7:1635; Harris to Stassen, 2 August 1953, DDEL, C. D. Jackson Records, box 1; HICOG Berlin to Department of State, 17 September 1953, NARA, RG 59, 862B.49/9-1753.

72. John A. Bross (Chief of CIA's Eastern Europe Division) to Director of Central Intelligence, 11 August 1953 (FOIA release to author); Allan A. Michie, *Voices through the Iron Curtain: The Radio Free Europe Story* (New York: Dodd, Mead, 1969), 139; Memorandum of Conversation between E. Williams (State Department) and M. Ruffin (French Embassy), 5 August 1953, NA, RG 59, 762A.00/8-553; HICOG Berlin to Secretary of State, 20 August 1953, NARA, RG 59, 762.0221/8-1752 (FPOIA release to author). —The Western Powers finally abandoned their requirement for interzonal travel passes on 14 November 1953. See HICOG Berlin to Secretary of State, 23 November 1953, NARA, RG 59, 762.0221/11-2353.

73. "Memorandum of Informal PSB Meeting, July 8," 8 July 1953 (FOIA release to author); Kirkpatrick to Foreign Office, 6 July 1953, PRO, FO/371/103843, CS 1016/158; HICOG Berlin to Secretary of State, 24 July 1953, NARA, RG 59, 862B.49/7-2453; HICOG Berlin to Secretary of State, 23 July 1953, NARA, RG 59, 862B.49/7-2353; HICOG Berlin to Secretary of State, 4 August 1953, NARA, RG 59, 862B.49/8-453; HICOG Bonn to Secretary of State, 9 August 1953 (FOIA release to author); Conant to Secretary of State, 11 August 1953, NA, RG 59, 862B.49/8-1153; W. Dowling, memorandum, 22 September 1953, NARA, RG 59, 862b.49/9-2253; Steere to Secretary of State, 24 September 1953, NA, RG 59, 862B.49/9-2453 (FOIA release to author); Jebb to Foreign Office, 9 September 1953, UK National Archives, FO/371/103846, CS1016/237.

74. C. D. Jackson to Walter Bedell Smith, 18 August 1953 (FOIA release to author); Conant to Eisenhower, 19 October 1953, DDEL, Dwight D. Eisenhower Papers, Administrative Series, box 10; "Nach den faschistischen Provokationen in Berlin und in der DDR: Auseinandersetzungen im Lager der Westmächte über Viermächteverhandlungen," 6 July 1953, enclosed in Busse/MfAA to Eisermann/Regierungskanzlei, 8 July 1953, SAPMO-BA, NY 90/463; HICOG Berlin to Secretary of State, 22 July 1953, NARA, RG 59, 862B.49/7-2253; Bohlen to Secretary of State, 5 August 1953, NARA, RG 59, 862B.49/8-553.

75. Conant to Secretary of State, 18 July 1953, NARA, RG 59, 862B.49/7-1853; *FRUS, 1952–1954*, 7:1632–33; Conant to Secretary of State, 8 August 1953, NARA, RG 59, 762B/8-853. Günter Buchstab, ed., Adenauer: *Es mußte alles neu gemacht werden." Die Protokolle des CDU-Bundesvorstandes 1950–1957*, (Stuttgart: Klett-Cotta, 1986), 585.

76. Conant to Secretary of State, 17 July 1953, NARA, RG 59, 862B.49/7-1753 (FOIA release to author); Steere to Secretary of State, 24 September 1953, NARA, RG 59, 862B.49/9-2453 (FOIA release to author); Conant to Bonn, 9 December 1953, NARA, RG 59, 862B.49/12-953; Department of State to HICOG Bonn, 9 December 1953, NARA, RG 59, 862B.49/12-953. The State Department had

specifically recommended against "detailed consultation" with the federal government in the initial stages of the program. See Riddleberger to General Smith, 6 July 1953, NARA, RG 59, 862B.49/7-653. As late as 24 July, Secretary of State Walter Hallstein "indicated that the chancellor had not been consulted." HICOG Berlin to Secretary of State, 24 July 1953, NARA, RG 59, 862B.49/7-2453.

77. Kirkpatrick to Foreign Office, 18 September 1953, British National Archives, FO371/103872; Conant to Secretary of State, 14 September 1953, NARA, RG 59, 862B.49/91453; see also Jacques Reinstein to General Smith, "Conversion of the Berlin Food Distribution Program," memorandum, 25 August 1953, NARA, RG 59, 762.0221/8-2553; Department of State to HICOG Bonn, 4 September 1953, NARA, RG 59, 862B.49/8-2053 [sic].

78. Department of State memorandum, 1 October 1953, *FRUS, 1952–1954*, VI, 678–81; Hershberg, *James B. Conant*, 660–62; Memorandum Prepared in the Department of State, 1 October 1953, *FRUS, 1952–1954*, 8:85; Berlin Element, HICOG, "Working Paper Prepared in the Eastern Affairs Division," 25 June 1953, *FRUS, 1952–1954*, 7:1598; HICOG Berlin to Secretary of State, 6 August 1953, NA, RG 59, 762B.00/8-653; Record of 6th CINCSAEUR-HICOG Commanders Conference, 29 June 1953, *FRUS, 1952–1954*, 7:1605; Conant to Dulles, 8 August 1953, *FRUS, 1952–1954*, 7:1640.

79. HICOG Berlin to Secretary of State, 17 August 1953, NARA, RG 59, 762B/8-1753; Sutterlin to Creel, memorandum, 20 August 1953, NRC, RG 466, HICOG Papers. There was also growing criticism of U.S. support for anti-communist, CIA-controlled organizations in West Berlin: "It is felt that the number of these organizations, type of activities they engage in and type of individual some of them may attract as co-workers, has created [a] situation fraught with both opportunity and risk. While we do not wish to exaggerate [the] possibility of serious trouble here, [the] very setting of West Berlin makes it vulnerable to mass action; and organizations mentioned have certain possibilities, difficult to calculate, of stirring up such action. It is felt that most careful consideration should be given to just what ends the activities in question are designed to achieve, and what methods should be prescribed to reach these ends . . . I feel that recent developments in East Germany call for some degree of reappraisal." HICOG Berlin to HICOG Bonn, 15 August 1953, NA, RG 59, 762A.0221/8-1553 (FOIA release to author).

80. "U.S. Policy on Unrest in Soviet Occupied Germany," Department of State Circular Airgram, 30 September 1953, NARA, RG 59, 762B.00/9-3053. On the Solarium reassessment, see John Lewis Gaddis, *Strategies of Containment: A Critical Appraisal of Postwar American National Security Policy* (New York: Oxford University Press, 1982), 145–46; Martin Beglinger, *"Containment" im Wandel: Die amerikanische Außen- und Sicherheitspolitik im Übergang von Truman zu Eisenhower* (Stuttgart: Steiner, 1988), 144–64; H. W. Brands, "The Age of Vulnerability": Eisenhower and the National Insecurity State," *American Historical Review* 94 (1989): 963–69; Marc Trachtenberg,

History and Strategy (Princeton, NJ: Princeton University Press, 1991), 132–41; James D. Marchio, *Rhetoric and Reality: The Eisenhower Administration and Unrest in Eastern Europe, 1953–1959*, Ph.D. diss., American University, 1990; James G. Hershberg, "'Explosion in the Offing': German Rearmament and American Diplomacy, 1953–1955," *Diplomatic History* 16, no. 4 (1992): 511–50, 527; Detlef Felken, *Dulles und Deutschland: Die Amerikanische Deutschlandpolitik, 1953–1959* (Bonn: Bouvier: 1993), 110–17; Robert R. Bowie and Richard H. Immerman, *Waging Peace: How Eisenhower Shaped an Enduring Cold War Strategy* (New York: Oxford UP, 1998), chapter 8.

81. Schenk, *Im Vorzimmer der Diktatur*, 226–31; HICOG Berlin to Department of State, 17 September 1953, NARA, RG 59, 862B.49/9-1753.

82. HICOG Berlin to Secretary of State, 28 August 1953, NA, RG 59, 862B.49/2853; Reinstein to General Smith, 25 August 1953, NARA, RG 59, 762.0221/8-2553; Probst D. H. Grüber (1891–1975), Plenipotentiary of the Council of the Protestant Church of Germany (EKD), had as early as 21 July 1953 indicated his opposition to the food program as a form of "psychological warfare." He publicly denounced it in a sermon on 26 July 1953 as "spiritual poison war." Church associates of Bischof Dibelius, the leading figure within the German Church, however, approved of the food scheme. Grüber to Beyling, 21 July 1953; Report by Grötschel on a conversation with Grüber, 22 July 1953, SAPMO-BA, NY 90/456. U.S. officials remarked that "it cannot be said with any definitiveness to what extent his ideas on this subject are shared." HICOG Berlin to Department of State, 11 August 1953, NA, RG 59, 862B.49/8-1153. For Adenauer's concern with Probst Grüber's criticism, see Otto Lenz, *Im Zentrum der Macht: Das Tagebuch von Staatssekretär Lenz 1951–1953* [Inside the Center of Power: The Diary of State Secretary Lenz, 1951–1953], ed. Klaus Gotto, Hans-Otto Kleinmann, and Reinhard Schreiner (Düsseldorf: Droste, 1989), 677.

83. HICOG Berlin to Secretary of State, 29 July 1953, NARA, RG 59, 762B.00/7-2953; HICOG Berlin to Secretary of State, 29 August 1953, NARA, RG 59, 862B.00/8-2953; HICOG Berlin to Department of State, 17 September 1953, NARA, RG 59, 862B.49/9-1753.

84. Ilko-Sascha Kowalczuk, Armin Mitter, and Stefan Wolle, eds., *Der Tag X. 17. Juni 1953. Die "Innere Staatsgründung" der DDR als Ergebnis der Krise 1952/54* (Berlin: Ch. Links, 1995); HICOG Berlin to Secretary of State, 6 August 1953, NARA, RG 59, 862B.00/8-653; HICOG Berlin to HICOG Bonn, 21 October 1953, National Security Archive, Soviet Flashpoints Collection; HICOG Berlin to Secretary of State, 18 November 1953, NA, RG 59, 762B.00/11-1853.

85. Heidenreich, Münkel and Stadelmann-Wenz, *Geheimdienstkrieg in Deutschland*, 266–324; Heidenreich, *DDR-Spionage*, 253–59; see also Karl Wilhelm Fricke, Roger Engelmann, *Konzentrierte Schläge: Staatssicherheitsaktionen und politische Prozesse in der DDR 1953–1956* (Berlin: Ch. Links, 1998).

86. CIA Records (FOIA release to National Security Archive).

CONCLUSION

1. Thomas A. Schwartz, *America's Germany: John J. McCloy and the Federal Republic of Germany* (Cambridge, MA: Harvard University Press, 1991), 66–67.

2. Memorandum for Mr. C.D. Jackson, 3 November 1953, Dwight D. Eisenhower Library (Mandatory Review release to author).

3. State Department to American Embassy Bonn, 7 June 1955, National Security Archive, Soviet Flashpoint Collection.

4. U.S. Mission Berlin to Department of State, 19 July 1955, NARA, RG 59, 762B.00/7-1955; American Embassy Bonn to Department of State, 10 August 1955, NARA, RG 59, 762B.00/8-1055; "Progress Report on "United States Policy Related to East Germany," by the Operations Coordinating Board, 17 May 1956, National Security Archive, Soviet Flashpoints Collection.

5. HICOG Bonn to Department of State, 13 April 1954 (FOIA release to author); HICOG Bonn to Department of State, 30 April 1954 (FOIA release to author); "Emergency Relief for the People of East Germany," memorandum from Livingston Merchant to Hoover, 26 April 1955, NARA, RG 59, 762B.00/4-2655; American Embassy Bonn to Department of State, 17 July 1956, NARA, RG 59, 511.62B/7-1756; American Embassy Bonn to Department of State, 22 October 1956, NARA, RG 59, 511/62B/10-2256.

6. "U.S. Policy Toward East Germany," memorandum for the National Security Council, 12 September 1956, National Security Archive, Soviet Flashpoints Collection; William Glenn Gray, *Germany's Cold War: The Global Campaign to Isolate East Germany, 1949–1969* (Chapel Hill: University of North Carolina Press, 2003), 21.

7. U.S. Mission Berlin to Department of State, 29 March 1956, NARA, RG 59, 762B.00/3-2956; "U.S. Policy Toward East Germany," memorandum for the National Security Council, 12 September 1956, National Security Archive, Soviet Flashpoints Collection.

8. Draft letter from President Eisenhower to Chancellor Adenauer, 20 July 1953, C. D. Jackson Records, box 3, DDEL; *New York Times*, 26 July 1953.

INDEX

Note: page numbers in italics refer to figures. Those followed by n refer to notes, with note number.

Social Democratic Party (SPD) (*continued*)
on, 60; defection of officials from, 94–95; and plebiscite against West German rearmament, 163, 165; and SBZ elections of 1946, 71, 72; Soviet revival of, in Berlin sector, 67; Soviet revival of, in SBZ, hopes for, 72, 73, 313n144; fusion with KPD, 58; Western efforts to revive in East, 67; and worker uprising in GDR (1953), 248. *See also* SPD-KPD merger

Socialist Unity Party (SED): blocking formation of, in Western zones, 66–67; and Bonn and Paris Treaties, pressure to prevent signing of, 231; call for conquest of West Germany, 140–42; call for unified Germany under SBZ model, 83, 84; Clay's refusal to recognize, 63; conquest of West Germany as goal of, 108; and creation of GDR, 102–3; decline in prestige, due to shortages, 89; defections from, 94–95; denunciation of European Recovery Program, 83; and Deutschlandtreffen rally, 121–22; and Eisenhower packages program, 261, 264; 15th Plenum, 260, 264; firm control of GDR by, 280; and Free German Youth, 106, 121; and GDR German unity efforts, 107; and New Course, 241–42; and illegal trade, encouragement of, 215; "Manifesto to the German People on the Occasion of the London Conference," 83; and movement toward East German government, 87; and nationwide referendum on future of German state, 80, 82, 84–86; and opposition to West German state, 94; Parteiaktiv, creation of, 94; and People's Congresses for Unity and Peace, 83–86, 277–78; political dominance of, as goal of People's Congress, 82; and potential for unified Germany, 99; purges in, 94; and SBZ elections of 1946, 68–70, 71–72, 73–74; Second Conference (1952), and isolation of GDR, 189; Second Conference (1952), announcement of GDR turn to full socialism, 234; Soviet concerns about failures of, 94; and Soviet line on Korean War, 138; SPD-KPD merger into, 60; Stalinist transformation of, 121; support for national unity, 80–81, 82; Third Party Congress, 107, 138, 140–42; U.S. efforts to undermine, 94–95; on U.S. imperialism, 138; worker uprising in GDR (1953) and, 254; and World Youth Festival, 176–82

Sokolovsky, Vasily: and Clay, friendship with, 27, 66; and Clay's proposed trade of economic unity for reparations, 74–75; on Clay's vision for postwar world, 33; on counterblockade, 200; and German central

administrations, 31, 32, 33, 35–36, 50; and interzonal trade, support for, 74; and joint export-import plan, 47; and level-of-industry agreement, 39; and reparations issue, 48, 51; and SBZ elections of 1946, 68; and Soviet withdrawal from Allied governance structures, 87; and SPD-KPD merger, 61, 64; and worker uprising in GDR (1953), 244, 245, 255

sovereignty, German, return of, negotiations on, 182

Soviet attack on Western Europe: fears of, after Korean War outbreak, 135–45; U.S. preparations for, 110; vulnerability of Berlin and, 142

Soviet Control Commission (SCC): creation of, 103–4; dismantling of, 241; and GDR transformation into communist state, 237; and plebiscite on West German rearmament, 163

Soviet Military Administration (SMA) in Germany: 44–45, 66; and CDU and LDP, turn to support of, 93; concerns about Soviet removal of German infrastructure, 14; head of, 14; and level-of-industry agreement, 41; as not fully functional until late 1945, 36–37; recruitment of reliable Germans for German central administrations, 37; renaming as Soviet Control Commission (SCC), 103–4; and trade within Germany, 41

Soviet occupation zone (SBZ): cultural renewal efforts in, 56–58; currency for, 87–89, 317–18n32; early satisfaction of Germans in, 57–58; economic decline in, 41, 51, 89; establishment of separate administration in, 297n30; internment camps, 91; lack of uniform administration of, 55; land reform, alienation of German public by, 59; police in, 108; political renewal in, 58; Radio Berlin broadcasts, 56, 57; rapid decline in public approval of Soviets, 59; repressive rule, groups working to expose, 91–92; Soviet autonomy in, as Soviet goal, 10, 11–12, 35, 38, 46; Soviets eliminate overt opposition, 93–94; and Soviet propaganda, effectiveness of, 57; transformation into people's republic, early debate on success of, 65; walling-off of, as Soviet goal, 45–46; and Western media, 38, 89, 90–91

Soviet occupation zone, anticommunist groups active in, 91–93; growth during Berlin Blockade, 94; U.S. support for, 92, 93–94. *See also* German resistance groups

Soviet occupation zone, elections of 1946, 67–74, 312n127; fallout from, 72–74; results of, 71–72; Soviet disappointment in, 74; Soviet interference in, 68, 69, 74; U.S. policy

INTERNATIONAL HISTORY
PROJECT SERIES

Edited by James G. Hershberg

A full list of titles in the Cold War International History Project Series is available online
at www.sup.org/cwihp